Christians and Jews in Angevin England

YORK MEDIEVAL PRESS

York Medieval Press is published by the University of York's Centre for Medieval Studies in association with Boydell & Brewer Limited. Our objective is the promotion of innovative scholarship and fresh criticism on medieval culture. We have a special commitment to interdisciplinary study, in line with the Centre's belief that the future of Medieval Studies lies in those areas in which its major constituent disciplines at once inform and challenge each other.

All enquiries of an editorial kind, including suggestions for monographs and essay collections, should be addressed to: The Academic Editor, York Medieval Press, University of York, Centre for Medieval Studies, The King's Manor, York, YO1 7EP (E-mail: gmg501@york.ac.uk).

Publications of York Medieval Press are listed at the back of this volume.

Christians and Jews in Angevin England

THE YORK MASSACRE OF 1190 NARRATIVES AND CONTEXTS

Edited by

Sarah Rees Jones and Sethina Watson

THE UNIVERSITY *of York*

YORK MEDIEVAL PRESS

MARC FITCH FUND

DAMUS·UT·DETUR

The publishers acknowledge the generous financial support of the
Marc Fitch Fund in the production of this volume.

First published 2013

A York Medieval Press publication
in association with The Boydell Press
an imprint of Boydell & Brewer Ltd
PO Box 9, Woodbridge, Suffolk IP12 3DF, UK
and of Boydell & Brewer Inc.
668 Mt Hope Avenue, Rochester, NY 14620-2731, USA
website: www.boydellandbrewer.com
and with the
Centre for Medieval Studies, University of York

ISBN 978-1-903153-44-4

A CIP catalogue record for this book is available
from the British Library

The publisher has no responsibility for the continued existence or accuracy
of URLs for external or third-party internet websites referred to in this
book, and does not guarantee that any content on such websites is, or will
remain, accurate or appropriate.

Papers used by Boydell & Brewer Ltd are natural, recyclable products
made from wood grown in sustainable forests

Printed and bound in Great Britain by
CPI Group (UK) Ltd, Croydon, CR0 4YY

CONTENTS

Contents

LIST OF ILLUSTRATIONS

Maps

Figures

CONTRIBUTORS

Anna Sapir Abulafia is Fellow, College Lecturer and Director of Studies in History at Lucy Cavendish College, Cambridge. She has published extensively on medieval Jewish history, including *Christians and Jews in the Twelfth-Century Renaissance* (London, 1995) and *Christian-Jewish Relations, 1000–1300: Jews in the Service of Medieval Christendom* (London, 2011)

Anthony Bale is Professor of Medieval Culture at Birkbeck, University of London. He has published widely on medieval representations of Jews, including in *The Jew in the Medieval Book: English Antisemitism 1350–1500* (Cambridge, 2006) and *Feeling Persecuted: Christians, Jews, and Images of Violence* (London, 2010). He has recently edited Mandeville's *Book of Travels and Marvels* and is now researching medieval travellers' accounts of Jerusalem and the Holy Land.

Heather Blurton is Associate Professor of English and Medieval Studies at the University of California, Santa Barbara. She is the author of *Cannibalism in High Medieval English Literature* (London, 2007) and co-editor, along with Jocelyn Wogan-Browne, of *Rethinking the South English Legendaries* (Manchester, 2012).

Carlee A. Bradbury is an Assistant Professor in Art History at Radford University.

Jeffrey J. Cohen is a Professor of English, Director of the Medieval and Early Modern Studies Institute, and affiliated faculty with the Program in Judaic Studies at the George Washington University in Washington, DC. *Stories of Stone*, his current project, is funded by fellowships from the ACLS and the Guggenheim Foundation.

Alan Cooper is an Associate Professor of History at Colgate University. He is currently preparing a book length study: *William Longbeard's Long Beard: Crusading Rhetoric, the Apocalypse and the Politics of the Poor in Medieval England*.

Eva De Visscher teaches medieval history at the University of Oxford. Her research focuses on cultural exchange between Jews and Christians in medieval Europe. She has recently published on the subject of multilingualism in Jewish-Christian encounters and cross-religious learning and teaching. A book on Christian Hebraism in the twelfth and thirteenth centuries is forthcoming. She is currently investigating Jewish self-perception in central and late medieval Germany.

Joe Hillaby is Honorary Research Fellow at the University of Bristol and has served as a JHSE Council Member since 1995 and President 2006–8. He has published detailed studies of the medieval Jewries of London, Hereford, Worcester, Gloucester and Bristol, the twelfth-century Jewish colonization of England, the English medieval synagogue, *mikva'ot* and ritual-child-murder accusations. A contributor to the *Encyclopaedia Judaica*, his *Dictionary of Medieval Anglo-Jewish History* will be published in 2013.

Paul Hyams is Professor of Medieval History at Cornell University. Much of his work focuses on the transition from a Europe of too few full time-lawyers to one with too many. His most recent book is *Rancor and Reconciliation in Medieval England: Wrong and its Redress from the Tenth to Thirteenth Centuries* (Ithaca, NY, 2003), but he works best at article length. His recurrent interest in freedom and servitude will shortly release *The Joy of Liberty and the Price of Respectability* on English manumission charters of the long thirteenth century.

Hannah Johnson is Associate Professor of English at the University of Pittsburgh. Her first book was *Blood Libel: The Ritual Murder Accusation at the Limit of Jewish History*(Michigan, 2012), and she is currently co-authoring a book entitled*Chaucer's Prioress and the Jews: Ethics, Criticism, and Antisemitism.*

Matthew Mesley (PhD, University of Exeter) is a Post-Doctoral Research Assistant at the University of Zürich. His current research is focussed on the construction and representation of clerical and episcopal gender in medieval Germany.

Robin R. Mundill is an Honorary Research Fellow at the School of History at the University of St Andrews and Head of History at Glenalmond College, Perth, Scotland. His published works include *England's Jewish Solution* (Cambridge, 1998) and *The King's Jews: Money, Massacre and Exodus in Medieval England* (London, 2010).

Sarah Rees Jones is Senior Lecturer in History, based at the graduate Centre for Medieval Studies, at the University of York. Her research and publications focus on medieval urban topography, culture and society.

Thomas Roche, a former teaching assistant at the Sorbonne (Université Paris-4), now heads the Archives départementales of Nièvre, in Nevers. His current research interests focus on legal history and charters in the Anglo-Norman world and also in Burgundy, during the high Middle Ages.

Pinchas Roth recently completed his dissertation, 'Later Provençal Sages: Halakhah (Jewish Law) and Rabbis in Southern France, 1215–1348', in the Department of Talmud and Halakha at the Hebrew University of Jerusalem.

Contributors

Robert Stacey (PhD, Yale), is interim Dean of the College of Arts and Sciences, and Professor of Medieval History at the University of Washington. Stacey's scholarly work has focused on medieval English history, eleventh–fourteenth centuries; Jewish history, particularly in England; and political, constitutional, and economic history.

Nicholas Vincent is Professor of Medieval History at the University of East Anglia, and a Fellow of the British Academy. His most recent book is *A Brief History of Britain, 1066–1485* (London, 2011).

Sethina Watson is Lecturer in History and member of the Centre for Medieval Studies at the University of York. She works on the church and laity in the twelfth and thirteenth centuries and has published on charity, towns and pastoral care. Her current book is a constitutional study of early hospitals and charities.

Ethan Zadoff is completing his doctoral dissertation, titled '"Therefore a man shall leave his father and mother and be joined to his wife": Medieval Jewish Marriage Law in Northern France and Germany in Comparative Perspective, 1140–1234' in the Department of History of the Graduate Center of the City University of New York. He is an adjunct lecturer in the Hebrew Division of Hunter College.

EDITORS' PREFACE AND ACKNOWLEDGMENTS

Many of the chapters published in this volume were first delivered at a conference held in March 2010 at the University of York on 'York 1190: Jews and Others in the Wake of Massacre'. We would like to thank Dr Hannah Meyer (Cambridge) and Dr Hugh Doherty (Oxford), who joined us in 2009 in planning the conference. Their influence can still be detected in several of the chapters.

The conference was supported financially by the British Academy. Generous further assistance was provided by The Jewish Historical Society of England (both the London and the Leeds branches), the Royal Historical Society and the Departments of English and History as well as the Centre for Medieval Studies at the University of York. Following the conference, the Leeds branch of the JHSE established an annual prize for student work on the history of Jews in Yorkshire (in any period). We would particularly like to thank Nigel Grizzard and Malcolm Saunders for their advice in developing the conference and ensuring that we could provide excellent hospitality for all our guests. The King's Manor and the hospitium of St Mary's Abbey proved ideal venues, while English Heritage provided access to Clifford's Tower with excellent stewardship for our groups. Under the direction of Professor Elisabeth Dutton (Fribourg), the Centre for Medieval Studies' own 'Lords of Misrule' enriched the event with their performance of the medieval *Croxton Play of the Sacrament* and Steven Berkoff's *Ritual in Blood*.

Every chapter in this volume owes a debt to Professor Barrie Dobson for his singular contribution to writing the history of the massacre and of medieval English Jewish communities more widely. The Borthwick Institute for Archives republished his essays on Anglo-Jewish history for the occasion: *The Jewish Communities of Medieval England* (2010). We are grateful to Dr Philippa Hoskin for managing that publication to press, to Dr Helen Birkett for taking the lead editorial role and to Timothy Rees Jones for his editorial assistance.

This collection of essays contains several new papers which were not delivered at the conference as well as developments of those that were. In preparing the collection for publication we owe a very large debt to Dr Robert Kinsey for his assistance in standardising the footnotes and preparing the bibliography and index, and to Cath D'Alton for preparing the map. Caroline Palmer has been a most patient and supportive editor at Boydell & Brewer, and Professor Peter Biller, general editor of the York

Medieval Press, has provided some extremely useful insights and advice about the range and organisation of the volume.

Finally the authors themselves have provided excellent fellowship through the process of turning our idea into a fully fledged book.

Sarah Rees Jones and Sethina Watson
University of York
19 June 2012

ABBREVIATIONS

AJSR	*Association for Jewish Studies Review*
BIHR	*Bulletin of the Institute of Historical Research*
BL	British Library
BN	Bibliothèque nationale de France, Paris
Bodl.	Bodleian Library, Oxford
Brakelond, *Chron.*	*The Chronicle of Jocelin of Brakelond, concerning the acts of Samson, Abbot of the Monastery of St. Edmund*, ed. H. E. Butler (London, 1949)
Canterbury, *Historical Works*	*The Historical Works of Gervase of Canterbury*, ed. W. Stubbs, 2 vols., RS 73 (London 1879-80)
CCR	*Calendar of Close Rolls*
CFR Henry III	*Calendar of the Fine Rolls of the Reign of Henry III: Preserved in the National Archives*, ed. P. Dryburgh and B. Hartland, 3 vols. to date (Woodbridge, 2007-)
CPR	*Calendar of Patent Rolls*
CPREJ	*Calendar of the Plea Rolls of the Exchequer of the Jews*, ed. J. M. Rigg et al., 6 vols. (London, 1905-2005)
CRR	*Curia Regis Rolls, Richard I–Henry III*, 20 vols. (London, 1922-2006)
CUL	Cambridge University Library
Devizes, *Chronicle*	*The Chronicle of Richard of Devizes of the Time of King Richard the First*, ed. J. T. Appleby (London, 1963)
Diceto, *Historical Works*	Ralph de Diceto, *The Historical Works of Master Ralph de Diceto, Dean of London*, ed W. Stubbs, 2 vols., RS 68 (London, 1876)
Dobson, *JMY*	R. B. Dobson, *The Jews of Medieval York and the Massacre of March 1190* (York: Borthwick Papers no. 45, 1974)
EHD	*English Historical Documents*
EHR	*English Historical Review*
EYC	*Early Yorkshire Charters*, ed. W. Farrer and C. T. Clay, 13 vols., Yorkshire Archaeological Society Record Series, Extra Ser. 1-10 (Edinburgh and Wakefield, 1914-65)
Foedera	*Foedera, Conventiones, Litterae, et Cujuscunque Generis Acta Publica*, ed. T. Rymer, 20 vols. (London, 1704-35)
Giraldi Cambrensis Opera	*Giraldi Cambrensis Opera*, ed. J. S. Brewer, J. Dimock and G. Warner, 8 vols., RS 21 (London, 1861-91)

Howden, *Annals*	Roger of Howden, *The Annals of Roger de Hoveden: Comprising the History of England and of other Countries of Europe from A.D. 732 to A.D. 1201*, ed. H. T. Riley, 2 vols. (London, 1853)
Howden, *Chronica*	Roger de Howden, *Chronica Magistri Roger de Houedene*, ed. W. Stubbs, 4 vols., RS 51 (London, 1868-71)
Howden, *Gesta*	*Gesta Regis Henrici Secundi et Gesta Regis Ricardi*, ed. W. Stubbs, 2 vols., RS 49 (London, 1867)
Itin.	*Itinerarium peregrinorum et gesta regis Ricardi* in *Chronicles and Memorials of the Reign of Richard I*, ed. W. Stubbs, 2 vols., RS 38 (London 1864-65), 1.
JAE Docs.	*The Jews of Angevin England: Documents and Records from the Latin and Hebrew Sources*, ed. J. Jacobs (London, 1893)
JMCE	*The Jewish Communities of Medieval England: The Collected Essays of R. B. Dobson*, ed. H. M. Birkett, Borthwick Texts and Studies no. 39 (York, 2010)
JHS	*Jewish Historical Studies*
JHSE Miscellanies	*Miscellanies of the Jewish Historical Society of England*
JHSE Transactions	*Transactions of the Jewish Historical Society of England*
JMB, ed. Skinner	*The Jews in Medieval Britain: Historical, Literary and Archaeological Perspectives*, ed. P. Skinner (Woodbridge, 2003)
JQR	*Jewish Quarterly Review*
JRUL	John Rylands University Library, Manchester
JSQ	*Jewish Studies Quarterly*
Kennedy, '"Faith"'	M. J. Kennedy, '"Faith in the One God Flowed over you from the Jews, the Sons of the Patriarchs and the Prophets": William of Newburgh's Writings on Anti-Jewish Violence', *Anglo-Norman Studies* 25 (2002), 139-52
King's Works	*The History of the King's Works*, ed. H. M. Colvin, 6 vols. (London, 1963-82)
Lipman, *JMN*	V. D. Lipman, *The Jews of Medieval Norwich* (London, 1967)
LPL	Lambeth Palace Library
Monmouth, *Kings of Britain*	Geoffrey of Monmouth, *The History of the Kings of Britain*, trans. L. Thorpe (Harmondsworth, 1966)
MTB	*Materials for the History of Thomas Becket Archbishop of Canterbury*, ed. J. C. Robertson and J. B. Sheppard, 7 vols., RS 67 (London 1875-85)
ODNB	*Oxford Dictionary of National Biography*
OMT	Oxford Medieval Texts
P & P	*Past and Present*
Paris, *Chronica Majora*	Matthew Paris, *Chronica Majora*, ed. H. R. Luard, 7 vols., RS 57 (London, 1872-83)
PG	*Patrologiae Cursus Completus s. Graeco-Latina*, ed. J.-P. Migne, 162 vols. (Paris, 1857-1912)
PL	*Patrologiae Cursus Completus s. Latina*, ed. J.-P. Migne, 221 vols. (Paris, 1844-64)

PR	*Pipe Roll* (as published by the Pipe Roll Society), cited by regnal year
PR 2-4 Henry II	*Great Rolls of the Pipe for 2, 3 and 4 Henry II*, ed. J. Hunter, Record Commission (London, 1844)
RCHME, *City of York*	Royal Commission on Historical Monuments, England, *City of York*, 5 vols. (London, 1962-81)
Richardson, *EJ*	H. G. Richardson, *The English Jewry under Angevin Kings* (London, 1960)
Roth, *HJE*	C. Roth, *A History of the Jews in England*, 3rd edn (Oxford, 1964)
Rot. Chart.	*Rotuli Chartarum in Turri Londinensi Asservati*, Record Commission (London, 1837)
Rot. Litt. Claus.	*Rotuli Litterarum Clausarum in Turri Londinensi Asservati*, ed. T. D. Hardy, 2 vols., Record Commission (London, 1833-44)
Rot. Litt. Pat.	*Rotuli Litterarum Patentium in Turri Londinensi Asservati, 1201-1216*, ed. T. D. Hardy, Record Commission (London, 1835)
Rot. de Ob. et Fin.	*Rotuli de Oblatis et Finibus in Turri Londinensi Asservati, tempore regis Johannis*, ed. T. D Hardy, Record Commission (London, 1835)
RS	*Rerum Britannicarum Medii Aevi Scriptores* (Rolls Series)
SS	Surtees Society
Statutes of the Realm	*Statutes of the Realm, 1101–1713*, 11 vols., Record Commission (London, 1810-28)
TNA	The National Archives
TRHS	*Transactions of the Royal Historical Society*
VCH	*Victoria County History*
VCH, City of York	*A History of the County of York: The City of York*, ed. P. M. Tillot, Victoria History of the Counties of England (Oxford, 1961)
VCH, East Riding	*A History of the County of York: East Riding*, 9 vols., Victoria History of the Counties of England (London, 1969-)
VCH, Yorkshire	*A History of the County of York*, ed. W. Page, 3 vols., Victoria History of the Counties of England (1907-74)
WAM	Westminster Abbey Muniments
Wendover, *Flowers of History*	Roger of Wendover, *The Flowers of History*, ed H. G. Hewlett, 3 vols., RS 84 (London, 1886-89)
WN, ed. Howlett	William of Newburgh, 'Historia Rerum Anglicarum', in *Chronicles of the Reigns of Stephen, Henry II and Richard I*, ed. R. Howlett, 4 vols., RS 82 (London, 1884-89), I-II
WN, trans. Stevenson	William of Newburgh, 'Historia Rerum Anglicarum', in *The Church Historians of England*, trans. J. Stevenson, 5 vols. (London, 1853-58), IV, pt. 2, 397-672

WN, ed. Walsh & Kennedy	William of Newburgh, *The History of English Affairs, Books I and 2*, ed. P. G. Walsh and M. Kennedy, 2 vols. (Warminster and Oxford, 1988-2007)
YAJ	*Yorkshire Archaeological Journal*
YAS	Yorkshire Archaeological Society
YCA	York City Archives
YMA	York Minster Archives
York Minster Fasti	*York Minster Fasti: Being Notes on the Dignitaries, Archdeacons and Prebendaries in the Church of York prior to the year 1307*, ed. C. T. Clay, 2 vols., Yorkshire Archaeological Society. Record Series 123 and 124 (Wakefield, 1958-59)

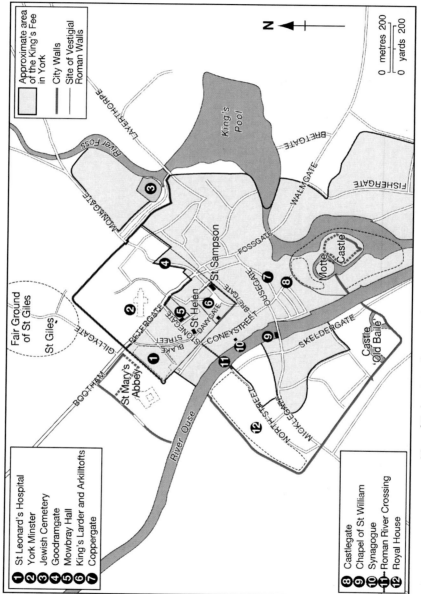

Legend:

Approximate area of the King's Fee in York

City Walls

Site of Vestigial Roman Walls

0 metres 200

0 yards 200

1. St Leonard's Hospital
2. York Minster
3. Jewish Cemetery
4. Goodramgate
5. Mowbray Hall
6. King's Larder and Arkilltofts
7. Coppergate
8. Castlegate
9. Chapel of St William
10. Synagogue
11. Roman River Crossing
12. Royal House

Map of York c. 1190 showing selected features mentioned in the text

Introduction

The Moment and Memory of
the York Massacre of 1190

Sethina Watson

During the course of one desperate night in March 1190, an estimated 150 Jewish men, women and children committed suicide or were murdered at the royal castle in York, where they had fled for safety. The York massacre horrified contemporaries, Christians and Jews, and is remembered today around the world. It is recalled in Jewish elegies and holds a singular, sad place in the English national story as 'the most notorious anti-Jewish atrocity' in its history.[1] Most particularly, the memory is tied to place. Clifford's Tower, the mid-thirteenth-century stone keep of the royal castle, has become its most enduring symbol.[2] Yet it is the city itself that is most profoundly identified with the massacre. Report ascribed a medieval 'Herem' (ban) to the city, that from that awful night no Jewish person should stay within its walls.[3] In fact, a medieval Jewish population returned to and for a short while flourished at York and a modern congregation emerged in the late nineteenth century. The rumour was less a response to historical circumstance than to the city's perceived silence, which was interpreted as a refusal to remember. This silence was broken in 1978 when the memorial plaque was unveiled at Clifford's Tower by leaders of the city and England's Jewish and Christian communities. In the following years York's Jewish past was more fully recovered through archaeological excavation of its Jewish cemetery, a four-day commemoration of the massacre's octocentenary, and revised guidebooks to Clifford's Tower.[4] Nevertheless, the

---

1   B. Dobson, 'The Jews of Medieval York in the Context of some other English Jewish Communities', in *JCME*, pp. xix–xxvii (p. xix). For the elegies of Joseph of Chartres and Menachem ben Jacob of Worms, *Clifford's Tower Commemoration: York 15–18 March, 1990*, ed. G. Hunter et al. (York, 1990), pp. 72–81.
2   An example of its modern iconic use can be found on the cover of S. Goldin, *The Ways of Jewish Martyrdom*, trans. Yigal Levin (Turnhout, 2008).
3   For a contemporary testimony, *Clifford's Tower Commem.*, ed. G. Hunter et al., p. 15.
4   B. Dobson, 'The Medieval York Jewry Reconsidered', in, *JMB*, ed. Skinner, pp. 145–56 (145). Dobson cites John Silkin's *c.* 1960 poem 'Astringencies: The Coldness' on the 'deadening' effect on the city of its failure to remember. The medieval Jewish community and the massacre feature in the current guidebook, J. Clark, *Clifford's Tower and the Castle of York* (London, 2010), pp. 3, 22–4.

rumour of the 'herem' lives on and was a warning that contributors to this volume can personally attest to hearing. The horrific events have become a traumatic memory, rooted geographically rather than historically.

As the bibliography at the end of this volume attests, scholarship on medieval Anglo-Jewry and on relations between Christians and Jews has been exceptionally rich over recent decades. Yet the timeless tragedy of massacre can still work to detach the violence of 1190 from its historical contexts. It has found a place within a wider history of Jewish martyrdom, of communities driven to that most desperate of acts, 'Kiddush ha-Shem' (literally, 'sanctification of the Name'): martyrdom in the name of God. Here it is recognized as the English expression of pogroms witnessed in France and the Rhineland, first in 1096 and 1146, at the launch of the First and Second Crusades, and (within living memory of victims, perpetrators and chroniclers of 1190) the murder of thirty Jews at Blois in northern France in 1171 and attempted violence in Mainz in 1188.[5] Despite Barrie Dobson's ground-breaking 1974 study, the massacre has not been integrated so readily into English or Anglo-Jewish history. Recent work, much of it by contributors to this volume, has thrown particular light on patterns of settlement from the arrival of Jewish communities in England after the Conquest; on relations between Jews and the English crown and the roles of Jews in economic life and urban life, especially from the mid-thirteenth century; and on the narrative and lived violence of accusations of ritual crucifixion.[6] The Expulsion of the Jews in 1290 now sits firmly incorporated into national, political and social histories of the late thirteenth century.[7] The contexts of the anti-Jewish uprisings of 1189-90 have not received such wide investigation and are usually confined to discussions of money-lending and debt. Scholars have yet to fully embrace

---

[5] Such connections were first made within years of the massacre. Ephraim ben Jacob of Bonn, author of an account of Jewish persecution during the Second Crusade, included the London and York massacres in his catalogue of anti-Jewish violence between 1171 and 1196, R. Chazan, 'Ephraim ben Jacob's Compilation of Twelfth-Century Persecutions', *JQR* 84:4 (1994), 397–416 (401–2). For modern studies, see Goldin, *Jewish Martyrdom*, pp. 85–112, 179–207 (where the York massacre is at pp. 85–6, 202–7); S. Einbinder, *Beautiful Death: Jewish Poetry and Martyrdom in Medieval France* (Princeton, 2002), pp. 29–31. A. S. Abulafia, *Christian-Jewish Relations 1000–1300: Jews in the Service of Medieval Christendom* (Harlow, 2011), pp. 93–5, 158–61 (for York). J. Riley-Smith, 'Christian Violence and the Crusades', in *Religious Violence between Christians and Jews: Medieval Roots, Modern Perspectives*, ed. A. Sapir Abulafia (Basingstoke, 2002), pp. 3–20 (p. 4), whose brief notice is the only reference to the English violence of 1189–90 in this rich volume. Also, J. Hillaby, 'Introduction', in *JCME*, pp. *viii–ix*.

[6] The essays that follow provide recent bibliographies of these rich fields. For an overview of patterns in scholarship, see P. Skinner, 'Introduction: Jews in Medieval Britain and Europe', in *JMB*, ed. Skinner, pp. 1-11; and R. R. Mundill, 'Out of the Shadow and into the Light – The Impact and Implications of Recent Scholarship on the Jews of Medieval England 1066–1290', *History Compass* 9:8 (2011), 572-601.

[7] R. C. Stacey, 'Parliamentary Negotiation and the Expulsion of the Jews from England', in *Thirteenth Century England* 6, ed. M. Prestwich et al. (Woodbridge, 1997), 77–101; P. R. Brand, 'Jews and the Law in England, 1275–1290', *EHR*, 115 (2000), 1138–58; and the work of R. R. Mundill in the bibliography.

Dobson's challenge to recognize the deep roots of the massacre in English government, society and cultural imagination.

The approaches of two foundational monographs on Anglo-Jewry illuminate the challenge that continues to haunt scholars. In 1960 H. G. Richardson chose to address neither the massacre nor the violent accusations of ritual crucifixion. 'Those incidents, atrocious as they were', had been recounted by others and 'are not inconsistent with a long, quiet history of friendly intercourse and business dealings between Jew and Gentile', the subject of his study.[8] In contrast, in Cecil Roth's 1948 chapter on 1189 to 1216 (revised in 1964) the massacre becomes the story of the Jews of England. It relates the course of the violence and what Roth interprets as the royal response, including intensive regulation and financial exaction.[9] Often retold, the story of the York massacre remains awkwardly situated within the society from which it erupted: a narrative either set apart, or quick to consume all that lies around it.[10] In part, the problem of integrating the violent and the routine stems from the surviving sources. These fall into two camps, both generated by the Christian majority. One is literary and ecclesiastical: the saints' lives, histories and dramas that, from 1144, related stories of anti-Jewish violence and perceived Jewish crime, often centred upon accusations of ritual child murder.[11] The other is bureaucratic, largely financial: the multiple series of royal records which include the plea rolls of the Jewish Exchequer surviving from 1219-20, 1244, 1253 and almost continuously from 1266.[12] Since English kings extended intrusive claims over their Jewish subjects, these records provide exceptional details of Jewish communities, at least as far as they were subsumed within and shaped by this governmental apparatus. With the exception of the pipe rolls, however, these records post-date 1199, and most draw our attention firmly into the mid to late thirteenth century. The first is most often studied using literary models of interpretation; the second remains decidedly historical. In time, sources, and contexts, the violence of 1190 straddles the two. Exploring its wider contexts demands interdisciplinary and multidisciplinary methodologies.

---

[8] Richardson, *EJ*, p. 46, and the brief observation on p. 22.

[9] Roth, *HJE*, pp. 18–37 (the build up and aftermath of the events are pp. 19–28).

[10] *JMB*, ed. Skinner, presents one of the more committed treatments, yet here, too, consideration is confined largely within Hillaby's chapter – in a section called 'The Jewry under attack, 1189–90' (pp. 29–31) – and Dobson's reflection on the treatment of York's medieval Jews thirty years after his defining work (pp. 145–8). See, too, A. Bale, 'Fictions of Judaism in England before 1290', in ibid., pp. 129–44 (139). For the most recent consideration of the events, within a chapter on anti-Jewish violence, see R. R. Mundill, *The King's Jews: Money, Massacre and Exodus* (London, 2010), pp. 75–81.

[11] In particular, see work by A. Bale, J. J. Cohen, and M. Rubin in the bibliography.

[12] P. Brand, 'The Jewish Community in the Records of Royal Government', in *JMB*, ed. Skinner, pp. 74–83 (p. 78).

The violence that reached its apogee in York in fact began at the doors of Richard I's coronation feast at Westminster on 3 September 1189 and spread immediately into London. In its aftermath, Richard issued a decree that all Jews were under his protection and must not be harmed, but by the end of the year he had left England on crusade and the violence reignited, spreading to towns across England between January and March and culminating in the massacre at York. Modern histories of Angevin England struggle to situate these attacks. They usually discuss them, if they do, within important but circumscribed discussions of anti-Semitism or debt.[13] Medieval chroniclers, on the other hand, recognised the anti-Jewish violence, and the challenge confronted by Christians living with Jews, as a defining element of their age. Some used it to structure their histories of Angevin England. Richard of Devizes (d. *c*.1200) opens his work with the violence that spread from the coronation across England, choosing his starting point 'so that this little book should have a beginning of some importance ('alicuius momenti habeat initium')'.[14]

News of the massacre at York travelled swiftly and haunted Christians and Jews. On the continent, Jewish writers captured the memory of the English martyrs in history and elegy; in England, Christian chroniclers struggled to give meaning to its events.[15] It is from one historian in particular that we draw our most detailed insights: William of Newburgh, one of the most admired historians of his age. His *Historia Rerum Anglicarum* ('History of English Affairs') offers a critical history of England between the Conquest and the end of Richard's reign.[16] Born *c*. 1136 in Bridlington, Yorkshire, William entered the Augustinian priory of Newburgh as a youth. It was here, 20 miles north of York, that he wrote his history between 1198 and 1201. The work is divided into five books: the first three cover 1066 to 1154, Henry II's coronation to 1174, and 1175 to his death (1189); the final two, more substantial, books extend from Richard's coronation to 1194 and then from 1194 to 1198.[17] William devoted a degree of attention to the events of 1189-90 that is

---

13 For two that engage with the issue, see R. Bartlett, *England under the Norman and Angevin Kings, 1075–1225* (Oxford, 2000), pp. 354–60 (esp. 358–60); and, in particular, D. Carpenter, *The Struggle for Mastery. Britain 1066–1284* (Oxford, 2003), pp. 248–52.

14 Devizes, *Chronicle*, pp. 2–4; A. Bale, 'Fictions of Judaism in England before 1290', in *JMB*, ed. Skinner, pp. 129–44 (pp. 133–4). For William of Newburgh, see below.

15 Dobson, *JMY*, pp. 21–4. For a thoughtful discussion of the Hebrew accounts by Ephraim of Bonn (d. 1200), Joseph of Chartres (*c*. 1200) and Menahem of Worms (d. 1203), see A. Bale, *Feeling Persecuted: Christians, Jews and Images of Violence in the Middle Ages* (London, 2010), pp. 171–4. Ephraim of Bonn is trans. in Roth, *HJE*, p. 272

16 K. Norgate, 'The Date of Composition of William of Newburgh's History', *EHR* 19 (1904), 288–97. For William, see J. Taylor, 'Newburgh, William of', *ODNB* (Oxford, 2004); N. F. Partner, *Serious Entertainments: The Writing of History in Twelfth-Century England* (London, 1977); P. Biller, 'William of Newburgh and the Cathar Mission to England', in *Life and Thought in the Northern Church c.1100–c.1700: Essays in Honour of Claire Cross*, ed. Diana Wood, Studies in Church History: Subsidia 12 (Woodbridge, 1999), pp. 11–30.

17 There is a modern edition and translation of Bks I and II: *WN*, ed. Walsh & Kennedy. For the

unique among his contemporaries. His account of 'The Destruction ('exitio') of the Jews at York' and its consequences extends to three chapters (9–11) of Book Four, over eleven pages in the Latin edition, with three further chapters on preceding events. As is the case with much of his later books, his account was drawn from another Yorkshire historian, Roger of Howden, whose outline of events he expanded.[18] For the anti-Jewish violence William's efforts go far beyond mere embellishment. He emphasizes that these events, in particular, are 'greatly worthy of remembrance', and stresses his responsibility to transform public knowledge of recent happenings into a full report to be transmitted beyond living memory and into posterity. Newburgh's preface to his history famously denounces the mythologizing 'history' of Geoffrey of Monmouth; but it ends, too, with his own task, which he affirms in the first sentence of his dedicatory letter: to take those things that are great and memorable in his own times and commit them, on the page, to lasting memory. Only on two occasions in his history does he discuss his role, and posterity, so explicitly in this way: before the York massacre and before the anti-Jewish riots at Richard's coronation (the opening of Book IV).[19] For Newburgh, the anti-Jewish violence looms large in his sense of the meaning of the age he lived in and of his own responsibility as an historian. To him, the moment of 1190 was undeniable, both in the sense of its cosmic importance and as a point in time, shaping his era.

The events in York began at an ominous moment: a few days before the Christian Palm Sunday (the week before Good Friday and Easter) and the Jewish 'Shabbat ha-Gadol' (The Great Sabbath), the Sabbath before Passover to commemorate the pascal sacrifice obtained by Hebrew slaves in Egypt. As a fire raged through the city, Newburgh relates, a band of 'armed con-

---

later books, we still rely on the Rolls Series edition (WN, ed. Howlett) and an earlier translation: WN, trans. Stevenson, repr. as *The History of William of Newburgh* (Felinfach, 1996).

18 J. Gillingham, 'Two Yorkshire Historians Compared: Roger of Howden and William of Newburgh', *Haskins Society Journal* 12 (2003), 15–37. For William's treatment of the Jews, see Vincent, in this volume, and Kennedy, '"Faith"'.

19. The language is duplicated in his prefaces of both the London and York uprisings, suggesting a link in William's mind in their historical meaning. He prefaces the York massacre (Bk IV, ch. 9): 'Quod nimirum, quia valde memorabile est, *pleniori ad posteros oportet relatu transmitti*' (For without doubt, because this is greatly worthy of remembrance, it ought to be transmitted to posterity by a very full report). And the London riot (Bk IV, ch. 1): 'Res quidem recentis memoriae est, nullique ignota praesentium; sed operae pretium est *pleniori relatu transmittere ad posteros* tam perspicui circa gentem perfidam et blasphemam superni judicii monumentum' (Though this event is fresh in our memory, and unknown to none who are now living, yet it is worth the trouble to transmit it to posterity by a very full report, as an evident judgment from on high upon that perfidious and blasphemous race). Later (Bk V, ch. 24), William compares the efforts of ancient authors to commit all that is worthy of remembrance to writing with his own decision to select stories of revenants as a warning to posterity. There are briefer mentions, too, of his obligation to record for posterity (Bk III, cc. 15, 18), but not in the emphatic terms above. Citations are from WN, ed. Howlett, with minor emendations to the translation of Stevenson.

spirators', indebted local lords under the leadership of Richard Malebisse, took advantage of the confusion to burst into the home of the late Benedict of York, in life York's leading and wealthiest Jew. The conspirators killed Benedict's widow and sons and plundered and burned the house. When this was discovered, many of the city's Jews took refuge, with their valuables, in the royal castle. The conspirators then plundered the home of York's other Jewish leader, Josce, killing those of his household who remained behind. At this moment the violence shifted. The angry pillagers were joined by others who, Newburgh tells us, had long regarded the Jews with malice and, with them, the targets switched from York's wealthiest Jewish creditors to the Jewish community itself. The crowd now raged through the city, offering any Jews they found the choice of baptism, or death. Some feigned the former, in order to live; others were 'butchered without mercy' ('sine misericordia vero trucidati sunt'). Meanwhile, the frightened community in the castle did not know whom to trust and, the following day, refused to readmit the castle's own constable who angrily complained to the royal governor of Yorkshire. Urged by the conspirators to see this as an action against the king, the governor, now angry, ordered an assault on the castle. As word spread of the impending attack, armed mobs from the countryside and workmen and youths from the city gathered. This worried the governor who, regretting his initial response, rescinded his order; but it was too late. Stirred by the preaching of clergy and, in particular, a fervent Premonstratensian hermit, the mob ignored the governor and, at the end of a long day, brought siege engines into place.

That night, 16 March, 'Shabbat ha-Gadol', the Jews debated their fate. On the Great Sabbath rabbis preached an extensive sermon[20] and those huddled in the castle had among them a celebrated continental scholar, Rabbi Yom Tob of Joigny. He urged them, in a speech imagined by Newburgh, 'to prefer a glorious death to an infamous life' of false conversion and so follow the precedent set 'by many of our people' when faced with tribulation.[21] Some preferred to risk the mob, but the scholar (aged and 'most insane' according to Newburgh) encouraged the others to set fire to their valuables and the castle. Many men, including Josce, slit the throats of their wives and children before killing themselves. The next morning survivors threw themselves on the mercy of the Christian mob, pledging to be baptised. On discovering what had happened, many of the mob were horrified, and moved to pity. But the original conspirators, encouraged by Malebisse, gave false assurances and murdered the survivors as they emerged from the castle. The conspirators then marched to the Minster church where they demanded, then burned, the bonds stored there, evidences of Christian debt to Jews.

The definitive scholarly treatment of the massacre remains Barrie Dobson's

---

[20] I am indebted to Anthony Bale for this point, and for his comments more widely on this introduction.

[21] 'Hoc enim et multi nostrorum in diversis tribulationibus laudabiliter fecisse noscuntur, formam nobis decentissimae electionis praestruentes' (Bk IV, ch. 10).

1974 study. This traced the origins of the Jewish community in York, the events and perpetrators of 1190, the 'halcyon years' of the rejuvenated community in the 1220s and 1230s and its 'pulverising' decline in the 1250s and 1260s.[22] In particular, Dobson illuminated the late arrival of the Jewish community in York in the mid-1170s, induced by demand for credit and a royal government offering protection. This was in the midst of a period of swift change in relations between the crown, moneylenders, and Northern debtors. In 1164 the crown had abruptly shifted its reliance from Christian to Jewish credit and in 1186 Aaron of Lincoln, the Jewish lender who dominated English credit, died.[23] Freed from Aaron's near-monopoly in the North and answering growing demands of Yorkshire landlords for credit, the Jewish community developed swiftly in York as its own credit nexus, under the leadership of Josce and Benedict of York. Pipe roll evidence supports Newburgh's report that indebted lords from the nearby countryside led the charge, supported by labourers and clerks, as the Christian notables of the city 'declined to take part'. Dobson also identified key factors that fanned the violence: a growing European climate of anti-semitism, ritual murder accusations against English Jews, and recent attacks on Jews in Northern France. More immediately, the Angevin build-up to the Third Crusade was underpinned by a policy of rapacious financial exaction. Other national policies had acute consequences in York, which was in the throes of a 'crisis of authority'. It had been without an archbishop for ten years, had lost its mighty sheriff, Ranulf de Glanville, in 1189 and now saw its key regional leaders abroad.[24] Dobson's work demonstrated how many threads from Angevin England, and Christendom more widely, wove together to give form to the York massacre.

In March 2010 a three-day conference in York drew together leading scholars from the US, the UK, Israel and France with the aim of following those threads back into the society from which they emerged. This volume is the fruit of that exchange. It explores the massacre not as an event that sits apart from the 'long, quiet history of friendly intercourse and business dealings between Jew and Gentile', but as a calamity – dissonant, shocking, yet readily imagined by those who participated and those who recorded it for posterity alike – that belonged to its time, that was created within and, in turn, acted to shape the society from which it so shockingly erupted. The essays here comprise a multi- and inter-disciplinary collection by historians, literary scholars, theologians and art historians. While contributions develop themes inspired by Dobson's work, the essays contribute new materials, interpretations and approaches that reflect the ways in which the humanities in general and scholarly research of this period in particular has changed in the last four decades. In addition to chronicle accounts and royal records,

---

22 Dobson, *JMY*, and his reflections, in *JMB*, ed. Skinner (2003) and *JCME* (2010).
23 Dobson, *JMY*, pp. 6–11; Richardson, *EJ*, pp. 60–6, 115–7, 161–3.
24 Dobson, *JMY*, pp. 24–37.

materials include Hebrew legal texts and primers, literary texts, charters, stained glass, miracle stories, and heritage plaques. Interpretations derive both from this new material and from the influence of new approaches to the past, which include here questions of narrative, memory, neighbourliness, bodies and space, post-colonialism and ethics. The essays are grouped here under three headings: the events of 1190 and their contexts; Jewish communities among Christians in England; and representations of Jews in text, image and memory. The essays speak to one another across these divides. Together, they explore the contexts – social, financial, governmental, theological, and literary – of the violence and its aftermath in England, as well as the problem of memory. In so doing they put anti-Jewish violence and the broader challenge (on both sides) of Jews living among Christians at the heart of the society and history of Angevin England. Our cover image depicts the scene at the rear centre of the Cloisters Cross, where a blind Synogoga pierces the Lamb of God. One of a number of anti-Judaic scenes that decorate this devotional object, it highlights how at the heart of medieval faith lay tense religious identities, framed in opposition, yet intertwined, and too easily suffused with the memory and threat of violence.[25] Produced in England *c.* 1150x70, it has been associated with Bury St Edmunds and so with a wider pattern of events there including the 'martyrdom' of little Robert (d. 1181), complaints about the access of Jewish moneylenders, the local massacre of 1190 and, later that year, the expulsion of the Jews from the town.[26]

As many essays stress, and the Cloisters Cross makes vivid, the York massacre was neither an isolated nor merely a local event. It was national in origin and reach, and it played out on an international (even cosmic) stage. Its first victim was not a member of Benedict's mourning family, but Benedict himself who, with Josce, had travelled to Richard's coronation. Caught in the ensuing riots, Benedict had been forced to convert but died of his wounds, depriving York of its wealthiest Jewish leader.[27] Its context, however, extended further even than London. Jerusalem itself had fallen out of Christian hands in 1187, prompting calls for a new crusade and hand-wringing about the state of Christian Europe. Contemporaries recognized York as the most appalling of a wave of anti-Jewish riots, which many were quick to associate with preparations for crusade. Joseph Hillaby charts the course of the violence as it spread through provincial towns in eastern England between January and March. He considers the evidence for each act or allegation and

---

[25] E. C. Parker and C. T. Little, *The Cloisters Cross: Its Art and Meaning* (London, 1994), p. 16, 35–42. Inscriptions along the cross's shaft and edges affiliate 'synogoga' with death and 'ecclesia' with life, and portray the Jews mocking the Crucifixion (and so denying Christ), ibid., p. 52.

[26] ibid., pp. 36-8; P. R. Hyams, 'The Jews in Medieval England, 1066–1290', in *England and Germany in the High Middle Ages*, ed. Alfred Haverkamp et al. (Oxford, 1996), pp. 173-92 (pp. 180-1).

[27] Dobson, *JMY*, pp. 8–9.

the consequences for the local Jewry of the town. He stresses the importance of local circumstances in constructing the motives, shape and reach (or limit) of the violence. Chief among these was the presence of episcopal or royal authority in the town to intervene swiftly or offer a castle as refuge. Alan Cooper compares the uprisings of 1189/90 with the 1196 revolt of William Longbeard to explore wider tensions between the powerful and the poor under the Angevin regime. His piece, as does that of Hillaby, reinforces the sense of danger created by a country preparing for crusade. Yet it thinks, too, about the emotional dramas that could be played out as crusaders of all classes returned, psychologically scarred and quick to feel betrayed by the corruption or simple failure of those in charge. As Sarah Rees Jones makes clear, the city of York had been a victim of extreme, but alternating, royal policies since the Conquest as the crown first brutally refashioned then largely abandoned the city. Politically frustrated citizens not only laboured under punishing royal exactions but now found themselves in competition with a newly-arrived Jewish community who were agents of royal moneylending and, after Aaron of Lincoln's death in 1186, the new hub of northern credit. Rees Jones' examination of those fined for the massacre reveals Anglo-Scandinavian families who had resisted royal authority in the past and led calls for the city's independence. Together these essays stress the very live question of royal authority at this time: its necessity, its heavy-handedness, the identity and powers of its agents and what this meant for those who lived, day by day, under its constraints.

Others take Newburgh's work as their subject, asking us to think about the ways in which texts remember and, in turn, act to create memory. Heather Blurton considers how after 1189/90 Christian chroniclers appropriated the language of Exodus and Lamentations instead of Christ's passion to explain anti-Jewish violence. To Newburgh, England itself was transformed 'into an Egypt where their fathers had endured harsh things'.[28] This language marked a wider shift in Christian thinking about the nature of Jewish crimes, from crucifixion to perfidy, and its inevitable remedy: Jewish exile. Nicholas Vincent unpicks Newburgh's account of the massacre itself to consider how Newburgh expanded Howden's text and how deeply two other sources underpin his embellishment: the account of Masada by the first-century Jewish historian, Josephus, and the Vulgate Bible, in particular Matthew 27. Reacting to the recent fall of Jerusalem in 1187, Newburgh sought meaning for contemporary events within a world chronology. The use of Josephus brought a sense of timelessness to the violence, casting it as a replay of Masada. Matthew 27, part of the liturgy on Palm Sunday, was employed to reflect upon (and denounce) the actions of the perpetrators. In so doing, Vincent challenges our own memory of the massacre, since this is based upon a text which finds the form and meaning of the violence in

---

[28] WN, ed. Howlett, p. 294.

liturgy and ancient history. We are left to ask not only what did happen but also what it is that we are remembering? This is a theme taken up by Jeffrey Cohen, who prompts us to read against Newburgh's narrative by recognizing his tales as narrative choices. Medieval Jews were trapped in text by narrative inevitabilities that cast them as a 'timeless and petrified type', so their future was pre-determined. By releasing them from these consuming narratives, we might glimpse historical Jews in their present, integrated into a wider story and the 'complicatedly multicultural' society it reflected. Here we might glimpse Jewish neighbours as adaptable participants in an urban economy, living with Christian servants, performing pranks, their children running through the house with Christian playmates. As many of the essays in this collection suggest, the models through which meanings are ascribed shape the telling of the events and so, in turn, the material that has been left to us. At times, a model or meaning can be so powerful that it can threaten to become the memory, subsuming events or circumstances.

Behind the horror of the violence of 1189/90 we can glimpse a more routine, but no less powerful, story of Christian-Jewish relations: one of financial, political and even religious interdependence. Members of Jewish communities were key components in the machinery of English state and economy. They linked government to localities and both to the credit necessary to lubricate the booming economy, taxation and property market of the late twelfth century. Robert Stacey overturns the idea of the 'archae' and the Jewish Exchequer as institutions born of the massacres of 1190. He argues that they had deeper roots, in the English royal claim of monopoly over the Jews, a claim which intensified under the Angevins to encompass legal monopoly in 1178 and political dominance under Richard and John. The 1194 regulation of Jewish debts, which inaugurated the 'archae', and the justices of the Jews from 1198 were the machinery of financial monopoly, informed by lessons learned in the administration of Aaron of Lincoln's debts and by the need for a robust apparatus to counter fraud and absorb expanding business. Yet these claims to monopoly cannot be divorced from the violence of 1190: new Jewish tallages in 1186 and 1188 had forced Jewish creditors to pressurize debtors while the intensifying political claim ended seigneurial Jewish communities and defined Jews as the king's men. Robin Mundill traces the workings of the 'archa' system, which recorded Jewish loans in chests administered by local Christians and Jews together. Mundill examines their range of duties, illuminating close working relationships among the leaders of both faiths and in towns across England. Here we see Christians and Jews forming contracts, collecting royal tallages, serving together on juries, and even conspiring in crime. Its innovations, Mundill argues, were later imitated for Christian creditors.

Interdependence was not limited to the realms of finance and government. Jews and Christians were confronted, intellectually as well as practically, with the challenge of living together. Pinchas Roth and Ethan Zadoff shed new light on the English tosafist community, Jewish scholars who moved between Northern France, Mainz and England from the later-twelfth century. In the work of Elijah Menahem of London (fl. 1250s–70s) they detect a distinctive identity within English Jewish scholarship and among English Jews. English tosafists were peculiarly practical in their approach. Drawn to Maimonides and the Mishneh Torah, they aimed to engage with the local customs and create a body of ritual law for daily practice and wide dissemination. The essay highlights the efforts of smaller Halakhic communities to adapt Jewish law to local circumstances and yet retain distinctive identities while engaging with neighbouring Jewish communities. It also underscores the reach of the tragedies of 1189/90, which killed two of England's three leading tosafists: Jacob of Orleans in London and Yom Tob of Joigny in York. Eva De Visscher examines primers that were made or adapted for Christians to learn Hebrew. Their interplay between script, language and faith suggests that Christians adapted material, perhaps to assert their own religious identity as they ventured into Jewish terrain. She evokes a complex multicultural society where Christians and Jews were aware of and responding to the other but always from a fundamentally different vantage point. Each inhabited a separate world, defined by their own faith. This is a point taken up by Matthew Mesley, who considers a twelfth-century miracle story of the healing and conversion of a Jewish woman from Lincoln. He situates the tale within wider patterns of anti-Jewish stereotypes, often textual constructions, and intensifying ecclesiastical concerns about sacred spaces where real Jews walked. The tale itself, as well as the Jewish woman in its service, reinforced for its Christian audience eternal boundaries that were in danger of being blurred through mundane social intercourse. Indeed, the challenge of different faith worlds sharing material spaces is one that echoes through the essays in this volume. Carlee Bradbury considers images of the Jew at the funeral of the Virgin Mary, in a psalter, books of hours and stained glass. In monocultural (here, Christian) spaces, so safely removed from the complexities of actual coexistence, images of the faithless other could be taken to an extreme. As the Jew becomes increasingly less human from the thirteenth century, these images lay bare the fears of intrusion, even violation that could underlie such coexistence.

The question of faith (and perfidy) was thus woven into the fabric of medieval law and society. As neighbours, financiers, business partners, servants, tradesmen, tenants and landlords, Christians and Jews were engaged in routine relationships whose small reciprocal gestures should have built trust but in fact, Paul Hyams argues, came to sow ever more suspicion and revulsion. He situates these quotidian encounters within a corrosive fabric that bound Christians and Jews. Each retained a faith identity that was assertive, and even violent, in its appraisal of the other. In Angevin England 'faith' became intertwined with 'making faith', that is the acts of fealty, oath and being 'fidelis', one who is loyal and trustworthy. By not being able to pledge their faith, Jews navigated daily life in Christian England with a social disability that challenged their status as landholders, lords, vassals and witnesses. It compromised their ability to give their word in matters great (conversion) and small (routine business transactions) and ate at the heart of their relationships with neighbours. The mechanisms for forming legal agreements are examined by Thomas Roche who situates several Cistercian charters not sealed 'because of the perfidy of the Jews' within the social rituals of trust that surrounded the making of an agreement. Jews and Christians responded, he argues, by creating a distinctive 'hybrid' diplomatic formed by tokens of faith (formulas and Latin that mimicked Hebrew) that one could make and the other acknowledge, and so receive. Anna Abulafia also stresses the 'lively interaction' and mutual adaptation of Jews and Christians as they navigated life in homes, on streets, in trade and finance or at table. These were conducted within two powerful frameworks: one theological; one political, regulated in law. These defined the role of Jews in (often conflicting) terms of their service or utility. Jews were defined by occupations that were permitted them, so when the crown redefined Jewish service, Jewish existence was turned upside down. Jews in Angevin England lived lives, to a large degree, defined by others. Many essays reflect the consequence of two faiths that were alien in concept but whose adherents lived their lives in routine proximity. This tension could find expression in the details of daily life. The nature and consequences of oaths, for example, were contentious issues for Jews in Christian society and for Christians making, or breaking, agreements with Jews.

At the heart of this collection lies the problem of memory: whose memories (and of what); how memories create models and how models, in turn, can define what is remembered; and the dialogues between history, memory and meaning that give shape to both the remembered past and possible futures. At times, this can be a question of literary models or cultural archetypes, which challenge us to ask how far a text has captured elements of the historical events it purports to discuss. At the very least, it captures one author's assertion of his idea of meaning over complex, chaotic events in his time. But the consuming narratives we find in histories (in part *through* those histories, but reinforced, too, by liturgy, elegy and drama) could lurk ominously behind the daily web of interactions that made up urban life. Models and memories could haunt events themselves. In offering a shared narrative, they can suggest a definition to confusing events as they are unfolding and so, in their way, give form to the present. And the more dreaded a 'memory', the greater its power might be. Could this have played a part in the violence of 1190? Newburgh thought so, judging that the citizens of Lincoln rose up, 'seizing the opportunity and animated by precedent' (Bk IV, ch. 9). Hyams suggests it is likely that report-chronicles of martyrdoms on the continent circulated among the English Jewish community 'to sharpen fears and exhort them to imitation of their forbears if the feared occasion arose' (p. 137). Might these have haunted the Jews of York in those terrifying days of March? Rabbi Yom Tob, the tosafist scholar identified as the elder who exhorted the Jewish community of York to self-martyrdom, was the author of an elegy for the martyrs of Blois in 1171.[29] Whatever the significance of 'eternal' models on the immediate events, the essays make plain that there was nothing inevitable about the course of the violence of 1190 nor simply 'timeless' in its meaning. The very challenge of Christian living with Jew, and Jew with Christian, in Angevin England ran far deeper than the horrific events of 1189/90. As Newburgh recognized, it sat at the core of Anglo-Christian as well as Anglo-Jewish history.

Nor can we leave the problem of memory solely to the past. Hannah Johnson's contribution directly confronts 'the work of memory' through the lens of ethics and methodology in historical scholarship. What are historians and their sources doing when writing the history of martyrdom and what are our responsibilities in reaffirming – or challenging – the memory of violence? When narrative and memory become intertwined, and together constitute a form of justice for the victims, questions of historical contingency become ethically difficult. Can we, Johnson asks, uncover an ethics of contingency? Finally, in an epilogue, Anthony Bale considers the modern memorial nature of 1190 to challenge us to think about Anglo-Jewry beyond trauma. What we choose to publicly remember, where, and why acts to construct a memory and our idea of the events. A contemporary pleasure in being smugly, safely shocked that 'on this spot, occurred something horribly medieval' can become the framework by which we publicly construct our past. While many pasts can be objects of this process, our Jewish past can fall too readily victim, a continuing sign of 'the unstable status of England's medieval Jewish community and the abiding memories, medieval and modern, surrounding it' (p. 304).

Together, the essays in this collection stress the complex challenge that confronted Christians and Jews living together in Angevin England. Theirs was a world that was in one sense routinely multicultural. Jewish communities lived in towns across England, carrying out professions that relied on Christians and on which Christians relied. Christians and Jews were neighbours, employers, servants, business associates, power-brokers and suppliants, even friends. They shared domestic and economic space, public and ceremonial space. The existence of each was framed by the presence of the other. Yet, as Hyams points out, each 'felt they lived in a religious monoculture' (p.133). Each faith-world, at best, struggled conceptually to accommodate the other; at worst, it could harbour an aggressive, even (and increasingly from the Christian side) violent sense of its identity in the face of the other. The relationship was thus intimate, yet alien; routine, yet eternal. The difficulty became most acute when spaces or moments were transformed from mundane to sacred. Since public space in Angevin England was largely Christian, and our sources overwhelmingly so, we see this most readily in terms of Christian shifts to which local Jews were subject. It might

---

[29] Dobson, *JMY*, p. 19.

happen when a public street became the site of a religious procession or during periods such as Lent, Easter or the build-up to crusade. At these moments a space could become timeless, as the boundaries between past, present and even eternity were elided. Then, the gaze of a known unbeliever became a vehicle through which participants could observe, and perhaps doubt, themselves. The problem of living, and believing, in the presence of the other raised questions of faith, identity, oaths, loyalty, leadership, and neighbourliness. As medieval chroniclers recognized, these may be played out locally or nationally but they challenged both Jews and Christians to see themselves in cosmic terms.

1

Neighbours and Victims in Twelfth-Century York a Royal Citadel, the Citizens and the Jews of York

Sarah Rees Jones

Barrie Dobson's wide-ranging and richly-detailed study of the massacre of the Jews of York in March 1190 remains the definitive history of that terrible event.[1] Most importantly he demonstrated that the massacre did not mark the end of a Jewish community in the city but rather occurred near its beginning: very soon after their first settlement under Josce and Benedict of York in the 1170s and 1180s. The return of Jews to York after 1190, and the new Jewish community which flourished in the early thirteenth century, was the subject of later papers by Dobson, now reprinted in a single volume.[2]

Here we do not try to cover the same ground. Where Dobson's history focussed on the Jews of York and the national context for the events in March 1190, this chapter deals in more depth with the city of York itself, both as a place and as a community in the later twelfth century. Modern memorialization of the massacre of March 1190 has become indelibly associated with Clifford's Tower, at the foot of which there is now a plaque of commemoration for the victims of 1190. Yet this stone structure was built some fifty years after the massacre and named another eighty years after that: it was not the structure in which the massacre occurred. The stone tower does stand on the site of a previous wooden castle keep, which stood on top of a smaller earth motte at the centre of a castle first constructed by William the Conqueror in 1068-69.[3] It is usually assumed that this was the site of the mass suicide and murder of the Jews in March 1190. However scholars have long known that even this is simply a best guess for identifying the royal 'arx' at the centre of William of Newburgh's narrative, and other interpretations have been sug-

---

[1] Dobson, *JMY*.
[2] *JCME*.
[3] RCHME, *City of York*, II, 57–89; T. P. Cooper, *York: The Story of its Walls, Bars and Castles* (London, 1904); T. P. Cooper, *The History of the Castle of York from its Foundation to the Present Day* (London, 1911); *King's Works*, II, 889–994; J. Clark, *Clifford's Tower and the Castle of York* (London, 2010).

gested.[4] It is clear that the story of York as the place of the massacre is more complex than the image of this single later solid stone structure.

The history of York as a city and community in the twelfth century has been little studied. In part this is because of the paucity of evidence. Archaeological work has focussed primarily on the city before the Norman Conquest, or on the period after 1300 from which standing buildings survive in abundance. Documentary sources are also problematic. No civic archives survive before the 1260s and references to York in the records of royal government do not easily provide a narrative of local people, places or events. Their focus is primarily on royal administration and so, too, is that of the chroniclers, such as Newburgh and Howden. The major local documentary sources for York in the twelfth century are charters recording land transactions in the city, which survive as originals and as copies in later cartularies.[5] This chapter will integrate the evidence of these charters with the better-known chronicles and royal records before 1200.

York and its inhabitants are even neglected in narratives of the 'York Massacre', largely due to the perception of them as both unimportant in and disengaged from the events of 1190. This can in part be traced back to the statement of William of Newburgh that 'the more noble and substantial citizens of the town, fearing the dangers of the king's reaction, cautiously declined to take part in such madness', a statement which makes an even greater impression when it is contrasted with his clear apportionment of blame to the citizens of Lincoln for the attack upon the Jewish community there.[6] As a result attention has instead focussed on those whom Newburgh did blame for the York attack; the Yorkshire knights Richard Malebisse, William Percy, Marmaduke Darrell and Philip de Fauconberg.[7] However, as Alan Cooper reminds us, it was not only knights, but also working men, youths and countrymen whom Newburgh blamed; only the more substantial citizens of York were exonerated by him.[8]

This focus on knights as the real leaders of an unruly 'mob' in 1190 should be treated cautiously for it was almost conventional by the later twelfth century to represent cities as a civilizing influence against the endemic vio-

---

4   Vincent, in this volume (p. 75); P. V. Addyman, 'Excavations at Baile Hill, York', *Château Gaillard. Etudes de Castellogie Médiévale* 5 (1972), 7–12 (pp. 7–10); P. V. Addyman and J. Priestley, 'Baile Hill, York', *Archaeological Journal* 134 (1977), 115–56, and see below p. 32.
5   Some 2,500 charters survive for York in the twelfth and thirteenth centuries: S. Rees Jones, *Medieval Title Deeds for the City of York, 1080–1530* (Colchester: UK History Data Archive, 1996), SN:3527; S. Rees Jones, *The Database of Medieval Title Deeds for the City of York: A Guide for Users, University of York Occasional Papers in History* 3 (York, 1996). A book length study of these materials is forthcoming: S. Rees Jones, *Medieval York: The Making of a City, 1068–1350* (Oxford University Press).
6   WN as translated in Dobson, *JMY*, p. 32. For Lincoln see Hillaby in this volume.
7   Dobson, *JMY*, p. 33.
8   Cooper, below p. 95.

lence of the knightly classes.[9] This rhetoric was influenced by real politics. Henry II (1154–89) and his sons Richard I (1189–99) and John (1199–1216) tried to build partnerships with major towns in the provinces throughout the Angevin realms in France as well as England in order to restrain the local power of the aristocracy.[10] In the north this meant building a relationship with the citizens of York and eroding the influence of local barons such as Roger de Mowbray and William, count of Aumale and earl of York, who had taken control of the city and its region during the wars of Stephen's reign (1135–54). As the chief city of the north, York was exceptionally important to the crown. It was the only city in the region under royal control and its strategic importance was pivotal in the wars between the kings of England and Scotland. The crown could not afford to alienate its leading citizens, but building a relationship with them was difficult too. This complex, often strained, relationship between crown and city provides a critical context for understanding both the arrival and reception of Jews in York.

The scale of the ambitions of William I, William II and Henry I in relation to York and their transformative impact on the city have not been fully appreciated. We know that substantial changes were made to other towns, such as the construction of the French borough in Nottingham or of the new town centre in Norwich.[11] In the cases of Lincoln and Exeter their elevation as new cathedral sees resulted in their major redevelopment.[12] In contrast, established interpretations of the topography of York argue that the medieval street plan was largely established before the Conquest, during the tenth and eleventh centuries, when a new pattern of markets and streets was superimposed upon the older Roman town plan.[13] After the Norman conquest two castles were constructed and York Minster was reconstructed on a new alignment by the first Norman archbishop of York, but it is usually argued that the overall street plan of the city remained largely unaltered.[14] However both new evidence, and a reappraisal of older knowledge, suggests that the Norman refashioning of York was much more extensive than this and that it reflected the ambition of the first Norman kings to turn York into a true royal capital in the North. This ambition ultimately proved unsustainable. Nevertheless it produced a set of consequences that were instrumental not

---

9   P. Godding and J. Pycke, 'Le Paix de Valenciennes de 1114: Commentaire et édition critique', *Bulletin de la Commission Royale pour la publication des anciennes lois et ordonnances de Belgique* 29 (1981), 1–142.

10   M. Aurell, *The Plantagenet Empire, 1154–1224* (Harlow, 2007), pp. 194–5.

11   D. M. Palliser, T. R. Slater and E. P. Dennison, 'The Topography of Towns 600–1300', in *The Cambridge Urban History of Britain I: 600–1540*, ed. D. M. Palliser (Cambridge, 2000), pp. 153–86 (p. 160); B. Ayers, 'The Urban Landscape', in *Medieval Norwich*, ed. C. Rawcliffe and R. Wilson (London, 2004), pp. 1–28.

12   M. Jones, D. Stocker and A. Vince, *The City by the Pool: Assessing the Archaeology of the City of Lincoln* (Oxford, 2003).

13   R. Hall, *English Heritage Book of Viking Age York* (London, 1994).

14   ibid.; D. M. Palliser, *Domesday York*, Borthwick Papers 78 (York, 1990).

only to the arrival of a Jewish community in York but also to the reception of that community by local burgesses.

The Norman transformation of York addressed the problem for the crown that before 1068 there was no direct royal presence in the city.[15] The first kings of England, from the reign of Edgar (959–75) to that of Edward the Confessor (1042–66), never visited York. Instead lordship over the city and its region was delegated to the archbishops of York and the earls of Northumbria. The ancient and extensive lordship of the archbishop of York centred on the two collegiate churches of St Peter (York Minster) and Christ Church in Micklegate, which were located respectively in the centre of the former Roman fortress and in the 'colonia', or civilian town, on either side of the river Ouse. This lordship probably originated with the foundation in the seventh century of York Minster around which a new town slowly developed outside the Roman walls, while the church also acquired estates incorporating much of York's rural hinterland. The earldom of Northumbria was established in the later tenth century and appears to have been endowed with urban and rural estates near York which were carved from those of the church. By the mid eleventh century its principal residence was in Bootham where there was also a new church dedicated to St Olave. In 1066 the combined rural estates of the Minster and the earl extended across most of York's immediate rural hinterland within a radius of about fifteen miles. In 1086 many of these villages also paid geld with the city and it was only later that they were assigned to separate hundreds or wapentakes.[16] There is no evidence for a royal residence in the city during the eleventh century and the crown controlled no rural manors close to York from which such an urban residence could have been supported.

This situation was dramatically altered after the Conquest. The first Norman kings transformed York into a royal capital as destruction in the years of conquest was followed by extensive redevelopment. William I built two castles in 1068-69, one on either side of the river Ouse, and his decisive suppression of fierce local resistance resulted in both the devastation of many houses in the city and a wholesale replacement of local landowners with Frenchmen. The 'harrying of the north' in the winter of 1069-70 extended into the countryside this policy of the appropriation of estates through which the king himself emerged as the largest new landowner in the county together with a small number of Norman barons.[17] The first Norman kings also constructed a royal house ('domus regis') in York. This occupied a very large site on the west bank of the Ouse close to the major approach road to

---

15 The following section discusses briefly materials which are laid out much more fully in Rees Jones, *Medieval York*. See also S. Rees Jones, 'Property, Tenure and Rents: Some Aspects of the Topography and Economy of Medieval York', 2 vols. (unpublished D.Phil. dissertation, University of York, 1987), I, 81–133.

16 Domesday Book, 298 b–d.

17 P. Dalton, *Conquest, Anarchy and Lordship: Yorkshire, 1066–1154* (Cambridge, 1994).

the town used by royal visitors.[18] It is probable that it occupied most of the area (some 300 m by 100 m) within the Roman walls of the former 'colonia' to the west of modern Tanner Row, and it perhaps extended as far as the banks of the Ouse. It had a chapel dedicated to Mary Magdalene and was used for meetings of the county court: the custodian of the York royal house was required to provide benches for these meetings and wax for the court's use was stored in the chapel.[19] It was regarded as one of the most important royal houses in England: in the early 1130s the hereditary custodian of the house was granted a fee of 5d. per day, just 2d. less than the keeper of the palace at Westminster.[20]

Such a royal residence needed to be supplied and much of the town and the surrounding countryside was turned into a supporting economic infrastructure. A royal larder was situated on the east bank of the river Ouse. It was close to the site of the original Roman river crossing, which may have survived in use as the most direct route between the royal house, the larder and the Minster.[21] The larder occupied a defensible site just within the walls of the Roman garrison, which at that time were still standing to a height of several metres.[22] The larder was also associated with an open area known as 'Arkilltofts', just possibly the site of the former residence of the Anglo-Scandinavian thegn, Arnketil, who was among the leaders of resistance to the Conquest in 1068 and 1069. Royal larderers sought to control local markets and Arkilltofts may well have developed into a marketplace under their authority, later becoming the civic market place, the 'Thursday Market', in the thirteenth century (now St Sampson's Square).[23] The larderer's authority also extended over the city's summer fair ground which was outside the walls and was shared with the archbishops.[24]

Norman authority over the site of the fair ground was further marked by a chapel dedicated to St Giles, a new cult brought to England by the French around 1100. Other new churches were dedicated to saints popular with the new Anglo-Norman and French elite, including the churches of St Helen (the mother of Constantine) in Stonegate and St Sampson, which were built near to the royal larder and in close proximity to the vestigial remains of the

---

[18] RCHME, *City of York* III, 53; *King's Works* I, 42–7.

[19] *EYC* I, pp. 405–6, nos. 525–6, whose date is corrected in *Rolls of the Justices in Eyre: Being the Rolls of Pleas and Assizes for Yorkshire in 3 Henry III (1218–19)*, ed. D. M. Stenton, Selden Society 56 (London, 1937), p. 420.

[20] *Rolls of the Justices in Eyre*, pp. 419–20; RCHME, *City of York* III, 53; *King's Works* I, 82.

[21] R. B. Pugh, 'Prisons and Gallows', in *VCH, City of York*, pp. 491–8 (pp. 494–7). For the river crossing see below, pp. 21–2.

[22] BL MS Cotton Nero D. III, fol. 115r; York Archaeological Trust, York Archive Gazetteer, '44, Coney Street/Feasegate, York. Site Code: 1998.2 YORYM, SE60305182', http://www.iadb.co.uk/gaz/gaz_details.php?SiteID=1055 [accessed 1 July 2008].

[23] *Charters of the Vicars Choral of York Minster*, ed. N. Tringham, 2 vols., YAS, Rec. Ser. 148 and 156 (Leeds, 1993–2002), I, 33–4.

[24] H. Richardson, *Medieval Fairs and Markets of York* (York, 1961).

Roman fortress walls and gates.[25] St Giles was particularly associated with hunting and the royal larderers also policed and defended the king's right to hunting in local forests. Indeed, in one of the most radical transformations of the landscape of kingship in England, the entire countryside surrounding York within a radius of fifteen miles had been turned into royal forest by around 1100.[26] Hunting was tremendously important to the display of king-ship in the twelfth century. It conveyed simultaneously territorial, military and economic dominance. So this transformation of the landscape in par-ticular was indicative of the early Norman kings' ambition for York.

The economic infrastructure for the royal house was further enhanced by the flooding of the river Foss and the creation of a royal fishpool in the city centre (also with a royal custodian) just upstream from the new castle in Nessgate (which was renamed Castlegate).[27] The tenants of the crown's nearest larger rural manors, at Boroughbridge some twenty miles upriver from York, were also freed from all tolls on the passage of their ships into the city. This was a privilege which later brought them into dispute with the city but it may originally have been intended to facilitate the supply of the royal establishment in York.[28]

The growth of the royal presence in York was at the expense of the earls of Northumbria. By 1086 the city itself was formally divided for administra-tive purposes between the fee of the archbishop and the fee of the king. The king's fee included all commercial districts alongside the two river fronts in the city which archaeological excavations have shown to have been urban-ized over the course of the tenth and eleventh centuries. There is no refer-ence to the earl's estate in York in 1086 because it was at that time in the process of being transferred to a new Norman foundation, the Benedictine monastery of St Mary. Indeed the transformation of York's religious insti-tutions further underpinned the new Norman colonization. In addition to the foundation of new parish churches and chapels, a number of major new religious foundations were endowed by the Norman kings and their French followers. The Minster was rebuilt and its community reformed while Christ Church in Micklegate was refounded as a Benedictine priory, now depend-ent on a French mother house and dedicated to Holy Trinity. A number of lesser religious houses and hospitals were established in the city's suburbs, including a convent for nuns in Clementhorpe. Most importantly, the hospi-tal of St Peter (later rededicated to St Leonard) was established on a promi-

---

[25] 'The Parish Churches', in *VCH, City of York*, pp. 365–404; RCHME, *City of York* V, 20a, 44a. The church of St Sampson is constructed on top of the Roman wall. The church of St Helen is constructed just within the site of the southern entrance to the former Roman fortress.

[26] *VCH, East Riding* III, 1–28; *VCH, City of York*, p. 501; C. R. Young, *The Royal Forests of Medieval England* (Leicester, 1979), p. 21.

[27] S. Rees Jones, with C. Daniell, 'The King's Pool', in *Medieval Urbanism in Coppergate: Refining a Townscape*, ed. R. Hall and K. Hunter-Mann (York, 2002), pp. 696–8.

[28] *Rolls of the Justices in Eyre*, p. 392.

nent site within the Roman fortress area not far from the royal larder and occupying an equally impressive corner of the surviving fortress walls.[29] St Leonard's, in particular, was patronized by the earliest Norman kings and was one of the largest hospitals in England, on a par with the great hospital of St Bartholomew in London. The hospital's cartulary later celebrated William I and II as its re-founders but memorialized King Stephen as a particularly important patron, together with many of the most prominent Yorkshire barons, knights and burgesses of early to mid twelfth-century York.[30]

Finally it is likely that the city defences were incorporated into this reconstruction of the city. The overall alignment of major sections of the defences may have originated in the Roman period but it is clear that the actual defences were frequently reworked, resulting eventually in long sections of the Roman walls being buried in an earth embankment with (at first) a timber palisade on top. Also, new sections of defences were added to the central core of the former Roman garrison area around York Minster connecting it to the two rivers (the Foss and the Ouse), while the two sides of the garrison area defences within this newly enclosed area were gradually abandoned. Houses, gardens and one church (the church of St Sampson) were constructed in their place. Two of the medieval stone gateways into the city at Micklegate Bar and Bootham Bar contain monumental early Norman stone arches, suggesting that they were part of a considerable strengthening of the defences around Micklegate and Petergate, as well as the confirmation of those streets as major routes into and across the city.[31] It is possible that they marked processional routes linking all the major churches (Holy Trinity priory in Micklegate, the Minster and St Mary's abbey) with the sites of royal power (the royal house, the royal larder, St Leonard's hospital, and the fair ground at St Giles). While we have no clear archaeological evidence for the date of this reconstruction or for the extension of the walls of the Roman garrison to the rivers Ouse and Foss, the latter must have been in place by 1177 when the Jewish cemetery was located outside.[32] Medieval Jewish cemeteries were always located outside city walls and the site of the York cemetery occupies what was probably the only such area which was both within the king's fee and not already developed.

If we take all these developments together we can see that the early Norman kings redeveloped the entire city as an extension of, and service centre to, a new royal palace: a royal citadel ('arx') indeed. Mapping these developments on to a base map of Roman York shows the extent to which these royal sites re-utilized still impressive, visible aspects of the city's Roman topography and architecture, which were clustered around a focus on the site

---

[29] RCHME, *City of York* V, 93–94.
[30] BL MS Cotton Nero D. III, fol. 3r; W. Page, 'Hospitals: York', in *VCH, Yorkshire* III, 336–52.
[31] RCHME, *City of York* II, 95–101, 116–120.
[32] S. Rees Jones, 'The Historical Background', in J. M. Lilley et al., *The Jewish Burial Ground at Jewbury* (London, 1994), pp. 301–12.

of the original Roman crossing over the river Ouse, suggesting that this was still in use in at least some form (whether as bridge or ferry). Coney Street, Blake Street and North Street all converge on the site of this crossing and were the only three streets in York in the early twelfth century whose names ended in the Latin (or English) suffix –street '–straet' or '–strata' rather than the Old Norse –gate or '–gata'.[33] They were part of a network of adjacent streets in the king's fee including Davygate (named after David the Larderer, *c.* 1135–80) and Castlegate which can only have acquired their names after the Conquest.[34]

Above all the refashioning of the entire city as a centre of Christian *imperium* reflected contemporary historical writing about York. Since the time of Bede this had always asserted the centrality of York's ecclesiastical mission: that royal authority was built upon Christian foundations, and that the city of York was a central monument to that imperial achievement.[35] And of course it was at just this moment, in about 1138, that Geoffrey of Monmouth was elaborating on that tradition in his inventive *History of Britain* which claimed a Trojan origin for the princes of Britain. Monmouth's *History* linked the origins of York in particular with the origins of the Christian faith itself. Ebrauc, the mythical Trojan prince who Monmouth claimed as the founder of York, lived in the time of David, king of Judea, whose own city, Bethlehem, was the chosen birthplace of Christ. According to Monmouth, York became the seat of one of the three pagan high priests of Britain, the archflamens, and was thus a natural choice for the seat of an archbishopric when Britain was converted to Christianity.[36] Indeed throughout Monmouth's *History* it is York's role as a centre of ecclesiastical government in the British Isles which is emphasized. Although frequently conquered by pagan invaders, York's supremacy as the metropolitan see of northern Britain is constantly reasserted in Monmouth's narrative, particularly in the story of King Arthur, who celebrated Christmas in York following his defeat of the pagan Saxons, Scots and Picts.[37] This was the moment when Arthur formally confirmed his hegemony over northern

33 Earliest recorded forms include 1108x14 'Blaicastret', 1153x8 'Cunegestrate', 1166x79 'Nordstreta'. For earlier discussion of the etymology of York street names see: A. H. Smith, *The Place-Names of the East Riding of Yorkshire and York* (Cambridge, 1937); D. M. Palliser, 'The Medieval Street-Names of York', *York Historian* 2 (1978), 2–16; G. Fellows-Jensen, 'The Anglo-Scandinavian Street-Names of York', in *Aspects of Anglo-Scandinavian York*, ed. R. A. Hall et al. (York, 2004), pp. 357–71 esp. pp. 360–3.

34 We could possibly add both Stonegate and Petergate to this list of names originating after the Conquest. The difficulty is that virtually all York's medieval street names are recorded for the first time in the early twelfth century. However the invention of both Castlegate and Davygate proves that the Old Norse suffix –*gata* does not have to denote a pre-Conquest origin for the name.

35 *Historia Regum Britannie of Geoffrey of Monmouth I: Bern Burgerbibliothek, MS. 568*, ed. N. Wright (Cambridge, 1985), pp. xix, xxxix–xl, xlvi.

36 Monmouth, *Kings of Britain*, p. 125.

37 Ibid., pp. 220–1.

mainland Britain before turning his attention to Ireland. These stories were certainly well known in York and Yorkshire.[38] Monmouth's patron, Walter Espec (d. 1147x58), was a great Yorkshire landowner, a patron of its new monastic houses and an influential figure in the city and region. The image of York as the great Christian capital of northern Britain was reflected in many cultural contexts from the choice of local church dedications (such as St Helen) to the depiction of the city on early maps.

The early Norman kings' ambition of creating a northern royal capital in York was reflected in their visits. Our sources are extremely slight but it is clear that royal visits were more frequent in the twelfth than in the eleventh century. Henry I visited at least four times (1100–35), and his successor King Stephen was a still more frequent visitor.[39] Henry II paid at least six visits to York as he fought to restore royal authority in the north against local barons and the king of Scotland. His crowning achievement came in 1175 when he staged in York Minster a public ceremonial humiliation of William I 'the Lion', king of Scotland, in the presence of the entire Scottish court. Henry also used his time in York to display his sovereignty in other ways: he went hunting, he presided over punitive sessions of the royal courts, he raised taxes and he affirmed himself as the royal patron of York's religious houses.

This refashioning of York as a royal citadel also fostered a transformation of the community resident in the city. Following the Conquest and continuing into the twelfth century a great deal of land in the city was transferred to French knights who owned their urban estates alongside burgesses of Anglo-Scandinavian descent. Indeed the description of York in the Domesday Book is largely a description of the eighty-two tenements within the king's fee that had been awarded to nineteen French knights.[40] The picture is too complicated to present in detail here, but the redistribution of lands also consolidated the integration of the landowning classes of the city and shire, tying the city into the politics of the county and its leading knights and barons.[41] This pattern continued into the twelfth century when new generations of servants of the king's household also acquired estates in and around the city.

Norman families who retained York estates from the time of the Conquest into the later twelfth century included the Percy family. Their ancestor, William Percy, one of the first Norman custodians of the castle, owned several properties in York, including most of the parish of St Mary in Castlegate, and the advowson of the church was still owned by Agnes de Percy in the

---

[38] J. Crick, *The Historia Regum Britannie of Geoffrey of Monmouth IV: Dissemination and Reception in the Later Middle Ages* (Cambridge, 1991), pp. 64, 196, 207, 209, 214–15.

[39] E. Miller, 'Medieval York', in *VCH, City of York*, pp. 25–116 (pp. 25–6), J. Green, 'King Henry I and Northern England', *TRHS* 6th s. 17 (2007), 35–55; D. Crouch, *The Reign of King Stephen 1135–1154* (Harlow, 2000), pp. 38n, 40–41, 200, 243–4, 286–7.

[40] *Domesday Book*, fols. 298 a, b.

[41] Dalton, *Conquest, Anarchy and Lordship*.

later twelfth century.[42] If this castle was the place of Jewish refuge in 1190, then any Jews approaching it would have had to pass through this estate in order to reach it. This is a chilling thought, especially since the head of a junior branch of that family, William Percy of Carnaby, was later charged with inciting the violence against them. Other important Norman landowners in York acquired their estates through service to the king in the twelfth century. Walter Espec, the patron of Geoffrey of Monmouth, owned land in Ogleforth, and others with York estates included household officials of Henry I such as Herbert the Chamberlain and Nigel d'Aubigny, a knight of the royal household who rose to become a 'provincial viceroy' in the north, a royal justice in Yorkshire and custodian of York castle until *c.* 1118.[43] Indeed the city estate of d'Aubigny and his son, Roger de Mowbray, included a large and prominent site in Stonegate, known as 'Mulbrai Halle', which dominated the central area of the Roman fortress and lay midway between the Minster and the royal larder.[44] Mowbray became a powerful figure in York politics in the 1140s and 1150s. He was a great rival to other local barons who were more favoured than he was by both Stephen and Henry II, and he was constantly thwarted in his desire to control the royal castle as his father had once done. He eventually joined the rebellion 'of the young king' against Henry II in 1173-74, holding the city for the rebels. A large hall in such a prominent site in the city centre would be appropriate for the man who was once described as the real 'lord of York'.[45]

Other royal officials rented or bought property in Coney Street. Coney Street literally means 'the king's street' in an amalgam of Old Norse and Latin. It connected the royal castle to the river crossing between the king's house and the royal larder and may have been so named because of its association with both offices and officers of the crown. Bertram of Bulmer (sheriff 1128/9–30 and 1154–63), Fulk Paynel I, Geoffrey Hageth, a royal justice, the infamous Richard Malebisse (alleged instigator of the attack on the Jews in 1190), Roger Batvent under-sheriff of Yorkshire in 1194–98 and William Stuteville, sheriff from 1201 to 1203, all either leased or owned houses in

---

[42] *Domesday Book*, fol. 298a; S. Rees Jones, 'Building Domesticity in the City: English Urban Housing before the Black Death', in *Medieval Domesticity: Home, Housing and Household in Medieval England*, ed. M. Kowaleski and P. J. P. Goldberg (Cambridge, 2008), pp. 66–91 (pp. 80–2).

[43] *Charters of the Honour of Mowbray, 1107–1191*, ed. D. E. Greenway, Records of Social and Economic History, n.s. 1 (London, 1972), pp. xvii–xxxii; J. O. Prestwich, 'The Military Household of the Norman Kings', *EHR* 96 (1981), 1–35 (pp. 24–5).

[44] Property at 35a–39 Stonegate was known as 'Mulberiahalle': *Mowbray Charters*, pp. xxiv n., lxxxii, 8; *York Minster Fasti* II, 51; *Abstracts of the Charters and Other Documents contained in the Chartulary of the Cistercian Abbey of Fountains*, ed. W. T. Lancaster, 2 vols. (Leeds, 1915), p. 274. 'Mulberiahalle' occupied a large area including the site of its modern namesake, Mulberry Hall, at 17 Stonegate.

[45] Jordan Fantosme, *Chronicle of the War between the English and the Scots in 1173 and 1174*, ed. F. Michel, SS 11 (London, 1840), 971–2; H. M. Thomas, 'Mowbray, Sir Roger (I) de (*d.* 1188)', *ODNB* (Oxford, 2004). Howden, *Chronica* II, pp. 79–80.

Coney Street and developed close links with a number of the wealthier burgesses who also lived in that neighbourhood.[46] The riverside location made
Coney Street one of the most important road arteries in the city and archaeological evidence provides further clues about the social transformation of
this neighbourhood. In neighbouring Coppergate, for example, the century
after 1000 saw a significant reduction in discarded metal objects associated
with metalworking and an increase in metal goods associated with riding
horses.[47] This suggests an elevation in the social status of the residents under
the influence of the new Norman settlement.

Here, too, the most powerful of York's Jews settled. When Benedict and
Josce, and, later in the thirteenth century, Aaron of York settled in Coney
Street, or the adjacent street of Bretgate (later known as Jewbretgate or
Jubbergate),[48] they were choosing to live in what was effectively a royal
quarter and one of the wealthiest neighbourhoods of the city, where their
daily lives were lived cheek-by-jowl with other servants of the crown and
the most prosperous members of the York mercantile elite. Coney Street
was close to the castle (a possible place of refuge) but perhaps more importantly it was close to the royal larder and market (Jubbergate led from
Coney Street to the market ground in Arkilltofts by the royal larder), and it
was alongside the river by which most travellers and much trade arrived
in the city. When a Jewish community resettled in York in the thirteenth
century, Coney Street was again the neighbourhood in which many of the
wealthiest members lived and where the *schola*, or synagogue, stood near
to the church of St Martin.

But the York in which Jews began to settle from the 1170s was very different from the York of the earlier Norman kings. For, despite those earlier
kings' ambitions, the twelfth century, like the later eleventh, turned into a
period of protracted local warfare, particularly after 1138. By the 1170s little
was left of the royal infrastructure put in place by William I and his two sons.
King Stephen was the last Norman king to seek to impose his personal authority in the city. As challenges to his rule increased after 1138 he reverted to
the older practice of appointing a local earl to represent the crown's interest
in the north.[49] Control of York was given to William d'Aumale who, as earl
of York, presumably took over the royal house as he did the castle. Aumale's
ascendancy, fiercely resisted by opponents such as Roger de Mowbray, pre-
cipitated the outbreak of private wars which were seen by local chroniclers
as a disastrous period of terrible anarchy in Yorkshire. The royal infrastructure crumbled and even the royal mint in York began issuing coins in the

---

46 BL MS Cotton Nero D. III, fols. 107r, 125r; JRUL MSS 220–1, fol. 1r; *Chartulary Fountains*, pp. 275, 279; *EYC* I, no 234: *EYC* IX, 18.
47 P. Ottaway and N. Rogers, *Craft, Industry and Everyday Life: Finds from Medieval York* (York, 2002), pp. 2956–67, 2996–7.
48 Dobson, *JMY*, p. 46.
49 R. H. C. Davis, *King Stephen, 1135–58*, 3rd edn (London, 1990), pp. 125–8.

name of local barons rather than the king.[50] Many new private castles sprang up around the county and private armies terrorized the local population; even Henry II did not bring peace to the north after his accession in 1154. The impact of this local warfare is perhaps reflected in the archaeological evidence of houseplots abandoned in some streets of central York for nearly a century after the Conquest.[51]

After 1154 Henry II thus adopted a very different policy towards Yorkshire from any of his predecessors. His first priority was to destroy the power of the earl of York with military force and several of the earl's strongholds in the county, such as Scarborough castle, were taken for the crown. In the case of the city of York, Henry II at first trod diplomatically. His first charter to York simply confirmed to the merchant guild all the privileges they had previously enjoyed under royal lordship, and he also took back custody of the royal castle and presumably of the royal house.[52] While Henry certainly visited York there is less evidence of the personal aspects of earlier Norman kingship in his patronage of local institutions. He confirmed Stephen's gifts to St Leonard's hospital, but he did not provide new endowments.[53] Nor are there any signs of investment in the royal buildings of York: by 1186 the sheriff was collecting rent for the abandoned site of the royal mint, and royal coin continued to be minted in forges in private workshops.[54] Rather surprisingly the castle remained a timber construction, unlike other royal castles in the north (such as Carlisle, Brough, Knaresborough, Pickering or Scarborough) whose keeps were rebuilt in stone. Indeed in contrast to the great sums which Henry lavished on some of his southern palaces, such as Clarendon, Woodstock or Westminster, in York there is just one payment for the construction of a gaol to hold those arrested under the Assize of Clarendon in 1165-66 and one other payment for work on the towers ('turris') of York overseen by David, the king's larderer, in 1172-73.[55]

Yet if Henry spent little on local royal buildings the financial records of royal government show that he substantially increased his financial demands on the local community. The annual farm (or rent) from York to the crown had been fixed at £100 by 1086 and was included in the farm for the whole county, but from the beginning of his reign Henry II regularly demanded substantial additional sums in the form of non-voluntary 'gifts', aids, fines and escheats. An annual gift of £133 was demanded of the city between 1155

50 Ibid., pp. 330–1.
51 *Medieval Urbanism in Coppergate*, ed. R. A. Hall and K. Hunter-Mann (York, 2002), pp. 705, 727, 756, 774–87, 859; N. McNabb, 'Anglo-Scandinavian, Medieval and Post-Medieval Urban Occupation at 41–49 Walmgate, York, UK', The Archaeology of York, Web Series 1 (York, 2003). http://www.iadb.co.uk/wgate/main/discuss.php [accessed July 2012].
52 *British Borough Charters, 1042–1216*, ed. A. Ballard (Cambridge, 1913), p. 6.
53 BL MS Cotton Nero D. III, fols. 3v–4r.
54 Miller, 'Medieval York', p. 30; *PR 33 Henry II*, p. 82. See below, pp. 30–1.
55 *PR 19 Henry II*, p. 2; RCHME, *City of York* II, 60. It is not clear whether these towers were part of the castle or city defences, or part of another structure.

and 1161, rising to the exceptionally large figure of £540 in 1161-2.[56] In the 1160s similar sums were demanded; in 1162-3 (50 marks), 1164-5 (£200), and in 1168-69 (£333 6s. 8d.).[57]

The size of these demands meant that the city did not always pay the whole sum demanded, but even these were supplemented from the mid 1160s by sometimes equally large demands placed on individual citizens or trading groups. From 1164 an annual charge of £10 was placed on the weavers of York, representing an extension north of the Trent of a policy of licensing craft groups which had started in southern towns in the previous decade.[58] More striking still, in the same year Lefwin of York, a prominent citizen, was put in mercy for the sum of 300 marks (£200) and the Dean (*decanus*) of York (possibly the secular reeve of the city) for another £100. Indeed from 1160, and particularly following the Assize of Clarendon in 1166 the steady expansion of royal law resulted in increasing numbers of York citizens appearing in the pipe rolls owing sums of money, ranging from 3s. 4d. to £66; which they and their families would often take many years to redeem. An early, but typical, case was that of William of Thixendale ('Sexdecimvallibus' or 'Sezevaux') who was first fined 100 marks (£66 13s. 4d.) for taking his wife ('mulier') by force in 1160-61. For the next thirty-five years first William and then his son appeared annually paying off this hefty fine in small instalments until eventually the debt passed to the third generation and on into the reign of King John.[59] This case illustrates well the impact of the expanding scope of royal government. It brought larger numbers of local people before the royal courts, resulting in demands for more and more money. However it was above all the use of novel written procedures of administration which meant that local offenders and their descendants could be subjected to demands from royal officers for decades. The vice of royal government gripped ever tighter, and must have seemed inescapable.

A further source of discontent, especially as these novel demands accumulated, was the subjection of York to the county sheriff. Other cities, such as Lincoln, were sometimes allowed to pay their own farm to the crown and from the beginning of Henry II's reign the citizens of York must also have known that burgesses in other (new) royal boroughs in the county such as Knaresborough (from 1156), Doncaster (from 1160) and Scarborough (from 1163) were allowed to account directly for their own farms.[60] It may be that this lay behind the demand of some of York's burgesses for a commune in 1173-74. In that year Thomas de Ultra Usam and his son were fined 40 marks 'pro communa quam dicti sunt velle facere'.[61] Thomas may be identified

---

56 *PR 8 Henry II*, p. 51; C. Stephenson, 'The Aids of English Boroughs', *EHR* 34 (1919), 457–73.
57 *PR 9 Henry II*, p. 58; *11 Henry II*, pp. 45–52; *15 Henry II*, p. 36.
58 *PR 11 Henry II*, pp. 45–52.
59 *PR 7 Henry II*, p. 37 and thereafter annually into *PR 2 John*, p. 102.
60 *PR 2–4 Henry II*, pp. 85–6; *7 Henry II*, pp. 35–6; *10 Henry II*, pp. 11–13.
61 *PR 21 Henry II*, p. 180.

with the Thomas son of Ulviet who had paid a fine to join the guild merchant in 1130 and certainly with the Thomas de Ultra Usam who was fined 10 marks in 1162-63.[62] 'Commune' is a word that has been used by modern urban historians with a particular technical meaning: it describes a sworn association of townsmen who organized themselves either for defence, for trade or to assert their independence from lords and princes in collective and semi-autonomous corporate self-government. However we know nothing more about this particular commune in York. It may be more sensible to put it in the context in which it appears in the pipe roll, which is among a long series of fines imposed on York citizens for their part in the major rebellion against Henry II known as the 'young king's revolt': the war of eighteen months' duration led by Henry's three sons and his wife Eleanor together with many rebel barons against his government in England and France. In the north one of the leading rebels was Roger de Mowbray and numbers of men in both York and the county were fined for communicating with the king's enemies ('quia communicavit cum inimicis Regis'), or for being in communion with Mowbray or the king's enemies ('pro communionem quam habuit cum Rogero de Molbrai').[63] It seems possible then that Thomas's 'communa', listed among these fines, was in fact just another way of describing a charge of conspiracy rather than a description of particular form of borough government.

Certainly several other leading citizens, including William of Tickhill, Gerard and Hugh the sons of Lefwin, William of Selby, Robert Brun of Coney Street and Alan son of Romund, were fined for conspiracy with the rebels in 1173-74 or for receiving fugitives, for receiving the chattels of Flemings (who were allied with the rebels and so banned from trade), for selling shields to the rebels, and/or simply forced to pay very large sums (£400 from Gerard son of Lefwin) in 'benevolences' to buy the king's good will. Many of these men had already appeared before the king's courts before 1173 for other reasons: William of Selby fined 10 marks for selling wine against the assize in 1165; William of Tickhill fined 10 marks for not wishing to stand as a pledge in 1168, Hugh son of Lefwin fined £5 for recovery of 60 marks.[64] Whether this was the reason why they were engaged with the rebels during the protracted revolt of 1173-74 we cannot tell, but almost certainly they could not carry out their normal business without so engaging and they paid heavily for that. Indeed the family of the sons of Lefwin paid nearly £1000 in fines and charg-

---

62 Miller, 'Medieval York', p. 32; *PR 31 Henry I*, p. 34; *9 Henry II*, pp. 57–60. Thomas's grandfather, Forne, was also named in 1106 as one of the four hereditary lawmen or judges who presided over the city's internal administration, a position that is first recorded in 1086: D. M. Palliser, 'The Birth of York's Civic Liberties, c. 1200–1354', in *The Government of Medieval York: Essays in Commemoration of the 1396 Royal Charter*, ed. S. Rees Jones (York, 1997), pp. 88–107 (pp. 90–1).
63 *PR 21 Henry II*, pp. 174–83.
64 *PR 12 Henry II*, p. 49; *15 Henry II*, p. 39; *17 Henry II*, p. 73.

es over the later years of the reign of Henry II, more than any other Christian family in the whole of England.[65] Nor were the immediate fines the end of their punishment. A punitive session of the forest eyre in 1175, over which Henry presided in person, raised over £1600 in fines, and the ceremonious humiliation of the king of Scotland and his court in 1175 in York Minster was surely intended to impress the citizens as much as its baronial participants.[66]

It is extremely significant that it was in the aftermath of the great revolt of 1173-74 and its emphatic suppression that Jewish moneylenders first settled in York. Some Jewish scholars may have been invited to attend the court of the archbishop of York for debate on matters of scripture earlier in the century, but the first Jewish families to settle in York almost certainly moved there from Lincoln and 'may have operated as an outlying agency of a national financial network dominated by Aaron of Lincoln until his death in 1186'.[67] Along with other provincial Jewries, the York community was granted in 1177 the right to maintain its own cemetery, and a site was provided outside the city walls on the banks of the River Foss.[68] We know relatively little about this first Jewish community. Most of our evidence about Jews in medieval York comes from the plea rolls of the Jewish Exchequer established after 1190 and it relates primarily to the second wave of Jewish settlement in the city in the thirteenth century (and especially in the reign of Henry III). However incontrovertible references to Jews in York begin from the early to mid 1170s: a purchase by 'Josce the Jew, son of David' of a burgage in Fossgate, a Hebrew bond referring to Aaron of Lincoln, Josce of York and six other Jews acquitting debts of 1260 marks due to them up to the feast of Michaelmas 1176, and references to Josce of York lending money to the king and receiving payments from the sheriffs of Berkshire, Oxfordshire and Yorkshire.[69] Josce was joined in the 1180s by Benedict, and both developed successful businesses building up portfolios of property across the county and beyond.[70] These two men were exceptionally wealthy, a fact that attracted comment: Newburgh described Josce's house as 'rivalling a noble citadel in the scale and stoutness of its construction'.[71] Dobson believes that the Jewish com-

---

[65] H. M. Thomas, *The English and the Normans: Ethnic Hostility, Assimilation, and Identity 1066–c.1220* (Oxford, 2003), p. 185.

[66] D. Crook, 'The Earliest Exchequer Estreat and the Forest Eyres of Henry II and Thomas fitz Bernard, 1175–80', in *Records, Administration and Aristocratic Society in the Anglo-Norman Realm*, ed. N. Vincent (Woodbridge, 2000), pp. 29–44 (pp. 33–4).

[67] R. B. Dobson, 'The Decline and Expulsion of the Medieval Jews of York', *JHSE Transactions* 26 (1979 for 1974), 34–52 (p. 35).

[68] Rees Jones, 'The Historical Background', in *Jewish Burial Ground at Jewbury*, ed. Lilley et al.

[69] Dobson, *JMY*, pp. 11–12.

[70] ibid., pp. 12–13. In 1200 and 1205 King John granted properties of Benedict the Jew of York in Northampton and York to new owners. His 'land and houses' in York were not described but had been acquired by the crown from Philip, bishop of Durham (1197–1208) and were granted to Richard de Richeford: *Rot. Chart.*, pp. 52, 150.

[71] WN, trans. Stevenson, p. 314.

munity before 1190 was 'a community dominated by a small and closely-integrated elite of money-lenders and dealers in bonds' of no more than 150 men, women and children. But he goes on to conclude that the community was also beginning to expand in new directions, in particular through the development of its scholarly and religious life, as it welcomed a group of prominent Jewish scholars including Rabbi Yom Tob of Joigny, Rabbi Elijah, a certain Moses and even Josce of York himself, who was notable for his learning as well as his financial skills.[72]

The arrival and documentation of York's first Jewish community coincided with, and may well have been the product of, increased efforts by royal government to regulate and profit from not only the financial activities of Jews but also many other aspects of local trade and commerce throughout England. Robert Stacey charts the growth of royal power over Jews and their financial transactions elsewhere in this volume. Over a similar period officials of the royal household also developed regulations for commodities purchased by the crown such as bread, ale, wine or cloth, and these eventually became the basis for national assizes governing the sale of these commodities.[73] In 1177-78 the sheriff collected 20 marks in York for infractions of the assize of measures and in 1179-80 the range of craft guilds amerced by the king extended to the glovers and cordwainers, saddlers and hosiers.[74] A particular problem was the regulation of moneyers in York, who towards the end of Stephen's reign, in the 1150s, had produced 'debased' coins in the name of the local barons Robert de Stuteville and Eustace fitz John.[75] Payments from the moneyers of York, and the associated exchange, to the royal sheriff are a regular feature of the pipe rolls only from 1164-65[76] but by the 1170s minting in the city was clearly being reorganized. In 1170-71 William de Brettegate paid 20 marks to be relieved of the custody of the mint and from 1176 to 1180 an allowance was made to the sheriff for the lack of payments from the city's moneyers (variously numbered from three to eight).[77] Nevertheless the York mint clearly participated in a great general recoinage of English coin in 1180 and it is likely that in York, as in Winchester, minting continued in a number of forges on private premises

72 Dobson, *JMY*, pp 14–15.
73 F. Sargeant, 'The Wine Trade with Gascony', in *Finance and Trade under Edward III*, ed. G. Unwin (Manchester, 1918), pp. 257–311; P. Grierson, 'Weights and Measures', in *Domesday Book Studies*, ed. A. Williams and R. W. H. Erskine (London, 1987), pp. 80–5; R. H. Britnell, *The Commercialisation of English Society, 1000–1500*, 2nd edn (Manchester, 1996), pp. 26, 94–5; J. M. Bennett, *Ale, Beer and Brewsters in England: Women's Work in a Changing World, 1300–1600* (Oxford, 1996), pp. 99–100; J. Davis, 'Baking for the Common Good: A Reassessment of the Assize of Bread in Medieval England', *Economic History Review* 57 (2004), 465–502.
74 *PR 24 Henry II*, pp. 71–2: 26 Henry II, pp. 71.
75 M. Blackburn, 'Coinage and Currency', in *The Anarchy of King Stephen's Reign*, ed. E. King (Oxford, 1994), pp. 145–205 (pp. 183–5).
76 *PR 11 Henry II*, pp. 49.
77 *PR 17 Henry II*, p. 73; 22 Henry II, p. 99; 26 Henry II, p. 61.

rather than at a single official site, although there may have been an unsuccessful attempt to establish such a site.[78] By 1181-2 the sheriff was renting out the land where the old building of the mint had stood ('terre ubi vetus fabrica monetariorium Eboraci fuit').[79] All these changes may have caught out older moneyers such as Gerard son of Lefwin who had paid 50 marks for the mint ('cuneo') of the king in 1165, but who was fined 200 marks for denying the possession of false money in 1184 along with his servant Everard Bradex who was fined 30 marks.[80]

After the great rebellion of 1173-74, then, the novel exactions of the crown only increased in their sophistication and range: the pipe rolls for the 1180s record ever lengthening lists of payments due from individuals. Demands on the city community as a whole also continued culminating in a new 'gift' of £226 6s. 4d. in 1186-87, and only one third of this had been paid before the next year when the special 'tithe of Saladin' was requested.[81] The arrival of wealthy Jewish financiers, speaking French, and protected and regulated by the crown, was most likely interpreted locally as part of this broader expansion of royal financial impositions in the city and its hinterland. Certainly the initial reception of Jews was not untroubled. In 1178-79 Ralph de Glanville, as sheriff of Yorkshire, arrested a man (unnamed) for the death of a Jew (unnamed), and in the same year for the first time several (non-Jewish) individuals in York and Yorkshire were fined as usurers: both signs, perhaps, that the crown intended to defend and protect its rights over the money lending activities of 'its' Jews against the non-Jewish population.[82]

The Jewish community in York was therefore less than one generation old at the time of the coronation of King Richard I in London on 3 September 1189 which, according to Newburgh, several of its leading Jews journeyed to attend. Here, Benedict of York was injured and converted to Christianity by the prior of St Mary's abbey in York (who was also in London) but recanted the next day before the king. He died of his wounds, but others returned to York. Richard I issued an injunction against further violence against Jews in England, but he and many of his leading officials soon left for France. Crucially, and thanks to new research by Dr Hugh Doherty, we now know that these officials included the new sheriff of Yorkshire, John Marshal, who was not (as earlier historians thought) present in York in early 1190.[83] This fact,

---

[78] M. Biddle and D. Keene, 'Winchester in the Eleventh and Twelfth Centuries', in *Winchester in the Early Middle Ages: An Edition and Discussion of the Winton Domesday*, ed. M. Biddle (Oxford, 1976), pp. 241–448 (pp. 396–421).

[79] *PR 28 Henry II*, p. 36; *33 Henry II*, p. 82.

[80] *PR 12 Henry II*, p. 49; *31 Henry II*, p. 69. York coins bearing Everard's name survive from *c.* 1180: Cambridge, Fitzwilliam Museum, Museum Accession Numbers: CM. 1250–2001 and CM. 1259–2001.

[81] *PR 33 Henry II*, p. 93; 'Ordinance of the Saladin Tithe (1188)', in *EHD, II: 1042–1189*, ed. D. C. Douglas and G. W. Greenaway, 2nd edn (London, 1996), pp. 421–2.

[82] *PR 25 Henry II*, pp. 23, 40.

[83] Hugh Doherty, 'The Sheriffs of Yorkshire and the Massacre of 1190', Conference paper, Uni-

as well as a vacant archbishopric, left a dangerous absence of royal authority in Yorkshire. By the beginning of March Jew-baiting had spread to York, starting with murderous attacks on the houses and families of the recently deceased Benedict and also Josce who is said to have led all York's surviving Jews into the royal 'arx' for protection. Whether this was the wooden keep later replaced by the stone Clifford's Tower is a matter of conjecture. Roger of Howden described the massacre as occurring 'in veteri castello' (which could refer to the 'vetus ballia', the second Norman castle, on the west bank of the Ouse), while Matthew Paris described some Jews as enclosing themselves within the 'domo regia' and setting fire to themselves together with the 'domibus regiis' which could refer to the king's house ('domus regis') on the west bank.[84] All three of these sites are possible candidates for the 'arx' at the centre of Newburgh's tale, but we cannot be certain which may have been the true site of that awful immolation, and no archaeological excavations in the present castle have yet revealed evidence to firmly support Newburgh's account.[85]

Apart from chronicles, the events of March 1190 are only documented in one surviving administrative source: the lists compiled of the men fined for the massacre in the years after 1190.[86] As Doherty has argued, royal reaction to this horrible lapse of its authority in Yorkshire was swift and decisive. It followed the pattern of other recent royal punishments by taking the form of financial penalties imposed on the local community as well as seizing the estates of the leading perpetrators. An initial list of those fined appears in the pipe roll for the second year of Richard I's reign but new names were added to the original list in later years. For this reason we do not know whether the citizens included in the lists were being punished because of their personal involvement in the violence of March 1190 or whether they were fined simply as the leading representatives of the city of York. Following Newburgh, Dobson concluded that these men were fined not because of their guilt but because of their wealth: that this was a list of York's richest inhabitants, not, as in Lincoln, of those engaged in violence against the Jews.[87]

Although it is impossible to know who was engaged in the events of March 1190 and how they were motivated we can flesh out the biographies of many of those on the lists using the evidence not only of the pipe rolls but also of title deeds recording property transactions which are among our

---

versity of York, 22 March 2010.

84 Howden, *Chronica* III, 34; Paris, *Chronica Majora* I, 359.

85 A quantity of burnt timbers were observed in archaeological excavations of the mound beneath Clifford's Tower in 1902 and were then interpreted as evidence of the destruction of the Norman keep in the revolt of 1069. The fire in 1190 has been speculatively suggested as an alternative explanation. The record of the observations is considered too sparse to support a definitive interpretation: J. Clark and Field Archaeology Services, *Historic Buildings Analysis: Clifford's Tower, York*, Report for English Heritage (London, 2005), p. 3.

86 *PR 2 Richard I*, pp. 68–70; *3–4 Richard I*, pp. 69–70, 215–16.

87 Dobson, *JMY*, p. 32.

most abundant surviving sources for York in this period.[88] Of the fifty-nine citizens of York named on these lists, at least fifty-one can be identified in charters as participants or witnesses in land transactions.

First, the names give us an insight into continuity with the past. Many of the patrilineal names suggest that these men were the descendants of Anglo-Scandinavian families and representative of a continuing population dating back before the Norman Conquest of 1068-69. Around 25 per cent of those fined were from the first generation to have been given French first names (such as Thomas son of Ramkill, or Robert and Serlo the sons of Wulfsi). In the names of their fathers and grandfathers they carried the memories of York's turbulent history over the period of the Conquest and its aftermath.

Indeed the impression of a group well acquainted with the city's past is reinforced when we collate references to them elsewhere in the pipe rolls and in charters of land transactions in York. At least eight of those fined in 1190 had already been fined by royal officers over the preceding decade for various offences from rape, infringements of the forest law, and trading infractions to offences related to the mint.[89] In addition more than half of those fined in 1190 seem to have been near to the end of their lives: evidence about them is relatively sparse, although it is often possible to find references to the property holdings of close relatives and descendants.[90] This generation included some of those fined the largest amounts in 1190, such as Warin of Cuningestrata who was fined 20 marks. Warin witnessed a number of charters between the later 1150s and the mid 1190s, but was then replaced in witness lists by his sons Thomas and Ambrose and his grandson Stephen (also known as Stephen Wariner) who lived around the corner from Coney Street in property between Ousegate and Coppergate in the early thirteenth century.[91] This would certainly support the idea that those fined in 1190

88   See note 5 above.

89   These eight men were Everard Bradex, Philip son of Baldwin, Robert son of Askell, Robert of Selby, Roger son of Gerard, Serlo the brother of Robert (son of Wulfsi), Simon Blund and Thomas of Bretgate. Robert son of Askell was fined 15 marks in 1179–80 for taking a woman by force: *PR 26 Henry II*, p. 62. Most of the other offences were clustered between 1184 and 1186: *PR 31 Henry II*, pp. 68–9; *32 Henry II*, pp. 68, 93–5.

90   Those fined in 1190 who appear to have been towards the end of their lives included Thomas son of Richard, Warin of Cuningestrata, William son of Otwy, Turkill and Gerard of Bretgate, Robert son of Liulf, John son of Goduse, Ralph son of Lundwar, Thomas son of Yol, Roger son of Bernulf, Walter son of Godfrey, Serlo Bella, Robert and Serlo the sons of Wulfsi, Roger son of Lemmar, Philip son of Baldwin, Simon Sakespee, Roger son of Gerard, Osbert Stutte, Avenel and Turstin Galien. Another eight men who have not yet been identified include William Deusanz', William son of Walkelin, Herbert brother of Walter, Galfridus carnifex (Geoffrey the butcher), Malgerus talliator (Malger the tax assessor), Roger son of Lemmar (although Lemmer the tanner is recorded as witness to a transaction in Skeldergate in *c.* 1148x75: *Cartularium Abbathiæ de Whiteby, Ordinis S. Benedicti fundatæ anno MLXXVIII*, ed. J. C. Atkinson, 2 vols., SS 69, 72 (Durham, 1879–81), I, 226), Elias clericus, Erkenbaldus Wesdier, Robert son of Askill and William of Buggeden.

91   *Chartulary Fountains*, pp. 268, 273, 275; York, YMA, Cartulary of St Mary's Abbey, York, fols.

included some of the most senior figures in the city. They also included the patriarchs of dynasties which continued to be an important presence in the city into the next century and beyond.

As well as providing links with York's past the list also gives us a glimpse of the future. It includes some men who survived into the next century. William son of Sigfrith (who was fined the largest sum of 100 marks in 1190) was one of these together with Thomas Palmer (also known as Thomas son of Hugh), Hugh son of Lefwin, Ralf the glover (le wanter), Thomas son of Ramkill and Daniel the oxherd (le buuier or bouarius) who all survived for long enough to be tallaged in 1204.[92] Of these men two (Thomas Palmer fined 25 marks and William Brinkelaw fined 1 mark) both went on to achieve office as mayor and bailiff of the city in the second and third decades of the thirteenth century.[93] Indeed both Palmer and Brinkelaw were associated with one of York's most prominent citizens in the reign of King John, William Fairfax, who was one of the last royal reeves of York, possibly an early mayor, a significant property owner and a major money-lender. Fairfax was also engaged in the military resistance against King John in the barons' war, leading an attack on the royal house in York during which he captured and imprisoned its keeper.[94] The group of men fined in 1190 therefore include not only those who had resisted royal authority and led demands for York's independence from the royal sheriff in the past, but also those who would continue to do so in the future.

Beyond this we can make some assessment of the wealth of the citizens of York who were fined after 1190 and identify the neighbourhoods within the city where they probably (or in several cases certainly) lived. That most of the citizens fined can be identified in charters as owners of property in itself makes a point about their wealth, since only a minority of the residents of medieval towns, probably less than 10 per cent, would have been landowners.[95] Also their property ownership was concentrated in those areas of the city where the king's influence was strongest. The largest number (seventeen individuals) were associated with properties in Coney Street, Coppergate, Ousegate and Castlegate, and the second largest group (ten individuals) with the neighbourhood of Walmgate.[96]

2r, 34r; JRUL MSS 220–1, fol. 58r; BL MS Cotton Nero D. III, fols 104r, 169r.

[92] *PR 6 John*, pp. 207–8.

[93] JRUL MSS 220–1, fol. 4r; BL MS Cotton Nero D. III, fol. 204r; *EYC* I, 177, 200.

[94] *Rolls of the Justices in Eyre*, pp. 423–4.

[95] S. Thrupp, *The Merchant Class of Medieval London, 1300–1500* (Chicago, 1948), p. 125; D. Keene, *Survey of Medieval Winchester*, 2 vols. (Oxford, 1985) 1, 218, 225.

[96] Those who can be identified as owners and residents in the streets between Coney Street and the Castle: William son of Sirith, Thomas son of Richard, Wain of Cunigestrata, Robert Glene, John son of Goduse, William of Otley, Thomas son of Yol, Serlo Bella, Malgerus Talliator, Simon and Thomas Blund, Thomas son of Ramkill, Philip son of Baldwin, William son of Constantine, Walter son of Reiner, Hugh son of Lefwin and Osbert Stutte. Those associated with Bretgate (now Navigation Road) off Walmgate: Turkillus of Bretgate, Everard Bradex,

In particular some of those who paid the largest fines in 1190 lived in and around Coney Street, where their neighbours included not only some of York's wealthiest Jews but also royal officials and Yorkshire barons. Apart from the eponymous Warin of Cuningestrata, William son of Sirith may have lived here, since he witnessed two charters in Nessgate (Castlegate) in the later twelfth century, although his son and grandson both lived across the city in Goodramgate.[97] Of several notable people in the area Hugh son of Lefwin was one of the most important. His father was active early in the reign of Henry II, owing the king the huge sum of £200 (£40 of which was assigned to one of his baronial neighbours in Coney Street, Fulk Paynel).[98] His stepfather, William Tickhill, was an equally prominent citizen and both were well connected with local knights and were owners of rural estates as well as York property. Hugh was also a minor royal office holder (in the king's exchange in York), and an alleged ally of the disgraced Roger de Mowbray during the revolt of 1173-74 together with William Tickhill and his brother Gerard, both of whom had probably died by 1190 leaving Hugh as the family head. Hugh son of Lefwin lived in a stone hall in Coney Street on the site of the later city Guild Hall.[99] He also owned other property in the same street, at the centre of a network involving several of those fined in 1190. His estate included a large house that Hugh had acquired from Richard Malebisse, the alleged leader of the mob attacking the Jews in 1190. This same house was first leased to John son of Goduse (another of those fined in 1190) and later leased to Roger Bavent the undersheriff of Yorkshire from 1194 to 1198.[100] It occupied a site beside the church of St Martin and thus near the synagogue and the homes of some of York's leading Jews, such as Aaron of York, that were first recorded in the early decades of the thirteenth century.[101] Other tenants of Hugh's in Coney Street included Thomas son of Ramkill who lived in a house and held three plots there, while near neighbours included Philip son of Baldwin and William son of Constantine.[102] Everard Bradex, the moneyer employed by Gerard son of Lefwin, was another member of this group. All four were witnesses to each other's charters and were fined along with Hugh in 1190.

William Deusanz, Thomas Palmer, Gerardus of Brettegate, Ralf son of Lundwar, Richard and Martin of Sezevaux, Daniel Bovarius and Simon Sakespee. Smaller groups of four or five individuals were associated with Bootham and Micklegate respectively, while one to three individuals were associated with Goodramgate, Petergate, the Shambles, Fishergate and Clementhorpe.

97 For William son of Sirith and family: BL MS Cotton Claudius D. XI, fol. 2r; BL MS Cotton Nero D. III, fol. 103r; Bodl. MS Dodsworth 7, fol. 22r; *Charters Vicars Choral*, I, 365.

98 *PR 11 Henry II*, p. 49; *12 Henry II*, p. 39.

99 *EYC* I, 198–200; York, YCA, G16; TNA, SC 6/708, m.10; Rees Jones, 'Property, Tenure and Rents', I, 72.

100 *Chartulary Fountains*, p. 274; JRUL MSS 220–1, fols. 3r, 4r, 10r.

101 Dobson, *JMY*, pp. 44–5.

102 YML, Cartulary of St Mary's Abbey, fol. 2r; JRUL MSS 220–1, fols. 1r, 5r, 74r; BL MS Cotton Nero D. III, fol. 107r.

A similar and equally robust network was based in and around Bretgate. Two streets in York shared this name. One, off Coney Street, later became Jewbretgate or Jubbergate because of its association with the homes of Jews living there in the thirteenth century. However the Bretgate of this group was undoubtedly off Walmgate as the description of the properties and their later history makes clear. Walmgate was a distinctive neighbourhood whose fortunes were recovering in the later twelfth century as properties abandoned since the Conquest were resettled and redeveloped with new industries. It was not yet enclosed within the city defences (that was to happen during the reign of King John) but it is clear that some of its residents were persons of substance, living in stone houses, building up estates of property across the city and county, holding public office and playing a leading role in city affairs. Thomas Palmer, the future mayor of York, makes some of his earliest documented appearances as a tenant in Walmgate.[103] The eponymous Turkill and Gerard of Brettegate were perhaps dominant members of the neighbourhood who were fined in 1190. It also included Simon Sakespee, the nephew of Walter son of Faganulf, whose family of hereditary priests owned the churches of St Mary and St Margaret in Bretgate within their patrimony in the early twelfth century: and Walter and Jordan Sakespee were celebrated as major patrons of the hospital of St Leonard in York to which they gave the advowson of those churches.[104] Like the Coney Street group this Walmgate group appears tightly knit, but its wealthier members were also linked with those in Coney Street, sometimes witnessing charters there. Indeed the wealthiest families used these connections to move out. Some of the earliest references to Richard and Martin of Thixendale ('Sezevaux') in York place them in Walmgate, but the family soon acquired property elsewhere in the city becoming, first, mayors of York and, eventually, county gentry in the later thirteenth century.[105]

The importance of these two neighbourhoods for the men first fined for the massacre of the Jews in 1190 may be significant. Both were neighbourhoods which lay within the king's fee in York, rather than in the fee of the archbishop and the Minster (centred around the Minster), or of St Mary's abbey (centred in Bootham). They were also both old industrial and commercial neighbourhoods which were being transformed by new prosperity in the last decades of the twelfth century. Given both the vigorous growth of new centres of industry and commerce and their location within the king's jurisdiction it is not surprising that it was the residents of these neighbourhoods who were particularly active in emerging new structures of civic government. Coney Street and Walmgate were also neighbourhoods where we know (at least from slightly later evidence) that Jews settled or had con-

---

103 BL MS Cotton Nero D. III, fol. 9r.
104 JRUL MSS 220–1, fol. 3r; BL MS Cotton Nero D. III, fol. 11r–v; *EYC* I, 240–51.
105 *Yorkshire Deeds*, ed. W. Brown et al., 10 vols., YAS, Rec. Ser. 39, 50, 63, 65, 69, 76, 83, 102, 111, 120 (Leeds, 1909–55) II, 203, no. 534. For the Sezevauz family see, Rees Jones, *Medieval York*.

nections, particularly in streets near Coney Street, but there is also the very early reference to Jewish property in Fossgate, which was an extension of Walmgate towards Ousegate and the city centre.[106] More important may be the evidence that a number of York citizens were indebted to Aaron of Lincoln (whose debts were administered by the crown following his death in 1186) and the two streets where properties are specifically identified as having been mortgaged to him were (again) Walmgate and Ousegate (by one Richard Blundus).[107] All this suggests significant engagement between wealthy Christian and Jewish residents in these neighbourhoods in particular. Might these debts have provided a motive for antipathy towards the king's Jews similar to that which has commonly been ascribed to the knights of the shire? Yet, to complicate this picture, there is evidence that the citizens fined in 1190 were themselves providers of credit. Hugh and Gerard the sons of Lefwin both acquired rural estates in this manner, while the growing practice of purchasing rent charges on property enabled many of this group (and their associates and descendants) to build up extremely valuable estates in the city.[108]

It is not possible here to explore all the possible connections between those fined in 1190. This was a tight-knit group, united by bonds of family, business and neighbourhood. Certainly they were wealthy and prominent citizens, but also they were associated with particular neighbourhoods sharing certain characteristics: of growing commercial prosperity, of strong networks around key individuals and of proximity to the institutions associated with royal government. They were also the neighbourhoods in which York's new Jewish families were most active and prominent. It was certainly to these neighbourhoods that Jews returned in their second settlement in the reign of Henry III.

Perhaps not surprisingly a final characteristic of the citizens fined for the attack on the Jews is the degree to which they were associated with local knights, barons and royal officials both before 1190 and afterwards. The importance of wealthy burgesses in the county communities of twelfth-century England has not been adequately recognized. However the close engagement of York men with the rebels in 1173-74 should come as no surprise; neither should their connections, through trade and ownership of property, with Yorkshire barons and knights. We have already seen that Hugh son of Lefwin acquired property in Coney Street from Richard Malebisse, and later

---

[106] See above, n. 69.

[107] *PR 9 Richard I*, pp. 46, 61–2. Richard Blundus was possibly a relative of Simon Blund, who was fined in 1190, although Blund was a common cognomen. Citizens of York are not explicitly identified as such in the lists of his debtors, but names which do appear such as 'Walter Aurifaber', 'William de Selby' and 'Nicholas de Buggethorpe' were all names of wealthier York residents occurring in other contemporary records and it is likely that they were citizens.

[108] For Hugh and Gerard, sons of Lefwin see: Miller, 'Medieval York', p. 26. For the trade in rents in the thirteenth century see: Rees Jones, *Medieval York* for more detail.

let it to the undersheriff of Yorkshire; the connections of Hugh and Richard with Roger de Mowbray are also well established. One of Hugh's other properties in Coney Street, inhabited by Thomas and William Ramkill and their families, and later by Hugh's wife's daughter, neighboured a house of William de Stuteville (a royal justice who married the niece of Ranulf de Glanville, sheriff of Yorkshire).[109] Philip son of Baldwin (fined in 1190) held land from Geoffrey Hageth the royal justice in Coney Street, while Avenel (fined in 1190) looked after the town house of Richard of Huddleston, owner of the manor of Huddleston in west Yorkshire where stone for York Minster was quarried.[110] These connections continued after 1190: both Warin of Cuningestrata and Henry of Fishergate (among those fined for the massacre) were employed on the works restoring and enlarging the castle after 1190.[111]

Perhaps the most important presence in York before 1190, and indeed a critical absence in 1190 itself, was Ranulf de Glanville, the former royal justiciar, sheriff of Yorkshire and close friend to Henry II, who had presided over several of the courts in which York citizens had been fined in the 1180s. Glanville was absent from York in March 1190, since he had left the government on the accession of Richard in 1189 and departed on the crusade.[112] Despite his association with the unpopular novel demands of Henry II's government he too had become an established presence in the city. In particular he had acquired a large stone house immediately before the west front of York Minster. The house had been forfeited to the king by Walter son of Daniel between 1178 and 1181 because Walter had murdered his wife (his guilt having been decided by a duel in the king's court). It would have made an imposing residence for Glanville's visits to York, but shortly before 1189 he granted it to William of Fishergate who in turn gave it to the hospital of St Leonard, a gift that was confirmed by Henry II.[113] It is notable, however, that Petergate was not one of the streets from which many citizen property owners were fined in 1190, perhaps because Petergate lay within the archbishop's jurisdiction, and to some extent was dominated by the community of the cathedral close. Whether by accident or design, Glanville's house lay away from the neighbourhoods of those citizens who were most strongly associated with events in 1190.

The months following the accession of Richard I were important in the lives of all these men, for a reason other than the massacre in March 1190. For it was in those same months that the citizens of York first won exemp-

---

[109] See above and also BL MS Cotton Nero D. III, fol. 107r; YML, MS Cartulary of St Mary's Abbey, fol. 2r; *EYC*, VII, 9.
[110] *EYC* I, 180, no. 216.
[111] *PR 3–4 Richard I*, p. 61.
[112] J. Hudson, 'Glanville, Ranulf de (1120s?–1190)', *ODNB* (Oxford, 2004).
[113] Between 1205 and 1214 the house was demolished in order to enlarge the Minster Close around the west end of the cathedral: BL MS Cotton Nero D. III, fol. 130v; BL MS Cotton Claudius B. III, fol. 40r; YML, L2/1, pt ii, fol. 45r–v, pt iii, fols. 42r, 62r, 67v; pt iv fol. 8r; Rees Jones, 'Property, Tenure and Rents', II, 206–9.

tion from taxes on their trade throughout the Angevin empire, and were also allowed to pay the balance of the annual farm due from the city directly to the crown, without the sheriff acting as intermediary.[114] The right to farm the city directly from the king lapsed after just one year. We do not know why, but might speculate that the massacre in March was the primary reason that the citizens failed to maintain this privilege which would not be confirmed again until 1212 when King John granted the city the right to pay its own farm in perpetuity by charter.[115] Instead of being the first county town to receive this privilege by charter, York became one of the last.[116]

This achievement of civic liberty needs to be placed in context. The inhabitants of York were already well used to managing their own internal affairs, regulating trade, and holding courts without any royal prescription and without keeping any records.[117] The new freedom to pay their own farm, acquired first in 1189-90 and again in 1212, did not therefore mark the beginning of local government in York, but it did represent a decisive moment in which that autonomy was extended and reinforced through the transfer of responsibilities for royal administration in the city from the royal sheriff of the county to the citizens themselves. Winning, but also then losing, the right to pay their own farm is a forgotten but crucial part of the civic context to the attacks on the king's Jews in York that year, in part because it perhaps reinforced a new emphasis being placed on the other cultural contexts through which York citizens were asserting their autonomy from royal administration around 1190, in particular the idea of York as a Christian city founded in the shadow of York Minster. The final context in illuminating the simmering cauldron which exploded in March 1190 is faith; in this case, the meaning and uses of faithfulness in both constructing and disrupting neighbourliness.

As Paul Hyams indicates 'faith' was a powerful concept which militated against the easy integration of new immigrants who were not Christian. In York the Christian faith had a strong historical resonance in a city which had developed in the shadow of its cathedral church and which had no long tradition of royal government. Indeed before 1200 the courts of York Minster and other religious institutions, such as St Mary's abbey and St Leonard's hospital often provided more effective and more local places of trust for residents than did the royal courts.[118] The flourishing cult of St William in York (a recent archbishop who had died in 1154 and was canonized in 1170) also provided a vehicle through which local people could organize them-

---

114 *PR 2 Richard I*, p. 59; Miller, 'Medieval York', pp. 30–1, 33.

115 *Rot. Chart.*, pp. 40b, 187.

116 J. Tait, *The Medieval English Borough: Studies on Its Origins and Constitutional History* (Manchester, 1936), p. 291.

117 Palliser, 'York's Civic Liberties', p. 89.

118 For what follows see: S. Rees Jones, 'The Cults of St William of York and St Kenelm of Winchcombe', in *Cities, Texts and Social Networks 400–1500: Experiences and Perceptions of Medieval Urban Space*, ed. C. Goodson et al. (Farnham, 2010), pp. 193–214.

selves and express their desires for good government in two ways. First, local saints' cults made it legitimate for local people to group together in order to raise and spend money on good causes, including the construction of a new stone bridge across the river Ouse. Second, through the recording of mundane miracles (the revival of children who had fallen down wells or of middle-aged men felled by strokes), the cults provided ordinary people with a public theatre in which they could articulate the things that really mattered to them: the health of their family, their problems with old age, difficult personal relationships, the sufferings and cruelties inflicted by war. These were the problems which affected their daily health, wealth and happiness. They were very far removed from the agenda of royal government but became one of the principal cornerstones of municipal self-government down to modern times. Certainly in York the cult of St William was in many ways more fundamental to the successful foundation of civic government than the acquisition of a commune and it is telling that the main offices of civic government were located in the chapel of St William built after 1170 on Ouse Bridge, where a fraternity of prominent citizens established both a hospital and other charities for the poor of the city. Such faith communities were formed around a concern for mundane domestic issues which should have provided the kind of motivation to enable Jews and Christians to live well together, to share their anxieties about child-care, poverty and old age. But by their very nature such fraternities excluded Jews, forcing them to develop separate public networks of mutuality and charitable assistance.

This powerful conjunction of resistance to royal interference and the embracing of local faith institutions is nowhere more evident than in York's common seal, one of the most remarkable survivals from York and one of the earliest surviving civic seals in England.[119] The seal is also attached to a charter containing one of the earliest references to the citizens acting together as a corporate body, a commonalty. It was issued not long after the momentous months in which York both first acquired the right to pay its own farm to the crown and just as quickly was plunged into the horrific events of 16 March 1190. The design of the civic seal imitated the royal chancery seal in size and colouring, being some 2.5 inches in diameter and made of green wax.[120] However the legends and iconography of its two faces give equal weight to king and church. One side depicts a walled city (or possibly, even, a castle) and the (now damaged) legend: SIG[IL]LUM CIV[I]VM [CIVIT]A[TIS...] FIDELES R[EG]IS (the seal of the citizens of the city of York, ... the faithful of the king). This is probably the earliest surviving view of York, and may provide a unique insight into the possible appearance of the castle, in par-

---

[119] BL Add. Charter 10636; *British Museum Catalogue of Seals*, no. 5542; R. B. Pugh, 'The Seals, Insignia, Plate and Officers of the City', in *VCH, City of York*, pp. 544–6.
[120] An impression of the royal chancery seal of Henry II is appended to the city's oldest surviving royal charter: YCA A1.

ticular, close to 1190.[121] On the other side the seal displays the image of St Peter flanked by two angels and the legend: [SIG]ILLUM ECL[ESI]E SAN[CTI PET]RI CAT[HEDRALIS E]BURAC[ENSIS] (the seal of the cathedral church of St Peter of York).[122] This new civic seal perfectly illustrates how York's development in the twelfth and thirteenth centuries was fundamentally shaped by both the ancient lordship of the church and the more recent lordship of the crown. It asserts that the development of a corporate civic identity was constructed within the context of faithfulness to both. Made not long after the citizens had won (but also lost) their long-sought status as a commune (a word that is not included in the legend as it is in other towns' early common seals), and before this title was officially regained in 1212, the seal perhaps betrays a determination to act as a body of citizens regardless of any formal concession of such privilege from the crown. The unique use of the term 'fideles' in the legend in the aftermath of 1190 is a particularly evocative (even chilling) word for a group of citizens in constant negotiation with the different authorities demanding their loyalty. It was a word used increasingly commonly at the time, in other legal contexts, as an alternative to 'barones': the king's barons also emphasized their faithfulness to the king (at a time when many had not been so faithful).[123] Since the citizens of London also described themselves (on their seal) as 'barones' it is possible that York's leading citizens were aware of the multiple claims they were making by using this word: as important as London, as faithful subjects of the crown (in the face of evidence to the contrary) and above all as a citadel of Christian government. The seal suggests an acute awareness within the city of its external and historical reputation, and also illustrates how much these citizens, living close to their new Jewish neighbours and in daily interchange with them, were at the same time constructing a sense of citizenship which drew explicitly on their faith.

So were the citizens of York who were fined in 1190 simply the most important citizens of York and innocent of any direct part in the violence unlike the working and young men of town and country and at least some knights of the shire, as Newburgh claimed, or were they (as the citizens fined at Lincoln were said to be) guilty of the massacre of the Jews in 1190? The evidence presented here offers no clear answer. It does demonstrate, however, that those listed in the pipe rolls in 1190 and 1194 were very closely associated as neighbours with both the leaders of the mob and their victims on that night

---

[121] The image is unlike those on other city seals and does not appear to be a walled city. It shows a central tall crenellated tower with a double-arched window, flanked by two shorter towers and surrounded by a curtain wall.

[122] See Pugh, 'Seals, Insignia, Plate and Officers', p. 544; S. Rees Jones, 'York's Civic Administration, 1354–1464', in *Government of Medieval York*, ed. Rees Jones, pp. 108–40 (p. 121).

[123] M. Gervers and N. Hamonic, '*Pro Amore Dei*: Diplomatic Evidence of Social Conflict during the Reign of King John', in *Law as Profession and Practice in Medieval Europe: Essays in Honor of James A. Brundage*, ed. K. Pennington and M. H. Eichbauer (Farnham, 2011), pp. 231–62 (pp. 251–2).

in March. Even if they did not reveal it, they certainly knew very well what had happened and who was responsible for it.

As Dobson so acutely concluded his study of the massacre in York in 1190 'it was the Jews who had to pay the harshest price for the unpopularity of royal government whose purposes they served'.[124] This chapter has in part developed that theme: the leading citizens of York were indeed feeling the grip of a new style of national bureaucracy which was replacing more personal aspects of royal government and beginning to invade many aspects of their daily life. The alternative framework on which they could, and did, construct a collective identity was that of their Christian faith. But this is only part of the story and in itself oversimplifies the many connections between citizens and knights, royal officials and merchants, Christians and Jews who lived in such very close proximity with each other in the small neighbourhoods of Coney Street and Walmgate. It is within those intimate, informal and complicated personal relationships, which can barely be recovered historically, that the real causes and consequences of the massacre of York 1190 should be sought.

---

[124] Dobson, *JMY*, p. 37.

2

Prelude and Postscript to the York Massacre: Attacks in East Anglia and Lincolnshire, 1190

Joe Hillaby

The York massacre on 'Shabbat ha-Godol', whilst by far the most disastrous attack on a Jewish community, did not occur in isolation. The widespread riots in London, following Richard I's coronation on 3 September 1189, led to a series of onslaughts on Jewish communities in the eastern counties of England, the heartland of the late twelfth-century English provincial Jewry.

Ralph de Diceto, dean of St Paul's from 1180 to *c.* 1200, has little to say about the events in London, probably because, the see being vacant, he took the place of the bishop of London at the coronation and subsequent festivities. For a detailed account of events in London we have to turn to William of Newburgh's *Historia*, which explains that the riot erupted when the press carried some Jews, who along with women had been forbidden entry, into Westminster Palace. The sources reveal that the London mob was predominant, with a sprinkling of retainers of nobles attending the ceremony, and a number of fire-raisers. Ultimately, as Newburgh points out, in the general desire for plunder 'neither friends nor companions' were spared.[1]

Attacks on Jewries spread to the provinces. According to Diceto, the first took place at Norwich on 6 February, followed by assaults at Stamford (Lincolnshire), York and Bury St Edmunds (Suffolk) on 7, 16 and 18 March respectively.[2] What follows is an attempt to trace their path and character, against the background of the emerging provincial Jewish communities concerned.

Lynn (Norfolk)

Richard I, Newburgh tells us, departed on crusade, 'holding a solemn conference with the French king', on 30 December 1189. The first attack was not,

---

[1]   Diceto, *Historical Works*; WN, ed. Howlett (Bk IV, ch. 1). For general discussion of the London riot, see J. Hillaby, 'The London Jewry: William I to John', *JHS* 33 (1995 for 1992–94), 1–44 (pp. 26–30).
[2]   Diceto, *Historical Works* II, 75–6.

as Diceto asserts, in Norwich, but on the Lynn Jewry, in January. Toponym
and other evidence indicates that this was an off-shoot of an earlier community at nearby Castle Rising, where in *c.* 1138 William d'Aubigny, first
earl of Arundel, had built a remarkable keep, a smaller version of Henry I's
castle at Norwich, to celebrate his marriage to the dowager queen, Adeli-
za.[3] Within its bailey of some twenty acres he founded a small town, where
Stephen granted him the right to establish a mint.[4] A Jewish presence may
have been essential for the mint's initial success, but the opening of Henry
II's reign witnessed its closure and the movement of members of the community from Rising to Lynn.

Lynn's development began with Henry I's grant to the d'Aubigny family of
'all the "misteria" of Lynn with a moiety of the market toll and other customs,
the port with its moorings for ships, the way of the water and the passage, with
all pleas'.[5] This port proved highly successful; down the Great and Little Ouse
came grain from some of the richest arable lands in England. The area between
the Millfleet and Purfleet, together with the church of St Margaret and a Saturday market-place, was granted by Bishop Herbert de Losinga to the monks of
his new cathedral church at Norwich in *c.* 1096. The prior of Lynn was a client
of Deulebene, a Jew of Rising. By 1146x50, a charter shows that the original settlement and port facilities had expanded north of the Purfleet into 'Newland',
where a second, Tuesday, market-place and a chapel dedicated to St Nicholas,
the saint of sailors, merchants and pawnbrokers, were established.[6] The pipe
rolls indicate the town's growth by 1176/7, when the borough aid for Lynn
was 80 marks; Norwich, 100 marks.[7] A survey of *Newelond* of *c.* 1279 refers to
'Jewislane', at the south-east corner of the Tuesday market-place, where boats
from Norway, the Baltic, Flanders and Italy anchored in the thirteenth century.
Only *c.* 1860 did it become Surrey Street.[8]

Events at Lynn in January 1190 are described in detail by Newburgh, who
stresses the size and wealth of Lynn and its arrogant or warlike ('feroces')
Jews. This description is probably more appropriate to the affluent York
community, only eighteen miles south of Newburgh Priory. Notable, too,
is his acceptance of the citizens' attempts to exculpate themselves.[9] Conflict
arose, he relates, when the Jews besieged a church, probably St Nicholas's

3 *King's Works* I, 39; R. A. Brown, *Castles from the Air* (Cambridge, 1989), pp. 80–2.
4 M. Blackburn, 'Coinage and Currency', in *The Anarchy of King Stephen's Reign*, ed. E. King
   (Oxford, 1994), pp. 145-205 at 154, 159, 161.
5 D. M. Owen, 'Bishop's Lynn: The First Century of a New Town?', in *Proceedings of the Battle
   Conference on Anglo-Norman Studies II, 1979*, ed. R. A. Brown (Woodbridge, 1980), pp. 141–53.
6 Ibid., p. 151.
7 *PR 23 Henry II*, p. 125.
8 E. Rutledge and P. Rutledge, 'Kings Lynn and Great Yarmouth, Two Thirteenth-Century
   Surveys', *Norfolk Archaeology* 37 (1978), 92–114 (pp. 92–7); *The Making of Kings Lynn: A Documentary Survey*, ed. D. M. Owen, *Records of Social and Economic History, n.s. 9* (London, 1984),
   pp. 44–51.
9 WN, ed. Howlett (Bk. IV, ch. 7).

chapel, where a convert had sought safety from members of his former community. When cries of 'Help for the Christian!' were heard, the townsfolk, Newburgh explains, 'acted negligently, for fear of the king', but young foreigners, sailors who had come there for trade, entered the fray with gusto, storming and plundering the Jewry, burning its houses and killing the inhabitants. Lacking the protection of a castle, many members of the community were slaughtered. The foreign sailors loaded their booty, boarded their ships and set sail. The day after, a well-known Jewish physician, 'honoured by Christians for his skill and behaviour', arrived in the town. Met by the grisly sight, and foretelling divine vengeance, he was the citizens' last victim. Questioned by the chancellor and his officers, the townspeople blamed 'the strangers' for the massacre.

Not all members of the former Rising community suffered this fate. Toponyms show that a number had moved not to Lynn but to Chichester[10] where d'Aubigny, confirmed in his earldom of Arundel by Henry II, had gained control of the town and castle, augmenting his position in Sussex.[11] Rising's Jews were well established here by 1186, the year of the Guildford tallage, for which the community still owed £285 in 1191/2. For the Northampton *Promissum* of 1194 Chichester, assessed at £26, ranked twelfth of the twenty-four Jewries.[12] In the 1197/8 pipe rolls one even finds a Solomon 'Jew of Arundel'.[13]

Norwich (Norfolk)

Newburgh makes no mention of an attack on the Norwich Jewry. Diceto alone reports that 'on 6 February 1190 as many Jews as were found in their houses were butchered; some took refuge in the castle', only some 200 yards from the Jewry, which was in the market-place, facing St Peter Mancroft church.[14] Although refaced in the 1830s, the castle built by Henry I was much as we see it today.[15] The pipe rolls indicate that the number slain was small, for the total value of their chattels was only £1 8s. 7½d.[16] The county's sheriff and castellan had already shown themselves well able to protect the Jews during a crisis.[17] Payments by the Norwich Jewry to the 1194 *Promissum* provide details of the families that found refuge in the castle. Twelve heads of households can be identified, including Jurnet of Norwich, one of the most prominent members of the twelfth-century English Jewry, and his brother,

---

10 *PR 3–4 Richard I*, p. 194.
11 *King's Works* II, 612.
12 I. Abrahams, 'The Northampton *Donum* of 1194', *JHSE Miscellanies* 1 (1925), lxvi–lxvii.
13 *PR 9 Richard I*, p. 224.
14 Diceto, *Historical Works* II, 75.
15 *King's Works* II, 753–5.
16 *PR 2 Richard I*, p. 1; not £28 7s. 2d. as in Lipman, *JMN*, p. 58.
17 *The Life and Miracles of St William of Norwich*, ed. A. Jessopp and M. R. James (Cambridge, 1896), pp. 43–9.

Benedict, one of the principal creditors of Bury St Edmunds abbey.[18] The brothers contributed all but £16 of the Norwich payment of £90 14s. 5d. in 1194. Others included the families of four exiles from the former seigneurial Jewry at Bungay in Suffolk; Abraham, Mosse, Ursell and his brother, Isaac. Norwich, which had stood first amongst the provincial Jewries in the 1159 *Donum*, was now merely sixth.[19] Who was responsible for the attack? Diceto attributes the assaults on the Jewries at Norwich, Stamford, Bury and even York to crusaders.[20] This is discussed in the conclusion, but the evidence suggests it was probably not the case at Norwich.

Jurnet's eldest son, Isaac, who succeeded to the business *c.* 1197,[21] would have been with his parents in 1190 when they fled to Norwich castle and no doubt watched their Jewry consumed by the flames. He was not inhibited by this experience. Imprisoned by John in 1210, he had the courage and skills to negotiate for his life, the king accepting his offer of 10,000 marks, payable at 1 mark per day.[22] In 1217 the Council of Regency released the more prominent Jews from prison so that, in Nicholas Vincent's words, they might be 'a prop to the hard-pressed Exchequer'. Isaac renewed his promise to pay the fine at 365 marks per annum. Between 1218 and 1220 he took full advantage of the support of the Exchequer of the Jews, whose plea rolls record some twenty-seven claims made by him for repayment.[23] Vincent refers to the possibility of a personal relationship between Isaac and Peter des Roches, the powerful bishop of Winchester. The fine rolls for 1221 and 1225 show that Isaac's payments were reduced from 365 marks, first to 250, then 200 marks and in 1225 to £100. Isaac felt confident enough *c.* 1225 to quit the Norwich Jewry and move to a riverside house, now Wensum Lodge, in King Street, almost a kilometre from the security of the castle. There he was to go from strength to strength, his payment being ultimately reduced in 1234 to 60 marks, a sixth of the original amount negotiated with John.[24]

Stamford (Lincolnshire) and Northampton

Only at Stamford does Newburgh attribute an 1190 massacre to crusaders. His extensive account describes how on 7 March 'a multitude of young men who had taken the sign of the cross and were ready to leave for Jerusalem'

[18] Brakelond, *Chron.*, pp. 5–6.

[19] *PR 5 Henry II*, p. 12; J. Hillaby, 'Jewish Colonisation in the Twelfth Century', in *JMB*, ed. Skinner, pp. 15–40 (p. 21); Abrahams, 'Northampton *Donum*', pp. lxvi–lxvii.

[20] Diceto, *Historical Works* II, 75.

[21] *PR 9 Richard I*, p. 233.

[22] *CPR 1216–25*, p. 180.

[23] N. Vincent, *Peter des Roches: An Alien in English Politics, 1205–1238* (Cambridge, 1996), pp. 177, 179; *CPR 1216–25*, pp. 98, 105, 179, 180; *CPREJ*, I, 13, 15.

[24] Vincent, *Peter des Roches*, p. 179; *Rot. Litt. Claus.* II, 67; *CFR Henry III*, II, 534, no. 134, 537, no. 157.

came to Stamford's Lent fair. Indignant that the Jews possessed so much whilst they, facing such a journey, had so little, they believed they would be serving Christ if they attacked his enemies, whose goods they coveted. None of the locals or others at the fair hindered them; some even helped. Several Jews were slaughtered; the rest, Newburgh reports, 'were received within the castle' overlooking the market-place. As at Lynn, the assailants left with no questions asked.[25]

Newburgh relates that one of them, John, 'a most audacious youth', fled to Northampton, where he was murdered and his corpse thrown outside the town walls. It was believed to be the body of a martyr, presumably of the Jews, and to have worked miracles, thus offering a lucrative cult for the town's tradesmen. Hugh of Avalon, bishop of Lincoln (1186–1200), hastened to Northampton, where an episcopal anathema and 'the protection of his guardian angels, ... [that] armed him with divine might, caused ... the burgesses ... to give way out of shame'. This was but one of many strange and informal cults that developed in the twelfth century, an era of irrational popular zeal. St William of Perth was a Scots baker, murdered on pilgrimage at Canterbury; in 1190 the pope outlawed the cult of a drunkard. In 1234, under Gregory IX, the papacy took control of the canonization process.[26]

Did the events at Stamford constitute a massacre? Certainly the killing was wanton, but were there, as Diceto records, 'many' ('multi') victims?[27] Newburgh, for Barrie Dobson 'perhaps the most incisive and critical of all English medieval chroniclers', refers to only 'aliquot' ('some' or 'several') victims.[28] Nor does Diceto mention the Jews taking refuge in the castle. The pipe rolls provide little evidence to indicate that Stamford was host to a sizeable Jewish community in the later twelfth century, despite its considerable economic importance and strategic links with the Wash. In the 1184/5 pipe roll Isaac 'son of Simon of Stamford ... remains at Stamford', possibly suggesting that other Jews were content to travel from their homes at Lincoln for the town's Lenten fair.[29] In the 1194 *Promissum* no Jews are recorded in the town, although a Manasser of Stamford paid £10 at Lincoln and Isaac of Stamford £3 at Northampton.[30] Had they found safety in the castle?

---

[25] Diceto, *Historical Works* II, 75; WN, ed. Howlett (Bk. IV, ch. 8).

[26] E. W. Kemp, *Canonization and Authority in the Western Church* (Oxford, 1948); *Magna Vita Sancti Hugonis*, ed. D. L. Douie and H. Farmer, 2 vols., OMT (Oxford, 1985), II, 17.

[27] Diceto, *Historical Works* II, 75.

[28] Dobson, *JCME*, p. 15; WN, ed. Howlett (Bk. IV, ch. 8).

[29] *PR 31 Henry II*, p. 94.

[30] Abrahams, 'The Northampton *Donum*', pp. lxx, lxiii.

Lincoln

Newburgh had no doubts who attacked this Jewry: 'Lincolnienses vero', 'to speak the truth, the people of the city'. Stirred by the news of events elsewhere, they 'broke out in a sudden commotion' against the Jews who, well aware of the recent fate of the communities at Lynn, Norwich and Stamford, were on their guard for any signs of trouble and quickly retired, with their valuables, to the walled upper city and its castle. For Newburgh, 'the slight commotion was soon quieted'.[31]

After his experiences at Stamford and Northampton, Bishop Hugh must also have been vigilant for any anti-Jewish activity in his cathedral city. The author of his *Life* refers to him 'bravely and intrepidly advancing unprotected into the midst of an armed band at his cathedral at Lincoln', and mentions later 'the enraged clerks and laymen of Lincoln'.[32] This is difficult to understand; the cathedral lay within the walled upper city, a short distance east of the castle. Possibly, seeking to calm the mob and prevent them plundering Jewish and other property in the town, Hugh advanced outside the south gate of the upper city, at the southern end of what today is Steep Hill. Certainly, Lincoln's Jews were convinced that Bishop Hugh had risked his life for them. At his funeral, ten years later, they 'came out weeping to render him what homage they could, mourning and lamenting him aloud as the faithful servant of the one God'. Their respect for this man of God made the people realize that the prophecy, 'the Lord has caused all nations to bless him', had been fulfilled.[33]

Richard received news of the York massacre whilst in Normandy, on the first leg of his journey to Palestine.[34] He was enraged, Newburgh tells us, at not only the treason against his royal authority but also the harm to his income. As recently as 23 March, he had granted Isaac, eldest son of Rabbi Josce, a charter of liberties for the English and Norman Jewries, the penultimate clause of which commanded royal officers 'to guard and protect' his Jews.[35] He immediately commanded his chancellor, William de Longchamp, to ensure that the perpetrators were punished.[36]

Longchamp went first to York, arriving about Ascension Day, 3 May. Malebisse and his fellow conspirators had fled to Scotland, but the chancellor sacked the constable and replaced the sheriff with his own brother, Osbert. The citizens attempted to distance themselves from the 'promiscuous and countless mob' over whom, they protested, they had no control.

---

31 WN, ed. Howlett (Bk. IV, ch. 9).
32 *Magna Vita S. Hugonis* II, 17.
33 *Magna Vita S. Hugonis* II, 228.
34 WN, ed. Howlett (Bk. IV, ch. 11).
35 *Foedera* I, 51.
36 WN, ed. Howlett (Bk. IV, ch. 11).

Longchamp apparently agreed, for, as Barrie Dobson observes, he imposed 'a series of heavy fines based on individual wealth rather than culpability'.[37]

Longchamp then proceeded to Lincoln, where sixty pairs of iron fetters had been despatched on his orders.[38] The leaders and participants in the riot were almost certainly well known to the sheriff, bishop and others, including Lincoln's bailiffs. William son of Warner was evidently held to have been ultimately responsible, for his fine was by far the largest: £100, a third more than that imposed on William son of Sirich at York. Hill, who provides a list of Lincoln bailiffs and mayors, had a remarkable knowledge of the city's leading families in the late twelfth and early thirteenth centuries.[39] Thus we know that William son of Warner was a member of one of Lincoln's major political dynasties. His father was a city bailiff in 1164/5, 1167/8 and 1169–73 but William never held this office even though he was a man of considerable substance, as rector of the ancient church of Saints Peter and Paul in the Bail (the upper city) and holder of half a knight's fee in Stow.[40] The family's political authority apparently passed to his cousin, 'William nephew of Warner', city bailiff in 1186/7, 1189/90 and 1216, and mayor in 1217/18, who significantly is not amongst those fined. The second largest penalty was imposed on Lefwin(e), the last of a long line of city moneyers of that name.[41] He paid 40 marks (£26 13s. 4d.), the same as Ralf son of Lambert, the draper. Ralf's brother, William, paid £5; another brother, Hamo, 6 marks; and their father 4 marks. Fined 20 marks each were Reinbald of Wicheforde, 'the Rich', and Hugh the Fleming, bailiff in 1182/3 and 1187/8. Reinbald was to pay an equivalent amount to the Lincoln tallage in 1202. Ulf de Hundegate was fined 12 marks, and Richard son of James, bailiff in 1201 and coroner in 1218, paid 10 marks with three others. Of the ninety-four Lincoln men fined, seventy-eight paid 5 marks or less, and forty-four paid £1 or less. Full details, from the pipe roll of 1191/2, are reproduced in the appendix to this essay.[42] In contrast to the fines imposed at York, those at Lincoln were based not on individual wealth, but on a hierarchy of guilt.

Bury St Edmunds

Diceto records that fifty-seven Jews were slaughtered at Bury, 'as it is said', on Palm Sunday, 18 March, 1190.[43] His qualification is notable, for no such

---

[37] *PR 2 Richard I*, p. 59; Dobson, *JCME*, p. 21.
[38] *PR 2 Richard I*, p. 3; Devizes, *Chronicle*, p. 11.
[39] J. W. F. Hill, *Medieval Lincoln* (Cambridge, 1948), pp. 379–96.
[40] Ibid., pp. 103, 223, 295, 389–90, 393, 397–8.
[41] One appears on the Lincoln reverse stamp of a coin of King Magnus the Good of Norway, 1035–47, Ibid., pp. 32, 53, 174 n. 3, 397; H. R. Mossop, *The Lincoln Mint c. 890–1279* (Newcastle-upon-Tyne, 1970), Pl. XCII, nos 7–21; Pl. XCIV, nos. 10–16, 22–4.
[42] *PR 3–4 Richard II*, pp. 15–16, 242–3.
[43] Diceto, *Historical Works* II, 75–6.

massacre is mentioned by Roger of Howden, in his *Chronica*, Newburgh or even Bury's own chronicler, Jocelin of Brakelond.[44] The Michaelmas 1190 pipe roll does refer to the chattels of Jews killed, but these were valued at a mere £1 8s. 2d. Whilst confirming there were deaths, this hardly supports a total of fifty-seven. However, the 1191 pipe roll for Cambridge and Huntingdon shows that a fine of 100 marks for 'the Jews slain at Bury' was imposed on a Thomas de Burgo.[45]

Before 1190, the community had experienced varied treatment at the hands of the abbots of the great Benedictine monastery. There was no Bury contribution to the 1159 *Donum*. The earliest reference to a Jewry is by Jocelin of Brakelond, who reports that in 'the time of troubles', when Robert earl of Leicester's Flemish mercenaries landed near Orford in 1173, during the abbacy of the aged Hugh I (1157–80), the Jewish womenfolk and children were sheltered in the pittancery.[46] After Hugh's death there was a bitter contest for the succession, between Samson of Tottington, the sub-prior, and William the sacrist. William, Jocelin attests, was 'referred to as the father and patron of the Jews'; under his protection they 'had free entrance and … went everywhere throughout the monastery, wandering by the altars and shrines while Mass was being celebrated. Their money was deposited in our treasury, in his custody.'[47] Samson prevailed, elected in 1182 on an anti-Jewish ticket. He persuaded Jocelin to write a *Life* of 'the holy boy Robert [who] suffered martyrdom and was buried in our church [where] many signs and wonders were performed'.[48] Shortly afterwards Sancto, a Bury Jew, was fined 5 marks by the crown for taking 'vessels used at the service of the altar' as pledges.[49] The abbey's principal creditors, however, were outsiders: according to Jocelin, in 1177 William son of Isabel, sheriff of London, was owed £1040; and Benedict, brother of Jurnet of Norwich, £1280.[50] The mountainous debt Samson inherited could only have inflamed his hostility towards Bury's Jewish community.

According to Jocelin, Samson insisted that the Jews were 'St Edmund's men', as they lived within the ancient liberty of his church, so he was not answerable to the king, or his chancellor, for the attack on the Jewry. Richard's ministers countered that since Henry I's reign 'the Jews and all they have are the king's', and that 'no Jew, without royal licence, may subject himself to any magnate'. In response, Samson banished all Jews from the abbey's liberty, but the king commanded that they should retain their movables and the

---

44 Howden, *Chronica*.
45 *PR 2 Richard I*, pp. 1, 116.
46 Brakelond, *Chron.*, p. 10.
47 Ibid., pp. 8–23; D. Knowles, C. N. L. Brooke, and V. C. M. London, eds., *Heads of Religious Houses, England and Wales I: 940–1216* (Cambridge, 1972), pp. 32–3.
48 Brakelond, *Chron.*, p. 16.
49 *PR 29 Henry II*, p. 14.
50 C. N. L. Brooke, *London, 800–1216: The Shaping of a City* (London, 1975), p. 373; Brakelond, *Chron.*, p. 2.

value of their houses. Contrary to the abbot's directions, the royal justices granted them the right to two nights' lodging in Bury when they returned to claim repayment of loans. Bury's Jews left the town with an armed escort.[51]

There are vestiges of the cultural heritage of Bury's Jewish community. Pembroke College Library, Cambridge, Manuscript 59 preserves a fragment of a Hebrew prayer book, used to line the front board of a glossed book of Isaiah. This can be dated to the twelfth century and, according to its original shelfmark, B [Bible] 61, and inscription, *Liber Sancti Aedmundi*, belonged to the Bury abbey library until the dissolution. The manuscript contains twenty-two lines of Hebrew text, of which only eight are complete, with part of the liturgy for Yom Kippur, including 'selihot', penitentiary prayers. For Moses Abrahams it was 'no hazardous suggestion' that it formed part of a 'siddur', a prayer book, in use at the Bury synagogue until the expulsion in 1190, when it passed into Christian hands.[52] The Bodleian Laud Manuscript Or. 174 is a Hebrew psalter divided into 131 chapters and probably of the end of the twelfth century. The 'Incipit' of each chapter is translated into Latin of the Vulgate in a thirteenth-century English hand. A note on fol. 62v by Richard Brinkley, the Benedictine monk who became professor of theology at Oxford in 1502, records that 'this Hebrew psalter is from the library of the ancient monastery of St Edmund'.[53]

Dunstable (Bedfordshire)

In the *Gesta Regis*, attributed to Benedict of Peterborough but now accepted as the work of Howden, a brief note records that 'the Jews and their wives in the town of Dunstable were converted to the Christian faith and baptized and similarly in many English cities'. Roth interprets this as 'the entire diminutive community [having] saved itself from massacre by submitting to baptism';[54] but it may represent distortions of popular stories about the small Jewry that was closely associated with the Augustinian priory founded by Henry I. Richardson describes how a certain Christian called William bought a corrody, granting the right to board and lodging in the priory, from Prior Richard de Mores (1202–42). Getting further into debt, he pledged the cor-

---

[51] Ibid., pp. 45–6.

[52] M. R. James records that the volume was given by William Smart of Ipswich to Pembroke College in 1599. J. Olszowy-Schlanger, *Les manuscrits hébreux dans l'Angleterre médiévale: étude historique et paléographique* (Paris, 2003), pp. 34–5, 262–5; M. Abrahams, 'Leaf from an English *Siddur* of the Twelfth Century' *Jews' College Jubilee Volume* (London, 1906), pp. 109–13; M. R. James, *On the Abbey of St Edmund at Bury* (Cambridge, 1895), pp. 11, 48.

[53] A later inscription on the verso of the first folio announces in a bold hand '*Liber Guilielmi Laud Archiepi Cantuar: et Cancellarii Universitatis Oxon. 1633*', Olszowy-Schlanger, *Manuscrits hébreux*, pp. 35, 266–70; B. Smalley, *The Study of the Bible in the Middle Ages*, 2nd edn (Oxford, 1952), p. 342.

[54] Howden, *Gesta* II, 84; Roth, *HJE*, p. 22.

rody to an unnamed Jew, to the scandal of the local bishop, who insisted it be bought back – at a considerable premium. Tovey recounts that, shortly after his election, Prior Richard issued a charter to two London Jews, Flamengo and his son Leon, and their servants, 'to come and remain in the town of Dunstable, peacefully, quietly and honourably enjoying all the customs and liberties of the town like other members of the town'. In return Flamengo and his son were to pay the prior annually two silver spoons, each to the value of 12d.[55] Were such episodes the basis for the claims of conversion?

Ospringe (Kent), Colchester (Essex) and Thetford (Norfolk)

Roth, echoing Joseph Jacobs, has suggested that further attacks may have taken place on Jews at Ospringe, Colchester and Thetford, where pipe roll entries refer to recent murders of individual Jews.[56] At Ospringe there was no such attack, but a fine of 10 marks was imposed on the vill for failing to take appropriate action on the discovery of 'one of the king's Jews discovered dead'. This entry was repeated as a result of non-payment.[57] Just ten miles west of Canterbury on the route between the shrine of St Thomas and the port of Dover, Ospringe was too small to sustain a Jewish community. Its only claim to fame was the hospital for needy pilgrims and lepers founded *c.* 1234 by Henry III.[58] Later the Canterbury Jews found clients amongst the hospital's tenants.[59]

The 1195 pipe roll records an apparent assault on the Jewry at Colchester, but there is no reference to a Jew being killed, as at Thetford, or even found dead, as at Ospringe. Nevertheless, 'the men of Colchester' were fined 50 marks for releasing those accused on bail and not proceeding to prosecution.[60] Here lived Isaac, one of the wealthiest Jews of late twelfth century England, who in 1177, with Isaac and Aaron, the sons of Rabbi Josce, stood as surety for le Brun of London's 3000 mark fine. He was effectively ruined by the 1186 Guildford tallage, still owing £390 some eight years later.[61] Whether or not Isaac's property was the object of the attack, such was his relationship with the crown that he could ensure the sheriff's intervention on the Jewry's behalf.

55 Richardson, *EJ*, pp. 259–63; D'Blossiers Tovey, *Anglia Judaica: or the History and Antiquities of the Jews in England* (Oxford, 1738), pp. 83–6 *Annales Monastici*, ed. H. R. Luard, 5 vols., RS 36 (London, 1864–69), III, x–xii.
56 Roth, *HJE*, p. 21 quoting *PR 3–4 Richard I*, pp. 147, 203, 313; *5 Richard I*, p. 145; *Three Rolls of the King's Court in the Reign of King Richard I, AD 1194–1195*, PRS 14 (London, 1891), pp. 15, 16; *JAE Docs.*, pp. 112–13.
57 *PR 3–4 Richard II*, pp. 147, 313.
58 E. Prescott, *The English Medieval Hospital, c. 1050–1640* (London, 1992), pp. 41–2, 135.
59 *CPREJ* II, 49, 105–6, 159, 180, 242.
60 *PR 6 Richard I*, p. 36.
61 *PR 6 Richard I*, p. 34.

The 1159 *Donum* records Jewries at Thetford and Bungay, yet neither appears in the 1194 *Promissum*. Were they also victims of the 1190 riots? Both were founded during Stephen's reign by Hugh Bigod, created earl of Norfolk in 1140/41, but were evidently in Henry II's hands by 1159.[62] A number of Bungay Jews are listed at Norwich in 1194, having apparently moved voluntarily to the larger and more prosperous Jewry, where they occupied a site in the great market-place adjacent to the existing community; others, identified by their toponyms, were living at Hereford, Lincoln and Northampton.[63] By contrast, not a single Thetford toponym is to be found in the *Promissum*, even though in 1159 the community had ranked fifth amongst the provincial Jewries, contributing only 1 per cent less than Winchester and Cambridge.[64] In 1086 Thetford ranked sixth amongst the English boroughs, after London, Winchester, York, Norwich and Lincoln.[65] Here, until 1095 the diocesan centre of East Anglia, the Bigod family founded a Cluniac priory in 1103x4, where its earls were buried. Thus the early twelfth century borough and castle with its enormous motte were Bigod foundations. Thetford had a mint throughout Stephen's reign.[66] As at Castle Rising, Jewish expertise in the provision of silver was probably significant.

At Thetford, as at Canterbury and Bury, the site of the former Jewry came to be known as Heathenman Lane. It appears as Heathenman Street on Thomas Martin's plan for his *History of Thetford* (1779). Now Guildhall Street, it stretched from the Grassmarket of the early borough to the outer bailey of the castle, where the medieval market was founded.[67] Overall the evidence suggests Thetford Jewry's demise was related to the conflict between Henry II and Bigod in 1174. Thetford castle, confiscated in 1157 by Henry II, was destroyed prior to Hugh's revolt of June 1173.[68] When civil war broke out again in June 1174, Hugh, who had shown himself remorseless in Stephen's reign, led his men against Norwich where they slaughtered many of its people, then sacked and burned the city.[69] The reference in the 1192 pipe roll to 'Ursell of Ipswich, Isaac of Bedford and Seigneured of Bury St Edmunds rendering 50 marks for custody of the chattels, valued at £120, of Isaac Jew of Bury', killed at Thetford,[70] suggested to Roth that the Thetford Jewry was possibly the scene of another of the 1190 massacres. Yet whereas the fines on the citizens of York and the assessment of the chattels of the dead Jews at Norwich and Bury are recorded in the 1190 pipe roll, the reference to the death of a single Jew, who was not a resident but from Bury, occurs three years later. If not in the same league as York and Lincoln, Thetford was

---

62 W. L. Warren, *Henry II*, new edn (New Haven CT, 2000), p. 235.
63 Abrahams, 'Northampton *Donum*', pp. lxiv, lxvii, lxix, lxxii.
64 Hillaby, 'Jewish Colonisation', p. 21.
65 Tait, *Medieval English Borough*, p. 76.
66 Blackburn, 'Coinage', pp. 154, 159, 176, 178; Brown, *Castles*, pp. 213–14.
67 A. Crosby, *A History of Thetford* (Chichester, 1986), p. 102, fig. 8, Pl. 1.
68 Brown, *Castles*, pp. 169–70; Crosby, *History of Thetford*, p. 27.
69 Diceto, *Historical Works* I, 381.
70 *PR 3–4 Richard I*, p. 203; *5 Richard I*, p. 145.

still a wealthy town. Given the £318 he had imposed on the citizens of York, and £352 on those at Lincoln, it is difficult to believe that Longchamp would miss a further opportunity to raise funds for Richard if he had evidence of a massacre here.

The Crusaders

What evidence is there of crusader participation in the events of spring 1190? Diceto prefaced his paragraph on the risings at Norwich, Stamford and even York, as well as the 'massacre' at Bury, with the sentence, 'many in England who were intent on going to Jerusalem hastened first to rise up against the Jews before they fell upon the Saracens'. His whole paragraph, carefully excluding his reference to York, was included by Wendover in his *Flores Historiarum* and, following his death in 1234, by Matthew Paris in his *Chronica Majora*.[71] Diceto concluded, 'wherever Jews were found they were killed by the hands of crusaders, except those protected by municipal officials', probably a reference to the castellans at Norwich and Stamford.

Appalled by the events that followed the anointing of Richard I as king, a ceremony in which he played a significant role, Diceto found great difficulty in reconciling the London massacre with the teachings of the church as expressed by Calixtus II (1119–24) in *Sicut Judaeis*, his bull of protection for the Jewry. His interpretation of that massacre is that 'the peace of the Jews ('pax Judaeorum') which had been maintained since ancient times was broken by foreigners ('alienigenis')'. Newburgh provides a more down-to-earth explanation: that there might be general rejoicings on his accession, Richard had issued a general amnesty. 'Gaolbirds went free to rob and plunder more boldly than previously'. Diceto's outrage evidently coloured his account of the attacks in the provinces, which he strongly condemns: 'we must not believe that such a massacre of the Jews was pleasing to wise men since it is written, "Slay them not, lest my people forget"', quoting part of David's prayer in Psalm 59. 11. This continues: 'scatter them by thy power; and bring them down, O Lord our shield'. Here Diceto is referring us to St Augustine who, in *Civitas Dei*, held that if the Jews were not permitted to live and were not dispersed throughout the world, the church would not have the benefit of their testimonies concerning those prophecies fulfilled by Jesus as our Messiah.

At Lynn Newburgh, seeking to play down the responsibility of the locals, stressed the role of the departed foreign traders but, in describing the murder of the celebrated Jewish physician, confirms the guilt of the townspeople.[72] At Norwich relations between townspeople and the Jewry had been tense ever since the ritual murder allegation of 1144, when John de Chesney,

---

71 Wendover, *Flowers of History* I, 176; Paris, *Chronica Majora* II, 358.
72 WN, ed. Howlett, Bk. IV, ch. 7.

the sheriff, leading the Jews from the cathedral to the safety of the castle, had to surround them with his armed guards to protect them from the ire of the citizenry. As Lipman shows, relations remained bad throughout the thirteenth century. In 1200, ignoring Calixtus II's often repeated bull, *Sicut Judaeis*, the burgesses broke into the Jewish cemetery.[73] Thirty years later, the claims of circumcision of a five-year-old led to fines when the townspeople obstructed the sheriff in the execution of his duty. Despite the appointment in 1234/5 of twenty-six prominent citizens as guardians of the Jews, in 1235 and 1238 there was arson and looting in the Jewry. In 1275 the patent rolls branded some Norwich Christians as 'Judaizantes', lending money at interest. Lipman points out that, during the coin-clipping crisis, the Jewry was 'reduced by half'. A few years before the expulsion Meir ben Elijah of Norwich, describing the life of Jews in the city in his poem, 'Put a Curse on my Enemy', wrote: 'the people's disgust is heard'; 'they make our yoke heavier ... and are finishing us off'.[74] There is reliable evidence of a crusader presence only at Stamford's Lent fair, were Diceto is supported by the more detailed account of Newburgh.

Nevertheless, the fear of 'crusaders' that Diceto so clearly expressed, perpetuated by Wendover and Paris, remained long in the memory of the officers of the Exchequer of the Jews. Twenty-eight years after the 1190 attacks, when the young Henry III's Council of Regency sought to restore the prosperity of the English Jewry after the long troubles during John's reign, orders were sent to the constables at Gloucester and Bristol, and sheriffs of Lincoln and Oxford, to supervise the appointment of 'the twenty-four better and more discrete citizens' who were to be 'custodians of our Jews', and protect them 'et maxime de crucesignatis'.[75]

---

[73] 'In opposition to the wickedness and avarice of evil men in these matters, we decree that no one shall presume to desecrate or reduce the cemeteries of the Jews or, with the object of extorting money, to exhume bodies there buried.' The bull had most recently been repeated by Innocent III in 1199, J. Parkes, *The Jew in the Medieval Community: A Study of his Political and Economic Situation* (London, 1938), pp. 211–12; *Pleas before the King or his Justices, 1198–1202*, ed. D. M. Stenton, 4 vols., Selden Society 67–8 and 83–4 (London, 1952–67), I, 295, no. 3110.

[74] Lipman, *JMN*, pp. 156–9; S. L. Einbinder, 'Meir b. Elijah of Norwich: Persecution and Poetry among Medieval English Jews', *JMH* 26 (2000), 145–62.

[75] *Rot. Litt. Claus.* I, 354b, 357a, 359b.

Appendix: Fines for Assault on the Lincoln Jewry, 1191
Source: PR 3-4 Richard I, pp. 15-16 and 242-3

£100
William son of Warner

40 m. = £26 13s. 4d.
Ralf son of Lambert
Lefwin the moneyer

20 m. = £13 6s. 8d.
Reinbald of Wicheforde
Hugh the Fleming

15 m. = £10
Martin son of Edric
William de Fiskerton

12 m. = £8
Ulf of Hundegate

10 m. = £6 13s. 4d.
Baldwin the tanner
Roger son of Brand
Thomas of Paris
Richard son of James

£5
William son of Lambert

6 m. = £4
Alan son of Brand
Hamo son of Lambert
Richard son of Sirild'

5 m. = £3 6s. 8d.
Godwin the rich
Robert of St John's
churchyard
Robert of Legerton
Hugh Painel
Osbert son of Turgar
Gerard the tailor

4 m. = £2 13s. 4d.
William son of Ougrim
Turgot the tanner
William son of Walter

Miles the porter
Ralf son of Walter
Marsilius the Fleming
Lambert the draper
Walter Dod

3 m. = £2
Hugh son of Ralf £2
Gundred the tanner
Robert son of Suartebrand
Simon son of Toke
AErnulf the little
Yuo son of Brand
Roger brother of William
John son of Hugh
William son of Orgar

2 m. = £1 6s. 8d.
John son of Suaue
Fulk the tanner
Nicholas son of Gunnilda
Roger son of the smith
William pes leporis
Robert son-in-law of Lambert
Richard son of Ase
Fulk son of William
Siward of Neweport
Adam Blund
Gilbert Gay
Robert son of Gamel

£1
Wiger the tailor
Roger the weaver
Wigot son of Wigot
Gamel canum
Robert son of Aumund
John son of Walter
Robert son of Emma
Constantius
John Ruffus

1 m. = 13s. 4d.
Ralf of Merston
William son of Brictiue

William the tailor
Richard the long
Robert nephew of Goscelin
William Collecnape
Robert son of Alnad
Herbert of Neweport
Martin son of Joscelin
Fulk the mercer
Arnulf the weaver
Simon son of Alan
Bonefacius

10s.
Richard Suaue

½ m. = 6s. 8d.
Goscelin the long
Robert son of Rumfare
Walter son of Wulmer
William of Kyrkested
Hugh son of John
Alan the dyer
Leuric of Potteregate
William nephew of James
Peter son-in-law of Lefric
Arnulf the tailor
Robert of Bongeia
Norman the weaver
William son of Gladew'
Ewan son of Walter
Robert of Geiton
Thomas son of Gode
Richard the villein
Warin the tailor
Arnald the sailor
Goscelin of Neweport
Peter Thore

Total 94 persons of whom:
79 paid 5 marks or less
66 paid £2 or less
44 paid £1 or less

Total £352 3s. 4d.
Average £3 15s.

3

William of Newburgh, Josephus and the New Titus[*]

Nicholas Vincent

The story that follows is to be read as an exercise in intellectual history, and in particular as an attempt to trace the debt owed not just by twelfth-century English chroniclers, but by English churchmen and kings, to the literary and historical traditions of a much more distant past. In pursuing this line of enquiry, I owe a special debt to two modern historians. The first, Barrie Dobson, in his study of the York massacre of 1190, has identified the chief contemporary witness to these events, the *Historia Rerum Anglicarum* of William of Newburgh, as a 'comparatively impartial and well-balanced if sometimes over-calculated' source.[1] The full extent to which Newburgh's account of the 1190 massacre is 'over-calculated' I shall in due course reveal. The second of my modern authorities is Peter Biller, whose study of Newburgh and the Cathars has revealed for the first time the extent to which Newburgh's historical writing was coloured by a profound familiarity with scripture and patristics, in this particular instance with Augustine, Jerome and Isidore writing on the heresies of the early Church.[2]

To state my thesis very briefly, I intend, by close analysis of his language and lexical peculiarities, to demonstrate that Newburgh depended heavily in his account of the York massacre upon careful and deliberate citation both of the Vulgate of St Jerome, and of the standard Latin translation of the *Bellum Judaicum* of Josephus, widely circulated in twelfth-century England. This dependence has previously been obscured by the fact that commentators on Newburgh's text have too often depended upon Joseph Stevenson's English translation, first published in the 1850s, without detailed recourse to New-

[*] For assistance, I am particularly grateful to Julie Barrau, Robert Bartlett, Hugh Doherty, John Gillingham, Tom Licence, Sarah Lipton, Nigel Morgan and Magnus Ryan. Karen Kletter most generously allowed me to consult her unpublished Ph.D. thesis.

[1] Dobson, *JMY*, p. 24.

[2] Peter Biller, 'William of Newburgh and the Cathar Mission to England', in *Life and Thought in the Northern Church c.1100–c.1700: Essays in Honour of Claire Cross*, ed. D. Wood, Studies in Church History, Subsidia Series 12 (Woodbridge 1999), pp. 10–30.

burgh's own Latin. From this solid and major key exposition, I shall then attempt a rather more subtle and enharmonic modulation. The evidence that Newburgh, like other English writers, was reading Josephus in the 1190s, leads me to question precisely why Josephus was so widely read, and what in particular might have inclined Englishmen of the 1180s and 90s to hang upon his words. Here I hope to produce new evidence of the image presented in the 1180s and 90s of the Roman emperor Titus, and in particular to suggest ways in which Titus and the portrait of him conveyed to and by the English chroniclers may have influenced perceptions of the Third Crusade, of the reign of Richard I, and of the succession and prospects of Richard's brother, the future king John.

Newburgh's *Historia*, preserved in a number of early manuscripts, has been widely used since the time of its first printing in the sixteenth century.[3] The standard modern edition, produced by Richard Howlett for the Rolls Series in the mid 1880s, appeared some years after the translation of the chronicle into modern English made by Joseph Stevenson in 1856, after the Latin edition of Newburgh's chronicle published in that same year by the English Historical Society.[4] In more recent times, commentators have also been able to draw upon John Gorman's 1960 edition of Newburgh's commentary on the Song of Songs.[5] Crafted as a thematic identification of the Virgin Mary as the beloved of the Song, Newburgh's commentary draws upon a quite remarkable range of scriptural quotations as well as upon knowledge of Augustine, Jerome, Leo, Ambrose, Gregory the Great and Paschasius Radbertus.[6] Despite his breadth of scriptural and patristic reference, Newburgh seems to have written his commentary with little or no knowledge of more recent exegesis or scriptural method. Thus he claims that his is the first commentary to offer a detailed exposition of the Song as celebration of the Virgin Mary, despite the fact that there were half a dozen such commentaries (by Rupert of Deutz, Honorius of Autun, Philip of Harvengt, William of Weyarn and Alan of Lille) available in the schools, in which precisely this identification between the 'Beloved' and the Virgin Mary had been made.[7] This,

---

3   First printed by William Silvius as *Rerum Anglicarum libri quinque* (Antwerp, 1567), repr. by H. Commeline, *Rerum Britannicarum … scriptores* (Heidelberg, 1587), and ed. (from another manuscript) Jean Picard, *Guilelmi Neubrigensis … de rebus Anglicis* (Paris, 1610). Re-edited, together with three sermons attributed to Newburgh, by Thomas Hearne, *Guilielmi Neubrigensis Historia sive Chronica Rerum Anglicarum, libris quinque*, 3 vols. (Oxford, 1719).

4   *Historia Rerum Anglicarum Willelmi Parvi de Newburgh*, ed. H. C. Hamilton, 2 vols. (London, 1856); WN, trans. Stevenson; WN, ed. Howlett with a brief survey of the nine surviving manuscripts in vol. 1, pp. xxxix–l.

5   *William of Newburgh's Explanatio sacri epithalamii in matrem sponsi*, ed. J. C. Gorman, Spicilegium Friburgense 6 (Fribourg, 1960).

6   ibid., noting the patristic quotations at p. 35. The quotation at p. 169, unidentified by Gorman, is from Ambrose, 'De Officiis Ministrorum', 1:30 (*PL* 16, col. 66A, 'Affectus tuus nomen imponit operi tuo').

7   ibid., pp. 21, 43–55.

together with Newburgh's ability to draw upon the Church fathers and the Bible, but not apparently upon the glosses offered by his contemporaries up to and including the *Glossa Ordinaria*, suggests learning and access to a collection of books that was itself rather old-fashioned by the time that Newburgh was writing, in the 1180s or 90s.

Newburgh's Song of Songs commentary was dedicated to the abbot of Cistercian Byland, before 1196. His *Historia* was dedicated to the abbot of Cistercian Rievaulx, before 1199, although perhaps still receiving additions as late as 1201.[8] As Nancy Partner, author of the most detailed of the Anglophone commentaries on William of Newburgh, points out, this suggests that, despite his membership of the convent of Augustinian Newburgh, half way between Rievaulx and Byland, William was a 'Cistercian' sort of thinker.[9] Far from being widely travelled in the schools of twelfth-century England or northern France, he was perhaps educated and depended upon the libraries of his own small corner of Yorkshire. The book collections upon which he could draw would have included not just his own convent's books at Newburgh (more or less entirely lost to us) but the far more extensive libraries of Byland and Rievaulx, for the second of which we have a detailed catalogue from the 1190s.[10]

Two other reflections here, before we pass on. Besides his indebtedness to scripture and to the Church fathers, William of Newburgh's historical writing demonstrates a particular reverence for the writings of the greatest of the historians of northern England, the Venerable Bede.[11] Hence, perhaps, the particularly rich and resonant Latin style in which Newburgh's history was composed. In addition, John Gillingham has for the first time made plain that Newburgh had access to the historical writings of his fellow Yorkshireman, Roger priest of Howden.[12] For a large part of his account of contempo-

---

[8]   ibid., pp. 3, 8–17. For the suggestion that William died or stopped writing shortly after October 1197, see J. Gillingham, 'William of Newburgh and Emperor Henry VI', in *Auxilia Historica: Festschrift für Peter Acht zum 90*, ed. W. Koch et al. (Munich, 2001), pp. 51–71 (pp. 68–70).

[9]   N. F. Partner, *Serious Entertainments: The Writing of History in Twelfth-Century England* (Chicago, 1977), p. 54. For an earlier, and in some ways more subtle study of William, see R. Jahncke, *Guilelmus Neubrigensis: Ein pragmatischer Geschichtsschreiber des zwölften Jahrhunderts* (Bonn, 1912).

[10] For the three surviving manuscripts attributed to the Newburgh library (including a twelfth-century manuscript of Augustine, now Winchester College, MS 20, and Newburgh's own copy of his chronicle, now BL MS Stowe 62), see *Medieval Libraries of Great Britain: A List of Surviving Books*, ed. N. R. Ker, 2nd edn (London 1964), p. 133. For the Rievaulx catalogue, see *The Libraries of the Cistercians, Gilbertines and Premonstratensians*, ed. D. N. Bell, Corpus of British Medieval Library Catalogues 3 (Oxford, 1992), Z19 at pp. 87–121.

[11] WN, ed. Howlett, I, 11–19, and cf. Partner, *Serious Entertainments*, pp. 52, 61–4.

[12] J. Gillingham, 'Royal Newsletters, Forgeries and English Historians: Some Links between Court and History in the Reign of Richard I', in *La Cour Plantagenêt (1154–1204): Actes du colloque tenu à Thouars du 30 avril au 2 mai 1999*, ed. M. Aurell (Poitiers, 2000), pp. 171–85, esp. pp. 179–85; Gillingham, 'Two Yorkshire Historians', 15–37.

rary events, from the 1170s onwards, Newburgh seems merely to be glossing Howden's histories, adding details from time to time, but for the most part merely rewriting and elaborating Howden's testimony in a richer and more resonant ecclesiastical Latin.

This is very much what happens in the case of Newburgh's account of the 1190 massacre, where very few of his broader details are not also to be found in Howden's *Gesta* and *Chronica*, but where Newburgh has rewritten in much greater detail (and at more than four times the length) what Howden disposes of in a few brief paragraphs.[13] In broad terms, Newburgh rehearses the same narrative as Howden, but with greater rhetorical flourish and with a richness of vocabulary that is quite beyond Howden's more staid and restrained register. The initial attack upon the houses of Benedict and Josce, the Jews' seeking refuge in the royal castle, the siege of the castle, the activities of the mob, the speech made by one of their leaders in which the Jews were urged to commit suicide rather than to surrender, the divisions within the Jewish community, the self-slaughter, its revelation to the besiegers, and the final massacre of the besieged by their persecutors, are described by Newburgh in roughly the same order as by Howden. Newburgh, however, adds details not present in Howden: the preaching of a Premonstratensian hermit (apparently neither quite hermit nor Premonstratensian canon) and his death before the castle walls; the mechanics of the siege engines and their assault, and above all the precise details of a speech made within the castle to the Jews sheltering there by a Jewish elder, none of these details present in Howden's account.[14]

The speech of the elder (named neither by Howden nor by Newburgh), presumably first 'imagined' by Howden, was further embroidered by Newburgh in line with classical ideas on the suitably of reported orations, found in Livy or Sallust or, as we shall see, most significantly in Josephus. It follows the same basic line of argument already advanced by Howden in a much briefer report of a speech that Howden attributes merely to 'a certain man learned in law' ('quidam legisperitus'), and that Howden records as opening with the words 'Ye men of Israel, listen to my counsel' ('Viri Israelitae, audite consilium meum'), themselves borrowed from the Vulgate, from Acts 2. 22, from Peter's sermon proclaiming the divinity of Christ to the Jews: not a source, one suspects, with which a Jewish elder would, in reality, have chosen to begin an oration.[15] As we shall see, such scriptural references, already present in Howden's account, are vastly amplified in Newburgh's rewriting of this same speech. Meanwhile, and give or take one or two for the

---

13   Compare WN, ed. Howlett, I, 308–22, with Howden, *Gesta* II, 107–8; Howden, *Chronica* III, 33–4.

14   WN, ed. Howlett, I, 317–22. For the Premonstratensian interests of Richard Malebisse, leader of the York riot and founder of Premonstratensian Newbo Abbey, see H. M. Colvin, *The White Canons in England* (Oxford, 1951), pp. 165–7.

15   Howden, *Gesta* II, 107; WN, ed. Howlett, I, 318–19; Acts 2. 22 ('Viri Israelitae, audite verba hec'), and cf. Acts 3. 12; 5. 35.

most part not particularly significant details, Newburgh seems to know little about the siege that was not already known to Howden.

Most historians who read Newburgh's account continue to do so not directly from the Latin (however much the Latin may be the only source that they cite) but via Joseph Stevenson's English translation. This may help to explain a fundamental misunderstanding about Newburgh's account that should be put to rest here. It has sometimes been asserted that Newburgh displays a keen anti-Jewish bias in his narrative, for all that he may appear to excoriate both the Jews and their attackers.[16] This perception, however, emerges not so much from Newburgh's own Latin words but from over-dependence upon Stevenson's English translation. As M. J. Kennedy has demonstrated, Newburgh is a subtly nuanced antisemite, as often to be found lamenting as praising anti-Jewish violence.[17] Stevenson's translation threatens to disguise this subtlety. In a longish digression, for example, towards the end of Newburgh's account of the 'audaces et cupidi', in Stevenson's words the 'bold and covetous men', whose zeal against the Jews resulted in the massacre at York, Stevenson ends in a way that appears to lend Newburgh's account a bitterly anti-Jewish slant: believing that 'they were doing service to God' ('obsequium se prestare Deo'), while they were despoiling or ruining men who were rebels against Christ, these men allowed their greed to run riot 'with joyful fury' ('hilare furore'): 'The justice of God, indeed, little approved of such deeds (i.e. persecution and massacre), but ordained them, as is meet, that by these means He might coerce the insolence of that perfidious people and bridle their blasphemous tongues'.[18] What Stevenson has missed here is the deliberately ironic juxtaposition of the false 'homage offered to God' ('obsequium se prestare Deo') proclaimed on behalf of the Christians who robbed and murdered the Jews, and their claim to have bridled the Jews' own blasphemy.[19] One set of false oaths was sworn by the rioters, without divine approval, by men who later in Newburgh's account are specifically described as conspirators ('coniurati'), bound together by oaths ('coniurarunt'), only so that those who swore such oaths might silence the false blaspheming of others.[20] In this equation, it is the

---

16 See here, although with admirable nuancing, Kennedy, '"Faith"', pp. 139–52, esp. 145–52.

17 ibid., pp. 146–8, 152.

18 WN, trans. Stevenson, p. 563.

19 WN, ed. Howlett, I, 308–9, and for 'obsequium se prestare Christo', see also p. 311, where it is applied to those at Stamford who believed that by attacking the Jews they were doing God's work. Elsewhere in Newburgh's work it occurs in an ironic context, as in his Commentary on the Song of Songs (*Newburgh's Explanatio*, ed. Gorman, p. 326), where the Jews, believing that they are rendering homage to God, stone Stephen, kill James and imprison Peter ('Ubi ergo Iudei insalubris verbi ministros aperte sevire ceperunt, et lapidando Stephanum, occidendo Iacobum, vinciendo Petrum arbitrati sunt obsequium se prestare Deo').

20 WN, ed. Howlett, I, 313 ('coniurarunt adversus Judaeos Eboracenses prouinciales plurimi'), 314 ('Cumque urbis pars non modica … a coniuratis immisso conflagrauit incendio'), 315 ('Tunc demum qui Judaeos prius inuisos habuerant, cum coniuratis … manifeste et profusa licentia in eos debacchari coeperunt').

anti-Jewish conspirators rather than the Jews themselves who are shown to be both deluded and hypocritical.

Such irony can be found elsewhere in Newburgh's account, if we pay close attention to his choice of words. Thus, for example, it is significant that he chooses the superlative form of the same word 'feroces' ('the fierce' or, according to Stevenson 'the arrogant') that he applies to the Jews of Lynn, grown 'wild through royal patronage' ('tuitione regia feroces'), and employs it to refer to King Richard I who at one point is the 'novus princeps vitae' ('the new prince of life', a title, 'princeps vitae', that Ambrose and Isidore had employed in referring to Christ himself) but at the next the 'ferocissimus princeps', the 'wildest' or 'fiercest' prince.[21] Typically, whilst Stevenson translates 'feroces' as 'arrogant' when referring to the Jews, he translates 'ferocissimus' as 'most courageous' when applying the superlative form to King Richard.[22] This is not to suggest that Newburgh is an apologist for the Jews: in their attacks upon the convert Jew of Lynn, for example, 'thirsting for blood' ('sanguinem sitientes'), they sought an opportunity to consummate their malice ('quaerebant opportunitatem malitiae consummandae'), raging with perverse fury ('saevientes ... peruicaci furore'), with Newburgh employing here a full range of anti-Jewish stereotypes.[23] Nonetheless, these remarks are set within a context that, as we shall see, is often intended to portray the Jews as the victims rather than as the persecutors of Newburgh's Christian contemporaries. In the very next chapter, after his description of the Jews thirsting for the blood of an innocent Christian convert, Newburgh deliberately inverts this stereotype, describing the Yorkshire mob 'without any scruple of Christian conscience thirsting, out of greed for booty, for the blood of these perfidious (Jews)'.[24] Once again, we are in the realm of the chiastic juxtaposition of opposites here, with greed preyed upon by the greedy, and with Christians shown behaving less like Christians than like stereotypical Jews.

Besides a distorted understanding of Newburgh's attitude towards the Jews of York, Stevenson's translation also threatens to deprive its readers of any access to the colour, range and extraordinary lexical variety of Newburgh's Latin. Here we find a profusion of unusual and often rather archaic vocabulary. Some of these archaisms will concern us much more in due course. For

---

21 WN, ed. Howlett, I, 309 ('tuitione regia feroces'), 312 ('non metus ferocissimi principis', noting that in one of the six manuscripts examined for the edition 'ferocissimi' appears as 'fortissimi'), 317 ('Propterea diebus noui principis vitae', trans. by Stevenson, p. 568, merely as 'in the days of the new king'). For Christ as 'princeps vitae', see Ambrose, 'In Psalmum XL' (*PL* 14, col. 1081C), and Isidore, 'In Genesin', 31.12 (*PL* 83, col.278C). For Newburgh earlier describing Richard as the 'rex nouus ... ingentis animi et ferocis', see WN, ed. Howlett, I, 298.

22 WN, trans. Stevenson, pp. 563–4 ('arrogant from their numbers, the magnitude of their riches, and the royal protection'), p. 565 ('neither by the fear of a most courageous prince').

23 WN, ed. Howlett, I, 309.

24 ibid., I, 313 ('et sine ullo Christianae conscientiae scrupulo, perfidum sanguinem predarum cupidine sitientes').

the present, let us merely notice verbs such as 'excandere', 'cruentare', 'abra-dere', 'debacchor' or 'fefellere', Sallustian nouns such as 'vecordia' ('frenzy'), classical sounding constructions such as 'caesis in fuga nonnullis', 'vel ignem vel gladium cruentarunt',[25] and the echoes of Horace on the fateful conse-quences of words once spoken.[26] Newburgh was a writer with a broad range of classical as well as of scriptural reference.

Having completed his account of the mass suicide at York, Newburgh himself offers one of his few direct references to a source or authority for his own understanding of events. 'Truly', he states, 'the person who reads Josephus' history of the Jewish War will gain sufficient understanding that such madness ('vesania'), arising from the ancient superstition of the Jews, has persisted down to our own times whenever any more tragic misfor-tune fell upon them.'[27] Most modern commentators have noted and re-marked this reference to Josephus. None of them has done much more than this, or attempted to investigate the precise parallels that might be drawn between Newburgh's account of events at York in 1190 and Josephus' ac-count of massacre and mass suicide during the Jewish rebellion of the AD 60s and 70s, and in particular of the mass Jewish suicide at Masada, gener-ally dated to AD 72.[28]

Josephus' writings – in essence, his two great historical works, the *Bellum Judaicum*, probably written in the late AD 70s, in seven books, telling the sto-ry of the Jews, their kings and their sufferings at the hands of Rome from the second century BC through to the sack of Jerusalem in AD 70, and the *Antiq-uities*, in twenty books, describing Jewish history from Adam and the origins of mankind through to the rebellion of Josephus' own lifetime but stopping short of the sack of Jerusalem, generally agreed to date from as much as twenty years after the *Bellum Judaicum* – were made available to the Middle Ages in at least two translations into Latin from their Greek versions, itself in

[25] ibid., I, 308 ('excandere'), 309 ('caesis in fuga nonnullis'), 310 ('vel ignem vel gladium cruen-tarunt'), 312 ('abradere'), 315 ('debacchere'), 321 ('vecordia'), 322 ('fefellere').

[26] ibid., I, 315 ('irreuocabile verbum', echoing Horace, *Epistulae*, 18:71), and cf. p. 306 ('fere per ora omnium volitabant rumores', which perhaps echoes Vergil, *Aeneid*, 4:174–5, 'Fama, malum qua non aliud velocius ullum').

[27] WN, ed. Howlett, I, 320, 'Verum qui Josephi de Judaico bello legit historiam satis intelligit ab antiqua Judaeorum superstitione cum forte tristior casus incumberet, illam nostri temporis manasse vesaniam', and note Newburgh's repeated use immediately thereafter of the word 'madness', applied both to the suicidal 'madness' of the Jews and to the 'madness' of the attacking crowd (p. 321, 'Sed seruauit nos Deus et a fratrum nostrorum vesania ... Talia illis lacrimose loquentibus, nostrorum plurimi et exstinctorum vesaniam cum ingenti stupore horrebant'), and cf. p. 310, where it is the Christians at Lynn who are said, in their murderous activities, to act with 'Judaica vesania'.

[28] For example, R. Davies, 'The Medieval Jews of York', YAJ 3 (1875), 147–97 (p. 170); Dobson, JMY, p. 27 n.84; Kennedy, '"Faith"', p. 148. The most detailed modern attempt to demon-strate correspondence occurs in Karen Kletter's thesis, K. M. Kletter, 'The Uses of Josephus: Jewish History in Medieval Tradition' (unpublished Ph.D. dissertation, University of North Carolina, 2005), pp. 240–7.

the case of the *Bellum Judaicum* merely a Greek translation from an Aramaic original.[29] The standard Latin version of Josephus, which I shall henceforth refer to as the 'Josephus Latinus' translation and whose text circulated in the Middle Ages under the name of Josephus himself, comprised a fluent and comprehensive Latin translation of the *Bellum Judaicum*, agreed to date from the fourth century AD (sometimes attributed to Rufinus of Aquileia, contemporary of Jerome and translator of Eusebius), together with a later and less fluent, though rather more widely read, Latin translation of the *Antiquities*, produced perhaps as late as the sixth century within the circle of Cassidorus of Vivarium.[30] Alongside these translations of the *Bellum Judaicum*, in seven books, and the *Antiquities*, in twenty, there circulated an abbreviated Latin digest of Josephus rendered into five books, compressing both the *Bellum* and the *Antiquities* together with other extraneous materials into a version that circulated almost as widely as the 'Josephus Latinus', but in this case known to the Middle Ages as 'Hegesippus' and to modern historians as the 'Pseudo-Hegesippus' (since the historical Hegesippus, a contemporary of Eusebius, played no part in its manufacture).[31]

This Hegesippus adaptation of Josephus was perhaps written in the fourth century, it has been suggested as part of the wider programme presided over by the emperor Julian in the 360s to rebuild Roman Palestine and with it the Temple in Jerusalem (one of the sites central to the whole of the Josephan canon).[32] The Hegesippus translation of Josephus circulated widely in twelfth-century England and is to be found in English medieval library catalogues as a regular companion to the longer and more informative 'Josephus Latinus' translation, not least at Rievaulx in the 1190s, where it occurs as a separate entity, some distance in the catalogue from the two volume copy of the 'Josephus Latinus' that the monks of Rievaulx possessed. Although it was used as a convenient source of Josephan lore by such writers as Gerald of Wales or Matthew Paris, monk of St Albans, in the 1230s and 40s writing his digest of world history, Hegesippus seems to have played little or no part in Newburgh's narrative of events at York in 1190 and will henceforth play

---

29   Amongst a vast literature on Josephus, to which there is an excellent annotated bibliography by L. H. Feldman, *Josephus and Modern Scholarship, 1937–1980* (Berlin, 1984) see, in particular, H. Schreckenberg, *Die Flavius-Josephus-Tradition in Antike und Mittelalter* (Leiden, 1972); H. Schreckenberg, *Rezeptionsgeschichtliche und Textkritische Untersuchungen zu Flavius Josephus* (Leiden, 1977); F. Parente, 'Sulla doppia transmissione filologica ed ecclesiastica del testo di Flavio Giuseppe: un contributo alla storia della ricezione della sua opera nel mondo Cristiano', *Rivista di Storia e Letteratura Religiosa* 36 (2000), 3–51.

30   *The Latin Josephus I: Introduction and Text: The Antiquities, Books I–V*, ed. F. Blatt, Acta Jutlandica 30 (Aarhus, 1958), pp. 17ff.; Schreckenberg, *Flavius-Josephus-Tradition*, pp. 56–61.

31   *Hegesippi qui dicitur Historiae Libri V*, ed. V. Ussani, 2 vols., Corpus Scriptorum Ecclesiasticorum Latinorum 66 (Vienna, 1932–60), II, xxv–viii.

32   A. A. Bell, 'Josephus and Pseudo-Hegesippus', in *Josephus, Judaism and Christianity*, ed. L. H. Feldman and G. Hata (Leiden, 1987), pp. 349–61.

only a tangential role in our story.[33] By contrast, as we shall see, Newburgh was very heavily dependent upon a knowledge of Josephus as transmitted via the 'Josephus Latinus' translation.

There have been a number of studies of the circulation and influence both of the manuscripts and the text of Josephus in twelfth-century England.[34] All of these studies suffer from the fact that the actual words of the 'Josephus Latinus' are for the most part unobtainable in any standard modern Latin edition. In 1958, Franz Blatt published an edition of the first five books of the 'Josephus Latinus' translation of the *Antiquities*.[35] But the remaining fifteen books of the Latin *Antiquities*, and all seven books of the Latin *Bellum Judaicum*, can only be consulted in England either by direct access to one of the twenty or so English medieval manuscripts, or from an edition first published at Basle in 1524.[36] It is perhaps not surprising therefore that even those historians who have written about the manuscripts and transmission of Josephus are by no means as familiar with the text of the 'Josephus Latinus' as might be wished. In consequence, unless a twelfth-century writer like Newburgh specifically refers to Josephus as one of his sources it is unlikely, in the vast majority of cases, that linguistic borrowings, or unattributed reworkings of Josephan material by twelfth-century writers, will have been identified by modern historians. Given, as I shall now show, that the 'Josephus Latinus' was a text widely known in twelfth-century England, the difficulty for modern historians in gaining access to the Latin text is highly regrettable and continues to ensure that what may be a very broad indebtedness to Josephus on behalf of twelfth-century writers remains to a large extent hidden.

Where might Newburgh have consulted Josephus? He could certainly have found it at Rievaulx, in two volumes, where together with Hegesip-

---

33 For early English manuscripts of Hegesippus, including those once belonging to Hexham, Llanthony and Rochester, see R. Gameson, *The Manuscripts of Early Norman England (c.1066–1130)* (Oxford, 1999), p. 61 no. 59, p. 87 no. 286, p. 120 no. 555, p. 123 no. 588, p. 124 no. 594. For the copy once at Rievaulx, see *Libraries of the Cistercians*, ed. Bell, p. 106 (Z.19.113). For citation by Gerald of Wales, Ralph de Diceto and Matthew Paris, see *Giraldi Cambrensis Opera*, VIII, 8, 77, 79 (incidentally revealing knowledge both of Hegesippus and of the 'Josephus Latinus'); Diceto, *Historical Works*, I, 25; Paris, *Chronica Majora*, I, 70, 76–7, 110–13.

34 For lists of the English manuscripts, see *Latin Josephus*, I, ed. Blatt, pp. 87–93 nos.154–70; Kletter, 'Uses of Josephus', pp. 124–37 nos. 1–20. For the use of Josephus by medieval English writers, see Schreckenberg, *Flavius-Josephus-Tradition*, pp. 107–9, 141–64; Kletter, 'Uses of Josephus', passim.

35 *Latin Josephus*, I, ed. Blatt.

36 *Flavii Iosephi, patria Hierosolymitani, religione Iudaei, inter Graecos historiographos, cum primis facundi, opera quaedam Ruffino presbytero interprete* (Basle 'apud Io(hannem) Frobenium', September 1524), with copies in the Cambridge University Library [CUL] (S*.2.23(c) and 4.36.10), further copies (at Aberdeen University, Chetham's Manchester, University College London and Merton College Oxford) being listed from the online COPAC catalogue. For this 1524 edition, see Schreckenberg, *Flavius-Josephus-Tradition*, pp. 58–9, also referring to a revised edition of 1534 by Sigmund Gelen, of which there is a copy in the BL (588.k.13), with copies of a 1540 reprint of this edition both in the BL (588.k.14), and the Bodl. (P.1.3 Th.Seld); Parente, 'Sulla doppia transmissione', p. 40 n. 57.

pus, the 'Josephus Latinus' translations both of the *Antiquities* and the *Bellum Judaicum* appear in a library catalogue of the 1190s.[37] It was also at Durham (whose manuscript survives), at York (which also survives, though incomplete), at Lincoln (again surviving, the gift of Bishop Robert Chesney before 1166), at Rochester and Canterbury (surviving, both early twelfth century), and then elsewhere in a large number of medieval religious houses whose library catalogues are preserved, although the books themselves have been scattered or lost.[38] In terms of surviving manuscripts, there are at least twenty produced in England, most of them certainly to be dated to the twelfth century. The manuscripts themselves have been listed and to some extent examined by Blatt and more recently by Karen Kletter.[39] Kletter has also drawn attention to a series of excerpts and florilegia that contain passages from Josephus, again widely scattered across twelfth-century England.[40] As early as the first decade of the twelfth century we find Herbert Losinga, bishop of Norwich, writing to an Abbot Richard (perhaps to be identified as the last of the independent abbots of Ely) asking him to send him a copy of Josephus which he had several times requested but which had thus far been retained on the grounds that the binding was in poor repair.[41]

The surviving manuscripts – and here I have paid particular attention to the copies in Cambridge, York and the British Library, including those that in the Middle Ages were housed at Canterbury Cathedral, York Minster and at St Albans – themselves testify to regular use and reading over the centuries after 1100. Most of them have marginal notations dating from the twelfth to the sixteenth centuries. Such notes draw attention to Josephus' world chronology, his attempts to measure the span of history from the creation to the flood and from the flood to the building and subsequently

37 *Libraries of the Cistercians*, ed. Bell, pp. 98 (Z.19.54–5), 106 (Z.19.113).
38 For lists of these manuscripts, see above n. 34. For the particular cases cited here, see Durham Cathedral Library MS B.II.1 (Durham, *Antiquities* and *Bellum*); YMA MS XVI.A.7 (?York, incomplete copy of the first ten books of the *Antiquities* only, apparently from what was originally a two volume set); Lincoln Cathedral Library MS. C.I.6 (Lincoln, *Antiquities* and *Bellum*); Cambridge, St John's College MS 8 (Canterbury, *Antiquities* and *Bellum*); CUL MS Dd.1.4 (Canterbury, copy of the first fourteen books of the *Antiquities*, from what was originally a two volume set).
39 Above n. 34.
40 Kletter, 'Uses of Josephus', pp. 151–6, with a particular emphasis here upon excerpts relating to Moses and to Alexander the Great, in both cases drawing upon information from the *Antiquities* rather than from the *Bellum Judaicum*.
41 *Epistolae Herberti de Losinga, primi episcopi Norwicensis*, ed. R. Anstruther (Brussels, 1846), p. 16, no. 10 ('Mittite mihi Josephum, de quo frequenter fecistis excusationem propter dissolutionem libri. Nunc autem correcto et ligato libro, nulla vobis relinquitur excusationis compositio.'), whence *The Life, Letters and Sermons of Bishop Herbert de Losinga*, ed. E. M. Goulburn and H. Symonds, 2 vols. (Oxford, 1878), I, 251, also requesting the letters of Augustine and of Jerome, and cf. p. 249n. for speculation as to the addressee. Drawn to my attention by Tom Licence.

to the destruction of the Temple.[42] Other marginalia (they are generally too brief to be considered 'glosses') highlight particular historical events; Josephus' description of the philosophical divisions within Judaism (widely rehearsed by twelfth-century writers, from Peter Abelard onwards), his account of the geography of the Holy Land, his narrative of the siege and destruction of Jerusalem in AD 70, and, in the case of the St Albans' manuscript of the *Bellum Judaicum*, his account of the siege and mass suicide at Masada, a few years after the destruction of the Temple, precisely the passage that seems to have been most significant for Newburgh in his description of events at York in 1190.[43] The St Albans marginalia are also worthy of notice for another reason. Some of those in the St Albans copy of Josephus' *Antiquities*, now British Library MS Royal 13 D.VI, recording chronology, regnal years and the sum totals for world history, are written in a cursive hand, within small rectangular boxes neatly inked, that can perhaps be identified as the work of Matthew Paris, very close or identical to the hand that Richard Vaughan has elsewhere identified as Paris's autograph.[44] If this is indeed the case, then it supplies further evidence that, apart from

---

[42] For example, on chronology, see below n. 44, and for further such calculations, see CUL MS Dd.1.4 (*Antiquities*, from Canterbury Christ Church) fol. 5v, this same manuscript being scattered with marginal notations, including ink dots intended to highlight particular passages (e.g. at fols. 5v, 25r, 35v, 36r, 48r, 55v), pointing fingers (fols. 94r, 129r), pen-shaped markings (fols. 22r, 23r, 33r, 34r), and regular notes of the transition in Josephus' narrative from one book of the Old Testament to the next (fols. 28r, 79v, 117v, 118r). The late twelfth century York manuscript of the *Antiquities* (YMA MS XVI.A.7) has restrained marginal notation, decreasing in frequency as the work proceeds, but including notes of the transition between books of the Old Testament (fols. 33r, 85v, 96v), a variety of 'nota' marks and occasional glosses, for example on the mountain where Abraham proposed to sacrifice Isaac (fol. 15r), on Moses' Ethiopian bride (fol. 36v, 'Moyses duc(it) uxorem Ethiopissam'), on the fate of Nadab and Abiud (fol. 55r, 'Nadab et Abiud cremantur') and on Josaphat and Achab (fol. 175r, 'Quomodo culpatus Iosaphat eo quod Achab imperio auxilium impendit. Deum placauit et Ammonitas ac Moabitas contra eum insurgentes, Deo iuuante, deuicit').

[43] For highlighting of divisions within Jewish schools of philosophy, see Kletter, 'Uses of Josephus', pp. 88, 207–8, 220–1, 230, and cf. BL MS Royal 13 D.VII (St Albans' copy of the *Bellum Judaicum*) fol. 118v (this same passage in the *Bellum Judaicum* 2:8, marked 'De Esseis'), noting Masada at fol. 206v ('Situs Masade').

[44] BL MS Royal 13 D.VI, fols. 5r ('Duo milia sesecenti quinquaginta sex'), 31v ('Post annos xxx. et cccc.'), 118r ('Refert Iosephus in primo libro. A conditione primi hominis ad tempora diluuii preterier(unt) anni duo milia sescenti quinquaginta sex. A tempore diluuii usque ad edificationem Templi mille quadringenti qui scilicet invicem coniuncti faciunt quatuor milia quinquaginta sex', this same gloss also appearing in CUL MS Dd.1.28 fol.111r, next to Antiquities 8:3), 152v ('ccc. et lxx. annos, menses vi. diesque x. mille lxii. menses vi., diesque x. Mille dcccclvii. mensium vi. dierum x. iii. milia d viii. menses vi. dies x'), 156r ('vix(it) Nabuchodonosor post euersione Ierlm' annis xxv. anno xvii. regni Baltiasar'), and cf. fol. 4r ('calmana', not in a box, but apparently in the same hand, also erased at fol. 3v), 26r ('cxlvii.' and 'cccc.'), and cf. R. Vaughan, 'The Handwriting of Matthew Paris', *Transactions of the Cambridge Bibliographical Society* 1 (1953), 376–94, noticing, amongst many other examples, Matthew's annotations to Comestor (BL MS Royal 4 D.VII) and Geoffrey of Monmouth etc. (BL MS Royal 13 D.V).

knowing Hegesippus, Paris also knew Josephus directly, from the 'Josephus Latinus' translation.[45]

Having established that Newburgh could easily have gained access to Josephus, which he himself cites as a familiar text, we might also note that a relatively large number of English, and even specifically northern English, writers had already displayed familiarity with Josephus and his writings. Josephus' *Antiquities* had constituted a significant source for the exegetical writings of the Venerable Bede, as long ago as the eighth century, and although Bede seems not to have direct access to the *Bellum Judaicum*, he undoubtedly used the Latin translation of Eusebius' *Ecclesiastical History*, in whose early chapters large fragments of the *Bellum Judaicum* are rehearsed or summarized.[46] Perhaps as a direct result of that determination to tread in Bede's footsteps which is one of the hallmarks of the monastic revival in northern England after 1066, at least one other northern English writer, besides Newburgh, shows signs of a direct familiarity with Josephus. Laurence of Durham in his *Hypognosticon*, composed in the 1130s, as Kletter suggests, may well have drawn on Josephus' *Antiquities* as well as upon the Old Testament for his account of Seth's progeny and their interest in natural history, and for his digressions on Abraham's expertise in astronomy.[47] Elsewhere in twelfth-century England or the Anglo-Norman realm, writers as diverse as Orderic Vitalis, William of Malmesbury, John of Salisbury, Gerald of Wales, Ralph de Diceto and Peter of Blois, all display knowledge of Josephus and his histories, even if several of them, including John of Salisbury, seem to have depended for such knowledge not upon Josephus directly but upon the excerpts from his work in the Latin Eusebius.[48]

---

45 For other apparent borrowings by Paris from the Latin Josephus, see Paris, *Chronica Majora* I, 64, 70, 88, 98. Since the Josephus marginalia in his hand are almost exclusively concerned with matters of world chronology, this would also enhance our understanding of Paris's particular interest in eschatology, prophecy and the calculation of time as a means of anticipating the end of days (originally calculated by Paris to be set for the year 1250), evidenced by his copying out of Bodl. MS Ashmole 304, his 'Book of Fate'. Cf. R. Vaughan, *Matthew Paris*, 2nd edn (Cambridge, 1979), pp. 257–8; D. K. Connolly, *The Maps of Matthew Paris: Medieval Journeys through Space, Time and Liturgy* (Woodbridge, 2009), pp. 66–70, and for his original calculation of 1250 as marking the end of the world, see Paris, *Chronica Majora* V, 197.

46 Schreckenberg, *Flavius-Josephus-Tradition*, pp. 107–8; Kletter, 'Uses of Josephus', pp. 31–2, 101–6, 175–82.

47 Kletter, 'Uses of Josephus', p. 231, drawing attention to passages in *Gottes Heilspan – verdichtet: Edition des Hypognosticon des Laurentius Dunelmensis*, ed. S. Daub (Erlangen, 2002), p. 79 (Bk. 1, l. 177ff, on Seth's progeny and interest in natural history), p. 97 (Bk. 3, ll. 22–4, on Abraham's interest in the stars).

48 Schreckenberg, *Flavius-Josephus-Tradition*, p. 141 (Orderic, William of Malmesbury), p. 144 (Geoffrey of Monmouth), pp. 145–6 (John of Salisbury), pp. 154–5 (Ralph de Diceto, Peter of Blois). For John of Salisbury's dependence on Eusebius' digest of Josephus, in John of Salisbury, *Policraticus* (2:4–6), see, *Ioannis Saresberiensis Policraticus*, ed. K. S. B. Keats-Rohan (Turnhout, 1993), pp. 77–86, from Rufinus' translation of Eusebius' *History* (3:5–10), itself available in *PG* 20, pt. 2, cols. 222–46, cf. Kletter, 'Uses of Josephus', pp. 33, 68–9, 232–8.

Newburgh would thus have been in good company both in reading and in recycling the Latin text of Josephus. Yet how did this reading and recycling affect his account of the York massacre of 1190? Here we need to to consider various peculiar features of Newburgh's vocabulary not generally noticed by modern writers who have depended upon translations for a knowledge of his text. Let us begin with some peculiar words that litter Newburgh's account of events at York and that Newburgh had clearly borrowed from the Vulgate Bible. Some of these were noticed by Howlett in his Latin edition of the 1880s. The echoes, for example, of the 'ancient of days' of Daniel (7. 9, 13, 22, 'antiquus dierum') in Newburgh's description of the elder ('infelicissimus ille senior', presumably a rabbi, elsewhere the 'master of error', ('magister erroris'), a term reserved in the *Decretum* for heretics and more generally for the Devil or AntiChrist) whose speech had persuaded the Jews to suicide.[49] The echoes of Ecclesiastes (8. 4, 'Quare ita facis?') and Daniel 4. 32 ('Quare fecisti?') in the opening words of the speech that Newburgh attributes to this same elder, 'Cur ita facis?'.[50] The insistence that by killing the Jews, the Christian mob perverted the intention of Psalm 58. 12 ('My God will let me look in triumph on my enemies. Slay them not, lest my people forget.').[51] Newburgh is no apologist for Judaism. The Jews are a people or race (a 'gens', like the 'gens Anglorum' whose history constitutes the chief theme of Newburgh's, as of Bede's much older history).[52] Their role in Christian society is to serve as reminders of the betrayal and sacrifice of Christ.[53] Their beliefs are mere 'superstition' when compared to the truth of the Gospels.[54] They should live in servitude, albeit honourable servitude, with their otherwise natural proclivity to tyrannize over others curbed by regulation.[55] To convert them to the faith of Christ would indeed be laudable, and such a conversion, as Newburgh makes plain in his commentary on the Song of

---

[49] WN, ed. Howlett, I, 320 ('Dictante vero inveterato illo dierum malorum … infelicissimus ille senior … magistro erroris'). For 'magister erroris' as a synonym for Antichrist in the Pseudo-Sibylline 'Tiburtine Oracle', an early Latin translation of a fourth-century Greek prophecy, widely circulated in the eleventh and twelfth centuries, in this telling to be looked for immediately after the conversion of the Jews to Christianity, see Paris, *Chronica Majora* I, 50; R. K. Emmerson, *Antichrist in the Middle Ages: A Study of Medieval Apocalypticism, Art, and Literature* (Manchester, 1981), pp. 48–9.

[50] WN, ed. Howlett, I, 318.

[51] ibid., p. 316.

[52] ibid., p. 309 ('Linna … ubi eiusdem gentis plurimi habitabant'), and for his intention to tell the 'historia gentis Anglorum', see ibid., p. 11, where in the opening words of his chronicle, Newburgh refers back to his principal model, the 'Historiam gentis nostrae, id est Anglorum' written by the Venerable Bede.

[53] ibid., p. 316 ('Quippe eadem Christianae utilitatis ratione perfidus Judaeus Domini Christi crucifixor, inter Christianos vivere sinitur, qua et forma crucis Dominicae in Christi ecclesia pingitur, ad continuandam scilicet cunctis fidelibus saluberrimam Dominicae passionis memoriam').

[54] ibid., p. 309 ('ex eorum superstitione'), p. 320 ('ab antiqua Judaeorum superstitione').

[55] ibid., 316–17, and for the Jews as potential 'tyranni', p. 313.

Songs, is one of the mercies that might be hoped for from the intercession of the Virgin Mary.[56] To convert them by the sword, however, by compulsion, or even worse by threats and lies, is an act of barbarism and butchery, specifically compared to the activities of the gladiators ('lanistae') of the Roman stadium and their massacre of those innocents who, in the centuries of persecution and martyrdom, had been baptized in Christ.[57]

Thus far, Newburgh's knowledge of the Bible and of Christian history has been identified. Others of his scriptural references, however, have not previously been remarked. Yet why else, for example, does he employ the bizarre and archaic form 'praeses' to refer to what is undoubtedly the sheriff ('vicecomes') of York, John Marshal? John Marshal is at least four times referred to by Newburgh as the 'praeses' or 'praeses provinciae', in a late-Roman vocabulary that is far distant from that of the twelfth-century in which Newburgh wrote.[58] 'Praeses provinciae' was the standard term applied to Roman provincial governors enjoying 'merum imperium', the full bundle of rights and powers including coercive capital punishment. As such it occurs in hundreds of late Roman imperial edicts including those of Justinian and others which found their way into medieval civil and canon law.[59] It was not as a jurist, however, that Newburgh lighted upon this term but via the Gospel of St Matthew, in whose twenty-seventh chapter the word 'praeses' is on half a dozen occasions applied to the person of Pontius Pilate, Roman governor of Judea.

The decision to clothe John Marshal, in 1190, in the guise of Pilate, and hence to draw comparisons between Pilate's refusal to exonerate Christ and John Marshal's failure to aid the Jews of York, is surely deliberate and takes us much closer to Newburgh's understanding of events at York and to his attempts to present the essential innocence of the massacre's Jewish victims. By the twelfth century, the received image of Pilate had entered a new and hostile phase, in which Pilate was depicted not merely as a corrupt or unjust

---

[56] *Newburgh's Explanatio*, ed. Gorman, pp. 301–2, 326–7, noted together with other such passages, by Kennedy, '"Faith"', pp. 150–1.

[57] WN, ed. Howlett, I, 321–2 ('Mox ut egressi sunt, hostiliter comprehensos et baptismum Christi constanter postulantes, lanistae crudelissimi peremerunt, et de his quidem, quos ita plusquam belluina illa confecit immanitas, incunctanter dixerim, quia si in petitione sacri baptismatis fictio defuit, eius nequaquam effectu fraudatos sanguis proprius baptizavit. Sive autem ficte sive non ficte sacrum petierunt lavacrum, inexcusabilis est execranda illa crudelitas lanistarum', listing further reasons why such behaviour was wicked). As pointed out to me by Julie Barrau, 'lanistae' is used by Rupert of Deutz of the persecutors of Christ (Rupert, 'De Trinitate', in *PL* 167, col.1569B, 'agnus, inter lanistas crudelissimos'), and by Herbert of Bosham for the murderers of Thomas Becket (MTB III, 492, 'antequam lanistae illi intrassent ecclesiam').

[58] WN, ed. Howlett, I, 315 ('Ille vero provinciae praesidem ... Indignatus praeses contra Judaeos infremuit ... iussit praeses convocari populum'), p. 316 ('Tum praeses, iussionis poenitentia stimulatus, frustraque conatus revocare sententiam, arcis oppugnationem voluit inhibere').

[59] I am indebted to Magnus Ryan for discussion here.

judge but, in many instances, as himself either Jewish or unduly influenced by the Jews who killed Christ.[60] By identifying John Marshal as Pilate, and by choosing vocabulary from precisely that part of the Gospel of St Matthew in which the Jews, led by their priests and elders ('seniores', cf. Matthew 27. 1, 12, 20), are most clearly shown mocking and spitting upon Christ, 'Whose blood be on us and on our children' (Matthew 27. 25), Newburgh walks a delicate tightrope and comes close to reversing the conventional stereotypes, placing the York Jews of 1190 in the role traditionally occupied by the unjustly persecuted Christ. As their elder later reminds them, urging mass suicide: to surrender to one's enemies is to risk death with mockery ('cum ludibrio moriemur') which in turn echoes Hebrews 11. 36, where St Paul refers to mockery ('ludibria') as one of the tortures that Jewish heroes of the past have undergone for their faith, closely related, of course, to the mockery inflicted on Christ ('inludebant') by the Jews in Matthew 27. 29.[61]

Why is Newburgh's account of the massacre so haunted by echoes of Matthew 27? We might recall here that the massacre at York took place on the Friday and Saturday before Palm Sunday and that, according to both Sarum and York use, on Palm Sunday the whole of Matthew 26 and 27.1–61 would have been intoned in semi-dramatized accents, with the reader using three different pitches of voice, low for the speeches of Christ, medium for the narrative and high or strident for the crowds, priests and judges.[62] On the day after the Jews were killed in the castle at York, the local clergy would have acted out precisely those passages of the Gospel of St Matthew later selected by Newburgh as central elements in his account of the massacre. Newburgh's choice of Matthew 27 as the theme around which to weave his own set of variations was thus a deliberate gesture, using not only scripture but the liturgy to drive home his message that at York the Jews were mistreated just as they themselves had once mistreated Christ. Recalling the Jews' own

---

[60] C. Hourihane, *Pontius Pilate, Anti-Semitism and the Passion in Medieval Art* (Princeton, 2009), esp. chs. 7–8.

[61] WN, ed. Howlett, I, 319 ('cum ludibrio moriemur'), and for the mocking ('inludebant') of Christ, cf. Mark 15. 31. For 'ludibria', cf. II Maccabees 8. 17.

[62] For the date of the massacre, see WN, ed. Howlett, I, 322. For the liturgy, see *The Sarum Missal: Edited from Three Early Manuscripts*, ed. J. Wickham Legg (Oxford, 1916), pp. 92ff, esp. pp. 97–8; *The Sarum Missal in English*, trans. F. E. Warren, 2 vols. (London, 1913), I, 217ff, esp. pp. 228–9, also followed in the use of York, for which see *Missale ad usum insignis ecclesiae Eboracensis*, ed. W. Henderson, 2 vols., SS 59–60 (Durham, 1872–4), I, 90, and cf. A. Hughes, *Medieval Manuscripts for Mass and Office: A Guide to their Organization and Terminology* (Toronto, 1982), p. 246, no. 903 for the Passions of Matthew, Mark and Luke recited respectively on Palm Sunday, and the Tuesday and Wednesday of Holy Week. For the dramatization of the reading, see K. Young, 'Observations on the Origin of the Medieval Passion-Play', *Publications of the Modern Language Association of America* 25 (1910), 309–54; O. B. Hardison, *Christian Rite and Christian Drama in the Middle Ages: Essays in the Origin and Early History of Modern Drama* (Baltimore, 1965), p. 115; *The Medieval European Stage, 500–1550*, ed. W. Tydeman (Cambridge, 2001), pp. 60–1, and more generally, B.-D. Berger, *Le drame liturgique de pâques du Xe au XIIIe siècle: Liturgie et théâtre* (Paris, 1976).

self-slaughter on the Friday preceding Palm Sunday, contemporaries might well have pondered the liturgy for that day and in particular the communion prayer: 'Deliver me not, Oh Lord, into the will of mine adversaries, for there are false witnesses risen up against me, and such as speak wrong'.[63] As we shall see, this reference to 'false witnesses' itself has echoes in Newburgh's account of events.

Meanwhile, let us take another of Newburgh's phrases, the 'precious vessels ('vasa concupiscibilia', themselves borrowed from I Maccabees 1. 24), which Newburgh tells us, being impervious to fire, were deliberately defiled before the Jews attempted mass suicide.[64] Stevenson's translation here 'their most valuable vessels and other things which could not perish in the flames were by an artful kind of scheme prevented from being used again by being thrown into a place which I am ashamed to allude to'[65] both misses the reference to Maccabees and represents a bowdlerization of Newburgh's Latin. Newburgh himself states that 'artificiosa invidia pudenda repositione damnavit': these vessels were 'defiled with artful envy by a shameful repositioning', the nature of this repositioning being left unspecified, although, since the adjective 'pudenda' here is also the noun for the female genitalia, it is possible that the repository where the holy vessels were placed was not the privy, as readers of Stevenson might suppose, but somewhere a great deal more intimate (a place, incidentally, into which, despite Stevenson's translation, it would be very difficult to 'throw' things).[66] There is no doubting Newburgh's sense of disgust at these actions. Indeed 'invidia' ('envy'), the word he uses to describe the Jews' motive, had been recognized as one of the deadly sins since at least the time of Gregory the Great.[67] It was precisely this same 'invidia' which according to Pontius Pilate in Matthew 27. 18 (a passage whose significance for Newburgh's reconstruction of events we have already highlighted) had first led the Jews to deliver up Christ for judgement.

In the background to Newburgh's account of the 'precious vessels' lie other Biblical references: to the exposed pudenda of the harlots of Nahum 3. 5, and to the holy vessels of I Maccabees 1. 24 which the Assyrian ty-

---

63 *Sarum Missal*, ed. Wickham Legg, pp. 90–1; *Missale Eboracensis*, ed. Henderson, I, 82–3: 'Ne tradideris me, Domine, in animas persequentium me: quia insurrexerunt in me testes iniqui, et mentita est iniquitas sibi', and compare the opening collect for this same Friday, 'Miserere michi, Domine, quoniam tribulor: libera me, et eripe me de manibus inimicorum meorum: et a persequentibus me, Domine, non confundar, quoniam inuocaui te', closely related to the Epistle for that day, Jeremiah 17. 13–18.

64 WN, ed. Howlett, I, 319–20 ('Mox ad arbitrium insanissimi senioris, ne suis opibus hostes ditarentur, vestes pretiosas in conspectu omnium ignis absumpsit; vasa vero concupiscibilia et cetera quae poterant per ignem transire, artificiosa invidia, pudenda repositione damnavit').

65 WN, trans. Stevenson, p. 570.

66 I am grateful to Robert Bartlett for saving me from a significant mistranslation here.

67 For example, in Gregory, 'Homiliae in Evangelia', 1:3 (*PL* 76, col. 1088D) and 'Expositio in Psalmos Poenitentiales', 4:12 (*PL* 79, col. 590C, and cf. *PL* 78, cols. 241D, 246C).

rant Antiochus carried off from Jerusalem after sacking the city in 169 BC. Yet once again, Newburgh's choice of words suggests a deliberate desire to cloak his account in scriptural references, and in this instance to compare the threatened attack upon the Jews with the pillage and criminal tyranny of a more ancient history. There are perhaps reminiscences here of Josephus' notorious account of the means by which the Jews had sought to swallow their treasure during the sack of Jerusalem in AD 70, an account recycled by numerous twelfth-century writers, not least by Fulcher of Chartres writing of the massacre of the inhabitants of Jerusalem in 1099 and the subsequent burning of their corpses to extract gold and silver, at the climactic moment of the First Crusade.[68] In the face of Assyrian, Roman, and now of Christian hostility, such accounts imply, it was the fate of their material possessions that particularly concerned the Jews.

There was also, I would suggest, a connection in Newburgh's mind between the 'vasa concupiscibilia' of I Maccabees and the 'concupiscientia' that occurs elsewhere in scripture in a specifically sexual context, not least in the story of Susannah and the elders, in Daniel 13. 20, 56. This of course involves the 'elders', the 'duo senes iudices' reminiscent of Newburgh's 'senior quidam … famosissimus legis doctor' elsewhere described as 'infelicissimus ille senior', at whose behest, at York, the Jews defiled their precious vessels.[69] As pointed out to me by Julie Barrau, the identification here between the York rabbi and the elders of the Susannah story is sealed by Newburgh's reference in this same passage to the rabbi of York as 'inveteratus ille dierum malorum', which itself is a phrase borrowed directly from Daniel 13. 52: 'Inveterate dierum malorum, nunc venerunt peccata tua que operabaris prius' ('You old relic of wicked days, the sins which you committed in the past have now come home'), the words addressed by the boy Daniel to the first of the Jewish elders who had spied on Susannah.[70] The crimes of this elder as specified by Daniel included pronouncing unjust judgments, condemning the innocent and allowing the guilty to go free, even though the Lord said 'Do not put to death an

---

[68] Schreckenberg, *Flavius-Josephus-Tradition*, p. 139; Fulcher 1:28, in *Fulcheri Carnotensis Historia Hierosolymitana (1095–1127)*, ed. H. Hagenmeyer (Heidelberg, 1913), pp. 301–2, and cf. *Flavii Iosephi … Opera*, pp. 802–3 (6:15).

[69] WN, ed. Howlett, I, 318 ('Erat autem ibi senior quidam … famosissimus legis doctor'), 319 ('Tunc senior … ad arbitrium insanissimi senioris'), 320 ('infelicissimus ille senior').

[70] ibid., I, 320 ('Dictante vero inveterato illo dierum malorum'). The Susannah story certainly circulated within the Cistercian milieu to which Newburgh was attached, forming the subject of a long poem by Alan of Meaux, himself described as a monk of Cistercian Meaux and as a 'Master' of Beverley: J. H. Mozley, 'Susanna and the Elders: Three Medieval Poems', *Studi Medievali* n.s. 3 (1930), 27–52, esp. pp. 28–9, 41–50, where the biographical details on Alan are not to be relied upon. They are nonetheless accepted by L. Staley, 'Susanna and English Communities', *Traditio* 62 (2007), 25–58, who adds little to Mozley's contribution and who seems to have looked at neither the Sarum nor the York Missal in claiming that Daniel 13 was read as the epistle for the Saturday before the third Sunday in Lent. Neither Mozley nor Staley notices the extraordinary range of classical allusions in Alan's poem, including direct quotation from Horace and Vergil.

innocent and righteous person' (Daniel 13. 53-4). The implication here, in the recycling of this story by Newburgh, is surely that these were very much the same crimes with which the York rabbi, with his incitement to suicide, could be charged. We seem to have returned here to the world of Pontius Pilate, of unjust judges condemning the innocent to death, both the pronouncers and the victims of such judgement being identifiable with the Jews.

Having opened with an echo of Ecclesiastes and of Daniel ('Cur ita facis?'), Newburgh's version of the speech of the Jewish elder, who persuades part of the refugee band at York to kill themselves rather than apostatize, itself continues: 'For behold our death is at the gates', with echoes here of the mourning of the women of Zion in Jeremiah 9. 21 ('ascendit mors per fenestras nostras', itself, in the commentary by Jerome, interpreted as the fate of those guilty of concupiscence), and even more clearly to be related to the 'death' threatened to the innocent Susannah when spied upon by the Jewish elders through the 'gates' of her garden.[71] As a whole, the elder's speech is introduced by William of Newburgh as the 'letter which kills' ('littera que occidit'), a phrase that first occurs in the Second Letter of Paul to the Corinthians (II Corinthians 3. 6) and which to Paul, as to later patristic writers, perhaps most notably to Gregory the Great, denoted the ancient law of the Jews now replaced by the new dispensation won for Christians by Christ.[72] Nonetheless, if 'the letter which kills' perhaps gives a pejorative view of Jewish law and authority, elsewhere it is worth remarking the way in which Newburgh applies vocabulary used by other writers as stereotypical proof of Jewish wickedness or contumacy, not to the Jews of York but to their persecutors. The Jews, according to Newburgh, remain 'rigid' ('fortes et rigidi', a familiar term in anti-Jewish rhetoric, in part derived from the report in Exodus 32. 9 of God's own description of the Jews as a 'stiff-necked' people), but only as a result of the terror inflicted upon them by their Christian foes.[73] Meanwhile, it is the members of the Christian

---

71 WN, ed. Howlett, I, 318 ('Et ecce mors nostra in ianuis est'); Jerome 'Interpretatio Homiliarum duarum Origenis in Canticum Canticorum', *PL* 23, col.1141A, 'Quando videris mulierem ad concupiscendum eam, iam mors ascendit per fenestras tuas', also echoed in Alan of Meaux's poem on Susannah: Mozley, 'Susanna and the Elders', p. 45, lines 183–4, 195–6 ('Mortis ad introitus illa fenestra patet … Ostia sunt oculi, sunt aures, sunt ea per que mors habet ingressum'), referring to the doors ('ostia') of Susannah's garden though which the 'duo senes' had spied upon her, leading Susannah to exclaim that, were she to give in to their invitation to sin, then 'mors mihi est': Daniel 13. 20–22.

72 WN, ed. Howlett, I, 318 ('Erat autem ibi senior quidam, iuxta literam que occidit, famosissimus legis doctor'), cf. II Corinthians 3. 6 ('Qui et idoneos nos fecit ministros novi testamenti, non litterae sed spiritus. Littera enim occidit. Spiritus autem vivificat.'); Gregory, 'Moralia in Job', 11:16, in *PL* 75, cols. 965D–6A, and cf. Paschasius Radbertus, 'Expositio in Matthaeum', 11:25 (*PL* 120, col. 857A); Rupert of Deutz, 'De Trinitate' (*PL* 167, col. 1435B); Abelard, 'Sic et Non' (*PL* 178, col.1529D).

73 WN, ed. Howlett, I, 318 ('Judaei, sola iam desperatione fortes et rigidi'), and cf. Exodus 32. 9, 'Populus iste durae cervicis sit', itself echoed in Newburgh's description of the Jews at the time of Richard's coronation in 1189: 'blasphemi illi, qui tempore superioris principis supra modum cervicosi et protervi in Christianos fuerant', WN, ed. Howlett, I, 299.

mob whose 'blinded spirit' ('caecato animo caligarent') leads them to pervert the meaning of King David's words in Psalm 58, and whose minds are so 'blinded' by prejudice ('caecata mente persuaserat') that they supposed their undertakings were inspired by religion rather than by greed, both greed and spiritual blindness of course being qualities that medieval writers (not least in the iconography of the blinded figure of Synagoga) were elsewhere much more accustomed to apply to Jews than to Christians.[74]

There is another noun, one of the most frequently used in Newburgh's narrative of the massacre, that is just as revealing, and that now, for the first time, begins to disclose the degree to which Newburgh was bathed not just in the spirit but the language of Josephus' writing on the Jews. Just as 'praeses provinciae' might seem a strangely archaic term by which to refer to the sheriff of York, so the castle over which the sheriff claimed authority is described on no less than a dozen occasions within Newburgh's account of 1190 not as a castle (a 'castellum') or even as a tower (a 'turris', although the word 'turris' does occasionally appear here[75]) but as an 'arx', a citadel, employing a noun 'arx/arcis' that is rare in twelfth-century usage.[76] In classical Latin, the 'arx' was the citadel of any major town, and specifically the Capitoline citadel of Rome. Isidore of Seville, in his *Etymologies*, had defined it as the high fortifications of a town, named from the ease with which such places could be protected against enemies ('arcere', from which verb, Isidore suggested, came not just the Latin 'arxa' but 'arcus', 'a bow', and 'arca', not just the Ark of Noah, or the Ark of the covenant, but any strong box or container, up to and including the 'archa' of English medieval towns in which the official copies of Jewish bonds were stored).[77]

Newburgh undoubtedly knew Isidore, whose *Etymologies* were readily available to him, not least in the library of Rievaulx, and who is cited by Newburgh elsewhere in the *Historia* for his lists of early Christian heresies, his

---

74 WN, ed. Howlett, I, 316 ('caecato animo caligarent'), p. 318 ('caecata mente persuaserat'), and for the theme of blindness in general, often shown in art via the figurative blinding of Synagoga, see G. Dahan, *Les intellectuels chrétiens et les juifs au moyen âge* (Paris, 1999), pp. 475–7. Newburgh himself applies it specifically to the Jews in his Commentary on the Song of Songs: *Newburgh's Explanatio*, ed. Gorman, p. 326 ('cecitate eorum pia mater indignata et conversa').

75 WN, ed. Howlett, I, 315 ('turris regiae occupationem'), 317 ('in turri regia'), 318 ('certa erat turris expugnatio'), 320 ('interiora turris'), 321 ('turris huius').

76 ibid., I, 314 ('arcis regiae custode exorato ... in arcem migraverat'), 315 ('extra arcem ... multitudo que in arcem confugerat ... arcis prepositus ... commissae sibi arcis a Judaeis fraudatum ... arcemque illis regiam extorquendam ... arcemque oppugnari'), 316 ('arcis oppugnationem'), 317 ('arcemque oppugnantibus'), 320 ('ad expugnandam arcem'), 322 ('circa arcem').

77 Isidore, 'Etymologiae', XV.ii.32, in *PL* 82, col. 539B ('Arces sunt partes urbis excelsae atque munitae, nam quaecunque tutissima urbium sunt, ab arcendo hostem arces vocantur, unde et arcus, et arca'), borrowed for the most part from Varro, *Lingua Latina*, 5:32. Cf. *The Etymologies of Isidore of Seville*, trans. S. A. Barney et al. (Cambridge, 2006), p. 307.

knowledge of demons, and his derivation of the word 'castrum' from 'casta'.[78] Attempting a deliberately 'archaic' description of London, in which London itself was portrayed as the new Rome and hence its greatest royal fortification as the rival of Rome's imperial palace, William fitz Stephen, writing in the 1170s, had referred in his *Life* of Becket to the Tower of London as the 'arx palatina', associating it with the imperial palace on the Palatine Hill of Rome.[79] But why, without this impulse for York to mimic Rome, is William of Newburgh's York castle an 'arx' rather than a 'castellum'? The answer is surely supplied by Josephus, who refers in his account of Masada to Masada itself not just as an 'arx', but as being surrounded by a royal wall ('regiae vero murus') approached by the King's road ('Fossae vero iter ex regia in arcem summam ducebant'), using precisely the same term for Herod's fortress at Masada that Newburgh later employs for Richard I's castle at York, Newburgh's 'arx regia'.[80]

There are other direct borrowings from the Latin of the 'Josephus Latinus' to which attention should now be drawn. They are not always easy to spot since, as Peter Biller has shown in his analysis of Newburgh's recycling of patristic commentary in his account of the English Cathars of the 1160s, Newburgh is generally careful to avoid direct lexical imitation and to rephrase thoughts in his own particular vocabulary.[81] Nonetheless, the 'machines' ('machinae'), the stones ('saxa') and the fire ('ignis') of Newburgh's account are all prominent in Josephus' report of Masada, although they go unmentioned in most other chroniclers' accounts of York in 1190.[82] The lack of alimentary provision

---

78 Biller, 'William of Newburgh', p. 14; Partner, *Serious Entertainments*, pp. 61, 67, 244 nn. 85–6, citing WN, ed. Howlett I, 92–3, where the juxtaposition of 'castra/casta' derives from Isidore, 'Etymologiae', IX.iii.44 (in *PL* 83, col. 346C, 'Castra sunt ubi miles steterit, dicta autem castra, quasi casta, eo quod illic castraretur libide. Nam nunquam iis intererat mulier.').

79 *MTB* III, 3 ('Habet ab oriente arcem palatinam, maximam et fortissimam').

80 Josephus, *Bellum Judaicum*, 7, in *Flavii Iosephi … Opera*, pp. 843–4 (7:28) ('Quin et regiam sibi aedificauerat ab occidentalis partis ascensu, intra moenia quidem arcis positam, vergentem autem ad septentrionem. Regiae vero murus erat magnus ac firmissimus, celsitudine quatuor sexagenum cubitorum. In angulis turres habebat … Fossae vero iter ex regia in arcem summam ducebant, quas foris nemo cernebat. Sed ne manifestae quidem viae facilem sui usum praebere hostibus poterant. Nam orientalis quidem via natura est inaccessa, ut supra memorauimus. Occidentalem vero, magna in angustia posita turri conclusit, quae non minore mille cubitorum spatio ab arce distaret, quam neque transire posse, neque capi facile videbatur … quod arcis altitudine ab omni terrena ac foeculenta materia sit remota'); WN, ed. Howlett, I, 314 ('arcis regiae custode exorato').

81 Biller, 'William of Newburgh', p. 23, 'William is not often a transparent and slavish copier, and betrays only by a nuance of rhetoric or an unusual choice of a word a dependence on sources, the tracing of which, therefore, is not a demonstrative science'.

82 For these three words in Josephus' account of Masada, see *Flavii Iosephi … Opera*, p. 843 (7:28) ('Saxum gyro non exiguum et excelsum, longitudine undique abruptis atque altis vallibus cingitur ex inuisibili … sunt animalium gressibus inaccessae, nisi quod duobus modis idem saxum in difficilem explicatur ascensum'), p. 844 ('columnis quidem et singularibus saxis undique substitutis … erat quaedam continentia saxi vastior latitudine, multumque porrecta'), pp. 844–5 ('Verum neque firma neque sufficiens machinis ferendis haec mensura videbatur, sed super eum tribunal, constructis saxis ingentibus … Erat autem aliarum machinarum fabrica illis assi-

(the 'externorum alimentorum penuria') against which Herod had guarded at Masada with a 'great, daily and opulent supply' ('apparatus magis et diurnitatem et opulentiam') both of food and of weapons ('armorum mulitudo') is deliberately contrasted in Newburgh's mind with the lack of a 'sufficient supply of food' ('sufficiens escarum apparatus') or of weapons ('sufficientem … armaturam') which condemned the besieged at York to be swiftly overwhelmed. In Josephus, in the same brief passage in which all these terms appear, it is the pathways leading to the heights of the fortress that no outsider ('foris nemo') might determine. In Newburgh, again in this same brief passage, no-one from outside ('nemo foris') needed to attack the castle, since starvation alone would have ensured the Jews' surrender.[83]

Even more clearly than these verbal echoes, the entire tone and pattern of Newburgh's report of the speech at York mirrors that of the speech which Josephus attributes to Eleazar at Masada. The bringing to bear of the siege engines, the final dashing of the hopes of the besieged, the night-time vigil in which the besiegers rejoice at their coming victory and the besieged lament their fate, the speech to them by an elder in which they are urged to suicide, but by which only some of them are persuaded, the elder's renewed insistence that suicide is the only option, breaking his speech into two distinct periods, and the final almost rapturous acceptance of this counsel by the majority in which they first destroy their property by fire and then submit themselves to the knife; every single one of these elements is shared in common between Josephus and Newburgh, even though the reported speeches, attributed by Josephus to Eleazar, and by Newburgh to his un-named Jewish elder, take very different forms, in Josephus with its key emphasis upon liberty and the inexorable power of Rome already demonstrated in the crushing of rebellion in Jerusalem and elsewhere, in Newburgh's account with its chief emphasis upon the horrors of apostasy from Judaism and the merciless nature of the Christian enemy.[84]

---

milis'), p. 845 ('ne machinis quidem simile aliquid pateretur … sed quod caedendi inferebantur machinarum ictus euanescebant … Ubi hoc Syluius considerauit, igni magis murum captum iri putans … ignem cito comprehendit … Incipiente quidem adhuc incendio, spirans aquilo Romanis erat horribilis, auertens enim desuper flammas in eos abigebat et pene machinas quasi iam conflagraturas desperauerant'), p. 846 ('sacratissimam vero urbem suam igni hostium excidioque prodidisset … Ignis enim qui ferabatur in hostes, in aedificatum a nobis murum non sponte reuersus est'), p. 847 ('Alii autem, cum mandata perceperint, igni traditis corporibus').

83 Compare here WN, ed. Howlett, I, 317 ('Igitur Judaei obsidebantur in turri regia, deeratque obsessis sufficiens escarum apparatus, sola proculdubio inedia mature expugnandis, etiam si nemo foris urgeret. Sed nec sufficientem, sive pro sui tutela sive ad hostes propulsandos, armaturam habebant, quos nimirum imminentes saxis tantummodo interiori muro detractis arcebant.'), with Josephus' account of Masada, in *Flavii Iosephi … Opera*, p. 844 (7:28) ('Fossae vero iter ex regia in arcem summam ducebant, quas foris nemo cernebat. … Intus autem repositi apparatus, magis et diuturnitatem et opulentiam iuuere … Inuenta est autem omnigenum quoque armorum multitudo, ab rege condita').

84 In the printed edition of the Latin edition, Josephus' account of Masada runs to more than 3000 words, over seven pages: *Flavii Iosephi … Opera*, pp. 843–50 (7:28).

Josephus, the Church fathers, and above all the Vulgate of Jerome maintain a constant whisper beneath the surface of Newburgh's account of the York massacre that, like the tuning in and out of radio stations, or the patterning and recycling of a series of quotations in poetry, was intended to alert Newburgh's readers to a deeper level of engagement and understanding. So subtle are these murmurings that they have proved inaudible to modern commentators. Yet these voices from the classical and early Christian past are crucial if we are to understand Newburgh's purpose and the extent to which he can be relied on as a 'historical' witness to events at York. It would henceforth be unwise to cite any detail in Newburgh's account as 'historical' reality, without first establishing whether or not such details have a tropological rather than a purely 'historical' purpose. Newburgh's borrowings from Josephus also invite a broader series of questions. Why was Josephus being read in northern England in the 1190s, and what, in turn, might this reading of Josephus have contributed to the prejudice of Newburgh and his contemporaries when writing of more recent events?

As has long been recognized, twelfth-century writers had any number of reasons for an interest in Josephus: as an independent account of Jewish history to be compared and contrasted with Scripture, as an outline of world chronology full of precise dates, for his relevance to crusading history and in particular to the Christian capture of Jerusalem in 1099, for his use as evidence that, after AD 70, the impetus in human history had passed from the Jews to a new dispensation, subsequently to be identified with Christianity, or merely as a teller or rattlingly good tales. To all of this, after 1187, could be added the potential usefulness of his account both of the rebellion against proper authority by the city of Jerusalem, and of the means by which such rebellion might be quashed and Jerusalem itself restored to specifically Roman rule. Josephus' *Bellum Judaicum*, after all, tells the story of a revolt by Jerusalem against Rome and of the just vengeance of Rome, led by Vespasian and his son, Titus. In 1187, another revolt in Palestine, this time led by the Moslem followers of Saladin, deprived Christianity of the city of Jerusalem, sparking a new crusade whose leaders hoped to emulate Vespasian and Titus, if not in the destruction of the city of Jerusalem then in its recapture and restoration to 'Roman' rule. Even the details that Josephus supplies of world chronology, in the Latin version of the *Bellum Judaicum* referring to a period of 1130 years between the first building of the Temple by Solomon and its destruction by Vespasian, and of 1174 or 1177 years from the accession of King David to the destruction of Jerusalem by Rome, would have been of keen interest to twelfth-century writers only too aware of the 1187 years that had passed between the birth of Christ and the fall of Jerusalem to Saladin. [85]

---

[85] Josephus in fact supplies two distinct calculations at the end of Book 6 of the *Bellum Judaicum*, whence the Latin versions in *Flavii Iosephi ... Opera*, p. 819 (7:10) ('Nam et mensem, ut dictum est, eumque diem seruauit quo primum ab Babyloniis Templum erat incensum. Et a prima structione Templi quam Solomon rex inchoauerat, usque ad hoc excidium, quod

English historians were aware, too, of Josephus' reputation as a seer and fortune-teller, capable of predicting the fall of Jerusalem, the death of Nero and the promotion of Vespasian to the imperial throne.[86] Vespasian and Titus, the first of the Flavians, were destined in due course not only to capture and sack Jerusalem, thereby bringing an end, in Christian eyes, to the old dispensation of the Christian law, but themselves to be seated on the imperial throne, dressed in the purple as the representatives of a new imperial dynasty prophesied by Josephus; a dynasty whose very name 'Flavius Josephus' himself adopted as a badge of personal dynastic allegiance.

There is no doubt that, as Newburgh makes plain, the coming crusade cast a shadow over events at York in 1190, with a large number of those who attacked the Jews being crusaders either hoping to plunder funds with which to undertake the journey to the East or determined to do the work of Christ by slaying Christ's enemies closer to home.[87] It is now time to suggest that it may also have cast a shadow over contemporary approaches to Josephus and the Roman imperial past. In the immediate aftermath of the fall of Jerusalem to Saladin in 1187, the German emperor Frederick Barbarossa and his son, the future Henry VI, both took the cross, potentially as modern embodiments of the spirit of Vespasian and Titus. So too did Henry II of England and his eldest son Richard. Is there any evidence here to suggest that the Plantagenets saw themselves or were seen by contemporaries as modern incarnations of the first-century Flavians?

Classical comparisons came easily to English or Anglo-Norman chroniclers, from William of Poitiers onwards, portraying the deeds of English

euenit secundo anno principis Vespasiani, mille centum triginta colliguntur anni, et septem menses, ac dies quindecim. A posteriore vero, quam secundo anno Cyri regis Aggaeus fecerat, usque ad excidium quod Vespasiano imperante sustinuit ciuitas, anni sexcenti trigintanouem, et dies quadragintaquinque'), p. 828 (7:18) (noting the fall of the city on 8 September 70 AD, 'Quinquies autem prius capta, tunc iterum vastata est. Aegyptiorum quidem rex Asochaeus, et post eum Antiochus, deinde Pompeius, et post hos tum Herodes et Sosius captum oppidum seruauere. Antea vero rex Babyloniorum eo potitus excidit, post annos ex quo aedificatum est, mille trecenti sexaginta, et menses octo, et dies sex … et quadringentesimo sexagesimo quarto anno post, ac mensibus tribus, a Babyloniis euersa est. A rege autem Leobio, qui primus Iudaeus in ea regnauit, usque ad id quod Titus fecit, excidium, anni mille centum septuagintaquatuor. Ex quo primum autem condita est, usque ad excidium, anni mille centum septuagintaseptem').

[86] For example, *Radulfi Nigri Chronica*, ed. R. Anstruther, Caxton Society 13 (London, 1851), p. 115. ('Josephus vicesimum librum Antiquitatum scibit. Hic multa predixit Vespasiano de eius imperio et morte Neronis, diem etiam irruptionis predixit ciuibus.'). Josephus, of course, was also widely famed for the so-called 'Testimonium Flavianum', by the fourth century AD interpolated into Bk 18 of the *Antiquities*, in which the coming of Christ is said to have been foretold to the Jews. The 'Testimonium' is specifically noticed by Ralph de Diceto (Diceto, *Historical Works* I, 25), and according to Gerald of Wales was the subject of controversy at Oxford where Master Robert, prior of St Frideswide's, accused the Jews of suppressing this passage from their own version of Josephus' histories (*Giraldi Cambrensis Opera* VIII, 65–6).

[87] WN, ed. Howlett, I, 313–14.

kings in the guise of Julius Caesar or the later heroes (and occasionally villains) of the Roman imperial past.[88] The so-called Monk of Caen in his obituary of William I of England famously adapted a description first applied by Suetonius to the drinking habits of the emperor Augustus and thereafter known through its recycling by Einhard in his description of the emperor Charlemagne.[89] The Flavian dynasty is briefly mentioned by William of Poitiers, who lists Titus as 'the darling of the world' ('orbis amor'), borrowing a phrase from Suetonius in order to compare Titus' triumphant reception in Italy after the fall of Jerusalem with William the Conqueror's reception in Normandy after his victory at Hastings.[90] William of Malmesbury also refers to Titus, though in much less flattering terms, in the same breath as Nebuchadnezzar and Hadrian, as one of those foreign conquerors whose victories over Jerusalem condemned the city's inhabitants to death among the ruins.[91] A more detailed or positive approach to Titus only began to emerge in England, from the 1130s onwards, when Henry of Huntingdon accorded a favourable notice to Titus amongst his lists of the Roman emperors and their qualities.[92] In John of Salisbury's *Policraticus*, composed in the 1150s, besides being praised for his role as divine scourge

---

88 See, for example, the numerous citations of Caesar's Commentaries or Suetonius on Caesar, conveniently listed in *The Gesta Guillelmi of William of Poitiers*, ed. R. H. C. Davis and M. Chibnall, OMT (Oxford 1998), p. 189.

89 'De obitu Willelmi', first edited by T. D. Hardy, *Descriptive Catalogue of Materials Relating to the History of Great Britain and Ireland*, 3 vols., RS 26 (London, 1862–71), II, 15, and cf. *The Gesta Normannorum Ducum of William of Jumièges, Orderic Vitalis and Robert of Torigni*, ed. E. M. C. van Houts, 2 vols., OMT (Oxford 1992–5), I, lxi–lxv at p. lxiii.

90 Poitiers, *Gesta Guillelmi*, pp. 174–5 ('Vespasiani filio Tito, qui dum recta vehementer amaret orbis amor dici meruit, nunquam Italia laetior quam Normannia occurrit Guillelmo regi principi suo').

91 William of Malmesbury, *Gesta Regum Anglorum*, ed. R. M. Thomson and M. Winterbottom, 2 vols. OMT (Oxford 1998–9), I, 640 ('Quis non audierit quotiens sub aduerso marte cadens ciues ruinis sepelierit suis, uel Nabuchodonosor uel Tito uel Adriano agentibus?').

92 Henry of Huntingdon, *Historia Anglorum: The History of the English People*, ed. D. Greenway OMT (Oxford, 1996), pp. 42–4, 532, to a large extent merely rehearsing Bede and Paul the Deacon, who themselves drew upon Suetonius and had in their turn been recycled in Landolfo's eleventh-century *Historia Miscella* and in the universal chronicle of Hugh of Fleury. For the principal earlier digests of information on the Roman emperors, ultimately derived from Suetonius and (for the Jerusalem episodes) from Josephus, upon which Henry and most of his successors depended, see *Pauli Orosii Historiarum adversum paganos libri VII*, ed. K. F. W. Zangemeister (Vienna, 1882), pp. 460–2; Bede's *Chronica Maiora*, in *Bedae Venerabilis Opera Didascalica*, vi, ed. C. W. Jones, 3 vols. (Turnhout, 1975–7), cc.298–300; Paul the Deacon, *Pauli Diaconi Historia Romana*, ed. A. Crivelucci (Rome, 1914), 7:19–21; *Hugonis Floriacensis monachi Benedictini Chronicon*, ed. B. Rottendorff (Munster, 1638), p. 65 (noting Titus' death at the age of 41, rather than 42 as reported by most English sources); *Landolfi Sagacis Historia Romana*, ed. A. Crivellucci, 2 vols. (Rome, 1912–13), I, 216–19. For a magisterial conspectus of twelfth-century knowledge of the Roman past (from which Josephus is nonetheless unaccountably absent), see L. B. Mortensen, 'The Texts and Contexts of Ancient Roman History in Twelfth-Century Western Scholarship', in *The Perception of the Past in Twelfth-Century Europe*, ed. P. Magdalino (London, 1992), pp. 99–116.

of the Jews, and for his innocence and 'piety' ('pietas'), compared to some of the greater qualities of Socrates, Scipio, Ulysses or other heroes of the ancient world, Titus is accorded a brief obituary, very similar to the notice in Henry of Huntingdon's chronicle but here apparently drawn directly from Suetonius rather than from intermediary sources. Here John of Salisbury reports Titus' generosity, his famous claim to have wasted any day in which he did not bestow gifts, his insistence that no-one leave his presence unrewarded, his deathbed penance for a single unnamed crime, his refusal to lay hands on the goods of his subjects, his clemency in matters of justice, and his pardoning even of those who conspired against him.[93]

Similar lists of the virtues of Titus are to be found in the writings of Ralph Niger (who adds various details including Titus' expertise in two languages and his death at the age of forty-two),[94] in Gerald of Wales (who to a large extent merely copies Hugh of Fleury and Henry of Huntingdon, but who repeats that Titus did penance for a single crime, and who adds a proverb , 'So limited were Titus' lands that it would take only two years to traverse them'),[95] in the verses 'In Praise of the Divine Wisdom' by Alexander Neckham (who as a writer is of particular interest here since his mother also served as wet nurse to the future King Richard I, born on the same day as Neckham, and who repeats the usual details of Titus' generosity, claiming that he was greater even than Augustus, comparing his riches to those of Croesus and his public works to those of Solomon, builder of the Temple),[96] and in the universal chronicle of Ralph of Diceto, who to a large extent merely rehearses the remarks made by earlier writers, but who, misunderstanding their insistence, itself borrowed directly from Suetonius, that Titus laid hands on no-one else's property ('abstinuit alieno') recasts this as a claim that Titus abandoned the use of dice ('abstinuit aleae').[97] There is little in any of this to suggest that Titus was singled out for particular attention in twelfth-century England, though plenty to demonstrate that the reputation that he enjoyed by the 1190s was a thoroughly heroic one.

How might this have impacted upon twelfth-century reading of Josephus or indeed of more recent English or Plantagenet history? The drawing of compari-

---

93 Salisbury, *Policraticus* (2:10, 3:9, 14), pp. 84, 89, 198, 227–8.

94 Niger, *Chronica*, pp. 24 (derived largely from Hugh of Fleury), 113–14.

95 *Giraldi Cambrensis Opera* VIII, 80–1 ('se semel in vita fecisse quod poeniteat … De quo et metrice scriptum est, "Ostensus terris Titus est breuitate bienni"'), the edition here noting Gerald's reliance on Hugh of Fleury, but failing to notice that it is Henry of Huntingdon, not Eutropius, who is copied for the rest of Gerald's notice.

96 Alexander Nequam, 'De Laudibus diuine sapientie', lines 213–30, in *Alexandri Neckam De Naturis Rerum Libri Duo*, ed. T. Wright, RS 34 (London, 1863), p. 445.

97 Diceto, *Historical Works* I, 62 ('Titus abstinuit aleae, qui culpatus quare plus promitteret quam dare posset, ait "non oporteret quemquam a sermone principis tristem recedere". Titus imperator tantae bonitatis fuit ut cum quadam die recordatus fuisset in coena nichil se in illa die cuiquam prestitisse, dixit "Amici, hodie diem perdidi".').

sons between modern kings and the emperors of antiquity was a common, even though a far from exact science. In England, if Julius or Augustus were to be identified with the first post-Conquest king, William the Conqueror, then problems arose further down the line, when it came to finding modern pairs for Julius' successors. William Rufus, after his death, might just about be paired with Tiberius, but what of Caligula and above all of Nero? What of the short-lived military tyrants Galba, Otto and Vitellius? With the arrival of a new dynasty on the English throne after 1154, it would be possible to detect parallels between the Plantagenets and the thrusting and militarily successful Flavian emperors, from Vespasian onwards. Of Vespasian, the first of the Flavians, Suetonius tells a story of the sprouting of an ancient oak tree that undoubtedly has parallels with the story of the green tree of England, reported in the early lives of Edward the Confessor and recycled by Ailred of Rievaulx, after 1150, as a prophecy of Henry II and his reuniting of the dynasties of England and Normandy.[98] It is interesting, though hardly conclusive, that Rievaulx's own copy of Ailred's genealogy of Henry II, in which this prophecy was reported, was by the 1190s bound up together with Josephus' *Bellum Judaicum*, perhaps in the very same manuscript of Josephus from which Newburgh was working for his recasting of the Masada narrative to fit the circumstances of the Jews of York.[99] Vespasian was also credited with visiting Britain (by Josephus, Suetonius, and hence by Geoffrey of Monmouth), and (as noted by John of Salisbury and Ralph Niger, in turn copying Suetonius), with miracles of healing of the blind and the lame.[100] Such miracles might be compared to the revival under Henry II of Edward the Confessor's practise of touching for the King's evil.[101] Set against this, however, Vespasian was generally dismissed as a skinflint and miser, a great general, but one who came to the imperial throne only late in life, aged almost sixty.[102]

---

[98] Suetonius, *Vespasianus*, 5, and for Edward the Confessor's prophecy of the green tree, as rewritten by Ailred of Rievaulx to accord with the accession of Henry II, see *The Life of King Edward Who Rests at Westminster*, ed. F. Barlow, OMT, 2nd edn (Oxford, 1992), pp. 118–19, 131–2; Ailred, 'Vita Sancti Edwardi', in *PL* 195, cols.773–4.

[99] *Libraries of the Cistercians*, ed. Bell, p. 98 (Z19.55), where Ailred on King David is identified as Ailred's 'Genealogia' (most readily available in *PL* 195, cols.711–38).

[100] For Josephus' notice, from *Bellum Judaicum*, Bk 3, see *Flavii Iosephi ... Opera*, 706 (3:1) ('armisque ante illud tempus incognitam, Britanniam vendicasset. Unde patri quoque ipsius Claudio praestiterat, ut sine proprio sudore triumpharet'). For Vespasian's supposed visit to Exeter, see Geoffrey of Monmouth, *The History of the Kings of Britain*, ed. M. D. Reeve, trans. N. Wright (Woodbridge, 2007), pp. 84–5, whence Gervase of Canterbury, *Historical Works* II, 13. Suetonius (*Vespasianus*, 4) credits him with the conquest of the Isle of Wight. For his healing miracles (Suetonius, *Vespasianus*, 7) as reported in England, see Salisbury, *Policraticus*, 2:10, p. 89; Niger, *Chronica*, p. 113 (Chronicle 2: 'factus imperator sanauit unum orbatum lumine et alterum debili crure').

[101] For Henry II's 'touching' for scrofula, see the references gathered by N. Vincent, 'The Pilgrimages of the Angevin Kings of England 1154–1272', in *Pilgrimage: The English Experience from Becket to Bunyan*, ed. C. Morris and P. Roberts (Cambridge, 2002), p.38 nn. 122–3.

[102] As, for example, by Salisbury, *Policraticus* (3:14), p. 227 ('eo quod natura cupidissimus esset pecunie nec auaritiam minueret processus aetatis').

Only with Titus did English historians once again encounter a Roman emperor whose achievements and qualities might readily be compared to those of English kings of recent vintage. Consider some of the more commonly reported aspects of his life: his mastery of poetry in both Greek and Latin, his musical expertise, his heroic exploits as a general and huntsman, his public declaration of penitence for an unnamed crime, his role in the capture of Jerusalem, his generosity to his followers, his pardoning of those who conspired against him, not least of his younger brother, the future emperor Domitian, his death at the age of only forty-two, even his role as scourge, albeit as pitying and reluctant scourge of the Jews as the crucifiers of Christ and as the representatives of a law and a covenant doomed by God to pass away from the world. Readers of Josephus' *Bellum Judaicum* would also learn of Titus' personal bravery and prowess as a leader of men, and of his reluctant massacre of prisoners during the siege of Jerusalem, who he feared might otherwise encumber his own troops.[103] It is not difficult to detect in this career a series of parallels that might be drawn with one particular English king, himself after 1190 embarked upon a venture for the reconquest of Jerusalem from rebellious local tribes.

Richard I, the son of the founder of a new imperial dynasty, wrote poetry in French and showed great eloquence in Latin, was a great general and huntsman, did public and notorious penance for unnamed crimes, hoped to conqueror Jerusalem, massacred 2600 Saracen prisoners at Acre rather than have them encumber his advance, was the most generous of patrons to those within his power, pardoned his own younger brother, John of Mortain, for rebellion in the 1190s, died in 1199 five months short of his forty-second birthday, and witnessed, both at his coronation in 1189, from which the Jews were deliberately excluded, and thereafter, at a pitying distance, the modern persecution of the Jews.[104] If Ralph of Diceto is to be believed, Titus also abandoned the use of dice. Why? I suggest because it was the abandonment of dice as of all games of hazard that was widely broadcast in the 1190s, by both Richard of England and Philip of France, as a means of earning divine favour for their forthcoming campaign to recover a rebellious Judea.[105] Even the details of Richard's campaigning in the Holy Land, his arrival at Acre,

---

[103] Josephus, *Bellum Judaicum*, Bk 5, in *Flavii Iosephi ... Opera*, 797(6:12) ('Tito quidem miserabilis videbatur ista calamitas, cum Iudaei in dies singulos quingenti, nonnunque etiam plures caperentur. Sed neque captos dimittere tutum erat, tantamque asseruare multitudinem custodum videbat esse custodiam, maxime vero propterea non prohibuit, citius eos existimans ea facie remissuros, tanquam similia passuros, nisi se dedidissent.'). For the plotting of Domitian, and Titus' forgiveness, see Suetonius, *Titus*, 9; *Domitianus*, 2.

[104] For all of these various characteristics, see the standard modern biography by J. Gillingham, *Richard I* (New Haven CT, 1999), pp. 168–71 (massacre of prisoners), 237–8, 256–7 (eloquence), 242–3, 254–5 (poetry, and for Titus as musician, see Suetonius, *Titus*, 3), 261–2 (largesse), 263–4 (penance), 284–5 (clemency to John).

[105] Diceto, *Historical Works* I, 62, and for the crusading regulations, see Howden, *Gesta* II, 130–1; Howden, *Chronica* III, 59.

his insistence thereafter on approaching Jerusalem only from the south and from the frontiers of Egypt, mirrored the events of Titus' Judean campaigns of the AD 60s, with his arrival at the port of Acre (known to Josephus under its former name as Ptolemais), and his final march on Jerusalem mounted from Egypt and the desert of Sinai.[106] Newburgh, whom we have already found assiduously reading his Josephus, refers to Acre throughout his narrative of the Third Crusade as 'Ptolemais', using its ancient Josephan name.[107]

Did other contemporaries pick up on these parallels? Did such parallels indeed play a role not only in the way that Richard was portrayed by the chroniclers but comported himself, in deliberate imitation of Titus, the 'darling of the world', Jerusalem's deliverer? There is certainly evidence that Titus' reputation was known in those parts of southern France over which Richard had ruled or sought to rule prior to his accession as king of England in 1189. Thus at Moissac, on the river Tarn, twenty miles to the east of Agen where Richard undoubtedly had dominion before 1189, the monks subscribed to the pious fiction, clearly known to John of Salisbury and cited in the *Policraticus*, by which Vespasian and Titus, for their subjugation of Jerusalem, were accepted as honorary Christians a century and a half in advance of the emperor Constantine. As a result, the porch to the church at Moissac had been built *c.* 1120 in deliberate imitation of the Arch of Titus, one of the most prominent of the surviving classical monuments of the city of Rome.[108]

The most clear-cut evidence that there were indeed comparisons drawn between Titus and Richard appears in the *Itinerarium Ricardi*, a biography of Richard, of disputed date but perhaps of *c.* 1220, and a work in which Titus

---

106 Josephus, *Bellum Judaicum*, Bk 3 (for Titus' arrival in Alexandria and march thence to Ptolemais), Bk 4, final sentences (for Titus' advance on Jerusalem from Egypt, via Gaza, Ascalon and Joppa).

107 WN, ed. Howlett, I, 259, 347.

108 For the church, see L. Seidel, 'Images of the Crusades in Western Art: Models as Metaphors', in *The Meeting of Two Worlds: Cultural Exchange Between East and West During the Period of the Crusades*, ed. V. P. Goss (Kalamazoo, 1986), pp. 377–91. For the Christianization of Vespasian and Titus, see the false encyclical attributed to Pope Sergius, apparently a forgery of the early twelfth century contrived at Moissac: A. Gieysztor, 'The Genesis of the Crusades: The Encyclical of Sergius IV (1009–1012)', *Medievalia et Humanistica* 5 (1948), 2–23; 6 (1950), 4–34, esp. 33–4, 'Spero, credo et certissime teneo qui per v(i)rtutem Domini nostri Ihesu Christi nostram erit victoriam sicut fuit in diebus Titi et Vespasiani, qui Dei filii morte vindicauerunt et adhuc baptismum non receperunt, sed post victoriam ad imperialis honorem Romanorum peruenerunt et de suis peccatis indulgentiam receperunt'. The Christian conversion of Vespasian and Titus also reoccurs as a theme in the so-called *Vindicta Salvatoris*, a cycle of stories dealing with the expiation of Christ's crucifixion, for which see H. Lewy, 'Josephus the Physician: A Mediaeval Legend of the Destruction of Jerusalem', *Journal of the Warburg Institute* 1 (1937–8), 221–42 (pp. 224–5, 230–1). I owe my knowledge of this literature to Karen Kletter. For the echoes of the *Vindicta Salvatoris* in John of Salisbury's account of Titus, see above n. 93. For the *Vindicta* itself, composed *c.* 700 and widely circulated, see S. K. Wright, *The Vengeance of Our Lord: Medieval Dramatization of the Destruction of Jerusalem*, Pontifical Institute of Mediaeval Studies, Studies and Texts 89 (Toronto, 1989), esp. pp. 28–32, citing the edition by C. von Tischendorf, *Evangelia Apocrypha*, 2nd edn (Berlin, 1876), pp. 471–86.

is twice referred to as a model for Richard of England: at his coronation in 1189, 'truly that day of wrath and great bitterness for the Jews of London', where Richard is compared to Hector, Achilles, Alexander, Roland and specifically to Titus 'whose right hand showered favours', and again, in Sicily, at the Christmas court of 1190, where Richard is said to have lamented any day on which he did not give gifts (a direct echo this of all English writers on Titus, themselves echoing Suetonius) and in which, once again, his right hand is said to have 'scattered favours'.[109] Even the physical description that the Itinerarium provides of Richard, 'in complexion half way between red and flame' ('inter rufum et flauum medie temperata cesarie') may contain a deliberate echo of Titus. Richard's father, Henry II, was widely known as 'Rufus' to his contemporaries.[110] The 'flauum ... cesarie' of the Itinerarium's description is not a million miles away from the flaming qualities of Titus Caesar and his dynasty, the Flavians.

Might this be one reason why writers such as Newburgh were, in the 1190s, so keenly reading Josephus' *Bellum Judaicum*, with its detailed account

---

[109] 'Itinerarium peregrinorum et gesta regis Ricardi', in *Itin.*, pp. 142–3 ('vere dies illa mala et valde amara fuit Iudeis Londonie qui eodem die destructi sunt'), 143 ('Huic autem virtus Hectoris, magnanimitas erat Archillis, nec inferior Alexandro nec virtute minor Rolando, immo nostri temporis laudabiliores facile multifariam transendens. Cuius, velut alterius Titi, dextra sparsit opes, et quod in tam famoso milite perrarum esse solet, lingua Nestoris, prudentia Ulixis in omnibus negotiis vel perorandis vel gerendis, aliis merito reddebant excellentiorem'), 173 ('Quinimmo inestimabilis pretii largitus est singulis rex Ricardus pro dignitate donaria ad perfecte consummandam festiuitatis gratiam. Diem nimirum se dolebat perdidisse qua nihil se contingeret donasse, Titi solius liberalitatis comparandus, cuius dextra sparsit opes'). Stubbs placed 'Dextra sparsit opes' within inverted commas, as if it were a direct quotation, but if so, its source remains untraced. Amidst a longstanding debate over the date and status of the 'Itinerarium', I accept John Gillingham's contention that it is in essence a Latin reworking of the earlier French verse chronicle of Ambroise and that it was in circulation early enough to serve as a source for the continuation of William of Tyre which Marianne Salloch dated to *c.* 1220, although Salloch was inclined to suppose that the shared material here proved dependence by the 'Itinerarium' upon an earlier, now lost recension, of the William of Tyre continuation: *Die lateinische Fortsetzung Wilhelms von Tyrus*, ed. M. Salloch (Leipzig, 1934), pp. 36–7; B. Hamilton, *The Leper King and His Heirs: Baldwin IV and the Crusader Kingdom of Jerusalem* (Cambridge, 2000), p. 13. For an alternative synopsis, construing Ambroise as a later French translation of an earlier Latin 'Itinerarium', see F. Vielliard, 'Richard Coeur de Lion et son entourage normand: Le Témoignage de l'Estoire de la Guerre Sainte', *Bibliothèque de l'Ecole des Chartes* 160 (2002), 5–52. Gillingham, 'William of Newburgh and Henry VI', pp. 56–7 n. 34, and 'Two Yorkshire Historians', pp. 23–4 n. 48, floats the possibility that it was Newburgh himself who wrote the Latin continuation of William of Tyre.

[110] *Itin.*, p. 144 ('erat quidem statura procerus elegantis forme, inter rufum et flauum medie temperata cesarie, membris flexibilibus et directis, brachia productiora, quibus ad gladium educendum nulla habiliora vel ad feriendum efficaciora, nihilominus tibiarum longa diusio, totiusque corporis dispositione congrua, species digna imperio cui non modicum competentie mores addebant et habitus, qui non tantum a generis dignitate sed virtutum ornamentis summam possit consequi vel laudem'), and for Henry II as 'Rufus' or 'the little fox' ('vulpecula'), see *Recueil des Actes de Philippe Auguste roi de France: Tome VI (Lettres mises sous le nom de Philippe Auguste dans les recueils de formulaires d'école)*, ed. M. Nortier (Paris, 2005), pp. 50–2, nos. 24–5.

of the exploits of the historical Titus: not just because Jerusalem itself was once again the focus of world-wide attention, or because of the parallels that might be drawn between the fate of the Jews at Masada and those at York, but because England's king was expected to enjoy a destiny no less heroic than that of Titus, reconqueror of Jerusalem? Like Newburgh, Ralph of Diceto was clearly reading Josephus in the 1180s or 90s, with the deliberate intention of drawing comparisons between ancient and more recent history. The crimes of Herod towards his sons, as reported by Josephus both in the *Antiquities* and the *Bellum Judaicum*, were cited by Diceto as one amongst many examples of strife between fathers and sons in the centuries prior to the great rebellion of 1173-4, in which Henry II's sons had risen in rebellion against their father.[111] Since the 1170s, indeed, it was the crimes of Herod the Great, as reported by Josephus, that almost certainly underlay the accusations that Henry II of England, for his murder of Thomas Becket, was guilty of 'Herodian cruelty'.[112]

King Richard's own interest in prophecy is well known, not least because of the detailed reports of his meetings in Calabria in the winter of 1190 with Joachim of Fiore, the greatest prophet of his age, said to have predicted that Richard would shortly recapture Jerusalem and that Richard's name would be 'exalted above all other princes of the world … glorified for evermore'.[113] This was, after all, a period acutely aware of signals and signs, not least those that had foretold the impending defeat of the crusader army at Hattin in 1187, disclosed by an eagle circling the Christian army, crying out words borrowed from the Apocalypse of St John (Revelation 8. 13) 'Woe, woe to you, Oh Jerusalem!'[114] For those who had read Josephus on the Jewish War, there were immediate echoes here both of the Roman eagle placed over the gate of the Temple by Herod, whose throwing down was one of the first signs of the Jewish revolt, and of the voice of the prophet said to have foretold the fall of Jerusalem in AD 70: 'Woe, woe, Oh Jerusalem!'[115]

After the failure of the Third Crusade, of course, with Richard I's withdrawal from Jerusalem and his subsequent capture and ransoming in

---

[111] Diceto, *Historical Works* I, 359–66, esp. pp. 359–60.

[112] *MTB* VII, 446, no. 743 ('a ministris Herodianae crudelitatis').

[113] Howden, *Gesta* II, 151–5, esp. p. 153 ('et Ipse nomen tuum glorificabit in aeternum, et tu Ipsum glorificabis, et in te Ipse glorificabitur'; Howden, *Chronica* III, 75–9, at p. 78 ('exaltabit nomen tuum super omnes principes terrae'); Gillingham, *Richard I*, pp. 138–9.

[114] *Itin.* p. 14 ('aquila Christianum transvolaret exercitum quae septem missilia et balistam gestans in pedibus voce terribili personabat, "Vae tibi Jerusalem!"'), also in Roger of Wendover, whence Paris, *Chronica Majora* II, 327, also in the continuation of William of Tyre, and cf. Revelation 8. 13 ('Et vidi et audivi vocem unius aquilae volantis per medium caeli, dicentis voce magna "Vae, vae, vae habitantibus in terra de ceteris vocibus trium angelorum qui erant tuba canituri!"').

[115] Josephus, *Bellum Judaicum*, Bks 1 and 6, in *Flavii Iosephi … Opera*, 653–5 (2:21) ('supra maximam portam templi rex aquilam collocauerat auream'), 821 (7:12) ('Vox ab oriente, vox ab occidente, vox a quatuor ventis, vox in Hierosolymam … Veh veh Hierosolymis').

Germany, there could no longer be any question of identifying Richard of England with the conquering Titus. Newburgh, indeed, reached not for a classical but a Biblical analogy for Richard, comparing Henry II to Solomon and Richard to Rehoboam, Solomon's son. Under Rehoboam (III Kings 12 and 14. 21-31, II Chronicles 10-12) the Jews were subjected to unprecedented levels of taxation, their Temple treasures were sacked by the Egyptians, and their land itself was divided into two parts, with Israel and the northern tribes breaking away from Rehoboam's Judah (for which perhaps read Richard's Aquitaine and the south). The most famous of Rehoboam's utterances, 'Whereas my father chastised you with whips, so shall I chastise you with scorpions' (III Kings 12. 11, II Chronicles 10. 14), specifically quoted by Newburgh, perhaps assists us to a clearer idea of precisely what Newburgh himself made of Richard I's record as king.[116]

Classical and Biblical analogies for the Plantagenets were no new thing. During the Becket dispute of the 1160s, Henry II had regularly been compared to Pharaoh.[117] Risen, like the earlier self-consciously classicized dynasty of Charlemagne, from origins that were far from imperial, the Plantagenets themselves were not averse to hearing their achievements lauded in terms normally reserved for Hector, Arthur or Roland.[118] Joseph of Exeter, author in the 1180s of a six-book epic poem on the Trojan War, was commissioned to accompany the English contingent on the Third Crusade to which he devoted another classicized epic, the *Antiocheis*, today known only from fragments dealing with King Arthur, preserved by William Camden.[119] Matthew of Rievaulx, writing *c.* 1220, not only described Henry II as 'another Charlemagne' but compared Henry to both Ulysses and Croesus, and Richard I to Hector. Not all such classical comparisons were flattering. Matthew of Rievaulx, for example, claims that though Henry II rivalled Ulysses in cunning and Croesus in wealth, in the end he came to resemble 'poor Amyclas', the fisherman in Book 5 of Lucan's *Pharsalia*, whose assistance was sought by Caesar, but whose squalor and poverty were notorious.[120] In the 1190s, Richard of Devizes, despite comparing Richard's reception at Acre to that of Christ come again to restore the realm of Israel, dismissed the fam-

[116] WN, ed. Howlett, I, 283.

[117] A. Saltman, 'John of Salisbury and the World of the Old Testament', in *The World of John of Salisbury*, ed. M. Wilks, Studies in Church History, Subsidia s. 3 (Oxford, 1984), 343–63, esp. 346–8.

[118] In general here, see N. Vincent, 'The Court of Henry II', in *Henry II: New Interpretations*, ed. C. Harper-Bill and N. Vincent (Woodbridge, 2007), pp. 278–334 (pp. 333–4).

[119] K. Bate, 'Joseph of Exeter', *ODNB* (Oxford, 2004), citing the fragments in William Camden's *Remaines Concerning Britain* (London, 1657), pp. 308–10, a reference which I owe to Hugh Doherty.

[120] A. Wilmart, 'Les Mélanges de Matthieu, préchantre de Rievaulx au debut du XIII siècle', *Revue Bénédictine* 52 (1940), 15–84 at pp. 65–6: 'Floruit Henricus quasi Karolus alter, Ulixes sensu, Cresus erat opibus, post pauper Amiclas'.

ily of Henry II in general as 'the confused house of Oedipus'.[121] Devizes was a monk who clearly knew his Statius.[122]

Meanwhile, one member of the Plantagenet family might have been expected to pay particular attention to such remarks, especially to any attempted comparisons between Henry II and Vespasian or Richard I and Titus. If Richard I was the new Titus, 'the world's darling', then where did this leave his younger brother, the future King John? Richard forgave John his plotting in the 1190s, just as Titus had forgiven the conspiracies of his younger brother, Domitian. According to Suetonius and his followers, after Titus' early death, Domitian, 'having promised well', embarked upon a career as imperial tyrant, butcher of the senatorial class, 'equal to Nero', persecutor of that early prophet of doom, St John of Patmos, who according to Eusebius and other early authorities had written his Book of Revelation whilst in exile imposed by Domitian. Domitian himself was doomed to be the last of the three Flavian emperors, chased ignominiously from his throne.[123]

Did contemporaries after 1199 remark these analogies? Certainly, they showed John beginning well but then declining rapidly into tyranny and murder.[124] Richard of Devizes' reference to Oedipus was drawn from the *Thebaid*, an account of the bloody warfare between the sons of Oedipus widely read as reflecting the strife that in the lifetime of its author, Statius, Domitian's court poet, had divided the sons of Vespasian, Titus and his paranoid younger brother, Domitian. Like Domitian with John of Patmos, so

---

[121] Devizes, *Chronicle*, p. 3 ('Edipode confusa domus'), p. 39 ('ac si esset Christus qui reuenisset in terram restituere regnum Israhel').

[122] Statius, *Thebeiad* 1:17, at the opening, of course, of yet another epic tale of civil war and family strife.

[123] Amongst remarks passed by the English chroniclers, note Henry of Huntingdon, *Historia*, p. 532 (that Domitian was better with a bow than in his acts, 'optimus arcu, pessimus actu'); Salisbury, *Policraticus* (3:14), p. 228 ('Domitianus, qui grauissimam theomachiam exercuit post Neronem, huius virtutis aliquid plerumque indulsit ciuibus, licet in eos gratis quandoque insaniret, homo quidem usquequaque inutilis et qui nichil aliud habebat virile nisi nomen imperii'); Niger, *Chronica*, p. 115 ('Domitianus frater Titi primo clemens fuit ... anno imperii eius xiiii. fit persequutio Christianorum secunda. Beatus Iohannes scribit Apocalypsim.'). Landolfo's *Historia Romana* (ed. Crivellucci, I, 219) sets the tone for the idea that Domitian began well (following Suetonius, *Domitianus*, 3, 'Circa administrationem autem imperii aliquamdiu se varium prestitit, mixtura quoque aequabili vitiorum atque virtutum, donec virtutes quoque in vitia deflexit'): 'Primis tamen annis moderatus in imperio fuit, mox ad ingentia vitia progressus liuidinis, iracundie, crudelitatis, auaritie tantum in se concitauit ut merita patris et fratris aboleret'. Domitian's persecution of the Church and of St John were well known too through the description supplied in the Latin translation of Eusebius, *Historia* (3:17), in *PG* 20, pt. 2, cols. 250–1 ('ad extremum Neroniane impietatis bellique et odii aduersus Deum, successorem seipsum professus est').

[124] For early accounts of John's accession and first years as king, see J. C. Holt, *King John* (London, 1963), pp. 18–20, and J. Gillingham, 'Historians without Hindsight: Coggeshall, Diceto and Howden on the Early Years of John's Reign', in *King John: New Interpretations*, ed. S. D. Church (Woodbridge, 1999), pp. 1–26, which although challenging Holt, agrees that there was a brief lull in the criticisms after 1199.

King John with Peter of Pontefract was widely advertized as a ruler who persecuted the prophets of doom. Like Domitian, 'equal to Nero', so King John was portrayed as a persecutor of the Church.[125] 'Equal to Nero' Domitian may have been, but as always, to anyone who had read Suetonius, the even more awful figure of Nero inevitably trumped the far paler portrayal of Domitian the tyrant. It is as a new Nero, murderer of his own kin, a tyrant doomed to suicide, that John appears in the most heavily classicized of all contemporary accounts of his reign, the *Philippidos* of the Capetian sycophant, Guillaume le Breton.[126] Elsewhere, contemporaries reached for apparently less inflammatory classical comparisons in describing John. According to the Barnwell chronicler, John enjoyed mixed fortunes, like Marius, sometimes up, sometimes down.[127] Modern commentators who cite this passage have generally failed to notice quite how bitter it was intended to be. It is Lucan that the Barnwell chronicler was citing here, and according to Lucan, Gaius Marius, the corrupt consul whose rivalry with Sulla first turned the legions against the Roman people, plunged Rome into that civil war that stained the very steps of the senate with Roman blood.[128] As any reader of Lucan would know – and who, in the twelfth century, had not read Lucan? – the civil war provoked by Marius led directly to the Caesars, to empire and to Lucan's own particular patron, the emperor Nero. The analogy between King John and Nero thus hovers in the mind of the Barnwell chronicler less obviously but every bit as significantly as in that of Guillaume le Breton.

Some talk of Alexander, and some of Hercules. By contrast, the gallery of role models available to English writers of the 1190s – Vespasian, Titus, Domitian – is much less familiar to a modern readership. To most modern

---

125 As, for example, in the work both of Matthew of Rievaulx, and in the later, anonymous 'Invective against King John': Wilmart, 'Les Mélanges de Matthieu', pp. 66–7; N. Vincent, 'Stephen Langton, Archbishop of Canterbury', in *Etienne Langton: Prédicateur, Bibliste, Théologien*, ed. L.-J. Bataillon et al. (Turnhout, 2010), pp. 51–123 (pp. 87–8).

126 'Philippidos' 6:567–75, in *Oeuvres de Rigord et de Guillaume le Breton, historiens de Philippe–Auguste*, ed. H. F. Delaborde, 3 vols. (Paris, 1882–85), II, 174 (referring to John's murder of Arthur: 'Ecce Neronis opus, quo post preclara virorum funera nobilium, post caros postque propinquos, tormentis variis quos interfecit, ut esset solus in imperio, materni visceris alvum findere presumpsit, forulumque propaginis in quo conceptus fuerat, de quo processit ad ortum, inspexit, tandem proprio se perculit ense, cerdonum metuens subulis incurrere mortem. Ecce Judas alter, Herodes ecce secundus', also noting that Judas' betrayal of Christ to the Jews' crucifixion merely brought down the vengeance of Vespasian upon them, condemning them to perpetual servitude).

127 *The Historical Collections of Walter of Coventry*, ed. W. Stubbs, 2 vols., RS 58 (London, 1872–73), II, 232, 'Princeps quidem magnus sed minus felix et cum Mario fortunam utramque expertus, munificus et liberalis in exteros, sed suorum depraedator, plus in alienis quam in suis confidens, unde et a suis ante finem derelictus est, et in fine modicum luctus', noticed, for example, by J. C. Holt, *The Northerners: A Study in the Reign of King John*, 2nd edn (Oxford, 1992), p. 143.

128 Lucan, *De Bello Civili*, 2:68–133, esp. lines 103–4 ('Stat cruor in templis, multaque rubentia caede lubrica saxa madent'), 131–3 ('Ille fuit vitae Mario modus, omnia passo quae peior fortuna potest, atque omnibus uso quae melior, mensoque hominis quid fata paterent').

historians, indeed, these are names known chiefly from the Cotton collection in the British Library, divided between classes named after the Roman emperors, rather than as living or breathing figures from the classical past. Even Mozart's operatic commemoration of the 'clemency of Titus' has failed to rescue the Flavians from obscurity. In the 1190s, however, the names of the Flavian emperors, and of their chief chronicler, 'Flavius Josephus', perhaps loomed rather larger in the imagination of William of Newburgh and his contemporaries. The reputations of Vespasian, Titus and Domitian, I suggest, played no small part in the self-perception of Richard I, of King John, and meanwhile in the portrayal of those most unfortunate figures, the victims of ancient prejudice, the murdered Jews of York.

4

1190, William Longbeard and the Crisis of Angevin England*

Alan Cooper

The brief life and abortive revolutionary career of William FitzOsbert, alias William Longbeard, came to a sad end, if our sources are to be believed, in a mad insurrection against the royal and municipal authorities in London in April 1196. His brief moment of fame or infamy can be used as a window into many aspects of late twelfth century culture. His life throws light on the experience of crusading and the possibly traumatic effects it could have; on the plight of the poor in a newly urbanized and monetarized society; and on the politics of London and of England as a whole. Indeed, a comparison of the events surrounding the massacre in York in 1190 and the events surrounding FitzOsbert's death provides a window into the tensions of Angevin England. This chapter will therefore consist of three parts. First, I provide a very brief narrative of the events of April 1196. Then I offer an extremely basic compare-and-contrast exercise between FitzOsbert's demise and the events of March 1190; and finally, I suggest what that comparison can say about the nature of English society in the 1190s.

Let me begin with a brief narrative of FitzOsbert's life. William FitzOsbert, the younger son of a rich London family, is first recorded as a participant on the Third Crusade.[1] Following the example of a previous generation of Londoners, he joined with some fellow citizens to fit out a ship as a communal undertaking. I have argued elsewhere that FitzOsbert may well have been traumatized by the experience of the crusade: the conditions of the campaign and his behaviour afterwards are certainly consistent with such a hazardous

---

* I have presented work on FitzOsbert at the Haskins Society (2005 and 2009), the Arizona Center for Renaissance and Medieval Studies (2006), Kalamazoo (2007), Leeds (2007) and Cornell (2008), as well as Harvard (2005), the Institute of Historical Research (2008) and York (2010). I would like to thank the commentators at the conferences and Robin Fleming, John Gillingham, Hugh Doherty, Paul Hyams, Ian Wei, and Caroline Palmer, in particular, as well as my colleagues and students at Colgate, for their encouragement.
1 For FitzOsbert as a crusader, see C. Tyerman, *England and the Crusades, 1095–1588* (Chicago, 1988), pp. 73–4, 183.

diagnosis.[2] Two points about the crusade might be emphasized above all. The first is the suffering of the crusaders outside the city of Acre. In the winter of 1190/91, the majority of the crusaders were stuck outside the city, encamped between the garrison inside the walls and Saladin's relief army. Trauma is usually a result of a slow erosion, of exhaustion and sustained passivity in the face of fear. Outside Acre, over the winter when King Richard had yet to arrive, the army suffered from disease and famine, and many people died, including the archbishop of Canterbury and Ranulf de Glanville. In this context, the bishop of Salisbury, Hubert Walter, later to become archbishop of Canterbury as well as Richard's great reforming justiciar, came to prominence, taking it as his task to raise funds for the relief of the poor. He preached to the army reminding them of their duty to succour their fellow Christians.[3] When King Richard arrived he brought relief, and eye-witness accounts make clear the utter devotion of the rank and file to the king as the result.[4]

Which brings me to my second point about the crusade: it ended in controversy. It achieved notable successes, such as the capture of the island of Cyprus and the great port of Acre; it failed, however, to recapture Jerusalem. The sources are clear in the sense they give of the arguments that must have broken out on the crusaders' return. The crusaders were subjected to derision.[5] In their eyes, however, Richard the Lionheart was a hero, and they would have been appalled to discover the stories that had been circulated – particularly by Philip Augustus – accusing Richard of conspiring with the Assassins in the murder of Conrad of Montferrat. And, of course, they would have discovered that on his return journey in 1192, Richard had been taken prisoner by the duke of Austria and held for ransom. In short, the returning crusaders would have felt a sense of betrayal. Trauma can be most particularly caused by a sense that what is right has been broken: that the proper order of things – including the correct reward for endurance and suffering – has been disturbed and can no longer be trusted.[6]

When FitzOsbert returned to London, he was shocked by what he found. While he had been away, London had achieved the goal it had been aiming at for fifty years, if not more: it had been granted recognition of its commune, and the self-governing status that this implied. But the commune had been granted under nefarious circumstances. In the political crisis of 1191, the justiciar, William Longchamp, had been removed

---

2   Most fully in a paper entitled 'Trauma and the Crusades' delivered at the Haskins Society Conference at Boston College in November 2009. For the best example of a historical reconstruction of the hardships of war that may lead to trauma, see E. T. Dean, *Shook over Hell: Post-Traumatic Stress, Vietnam and the Civil War* (Cambridge MA, 1997), esp. cc. 3–4.

3   *The History of the Holy War: Ambroise's Estoire de la Guerre Sainte*, ed. M. Ailes and M. Barber, 2 vols. (Woodbridge, 2003), II, 92–3.

4   *History of the Holy War* II, 95.

5   ibid., II, 192.

6   See J. Shay, *Achilles in Vietnam: Combat Trauma and the Undoing of Character* (New York, 1994), esp. ch. 1.

from office, the key moment coming when the Londoners were forced to choose between supporting Longchamp or the king's brother, John. The city was divided, but eventually the faction that supported John prevailed: Longchamp was deposed, and, in reward for their support, John awarded the Londoners recognition of their commune. Meanwhile, the crusading sources make it perfectly clear that Richard abandoned the crusade, rejecting the army's desperate desire for an assault on Jerusalem, because of events at home. Again, betrayal: the army knew that but for the failure of their fellow Christians to support them, the crusade might have achieved its goal. One source even hints that Richard planned to continue his crusade back home.[7] Events in London would have fueled FitzOsbert's anger. All of England was taxed to pay King Richard's ransom, but London had a particularly large sum to pay. Even the sources that are hostile to FitzOsbert agree that the way in which the city fathers went about collecting the money was wholly corrupt. Not only did they use the opportunity to line their own pockets, but they tried to shift the burden of the taxes onto the poorest parts of the city's population.[8]

It is in this context that FitzOsbert comes to our attention.[9] All the sources agree that by April 1196 he had made himself the champion of the poor, even if they disagree about his motives. By now he had grown a long beard and acquired the pejorative nickname Longbeard. He spoke out at the thrice-yearly meeting known as the Folkmoot, which was a compulsory meeting for all the citizens of London, held in the churchyard of St Paul's, where a pulpit used for proclamations and oratory stood until it was destroyed by Puritans in the 1640s. FitzOsbert then went beyond oratory, travelling to Normandy to visit King Richard. Here he took advantage of his status as a fellow crusader of the king to give him a direct report on the corruption of his officers, which the king took seriously enough to appoint the abbot of Caen to examine the situation. Unfortunately, the abbot died within a few days of his arrival in England. 'Those people who had dreaded his arrival were not saddened by his passing',[10] says William of Newburgh.

---

7   *History of the Holy War* II, 147. For London's role in the political crisis of 1191, see C. N. L. Brooke, *London, 800–1216: The Shaping of a City* (London, 1975), pp. 45–6.

8   The sources for the immediate events of April 1196 can perhaps be found most conveniently collected in *English Lawsuits from William I to Richard I*, ed. R. C. van Caenegem, 2 vols, Selden Society 106 and 107 (London, 1990–1), II, 687–94.

9   The story of William's protest and death has been told in many books, mostly, however, in ones that are not concerned with the main political narrative of Richard's reign; see, for example, M. Mollat, *The Poor in the Middle Ages: An Essay in Social History* (New Haven CT, 1986), pp. 83–4; Brooke, *London*, pp. 48–9. John Gillingham's biography of Richard I does not mention FitzOsbert at all. The only works particularly on Longbeard are G. W. S. Barrow, 'The Bearded Revolutionary: The Story of a Twelfth-Century London Student in Revolt', *History Today* 19 (1969), 679–87, and J. McEwan, 'William FitzOsbert and the Crisis in London in 1196', *Florilegium* 21 (2004), 18–42.

10 'illi qui introitum ejus expaverunt, exitum ejus non fleverunt', WN, ed. Howlett, II, 465 (translations are my own). Newburgh is the most vivid source for the life and death of Wil-

That left Longbeard himself, as well as his associates. All the chroniclers seem in agreement that William FitzOsbert was the head of a party bound by an oath. The numbers are certainly exaggerated, and the accusations of their actions and motives should be taken with more than a pinch of salt, but there seems no reason to disbelieve that William might have been the head of such a subversive movement. Whatever he was up to, it aroused the suspicions of Hubert Walter, archbishop of Canterbury, justiciar of England, the saviour of the poor outside Acre. He placed limits on the movements of the common people of London and even had two of them arrested in Lincolnshire; then he acted against their leader, trying to arrest FitzOsbert on charges of sedition. According to Newburgh, the arrest proved impossible because of FitzOsbert's crowd of supporters. When Hubert Walter's men did finally get close enough, FitzOsbert killed one of them with an axe. Then he and his confederates fled to the church of St Mary-le-Bow on Cheapside, the commercial heart of the city. Although they claimed sanctuary, fires were set at the archbishop's command, and the fugitives were smoked out. William was then taken via the Tower, where a summary trial took place, to Smithfield, outside the walls, where he and nine supporters were hanged. Although the common people tried to venerate him as a saint after his death, FitzOsbert may appear a rather pathetic figure: a rebel for a misconceived cause, destined to die a brutal death that put an end to his movement, such as it was.

So – to turn to my second point – what similarities can be seen between the violence of March 1190 in York and the violence in London in April 1196? To set up the comparison we might look at an event that bridges the gap between them, namely the anti-semitic violence in London in 1189 after Richard's coronation. The sources are adamant that the violence was initiated and carried out by the 'common people of the city of London' ('plebs civitatis Londoniae'),[11] 'the common people with arrogant eye and insatiable heart' ('plebs superbo oculo, et insatiabili corde')[12] or 'the unruly mob in a fury' ('indisciplinata cum turbine turba')[13] as well as 'households of the nobles' ('nobilium familias')[14] who were attending the coronation. Roger of Howden presents the city as divided between the poorer classes and those in the city who were personal friends with Jews.[15] While in other contexts, London is presented as a happy

liam FitzOsbert; on the problems that Newburgh's style and intentions present to the historian, see Vincent, in this volume.

11 Howden, *Gesta* II, 84 (i.e., the earlier annals composed by Howden that he later expanded into his chronicle).
12 Howden, *Chronica* III, 12.
13 WN, ed. Howlett I, 295.
14 ibid., I, 299; similarly, Howden, *Gesta* II, 83–4.
15 Howden, *Gesta* II, 84; Howden, *Chronica* III, 12. In the later version in the chronicle, Howden confuses matters a little by changing 'plebs civitatis Londoniae' to 'cives Londonienses', but he adds the phrase 'plebs superbo oculo, et insatiabili corde', so that context continues to suggest the lower classes; in both versions Jews are saved by their friends in the city, but the annals include the detail that they were hidden in their friends' houses.

unity,[16] in 1189 we see fissures within the population. Likewise in York: 'The elite of the city and the more important citizens ... cautiously declined to join such a frenzy', but the massacre was carried out by 'all the working sort and all the young men of the town as well as a large crowd of countrymen and not a few military men'.[17] Placed together then, the events of 1189/90 and 1196 may be a window into the politics of the lower classes.

If we try to identify the various strands of this political discourse, the most obvious starting place suggested by a comparison of 1189/90 and 1196 is the effect of the crusades on domestic politics. The connection between the crusades and the massacres of 1189/90 is obvious enough: the preaching of a crusade stirred up hatred against non-Christians. Newburgh, while criticizing the London mob, cannot help injecting a note of sympathy with their actions, saying that the massacres showed 'the new confidence of the Christians against the enemies of the cross of Christ'.[18] Indeed, many of the perpetrators of the York massacre left the country afterwards on the Third Crusade.[19] The connection between the crusade and FitzOsbert's protest is more complicated. As I suggested before, William FitzOsbert suffered from trauma after his own experience of the Third Crusade. The political connection goes deeper, however: the preaching of the crusades always included appeals to the notion of Christian brotherhood. This aspect was at its strongest in the aftermath of the fall of Jerusalem in 1187, which was interpreted as a punishment for the collective sins of Christendom. The preparations for the Third Crusade included promises of a reformed and frugal lifestyle on the part of the leaders.[20] And the experience of the conditions outside Acre may have inspired FitzOsbert's call for succouring the poor of London.

That the crusades did indeed have a profound impact not just on the knightly class but also on the poorer members of society is confirmed by an extraordinary document from the 1190s. It is a list of people who had taken the crusading vow and then failed to travel to the Holy Land. The document was produced as part of a general investigation into such cases, which was ordered in January 1196 and continued until March 1196. The timing makes me wonder whether the investigation itself might not have been another element stirring in the tensions that led to FitzOsbert's protest. The surviving document concerns Lincolnshire and lists twenty-nine people, twenty of whom are listed

---

[16] See, for example, Richard of Devizes' account of the events of 1191; Devizes, *Chronicle*, pp. 46, 49. Compare Brooke, *London*, pp. 45–6.

[17] 'urbis nobilitas et cives graviores ... tantam vecordiam caute declinarunt ... omne genus opificum, atque universa juventus urbana cum plurima provincialium turba, et militaribus viris non paucis', WN, ed. Howlett, I, 316.

[18] 'nova Christianorum contra inimicos crucis Christi fiducia', WN, ed. Howlett, I, 297.

[19] WN, ed. Howlett, I, 322; Dobson, *JMY*, p. 28.

[20] Tyerman, *England and the Crusades*, p. 61. For the ideological connection of crusading and care for the poor in the lead-up to the Third Crusade, see M. Markowski, 'Peter of Blois and the Conception of the Third Crusade', in *The Horns of Hattin*, ed. B. Z. Kedar (Jerusalem, 1992), pp. 261–9, esp. p. 265.

as poor. Alongside them are people of various poorer professions such as skinners and cobblers,[21] which would seem to be reasonable evidence that even as late as the Third Crusade the 'poor' of the crusade did include genuinely poor people, not just knights who had fallen on hard times.

The connection to the crusades leads to another strand of the political discourse of the 1190s that is suggested by the two events: apocalypticism. The massacre of 1190 was incited in part by a Premonstratensian hermit. That FitzOsbert fulfilled the familiar role of a millenarian social critic is confirmed not only by the apocalyptic language put into his mouth by Newburgh, who was utterly hostile to FitzOsbert, but also by the unanimous opinion of the chroniclers that Longbeard had not just a beard, but a 'barba prolixa', an unkempt, shaggy beard that was the distinctive mark of would-be holy men.[22] It is worth noting that the 1190s were a time of heightened apocalyptic mood: the fall of Jerusalem and the preaching of the crusade had been greeted with various predictions of the coming end, many swirling around the troubling success of Saladin and thus his status as a forerunner of Antichrist.[23]

If the apocalyptic side of both moments of violence can serve to emphasize their irrational qualities, it is possible to see through these qualities to find genuine social protest. Newburgh quotes Longbeard as saying: 'I am the saviour of the poor, and you, poor people, who have experienced the hard hand of the rich, drink the waters of the doctrine of salvation from my springs, and you should do this with joy for the time of your visitation is come.'[24] This is almost certainly language invented by Newburgh, but its allusions both to injustice – 'the hard hand of the rich' – and governance – the word 'visitation' – pick up a theme in all the accounts of FitzOsbert's career that his furious denunciations of the London oligarchy were justified. The rich London citizens were exploiting the poor. We will certainly feel less sympathy with the perpetrators of the violence in March 1190, but we may follow Barrie Dobson in reading events there as 'a deliberately violent protest against the financial oppression of the Angevin government' and 'a deliberate reaction on the part of discontented northerners against what they regarded, with some justification, as victimization at the hands of a Westminster government which refused to take them into partnership'.[25]

---

21 C. R. Cheney, *Hubert Walter* (London, 1967), p. 132. See also N. Orme and O. J. Padel, 'Cornwall and the Third Crusade', *Journal of the Royal Institution of Cornwall*, 142 (2005), 71–7. I am indebted to Hugh Doherty for this reference.

22 G. Constable, 'Introduction', in *Apologiae Duae*, ed. R. B. C. Huygens (Turnhout, 1985), pp. 47–130 (p. 53).

23 B. McGinn, *Antichrist: Two Thousand Years of the Human Fascination with Evil* (New York, 2000), p. 141.

24 'Salvator pauperum ego sum. Vos pauperes duras divitum manus experti, haurite de fontibus meis aquas doctrinae salutaris, et hoc cum gaudio quia venit tempus visitationis vestrae.', WN, ed. Howlett, II, 469.

25 Dobson, *JMY*, pp. 36–7.

In other words, just as personal circumstances caused the wealthy Fitz-Osbert to make common cause with the poorer classes in London, so a sense of political exclusion allowed the disillusioned knights of York to unite in genocidal hatred with the workers and peasants against the Jews. Moreover, we might see the two moments of violence together as a protest against the very success of the Angevin Empire. The bringing together of England with the north and west of France had helped to make a lot of people very wealthy. The result was, in John Gillingham's words, that: 'One of the most striking facts about Angevin political history is the consistent loyalty of the towns', because '[p]robably what really counted was that the urban ruling elites believed that the Angevin Empire was in some sense "good for business" and should, therefore, be supported. They were likely right'.[26] In the pogroms of 1189/90, the ruling class of London and Winchester, the two sets of burgesses who are represented as closest to the king and were given the honour of serving him at the coronation, protected the Jews.[27] The followers of Longbeard objected to the wealth and civic power of London's merchant elite; the antisemitic mob in York identified – rightly or wrongly – the Jews as winners in the Angevin Empire's economic system.

Reading the two moments as being protests of such ambitious scope highlights another point of comparison between them. Both outbreaks of violence were of broad national significance. The antisemitic attacks broke out in London, King's Lynn, Norwich, Stamford, Bury St Edmunds, Lincoln, Colchester, and perhaps Thetford in Norfolk, all of this despite the king sending out letters across the whole country forbidding further violence after the incident at his coronation.[28] In the case of FitzOsbert, the brief moment of violence was confined to London itself, but there are reasons to believe that the royal authorities feared a wider uprising. Hubert Walter forbade the poor of London to travel and had two of them arrested in Stamford. After FitzOsbert's death, he acted to suppress a cult that arose

---

[26] J. Gillingham, *The Angevin Empire*, 2nd edn (London, 2001), pp. 64–5. Gillingham emphasizes the granting of independent commune status to many towns across the Angevin realm as well as the business advantages brought about by having trade routes under a single prince.

[27] The bitter comments by the thoroughly unpleasant Richard of Devizes suggest the tensions provoked by this protection: 'Winchester alone spared its worms. They were a prudent and far-sighted people and a city that always behaved in a civilised manner. They never did anything over-hastily, for fear they might repent of it later, and they looked to the end of things rather than to its beginnings. They did not want partially to vomit forth the undigested mass violently and at their peril, even though they were urged to do so, when they were not ready. They hid in their bowels, modestly (or naturally) dissimulating their disgust meanwhile, till at an opportune time for remedies they could cast out all the morbid matter once and for all'. Devizes, *Chronicle*, p. 4; and see the subsequent absurdly concocted and elaborately embroidered story told by Richard of a ritual murder by the Jews of Winchester, pp. 64–9. On the protection given to the Jews of London, see above, n. 16. For the coronation, see P. E. Schramm, *A History of the English Coronation* (Oxford, 1937), pp. 68–9.

[28] Dobson, *JMY*, p. 25; and see Hillaby's essay in this volume.

proclaiming FitzOsbert a martyr, a cult that included people coming to London for business from around the country.[29]

It is also instructive to compare FitzOsbert to the victims of the massacre, since both he and the Jews in York, when their moment of crisis came, fled towards royal authority. In the case of the Jews, this is obviously connected to the well-established status of the Jews as under royal protection, a status further guaranteed by Richard after his coronation even though he was a crusader (a fact that encouraged the London mob to think their actions might find his favour).[30] In the case of FitzOsbert, the situation is more complicated. After he killed a man seeking to arrest him on royal authority, one might expect him to flee. Instead, he chose to seek sanctuary in the church of St Mary-le-Bow, a church under the special jurisdiction of Hubert Walter as archbishop of Canterbury. This seems to have been a deliberate choice: Newburgh says that FitzOsbert and his associates fled to the 'neighbourhood' ('vicinia') of St Mary's,[31] and, from what we know of FitzOsbert's family, he lived in the parish of St Nicholas on Lombard Street, not next to St Mary-le-Bow.[32] This choice of sanctuary suggests that FitzOsbert may again have put faith in his own status as a former comrade-in-arms of the justiciar – perhaps even particularly remembering Hubert's concern for the poor outside Acre – but also that he suspected that the attempt to arrest him was a plot on the part of the London authorities and so thought that the king's representative would side with him. Both efforts to seek justice, however misguided they were, may have been encouraged by the heightened expectations surrounding King Richard. On his accession, he fashioned an image of himself not just as a crusader king but as a king who would bring new justice, in contrast to his father. A song composed for his coronation declared: 'The age of gold returns/ The world's reform draws nigh/ The rich man now cast down/ The pauper raised on high'.[33] Throughout all the troubles of the 1190s, Richard's personal reputation remained undimmed.

To conclude my compare-and-contrast exercise, let me suggest what the two outbreaks of violence, if taken together, indicate about the political discourse of the poorer classes. The limited evidence for 1196 demonstrates a well informed opposition to what was seen as novel, unjust and repressive taxation; if we include the earlier events, we might also identify a strong xenophobia combined with a sense of alienation against the new wealth generated by an international economy. All that said, however, the comparison does also point out a further, more obvious strain in twelfth-century society

29 WN, ed. Howlett, II, 473.
30 See ibid., I, 295.
31 ibid., II, 470.
32 Tyerman, *England and the Crusades*, p. 74.
33 'Redit aetas aurea/ Mundus renovatur/ Dives nunc deprimitur/ Pauper exaltatur', quoted in Gillingham, *Richard I*, p. 108. On contemporary comparisons between Richard and Emperor Titus, see Vincent, in this volume.

that should not be underplayed. Simply put, the society had plenty of violent and broken individuals. Richard Malebisse at York comes across as an odious individual, predisposed to violence: Hugh Thomas suggests that the unusual family name 'advertised their potential for violence' and that 'Richard's forebears had destructive and violent attitudes that may have shaped Richard's upbringing and training'.[34] With FitzOsbert we might have more sympathy, as someone traumatized by war and seeking justice for the oppressed; but who, in the moment of crisis, snapped and turned to violence before falling victim to ruthless judicial violence himself.

And so let me turn to my third part: what do these two moments of violence when put together tell us about English society in the 1190s? In short, they show us the tensions of a society in transformation and under considerable pressure. There were both long-term changes underway in the economy and society and short-term financial exigencies that helped fuel a sense of crisis. Such changes have often been discussed as part of a narrative of economic growth and governmental innovation. These narratives are certainly true, but in setting aside the effect of changes on the poorer elements of society they are incompletely true. The brief moments in 1189/90 and 1196 when social tensions erupt into the political narrative demand a reassessment.

The long-term context of the 1190s may be summarized quite briefly: society was undergoing profound and rapid changes. The monetarization of the rural economy was increasing disparities between rich and poor in the countryside: after about 1170 the previous trend of the reduction of demesne was reversed and landlords increasingly brought land under their own control.[35] While growing amounts of cash in the countryside stimulated a land market among the peasants that allowed the prosperous to benefit, a simultaneous increase in wage labour – in place of payment in kind – reduced the traditional safety nets.[36] Even the legal status of peasants was under threat; as Rodney Hilton puts it, the 'last two decades of the [twelfth] century were the crucial period for the depression of the majority of the rural population'.[37] R. H. Britnell, looking at the long thirteenth century, sums up the situation thus:

> the economic developments of the period were not analogous to modern growth, and did not promote general improvement in material standards of living. The favourable interpretation that can be placed on the institutional devel-

---

[34] H. M. Thomas, 'Portrait of a Medieval Anti-semite: Richard Malebisse "vero agnomine Mala Bestia"', *Haskins Society Journal* 5 (1993), 1–15 (pp. 2, 3).

[35] B. Geremek, *Poverty: A History*, trans. A. Kolakowska (Oxford, 1994), p. 55; Britnell, *Commercialisation*, p. 109; E. Miller and J. Hatcher, *Medieval England: Rural Society and Economic Change, 1086–1348* (Harlow, 1978), pp. 209–10.

[36] Britnell, *Commercialisation*, pp. 102–5, 126–7 and 145.

[37] R. H. Hilton, 'Freedom and Villeinage in England', *P & P* 31 (1965), 3–19 (p. 13).

opment of English society has accordingly to be dampened, at least with respect to the bottom third of the population, by the reflection that thousands of families were left free to be hungry.[38]

One way for the rural poor to escape this plight was to migrate to the cities. At the end of the twelfth century cities across Europe were becoming large enough for urban poverty to become endemic for the first time.[39] The newly-arrived poor from the countryside were easily pushed to the margins of urban society: as guilds and communes secured powers for the established merchants of the city, they limited outsiders' opportunities to prosper, forcing unskilled, unrepresented workers to the periphery where they were confined to temporary employment.[40] And even this supposes that urban immigrants survived the epidemiological imbalance between country and city that killed many newcomers[41] and must have wrecked many dreams of betterment.

Moreover, if the period around 1200 may generally be characterized as a period of economic growth, the moment of FitzOsbert's protest was not. It was, in fact, one of particular tension, because it was a period of famine. Across Europe, the years from 1194 to 1196 were marked by heavy rains and flooding, which ruined crops and caused food prices to rise even faster.[42] This situation can be demonstrated both by the written evidence collected from narrative sources across Europe by Fritz Curschmann in the late nineteenth century[43] and by new evidence of the growth of oak trees and the development of glaciers that shows that the 1190s were a decade that was markedly colder and wetter than those that preceded it.[44] In France at least the situation was so bad that we are told that popular rumour told of the birth of Antichrist

---

[38] Britnell, *Commercialisation*, pp. 150–1.

[39] Mollat, *The Poor in the Middle Ages*, pp. 61, 63. For a summary of urban growth in England in this period, see E. Miller and J. Hatcher, *Medieval England: Towns, Commerce and Crafts, 1086–1348* (London, 1995), pp. 263–79.

[40] Mollat, *The Poor in the Middle Ages*, pp. 68–9; Geremek, *Poverty*, pp. 64–6.

[41] R. Fleming, 'Bones for Historians: Putting the Body back into Biography', in *Writing Medieval Biography, 750–1250: Essays in Honour of Professor Frank Barlow*, ed. D. Bates, J. Crick and S. Hamilton (Woodbridge, 2006), pp. 29–48 (pp. 41–3).

[42] Mollat, *The Poor in the Middle Ages*, p. 62. Mollat also writes: 'The drama [of social disorder] was played out against a background of sporadic scarcity and famine: the darkest times came at the end of the eleventh century and then again in 1125, 1144, 1161, and 1191–97', p. 57.

[43] F. Curschmann, *Hungersnöte im Mittelalter: ein Beitrag zur deutschen Wirtschaftsgeschichte des 8. bis 13. Jahrhunderts* (Leipzig, 1900), pp. 155–61.

[44] Personal communication from Prof. Michael McCormick, Harvard University. Some of this data and the conclusions drawn from it are not yet published, but see U. Büntgen et al., '2500 Years of European Climate Variability and Human Susceptibility', *Science* 331 (2011), 578–82 and links at http://www.ncdc.noaa.gov/paleo/pubs/buentgen2011/buentgen2011.html [accessed 26 May 2011].

and the imminent end of the world.[45] The language put into the mouth of William Longbeard by unsympathetic chroniclers may suggest that he preached about starvation. He uses metaphors of consumption and takes the title 'saviour of the poor'. Newburgh writes of the 1190s that:

> Moreover, the hand of the Lord lay heavy on the Christian people at this time, as the insanity of the princes was destroying the lands alongside pestilence and famine ... Indeed, the famine, produced by unseasonable rains, had for several years vehemently worn down the people of France and England, but with kings raging between themselves, it increased more than usual. And when the impoverished common people were dying everywhere from starvation, there followed in famine's footsteps a very cruel pestilence, as if the air had been corrupted by the corpses of paupers, which hardly spared those for whom food was plentiful, but did shorten the long agony of hunger for the poor.[46]

Newburgh's emphasis on the way in which war exaggerated the accidents of climate and disease is instructive, as are his comments on the disparities between rich and poor.

For, indeed, the 1190s were a period of contrasting fortunes, especially as they came in the middle of a period of great inflation.[47] This inflation has been much debated since P. D. A. Harvey first suggested that 1180–1220 'take its place beside the sixteenth and the twentieth centuries as one of the three great inflationary periods of recorded English history'.[48] Notably, Paul Latimer places a greater emphasis on the years immediately after 1200, arguing that the principal cause of the inflation was a loss of confidence in the coinage that caused the sudden release of hoarded wealth.[49] Nevertheless, prices of wheat and livestock doubled or even trebled in a fifty-year period covering 1200 and, more importantly, as Latimer's evidence shows, between 1192 and the first decade of the thirteenth century,

---

[45] *Oeuvres de Rigord* I, 141. See W. L. Warren, *King John*, 2nd edn (New Haven CT, 1997), p. 63.

[46] 'Aggravata est etiam ipso tempore manus Domini super populum Christianum, vesaninae scilicet principum vastanti provincias jungens famem et pestem ... Et quidem fames intempestivis edita imbribus, per annos jam aliquot Galliae Angliaeque populos vehementer attriverat, sed regibus inter se debacchantibus plus solito invaluit. Cumque vulgus pauperum passim inedia deperiret, secuta est e vestigio, tanquam ex pauperum mortibus aere corrupto, pestis saevissima, quae et illis quibus alimenta abundabant minime parceret, et indigentibus longum famis cruciatum breviaret.' WN, ed. Howlett, II, 484.

[47] P. D. A. Harvey, 'The English Inflation of 1180–1220', *P & P* 61 (1973), 3–30.

[48] Harvey, 'English Inflation', p. 30.

[49] P. Latimer, 'The English Inflation of 1180–1220 Reconsidered', *P & P* 171 (2001), 3–29, esp. 3–4, 19–23.

the price of wheat rose from just under 20d. per quarter to over 60d.[50] It would make sense to connect such a spike in wheat prices to the bad harvests of the late 1190s, not to mention the demands of feeding armies – that is, the same connections made by Newburgh. A period of inflation tends to hit the poor hardest, as the prices of basic staples outstrip their spending power. Moreover, looking over the longer term, wages, adjusted for inflation, would decline throughout the thirteenth century.[51] That said, England was unquestionably an enormously wealthy country, as shown by Newburgh's own story of the German ambassadors, astonished by the wealth of London, wishing they had charged a larger ransom.[52] Harvey's argument that longer-term inflation may have been caused by an influx of foreign silver used to pay for England's wool still has merit; money was flowing, and fortunes were being made.[53] In such a situation the disparities between rich and poor would have been accentuated and rendered much more obvious in a crowded city like London.[54]

The high politics of England helped to increase economic and social pressures. Henry II's reign ended with the Saladin Tithe, a crusading tax collected at unprecedented rates and with unprecedented zeal which, as a new tax on moveable goods, brought direct taxation into the countryside in a new manner.[55] On his accession, Richard I's first thought too was of crusade, and he set about collecting money in what Christopher Tyerman calls a 'spectacular spree of venality and extortion'.[56] The end of the crusade, of course, brought about Richard's imprisonment and ransom, for which in 1193 England was assessed an extraordinary tax of a quarter of revenues, and the whole Cistercian wool clip was seized.[57] And after the ransom came Richard's wars

---

[50] W. H. Beveridge, 'The Yield and Price of Corn in the Middle Ages', *Economic History* 1 (1927), 155–67 (pp. 162–4 and n.164); P. Latimer, 'Early Thirteenth-Century Prices', in *King John: New Interpretations*, ed. Church, pp. 41–73 (p. 57 Table 3). Latimer's own conclusions sometimes seem at variance to his tables, and the tables are hard to use; these difficulties are certainly due to the fundamental problems of the evidence, which picks up in quality and quantity right after 1200. It is noticeable that Latimer's best evidence for chronology is the rise in wages paid by King John: modern parallels suggest that wages lag behind inflation. See Latimer, 'English Inflation Reconsidered', pp. 6–7. See also Miller and Hatcher, *Medieval England: Rural Society*, pp. 65–8. Finally, at the same time a new assize of bread and ale was introduced that sought to regulate the size of loaves, a regulation that may well be seen as a response to difficult times, Britnell, *Commercialisation*, pp. 94–5.

[51] C. Dyer, *Standards of Living in the Later Middle Ages: Social Change in England c. 1200–1520* (Cambridge, 1989), p. 216.

[52] WN, ed. Howlett, I, 406.

[53] Harvey, 'English Inflation', pp. 81–3. For the increase in overseas trade in the twelfth century and particularly the connection to Flanders, see Miller and Hatcher, *Medieval England: Towns, Commerce and Crafts*, pp. 190–4.

[54] On the way in which medieval cities pushed the poor into certain districts and eventually into suburbs, see Geremek, *Poverty*, p. 69.

[55] Tyerman, *England and the Crusades*, pp. 75–80; Britnell, *Commercialisation*, p. 105.

[56] Tyerman, *England and the Crusades*, p. 77.

[57] Gillingham, *Richard I*, p. 271.

on the Continent, which he fought with a savage new ferocity, expending fortunes on mercenaries, fortifications and diplomacy. Crusade, ransom and war each demanded finance.

Richard pushed as hard as he could on every possible source of money. The list of financial measures is truly mesmerizing. In 1189, he systematically sold offices for profit, replacing all but five of the sheriffs, leading to the frequently quoted story that he would have sold London if he could have found a buyer.[58] John Gillingham defends Richard's actions in this period as routine business made unusual only in that 'those transactions which were usually spread over several years were concentrated into just one in order to meet the demands of an overriding need: the crusade'.[59] Gillingham, however, also suggests that Richard sold offices shrewdly and that soon the holders of the offices realized that they had been duped.[60] But, in that case, we can well imagine the ends to which the new sheriffs would turn to make up their losses. In 1194, on his brief return to England, Richard dismissed almost all the sheriffs again in order to sell the offices once more, while introducing increments on top of the traditional sheriffs' farms. He also revived the danegeld under the name of carucage, ordering a payment of 2s. per hide and demanded scutage to help with his campaign in Normandy.[61] A judicial eyre was ordered, which was in effect a search for revenues for the king: the instructions contain the far too honest statement that the justices should 'put their powers into legally restoring the lord king's wards and escheats, and to valuing them to the advantage of the lord king'.[62] A new customs system was introduced which sought to give the king access to the mercantile wealth of the Angevin empire.[63] Furthermore, Richard changed the Great Seal and caused everyone holding charters sealed with the old one to pay for new ones.[64] Finally, in my favourite revenue-raising measure, Richard reversed his father's policy on tournaments, allowing them to happen – for a fee, of course.[65] Doris Stenton remarks that the pipe rolls of the 1190s 'give the impression of a country taxed to the limit'.[66] Gillingham, by contrast, sees the excellence of the achievement concluding that the 'steady flow of cash into

---

[58] Devizes, *Chronicle*, p. 9.

[59] Gillingham, *Richard I*, p. 116.

[60] ibid., p. 118.

[61] ibid., pp. 270–1.

[62] 'legale posse suum ponent ad wardas exchaetas domini regis instaurandas, et adpretiandas ad commodum domini regis'. Howden, *Chronica*, III, 264.

[63] Gillingham, *Richard I*, p. 277.

[64] Lewis Warren calls this action 'a sign that responsible government was on the verge of collapse', Warren, *King John*, p. 62. Gillingham only comments that by 1198 'there was undoubtedly discontent in England at the weight of the king's financial demands', Gillingham, *Richard I*, p. 343. For details of re-issues, see J. H. Round, 'Richard the First's Change of Seal (1198)', in his *Feudal England: Historical Studies on the XIth and XIIth Centuries* (London, 1895), pp. 539–51, esp. pp. 549–51.

[65] Gillingham, *Richard I*, pp. 278–9.

[66] quoted in J. C. Holt, *Magna Carta*, 2nd edn (Cambridge, 1992), p. 43n.

the treasury after 1194 is fairly impressive': Hubert Walter informed the king that he had sent him 1,100,000 marks.[67]

The financial achievement was necessarily accompanied by the great revolution in record keeping. Historians obviously have a bias in favour of record keepers, and it is hard not to be impressed by the innovations brought in by Hubert Walter in his years as justiciar. For contemporaries, however, it meant further pressure. The most complex new accounting system was demanded in 1198, when the carucage was to be accompanied by a new assessment; rolls to be made in quadruplicate: one copy each for the clerk and knight as collectors, one for the sheriff, and one for baronial steward.[68] It is doubtful if these rolls were ever made, but other, earlier innovations left definite traces. In 1195, Hubert Walter initiated the procedure of keeping the 'foot of the fine'. that is to say a third copy of an agreement to be kept in the royal archives while the parties kept the other two parts. Local record-keeping was forced to keep pace: in 1194, Hubert Walter instituted the system of coroners in each county, together with clerks to keep coroners' rolls.[69] At the same time he ordered the establishment of Jewish 'archae', chests locked with three locks – one for the Jews of a community, one for the royal authorities and one for the local Christians – into which would be put one part of the bipartite chirographs that recorded every loan made by the Jews.[70] Michael Clanchy, in his study of the origins of English record-keeping, further suggests that the appearance of the earliest borough records, also in the 1190s, was a reaction to such innovations. Clanchy concludes: 'the Jewish archives of 1194, the feet of fines of 1195, the rolls of plough teams of 1198, and the Chancery rolls of 1200 were all products of a consistent purpose in making records, pursued by Hubert throughout his years of office'.[71] Hubert Walter himself eventually resigned, exhausted by the strains of administration, the incessant demands of the king and the vituperative opposition he had encountered.[72] Roger of Howden, commenting on the new judicial eyre, sums up the innovations in government in language reminiscent of that used to describe the humiliations of the Domesday Inquest: 'by these and other vexations, whether justly or unjustly, all England from sea to sea has been reduced to destitution'.[73]

And England was under one last strain in the 1190s: the king was absent. Of course, there were degrees of absence, and Richard could have an active

---

[67] Gillingham, *Richard I*, pp. 277–8.

[68] M. T. Clanchy, *From Memory to Written Record: England 1066–1307*, 2nd edn (Oxford, 1993), p. 72.

[69] ibid., pp. 68, 70–1.

[70] ibid., p. 71. For increasing royal pressure on Jewish money-lenders and the administrative mindset behind the creation of the 'archa' system, see Stacey in this volume.

[71] Clanchy, *From Memory to Written Record*, pp. 71–2, 73.

[72] Cheney, *Hubert Walter*, pp. 96–100.

[73] 'His igitur et aliis vexationibus, sive juste sive injuste, tota Anglia a mari usque ad mare reducta est in inopiam'. Howden, *Chronica*, IV, 62.

role in administration from the Continent in a way he could not from the Middle East. But regardless, the absence of the king helped upset the balance of governance. J. E. A. Jolliffe notes that: 'Royalty, being essentially *Dei gratia*, could not be conceived apart from those limiting graces without which its exercise would be intolerable to the Christian conscience'.[74] All worldly authority thus came from God, a king was merely his agent. There was one way someone could have unchecked worldly authority, though, and that was by being the agent of an absentee king.

I would emphasize here that my interest is in power as experienced by those without power. Historians have rightly corrected the image of Richard I as an absentee, uninterested king. Richard was passionately interested in England, but his interest was – unsurprisingly – in what he could get out of England. Evidence of his own personal interest in the administration of England after 1194 shows it focused almost exclusively in the south-east and in particular the routes to the Channel ports for money and supplies.[75] The achievement of raising such huge sums of money from England was extraordinary. It can, however, lead historians into assessing the reign solely on the basis of the administrative innovation. Richard Heiser, for example, in his work on the appointment of sheriffs, writes that 'medieval monarchs, confusing private and public sectors, viewed government offices as their property, to be auctioned off as they pleased' – no argument there, but he continues: 'In the eyes of their subjects, these offerings were opportunities to be seized, not vices to be denounced'.[76] 'Which subjects?' I would ask.

In conclusion, pausing to take the violence of 1189/90 and 1196 seriously allows us to appreciate the tensions of a society running very hot. Putting the massacres of 1189/90 next to the upheaval of 1196 shows the significance of the massacres beyond the long, horrible story of medieval antisemitism. Putting FitzOsbert's protest next to the massacres shows that he was more than one isolated maniac and perhaps a voice for an undercurrent of the whole of the 1190s. Extreme financial demands, fast societal change, economic strain, and an increasingly unforgiving governmental machinery created a country that was angry, anxious and divided against itself. The crisis of Angevin England first erupted to the surface in 1189; it would not burn itself out until after Magna Carta.

---

[74] J. E. A. Jolliffe, *Angevin Kingship*, 2nd edn (London, 1963), p. 15.

[75] See J. C. Holt, '*Ricardus Rex Anglorum et Dux Normannorum*', in J. C. Holt, *Magna Carta and Medieval Government* (London, 1985), pp. 67–83. Holt concludes that 'Richard intervened frequently and persistently in the control of English affairs … That intervention, where it was initiated by the King, was concerned with one object: war and the organization of war. That was natural enough. Quite apart from his own bellicose instincts, Richard had a war on his hands. This coloured both his own view of his role in government and the attitude of his subjects towards him' (p. 82).

[76] R. R. Heiser, 'Richard I and his Appointments to English Shrievalties', *EHR* 112 (1997), 1–19 (p. 10).

5

The Massacres of 1189-90 and the Origins of the Jewish Exchequer, 1186–1226

Robert C. Stacey

The Jewish Exchequer is not a new subject. William Prynne in the seventeenth century, and Thomas Madox a century later, were the first scholars to devote sustained attention to the institution.[1] In their wake, a series of twentieth-century historians have followed, each making valuable contributions.[2] But despite the attention that has been devoted to the workings of the institution, the historical context within which we should understand the Jewish Exchequer's emergence, and the significance of its emergence for the subsequent history of the medieval English Jewish community, are subjects that will still repay more careful investigation. Three points in particular deserve our attention, and will be the focus of this paper. First, the jurisdictional monopoly that thirteenth-century English kings claimed and exercised over their Jewish subjects is unique among contemporary European monarchies. How this royal jurisdictional monopoly came to exist is therefore an important question, to which historians have devoted too little attention. Second, this jurisdictional monopoly developed gradually in England between the 1170s and the 1230s. Although this monopoly was substantially in place by the end of John's reign, the last seigneurial Jewish communities in England did not disappear until the 1230s. Third, the emergence of the Jewish Exchequer during the 1190s, including the creation of the 'archae' system for enrolling Jewish debts, needs to be understood against the background of

---

1   W. Prynne, *A Short Demurrer to the Jewes long discontinued barred Remitter into England* (London, 1656); T. Madox, *The History and Antiquities of the Exchequer of the Kings of England*, 2 vols., 2nd edn (London, 1769).

2   The pioneering modern work on this subject was the contribution by C. Gross, 'The Exchequer of the Jews of England in the Middle Ages', in *Papers Read at the Anglo-Jewish Historical Exhibition*, ed. J. Jacobs and L. Wolf (London, 1888). Since that time, the most important contributions have been by H. Jenkinson, 'The Records of Exchequer Receipts from the English Jewry', *JHSE Transactions* 8 (1915–17), 19–54; A. C. Cramer, 'The Jewish Exchequer: An Inquiry into its Fiscal Functions', *American Historical Review* 45 (1940), 327–37; A. C. Cramer, 'The Origins and Functions of the Jewish Exchequer', *Speculum* 16 (1941), 226–9; Richardson, *EJ*, esp. pp. 135–60; P. Brand, 'Introduction', in *CPREJ*, VI, 1–73.

this evolving royal claim to sole lordship over all the Jews of England, rather than being seen as a fiscally-driven response to the destruction of Jewish debt records during the massacres of 1189-90.

Let me begin, then, by emphasizing the peculiarity of this English claim to a royal jurisdictional monopoly over all the Jews of the kingdom. Although a number of twelfth- and thirteenth-century kings claimed to exercise an exclusive legal jurisdiction over the Jews within their territories, in fact no other European monarchy actually did so. In France, the expulsion order of 1306 was arguably the first royal decree that applied without qualification to all the Jews who resided within the kingdom of France; and even then, the decree did not apply to the kingdom of Navarre or to the counties of Provence and Franche-Comté, even though each of these territories was ruled by a son or a cousin of King Philip IV. Prior to 1306, the continuing existence of seigneurial Jewish communities throughout France made royal jurisdiction over the French Jews a patchwork, haphazard affair in practice, subject (like so much else in medieval French political life) to endless negotiation and compromise between the king and his great lords.[3]

Much the same situation existed in Germany, where Frederick II's famous declaration that the Jews were 'servi camerae nostrae' ignored the reality that most of the Jews of Germany lived in effectively autonomous cities and towns, where they were subject to a continuous (and for Jews, dangerous) jurisdictional tug-of-war between 'town' and 'crown'.[4] Similar points might be made about the Jewish jurisdiction of the kings of Castile and Aragon. Only in England did the crown successfully establish a claim to be the sole protector of its Jewish subjects and the sole judicial arbiter of legal cases in which Jews and Christians clashed. How, then, did this peculiarly English royal jurisdictional monopoly over Jews come about?

The background to this development is of course the rapid development of English common law under the Angevins. That said, the parallels between the growth of common law jurisdiction and the developing royal jurisdictional monopoly over Jews are far from exact. This was most obviously because, by 1226, the king's claims to be the sole judge over Jews and Jewish cases had evolved so far as to effectively exclude Jews from utilizing the common law remedies that were increasingly available, as a matter of course, to the king's free, male, Christian subjects. By the mid-1230s, indeed, the king's jurisdictional monopoly over Jews, and the consequent 'rightlessness' of Jews under the common law of the kingdom, was sufficiently com-

---

3   W. C. Jordan, *The French Monarchy and the Jews: From Philip Augustus to the Last Capetians* (Philadelphia, 1989); W. C. Jordan, 'Jews, Regalian Rights, and the Constitution in Medieval France', *AJSR* 23 (1998), 1–16.

4   A. Patschovsky, 'The Relationship between the Jews of Germany and the King (11th–14th Centuries): A European Comparison', in *England and Germany*, ed. A. Haverkamp and H. Vollrath (London, 1996), pp. 193–218; M. Rubin, *Gentile Tales: The Narrative Assault on Late Medieval Jews* (New Haven CT, 1999).

plete that it could be cited by the author of *Bracton* as evidence that the Jews of England were, in effect, serfs, insofar as both Jews and serfs depended utterly for their 'rights' upon the will of their lord, and so could own nothing that was truly their own.[5]

How, then, did the Jews of England reach this point? The story begins with that traditional Carolingian legal device, the 'tuitio'.[6] These charters of protection were issued to a variety of favoured individuals and groups by the Carolingian kings and their successors. Their effect was to place the recipients (Jews, merchants, townsmen, monasteries, or whomever) under the direct protection of the king, thus establishing their legal freedom. Nothing in a 'tuitio' charter presumed, however, that the king had an exclusive right to judge legal cases involving Jews or merchants, or that the king alone was entitled to exercise rights of lordship and protection over all the Jews or merchants within his kingdom. A 'tuitio' charter simply defined some basic procedural safeguards that should be followed should the possessors of such a charter find themselves involved in a legal case before a judge.

For the Jews of England and Normandy (who were treated for this purpose as a single community), three 'tuitio' charters survive: two granted by King Richard I in 1190, which confirm the customs and liberties held by the Jews under Henry II; and a 1201 charter from King John, which claims to guarantee the liberties and customs held by the Jews during the reign of King Henry I.[7] The provisions of all three surviving charters are for the most part strikingly similar, making it likely that the missing charters of Henry I and Henry II were indeed the models for the later charters of Richard and John. There is, however, one significant difference between them. Whereas Richard's charters declare that Jews 'shall not enter into judgment except before us or before those who have charge of those lands in which the Jews reside or where the Jews might be,' John's charter declares that 'Jews shall not enter into judgment except before us or before those who have custody of our castles, in whose bailiwicks the Jews live.' John, in other words, is claiming an exclusive legal jurisdiction over Jews that finds no place in his brother's charters only a decade before.[8]

---

5   H. de Bracton, *On the Laws and Customs of England*, ed. S. E. Thorne, 4 vols. (Cambridge MA, 1968–77), I, vii–xii, 349, 417; III, xliv–l; J. A. Watt, 'The Jews, the Law, and the Church: The Concept of Jewish Serfdom in Thirteenth-Century England', in *The Church and Sovereignty c. 590–1918: Essays in Honour of Michael Wilks*, ed. D. Wood, Studies in Church History, Subsidia s. 9 (Oxford, 1991), pp. 153–72.

6   K. R. Stow, *Alienated Minority: The Jews of Medieval Latin Europe* (Cambridge MA, 1992), pp. 62–4.

7   King Richard's 1190 charter to the Jews of England and Normandy is contained in *Foedera* I, 51; his unpublished charter from the same year granted to Isaac son of Rabbi Joseph is in TNA, C 52/21, m. 3. King John's 1201 charter to the Jews of England and Normandy is in *Rot. Chart.*, p. 93.

8   Translations from *Church, State and Jew in the Middle Ages*, ed. R. Chazan (New York, 1980), pp. 68 (1190, cap. 10), 78 (1201, cap 10), with minor emendations.

This striking contrast suggests that something quite dramatic occurred to make John's assertion of an exclusive royal jurisdictional monopoly over all the Jews of England and Normandy credible by 1201 in a way that it would not have been in 1190. We must, of course, concede the possibility that John's claim in 1201 was less descriptive than it was programmatic. John may, in other words, have been claiming an exclusive royal jurisdiction over Jews that he could not in fact exercise. In Normandy, we know this was the case. John's order was a dead letter from the moment it was issued. By 1204, John's control over Normandy had collapsed, ensuring that seigneurial Jewish communities in Normandy would continue to exist under the Capetians just as they did elsewhere in thirteenth-century France.[9] In England, however, John's 1201 claim to be the sole lord of all the Jews of England was already an essentially accurate description of the legal realities of Jewish life – realities that would continue to characterize Jewish life in England for the rest of the thirteenth century. How then did this sudden change come about?

Two developments during the 1190s appear to have been of fundamental importance: the rapid disappearance of seigneurial Jewish communities in England; and the creation and growth of the Jewish Exchequer. Let us take these points in order.[10] Although the Jewish communities of Rouen and London were under the direct and exclusive jurisdiction of the crown from the eleventh century on, the provincial Jewish communities that grew up in England during the troubled reign of King Stephen were not so exclusively royal. At Dunstable, Coventry, Leicester, Bungay, Thetford, Castle Rising, and Bury St Edmunds, it seems clear that there were by the 1150s seigneurial Jewish communities in existence in England just as there were in France, and that, as in France, these communities looked to their lord, and not to the king, for protection when danger threatened.[11]

King Henry II did not initially challenge the independence of these seigneurial Jewish communities from royal control. In 1159, when he assessed a *donum* on the Jews of England, only communities located in towns that were then in the king's hands were required to pay it.[12] In 1168 when Henry levied

---

9   Jordan, *French Monarchy and the Jews*, passim; E. Taitz, *The Jews of Medieval France: The Community of Champagne* (Westport CT, 1994), pp. 179–83.

10 Portions of the argument that follows appear also in R. C. Stacey, 'Jews and Christians in Twelfth-Century England: Some Dynamics of a Changing Relationship', *Jews and Christians in Twelfth-Century Europe*, ed. M. A. Signer and J. van Engen (Notre Dame IN, 2001), pp. 340–53 (pp. 348–51).

11 For the Jews of Bury, who in 1173 sought refuge with the abbot of Bury when civil war threatened them, see Brakelond, *Chron.*, p. 10. For Dunstable, see Howden, *Gesta* II, 83; *PR 34 Henry II*, p. 127; Richardson, *EJ*, pp. 259–63. For Castle Rising, see *Red Book of the Exchequer*, ed. H. Hall, 3 vols., RS 99 (London, 1896), app. A, pp. llxxvii–llxxx; *PR 31 Henry II*, p. 40; *33 Henry II*, p. 55. For Coventry, see *PR 26 Henry II*, p. 153; *28 Henry II*, p. 161; *32 Henry II*, p. 128; *Rot. Litt. Claus.* II, 123. For Leicester, see *PR 2–4 Henry II*, p. 56; *31 Henry II*, p. 104; *Rot. Litt. Claus.*, II, 123.

12 *PR 5 Henry II*, pp. 3 (London), 12 (Norwich, Bungay and Thetford – the latter two boroughs belonging to Earl Hugh Bigod, but in the king's hands in 1159), 17 (Northampton), 24

his first Jewish tallage, the levy applied only to the Jews of London.[13] He made no attempts to levy any further tallages upon the English Jews until 1186. Instead, he borrowed money from both Jewish and Christian lenders, which he seems to have repaid.[14]

The *Dialogue of the Exchequer*, written around 1178, says nothing to suggest that the Exchequer exercised even a regular, much less an exclusive, jurisdiction over legal cases involving Jews. In 1179-80, however, the Exchequer may have begun to assert such a claim. No plea rolls survive for such an early period; but from 1179 onward, for the first time, the pipe rolls show plentiful evidence that the Exchequer was hearing and determining Jewish legal cases.[15] Some sense of the direction in which royal policy was moving may also be gleaned from a revised version of the *Leges Edwardi Confessoris* that was circulating around Henry's court during the 1170s, which stated flatly that all Jews were under the liege guardianship and protection of the king, and that they and all their property belonged to the king.[16] By contrast, an earlier version of the *Leges*, from the 1140s, had declared only that all Jews should be under the king's protection, and that he could claim them as his property if he wished and could.[17]

Only in 1186, however, did Henry give concrete expression to such claims. In the spring of that year, he confiscated the entire estate of Aaron of Lincoln, the wealthiest English Jew of the twelfth century, and promptly began constraining Aaron's debtors to pay their debts directly to the king himself. At Christmas time in that same year, for the first time, he levied an enormous tallage of sixty thousand marks upon the Jews of England as a single community. He imposed a further tallage on the entire Jewish community, this time of ten thousand marks, in 1188; and yet another tallage on the Jews of London that reportedly amounted to a quarter of their chattels.[18] These events marked a sea change in the relationship between the English crown and Jewish moneylending. By identifying the crown directly with Jewish lending, and by placing the Jews' debtors under enormous pressure to repay their debts directly to the king's government, they contributed in no small measure to the widespread attacks on Jewish communities that erupted in 1189 and 1190.

(Worcester, but not certainly a *donum* payment), 28 (Gloucester), 35 (Oxford), 46 (Winchester), 53 (Cambridge), 65 (Lincoln).

13 Canterbury, *Historical Works* I, 205.

14 On the king's borrowing during these years, see Richardson, *EJ*, pp. 50–66.

15 *PR 26 Henry II*, pp. 32, 153; *27 Henry II*, p. 134; *28 Henry II*, p. 162; *29 Henry II*, p. 159 (2); *30 Henry II*, p. 149; *31 Henry II*, p. 91. This change may have coincided with the appointment of Ranulf de Glanville as justiciar, in place of Richard de Lucy.

16 Howden, *Chronica* II, 231.

17 B. O'Brien, *God's Peace and King's Peace: The Laws of Edward the Confessor* (Philadelphia, 1999), p. 184–5 (text), 93–7 (discussion).

18 Richardson, *EJ*, pp. 161–3, collects the references. It is not clear whether the tallage of one-quarter of their chattels on the Jews of London was an additional imposition or simply a chronicler's description of the impact of the Guildford Tallage.

This intensification of royal fiscal pressure upon the Jews' Christian debtors was matched by growing royal pressure upon lords who claimed jurisdiction over seigneurial Jewish communities. Conventionally, the disappearance of the Jewish communities at Lynn (later King's Lynn), Thetford, Bungay, Castle Rising, and Bury St Edmunds has been seen as one of the consequences of the assaults against Jewish communities that swept across East Anglia during the spring of 1190 and that culminated in the massacre at York. I do not wish to minimize the severity or the consequences of these attacks; but although they may have contributed to the disappearance of these East Anglian Jewish communities, these attacks cannot be the sole explanation for their demise.[19] Only at Lynn is it possible to draw a nearly certain connection between the assaults of 1190 and the disappearance of an entire Jewish community. At Norwich and Colchester massacres were reported, yet Jewish communities survived. At Castle Rising we know of no attacks, yet the Jewish community disappeared. At Bungay and Thetford attacks also occured, but nothing suggests they were on any large scale. Yet the Thetford community pretty clearly disappeared entirely; and although some individual Jews may have continued to reside in Bungay, there is no evidence after 1190 of any organized Jewish community there either.

Even at Bury St Edmunds, where fifty-seven Jews were killed in March 1190, the community itself came to an end only in October of that year, when Abbot Samson of Bury sought and received King Richard's permission to expel the abbot's own long-established seigneurial Jewish community from the town, declaring as he did so that 'everything in the town and within the "banlieu" belonged by right to St Edmund; therefore, either the Jews should be St Edmund's men or they should be banished from the town'. And why was it that the Jews of Bury were no longer St Edmund's men? Because by 1190, Jews throughout England were being claimed by the crown to be the king's men; and as such, their presence in Bury was now a threat to the jurisdictional integrity of the abbot's liberty.[20]

Similar considerations probably lay behind the disappearance of the Jewish communities at Castle Rising, Thetford and Bungay. All three were seigneurial towns by 1190. Bungay and the suburbs of Thetford were held by the Bigod Earls of Norfolk; the royal half of Thetford now belonged to the Earl Warenne, who acquired it from King Richard in July 1190 in exchange for the Warenne lands in the Touraine. Castle Rising belonged to the earls of Arundel.[21] We know that the possession of such seigneurial Jewish commu-

---

[19] See Hillaby in this volume.

[20] Brakelond, *Chron.*, pp. 45–6; the translation is from Diana Greenway and Jane Sayers in Jocelin of Brakelond, *Chronicle of the Abbey of Bury St Edmunds* (Oxford, 1989), pp. 41–2. The date of the Bury expulsion is given in *Memorials of St. Edmund's Abbey*, ed. T. Arnold, 3 vols., RS 96 (London, 1890–96), II, 5. For further discussion, see Stacey, 'Jews and Christians', pp. 348–51.

[21] On Bungay and Thetford, see R. A. Brown, 'Framlingham Castle and Bigod, 1154–1216', *Pro-

nities was profitable: at Castle Rising, William d'Aubigny (d. 1176), the first earl of Arundel, had taxed the Jews of Castle Rising at will, and regularly borrowed money from them which he compelled his Christian tenants to repay.[22] There is every reason to presume that Earl Hugh Bigod of Norfolk (d. 1177) would have done similarly at Bungay and Thetford. Why then did the heirs of these lords assist in the dissolution of these Jewish communities during the 1190s?

The answer seems to lie in the same considerations that drove Abbot Sampson to expel the large and apparently prosperous community of Jews from Bury. Both the Bigod and Arundel earldoms had been in royal hands continuously since the 1170s; both were returned to their rightful heirs by King Richard I within months of his accession to the throne. Expulsions of Jews were an obvious way for a new lord to curry favour with his tenants, especially where those tenants had been compelled in the past to pay their lord's Jewish debts. Even more importantly, however, these expulsions helped to protect the jurisdictional rights of these newly-re-established lords from royal encroachment. This was a particularly important consideration in a liberty like Bury St Edmunds, where the abbot claimed a variety of sweeping seigneurial rights, including return of writs. But it was no less important at Bungay, Thetford, and Castle Rising. Royal officials were notorious for their efforts to extend their authority wherever they could and on whatever pretexts they could find. So long as 'the king's Jews' resided in a town, the king's officials would have ample cause to interfere there, thus eroding the jurisdictional autonomy of the town and establishing precedents that might in turn threaten a lord's other rights over his lands. Like the newly-restored Simon de Montfort, who in 1232 expelled the Jews from his half of Leicester for precisely such reasons, Bigod, d'Aubigny, Warenne and Abbot Sampson would all have had good reason by 1190 to do what they could to force these formerly seigneurial Jewish communities to leave their lordships.[23]

The king's government continued to tighten its grip over legal cases involving Jews throughout the 1190s. A significant milestone was reached in 1194, when legal cases involving Jews were removed from the ordinary jurisdiction of the justices in eyre and transferred to Westminster, where the cases were heard by an evolving group of professional justices gathered around

---

ceedings of the Suffolk Institute of Archaeology and Natural History 25 (1950), 128–48 (pp. 129–40) and reprinted in his volume of collected essays, *Castles, Conquest and Charters* (Woodbridge, 1989), pp. 189–200; Crouch, *Reign of King Stephen*, p. 120; *EYC* VIII, pp. 124–5. Clay dates the grant of Thetford to between 3 July 1190 and 29 September 1191. It is much more likely to be from the summer of 1190, however, when Richard was travelling through central France, than from 1191, when he was in the Holy Land.

[22] *Red Book of the Exchequer*, ed. Hall, app. A, pp. cclxvii–cclxxx. For evidence of other lords on the Arundel honour levying aids upon their tenants to acquit debts to Jews, see pp. cclxxiv–cclxxvii.

[23] On Montfort's decision to expel the Jews from Leicester, see J. R. Maddicott, *Simon de Montfort* (Cambridge, 1994), pp. 15–16.

the newly-appointed justiciar, Hubert Walter.[24] Some Jewish cases were still heard in the county courts even after 1194;[25] but it appears that Jews were no longer required to submit themselves to civil judgment except before the king's justices at Westminster or else, for minor cases, before the royal sheriffs and castle constables.

Further evidence of the king's growing claims to exercise a jurisdictional monopoly over Jews also emerges in 1194, when for the first time Hubert Walter issued regulations governing Jewish moneylending throughout England. Significantly, these regulations made no mention whatsoever of the existence of any seigneurial Jewish communities in England. They applied equally to all Jews in the kingdom, regardless of their place of residence. They established a nation-wide system for registering and recording debts owed to Jews, a system that was to be administered by local Christians and Jews working under the supervision of a royally-appointed clerk.[26] Unregistered debts were no longer to be legally enforceable. The system thus brought all Jewish financial transactions under the jurisdictional authority of the crown, strengthening decisively the king's claim to be the direct lord of every English Jew.

Historians are divided as to whether these 1194 reforms mark the beginning of the institutional history of the Jewish Exchequer. There is much wider agreement, however, that the need for some such system to register and record Jewish debts was a conclusion driven home to the royal government by the losses to the king's coffers resulting from the widespread destruction of Jewish bonds during the 1189-90 massacres. But despite this consensus among its historians, a careful look at the context in which the decision to create this system was made and at the way in which the system itself was designed to operate may suggest a different conclusion as to the motivations and purposes behind these reforms.

King Richard taxed his Christian subjects in England extremely heavily during his ten-year reign, first for his crusade, then to raise his ransom payment, and then to support his war with King Philip II of France. In comparison, the English Jews escaped rather lightly: a three thousand mark tallage toward the king's ransom in 1193, a five thousand mark tallage for the same purpose in 1194, and perhaps one further tallage of two thousand marks near the end of the reign.[27] Even allowing for unrecorded acts of royal extortion (some of which we can document), the Jews of England probably paid

---

24 The evidence is mostly negative: the fairly plentiful evidence on the PR of justices on eyre hearing cases involving Jews suddenly disappears after 1193. For examples of justices on eyre hearing pleas involving Jews, see *PR 31 Henry II*, p. 121; *34 Henry II*, pp. 37, 168, 177, 199, 207; *2 Richard I*, pp. 13, 129, 134, 149; *5 Richard I*, pp. 5, 11, 28, 92, 138, 171.

25 *PR 9 Richard I*, p. 114; Richardson, *EJ*, pp. 156–8.

26 For the operation of this system during the thirteenth century, see Mundill in this volume.

27 *The Memoranda Roll for the Michaelmas Term of the First Year of the Reign of King John (1199–1200)*, ed. H. G. Richardson, PRS 59 (n.s. 21) (London, 1943), pp. 69–72.

King Richard considerably less in taxation, fines, and other levies than they paid either to King Henry II during the 1180s or to King John.

Nevertheless, keeping track of the king's Jewish revenues was becoming a more and more demanding task. Apart from Richard's own tallages, large debts remained outstanding from the Guildford Tallage of 1186 and from the ten thousand mark tallage of 1188.[28] Aaron of Lincoln's debts were still being collected and disputed; his property still had to be managed; while so too did the entirely new set of Jewish debts and properties that fell into the king's hands as a result of the massacres of 1189 and 1190. By 1194, however, the dissolution of the Exchequer of Aaron had left the Exchequer without a formally constituted group of specialists in Jewish affairs to handle such tasks.[29] The need to reconstitute such a group must have become obvious to the beleaguered Exchequer officials as they struggled to keep up with the increasing press of Jewish business around the court. It must have been particularly obvious to Hubert Walter, who from December 1193 was not only archbishop of Canterbury but also the king's justiciar. From at least Longchamp's day, and probably since 1179 when Ranulf de Glanville became justiciar, the justiciar had had a particular responsibility for matters pertaining to Jews. Never before, however, had anyone tried simultaneously to be justiciar of England and archbishop of Canterbury. The burden was crushing, as even the king himself acknowledged.[30] Shifting the justiciar's day-to-day responsibility for Jewish affairs to a specially appointed group of Exchequer officials was an obvious way in which some of the burdens on Hubert Walter could be lessened.

With the outbreak in April 1194 of what promised to be a long-term war with France, the necessity for such a shift in responsibilities suddenly became acute. Charged to provide the revenues necessary to conduct this war, Hubert Walter embarked upon a systematic reorganization of the king's financial resources.[31] Sheriffs were dismissed and their offices put up for sale, as they had been in 1189. The annual fees sheriffs paid the king for holding their shires were increased, at the same time that many of the sheriffs' traditional sources of revenue were taken away from them and assigned to be collected by other men. Coroners were appointed to look after the king's judicial rights in each shire, and to act as a check upon the judicial powers of

---

[28] Arrears of these taxes are recorded on *PR 2 Richard I*, p. 159; *3–4 Richard I*, pp. 32, 50, 60–1, 139–40, 148; and on *Mem. Roll 1 John*, pp. 69–72.

[29] The Exchequer of Aaron was the name given to the group of Exchequer officials temporarily deputed to inventory and collect the properties and debts belonging to Aaron of Lincoln. For a discussion of this group, see Richardson, *EJ*, pp. 115–17, 120.

[30] C. R. Cheney, *Hubert Walter* (London, 1967), pp. 96–7, 99.

[31] For the articles of the 1194 eyre, from which much of what follows is taken, see Howden, *Chronica* III, 262–7, from which the version found in *Select Charters and Other Illustrations of English Constitutional History from the earliest times to the Reign of Edward the First*, ed. W. Stubbs, rev. by H. W. C. Davis, 9th ed. (Oxford, 1913), pp. 251–7, is derived. For an English translation of this well-known text, quoted in this and the next paragraph, see *EHD* III, 303–6.

the sheriff. Searching inquiries were also launched into the state of the royal demesne manors, heretofore an important element in the sheriffs' revenues. These manors' fixed rents, present stock levels, and economic potential if fully and properly stocked were all recorded and revised where necessary, and the manors themselves entrusted to specially appointed custodians, who accounted directly at the Exchequer for their receipts and expenditures. Inquiries were also launched into lands that came into the king's hands as a result of the death of their previous holders. These lands too were surveyed, restocked and removed from the sheriffs' hands. In their place, 'escheators' were appointed to manage these lands to the king's profit. Hugh Bardolf became the escheator in the northern counties. William of Sainte-Mère-Église took charge of the southern and western counties, with the assistance of two of his clerks, Master William of Chemillé and Hugh Peverell.[32]

Interestingly, the escheators were also given responsibility for the revenues arising from the Jewish communities within their respective areas.[33] As escheators, they would have handled a certain amount of Jewish property anyway.[34] Their responsibilities for Jewish affairs, however, were clearly not limited to escheated Jewish property. Rather, they seem to have exercised a general financial and administrative authority over revenues arising from the Jewish communities of their respective areas.[35] Previously such revenues would have been collected by the sheriffs; the escheators' responsibility for Jewish receipts was thus another example of revenues being removed from the sheriffs' hands in 1194 for separate accounting.[36] Hubert Walter also intended, however, to centralize the collection and accounting of Jewish receipts. To this end, William of Sainte-Mère-Église was charged to account at the Exchequer for all revenues arising from the Jews of England from 1194 until 1198, when he retired from his Exchequer duties. In handling Jewish receipts, and perhaps in their management of escheats and custodies also, Hugh Peverell and Hugh Bardolf were regarded by the Exchequer as his deputies.[37]

---

[32] *PR 6 Richard I*, pp. xx–xxij, 1–27; 1194 eyre articles, cap. 23. The appointments took effect at Easter 1194.

[33] *Mem. Roll 1 John*, pp. xcj–xcij, 72; *PR 6 Richard I*, pp. 1–27; Richardson, *EJ*, pp. 117–20. Similar arrangements also existed in Normandy, where in 1203 King John gave Richard de Villequier custody over the escheats of Normandy and the Jews of Normandy, excepting the Jews of Rouen and Caen: *Rot. Litt. Pat.*, p. 37; Richardson, *EJ*, pp. 206–10.

[34] See, for example, *PR 6 Richard I*, pp. 12, 27; *7 Richard I*, pp. 27, 53.

[35] *Mem. Roll 1 John*, p. 72, shows Hugh Peverell responding for receipts from the five thousand mark tallage of 1194 from Norfolk and Suffolk; *JHSE Miscellanies* 1 (1925), p. lxx, shows Hugh Bardolf accounting for receipts from the same tax from Lincolnshire.

[36] In Essex and Hertfordshire, for example, receipts from Jewish pleas were clearly a traditional part of the sheriff's revenues from the shires: see *Rot. Chart.*, p. 125b.

[37] *Mem. Roll 1 John*, p. 72. Peverell was clearly subordinate to William of Sainte-Mère-Église for the escheated property in his custody also: *PR 6 Richard I*, pp. 10–11. So too was Master William of Chemillé. Although Bardolf accounted independently for the escheats of the northern counties (*PR 6 Richard I*, pp. 11–15), he accounted together with William of Sainte-Mère-Église for his Jewish receipts from Lincolnshire.

Hubert Walter combined these new administrative arrangements with a sweeping set of changes in the way the royal government dealt with Jewish moneylending. Together, these measures mark the beginning of a new era in the administrative history of English Jewry. The justiciar's intention in 1194 was to bring all transactions arising out of Jewish moneylending under the immediate supervision of the king's government. To accomplish this, the archbishop ordered first that a written record be made 'of all Jews' debts and pledges, lands, houses, rents and possessions. And a Jew who conceals any of these things shall forfeit to the lord king his body and what he has concealed, and all his possessions and all his chattels, and no Jew shall ever be allowed to recover what he has concealed.'[38] This survey would provide the king with a complete inventory of Jewish property in England; to this extent, it bears obvious similarities to the surveys Hubert Walter was simultaneously commissioning into the king's escheats, custodies, and demesne manors. Its more important purpose, however, was to provide a 'baseline' from which the regulation of future Jewish moneylending could proceed. After 1194, Jews were to lend money only in specially designated towns, where all transactions relating to such loans would be carefully supervised and recorded by royal officials appointed for this purpose: two Christians, two Jews, and two scribes, all drawn from the town, and a supervisory clerk appointed by William of Sainte-Mère-Église and his clerk, Master William of Chemillé.[39]

> And in future no loan shall be made, no payment made to
> Jews, no alteration of charters made, except in the presence
> of the aforesaid [local officials], or of the greater part of them
> if all cannot be present.[40]

Along with his responsibility to account for all receipts from Jews, William of Sainte-Mère-Église was thus given overall administrative responsibility for the new arrangements regarding Jewish loans also. He was clearly being established as a kind of administrative plenipotentiary in charge of Jewish financial affairs. It was at the local level, however, that the new arrangements brought the most decisive changes in practice. Under the supervision of both Christian and Jewish officials, scribes were ordered to record the terms of each Jewish loan in chirograph form. One part of the chirograph, sealed by the debtor, went to the Jewish creditor; the other part went into a common chest (known in Latin as an 'archa'), where it was kept

---

38 *EHD* III, 305; and see n. 31 above.
39 On Master William of Chemillé, archdeacon of Richmond, see Howden, *Chronica*, vol. 3, pp. 16–17, 266; vol. 4, pp. 12, 37; *PR 8 Richard I*, pp. 175 (where he is referred to as bishop-elect of Avranches), 208; *9 Richard I*, p. 61; *10 Richard I*, p. 40; *Mem. Roll 1 John*, p. 32. There is no evidence that Master William ever played the role envisioned for him in 1194.
40 *EHD* III, 306.

under triple lock and key.[41] Only if both Christian and Jewish representatives were present, together with the supervising clerk, could the chest be opened and business transacted. For additional security, the supervisory clerk also kept a roll containing transcripts of all the charters deposited in the 'archa'; if changes were made subsequently in the terms of any charter, the changes had to be entered on the clerk's roll also.[42] Payments made by debtors to their creditors were also recorded, on no less than three separate receipt rolls, one kept by the two Christians, one by the two Jews, and the third by the supervising clerk.

Historians have been curiously cynical about these arrangements, portraying them as an attempt by the king to guarantee that if another massacre occurred like the one at York in 1190, he would still be able to collect the Jewish debts that ought to have fallen in to him, because he would now have a record of who had owed what and to whom.[43] Certainly the 1190 massacres were on the minds of the king's administrators at this time. When Hubert Walter sent royal justices through the countryside in the summer and fall of 1194, he commissioned them specifically to determine who had been responsible for the killing of Jews, and the whereabouts of deceased Jews' debts and property.[44] There is little in the regulations of 1194, however, that would in fact have prevented a repetition of the losses of 1190. A wooden chest containing Jewish chirographs would, after all, burn just about as easily as a pile of parchment charters and wooden tally sticks if set alight on the floor of York Minster. Moreover, although the 1194 survey of Jewish debts and property would tell the king how much was owed to Jews at that moment, it would become an outdated record almost immediately thereafter. Only if the supervisory clerks in charge of the local 'archae' sent periodic copies of their transcripts and receipt rolls to Westminster would the king in fact have had a riot-proof record of Jewish moneylending in his kingdom. No such requirement is mentioned in the 1194 regulations, however. Nor is there any other evidence to suggest that copies of these records were sent up to the government at Westminster on any regular basis. There is some doubt, indeed, whether the transcript and receipt rolls were ever systematically kept

---

[41] Later on, when three-part chirographs became common, the debtor would be given one part of the document also, so that he too would have a record of the terms. Three-part chirographs were utilized to record legal agreements in the royal courts from 1195 on: see *Feet of Fines of the Reign of Henry II and of the First Seven Years of the Reign of Richard I, A.D. 1182 to A.D. 1196*, PRS 17 (London, 1894), p. 21, and commentary in Cheney, *Hubert Walter*, p. 96. Tripartite chirographs were required for Jewish lending starting in 1233: Richardson, *EJ*, p. 294; Brand, 'Introduction', in *CPREJ* VI, 6–7.

[42] *EHD* III, 305–6.

[43] Roth, *HJE*, pp. 28–9 and R. Huscroft, *Expulsion: England's Jewish Solution* (Stroud, 2006), pp. 55–6 represent a much wider consensus.

[44] 1194 Eyre Articles, cap. 9; trans. *EHD* III, 303. Fines and amercements arising from this commission appear frequently on the PR: see for example *PR 5 Richard I*, p. 51; *6 Richard I*, pp. 36, 46, 161; *7 Richard I*, pp. 91, 92.

at all, even by the local 'archae' officials. Only at Norwich do any such records survive, and then only for the years between 1225 and 1227.[45] If these
1194 measures were principally intended to protect the king against losses
arising from another massacre, they were poorly designed and haphazardly
executed. Neither is a hallmark of Hubert Walter's administrative style.

I am inclined therefore to see the 1194 reforms not as a way to protect
the king's reversionary interest in Jewish property should another massacre
occur, but rather as an attempt to bring Jewish moneylending under much
closer royal supervision, and so to reduce the possibilities of fraud on all
sides. The survey of pre-1194 debts would make it nearly impossible thereafter for unscrupulous lenders to forge charters of indebtedness and present
them for collection as if they were legitimate pre-1194 debts.[46] After 1194, all
new debts would be contained and enrolled in the 'archae'. Once a debt had
been deposited in the 'archa', the receipt rolls would prevent dishonest borrowers from claiming falsely to have paid it. At the same time, debtors who
had indeed paid off their debts would now have easily verifiable evidence
that they had done so. This in turn would help to ensure that paid-up debts
would not pass into the king's hands as if they were unpaid, and be sum-
moned again for collection by the Exchequer (something that had caused no
end of trouble in trying to sort out Aaron of Lincoln's estate). When royal
officials assisted Jews in collecting their debts, they would know that the
debts being exacted were just and legitimate ones. And if debts subsequently
did fall into the king's hands, he could be sure that they were good debts, on
which he had a right to collect. Behind the reforms of 1194, in other words,
lay much more than the massacres of 1190. More importantly, I would suggest, lay the Exchequer's unhappy experience in attempting to collect the
debts of Aaron of Lincoln.[47]

The system established by Hubert Walter in 1194 for recording and registering Jewish debts probably never worked exactly as he had intended.
Communal chests were certainly established, and local committees of Christians and Jews were appointed to administer them. By the 1220s such chests
existed in more than twenty towns around the kingdom. But it was probably

---

[45] On the so-called Norwich Day Book, see Lipman, *JMN*, pp. 84–6, 187–225.

[46] Fraud was clearly a matter of some concern at this time: in 1194, Jews were ordered to swear
on their Torah scrolls that they would name all forgers of charters and clippers of coins, and
point out all forged charters: *EHD* III, 306. For another example of the concern with fraudu-
lent charters at this time see *PR 7 Richard I*, p. 8, in which Stephen de Turnham pays half a
mark to record on the Pipe Roll his acquittance from all Jewish debts owed either by him
or by his father up to Tuesday, 11 July 1195, 'so that if any Jew should exact any debt from
Stephen or his heirs by any charter which is from any date prior to the aforesaid Tuesday,
that charter shall be held to be a forgery and whoever presents it shall be seized as a forger
and all his chattels shall be seized into the king's hands and shall belong to the king'.

[47] For evidence of the Exchequer's difficulties during these years in collecting Aaron's debts,
and its uncertainties whether debts had been paid or not, see *PR 7 Richard I*, pp. 86–7; *9 Richard I*, p. 11; *10 Richard I*, pp. 57, 98.

as a local institution that the 'archae' system functioned best. The Jewish and Christian officials who administered each 'archa' quickly became, if they were not already, important and respected local figures, who acted frequently as witnesses to agreements or as intermediaries between contracting parties. Records of debts and acquittances were the main types of documents stored in the chests, but a variety of other documents were also deposited there, including many agreements, such as betrothal contracts, that were internal to the Jewish community itself and in which the king can have had no conceivable interest.[48] The presence of such documents in the chests shows clearly the extent to which the 'archae' system became an essential and thoroughly integrated feature of English Jewish life.

The system was less successful, however, in providing the king with an overview of Jewish financial activity. We do not know whether the survey of pre-1194 debts was ever in fact carried out. If it was, no reference to the existence of any records deriving from it has survived. Similar uncertainty surrounds the supervisory clerks, whom William of Sainte-Mère-Église and Master William of Chemillé were supposed to appoint to each of the local 'archae'. If these clerks were ever in fact appointed, they had disappeared without trace by the 1220s, when we begin for the first time to have evidence about the local operation of the 'archae'. Some of the transcripts of charters and the records of payments required in the 1194 regulations were still being kept in the 1220s, at least at Norwich. By the 1230s, however, these records too had apparently ceased to be kept.[49] We cannot be sure about this; it is impossible to prove a negative, especially across the span of eight hundred years. Had such records been kept, however, it would not have been necessary for Henry III and Edward I to send special teams of officials out from Westminster to conduct an inventory of the chests whenever they wished to know the total value of Jews' bonds.[50] They could simply have had copies of the transcripts and receipt rolls sent up to Westminster from each of the 'archae', a far easier and quicker procedure that would not have necessitated the closure of the 'archae' while these inventories were being carried out. The fact that neither Henry nor Edward could do this, and that from the 1230s on teams of royal officials toured the 'archae' every time the king

---

[48] For example, see *Shetaroth: Hebrew Deeds of English Jews before 1290*, ed. M. D. Davis (London, 1888), no. 15 (pp. 32–35), a betrothal contract between the father of the intended bride and the intending bridegroom. This document wound up in Westminster Abbey Muniments, 6847, probably during the early fourteenth century, when the contents of a number of provincial 'archae' were brought to the abbey for storage after the expulsion of the Jews from England in 1290.

[49] Although Brand, in *CPREJ* VI, 7, has a reference from *c.* 1270 that suggests that the chirographers were expected at that date to keep a roll 'recording the names of debtors and creditors, the total owed, the year and day of payment and the names of the witnesses'.

[50] For discussion of procedure on such 'scrutinies', see R. C. Stacey, 'Royal Taxation and the Social Structure of Medieval Anglo-Jewry: The Tallages of 1239–42', *Hebrew Union College Annual* 56 (1985), 175–249.

wanted an inventory of their contents, suggests strongly that transcripts of charters and records of receipts were no longer being kept in any reliable way by the 'archae' officials.

Nor did the 1194 reforms succeed entirely in regularizing the mechanics of Jewish moneylending. Many debts continued to be negotiated and retained outside the 'archae', despite repeated prohibitions.[51] Nor were all debts recorded in chirograph form, or even reduced to writing. Even for loans deposited in the 'archae', many debts and payments on debts continued to be recorded on notched tally sticks rather than in writing on parchment. We should not make too much of such practices, however. After 1194, the vast majority of Jewish bonds were recorded in proper chirograph form and deposited in the 'archae' as required. For borrowers, the system provided useful guarantees against fraud; for lenders, it was only by complying with these requirements that they could get the assistance of royal officials in collecting the debts they were owed. Everyone gained something from the new arrangements. That is probably why they worked so well.

Why these 1194 reforms were not carried through more fully is not entirely clear. The press of other business must certainly be part of the explanation. The king was fighting an all-out war in France, and Hubert Walter had a host of other responsibilities. The survey of Jewish debts and property he proposed in 1194 would have been an enormous undertaking. Hubert Walter was no doubt serious in ordering it, but he commissioned no one actually to carry it out.[52] If in fact he did abandon it, it would not have been the only such survey to suffer this fate. The final article of the 1194 eyre tells us that the archbishop had already given up an attempt to inquire into corruption by royal officials that he had ordered only a few months before.[53] Nor does every change in administrative plan necessarily constitute a failure. Angevin government was notoriously adaptive and experimental, never more so than between 1194 and 1216. Innovations were attempted and expedients tried. Some worked and became institutionalized through repetition. Some did not work, and were abandoned. Some worked too well and were abandoned under pressure from their outraged victims. For others, there simply was not enough time to carry them through. Not all the records Hubert Walter envisioned in 1194 were created and maintained. The 'archae' themselves, however, were successfully established; William of Sainte-Mère-Église was put in charge of Jewish debts at the Exchequer; and Jewish moneylending was brought more closely under royal supervision than it had ever been before. The creation of the 'archa' system thus marked a decisive moment in

---

[51] For an early example, see *CRR* I, 390–1.

[52] It is possible that the justices on eyre, together with the sheriffs and the escheators, were supposed to carry out this survey together with their survey of the royal demense lands, custodies, and escheats: see 1194 Eyre Articles, cap. 23, trans. *EHD* III, pp. 304–5. But cap. 23 says nothing directly to this effect.

[53] 1194 Eyre articles, cap. 25; trans. *EHD* III, 306.

the evolution of the king's claim to be the direct and exclusive lord of every English Jew in his kingdom.[54]

Some of the legal cases involving Jews that came before the Exchequer after 1194 were handled personally by the justiciar, Hubert Walter.[55] Others were decided by the justices of the Exchequer, with or without the justiciar's presence.[56] Prior to 1198, however, there were no justices at the Exchequer whom we know to have specialized specifically in hearing legal cases involving Jews. The only possible candidate for such a role is William of Sainte-Mère-Église. William's predecessor at the Exchequer, Hugh de Nonant, bishop of Coventry, had performed similar duties; and in Hugh's case we know that he sat with the regular Exchequer justices in hearing at least some Jewish cases.[57] For William, however, there is no such evidence. Although William served as an eyre justice in 1194, and sat regularly as a justice of the bench in 1195 and 1196, I cannot find a single legal case involving Jews or Jewish moneylending in which he was clearly involved during his time at the Exchequer.[58] Nor, for that matter, can I find any evidence that he actually exercised the kind of supervisory responsibility over the system for registering Jewish debts that the 1194 reforms envisioned for him, although he clearly did act as the king's principal accountant for Jewish receipts. I am reluctant, therefore, to follow H. G. Richardson in regarding either Hugh de Nonant or William of Sainte-Mère-Église as the first justices of the Jewish Exchequer.[59] There simply is not adequate evidence that so formal a body of Exchequer officials existed before 1198.

In February 1198, Benedict of Talmont, a Jew from Poitou, took over from William of Sainte-Mère-Église as the man in charge of collecting and accounting for the king's Jewish receipts.[60] Benedict was assisted in these tasks by Joseph Aaron, a clerk formerly in the service of Hubert Walter; by Jacob, the royally-appointed head of the English Jewish community; and by Jacob's clerk, a Jew named Abraham.[61] In contrast to William of Sainte-Mère-Église,

---

[54] As Dobson, in *JMY*, p. 30, has noted.

[55] *Mem. Roll 1 John*, p. 70; Cheney, *Hubert Walter*, p. 73. As Cheney noted, however, 'final concords which record him as presiding judge do not in themselves prove his presence; for in some of them his presence is demonstrably a fiction', ibid., p. 95 n. 3.

[56] *PR 3–4 Richard I*, p. 301, for an example from 1192.

[57] *Mem. Roll 1 John*, pp. xcj, 72; *PR 3–4 Richard I*, p. 301.

[58] For his judicial service, see D. Crook, *Records of the General Eyre* (London, 1982), pp. 57–8; R. V. Turner, *Men Raised from the Dust: Administrative Service and Upward Mobility in Angevin England* (Philadelphia, 1988), pp. 23–5. As Turner notes, during much of 1196 and 1197 William was in Normandy with the king, and so removed entirely from both the Exchequer and the bench.

[59] *Mem. Roll 1 John*, pp. xc–xcii, 72; Richardson, *EJ*, pp. 118–20. That Hugh Bardulf and Hugh Peverel were also justices of the Jews seems even less likely, although both did act as justices on eyre in 1194: see Crook, *Records of the General Eyre*, pp. 57–8.

[60] *Mem. Roll 1 John*, p. xc and n. 4.

[61] ibid., pp. xc–xcii, 69–72. Lady Stenton's claim, followed by Richardson, that Joseph Aaron was a convert from Judaism to Christianity rests solely on his name (*PR 10 Richard I*, p. xxix).

who frequently exercised his duties at the Exchequer through a deputy,[62] Benedict of Talmont and his team were continually and personally involved in their work at the Exchequer. For so long as Hubert Walter remained justiciar, however, their work was strictly financial rather than judicial.

On 11 July 1198, however, Hubert Walter stepped down as the king's justiciar, to be replaced by Geoffrey fitz Peter, a long-serving royal administrator who was one of the justices of the Exchequer.[63] Soon thereafter, we see for the first time the emergence of a specialized group of four officials charged specifically with hearing and determining legal cases involving Jews or Jewish debts. Two of the newly appointed 'custodians of the Jews',[64] Benedict of Talmont and Joseph Aaron, were already involved in Jewish business around the Exchequer. But the other two custodians of the Jews appointed in 1198, Simon of Pattishall and Henry of Whiston, were men of wide experience in the common law courts. Pattishall, indeed, has been described by Paul Brand as 'the first royal justice to be a career legal specialist'.[65] With their appointment, the history of the Jewish Exchequer can be properly said to begin.

Initially, the new justices of the Jews seem to have been regarded as a specialized committee of the Exchequer, exercising an authority delegated to them by the justiciar. Even when fitz Peter did not sit with them, enrollments of their decisions usually specify that the decisions were made by authority of the justiciar; and when new justices of the Jews were appointed by King John in 1200, the justiciar's role in these new appointments was emphasized.[66] Thereafter, however, the justiciar's direct responsibility for the justices of the Jews appears to have waned. Partly this was a consequence of the extraordinary personal interest King John took in the workings of his own administration. Partly too it may have been the natural result of the Jewish Exchequer itself becoming more firmly established with the passage of time.

We should not, however, overestimate the extent to which the Jewish Exchequer emerged during John's reign as a separate institution of government. After 1200, John appointed no new justices to it, and of the four whom he did appoint in 1200, one at least may never have taken up office.[67] Al-

---

This is, at best, very uncertain evidence.

[62] *Mem. Roll 1 John*, p. 72.

[63] For his career, see Turner, *Men Raised from the Dust*, pp. 35–70.

[64] *Custodes Judaeorum*: for the phrase, see *PR 10 Richard I*, pp. 125, 165–6. When a new group of officials was appointed in 1200, they were called 'bailiffs of the English Jews' (*Rot. Chart.*, p. 61).

[65] P. Brand, *The Origins of the English Legal Profession* (Oxford, 1992), p. 127.

[66] *PR 10 Richard I*, pp. 165–166, 210, 214; *Rot. Chart.*, p. 61.

[67] William d'Aubigny, baron of Belvoir. There may have been some trouble between d'Aubigny and King John in 1201 (Howden, *Chronica* IV, 161). His career can be pieced together from S. Painter, *The Reign of King John* (Baltimore, 1949) and J. C. Holt, *The Northerners: A Study in the Reign of King John*, 2nd edn (Oxford, 1992).

though William de Warenne of Wormegay, a cousin to the Earl Warenne, served as chief justice of the Jewish Exchequer until his death in late 1208 or early 1209, he was never replaced.[68] Thereafter, only two royal clerks remained as justices. One, Geoffrey of Norwich, left office in 1212 after having been implicated in a plot to assassinate the king. He died in prison.[69] The other, Thomas de Neville, then served as the sole justice of the Jews until 1215, when the institution collapsed, along with the Exchequer itself, in the anarchic conditions arising out of the Magna Carta revolt. It may not have been until the early years of Henry III's reign, therefore, when the Jewish Exchequer was re-established and reorganized, that it emerged as a fully defined institution in its own right, with its own 'plea rolls', its own office, and exercising an authority that did not derive by delegation from either the regular Exchequer or the justiciar.[70]

Like many of the officials around Richard's and John's courts, the justices of the Jews exercised a combination of financial, judicial, and administrative responsibilities that is not easily categorized. In 1198 and 1199, there may have been some modest degree of specialization between the four justices, with Benedict of Talmont and Joseph Aaron handling financial matters, and Simon of Pattishall and Henry of Whiston being principally in charge of legal matters.[71] But the divisions cannot have been absolute, and after 1200

---

[68] Richardson, *EJ*, p. 136 n.5; I. J. Sanders, *English Baronies: A Study of their Origin and Descent, 1086–1327* (Oxford, 1960), p. 101.

[69] Holt, *Northerners*, pp. 79–84; Painter, *King John*, pp. 270–2. Wendover reported that Geoffrey was crushed to death by the weight of a leaden cope.

[70] The fact that in 1218, when new justices of the Jews were appointed, these appointments were made by the common counsel of the realm and not by the justiciar or the justices of the Exchequer suggests this conclusion: *Rot. Litt. Pat.* II, 154; *Rot. Litt. Claus.* I, 370b; D. Carpenter, *The Minority of Henry III* (London, 1990), p. 83. By the mid-1220s, the Exchequer of the Jews was sufficiently well-established to have its own room at Westminster, separate from the offices of the regular Exchequer: *Rot. Litt. Claus.* II, 47. The first surviving 'plea roll' from the Exchequer of the Jews is from 1219–1220: see Brand, 'Jewish Community', p. 78. As Brand notes, the so-called 'plea rolls' of the Jewish Exchequer include not only records of legal decisions, but also memoranda and lists of recorded deeds.

[71] Benedict of Talmont and Joseph Aaron accounted at the Exchequer for debts owed by Jews to the crown. They kept a separate receipt roll and also maintained a separate treasury, from which they expended money on command of the king or the justiciar (*Mem. Roll 1 John*, p. xcii; *Rot. Litt. Claus.* I, 76, 87, 103b). Simon of Pattishall and Henry of Whiston do not seem to have shared in these duties, and their names do not appear on Benedict of Talmont's surviving account roll. Benedict seems also to have taken the lead in arranging for the sale or lease of escheated Jewish property (*Mem. Roll 1 John*, p. 24). The four justices acted together, however, in adjudicating disputes between Christians and Jews, whether these concerned Jewish debts or escheated Jewish property (*PR 10 Richard I*, pp. 125, 165–6; TNA, E 368/13, m. 4d, discussed in C. A. F., Meekings, 'Justices of the Jews, 1216–68: A Provisional List', *BIHR* 28 (1955), 173–88, repr. in his *Studies in Thirteenth-Century Justice and Administration* (London, 1981). They also acted together in ordering enquiries throughout the Jewish communities of England to determine whether a debtor owed any further Jewish debts, a fact that suggests they were now exercising some degree of supervision over the 'archae' also (*PR 10 Richard I*, pp. 210, 214).

there are no clear signs of any such specialization between the justices.[72] As Paul Brand has shown, the justices of the Jewish Exchequer would continue to exercise this characteristically Angevin combination of financial, administrative, and judicial powers over Jews and Jewish debts right up until the dissolution of the institution in 1290, following the expulsion of the entire Jewish community from England.[73]

If the argument of this paper is correct, then the creation of the 'archae' system in 1194 and the emergence of the Jewish Exchequer in 1198 were less directly responses to the massacres of 1189-90 than has sometimes been suggested. Certainly there were links between them, but all three developments are better understood as reflections of an increasingly aggressive royal claim to exercise exclusive lordship over all the Jews of the kingdom. This claim to an exclusive royal jurisdiction over all the Jews of England emerged during the 1170s and expanded in scope during the 1180s. Only in the 1190s, however, did it become a widely accepted element in the king's regalian rights. The emergence of the Jewish Exchequer during the 1190s, together with the success of the 'archae' system, both marked and made possible the full administrative realization of this peculiarly English claim to an exclusive royal jurisdiction over Jews, the history of which this paper has attempted to trace.

---

[72] In 1208, William de Warenne, Geoffrey of Norwich, and Thomas de Nevill accounted jointly for their receipts to the Exchequer. They acted together in legal cases also, although Warenne seems to have been regarded as the senior justice until his death. See *The Memoranda Roll of the Tenth Year of the Reign of King John (1207–8)*, ed. R. A. Brown, PRS 69 (n.s. 31) (London, 1957), p. 64 for the justices' Michaelmas 1208 account, and *Rot. de Ob. et Fin.*, p. 424, for the transferral of a case from the justices of the Jews to the king's own court, with references to 'William de Warenne and the custodians of the Jews'.

[73] *CPREJ* VI, 2.

6

Faith, Fealty and Jewish 'infideles' in Twelfth-Century England

Paul Hyams

The 1190 events in York make a powerfully moving tale, especially when recounted by thoughtful and articulate Yorkshiremen like William of Newburgh and Barrie Dobson. Nothing remotely comparable in savagery had previously occurred in this first century of the medieval English Jewry.[1] Every historian experiences a kind of pull to see this as a watershed moment in the limited presence of Jews in England. It has seemed to cry out to be fitted into the once familiar opposition between the 'open' twelfth century and the 'closed' thirteenth.[2] The contrast between the relatively accommodating regimes before 1200 and the harsher atmosphere of the thirteenth century, with the Expulsion of 1290 looming ever more clearly on the horizon, seem an attractive way to contrast the two centuries. One might see, for example, the smaller Jewish community of the twelfth century as just one among several collective 'others' within the realm, alongside Flemings as well as the dominant Normans and Angevins themselves, each respected and protected by kings to the extent that their links were relished. The differences between this and the much more sharply confrontational atmosphere in Plantagenet England must necessarily stand out to all students of Jewish history.

Those who have organized their narratives around some such turning point present a case to be respected.[3] England is in Jewish history at the end of the line in Western Christendom, having received its Jews and much of the context for their reception entirely from Continental Europe. One should expect it to follow its neighbours from across the Channel after a small time lag. The English timeline should be measured against the master narrative of Ashkenazi Jewry, whose traditional watershed was long ago placed at the launch of the First Crusade. But that watershed too is now viewed critical-

---

[1]   Students of the Norwich case of Little St William's murder in 1144, a first appearance of themes that soon developed into the tragic blood libel, now acknowledge that no actual pogrom resulted.

[2]   F. Heer, *The Medieval World: Europe, 1100–1350* (New York, 1962).

[3]   I have in mind especially Richardson, *EJ*.

ly.[4] It is perhaps time that all such questions on both sides of the Channel be revisited and placed in the context of new understandings not just of Jewish history but of that of Western Europe as a whole, including England.

This is not the place for so taxing a task, but I hope to make a modest contribution to the challenge by testing the hypothesis of a change of tone around the turn of the twelfth and thirteenth centuries against a factor that has to date been little considered, understandings on both sides of the religious divide of Faith. It may reveal as much about the Christian host community as its Jewish minority. In addition, this approach through faith inevitably raises some interesting and under-discussed questions about trust within and between both communities.

In the troubled decade of the 1260s, a Franciscan friar named Henry of Wodstone set out to lobby some sympathetic bishops to introduce legislation through the royal council against the freedom of the Jews to harm Christians. They were after all permitted in Christian lands solely by the grace of the princes who ruled them. The capacity to hold land in freehold, which enabled them 'to oppose the Christian <u>faith</u> was', in his view, 'very obviously contrary to the sacred regulations of Christian law and *faith*'. As he saw the situation,

> they [the Jews] if they can manage it, strive to exercise the lordship they enjoyed from their freeholds, to make 'fideles' [i.e., their Christian tenants] swear for these freeholds a corporal oath to keep faith ('de fidelitate facienda') to themselves, 'infideles', [and compel] other 'fideles' to do homage to them.[5]

His references to the 'fealty' and homage customarily done to a (land-) lord by his tenants are utterly commonplace. This was simple business language, which carried for the most part absolutely no religious message. But the fact that it was expressed in faith words enabled the friar to play on the wording to make his rhetorical point. 'Fidelis' is usually translated as 'vassal', one who is bound in loyalty to a lord. But Friar Henry makes it denote a believer, to sharpen the contrast with the Jewish unbelievers, who by acquiring free-

---

4 Often critiqued, 1095 has not to my knowledge been replaced within the new narrative of a fine new generation of medieval Jewish historians equipped now with good Latin to match their Hebrew.

5 A. G. Little, 'Friar Henry of Wodstone and the Jews', in *Collectanea Franciscana II*, ed. C. L. Kingsford (Manchester, 1922), pp. 150–6 (pp. 153–4): 'quod si optinere potuissent, racione liberorum tenementorum fideles in liberis tenementis ipsis infidelibus corporale sacramentum de fidelitate facienda alii fideles ipsis infidelibus homagium facerent ... quod manifeste est contra sacrosanctas christiane legis et fidei sanxiones.' The upshot seems to have been a statute on 25 July 1271 which prohibited Jews from holding land in freehold. The statute is *Foedera*, I, pt 1, 489.

hold land became lords over good Christians in a reversal of the way matters ought to have been. Already at the Third Lateran Council of 1179, the Church had proclaimed the moral wrongness of Jewish 'servi' lording it in any way over Christians.[6]

There is nothing in Friar Henry's statement that could not have been said in 1190 or the decade before. His message prompts me to investigate the role of faith words in the discourse on the Jews in the later twelfth century in order to assess what part they may have played in sharpening relations with their Christian hosts. The nub of security concerns within any community is the degree of trust individuals feel they can place in their neighbours, whom they identified as neighbours, and what defined neighbourliness. With a seemingly alien minority like twelfth-century Jews, their position immensely complicated by their religion, these concerns become fears that gnaw away at trust and cooperation with the relations that might otherwise grow into trust and friendship.

Would any twelfth-century Jew think to call himself an Englishman? Surely not. He and his family were, I shall argue, *in* but never quite *of* England. When the Angevins began in the last decades of the century to think of all inhabitants of the realm as its 'subjects', they would surely not include Jews. They remain a category apart, across a gap that widened with every advance of Englishness.

I advocate this approach to the comprehension of English Jewry without any direct attempt at proof. I will attempt instead to raise four issues to suggest how this community became different from all others. The first and last are quite technical questions. First, I ask whether Jews were able legitimately to hold land in fee, the standard entry ticket to knightly society. I then examine briefly the use of faith words by William of Newburgh, our fullest and most illuminating witness to the events of 1190, to illustrate how one intelligent and thoughtful observer viewed them. I go on to review some conventional evidence on the way Jews and Christians seemed to each other in the 1180s. And fourthly, I consider one important way in which the Christian English used faith to encourage mutual trust in their business dealings with each other, and ask what this might mean in their practical relations with Jews.

---

6   Bishop Thomas Cantilupe spoke at a council meeting about this time against the award of royal judicial office to Henry of Winchester, a convert to Christianity but still apparently regarded as a Jew. This drew editorial comment as follows, in the early fourteenth century proceedings for Thomas' canonization. 'Scilicet quia indignum Deoque minime gratum judicabat, Christi fideles e[t] Christianis natos parentibus homini a Judaismo ad Christum nuper converso subjacere, eorumdemque vitam & membrorum integritatem in potestate esse ejusmodi viri, cujus conversionem *æquitatemque* forsitan suspecta habebat ex Judaica perfidia veterique gentis in Christianos odio', *Acta Sanctorum, Octobris* (Paris, 1856), I, 547–8, trans. by R. C. Stacey, 'The Conversion of Jews to Christianity in Thirteenth-Century England', *Speculum* 97 (1992), 263–83 (pp. 277–8).

Jewish Freehold

Jews had to live somewhere. In England, they chose, with few exceptions, that this would be in a town and usually within easy reach of a royal castle and the main market.[7] They also acquired town houses to rent out to others, and they received a fair number of charters of rural property, indistinguishable in their form from the many thousands of land grants that survive from the twelfth and thirteenth centuries. Very few of these, however, were the full grants which great men and religious houses were busy confirming and distributing to their knights during the twelfth century, and which therefore formed the basic tenure of gentry society. The vast majority of the grants received by Jews were security for loan deals of one kind or another. I know of no good indication that any Jew established himself as resident lord on a country manor in the way successful knights expected to do.[8] This does not mean that they neglected to take full legal possession (seizin) of the properties they acquired, as was essential if they were to receive their rents and other dues. They must often have operated through a Gentile agent and with the sheriff's help to obtain the all-important acknowledgement of their lordship at the start of their tenure. It is hard to document exactly how they did this. But in 1208, for example, Moses son of Brun, a London Jew, sent his Gentile servant, Richard, along with the sheriff and a court order to take 'simple seizin' of the manor of Standon, Hertfordshire, which he then held in gage. They had the men of the village come along 'ad faciendum fidelitatem'. This must mean that they swore an oath of fidelity to perform on time all services due for their holdings, and it is exactly the formula which Friar Henry was later wilfully to misread.[9]

By 1190, most reasonably well educated churchmen, at least, would have been aware of a growing body of opinion that Jews were to be regarded as fit only to be servants to Christians and not their lords or masters, something which the Lateran Council of 1179 had explicitly forbidden.[10] They will also

---

7   See n. 30 below.
8   The literature does not seem to have noticed a 1213 inquiry into official corruption in Yorkshire and Lincolnshire, one of whose targets was: 'Et scire nobis faciatis domos et dominica judeorum, et que dominica tenuerint ad feodum …', *Rot. Litt. Pat.* I, 97. P. Hyams, 'Notes on the Transformation of the Fief into the Common Law Tenure in Fee', in *Laws, Lawyers and Texts*, ed. S. Jenks et al. (Leiden, 2012), 21–49.
9   This case, *CRR* V, 169 is cited by Richardson, *EJ*, ch. 5, see esp. pp. 83–6.
10 Canon 26 prohibits Jews to have Christian servants in their houses, and appears also to favour any Christian testimony over that of a Jew. The reasoning is that 'Jews ought to be subject to Christians and to be tolerated by them on grounds of humanity alone'. I tried to puzzle out the matter of Jewish 'servitude' in P. Hyams, 'The Jewish Minority in Medieval England, 1066–1290', *Journal of Jewish Studies* 25 (1974), 270–93 (pp. 287–8). My effort should be compared with that of A. Patschovsky, 'The Relationship between the Jews of Germany and the King (11th – 14th Centuries): A European Comparison', in *England and Germany in the High Middle Ages*, ed. A. Haverkamp and H. Vollrath (London, 1996), pp. 193-218.

have known plenty of lands and people under Jewish control and thus in some sense subjected to their service. Some monasteries in need of money had begun to take loans from Jews uninhibited by the recent canons against permanent alienation of Church property, handing their saint's lands over as security for repayment. And other churches with investment money to spare found they could profitably seek out estates encumbered by gages in the hands of Jewish lenders and so available for purchase, without any noticeable concern for the taint of usury.[11] Much of the documented monastic commerce in such land comes, as it happens, from Yorkshire and nearby Lincolnshire, a fact which may or may not be significant as a preparatory factor in the York riots of 1190. However that may be, local lords and gentry in the 1180s must have known at least something of the realities of debt and the land market. The way that Richard Malebisse and his fellows in 1190 targeted the chest of Jewish debt bonds deposited in the Minster comes close to proving this point. A few of the better advised lords had already started to instruct their clerks to include in their charters to their knights a prohibition of grants to either religious or Jew.[12]

Lordship, Fealty and Faith

Friar Henry knew what he was doing. He was undoubtedly aware that most people most of the time thought as little on the religious implications of faith as we do today, when we, devout believers, agnostics or atheist infidels, say 'Bless you!' after a friend's sneeze. 'Fideles' were by 1190 for the most part simply ordinary free men with obligations to the lord of their land. They owed 'fides' or 'fidelitas' to these lords, but what did that mean to them? In the past, there was an uncomplicated textbook answer to this question. Having sworn an oath to their lord at the time they became his 'man', they owed him fealty and all the various 'feudal' services and incidents that they and their peers customarily owed. By Friar Henry's time, this is a tenable position. The lawyers had reified the promise affirmed in their oath and Frenched the faith by which they made it.[13] But when historians read in twelfth-century texts of oaths 'fidelitatis', they should probably not assume such a meaning too quickly. 'fidelitas' is just as likely at this date to refer to the promise to behave as a man should to his lord as to a continuing relationship of vassalage.[14] We

11 M. G. Cheney, 'Inalienability in Mid-Twelfth-Century England: Enforcement and Consequences', in *Proceedings of the Sixth International Congress of Medieval Canon Law*, ed. S. Kuttner and K. Pennington, Monumenta Iuris Canonici s. C: Subsidia 7 (Vatican City, 1985), pp. 467–78, and Richardson, *EJ*, do not quite make this connection.

12 The earliest Yorkshire charter to warn of any Jewish 'machinamentum' refers to urban property: Hyams, 'Jewish Minority', p. 292.

13 J. Le Goff, 'Le rituel symbolique de la vassalité', in J. Le Goff, *Pour un autre Moyen Age* (Paris, 1977), pp. 349–419; P. Hyams, 'The End of Feudalism?', *Journal of Interdisciplinary History* 27 (1997), 655–62.

14 I intend to argue this case at length in a future study that will start by summarizing my view

need to test their assumption against context and contemporary lexicography. William of Newburgh may suffice as a demonstration for present purposes.[15]

Newburgh was particularly meticulous in describing the establishment of trust in political situations. He gives a good deal of detail on the various techniques, oaths, guarantees of different kinds, hostages and textual treaties and 'amicitiae', by which men from kings down attempted to establish, re-establish or confirm trust. He presents himself in his writing as honest to a fault, always careful, for example, to identify which information that he knew only by hearsay.[16] It is in this light that one has to tease out his own reading of the various faith words, of which I have noticed more than fifty examples in his chronicle, 'fides, fidelitas, fidelis/infidelis, perfidus/perfidia, infidus' etc.

I begin with the worst kind of bad or missing faith, 'perfidia'. This word has by Newburgh's time quite a history with regard to both Jews and others. It often goes beyond mere unbelief to imply a refusal of belief or even a malevolent and persecuting unbelief.[17] In Newburgh's work, it certainly means a belief that is more than just mistaken, an evil belief that can harm believers. He uses it freely of Jews and heretics too. When he summarizes Henry II's life and achievements, he chides him for having fostered the Jews 'more than was just', this 'people, perfidious and inimical to Christians'. He condemns the initial London rioters after the coronation banquet, noting that God reserves for himself 'divine vengeance'[18] on blasphemers and the perfidious', and wishes after the York massacre that 'the perfidious Jew [remain] as a most salubrious memorial to the Lord's Passion'.[19] Others he terms perfidious include Richard I's royal but dangerous brother, John, and Richard's own captor, the Emperor Henry VI.[20]

When we turn to a more positive view of faith, the central notion appears to be one of loyalty and trustworthiness, along with the faithful vassals who

of 'homage', since the two terms are obviously very often linked, and will overlap with the final section of the present chapter. I hope there to produce lexicographical evidence to suggest that fealty in its modern sense was rare for the twelfth century in Old French and Latin, and emerges in Middle English only after 1300. P. Hyams, 'Homage and Feudalism: A Judicious Separation', in *Die Gegenwart des Feudalismus*, ed. N. Fryde et al. (Göttingen, 2003), pp. 13–49.

15 For Bks I and II of Newburgh's work, I have supplemented WN, ed. Howlett, with WN, ed. Walsh & Kennedy.

16 One illustration is his disapproving account of the substitution of secular canons for monks at Canterbury and Coventry, WN, Bk IV, chs. 35–6.

17 B. Blumenkranz, 'Perfidia', *Archivium Latinitatis Medii Aevi, Bulletin Du Cange* 22 (1952), 157–70. The beginning of H. D. Schmidt, 'The Idea and Slogan of "Perfidious Albion"', *Journal of the History of Ideas*, 14 (1953), 604–16, makes especially interesting reading for English medievalists.

18 He honours the rioters with the label of 'divinae ... ultionis ministri'. This becomes even less condemnatory if one translates 'ultio' here as 'punishment'. But I show the word's ambiguity in the twelfth century in my 'Afterword: Neither Unnatural nor Wholly Negative: The Future of Medieval Vengeance', in *Vengeance in the Middle Ages: Emotion, Religion, and Feud*, ed. S. Throop and P. R. Hyams (Farnham, 2010), pp. 203–20 (pp. 215–18).

19 WN, ed. Howlett, II, 280, 299, 316.

20 ibid. II, 302, 404–5.

are expected to personify this virtue. In the aftermath of the civil war of 1173-74, for example, the former rebels, frightened after royalist successes, offered terms including security 'de pace et fidelitate', meaning a promise to keep the peace and maintain their own future loyalty.[21] The king in due course had his son, Henry, give to guarantee his future loyalty 'the security of many men as sureties' but also extracted as a 'nova … cautela' a solemn and public acknowledgement of lordship.[22] Newburgh describes this in a telling image as nature's strongest bond, torn apart as if it were a mere spider's web, in a phrase that echoes Ecclesiastes 4. 12: 'And if a man prevail against one, two shall withstand him; a threefold cord is not easily broken'.[23] In a perfect world, he seems to say, each should be able to rely on the other's word. In this one, the best safeguard was to tie individuals into webs of trust, which could where necessary hold them to their word. This widely accepted principle lies behind familiar processes like the tithings of the frankpledge system and the listing of witnesses on charters. If these institutions affected Christians only, they were as readily understood by Jews too. So when the York mob outside the castle persuaded surviving Jews to emerge, Newburgh has them promise them safety 'sub fidei testificatione', which must mean that their superior religious faith should guarantee their word.[24] The treacheries that ensued should warn prudent men and women to take careful stock of those who speak words of faith and trust, for words are cheap.[25]

Given the rhetorical demands of any effort to convince others that one can be trusted, it is natural that 'fides' comes to be associated with proof. To return to those optimistic Jewish survivors after the mass suicide, some of them threw out of the castle windows to the waiting mob a few of their Jewish dead as an 'occulatam … fidem', visible attestation to what had happened out of eyesight.[26] But the association with the supreme exemplar of Faith, Loyalty, and Devotion, the Christian religion itself, is stronger still. When a miraculous crucifix was seen in the sky at Dunstable, it clearly represented

---

[21] WN, ed. Walsh & Kennedy, II, 150.

[22] This act, referred to as 'hominium', presumably centred on the hand-having 'homage' ritual.

[23] WN, ed. Walsh & Kennedy, II, 155: 'Volebat enim pater ut qui fortissimum naturae vinculum tanquam telam araneae irreverenter diruperat, saltem iure civili vel gentium ad honestum et utile teneretur.' Ecclesiastes 4. 12: 'Et si quispiam praevaluerit contra unum, duo resistunt ei; Funiculus triplex difficile rumpitur.' Cf. further gloss to v. 13 'melior etc.', which expands upon the general theme of vv. 9–16 headed in the Vulgate 'utilitas societatis'.

[24] WN, ed. Howlett, II, 321. This passage should perhaps, however, be set into the context of the making of faith, discussed below.

[25] ibid. II. 464.

[26] ibid. II, 320–21. Then there was the pilgrim to Compostella, whose miraculous escape from the Devil left him with a burnt head, which he could later show off 'in argumentum fidei', ibid. II, 434, 436. The Old French word 'enseigne', cognate with our ensign, flag, often used at this time to mean something close to 'evidence', confirms that people found it much easier to trust their eyes than any other sense, as I show in my 'The Legal Revolution and the Discourse of Dispute in the Twelfth Century', in *The Cambridge Companion to Medieval English Literature*, ed. A. Galloway (Cambridge, 2011), pp. 43–65 (p. 43).

to Newburgh 'the devotion of the faithful', but the crusade was to regain the Holy Land from 'the control of the unfaithful' and reinstall the faithful.[27] Newburgh specifies that sincerity would require that the violence was 'just for the sake of *the* Faith', a proviso that explains why he tended to dismiss the Lynn pogrom on the ground of insincerity.[28] Evidently, Newburgh would like to encourage his readers to narrow the gulf between divine and human standards of trust as guarantees of lasting social and legal relations. Only those readers who believe in advance that the textbook oath of 'fealty' is fundamental to this society in a history, are likely to find it in this history, for all its intimate concern with trust between king, lords and vassals.[29]

How Would Jews Appear to Their Gentile Neighbours?

Newburgh's use of faith words can be no more than a first step towards the more comprehensive understanding of the role of faith in the daily discourse of the Gentile host community in England during the generation before 1190. The next requirement for present purposes is to set his usage into the context of the actual social relations between Jews and Christians in general within England, and more broadly over Western Europe, in the areas of Ashkenaz. This is a topic on which our knowledge has advanced so significantly over the last generation that it demands specialist knowledge to summarize it accurately. I therefore restrict my own effort once more to a series of suggestions.

Twelfth-century Jews were very much town-dwellers.[30] Many of them owned house property, both to live in and to rent out and most Jews lived in and amongst Christians, a somewhat double-edged privilege. This integrated them into urban life and culture no more effectively than it does recent immigrants in our own cultures. They can never have won a place within the urban patriciate or, so far as one can tell, fitted comfortably into the company of humbler neighbours and townspeople.[31] Since they had to do busi-

---

[27] WN, ed. Howlett, II, 268 (papal letter), 307.

[28] ibid. II, 308. I translate 'causa fidei tantum' with a definite article and capitalized initial letter.

[29] One likely instance is ibid. II, 244.

[30] The evidence adduced for rural resident communities no longer seems convincing, beyond the occasional existence of temporary residences as branch offices for business purposes. Quite apart from security concerns, the need for a *minyan* (ten adult males to make religious services possible) and the other accoutrements of religious observance makes it hard to believe that viable settlements could subsist outside towns. Within the Jewish community, it was apparently common enough for one Jew to maintain against his co-religionists a unique relationship with a particular Gentile. I refer below, at n. 58, to the *ma'arufiyah* arrangements by which this was done. It seems logical that the enterprising might seek to establish a similar dominance in promising rural areas in which they might find potential customers among the gentry, but I know of no pertinent evidence or studies.

[31] One test was guild membership. The only known Jewish gildsman remains Benedict of Winchester two generations after 1190. It is anyone's guess whether either he or his fellow gilds-

ness with their Gentile neighbours, the rabbis relaxed ancient Talmudic rules where necessary, the obvious example being those concerning drinking wine (and, in England, beer) with Gentiles.[32]

The harshest representations bubbled out of the ground at special times, such as Easter or during crusading preparations. Community relations may have operated in a kind of punctuated equilibrium, settling down between shocks as incidents receded in the memory, only to heat up again with some fresh crisis. In this light, 1190 was a moment of major disequilibrium whose memory might be expected to last longer than most. Yet Barrie Dobson has taught us to see the massacre changing relatively little in the short to medium term. Jews were soon back doing business in York. Within a decade or so, they were recognized to constitute an effective commonality of some kind. Their most prosperous days still lay ahead.[33]

But could any Jews really 'pass', in the sense of moving unremarked through the streets of the town where they and their parents had long dwelt, let alone in the deeper sense of being one of them?[34] Judging from the way an apostate was recorded in the Latin records as '*le Convers*', it will have taken even new Christians a while to gain real acceptance.[35] It seems unlikely that either Jew or Christian thought in such terms.[36] Few Gentile townsmen can have known a Jew well. Quite a number even in towns with a functioning synagogue and community may never knowingly have got to converse with one. They and their countrymen will have gained their image of the Jew very much from report or story, from a literature, that is, which did not tend to favour warm relations with such folk. Both Christians and Jews felt they lived in a religious monoculture, without alternatives worthy of consideration.[37] England hardly even experienced any heresy before the 1160s.[38]

men were comfortable in each other's company at the all-important feasts. His membership was perhaps purely formal, in the expectation, perhaps, that he would do mutually profitable business but never turn up to dine. M. Adler, 'Benedict the Gildsman of Winchester', *JHSE Miscellanies* 4 (1942), 1–8.

[32] H. Soloveitchik, 'Religious Law and Change: The Medieval Ashkenazic Example', *AJSR* 12 (1987), 205–21 (pp. 217–18): D. Malkiel, *Reconstructing Ashkenaz: The Human Face of Franco-German Jewry, 1000–1250* (Stanford CA, 2009), pp. 203–4.

[33] Dobson, *JCME*, esp. pp. 24–7, 53–86, 87–99.

[34] Patschovsky, 'Jews of Germany and the King', p. 209 is able to write of Germany: 'The inclusion of the Jews in the *treuga Dei* of 1103 provided a chance that Jews might become citizens among citizens, equals among equals...' I doubt any scholar could speak of England's Jews in similar terms.

[35] Stacey, 'Conversion of Jews'; L. Fogle, 'Between Christianity and Judaism: The Identity of Converted Jews in Medieval London', *Essays in Medieval Studies* 22 (2005), 107–16, esp. p. 110

[36] Among the very few anecdotes that might be read in this way, consider the one about the cheeky Francophone punster travelling in clerical company along the Welsh border, Roth, *HJE*, p. 279 (h).

[37] Soloveitchik, 'Religious Law', p. 214.

[38] Biller, 'William of Newburgh', pp. 11–30, esp. 23 sq., argues persuasively that we have

When considering the causes of the attack on York's Jews in 1190 it seems premature to focus too exclusively on the debt bonds housed in York Minster or the possible attractions of political action to gentry suffering from a liquidity crisis. Rather we should weigh these carefully against the known truth that Jews, simply by not being Christians, posed a troubling discord both to religious faith and to the whole cultural cohesion of everyday life in Angevin England. The most obvious fact about Jews was that that they were not Christian, they were unbelievers, already identified as Christ-killers. Churchmen like William of Newburgh might consider their visible presence in York and elsewhere to be 'a continual and most helpful remembrance ... of our Lord's Passion'.[39] Others did not.

It is true that only the most basic of the three forms of blood libel was as yet in circulation in England.[40] But this, the sacrifice of young boys so that their blood might be used in the celebrations for Passover, was horrifying enough. It certainly seems to have caused enough trouble for Jews and saints in their neighbourhood to have made deep impressions on ordinary townsmen during the generation before 1190. While it seems almost impossible to measure the power of such stereotypes, one cannot totally exclude the suspicion that some Jews may themselves have been influenced by the tales told about their co-religionists.[41] Fear of conversion was surely two-way, as important to Jews fearing apostasy as to their neighbours in the host community. Each community agonized in its own way over the durability of Jewish conversions, which mostly occurred only in situations of tension and violence. Rabbis like Rashi had softened the ancient rejection of apostates, holding that 'although he has sinned he remains a Jew'. It is hardly surprising if Christians, already on edge from the sense that the Jews were masters of the biblical letter, were drawn to associate converts with the tag 'as a dog that returneth to his vomit, so is the fool that repeateth his folly', a nastily emotive image.[42] Or that some wondered if they could ever trust the convert's word on such a matter.[43]

---

missed hints of a good deal of heretical activity by not considering the basic methodological truth that absence of evidence is not evidence of absence. Newburgh writes of the 'virus suae *perfidiae*' and the way they hid when '*fidelium* zelus succenditur' (my emphasis). WN, ed. Walsh & Kennedy, II, 56–60.

39   WN, ed. Howlett, II, 316.

40   G. I. Langmuir, 'The Knight's Tale: Young Hugh of Lincoln', *Speculum* 47 (1972), 459–82, repr. in his *History, Religion, and Anti-Semitism* (Berkeley CA, 1990).

41   No scholar sees any plausibility in the accusations made during this period. I wish I could be certain that no mentally unbalanced Jew was ever drawn to consider acting out Gentile fantasies.

42   Proverbs 26. 11; cf. II Peter 2. 22. Interestingly, the twelfth-century Glossa Ordinaria does not connect either verse with the Jews. A quick Google search for 'a dog that returneth to his vomit' with the addition of the word 'Jews' sadly reveals that the association retains its attractions for anti-semites to this day.

43   J. Katz, *Exclusiveness and Tolerance: Studies in Jewish-Gentile Relations in Medieval and Modern Times* (London, 1961), ch. 6. For Benedict of York's retracted conversion see below at n. 93.

All this is well enough known. The aspect of Jewish relations with the host community that remains almost untouched is the Jewish side of the confrontation. I still have little sense of how twelfth-century English Jews might have seen themselves, and what stereotypes they perhaps held of their Gentile neighbours.[44] It would for one thing embed the better understood Christian stereotypes in the context that could best bring them to life. What Christians were prepared to believe of Jews could well have contaminated the Jewish self-image. Most Jews will have been aware that they were considered enemies of Jesus and the Christian religion. They were probably not unwilling on safe occasions to admit this or even glory in the status it afforded them. But they cannot have felt neutral about being categorized as friends of the Devil, *the* Enemy of humankind.[45] Roger of Howden, the other Yorkshire chronicler of 1190, compounds the injury by making the Jewish rabbi, their 'jurisperitus', as Roger calls him, describe Christians as 'enemies of our law' (surely here meaning religion), the same old trick of imposing a mirror view of his own people's prejudice on the 'Other'.[46]

One Jewish response to such slurs was to retreat into a sense of themselves as the suffering elite with a sense of superiority over the Gentile they could not always conceal. Since Hebrew writings from twelfth-century England are in such sparse supply, the best we can do is turn to the rich documentation from across the Channel in the Tosaphist writings[47] of Ashkenaz. Among these, the martyrological chronicle narratives of the massacres consequent upon the first two crusades amply confirm the basic point, their general tone being rather more aggressively contemptuous of the Christian enemy than I for one would have expected.[48] Given their exceptional value as a testimony to Jewish faith in God, I turn briefly to consider the direction of change in the twelfth century.

To the generation caught up in the events of 1190, the story of past crusades has to have been one of the pieces of historical information most widely shared among Gentiles and Jews all over Western Christendom.

---

[44] I should like to hope that the present generation of Jewish historians might now take this task on, a hope already expressed in my 'Jewish Minority', p. 283.

[45] Jews' strictly monotheist views on Satan and his doings are different enough from the Christian ones to leave much room for misunderstandings. But no Jew could be unmoved by an accusation of serving the 'Adversary' or 'Hinderer', who was responsible for the evil inclination,'yetzer hara', that exists in every person and tempts us to do wrong.

[46] Howden, *Chronica* III, 33–4; Howden, *Gesta* II, 107. The *locus classicus* for this representation of the other as mirror image is perhaps that of the Saracens as having their own evil Trinity of Gods in the *Chanson de Roland*.

[47] The Tosaphists were so named because their commentaries and other writings 'added' to the Talmud. Their work during the high Middle Ages is said to have set the enduring pattern of Western Ashkenazi Judaism and its practices in such matters as dietary laws and the patterns of daily life.

[48] *The Jews and the Crusaders: The Hebrew Chronicles of the First and Second Crusades*, ed. S. Eidelberg (Madison WI, 1977); E. Haverkamp, *Hebräische Berichte über die Judenverfolgungen während des Ersten Kreuzzugs* (Hannover, 2005).

Members of both populations were uncomfortably aware at such times as the death of a king and the call to a new crusade that some of God's enemies and the king's were all too close to hand without any need to travel to the distant East. England's growing Jewry cannot but have heard of the massacres that accompanied the crusades in 1096 and 1147. That some at least of their number had seen one or another of the Hebrew reports of the pogroms seems almost as likely. The long-held view that 1095-96 marked a watershed moment in the course of Jewish history may now be contested, but the case for its continuing value in respect of Jewish doctrine on martyrdom, self-slaughter and suicide in the face of attempts to compel conversion by force remains powerful.

The law of the Talmud did not crown as martyrs those who committed suicide, which it treated always as a grave sin. Still less did it encourage men to kill their wives and children to avoid them apostatizing. On the contrary, apart from a very few cases in which martyrdom was mandatory, the rabbis honoured the sanctity of life and forbade its surrender. They further taught that 'one who suffers voluntary martyrdom should be viewed as having committed voluntary suicide'.[49] And all suicide was strictly forbidden, forced conversion being no excuse. This is not to say that it had not happened from time to time over the past centuries as a natural response to the impossible situations in which persecution had occasionally placed Jews, but the rabbinic ban on unnecessary deaths remained firm in 1096.

The pathbreakers were, it is argued, women. Normally, the rabbis paid little or no attention to females. Yet they were to pioneer the new view of martyrdom, as they had already quietly done with more mundane topics. They are said by the Hebrew chroniclers to have encouraged their husbands to seek death for the whole family, not just to kill women and children first but to say a blessing first and thus proclaim the act a *mitzvah*, performed in obedience to divine commandment. This in itself constituted a holy act, and made the actors *qedoshim*, holy men.[50] Given the timing of this development, one should consider the possibility that the new Christian view of martyrdom that emerged in the wake of the First Crusade had influenced the rabbis as well as the Jews' own experiences of crusader action, an uncomfortably intriguing thought. The impact of the massacres was so powerful that the rabbis, it is contended, found themselves drawn to augment their traditional interpretative techniques with assistance from the new dialectic methods,

---

[49] Soloveitchik, 'Religious Law', p. 208. It is at almost exactly this time that suicide becomes one of the early felonies in the English common law, R. Groot, 'When Suicide became Felony', *Journal of Legal History* 21 (2000), 1–20.

[50] Soloveitchik, 'Religious Law', p. 209; *Jews and Crusaders*, ed. Eidelberg, pp. 22, 80. If Newburgh was so influenced by what he read in Josephus, as Vincent shows above, ch. 3, it would be very extraordinary if the first-century suicides etc. at Massada did not weigh at least as heavily on Jewish minds.

as practised in the Christian schools of Northern France.[51] Both faiths demanded a holy act of their candidates for martyr, as evidence that they died in a holy cause and not merely in the course of a war, however just.[52]

Haim Soloveitchik contended that the results of this innovation were deep and long-lasting. He depicts the legal changes on martyrdom as one of those highly significant cultural choices made by Ashkenaz where other Jewries, in Spain and Provence (meaning Mediterranean France and Italy) remained unmoved.[53] Tosaphist thought on the subject was, he says, 'percolating downwards' to be internalized by ordinary men and women living in French and German communities. Thus it was they, rather than their religious leaders, who took the initiative and turned Ashkenazi culture in a new direction developing 'an idealized vision of itself': and, if Ashkenaz, surely also the Jewry of twelfth-century England.[54] It is likely that most English Jews knew stories about the crusading massacres, and passed them on from parent to child. This can only have quickened their response when preparations for a second major expedition began in the late 1140s. Copies of the martyrological report-chronicles may have circulated and remained around in 1190 to sharpen fears and exhort them to imitation of their forbears if the feared occasion arose. Perhaps such thoughts were among those that impelled the Jewish leaders to make their ill-fated trip to Westminster to offer their congratulations to the newly crowned king.

Trust and the Jews

For the historian of 1190, all this must raise questions concerning trust, between individuals both within and beyond their own religious communities. This is a topic which still awaits a detailed study in the English host community. In its absence I shall spend most of the rest of this chapter sketching a rough comparison of some different ways in which Christians and Jews sought to understand and foster trust. Since much of what I have to say centres on what each community understood by faith, my main focus will continue to be on the way Latin words like 'fides' and 'fidelitas', their cognates, and their vernacular equivalents, describe and shape human relationships with each other and with God.[55]

---

[51] Malkiel, *Reconstructing Ashkenaz*, pp. 152–6 and ch. 6.

[52] H. E. J. Cowdrey, 'Martyrdom and the First Crusade', in *Crusade and Settlement*, ed. P. Edbury (Cardiff, 1985), pp. 46–56.

[53] Soloveitchik, 'Religious Law', pp. 211–12, 217–18.

[54] Solovietchik, 'Religious Law and Change', p. 221. Where Malkiel, *Reconstructing Ashkenaz*, p. ix, dismisses England at the beginning of his study as 'largely irrelevant'; Stacey, 'Jews and Christians', pp. 340–53, considers the English Jewry both 'an archetypal medieval Ashkenazic community' and, because of this very characteristic, also quite exceptional.

[55] P. Biller, 'Words and the Medieval Notion of "Religion"', *Journal of Ecclesiastical History* 36 (1985), 351–69, shows that there were from at least the thirteenth century a number of Latin

One can easily see that the best people to trust are one's peers and rough equals or those with whom one enjoyed the recognized and socially sanctioned relationships of kinship, lordship and such-like. One's friends, 'amici', were at the time defined broadly as close blood relatives (perhaps extending into the ranks of baptismal kin, God-parents and 'gossips'), lords and vassals, and perhaps also neighbours and even the occasional 'plain-vanilla' friend. From most of these categories (the last excepted) Jews were by definition excluded; institutional friends were precisely what they were not. This nicely demonstrates why their acquisition of land in the countryside could never serve as an entrée into gentry society. Nor, of course, could they use marriage to co-opt allies who would stand surety for them in any hour of need, as others habitually did. The only exception was perhaps situations where money trumped affect, though there the resulting trust was brittle at best and as double-edged as the odds on mutual profit. And it could turn brutally against the Jews, as Newburgh believed it had in York.[56]

However 'fides' and 'fidelitas' played an ambiguous role in contemporary linguistic culture. Often, certainly, these terms refer to religion, always potentially the major parameter of difference and mistrust between Jews and Christians. But much of the time and for most ordinary folk, they were drained of religious content. Speakers and writers of Latin, like modern English speakers, comfortably use the same faith vocabulary in two linked but distinct contexts. They speak of their faith in God, and fight for *the* faith, meaning Christianity. But they also declare their faith in their *amici*, in all the various secular senses just listed. This is a feature of the Western European Romance languages, and with them of English. It is worth asking, then, if Hebrew does the same. If it turns out not to, this rich source of misunderstanding should certainly be factored into our analyses. But that is for the specialists to consider.[57]

It is these relations between men and women that are most directly to the present purpose. Twelfth-century Ashkenaz, including England, was a tense place for Jews to reside. It was a rare Jew who felt totally confident in these circumstances that his English neighbours were fully reliable in a time of unrest.[58] Diasporan life had therefore generated a number of devices

---

nouns available to indicate the notion of a 'religion' in much the modern sense. Among them were 'fides' and 'lex' as well as 'religio', each of which often carried other meanings.

56 WN, ed. Howlett, I, 322, describes the way the conspirators went off to the Minster as soon as the bloodshed was finished, to destroy the 'monumenta debitorum … tam pro sue et quam et aliorum multorum liberatione'.

57 I have bothered various Hebraists on this question, without clear results. I am grateful to David Malkiel and my good friend, Susan Einbinder, for their help, also to Carol Rosen for encouraging my speculation concerning the Romance languages.

58 One responsum does, however, call a Christian 'rich and trustworthy', I. A. Agus, *Urban Civilization in Pre-Crusade Europe: A Study of Organized Town-Life in Northwestern Europe during the Tenth and Eleventh Centuries based on the Responsa Literature*, 2 vols. (New York, 1965), I, 323–4. There must have been others.

to bolster security. The most common of these for business purposes was the 'ma'arufiyah', a monopoly relationship with a Christian partner, a valuable item resulting from careful preparation and so one to be defended against encroachment by co-religionists.[59] Jews were a safer bet. Merchants almost always relied on other Jews for sensitive tasks, such as looking after the spare cash they did not need or feared to carry with them on business trips. Yet there were limits to trust even within their own families.[60] Like their Christian neighbours, Jews were driven to strengthen agreements and promises in whatever acceptable way they could. So they made their agreements visible through ritual (at its simplest just a hand-clasp) and had them properly witnessed.[61] Or the terms of the agreement stated that each party must accept the other's word, as if it had been confirmed by the required biblical witnesses.[62] Or they sought to put the fear of God, quite literally, in their contractual partners by engaging a 'minyan' of ten adult males to lay a 'herem' that is, a public anathema like an excommunication.[63]

Among Christians the best known way by which ordinary folk set out to strengthen their word was to swear an oath. Oaths were, however, a sensitive area, in which churchmen saw all kinds of potential moral pitfalls. Jews too saw pros and cons in the oath. The rabbis worried especially because they took the sin of perjury so seriously. This impelled them to be very strict in wording oaths and backing them up with heavy sanctions including the threat of a 'herem'. They feared both false oaths that risked the souls of those who swore them and the risk that, for example, bullies would compel people to pay money they did not owe, because the bullied thought it sinful to take an exculpatory oath.[64] Perjurers had much to lose in everyday life too. Failure in an oath, whatever the reason, seriously damaged a man's ability to live a normal life afterwards.[65] It ruined his reputation and marked him out as one who could not be trusted. Even an apparently successful and justified oath might have bad consequences. The community might all too easily read a later accident or disaster as a sign that God was punishing him for perjury.

---

[59] ibid., I, 195–203, 266–9, 272–2 etc.

[60] ibid., I, 59, 62–5. One complainant is quoted as saying, in a case where two parties accused each other of lying about a money deal, 'for he was my elder brother, and I trusted him from the day I was born until now'!

[61] The 'kinyan', for example, was something like the Old English 'wed' or a transfer of seisin over a material object as gage or pledge, ibid., I, 357; I, 160–3 documents the hand-clasp.

[62] ibid., I, 310–2.

[63] Later, in the 1270s, there are instances of royal implementation of this *herem* procedure, as if it were indeed an excommunication. Known cases, however, involve a royal interest, since the debts to be enforced were ultimately due to the queen. F. D. Logan, 'Thirteen London Jews and Conversion to Christianity: Problems of Apostasy in the 1280s', *BIHR* 45 (1972), 214–29 (pp. 224–9 sets out some of the evidence).

[64] Agus, *Urban Civilization*, I, 147 gives an illustration; II, 794 for Rashi's willingness to threaten but not actually exact an oath from a Gentile suspected of lying.

[65] ibid., I, 405–6.

Oaths were, then, a blunt instrument best kept by Jews for use among themselves only as a last resort. They were harder to avoid when it came to relations with the Christian host community, which was less inclined to accept the unsupported word of a Jew even in a simple situation. The best documented are disputes leading to litigation. Jews are seen from the late 1160s both suing and being sued (or prosecuted) for a variety of alleged wrongs. They thus come into view during the same years after 1166 that saw a massive expansion of business in royal courts. By 1190 they were not to be impleaded outside a royal court, a lesser version of the similar privileges commonly granted to favoured individuals and religious houses.[66] There is very little here to mark a distinction between Jew and Christian in the eye of the law.[67]

But litigation required oaths at various stages of the proceedings. Initiators of lawsuits normally had to produce suit, that is, a sworn witness to attest to the basic validity of the suit. A Jew could use a lawful Jew to perform this office on his behalf, unless he had a royal writ to do the job instead. When sued by Christians, he was to be judged by a jury of co-religionists on their oaths. And he could when necessary 'make his law', by swearing an oath of purgation. He would not of course swear any such oaths on the Gospels as Christians did. Instead he was permitted to use for the purpose the Jews' own 'roll' or 'book', meaning a Torah scroll. Hence the need for the new Jewish Exchequer, formed in 1194, to acquire such a scroll for its own use. All this is perhaps more remarkable than has been allowed. It largely accepted the Jews on their own word, in sharp contrast to the special forms of humiliating oath 'more judaico', which were later imposed in many areas on the Continent. How significant one judges the timing of this concession will remain a matter for conjecture, unless we learn more about the lost royal charters.

The early date of this system was rather fortunate for the Jews. It preempted discussion of whether they were to be trusted even when they had sworn an apparently solemn oath. Since Jews were thus regarded as a people wedded to the literal truth of their bible and too articulate for their own good, it was perhaps inevitable that they would be thought liable to seek out cunning ways of circumventing, with verbally accurate statements designed to mislead, even the Second Commandment against taking the Lord's name in vain.[68]

Suspicions of this kind were almost certainly encouraged by rumours circulating about the way that Jews behaved at their annual Day of Atonement (Yom Kippur). The ceremonial declaration with which this solemn fast opens in synagogues is called from its first two words Kol Nidrei, meaning

---

66 The two royal charters of 1190 and 1201, *Foedera*, 2nd edn, I, pt 1, 51; *Rot. Chart.*, p. 93, claim that they are confirming an earlier lost charter of Henry II. The charters say they are only to enter pleas 'coram nobis' or before the castle constables where they lived. The noble privileges offered more, trials before the king himself or his chief justiciar.

67 Richardson, *EJ*, pp. 112–15.

68 Hyams, 'The Legal Revolution and the Discourse of Dispute in the Twelfth Century'.

'all vows'. It introduces a litany of exactly the kind that Christians feared most: a solemn string of terms meaning oaths and various other ways in which people strengthen their promises. It declares null and void all these made during the year since the last Yom Kippur.[69] Technically, Kol Nidrei is not a prayer; it does not beg for God's forgiveness, but asserts it. The text is so legal in tone and vocabulary that it has received much lawyerly reformulation involving careful distinctions between vow and oath and their revocation or nullification. But, originating in Palestine or Mesopotamia in the eighth or ninth centuries, it comes from a culture in which people believed in and cherished magic and incantations alongside the law of the Talmud. And, though most Jews today regard it as one of the most memorable readings of the liturgical year, it has been from the start a contested text. Some rabbis debated its wording, and thought up subtle amendments to make its message more acceptable. Others simply rejected it for use within their communities.

One of several reasons for the differences of opinion was the tendency for unlearned people to take it in a literal sense as a nullification of oaths, vows, and promises they did not wish to perform, not merely the promises individuals made about themselves to God, but those offered before courts or to business partners and associates. Historians must deduce much of this persistent misreading of Kol Nidrei from the rabbinic responses they provoked. One of these very much relevant to our subject occurred within the same generation as the 1190 massacre, in France.

Rabbenu Tam (d. 1171) is regarded as one of the great Tosaphist authorities, striving to modernize Jewish law. He argued from a close textual reading of Kol Nidrei that it could never have been intended to nullify vows already made in binding form. It made no sense to him, for example, to seek divine atonement and forgiveness for a vow made and broken in the past. It could not be nullified 'ex post facto', and it was now too late to revoke it. The idea that Kol Nidrei could *nullify* past vows he derided as palpable nonsense. He therefore proposed to amend the text so that it referred to vows that might be made and perhaps then neglected over the next year. It is only for these future vows, he thought, that it made sense to seek God's forgiveness. At the same time, he forthrightly declared that the revocation covered only self-made vows addressed to God. 'But for interpersonal vows [such as] oaths made before a Beth Din [Jewish court], oaths made to a widow, and *mitzvah* obligations, it has no power,' he concluded.[70]

It is hard to believe that so authoritative a statement was unknown to English rabbis and communal leaders. Even without supportive evidence, it feeds suspicion that the occasional Jewish rogue could have used Kol Nidrei as his excuse to renege on some debt or other obligation. If this is so, we may reasonably guess that such facts were known in a Christian com-

---

[69] I take most of my information in the next paragraphs from S. W. Gershon, *Kol Nidrei: Its Origins, Development, and Significance* (Northvale NJ, 1994).

[70] Gershon, *Kol Nidrei*, pp. 78–81, 126–8 (esp. pp. 81, 82 n. 14).

munity that was predisposed to think contemporary Jews as capable of wrongful acts as their forefathers had been when they denied the incarnate Christ. Speculative though this argument is, it supports a plausible view of the expectations of the host community when its members were asked to trust the word of a Jew.

'Making Faith'

Solemn vows required too much formality and fuss to be widely used in everyday matters, especially since religious leaders on both sides warned against a too frequent recourse to oaths. It is in the light of this likely Christian scepticism about the reliability of Jewish promises that I now turn to consider a practice that may have been much more routine than scholars have realized.

Medieval Englishmen, like modern ones, struggled to find effective ways of keeping people to their word. They extracted public performances of their contractual promises before a variety of audiences, and invented or borrowed a number of different devices. A number of twelfth-century charters added to their mix a practice called the making or giving of faith, in the hope of rendering the grants they recorded beyond challenge. They state that one of the parties made or gave faith to the other one, sometimes directly but frequently into the hands ('per manus') of a named third party.[71] Many others seem to refer to the same kind of ritual act alongside others such as an oath, when they describe the grant as made 'fide interposita' or something similar.[72] More than eighty charters from Yorkshire during the twelfth century and the first half of the thirteenth contain such references.[73] The practice was very ordinary in the country round York, as it was in most parts of England and a good deal of Northern France, from where it was presumably introduced after the Norman Conquest.[74] There has never been a comprehensive study of the practice.[75]

---

[71] J. A. Burrow, *Gestures and Looks in Medieval Narrative* (Cambridge, 2002), pp. 11–16, 34–9, 48–50 covers hand gestures.

[72] e.g. *Early Yorkshire Families*, ed. C. T. Clay, YAS, Rec. ser. 135 (Leeds, 1973), no. 13 (1179/1200); Glanvill, *Tractatus de legibus et consuetudinibus regni Angliae* vii.18 (*The Treatise on the Laws and Customs of the Realm of England commonly called Glanvill*, ed. G. D. G. Hall, OMT, rev. edn (Oxford, 1993), p. 92).

[73] *EYC.*

[74] J. Yver, *Les contrats dans le très ancient droit normand (xie-xiiie siècles)* (Domfront, 1926), pp. 44–57, and E. Tabuteau, *Transfers of Property in Eleventh-Century Norman Law* (Chapel Hill NC, 1988), pp. 138–9, make the case for Normandy. *The Anglo-Norman Dictionary*, ed. W. Rothwell et al., 2nd edn (London, 2005–). http://www.anglo-norman.net [accessed September 2010], s.vv. 'main-foi' and 'entrechangablement', confirms usage in the French of England and distinguishes the words from other hand gestures, 'par mene foi entrechonblement doné'.

[75] F. Pollock and F. W. Maitland, *History of English Law before the time of Edward I*, 2 vols., 2nd edn (Cambridge, 1898), I, 128–9; II, 190–2, 197–8. Yver, *Les contrats*, ch. 2, helpfully sets out Norman evidence with some reference to the English material.

If the challenge of bolstering trust is ubiquitous in an insecure world, it seems that much more pressing when the partner is an unbeliever with a gift for words and a reputation for shiftiness. But the device I describe here quite explicitly raised the question of faith, like the oaths with which it was frequently coupled.[76] It was similarly described with care, sometimes in charters that promised in explicit terms to exclude trickery.[77] Full descriptions of the hand ritual are much rarer.[78] But it is possible to deduce from a comparison of many accounts that one performed the act one handed, unlike the hand-having episode in the homage ritual, and with the right (not the sinister) hand, usually into that of a third-party guarantor or 'fideiussor'. It was apparently a simple hand-clasp, requiring no Gospel book or relic. And there is no indication that any object was passed, no *wed* to symbolize the invisible and intangible faith, as one might perhaps have expected. The onlookers could easily see it, and would know what it meant. The resulting publicity intensified pressure on the parties to stay true to their word, or suffer damage to their reputation. The 'fides' involved certainly implies trust between the human parties. But in its giving or making, it must mean more than that. It denotes a promise given on faith, one with putative Heavenly as well as human witnesses. On its breach, 'fidei laesio', the injured party (or, more likely, his third-party middleman) could seek ecclesiastical help; he could sue before an ecclesiastical judge. The focus was on conscience and penance, not rules and damages. The important exception was debt, over which the king retained jurisdiction, in theory; in practice creditors often sought to enforce debt promises too through the church system.[79] The difference when the potential dispute was between Christians became mostly a matter of wording. It was rather more than this when the contractual partner was Jewish.

[76] The coupling was performed enough times by the conjunction 'et' as to make it clear that that the more routine 'vel' is also to be read in a conjunctive not disjunctive sense. T. Madox, *The History and Antiquities of the Exchequer of the Kings of England*, 2 vols., 2nd edn (London, 1769), II, 182, was 'inclined to think ['fides'] was rather a Voire Dire, or a declaration upon their faith and allegiance, than an oath'.

[77] The common formulas are 'sine omni malo ingenio' or 'sine dolo', *EYC*, II, 719; III, 1526, 1797; IV, 91; V, 287; X, 113; XI, 68, 236.

[78] I have looked in a non-specialist fashion for any possible Roman law model. This seems unlikely, though several Roman rituals routinely used hands. 'Manus iniectio', for example, denoted the act of laying a hand on a debtor's shoulder to summon him into court. The 'dextrarum iunctio' by which the concord of the couple was signified in a Roman marriage was more likely, since this seems to have passed into Early Christian rituals and is illustrated in Renaissance art.

[79] Already in 1164, it seems accepted even by Henry II that 'fides' established ecclesiastical jurisdiction, except, according to the Constitutions of Clarendon, c. 15 and *Glanvill* x.12 (126), when used for debt, R. H. Helmholz, *The Oxford History of the Laws of England: Volume 1: The Canon Law and Ecclesiastical Jurisdiction from 597 to 1640* (Oxford, 2004), pp. 358–61. Pollock and Maitland, *History of English Law*, II, 191, thought that the third-party recipients were chosen for the 'coercive power' they already held over the parties. This is not obviously true in all cases, and their power of persuasion was more likely moral plus the potential to seek ecclesiastical censures.

This abundantly documented practice of making faith neatly leaps the gap, then, between human trust and faith in God. In the act of giving faith, promisors are sometimes said to have handed over their Christianity itself to a priest or even a bishop.[80] Henry II's Treasurer, himself a bishop, explained the point of the act in New Testament biblical terms as to bring the parties into unity 'because they are one in the confession of one faith'.[81]

How, indeed, could one give faith to or receive it from unconverted infidels? Orderic Vitalis was one historian earlier in the century to display no difficulty with the notion of giving faith *to* an unbeliever. He tells of Bohemond of Antioch, asked by a Muslim woman *c*. 1100 to promise that he would act by her advice alone: 'Spondete michi per fidem qua Christiani estis', and 'Hoc itaque michi *fide* pollicentes confirmate'; 'Promise me on the faith by which you are Christians', and confirm your promises to me 'on faith'. Bohemond, Orderic says, duly complied 'per fidem suam', and his men did likewise.[82] As a Norman, he will have known the same ritual as our Yorkshiremen. But this is the easy part of the theorem. Naturally, the superior Christian expects unbelievers to accept his word on *his* faith. The difficult part is when a Christian is asked to accept the word of an unbeliever, 'infidelis', on his faith, while understanding it to be inferior if not non-existent.

The issue arose most pressingly in wartime truce proposals, and so appears in some of the French chansons de geste that were read as much in England *c*. 1190 as anywhere else. The dilemma appears most accessibly in texts that depict Franks and Saracens agreeing to swear oaths to each other, each by his own 'law'.[83] In the twelfth-century poem, *Le Charroi de Nimes*, for instance, the Saracens challenged to swear to facts 'par ta loi', are made to use a parody of the Christian routine.[84] The instances I have

---

80 Pollock and Maitland, *History of English Law*, II, 190 n. 5, cites a Yorkshire confirmation charter whose grantor is made to say 'et primum haec omnia sacramento firmavit, deinde Christianitatem in manu mea qua se obsidem dedit et me plegium constituit de his omnibus'. M. G. Cheney, *Roger, Bishop of Worcester, 1164–1179* (Oxford, 1980), pp. 235–6, prints Maitland's other illustration, another confirmation from 1178.

81 *Dialogus de Scaccario: The Course of the Exchequer*, ed. C. Johnson, OMT, revised edn (Oxford, 1983), p. 126. The allusion is to Ephesians 4. 5.

82 *The Ecclesiastical History of Orderic Vitalis*, ed. M. Chibnall, 6 vols., OMT (Oxford, 1968–80), V, 360. The translation is mine, for the excellent editor cannot resist having Bohemond 'swear on oath'.

83 I owe the following references to my former Cornell student, Dr Tom McSweeney. Oaths present the same difficulty as the giving of faith; I discussed Jewish oaths, above at pp. 139–42.

84 *Le Charroi de Nimes: chanson de geste du XIIe siècle*, ed. D. McMillan (Paris, 1972), laisse XXII, l. 888; XLVIII, l. 1196; XLIX, ll., 1217-19, 1223-9. One might object that the oath-swearing character here is actually William of Orange in disguise! But there are similar passages, for example, in *La Chanson de Roland*, ed. G. Brault, student edn (University Park PA, 1984), laisses 46, ll. 605–8; 47, ll. 610–2. After Ganelon had sworn once on the relics in his sword, the Saracen king proffered to him a book of the 'lei' of Mohammed and Tervagant, and in laisse 48, another Saracen gives him a new sword. For 'loi' meaning religion, see Biller, '"Religion"'. In Iberia, the 'convivencia' must have raised such questions more frequently than elsewhere and perhaps dictated an easier acceptance of the words of people from the

noticed all concern Saracens. I know of no case in England or elsewhere of a Jew swearing on his faith in this way or giving faith with his right hand in the manner I have been discussing.[85] Nor do I know of any private citizen who adopted the procedure by which Jews were permitted to swear oaths before royal justices on their own Torah scrolls. There are, moreover, notably few occasions when a Christian gave his faith to a Jew. The only Yorkshire instance I have noticed is that of a minor baron called Amfrey de Chauncy, who 'affidavit' 'on my faith and charter' to Benedict and Josce of York just a few years before the dramatic events in London that led to Benedict's death.[86]

This evidence indicates a serious defect in the legal and everyday social capacity of English Jews to pursue their business activities with their Gentile neighbours. It would have been bad enough had this disability been confined to land transactions. But the *Dialogue of the Exchequer* (c. 1179) tells us enough about the device's frequent use in the king's financial business as to suggest that giving faith with one's hands was more widely used to seal all kinds of financial deals and even in such matters as the attempts lords made to hold their officials to the rules.[87]

The speculative edge to all this is undeniable. Let us build further upon it. If one goes back to reread standard chronicles and constitutional documents without the incubus of the belief that feudalism rules all, one may suspect that even in the higher reaches of political negotiation a reliance on trust conveyed through the giving of faith was not unknown.[88] Might it not

other two religions. D. Nirenberg, *Communities of Violence: Persecution of Minorities in the Middle Ages* (Princeton, 1996), p. 39 n. 72, mentions a confraternity of smiths in Segovia whose Christian and Muslim members swore their oaths to the patron saint, each on their own faiths.

[85] Yet Jews themselves used the hand-clasp, above at p. 139. This will have rendered their exclusion from making faith even more noticeable and annoying to them.

[86] *EYC* II, 841. Amfrey II de Chauncy came into his five-knight lordship before 1165 and was dead by 1190. He made a series of grants to religious houses, some of them related to his steadily increasing debts to Jews, *Early Yorkshire Families*, ed. Clay, p. 16; *EYC* II, 828, 831, 838–41. His friends appear to have tried to assist him. Thomas son of Richard acquitted him of 41 marks of Jewish debt 'super fidem meam', and arranged for him a settlement with St Peter's sealed by livery of seisin on the altar with an affidation and oath 'tactis sacrosanctis' there, *EYC* II, 841–4, mostly from the 1180s.

[87] *Dialogus de Scaccario*, pp. 10, 46, 80, 81, 113–4, 116–8. In a ducal grant of customs to Rouen, *Recueil des actes de Henri II*, ed. L. Delisle, 3 vols. (Paris, 1916–27), I, no. XIV, officials are to 'affidare'. *Glanvill* x.3 (117) says that a consumption loan can be made 'sub fidei interpositione'.

[88] When each free man is ordered to swear that: '*fidem portabit domino* Ricardo regi Angliae, filio domini regis Henrici, et dominae Alienor reginae, de vita et membris suis, et honore terreno, sicut ligio domino suo contra omnes homines et foeminas qui vivere possunt et mori et quod ei justitiabiles erunt, et auxilium ei praestabunt ad pacem et justitiam suam per omnia servandam', Howden, *Chronica* III, 5. The italicized words seem to me to be used in the same sense of firming up a promise as in the giving of faith. Cf. similarly *Glanvill* ix. 1 (104), where the notion of carrying or bearing faith is even more closely tied to what the textbooks deem to be homage and fealty.

be, therefore, that good Christians already in the later twelfth century felt a revulsion at the prospect of going through a ceremony of 'homage' and swearing an oath of fidelity to a Jew, or his representative, because of this question of faith?[89] I suggest that this emotional twist is likely to have proved at least as effective at moving opinion against the more friendly coexistence that Henry II is said to have favoured as the Church's remonstrations against the idea that Jews could be lords over Christians.

Even if issues of trust, and the vocabulary of Faith in which they were often couched, can be shown in this way to have been live already in the decades preceding the York tragedy, this does not of course supersede the various other factors previously adduced to explain the sharpening of community relations between the 'open' twelfth and the more 'closed' thirteenth centuries. But the addition of Faith to the mix does complicate the historian's task, and should compel some adjustments to our analysis. And should this view win acceptance for England, it will surely need investigation further afield, for the argument of this chapter rests in principle on a hypothesis about Ashkenaz as a whole, which the specialists will need to test for themselves.

But the reverberations may not stop there. Some very distinguished scholars have in recent years situated a 'crisis of truth' around 1200. Their arguments are based on setting the actions of the Lateran Council of 1215 that were designed to curtail the ordeal into a context of intellectual doubt in the schools and the subsequent wave of criticism that reached the highest circles of the Church to influence pope Innocent III.[90] They imply that the Lateran Council's action to restrain the use of ordeals resulted from mistrust not merely of the expectation that God would give His judgment through the ordeal, but of the prospects of human beings reaching truth at all in the difficult cases where the ordeal had seemed most useful. But truth as such looks to me no more at risk around 1200 than at any other time. It may seem so, because of the much larger volume of discussion of the issues by concerned writers from within and beyond the schools.[91] But disgruntled litigants had always railed against the system when it found against them.

---

89 This suggests that the terms 'fides' or 'fidelitas', which figure in descriptions of such oaths of fealty or fidelity, are perhaps used to denote a current strengthening of the promise when made than the long-term loyalty to which traditional accounts bind them. I hope to present more detailed argument for this case, expanding on the view of lordship custom presented in my 'Homage and Feudalism'.

90 The basic and strongest presentation of this view by J. W. Baldwin, 'The Intellectual Preparation for the Canon of 1215 against Ordeals', *Speculum* 36 (1961), 613–36, is very widely cited. S. D. White, 'Imaginary Justice: The End of the Ordeal and the Survival of the Duel', *Medieval Perspectives* 13 (1998), 32–55, presents a contrary view similar to the present one.

91 See Hyams, 'The Legal Revolution', pp. 43–65; P. Hyams, 'Trial by Ordeal: The Key to Proof in the Early Common Law', in *Of the Laws and Customs of England: Essays in Honor of Samuel E. Thorne*, ed. T. A. Green et al. (Chapel Hill, 1981), pp. 90–126, needs some adjustment to take account of recent literature, but I stand by its main contentions.

And more to the present point, the ecclesiastical intellectuals had long recognized that certain groups were less to be trusted than others, so that they required special attention to make them keep their word. Where the Vikings had once figured prominently, one found in the twelfth century heretics, Saracens, and of course Jews, who can often be identified by the 'perfidia' attributed to them.[92] We have already seen William of Newburgh illustrate this association of Jews with 'perfidia' as well as anyone. In its light, his account of the apostasy and demise of Benedict of York reads almost like an exemplum of why one cannot trust a Jew. William never doubted that Benedict had acknowledged Christ and received baptism only under compulsion and to 'put off death'.[93] He did this, says William, not at heart as a believer 'ad justiciam', but as one 'beating the air with a vacuous confession of the mouth alone'. Interviewed the next day, the new king asked him whether he was now a Christian, a question already indicative of doubt and suspicion. The dying Benedict answered that he had undergone a baptism forced by Christians, but (as William reports him) 'he always remained a Jew in his heart, and would have preferred to die as one, now that the wounds suffered on the previous day were driving him towards death, and he could live no longer'.

How Benedict might have expressed such thoughts in Hebrew is impossible to say. But it is a fair bet that the word 'emunah', faith in God, would have been part of his explanation, his dying confession of faith. Sarah Rees Jones describes elsewhere in this volume how the first known seal of the city of York found attached to a document dated between 1191 and 1206 bears a mysterious legend, sadly not quite complete. The full thought behind the words 'SIGILLUM CIVIUM CIVITATIS...FIDELES R...IS' is perhaps gone forever. Whatever it was, it almost certainly did not intend to include those Jews still resident in the city among the 'fideles'. Living within without being of the York community, they were set apart as unworthy of faith and trust, because their faith was different and so patently strange and inferior to that of the main body of citizens. I have shown here how real and all pervasive this gulf of faith was at the time, and suggested ways in which the gap is likely to have been widening.

---

[92] One illustration is the way Newburgh refers to Turks: WN, ed. Howlett, II, 328.
[93] ibid. II, 295, 299.

7

The 'Archa' System and its Legacy after 1194

Robin R. Mundill

On 17 March 1190, as the ash turned to dust at the top of the motte which is now known as Clifford's Tower, the government knew that it had lost control and would have to react to the spoliation of the York Jewry.[1] In the first case a riot had taken place and this did not please the new king, Richard I, and could not go unnoticed or unpunished. In the second case, because of the profits the crown drew from Jewish money lending, the government needed to put a system in place to protect its income from Jewish lending, particularly in York.[2] The unique solution to the latter marked a major step forward in the development of medieval commerce. The punishment came swiftly.[3]

The response to the second problem, that of protecting Jewish money lending, took the government a little longer to solve and, when it came, the repercussions were national rather than local. In September 1194, itinerant justices were sent around the country to reclaim and reorganize royal rights. Howden claimed that one of their briefs was to record in writing all lands, houses, rents and possessions of the Jews. They were also to provide six or seven places in which the Jews should deposit all their contracts and to appoint officials, two Jewish, two Christians and two scribes before whom all contracts were now to be made.[4] It is widely accepted that the *Ordinances of the Jewry* were the brainchild of Hubert Walter.[5] Walter's solution provided a closely scrutinized system of recording all Jewish business transactions which was run and administered by local official scriveners or notaries. From now on, all official business transactions between Christians and Jews were to be formally recorded on parchment and sealed.[6]

---

[1] Indeed the charred remains of the wooden fortress were found twelve feet underground by an excavation which took place in 1902–03. Dobson, *JMY*, p. 31. K. Jeffery, *Clifford's Tower and the Jews of Medieval York* (London, 1995).

[2] See Stacey in this volume.

[3] Dobson, *JMY*, p. 30.

[4] Howden, *Chronica* III, 266; *JAE Docs.*, pp.156–8.

[5] M. T. Clanchy, *From Memory to Written Record: England 1066–1307*, 2nd edn (Oxford, 1993), pp. 71, 103, 307; Dobson, *JMY*, pp. 28–30.

[6] For a discussion of sigillography and Jewish bonds see R. R. Mundill, *England's Jewish Solution: Experiment and Expulsion, 1262–1290* (Cambridge, 1998), pp. 217–19.

Such transactions were recorded by men of both Jewish and Christian faith. Hubert Walter's Ordinances added an early, local civil service to the administration of crown affairs.[7] If, in 1194, a system was created which at its height was to cover some twenty-six towns it required a small body of lay civil servants to administer them.[8] Over a century, these positions were the concern of a small but important group of citizens of the towns and cities of medieval England. As Dobson has noted for York, 'it may be significant that the two Christian chirographers were usually individuals who went on to become mayors, bailiffs or other office holders'.[9]

The appointment of a chirographer was the sheriff's responsibility. It was normally made by a jury consisting of six Christians and six Jews who then elected an office holder. The candidate had to find two pledges for the faithful performance of his duty. He then took an oath, probably in front of the sheriff. Clerks to the chest were appointed in the same way. There were at least two or three key holders for the chests.[10] Who exactly were the type of men who made up this small, élite group of officials, which, within the study of urban history, has tended to be ignored? A chirographer obviously had to be literate. The Christian chirographer was well versed in Latin and French; the Jewish chirographer probably had a smattering of legal Latin terms, spoke French and was able to write in Hebrew.[11] Whether Christians or Jews, they were obviously men who were prominent in their local community. They were to become a class of urban 'kulaks' responsible to the crown's representatives and dependent on government orders. They were men who had both local and national information at their beck and call; they were men with a degree of local power.

What exactly was their work? These men had total control of the local chest or 'archa'. They were the early archivists as we know them and their main duty was to keep a record of local business transactions. They could broker and discharge loans and might also be called upon to keep other forms of documents and pledges under their care.[12] They were clearly aware of the permitted interest rate for money lending, even of the types of articles that could be pledged as pawns and they would also be aware of the market prices of commodities, the silver content and state of the local coinage; they

---

7   *JAE Docs.*, pp. 156–9. Howden, *Chronica* III, 263.
8   V. D. Lipman, 'The Anatomy of Medieval Anglo-Jewry', *JHSE Transactions* 21 (1968 for 1962–67), 64–77 (pp. 65–6).
9   R. B. Dobson, 'The Decline and Expulsion of the Medieval Jews of York', *JHSE Transactions* 26 (1979 for 1974), 34-52 (p. 38).
10 R. R. Mundill, *The King's Jews: Money, Massacre and Exodus in Medieval England* (London, 2010), pp. 43–9.
11 P. Slavin, 'Hebrew Went Latin: Reflections of Latin Diplomatic Formulae and Terminology in Hebrew Private Deeds from Thirteenth-Century England', *Journal of Medieval Latin* 18 (2008), 306–25. For fuller discussion see Roth and Zadoff in this volume.
12 TNA E 101/249/10 shows that the chirographers kept details of different types of contract in the form of charters and tallies as well as agreements for annuities.

possibly even knew the royally appointed local minters who inscribed their name on each coin that was struck. The relationship between the Christian and Jewish officials must have provided a bridge between the communities. We know that business was often conducted in their own houses. As Vivian Lipman observed, they were used for a number of tasks.[13] Amongst other duties the chirographers were part of the mechanism in which the crown collected the Jewish tallages or taxes. Such was the case when, in 1269, John le Especer, chirographer of the York 'archa', made an oath to the Marshall of the Exchequer for £59 6s. 8d. of the tallage of the Jews of York.[14]

In the main, we know very little about these men although their names feature in the records. Vivian Lipman was able to construct a list of Norwich chirographers who were appointed between the 1220s and the 1280s. He found that the Jewish chirographers were important men of their community like Moses and Samuel, the sons of Isaac son of Jurnet, and Abraham son of Deulecresse, a Jew who dominated local transactions.[15] Amongst the eighteen Christian chirographers identified by Lipman, six were also bailiffs of Norwich and Robert of Coventry was a member of the town council.[16] In most towns they were clearly considered to have local importance. Canon Stokes drew attention to Josce son of Samuelotus, a Jewish chirographer in Cambridge whose 'archa' was moved in 1275 to Huntingdon by order of the queen mother who held the town as a dowry.[17] Josce was later appointed chirographer in Huntingdon and clearly used the 'archa' there to record his own business transactions. Eventually, Josce was able to get permission to live in Chesterton in order to supervise his property in Cambridge.[18] We also have a pretty complete set of names of the last serving officials from the towns which had 'archae' in 1290, as during the Expulsion they were charged with the final sealing of the 'archae' and, with the aid of the sheriff, of organizing the final removals of the 'archae' to Westminster before the Dissolution of the Jewries began. Over forty Christian officials are named on the list of twenty towns whose 'archae' made their last journey to Westminster.[19]

We know a little more detail of the types of duties these men undertook. There were times when they were asked to provide a full inventory of the

---

13 Lipman, *JMN*, p. 77.
14 *Medieval English Jews and Royal Officials: Entries of Jewish Interest in the English Memoranda Rolls, 1266–1293*, ed. Z. E. Rokéah (Jerusalem, 2000), p. 47.
15 The most recent assessment of Abraham son of Deulecresse's career is in R. R. Mundill, 'Edward I and the Final Phase of Anglo-Jewry', in *JMB*, ed. Skinner, pp. 55–83 (pp. 63–70).
16 Lipman, *JMN*, p. 77.
17 H. P. Stokes, *Studies in Anglo-Jewish History* (Edinburgh, 1913), pp. 190–2; Mundill, *King's Jews*, pp. 16–17.
18 Stokes, *Studies*, pp.190–2; TNA E 101/250/3; R. B. Dobson, 'The Jews of Medieval Cambridge', *JHS* 32 (1993 for 1990–2), 1–24 (pp. 18–20).
19 TNA E 101/249/29.

contents of their respective chests and to send these to Westminster.[20] There were other instances when they were given separate orders. Some indication of the routine business carried out by them is given by the Norwich Day Book, a set of four rolls which record the business transactions of the Norwich 'archa' from 1225 to 1227.[21] For the two-month period from February to March 1227, business was transacted every day of the week and may well have been at differing hours of the day, and four or five transactions were probably registered in a week. An extant roll from Norwich gives a daily breakdown for the period 11 December and 20 December 1224. During that time the chirographers, Geoffrey Edward, Simon Le Mercer, Moses son of Abraham Mocke and Meir son of Josce of Oxford handled about three or four transactions a day.[22] The chirographers, be they Christian or Jewish, were also men who probably conducted business of their own and saw their remit as an added responsibility to be carried out when necessary. When the creditor and debtor had come to an agreement it was required be made official. Both parties would arrive together at the 'archa' with chirographers present and the contract would be written up and then attested by witnesses, sealed and recorded. The whole process of writing up the contracts and attesting them could perhaps have taken as much as three quarters of an hour.

On some occasions, the 'archa' was opened for taking bonds out and notes were made of when exactly the chest had been opened. Debts were sometimes extracted from the chest, listed and sent to the Justices of the Jews in London.[23] On 11 November 1259, the Norwich chirographers, Roger of Tolhus, Nicholas of Burg, Abraham son of Deulecresse and Abraham son of Ursell of York, were ordered to send the debts of Jacob son of Fluria and his son Abraham to Westminster. On 18 February 1260 the 'archa' was again opened but, by this time, the Jewish chirographer, Abraham son of Ursell had been replaced by Abraham son of Isaac of Oxford.[24] Occasionally, bonds were misplaced or even registered in other 'archae'. On 20 November 1259, the Norwich chirographers were ordered to place two chirographs which had been found amongst the chattels of condemned Jews of Lincoln in the Norwich 'archa' where Abraham son of Deulecresse was to have free administration of them.[25]

We have some idea of the payment that chirographers received for actually drawing up the bonds. They were allowed to make a standard charge of 3d. for each bond; the two scribes were to receive 2d. and the keeper of the roll 1d. It seems they were also paid at other times. In December 1260, the king wrote to the Norwich chirographers and declared:

20 Mundill, *England's Jewish Solution*, pp. 205–6.
21 Lipman, *JMN*, pp. 84–9; WAM 6686, 6687, 6693, 9012.
22 WAM 6278; Lipman, *JMN*, pp. 226–7.
23 WAM 6983, 6997, 9006, 9009.
24 WAM 6689; Lipman, *JMN*, p. 279.
25 WAM 6906, Lipman, *JMN*, p. 282.

since it is the custom throughout the land of England, in whatever cities, boroughs or towns there are chirograph chests,
that the Jewish, as well as the Christian chirographers should
have their share of the pennies accruing on the removal of
chirographs and instruments from the 'archa' we order you
to allow Abraham of Saddlegate, son of Isaac of Oxford, who
holds a key of the chest his portion namely a quarter of all
pennies arising from the office of chirographer.[26]

The penalties for being involved with forgery or false charters were severe. In 1244, Hugh Le Brun was arrested with a false charter in Hereford. He claimed that he had been asked by Josce son of Aaron of Hereford, to go to the house of Thomas the chirographer and to make a false chirograph for £12 between Robert of the Berwe and Moses son of Abraham. Accompanied by Josce, Hugh went to the chirographer's house and then posed as Robert of the Berwe. When asked what he had been offered for his part in the forgery, Hugh replied that Josce had promised him a writ from the king for the withdrawal of one of his own debts from the Hereford chest. When Josce was examined he claimed that Moses had asked him to organize the forgery. Moses denied this. When Thomas the chirographer was examined, he claimed that Moses, Josce and Hugh came to his house but Moses left before the charter was made and that Josce and Hugh told him to make the charter and Josce even gave him the wax with which it was sealed. Hugh eventually acknowledged that he had made the charter. Both were sentenced to be hanged.[27]

Sometimes false accusations were made against the chirographers. Such was the case in 1274 in Exeter when Adam, the clerk of the chest, was arrested in a case brought by Hugh Fitchet. After the death of Hugh's father, Robert, Adam was accused of having fraudulently and maliciously written a charter for £80 between Robert and Salamon son of Salamon of Ilchester. An inquest was held in the presence of twelve Christians and eight Jews of the city of Exeter. The members claimed that the bond was good and lawful. They even swore that Robert Fitchet of Spaxton (some five miles west of Bridgewater and over forty miles north of Exeter) was at Exeter on the day the bond was dated because one of the members of the inquest claimed to have drunk with Robert after the bond had been deposited. In this particular case the clerk, Adam, was acquitted of the charge.[28]

The government kept a close eye on the actions of the chirographers. In 1271, the York chirographers incurred the wrath of central government. In mid-December, the sheriff of York, Roger Extraneus, was ordered to seize John

[26] WAM 6976; Lipman, *JMN*, p. 284.
[27] *CPREJ* I, 75.
[28] *CPREJ* II, 193–4; *Select Pleas, Starrs and Other Records from the Rolls of the Exchequer of the Jews, 1220–1284*, ed. J. M. Rigg, Selden Society 15 (London, 1902), pp. 83–4. Mundill, *England's Jewish Solution*, p. 214.

the Spicer, Stephen Sperry and all the Christian and Jewish chirographers who had held office from 1268 and to produce them at Westminster on 3 February 1273.[29] Some chirographers behaved illegally. In 1273, William of Tansterne and Walter of Ruddestan brought a writ against Jacob of the Cemetery and German of Luda, clerks of the York 'archa', for unlawfully accepting Hebrew 'starra' (quitclaims). It seems that at this point Jacob was also 'in mercy for other divers defaults'.[30] Certainly he was removed from office. Jacob appealed the decision when, later in the year, he gave five gold coins to the king to ask that the sheriff hold an enquiry by oath that he was fit for office and so be re-instated.[31] He clearly was not penalized, as in 1274, when an inquest was taken into properties in York which had been owned by Jews, he was mentioned and later that year he paid a fine of 13s. 4d. to keep a house in York which had belonged to Ursell, Fade Gendre, which the king had claimed as escheat.[32] It was not just the Jewish chirographers who were accused of unlawful practice. In 1275 William of Middelton of Sutfeud, William of Howden and Thomas Wycherche accused German of Luda, clerk of the York 'archa', of unlawfully holding back a 'starrum'. Again, in 1276, Robert of Cawode accused German of Luda of the same wrong-doing and the sheriff was ordered to seize him, but the writ came too late to be executed.[33]

Lesser malpractices were fined. In 1266, Henry III reproached three of the Norwich chirographers and fined them £10 for having disobeyed his command by putting in and removing charters from the 'archa' when the fourth chirographer, Simon of Paumer, had been captured and held in a raid by the 'Disinherited', rebels who terrorized the eastern counties during the civil war.[34] Norwich was perhaps relatively lucky to only have had a chirographer captured by this set of bandits. In other towns, groups of de Montfort supporters actually targeted and carried off the whole 'archa'.[35]

Much of the everyday business of the Nottingham chirographers can be gleaned from the lists of orders given to them. In February 1230, the sheriff was ordered to remove Manasser of Nottingham from office as he was considered unsuitable for the post. He was no longer allowed to hold a key to the 'archa'. The sheriff was also ordered to gather together 'upright Christians and Jews' to accept the oath of Manasser, the son-in-law of Ivette, that he 'will carry out that office and that all chirographs and tallies will be faithfully enrolled in their chest'.[36] Persistent orders concerning the taking out and putting in of chirographs and deeds came from Westminster. Some debtors had clearly

---

[29] *Medieval English Jews and Royal Officials*, ed. Rokéah, p. 110.
[30] *CPREJ* II, 89.
[31] *CPREJ* II, 89, 103
[32] *CPREJ* II, 156, 173.
[33] *CPREJ* III, 20, 156.
[34] WAM 6921; Lipman, *JMN*, pp. 296–7.
[35] Mundill, *King's Jews*, pp. 88–90.
[36] WAM 6889; *Medieval Jewish Documents in Westminster Abbey*, ed. A. Causton (London, 2007), p. 83.

taken to getting others to register their debts for them and this was henceforth forbidden – only the debtor to whom the debt was owed could now officially register transactions.[37] This was made clear in 1237 when the London chirographers were ordered that 'they should not replace any feet of chirographs in their chest unless in the presence of the Christian who has accepted the debt'.[38] Procedural instructions flew thick and fast. In the early 1230s, the officials were commanded not to replace any chirographs in their chest unless two Christian and Jewish chirographers were present and never to receive one unless from the hands of the debtor and they were to 'beware of leaving any chirograph out of the 'archa' for more than five days'.[39] There were also times when the officials were commanded to help sort out the estates of deceased lenders.[40] The officials were also ordered that they should not levy charges for replacing chirographs in the 'archa'.[41]

From time to time chirographers also received instructions from Jews or their agents. Sometime about 1250, David Lumbard wrote to his son, Moses, who lived in Nottingham, giving him instructions:

> May thy welfare increase son Moses, 'live long'. I am writing to inform thee that Nicholas of Wilton hath settled with all the Jews who shared his debts, and hath paid up the full sum. I desire thee therefore to deliver up to the bearer the three bonds and the corresponding indentures that are in the 'archa' – two of my own, and a third from Deulecresse for £2 13s. 4d. which thou wilt find amongst mine. Have thine eyes about thee, then and give them up to the person bearing this letter without delay, for so I have promised the Justiciars. There is no need for me to write more, excepting to wish thee peace, according to my desire – Father. Shew the chirographers this acquittance of Deulecresse and his instructions to withdraw the indenture from the 'archa'.

Although the bond had been deposited in Nottingham, it seems that Nicholas of Wilton paid David the money elsewhere. David's attorney or the bearer of the letter was entrusted to get Moses to secure the acquittal with the chirographers of Nottingham.[42]

There were times when Westminster thought that the system needed adjusting. In a detailed set of orders issued in Nottingham in 1241, follow-

---

37 WAM 9082.
38 WAM 6986.
39 WAM 9081.
40 WAM 9079.
41 WAM 9077.
42 WAM 6744. Printed in *Letters of Jews through the Ages, from Biblical Times to the Middle of the Eighteenth Century*, ed. F. Kohler, 2 vols. (London, 1952) 2, pp. 223–4.

ing on the great tallage of 1240, the sheriff was ordered to go to the 'archa' with four upright and lawful men of Nottingham and having broken the seals they were to list, separately and clearly, the witnessed feet of chirographs and chattels of each Jew. The instructions also stipulated that 'for the improvement of the realm and the suppression of the wickedness of the Jews … the Council and magnates demanded that new Christian and Jewish key holders be appointed'. From henceforth all bonds were to be made in the presence of the Christian borrowing the money and of the Jew lending it. The part of the agreement with the seal attached should be deposited in the 'archa' within ten days of the agreement being made, and, if delayed by a Christian chirographer, then a fine would ensue but, if delayed by a Jewish chirographer they would forfeit their goods. The debtor was to keep the top of the chirograph and the Jew the foot. The interest rate was now set at 2d. in £1 per week.[43] There were times when the officials received other orders which had been decided on elsewhere, as in late 1242, when Robert son of David of Calfhover wrote to say that he conceded to Moses son of David Lumbard that if any chirograph that had been made in his name in the borders of England was to be found in any chest after Michaelmas 1242 it was false and 'should be held for nothing'. For greater security he even added his seal.[44] The same Robert also sent a sealed writ to the Nottingham chirographers explaining that he had quitclaimed Deudon, a Jew, forever.[45]

The 'archae' needed to be under lock and key as the bonds and tallies themselves were not simply archival records; from the crown's point of view they could be used to raise revenue and to pay royal taxes. An 'archa' might simply be declared closed at any time and the bonds taken to Westminster.[46] The debts could then be called in and used by the crown. Alternatively, the crown could simply dip into the transactions in the 'archa' at will. Such was the case in 1246 when the Justices of the Jews in London sent twelve chirographs which were owed to Rachel, daughter of David Lumbard, to be replaced in the Nottingham 'archa' in order that they be repaid. The chirographers and the sheriff were told to 'arrest in any ways you know those debtors named in the chirographs'. The proceeds were to go towards the £12 which Rachel owed the king for her portion of the tallage of £4000.[47] In 1250, all tallies of Jews who had not paid their portion of the 1250 tallage were taken out of the 'archa' and sent to Westminster.[48]

---

43 WAM 9002. See also WAM 6719.
44 WAM 9113; *Medieval Jewish Documents*, ed. Causton, p. 88.
45 WAM 9112; *Medieval Jewish Documents*, ed. Causton, p. 89.
46 Mundill, *England's Jewish Solution*, pp. 150–3.
47 WAM 9080; Mundill, *England's Jewish Solution*, pp. 76–7; R. C. Stacey, 'Royal Taxation and the Social Structure of Medieval Anglo-Jewry: The Tallages of 1239-42,' *Hebrew Union College Annual* 56 (1985), 175-249.
48 WAM 6968; *Medieval Jewish Documents*, ed. Causton, p. 93.

Another part of the legacy of the 'archa' system can be evidenced by the deeds and contracts themselves which were kept under lock and key. Their different types show an important development in commercial transactions. As time went by many varied types of transactions were held in the 'archae'. In a broader sense the 'archa' became a legal repository.[49] It could contain Hebrew quitclaims or *starra*, mortgages, land deeds and conveyances, tallies, fee debts and bonds as well as commercial transactions.[50] These strong boxes became public treasuries and provided a safe haven for many types of local commercial transactions. Even before the 'archae' system was founded, Aaron of Lincoln had shown that diversity in financial dealings could lead to economic success by buying the debts of other Jews, lending both large and small sums, securing rent charges, pawn broking and even speculating in cereal crops.[51] Over the years that the 'archae' system existed it contained many different forms of agreements. New types of financial transactions were regularly developed and refined. One such development was the fee debt, a perpetual agreement to alienate or give the revenue from a portion of land in exchange for a cash advance.[52] Preferable to simply using the land as security, it was in effect an agreement for the creditor to buy an annual rent as part of their income.

By the 1260s some of the Jews' debtors were thus providing annual lump sums in return for cash in advance and these bonds were being sold on the open market. As early as June 1267, Robert Burnell invested in the growing market in fee debts when Master Elias Menahem granted him two yearly fees worth £31 'with the usuries and penalties'.[53] Some Jewish entrepreneurs seemed to specialize in fee debts. Between 1261 and 1262, Cresse son of Gente, a London Jew, made five agreements with Christians which were to yield him an annual income of £29. In return for an advance, William son of Stephen of Kineston (Nottingham) and John Meynel Scot of Leicestershire promised him £1 annually. Similar agreements for further unknown advances were made by Henry of Waltham in Sussex and Roger the Smith of Stratford in Middlesex. A higher payment of £6 per annum was agreed by Robert Hermer of Hancaster in Essex whilst Simon of Insula, a knight from Somerset, agreed to pay Cresse £20 per annum.[54] Thus, from five different cash advances, Cresse was to receive £29 annually – a good annual income when a knight might earn £55 or a stone mason £5 4s. 0d. per annum. As we have seen from Robert Burnell's investment these fee debts could be bought

---

49 Mundill, *King's Jews* pp. 21–42.
50 WAM 6106.
51 Mundill, *England's Jewish Solution*, pp. 108–45.
52 S. T. Lieberman, 'English Royal Policy towards the Jews' Debtors, 1227–1290' (unpublished PhD. dissertation, University of London, 1983), p. 53.
53 *CPR 1266–72*, p. 67. See dispute over one of these *CPREJ* I, 162. Burnell also bought up two debts owed to Jews Isaac de Provyns and Aaron de la Rye by Master John de la Lade deceased *CPR 1272–75*, p. 98; R. R. Mundill, 'Rabbi Elias Menahem: A Late Thirteenth-Century English Entrepreneur', *JHS* 34 (1994–96), 161–87 (p. 165).
54 TNA E 101/249/10.

or sold and thus a type of pyramid selling had started. Fee debts were finally banned in England in 1269.[55] In 1271, with a fairly forthright order, the king warned the sheriff of Essex and Hertfordshire, Walter of Essex, over the use of fee debts:

> We and our council issued an ordinance concerning those fees owed by Christians to Jews which were not given, sold, confirmed by us, nor enrolled in the rolls of the Justices of the Jews before the date of the said ordinance. We then ordered the chirographers of Colchester to produce such charters of fees to be dealt with by the Exchequer. The order was not implemented fully ... Inquire who the Christian and Jewish chirographers were on 13 January 1269, arrest them and have them before the Barons at Westminster on 13 April 1271 to answer us about this contempt and trespass .... if you do not execute this order in full we will act against you with severity. Bring this writ with you.[56]

A further legacy of the 'archa' system was the development of the commodity bond, particularly after the issue of the *Statute of the Jewry* in 1275. It is well documented that this Statute brought a major change in the way Jews could advance loans, a form of 'economic redirection'.[57] However, it was to lead to even tighter regulation, more use of the 'archae' and a growth in recording debts in general. In about 1279 Giovanni of Bologna, a notary on Archbishop Pecham's staff, made the observation that

> Italians, like cautious men, want to have a public instrument for practically every contract they enter into; but the English are just the opposite, and an instrument is very rarely asked for unless it is essential.[58]

As we have seen the deeds of the Jews of medieval England were the exception to the rule. Yet other lenders were also starting to enrol their loans and agreements and there had been a rise in what contractual details needed to be kept and written down. Such contracts were abundant in the late thirteenth century and were enrolled in a variety of places such as letter books,

---

[55] S. Cohen, 'Plea Rolls of the Exchequer of the Jews, Michaelmas 1277–Hilary 1279' (unpublished Ph.D. dissertation, University of London, 1951), p. xlviii.

[56] *Medieval English Jews and Royal Officials*, ed. Rokéah, pp. 71–2.

[57] Roth, *HJE*, pp. 70-3. For tables which illustrate the change in bonding preferences after 1275 see Mundill, *England's Jewish Solution*, pp. 108–45, tables on pp. 126–7; R. R. Mundill, 'Clandestine Crypto-Camouflaged Usurer or Legal Merchant? Edwardian Jewry, 1275–90', *Jewish Culture and History* 3 (2000), 73–97 (pp. 83, 85).

[58] Cited by Clanchy, *From Memory to Written Record*, p 52.

cartularies, the rolls of Chancery and the Jewish plea rolls. The London letter books of 1276 and 1284, show a significant rise in the number of English contracts between these dates.[59] Between, 1268 and 1292, Bishop Robert Burnell himself enrolled over 145 debts on the close roll, worth almost £5400.[60] Englishmen had begun to forget that their word was their bond and had started to secure their debts. Less than six years after Bologna's comment, there were for a brief period between 1285 and 1290 two different sets of registries for depositing and recording transactions – one for Jews and the other for Gentile merchants.[61]

The major legacy of Hubert Walter's original Jewish 'archae' system was the advent of Chancellor Robert Burnell's Christian registry system almost a century later. Before examining this, it is useful to delve a little deeper into the similarities between Jewish and Christian commercial contracts in the period 1275–90. In July 1283, a bond, which was made at Shrewsbury, was deposited in the 'archa' at Hereford for safe keeping. There it remained, presumably unpaid, until it was written down on a list of bonds which came into the king's hands in 1290.[62] This transaction can be cross-referenced by a more detailed entry on the plea roll of the Exchequer of the Jews which was then sitting in Shrewsbury in 1283. On 15 July 1283, Peter of Grenham came before the Exchequer of the Jews in Shrewsbury and recognized that he was bound to Isaac Le Eveske, a Jew of London, for eight sacks of wool at £6 13s. 4d. per sack to be delivered in two instalments in January and April 1284. If Peter could not deliver, it was agreed that the debt was to be raised on the security of his lands in Devonshire.[63] The consequences of such a penalty were possibly the sign of a desperate man. Peter of Grenham was indeed a man in financial difficulty and he borrowed again in 1285 from a Christian. In December 1285, possibly because of indebtedness, he granted away his manor of Oburnford, in Devonshire, to Sir Adam of Cretting.[64]

This method of making a formal recognition of debt was not so different from normal business practices in the Christian sphere of commercial activity. On 12 May 1287, the abbot of Meaux came before the Exchequer and formally recognized for himself, his convent and his successors, that he was bound to 'Ricardo' and 'Reynerio Guidicionis, Henrico of Podio, Thomasino Guidicionis', and their fellow merchants of Lucca, for eleven sacks of the

[59] W. R. Childs, *Anglo-Castilian Trade in the Later Middle Ages* (Manchester, 1978), p. 16.

[60] These are enrolled on the *CCR 1268–92* and are clearly not a complete sample of all Burnell's advances but serve to illustrate his involvement in 'low level' finance.

[61] R. R. Mundill, 'Christian and Jewish Lending Patterns and Financial Dealings during the Twelfth and Thirteenth Centuries', in *Credit and Debt in Medieval England c.1180–c.1350*, ed. N. J. Mayhew and P. R. Schofield (Oxford, 2002), 42–67 (pp. 52–3).

[62] TNA E 101/250/5.

[63] TNA E 9/43. The enrolment also records that a third part of the debt was owed to Josce son of Manser a prominent Hereford financier.

[64] C. Moor, *Knights of Edward I*, 5 vols., Harleian Society Publications 80–4 (London, 1929–32), II, 143; *CCR 1279–88*, pp.181–2.

better wool of his house. The wool was to be pressed and packed into round bales and weighed according to the ancient custom of the house and to be delivered to the merchants on 8 July 1289 in Hull. For this wool, the abbot acknowledged that he had received the full price of £10 per sack in advance. It was recorded that if the abbot could not deliver the wool to the merchants at the specified term, he agreed that the Exchequer might levy the wool or its value from the lands, tenements, goods and chattels of the house.[65] Although the Meaux transaction carries more detail and is contracting wool on a larger scale and probably of a higher quality, it is still secured by a prejudgement which offered recourse to its land and chattels in default of debt. Such a transaction offered a way of coping with default of repayment and from the creditor's point of view was a highly desirable inclusion. Thus, in the latter half of the thirteenth century, the 'archae' became even more important repositories for written contracts that kept the wheels of commerce turning.

There are also similarities to be drawn between Christian and Jewish agreements for grain. On 14 April 1275, the priory of Luffield in Buckinghamshire made an agreement with William of Plumpton, a clerk, that wheat received from him should be paid for on 17 June 'according to what a quarter of that wheat happened to be sold for in Towcester on three market days preceding the feast of St John the Baptist'.[66] Also in 1275, John of the Hethe of the parish of Laysters made a contract with Josce son of Manasser of Hereford. John promised to pay Josce sixty soams (horse loads) of 'good, dry and winnowed corn' or half a mark of silver for each soam. The grain was to be delivered to the Jew or to his attorney at his house in Hereford at Michaelmas 1275. The document was witnessed by the sheriff of Herefordshire and the bailiffs of Hereford.[67] It is also evident that, in 1277, Master Elias Menahem of London was contracting for wheat. Robert Springhald and Bartholomew Le Cryur, his son, were in debt to Master Elias for seventy quarters of 'good, dry and pure wheat', which were payable to any merchant according to the measurement of the queen's bushel. The delivery or consignment of grain was to be made to Elias or his attorney at his house in London.[68]

The development of such commercial transactions was the prelude to the development of the recognisance. Long ago, Michael Postan defined the recognisance as a prejudgement of a broken contract.[69] Such binding agreements made it even more important for creditor and debtor to record their transactions. The later Edwardian Jewish bonds were distant cous-

---

65 TNA E 159/60, rot. 18, 12 May 1287; *Advance Contracts for the Sale of Wool c. 1200–c. 1327*, ed. A. R. Bell et al. (Kew, 2006), p. 5.
66 Britnell, *Commercialisation*, p. 100.
67 R. R. Mundill, 'Anglo-Jewry under Edward I: Credit Agents and their Clients', *JHS* 31 (1990), 1–21; Hereford, Herefordshire Record Office, MS AH81/34.
68 *CPREJ*, III, pp. 309–10.
69 M. M. Postan, 'Private Financial Instruments in Medieval England', *Vierteljahrschrift fur Sozial und Wirtschaftsgeschichte* 23 (1930), 26–75 (p. 35); Mundill, 'Lending Patterns', p. 50.

ins to the Christian recognisance. In the case of default of debt, the action which a recognisance allowed was eminently desirable by the creditor and gave them security. It became easier for purposes of economic security to make or recognise a prejudgement and thus a conviction for debt so that, in case of default, the debt could still be collected. Such commercial advances led to the 'archae' system being copied in its entirety by Edward I's chancellor, Robert Burnell.

There was a growing need for aiding Christians who were owed debts.[70] The 145 debts or recognisances owed to Robert Burnell are merely one instance. The close rolls also reveal that immediate members of Robert Burnell's family such as his nephew William, dean of Wells; Philip, his brother; Richard Burnell and Sir Hugh Burnell of Shropshire had also enrolled their debts.[71] Members of the bishop's entourage and household included his attorney, William of Hamelton, archdeacon of York, and even his own cook also recorded their business. Similarly, many of the royal Exchequer clerks who came into everyday contact with Burnell, such as Thomas of Louth, William of Middleton, Hugh of Kendal and Henry Lenn, recorded their own transactions on the close rolls.[72]

Burnell had learned much from the activities of Jewish and Italian moneylenders. His connection with the Jews was a strong one; he certainly knew or had met many of the leading Jewish London financiers. Burnell was present when in August 1272 Master Elias Menahem and Floria his wife came into the Exchequer and, before the bishop and others, quitclaimed William of Hecham, knight of Suffolk, of a debt of £70.[73] In 1273, Burnell was used as an agent by Benedict of Winchester for the Jew's tallage payment which was secured by a promise of monies to help maintain Winchester castle.[74] In 1275, Hagin of Lincoln made a *starrum* in front of the bishop. In 1276 Burnell was granted a licence to buy a debt which was owed to Isaac of Provincia for £20 which was owed to him by John of Lade.[75] Later in the same year 'when Burnell had retired from court' he personally acknowledged twenty-two Jewish *starra* whilst he was staying at Beaulieu.[76] Indeed, the relationship between Burnell and Master Elias Menahem was so strong that the latter applied directly to the chancellor for permission to have safe passage to go to France to treat the Count of Flanders, Jean d'Avesnes, for a malady which could not

[70] Much of what follows comes from an unpublished paper 'Bishop Burnell and Big Bang in the Thirteenth Century' given at the International Medieval Conference, Leeds, 2007.
[71] *The Visitation of Shropshire, taken in the year 1623*, ed. G. Grazebrook and J. P. Rylands, 2 vols., Harleian Society Publications 28 and 29 (London, 1889), I, pp. 92–3; *CCR 1279–88*, pp. 131, 305, 387.
[72] *CCR 1279–88*, pp. 131, 305, 525; *CCR 1288–96*, pp. 118, 204, 248, 314, 414, 418, 472, 483; Mundill, 'Anglo-Jewry under Edward I', pp. 1–21.
[73] *Medieval English Jews and Royal Officials*, ed. Rokéah, p. 100.
[74] ibid., p. 111.
[75] *CPR 1272–81*, p. 142.
[76] *CPREJ* III, pp. 141–6. Burnell retired from court on 7 September 1276, *CPR 1272–81*, p. 160.

be treated locally.[77] Finally, in 1286, when Master Elias had died, the Exchequer was ordered to cancel some old debts owed by Richard of Coleworth to Robert Burnell and his brother Hugh who were now tenants of the deceased Richard of Coleworth's lands in Essex.[78]

In October 1283, Burnell entertained Edward I and the royal court at his manor of Acton Burnell in Shropshire. Amongst the festivities which accompanied the royal visit, the Statute of Acton Burnell was passed; it was amended by the Statute of Merchants two years later.[79] These statutes opened the doors for both overseas and native merchants to enrol their debts in state registries. They represented a radical change to money lending as they legitimized and gave new protection for reclaiming debts and provided a mechanism for prosecuting defaulting debtors. Burnell's system was to produce a legal recognisance with 'vicious teeth', as Richard Bowers has put it.[80] In his enactments Burnell provided a secure method of lending for Christians. The creditor now knew that there was more chance of reclaiming unpaid debts if a debtor failed. He also provided a system for safely recording such transactions.[81] The 1283 Statute set up several centres for the registration of debts at London, York and Bristol; and its re-enactment in 1285 extended this to Newcastle, Lincoln, Nottingham, Northampton, Shrewsbury, Exeter, Southampton, Norwich and Canterbury.[82] With the exception of Newcastle and Shrewsbury, these centres also had Jewish 'archae' with officials for recording Jewish debts. Burnell now appointed officials to keep rolls of debts and to produce 'lettres de obligaciun' or Certificates of Statute Staple affixed with both the seal of the debtor and the royal seal.[83] This new system did not however apply to Jews who were to continue to use the 'archae' and the Exchequer of the Jews to reclaim their debts which they continued to do until their expulsion in 1290.[84]

Thus the legacy of the 'archae' after 1194 can partially be seen in the development of a new type of lay civil service in the provincial towns of England in the personnel, who for just under a century, worked as guardians of the chests. These public notaries, both Christian and Jewish, were more liter-

[77] Mundill, 'Elias Menahem', p. 170.

[78] ibid., p. 173.

[79] T. F. T. Plucknett, *Legislation of Edward I* (Oxford, 1949), pp. 138–147; *Statutes of the Realm*, I, 53–4, 98–100.

[80] R. H. Bowers, 'From Rolls to Riches: King's Clerks and Money Lending in Thirteenth-Century England', *Speculum* 58 (1983), 60–71 (p. 63). Bowers also notes that it provided a system for recording the transaction as well as immediate recourse backed by the weight of the Exchequer and debt collectors.

[81] ibid., p. 63; J. Kermode, *Medieval Merchants: York, Beverley and Hull in the Later Middle Ages* (Cambridge, 1998), p. 238.

[82] *Statutes of the Realm*, I, pp. 53–4, 100; Plucknett, *Legislation of Ed. I*, pp. 139–48.

[83] ibid., p. 140; C. McNall, 'Some Aspects of the Business of Statutory Debt Registries, 1283–1307', in *Credit and Debt in Medieval England c.1180–c.1350*, ed. P. R. Schofield and N. J. Mayhew, pp. 68–88 (pp. 68–9).

[84] Mundill, *England's Jewish Solution*, pp. 121–2.

ate than their fellow townsmen and were not from the ranks of the clergy. The legacy of the 'archae' can also be measured by the subtle changes of the range, type and development of written contracts and other devices which were deposited in the 'archae' between 1194 and 1290. A further legacy was the recognisance or 'letter de obligacioun' and the system copied by Robert Burnell when he rolled out his debt registries for recording certificates of Statute Staple at Acton Burnell.[85] The legacy of the recognisance or the promise or contract secured on lands and chattels survived through the centuries. It was even transmitted across the Atlantic to America as a type of bail bond.[86]

What was a new departure in 1194 - the innovation of the 'archae' system - has influenced modern society in many ways. It may even have been a larger catalyst in the development of commerce than has hitherto been acknowledged. In some ways what stemmed from the massacre of 'Shabbat ha-Gadol' in 1190 has touched all of our lives in one way or another. 'My word is my bond', 'I promise to pay' and indeed the soon-to-disappear cheque all have some of their origins in the ash and dust of the York massacre in March 1190.

---

[85] Mundill, 'Lending Patterns', pp. 52–4.
[86] J. Chipp, 'Recognizance for Solomon Gidney, 1828', New Paltz, Ulster County, New York. http://www.co.ulster.ny.us/archives/documents/recog.html [accessed 12 April 2012].

8

Making agreements, with or without Jews, in Medieval England and Normandy

Thomas Roche

The abbey of Flaxley, or Dene, in Gloucestershire, was a small Cistercian house, founded between 1148 and 1154 by the earl of Hereford, on the exact place where his father had died while hunting. Its historian would be short on records: a handful of charters, a few references in royal records, and one cartulary, written in the early thirteenth century, peculiar in its form. It is a roll, measuring 0.18 by 6.3 metres, recording ninety-seven items. This document provides a list of books preserved in the abbey's library, and it has been well studied.[1]

The first student of the roll was Sir Thomas Phillips, who described it to the Royal Society of Literature, transcribed it and published a few charters.[2] The cartulary was later edited by A. Crawley-Boevey, whose family had bought the remains of the abbey, from Phillips's transcripts.[3] The original roll seemed to have disappeared at the time, but it was rediscovered in Phillips's papers and eventually acquired by the British Museum. It is now kept at the British Library under the shelfmark Additional Manuscript 49996.[4]

The term 'cartulary' could be misleading. At first sight, we do not find in this roll what we could expect from a twelfth-century Cistercian cartulary. The house was only fifty years old at the time of its writing, yet no narrative or transcription of the charter of foundation can be found therein. It looks actually rather like a management roll: it opens with lists of rents, referencing some of the charters transcribed later on. The deeds are rarely dated, but clues narrow the chronological span to the years from the 1180s to the 1200s.

In his short notice, Phillips did mention the occurrence of an unfamiliar formula: three charters from the abbot are said 'not to have been sealed,

---

1 D. N. Bell, 'The Books of Flaxley Abbey', *Analecta Cisterciensia* 43 (1987), 92–110.
2 T. Phillips, 'On the Cartulary of Flaxley Abbey, in Gloucestershire', *Transactions of the Royal Society of Literature of the United Kingdom* 1 (1829), 53–6.
3 *The Cartulary and Historical Notes of the Cistercian Abbey of Flaxley*, ed. A. W. Crawley-Boevey (Exeter, 1887).
4 G. R. C. Davis, *Medieval Cartularies of Great Britain: A Short Catalogue* (London, 1958), no. 407.

because of the perfidy of the Jews'. The wording is indeed uncommon: no other instance could be found, for example, in the diplomatic databases such as DEEDS or CBMA.[5]

What did it mean? Did the abbot fear – or wish to spread the idea – that Jews could have used his seal to forge bonds? Could the phrase mean that the matrix had been pawned to a Jewish moneylender, thus making it impossible to seal charters?[6] Phillips provided no explanation, but pointed to the connection between the violence, whether verbal or physical, against Jews and the fear of the misuse of the written word: the York massacre, to which he alluded, is a good example. Is the Flaxley formula only a 'hapax', or did it echo common contemporary patterns of thought? A clear answer is difficult to reach, but I will use this case to investigate three issues; the use and value of seals in transactions, the notion of 'perfidia' in charter-drafting and agreement-making, and the accusation of tampering with seals and documents.

The Credit of Seals

The growing use of seals, especially in the twelfth century, is a traditional topic in diplomatics, and so is its significance in cultural history.[7] As to the legal connection of sealed documents and financial transaction, the recent survey by

---

5   University of Toronto, 'Documents of Early England Data Set (DEEDS) Research Project'. http://res.deeds.utoronto.ca:49838/research/ [accessed April 2012]; *Centre national de la recherche scientifique*, 'Chartae Burgundiae Medii Aevi Project'. http://www.artehis-cbma.eu/La-base-de-donnees-CBMA [accessed April 2012].
6   Paul Hyams suggested this hypothesis in discussion at the York conference. The evidence is unclear. Of the charters transcribed in the roll, twelve, undated, were written in the name of the abbot only (and not the community): two for Abbot Alan (elected 1187), nine for Abbot Richard (attested *c.* 1200), one for an Abbot 'R'. The 'perfidia' formula can be found in three of Richard's charters, but his other six did not mention any sealing; five of his nine charters, including the three 'perfidia' documents, mentioned their drafting as a chirograph. There is nothing to distinguish the three 'perfidia' charters: the other charters dealt with similar matters (grants, sometimes in fee, with homage). This is all the more strange, since Alan's charters did mention their sealing. The charter by Abbot 'R' follows a distinctive style and so cannot be securely attributed to our abbot Richard; it mentioned its sealing. The only conclusion that can be drawn is that the formula on sealing was not part of the standard style Richard followed. Yet a chirograph (dated 1195, so very likely from Richard's rule) explicitly mentioned a seal on the monks' behalf. The abbot might not have used the convent's seal for the charters written in his own name; did he have a distinctive seal? If so, which would seem likely by 1200, then Hyams' hypothesis would be consistent with the simultaneous use of two matrices, one for the abbey, the other for the abbot; the latter could have been temporarily pawned. In the case of the land of Ragel, discussed below, the monks were able to raise a huge amount of money to pay off a layman's debt. This might cast doubt on the idea that the abbot had been reduced to pawn his matrix; on the other hand, the pawn could explain where so much cash came from.
7   M. T. Clanchy, *From Memory to Written Record: England 1066–1307*, 2nd edn (Oxford, 1993), pp. 51, 310–17; R.-H. Bautier, 'Le cheminement du sceau et de la bulle', *Revue française d'héraldique et de sigillographie* 54–59 (1984–89), 41–84.

Paul Brand about law and credit is useful.[8] The treatise commonly called *Glanvill* stressed the value of the written word, which is the most secure means to enforce debt obligation, compared with a mere oral transaction. But the seal is the key to the validity of a written bond. If the debtor denied the genuineness of the bond, but not of the seal, his cause would be lost. He had to deny the authenticity of both text and seal to have them tested, that means the alleged forged seal would be compared with others, or to prove his right by battle. The legal value of the seal in this matter resonates with the fear of its misuse.

Yet if we sum up studies on the use of seals by Jews, two points can be made. First, that Jews themselves had seals. They have been studied, in the case of France, by Brigitte Bedos-Rezak.[9] Her conclusion is that even if they use Hebraic characters and iconography, they have no other distinctive elements. Normandy (and, by extension, England) are an exception, in that seals are bilingual there. An explanation could be that they are more often, if not always, used externally to the Jewish community. Second, the end of the twelfth century witnessed the fact that, from a legal point of view, the use of seals by Jews and, more generally speaking, the drafting and keeping of credit records, was becoming more and more shaped by royal legislation. In France an order of Philip Augustus, which may date from 1219, ruled that in each major city two designated citizens were to keep the matrix of a special seal meant to be used with bonds involving Jews. It showed the legend 'SIGILLUM JUDÆORUM' and a Star of David. A roll should also be kept to record these transactions.[10] In England, a similar practical attention to the legal framework of dealing with Jews led to the development of the 'archae' system. Bonds were drafted as bipartite chirographs. The creditor was to have one half, the other being kept in a public chest, whose three keys were to be held respectively by a royal officer, a deputy of the Jews and a Christian deputy. Also, a list of all chirographs was to be made.

In the 1190s, had what *Glanvill* reported as legal practice effectively found its way into the habits of making bonds? At first sight, actual cases tend to support a positive answer. The fact that credit transactions are recorded on sealed documents was stressed. A common formulation of a bond is the notification that the debtor would pay his due to anybody that would present him with the sealed charter itself. That is indeed for instance the formula used in 1205 in an agreement made between Miles de Bray and Leo of York to settle the debt of the former's father.[11]

---

8   P. Brand, 'Aspects of the Law of Debt, 1189–1307', in *Credit and Debt in Medieval England, c.1180–c.1350*, ed. P. R. Schofield and N. J. Mayhew (Oxford, 2002), pp. 19–41.

9   B. Bedos-Rezak, 'Les sceaux juifs français', in *Art et Archéologie des Juifs en France médiévale*, ed. B. Blumenkranz (Toulouse, 1980), pp. 207–28.

10 E. Castaigne, 'Note sur le sceau que l'on apposait du temps du roi Philippe Auguste sur les obligations dues aux Juifs', *Bulletin de la Société Archéologique et Historique de la Charente* (1863), 53–8.

11 *Early Charters of the Augustinian Canons of Waltham Abbey, Essex (1062–1230)*, ed. R. Ransford (Woodbridge, 1989), no. 239.

Supporting this, charters of quittance by Jewish creditors stress that even a sealed document would have no value in the future. A chirograph recording a quittance of Abraham son of Moses to the abbot and monks of Gloucester explains that neither any heir to Abraham, nor anyone else, could in the future claim anything on the abbey's debt, even if providing a sealed charter as proof.[12] A Norman document, involving Samuel son of Abraham, as creditor, and Ralph Taisson, as debtor, included a similar clause.[13] The Gloucester charter had probably been sealed by Abraham (who introduced himself in the text as 'I, whose seal is below'). A chirograph between William the Cooper and Isaac son of Moses of Winchester included a formula of sealing; if the seal is not extant, the fact that William did have a seal is well attested by contemporary documents.[14] But the evidence for systematic sealing is not clear. The group of charters recording the arrangements between the Wanchy family and their Jewish creditors included no mention of seal, but, as they are only known by a later cartulary copy, the fact is not conclusive.[15] Nevertheless, the Norman document is only signed by Samuel, and then sealed with the seal of the City of Rouen. Is this practice a Norman version of the 'archae' system? Or an indication that a signature, even written in Hebraic letters, had more weight than a seal, when it comes from a Jew?

Moreover, an interesting case mentioned by Michael Clanchy shows that the value of a seal can be contested in a peculiar way. Sewal son of William de Spineto contested a bond against Samuel son of Aaron of Colchester. He expressed his doubts on the genuineness of the seal – just as explained in *Glanvill*. However, Samuel answered that the handwriting of the chirographer was easily recognizable, and that no suspicion could then be thrown on the validity of the text.[16]

We may not draw hasty conclusions from this case, but, nevertheless, this attention to the materiality, and to the personal character, of handwriting, from a Jew, does echo Bedos-Rezak's thought that medieval Jews shared a more intimate knowledge and use of the written word than Christians.[17]

[12] *The Original Acta of St Peter's Abbey, Gloucester, c. 1122 to 1263*, ed. R. B. Patterson (Gloucester, 1998), no. 243.

[13] N. Golb, *The Jews in Medieval Normandy: A Social and Intellectual History* (Cambridge, 1998), p. 376 (facsimile), from an original formerly kept in the Archives départementales of Manche and destroyed in 1944. This was according to Golb the only then extant original of a Jewish Norman charter.

[14] *A Cartulary of the Hospital of St John the Baptist*, ed. H. E. Salter, 3 vols., Oxford Historical Society 66, 68–9 (Oxford, 1914–17), III, no. 352; compare with no. 351, a grant of land which is sealed by William.

[15] *Charters Waltham Abbey*, nos. 356, 357, 359; there is similarly no mention of sealing in no. 603, a transaction between Robert Benne and Jurnet of London.

[16] Clanchy, *From Memory to Written Record*, p. 307.

[17] B. Bedos-Rezak, 'Les Juifs et l'écrit dans la mentalité eschatologique du Moyen Age chrétien occidental (France, 1000–1200)', *Annales* Économies. Sociétés. Civilisations. *HSS* 49 (1994), 1049–63.

Agreeing, with Trust

On the one hand, analysis of theological sources has clarified the use of the word 'perfidia'. According to Blumenkranz, for example, the term conveys two meanings: it is the fact of not being faithful, or of refusing faith, even persecuting because of it.[18] However, the word is uncommon in diplomatic documents. The Flaxley charters are the only ones to associate 'perfidia' with the Jews, generally speaking. Indeed, in formulas of malediction, frequently used in the eleventh and the first half of the twelfth century, 'perfidia' qualifies only certain Jews, such as Judas, Dathan or Abiron.[19]

If rarely used, 'perfidia' nevertheless echoes 'fides' and 'fidelitas', the trust and faith on which agreements and transactions were built at that time.[20] It is indeed now commonly held by medievalists that there is more in the written word than just the written word, and that every charter is part of a broader social process, of a 'conventio', as Paul Hyams suggested.[21] Yet studies have focused mainly on specific transactions, especially gifts. The recourse to anthropological models has helped to provide new analysis of the process of donation to monasteries. Charters there are just tokens in a complex relationship between the donor, the monks, their saint, and God himself, a relationship enlightened by 'caritas', the divine love between Christians, and highly ritualized. But donation is not the only social process we can study, though it is the one on which historians have focused, and might be seen as a 'rather special kind' of transaction.[22]

But if any charter is to be regarded as a 'conventio', then what are we to understand of charters that labelled themselves conventions, as was the case of those recording credit arrangements? They are often put aside in legal or diplomatic studies, because of their peculiarity. They did not fit any established diplomatic form, and are usually labelled as 'miscellaneous documents' in introductions to editions of cartularies.[23] Since they do not illustrate a particular facet of legal development, clearer, simpler documents on specific legal actions get the attention of legal historians. Eventually, the complexity of the transactions they record, and the variety of gestures or rituals they report mean that they cannot be analysed as a whole, according to a simple sociological model. Yet, they open a unique window into rela-

---

[18] B. Blumenkranz, 'Perfidia', *Archivium Latinitatis Medii Aevi, Bulletin Du Cange* 22 (1952), 157–70.

[19] L. K. Little, *Benedictine Maledictions: Liturgical Cursing in Romanesque France* (Ithaca NY, 1993).

[20] Hyams in this volume.

[21] P. Hyams, 'The Charter as a Source for the Early Common Law', *Journal of Legal History* 12 (1991), 173–89 (p. 174).

[22] ibid., p. 176, warning against the 'distorting lens' of the grant in alms.

[23] 'There is the inevitable class of miscellanea not fitting into any of the above [categories]. These are not amendable to diplomatic generalisation'; *Leiston Abbey Cartulary and Butley Priory Charters*, ed. R. Mortimer, Suffolk Charters 1 (Woodbridge, 1979), p. 39.

tions between the written word and the social processes of documents while being a part of an ordinary, 'low-scale', preventive legal practice.

Let us take an example, far from credit business, but from South Yorkshire, an agreement made in 1161 between the Norman monks of Saint-Wandrille, who possessed a priory at Ecclesfield, and Richard of Louvetot.[24] Diplomatically, it is a notice, opening with an invocation then the formula 'Hec est conventio (inter A et B)', that is quite usual in such documents though not in the formulary of final concords. It is a chirograph, unsurprisingly as it records mutual obligations and promises – this feature is not systematic though. It also includes long and detailed witness-lists, distinct for each party: agreements involved more than the two main actors, as they acted as part of a 'small world', but their witnesses should not be seen as their supporters so much as possible negotiators and sponsors of the compromise.

The agreement records several legal actions; a division of lands, the grant of a tithe, the assertion of mutual rights on wood use. But these operations are part of a multifaceted transaction which aims at dealing with an uncertain and hazardous situation, by clarifying the norms to be followed, by adjusting the status of partners, in order to prevent any future conflict. In our case, uncertainty had arisen from the clearance, by fire, of woods at Ecclesfield, on the road from Sheffield to Blackburn. The respective rights of the monks and Richard on these woods were settled 'from all antiquity' (actually, only for one generation, in all likelihood), but how to deal with the new situation? The clear ground was divided between the two lords; a still extant wood kept its shared status, and its use was regulated. Furthermore, Richard gave to the priory the tithe of his hunts in Hallamshire.

But what made the agreement was also the rituals employed to enforce it. They are not easy to apprehend because the charter is both a part of this process and our only source to document it. Indeed, the drafting and the validation of the written 'conventio' are part of a broader process. The detailed boundary clause in the Ecclesfield agreement is probably the trace left by the performance of a 'perambulatio', an inquest on the ground by representatives of the local community, of the 'small world' of the place. But the gestures related to the written word, here the apposition of 'signa' (but that could apply to sealing) and the division of the chirograph, are also devices of trust, as well as the public performance of a whole range of rituals; homage, kiss of peace etc., or the 'affidatio', the proclamation of mutual trust. 'Affidatio', in all its variations, as it could be given from either of the two parties to the other, as was most common, or from one of the two parties to a third person, usually invested with public authority, a prelate, a magnate or a royal officer; or from the sureties of one party to the other or to the third person. Even if commonly used, even if the gesture of 'affidatio'

---

24 *EYC* III, no. 1268; see also T. Roche, '"Des conventions infiniment variées": normes et coutumes dans les concordes des moines de Saint-Wandrille (XIe–XIIe siècles)', in *Coutumes, doctrine et droit savant*, ed. V. Gazeau and J.-M. Augustin (Poitiers, 2007), pp. 13–42.

was as simple as shaking hands, the religious aspect of these devices of trust cannot be ignored. Even the slightest detail could be significant, such as the choice of payment terms.[25] Moreover, the theatre of these ceremonies is usually a church or its vicinity, after mass or on a feast day, on days of social gatherings.

Such agreements are 'concordie', they are instances of concord, the social harmony brought about by divine love in a Christian society. By diplomatic devices of validation, and by sworn promises and performance of rituals, trust and faith have been settled in them. Indeed Frederic Cheyette has proposed to give up the phrase 'feudal society' and to promote rather the notion of 'oath society' as the notion to highlight is no longer the fee, but the issue of swearing and trusting.[26] Nevertheless, neither the witnesses nor the parties were naïve. Even if the text of an agreement stressed that all tokens of concord were given, they knew that it was meant to be temporary. It could prevent conflicts born out of uncertainty, but not suppress them. Any change regarding the parties, the object of the arrangement, or its context would bring the necessity of a new agreement, even if it could largely draw on its predecessor.

Credit transactions, if simpler than most agreements, were played according to the same rules. They were not only a financial operation, with money at stake, but also a social, normative and ritual building one. Social, as they involved two partners, who could not be but parts of a 'small world', itself permeated by public institutions. Normative, as they used a grammar of clauses to deal with hypotheses and promises. Ritual, eventually, because the agreement came not so much from the common will of both parties as from the shared value of 'concordia', expressed in gestures and words.

So could Jews fit in this picture? Could 'perfidious' Jews (as they would appear not only to the reader of the Flaxley roll, but more generally to the audience of contemporary liturgies) join in an agreement based upon mutual trust and faith? The issue is indeed not only a technical matter on the way of taking oath, but a cultural one.

Most charters recording credit transactions demonstrate no suspicion towards Jews. 'Affidatio' is used, whether from a Christian borrower or from his pledge, to the Jewish moneylender, with no apparent uneasiness.[27] Moreover, what appeared in documents was rather a mirrored exchange of

---

[25] For instance the feast of St Modwenna at Burton Abbey (Geoffrey of Burton, *Life and Miracles of St Modwenna*, ed. R. Bartlett (Oxford, 2002), app., no. 3), of St Edmund at Eye Priory (*Eye Priory Cartulary and Charters*, ed. V. Brown, 2 vols., Suffolk Charters 12–13 (Woodbridge, 1992), I, no. 89), or of St Wandrille in the Norman abbey of the same name (F. Lot, *Études critiques sur l'abbaye de Saint-Wandrille* (Paris, 1913), nos. 68. 82).

[26] F. L. Cheyette, *Ermengard of Narbonne and the World of the Troubadours* (Ithaca NY, 2001).

[27] 'Affidatio' of the pledger: *Charters Waltham Abbey*, nos. 239, 356, 357, 359, 603; *Cartulary Hosp. S. John*, no. 352; Richardson, *EJ*, app. 3, nos 3, 4. 'Affidatio' of the pledge: ibid., app. 3, nos 1, 2, 5, 6, 8, 9; also app. 4 (1183). Another charter records the 'affidatio' of both the borrower and his pledge: ibid., app. 3, no. 11.

trust. Indeed, when a Christian borrowed from a Jew, the bond was drafted as an agreement: the word 'conventio' could be used,[28] there were gestures of 'affidatio', terms of payment were given according to the Christian calendar. The charter was validated with a seal,[29] or as a chirograph. They did not diverge from bonds between Christians.[30] But when a Jew quitclaimed a debt a Christian owed, the charter of quittance used distinctive formulas recording the end of 'all debts since the creation of the world to today',[31] or in other words their quittance 'until the end of the world';[32] names of months were given in their Hebraic form;[33] the creditor signed using the Hebraic alphabet,[34] but this validation could be supported by a 'standard' confirmation by seal or chirograph.

Trust was established in both cases because each partner provided tokens of his own involvement in the transaction, tokens the other *could* receive. I would say that in the case of Jews, indeed we rather deal with 'hybrid' trust and 'hybrid' diplomatics: quittances are not given in Hebrew, but in a Latin coined to sound like Hebrew. This did not prevent Jewish moneylenders, for practical reasons, from endorsing and annotating their bonds in Hebrew.[35] Moreover, even if there was a gap between Christian and Jewish notions of trust as faith, they nevertheless shared common devices of trust when it came to the validation of a charter. Jewish diplomatic was a real part of English diplomatic. Jews were not outsiders, but insiders regarding the use of written word and its trust as validity.

Cistercian Perfidies

Did the abbot of Flaxley fear that Jews might forge charters with his seal? He did not explicitly accuse them. Yet monks were accustomed to argue against the validity of their opponents' charters, and forgery was, for them, an old

---

28 *Charters Waltham Abbey*, nos 239, 356 labelled themselves 'conventio', nos. 356, 357 *pactum*. Richardson, *EJ*, app. 3, nos. 9, 10; and app. 4, are named 'conventio'.

29 Whether by the borrower (*Cartulary Hosp. S. John*, no. 352; Richardson, *EJ*, app.. 3, nos 3, 11) or his pledge (ibid., app. 4).

30 See for instance *Ancient Charters, Royal and Private, prior to A.D. 1200*, ed. J. H. Round, PRS 10 (London, 1888), no. 54 (1188).

31 Golb, *Jews in Medieval Normandy*, p. 376; *Original Acta S. Peter's Abbey*, no. 243; Richardson, *EJ*, app. 9, no. 2 (1209).

32 Richardson, *EJ*, app. 9, nos. 1 (*c.* 1208), 4 (1209–10); later occurrences can be found in the appendix.

33 *Original Acta S. Peter's Abbey*, no. 243: the date is given as the '17th day of the month called in Hebrew *Elul*, in the 955th Hebraic lunar year'.

34 So did Samuel, son of Abraham, in the aforementioned Norman charter: Golb, *Jews in Medieval Normandy*, p. 376; later documents included a specific formula, recording the creditor confirmed his quittance with his signature in Hebrew (*littera mea hebrayca* 'signa'*vi*): Richardson, *EJ*, app. 10, nos. 2, 3, 4, 6 (1242–43).

35 Richardson, *EJ*, app. 4; see also Clanchy, *From Memory to Written Record*, p. 201–2.

habit. The notion of tampering became a greater issue as the value of the written word rose. John Hudson has noted an odd miracle story of a Robert *Putridus*, struck with terror as he saw his name written down on a list of criminals by royal officers, and praying to Saint Edmund to have him released from this perilous situation; on the following morning, as the list was read to summon the suspects for an ordeal, his name had disappeared.[36] The same fear that shook this Robert facing the written list probably seized the people of York on the verge of burning 'Jewish' papers in 1190. Just like their contemporaries, while not ignoring the written word, they were people of whom the majority did not have a rational, legally-minded view of it, but rather an emotional fascination for the might or the threat it bore.

Whether they came from this emotional fear of the written word, or on the contrary from ecclesiastical actors used to it and to its tricks, accusations of tampering documents were made against Jews. Sometimes on solid grounds: the prior of Dunstable faced in the 1220s a spurious bond presented by Moses, son of Le Brun.[37] But these accusations are anything but exclusive; as I said, it was a common feature in litigation. And in documents from around 1190, we can see they are even more plainly brought against another group: Cistercian monks. Walter Map, for instance, evoked jokes about Cistercians, especially against Bernard of Clairvaux. He then ironically added that he may be wrong, that Cistercians might be the chosen people, the 'Hebrews', whereas he himself and the other, sinful, Christians could only be 'Egyptians'.[38] Reversing the rôles, he went on then with narratives of 'Hebrew' abuses against 'Egyptian' knights. Three instances ought to be further examined.

Map first recalls 'the incident of the tree which marked their boundary and was removed by night far into the property of their neighbour, an Egyptian knight, at Coxwold'.[39] What the monks tampered with was the physical landmark that traditionally marked the borders of two pieces of land, and was used by local inquests ('perambulatio'), and also in charters as the drafting of their boundary clauses usually followed the route of the jury, as noted above. The editor of the Mowbray charters believed also that a charter relating to Coxwold may have been tampered with by the monks of Byland.[40]

In addition to altering a natural object which had a legal value, Cistercians could also play with the written word. Map goes on, evoking a

> duplicate charter ('de carta dupplici'), expressed in identical words and referring to the same land, which was fraudulently obtained from a stupid chancellor without his lord's

---

[36] J. Hudson, 'L'écrit, les archives et le droit en Angleterre (IXe–XIIe siècle)', *Revue Historique* 315 (2006), 3–35 (pp. 33–4).
[37] Clanchy, *From Memory to Written Record*, p. 307; Richardson, *EJ*, pp. 259, 287.
[38] W. Map, *De Nugis Curialium: Courtiers' Trifles*, ed. M. R. James, et al., OMT (Oxford, 1983), p. 96.
[39] ibid., p. 104.
[40] *Mowbray Charters*, no. 44.

knowledge to replace (so it was said) another that had been lost. They then exchanged that land for another piece, but from the same lord, and gave up one copy, keeping the other.

The fraud was eventually discovered by the king's court.[41] But the accusation of altering a charter is clearer in another anecdote:

… at Neath they were found to have had a conveyance from William, earl of Gloucester, of sixteen acres, which number, after the delivery of the deed, they had increased to 100'[42]

Map completed his tales with accusations of murder. He appears as a harsh critic of Cistercian 'politics' in managing, and enlarging, their estates. His bitterness would have come, according to Gerald of Wales, from his dispute with a Cistercian abbey refusing to pay him a tithe: Flaxley abbey. So are these nasty anecdotes, from such a prejudiced opponent, to be believed? Could Cistercian monks be more perfidious than the Jews they disdained in their charters?

A charter from the cartulary of Waltham abbey includes an interesting case, involving the Cistercian monks of Sawtry abbey. In 1184x1194, Geoffrey II of Scalers confirmed by it to the canons of Waltham the church of Babraham and its advowson; the gift was made at the request of King Henry with the assent of Geoffrey's lord, the duke of Brittany. The charter includes a special warranty against the monks of Sawtry: indeed, the donor's father, another Geoffrey, had entered this house, and if he had then given up any rights in Babraham, he had kept his seals and ring. By this remark, Geoffrey II as well as the canons wished to undermine the legal value of any charter granting the church of Babraham to Sawtry abbey, sealed by Geoffrey I, if one were ever to be found and used against them.[43] It was a wise move, as the gift was contested by the Sawtry monks, and the rights of the canons were recognized only after a long procedure before papal judges delegates, ending in 1195x1197.[44]

The Babraham case might only be an oddity; however, it came not from a writer's fantasy but is documented by diplomatic evidence. It is striking that Cistercian monks were involved, and that their opponent feared the misuse of a seal. In other words, this case could mirror perfectly the Flaxley formula: beware Cistercian, not Jewish, perfidy, these monks cannot help forging charters!

---

41 Map, *De Nugis Curialium*, p. 104; the editor believed 'duplicate charter' means 'chirograph'; I think it rather means here an actual 'duplicata', a copy of an (allegedly, here) lost charter, made by the same authority (the chancellor, here) that first delivered it.

42 ibid., p. 106.

43 *Charters Waltham Abbey*, no. 126.

44 ibid., no. 127.

The fear of false charters, the aggressive caution towards Jews and Cistercians, may be better understood if put in a wider context. The pressure of royal government, by its justice and its taxes, increased the competition in money-lending and land-gain. In this process, even the Cistercian monks of Flaxley played their card: against Walter Map, as noted above, but also gaining from the misfortune of indebted Christians. Indeed, they received the land of Ragel from a William, who had it from Philip of Burc, whom he helped to redeem his huge debt from the Jew Manasses of Bristol, actually 'with the monks' pence', as the charter read.[45] In the 'market for encumbered estates', as Henry Richardson has put it, religious houses, and especially Cistercians, bargained and competed with Jewish moneylenders. The ten abbeys indebted to Aaron of Lincoln at his death in 1186 all belonged to the Cistercian order; their debts should rather be seen as payments due in transactions over mortgaged lands, as in the Flaxley case, rather than stemming from money borrowed.[46]

But this competition for money and land, stressed by the growing weight of royal administration, met another long-term trend by which Western society was defining itself: its Christian identity, achieved through rejecting other communities, whether Jews, lepers or heretics, at its margins.[47] Cistercians were also active in this definition, as shown by their involvement in the move against heretics, another kind of 'unfaithful', 'perfidious' people to their eyes. In 1190, they were, and so were the Jewish moneylenders in another role, at the crossroads of those trends.

---

[45] *Cartulary Flaxley Abbey*, no. 84; see also nos. 81–3 for the transaction between William and Philip.

[46] Richardson, *EJ*, pp. 86–92.

[47] R. I. Moore, *The Formation of a Persecuting Society: Power and Deviance in Western Europe, 950–1250* (Oxford, 1987).

9

An *Ave Maria* in Hebrew: the Transmission of Hebrew Learning from Jewish to Christian Scholars in Medieval England

Eva De Visscher

An increasing emphasis on the otherness of the Jews in twelfth- and thirteenth-century ecclesiastical sources seems to coincide with a revival of the study of Hebrew among Christian scholars. While this revival, which forms part of a wider intensification of interest in language, rhetoric and the study of the biblical text, is visible all over Western Europe, scholars and texts of English origin are particularly well-represented in the extant source material.[1] This chapter focuses on the learning process involved in this type of cross-religious language acquisition. Examining Hebrew and Hebraist texts from pre-expulsion England, it aims to reconstruct, in so far as this is possible, how and from whom its Christian readers learnt Hebrew, and what methods and reference tools they had at their disposal.

Sources

Hebrew did not yet form part of the curriculum at the schools and fledgling universities and those Christian scholars setting out to learn it seem to have been few in number. Their aim was to be able to read the Hebrew Old Testament, at least in part in the original language, for exegetical as well as polemical reasons. 'This reading reflects the Hebrew better/less' ('hebreo plus/minus consonat')' is a recurring phrase in the work of one such Hebraist, Herbert of Bosham (c.1120–c.1194).[2] His knowledge of Hebrew, which

---

1 R. Loewe, 'The Mediaeval Christian Hebraists of England: Herbert of Bosham and Earlier Scholars', *JSHE Transactions* 17 (1953), 225–49; R. Loewe, 'The Mediaeval Christian Hebraists of England: The "superscriptio" *Lincolniensis*', *Hebrew Union College Annual* 28 (1957), 205–52; R. Loewe, 'Alexander Neckam's Knowledge of Hebrew', *Mediaeval and Renaissance Studies* 4 (1958), 17–34; J. Olszowy-Schlanger, *Les manuscrits hébreux dans l'Angleterre médiévale: Étude historique et paléographique*, Collection de la Revue des Études Juives 29 (Paris, 2003).
2 London, St Paul's Cathedral Library, MS 2; two examples out of over thirty are Psalm 26 (27), fol. 29r and Psalm 34 (35), fol. 35r.

he claims to have learnt from an early age ('a primis adolescentie annis') enables him to revise Jerome's translation of the Hebrew Psalms against the Masoretic text and to challenge scribal errors and what he considers to be erroneous allegorical exegeses.[3] According to his older contemporary Odo, in a polemic composed half a century earlier, it also provides Christians with the means to refute the Jews in their own language: 'Let the unbeliever become still when he hears faithful witnesses assert the same in Hebrew, Chaldean (i.e. Aramaic) and Greek'.[4]

Given the small numbers involved, it is probable that pupils were taught privately, in small groups or on a one-to-one basis.[5] Their Hebrew teachers may have been Jews, Jewish apostates or fellow Christian Hebraists at a more advanced learning stage. Jerome, as translator of what would later be called the Vulgate and author of several tracts on the Hebrew language, features as *the* main example to Christian Hebraists. His tracts and the prefaces to his Bible translation discuss the concept and methodology of textual criticism, and freely admit that he learnt Hebrew from Jewish tutors, something which to a certain extent offered legitimacy to medieval Hebraists' initiatives on that front.[6]

In his commentary on the Psalms according to the literal sense of scripture, Herbert of Bosham refers to his Jewish teacher as 'litterator meus' ('my peshat-teacher').[7] Although not afraid to voice strong and on occasion angry disagreement with the rabbinic exegesis of some Psalms, and no different from his Christian peers in stereotyping Jews in general as 'blind' ('caecus') and 'stubborn' ('pertinax') because of their 'hatred of the truth' ('odio

---

3 ibid., fol. 1r. On Bosham, see B. Smalley, 'A Commentary on the *Hebraica* by Herbert of Bosham', *Recherches de Théologie Ancienne et Médiévale* 18 (1951), 29–65; R. Loewe, 'Herbert of Bosham's Commentary on Jerome's Hebrew Psalter', *Biblica* 34 (1953), 44–77, 159–92, 275–98; D. Goodwin, *'Take Hold of the Robe of a Jew': Herbert of Bosham's Christian Hebraism* (Leiden, 2006); E. De Visscher, 'Putting Theory into Practice? Hugh of Saint Victor's Influence on Herbert of Bosham's Psalterium cum commento', in *Bibel und Exegese in der Abtei Saint-Victor zu Paris: Form und Funktion eines Grundtextes im europäischen Rahmen*, ed. R. Berndt (Münster, 2009), pp. 491–502; E. De Visscher, '"Closer to the Hebrew": Herbert of Bosham's Interpretation of Literal Exegesis', in *The Multiple Meaning of Scripture: The Role of Exegesis in Early-Christian and Medieval Culture*, ed. I. van 't Spijker (Leiden, 2009), pp. 249–72.
4 *Écrits théologiques de l'École d'Abélard*, ed. A. Landgraf (Louvain, 1934), pp. 126–7, 279; A. Sapir Abulafia, 'Jewish Carnality in Twelfth-Century Renaissance Thought', in *Christianity and Judaism*, ed. D. Wood, Studies in Church History 29 (Oxford, 1992), pp. 59–75 (p. 71).
5 J. Olszowy-Schlanger, 'The Knowledge and Practice of Hebrew Grammar among Christian Scholars in Pre-expulsion England: The Evidence of "Bilingual" Hebrew-Latin Manuscripts', in *Hebrew Scholarship and the Medieval World*, ed. N. de Lange (Cambridge, 2001), pp. 107–28 (p. 126).
6 D. Brown, *Vir Trilinguis: A Study in the Biblical Exegesis of Jerome* (Kampen, 1992).
7 St Paul's Cath. Lib. MS 2, Psalm 23 (24): 1–2, fol. 26v; Psalm 67 (68):14, fol. 72r: 'litterator meus dicebat…'. The semantic field of the term 'litterator' ranges from 'elementary teacher' to 'grammarian', but in Bosham's commentary its meaning is restricted to that of a Jewish authority on the literal sense of scripture.

veritatis'),[8] Bosham is never derogatory about *his* 'litterator'. He treats him, rather matter-of-factly, as a Hebrew language tutor whose authority on the literal meaning of the text he accepts. Bosham's contemporary Ralph Niger (1140–99) engaged a Jewish apostate called Philip to help him with the composition of a treatise on Hebrew names, and Alexander Neckam (1157–1217) describes in his commentary on the Song of Songs, written at the turn of the thirteenth century, how he attended rabbinical discussions on matters of biblical exegesis. It is unclear whether he is referring to a 'yeshiva' in Paris or in Oxford since he studied at both places.[9]

These glimpses into various tutor-pupil arrangements and learning environments suggest that some Jews and Christians entered into relationships which were amiable enough to allow for cross-religious intellectual exchange and scholarly collaboration. However, the most revealing witnesses to the Christian Hebraist learning process itself are to be found in a second set of sources: a small but fascinating collection of Hebrew books. Scattered around in manuscript libraries in Britain and continental Europe, and not studied comprehensively until the beginning of this century, twenty-seven Hebrew codices and one fragment, either of English provenance or proven to have been circulating in pre-expulsion England, have come to light so far. In her monograph on the subject Judith Olszowy-Schlanger has established that only three of these codices do *not* contain evidence of having been used by Christians of the period.[10]

The other twenty-five fall into two categories: the majority (sixteen codices) were purpose-made for Christian study by Jewish and Christian scribes, and the minority (nine codices) were produced by and for Jews, and later re-used by Christians. Taken together these groups comprise thirty-three codicological units. They include biblical books, with the Book of Psalms strongly represented (fourteen units); two prayer books; two grammatical treatises; a word list, and a fully fledged Hebrew-Latin-French dictionary, the first one of its kind to be composed for Christian use. In the first group the codices may open the Christian way, with the spine to the left, and Bibles follow the Christian biblical canon. Hebrew text and Latin translation are either juxtaposed, or the Latin appears in interlinear glosses above the Hebrew in so-called 'superscriptio'. Often large margins are provided (but not always used) for glosses and note-taking.[11] The latter group contains Latin annotations, usually in the margins.

---

8 ibid., Psalm 2, fol. 3v; Psalm 20 (21), fol. 24r.
9 G. B. Flahiff, 'Ralph Niger: An Introduction to his Life and Works', *Mediaeval Studies* 2 (1940), 104–36; R. W. Hunt, *The Schools and the Cloister: The Life and Writings of Alexander Neckam, 1157–1217*, ed. M. Gibson (Oxford, 1984), p. 96.
10 An inroad into the subject was made by B. Smalley, *Hebrew Scholarship among Christians in 13th Century England: As Illustrated by some Hebrew-Latin Psalters* (London, 1939); Olszowy-Schlanger, 'Knowledge and Practice'; Olszowy-Schlanger, *Manuscrits Hébreux*, p. 29.
11 Olszowy-Schlanger, *Manuscrits Hébreux*, pp. 15, 147-237.

Alphabets, Psalms and Prayers

Taking into account that the learning process crossed religious and to some extent also cultural boundaries, the question remains what teaching and learning methods were used. Both Jewish and Christian acquisition of literacy followed educational models which were intertwined with each group's own belief system and based upon their own sacred texts. What do the sources tell us about the learning of Hebrew as a language of foreign faith?

Almost half of the Hebrew books extant contain the Psalms: ten are Psalters, and a further five count the Book of Psalms amongst their codicological units. This should not surprise us since the Psalter was the most studied biblical text among medieval Christians, and the one most commonly glossed. It was also pivotal in early education; from late antiquity until at least the thirteenth century it was the book through which Christians learnt to read. Its association with basic literacy even produced its own term, 'psalteratus'. While 'litteratus' meant 'learned', the term 'psalteratus' referred, sometimes in a pejorative sense, to someone with basic reading skills (i.e. someone who knows how to read the Psalms but perhaps not much else).[12]

The method of learning a biblical language with the aid of glossed translations also has a long tradition in England. Latin Psalters with interlinear and marginal glosses in Anglo-Saxon emerge as early as the ninth century, and the magnificently illuminated Eadwine Psalter, a late example dating from the early twelfth century, contains Jerome's first revision of the existing Latin translation of the Psalms (the so-called *Psalterium Romanum*) with Anglo-Saxon, and his translation from the Hebrew (referred to as *Psalterium Hebraicum*) with Anglo-Norman 'superscriptio'. Judging from their size, format and execution, some of these Latin-vernacular Psalters were designed for teaching, others for private study. The same holds for their Hebrew-Latin equivalents, which range from very large to pocket sized. The largest Psalter (Oxford, Corpus Christi College MS 10) is larger than A4 size at 330 mm x 250 mm and, with its neatly laid-out Latin and Hebrew juxtaposed columns and large script, which would easily allow two or three people to study it at the same time, seems to have been designed as a teaching aid for Christian Hebraists. The smallest one (Bodl. MS Or 3), which has the size of half a postcard (103 mm x 750 mm), was produced for Jewish private use. Somewhere in the thirteenth century a Christian studied it, and scribbled Latin annotations in its narrow margins.[13] Of crucial importance is a note on one of the end flyleaves (fol. 69v), in a fourteenth-century hand, listing tax revenue

---

12 G. H. Brown, 'The Psalms as the Foundation of Anglo-Saxon Learning', in *The Place of the Psalms in the Intellectual Culture of the Middle Ages*, ed. N. van Deusen (Albany NY, 1999), pp. 1–24 (pp. 2–5).

13 Olszowy-Schlanger, *Manuscrits hébreux*, pp. 70–1.

for the diocese of Canterbury going back as far as 1292.[14] As is the case with the other codices re-used by Christians, the book's journey from Jewish into Christian hands is an obscure one, yet this date suggests that its first Christian owner may have acquired it as a result of the expulsion.

Although evidence is scarce, it seems that Jews as well as Christians of the period took the first step towards literacy by learning the alphabet. Children's exercise books found in the Cairo Geniza as well as a fragment of an alphabet primer in the twelfth-century Reggio Manuscript of the Mahzor Vitry contain the alephbet in various combinations: forwards, backwards, in so-called 'atbash' (the first letter ('aleph') followed by the last ('tav'), followed by the second letter ('beth') followed by the penultimate (*šin*) etc.) and in sequences of numerological significance.[15] No Christian Latin primers from pre-expulsion times are extant but as early as the tenth century alphabets would be added to Latin books, usually at the front, and may be followed by the beginning of the Lord's Prayer.[16] In the course of the thirteenth century Christian ABC primers in a more or less fixed form emerge and begin to serve alongside Psalters as entries into the world of literacy. They usually begin with three basic prayers; the *Pater Noster*, the *Ave Maria* and the *Credo*.[17]

Interestingly, several of the Hebrew books from thirteenth-century England display primer-like features. Hebrew alphabets appear in four of the Psalters,[18] in a book of the Prophets,[19] and in one of the Prophets and the Hagiographical writings.[20] Latin and Greek alphabets feature too,[21] and one Psalter even contains a runic, another one a Cyrillic and an Arabic alphabet.[22] These alphabets are added to what for Christians would be the front of the book, regardless of the manuscript's intended reading order. Further

---

14 ibid., p. 36.

15 I. G. Marcus, *Rituals of Childhood: Jewish Acculturation in Medieval Europe* (New Haven CT, 1996), pp. 32, 39; J. Olszowy-Schlanger, 'Learning to Read and Write in Medieval Egypt: Children's Exercise Books from the Cairo Geniza', *Journal of Semitic Studies* 48 (2003), 47–69.

16 N. Orme, *Medieval Children* (New Haven CT, 2001), pp. 246–7; 263–4; M. T. Clanchy, *From Memory to Written Record: England 1066–1307*, 2nd edn (Oxford, 1993), pp. 111, 214.

17 E. Duffy, *The Stripping of the Altars: Traditional Religion in England, 1400 – 1580* (New Haven CT, 1994), p. 53.

18 BN MS Héb. 113; London, Lambeth Palace Library [LPL] MS 435; Bodl. MSS Or 3, Or 621; for descriptions and images, see Olszowy-Schlanger, *Manuscrits hébreux*, pp. 181–7, 220–3, 271–7, 278–82.

19 Oxford, Corpus Christi College [CCC] MS 7, for a description, see Olszowy-Schlanger, *Manuscrits hébreux*, pp. 289–94.

20 Cambridge, Gonville and Caius College [GCC] MS 404 / 625; for a description, see Olszowy-Schlanger, *Manuscrits hébreux*, pp. 201–4.

21 BN MS Héb. 113 and CCC MS 7.

22 BN MS Héb. 113 and Bodl. MS Or 3. The Cyrillic alphabet has the name of each letter written underneath in Hebrew and it is unclear whether its scribe was Jewish or Christian; the dating, relationship to the body text and overall context are problematic, see Olszowy-Schlanger, *Manuscrits hébreux*, p. 271.

'primerization' occurs in two manuscripts in particular. The Hebrew Psalter with the Latin, Greek, Hebrew and runic alphabet (BN, Héb.113) also includes a *Pater Noster* in Greek and in Latin, and the one with the Cyrillic and Arabic alphabets contains the Inscription on the Cross in Hebrew, Aramaic and Latin, all in Hebrew characters.[23] In the codex containing the Prophets and Hagiographical writings we find, underneath the Hebrew alphabet complete with its vowels except for 'qamets', a short prayer to Christ and a Hebrew translation of the *Ave Maria*, the text of which is worth quoting in full:[24]

'Ĕlohey 'avrāhām bə'ēzrī yēšū hanōṣ rī melekh hayahūdīm
God of Abraham [is] my helper; Jesus of Nazareth, king of the Jews
(John 19. 19)

rah.mēynū šalōm miryam ḥēn məlē'ah 'adōn 'imakh bərūkhah 'ath
have mercy on us; hail Mary full of grace, the Lord [be] with you, blessed [are] you

bə'išōth ūvarūkh pərī vitnekh 'amen
among women and blessed [is] the fruit of your womb, amen

Alphabet and prayers are in the same, Christian, hand and the vowel-pointing conforms to the simplified system used by Christians at the time25 On one level the occurrence of a Pater Noster or Ave Maria should not surprise us. The acquisition of literacy was for both Jews and Christians tightly bound up with religious education and the initiation into scripture. After all, it would only be logical for aspiring Hebraists who were adult learners to seek to replicate the method by which they themselves had learnt to read. However, on a second level, it is worth asking if this primerization according to the Christian model could serve another purpose too. It is well-established that Ashkenazi communities adhered to the Hebrew script, whether the language expressed in it was Hebrew or the vernacular. As the numerous Hebrew parts of chirographs and Hebrew signatures on sales deeds of the period testify, this custom was upheld even when dealing with Christians, and reflects the notion that the Hebrew script, more so than the language, constituted a marker of Ashkenazi religious and cultural identity.[26] Because

---

[23] ibid., pp. 20, 36.

[24] GCC MS 404/625

[25] For an analysis of Christian vocalization, see J. Olszowy-Schlanger, 'A Christian Tradition of Hebrew Vocalisation in Medieval England', in *Semitic Studies in Honour of Edward Ullendorff*, ed. G. Khan (Leiden, 2005), pp. 126–46

[26] On the use of the Hebrew script, see C. Sirat, *Hebrew Manuscripts of the Middle Ages*, ed. and trans. N. de Lange (Cambridge, 2002), pp. 29–30, 232; on language and medieval Jewish

of this association between Hebrew script and Jewish territory, Christian Hebraists may have felt the need to emphasize their Christian identity while practising the reading and writing of Hebrew characters. A prayer to Christ, taken from the Gospel, and the Ave Maria are unambiguously Christian and more explicitly so, one can argue, than the Lord's Prayer. Thus, together with the primerization of this Hebrew-Latin codex we also see a christianization of what was considered Jewish territory.

Yet, as the image shows, the learning method of the Gonville and Caius codex does not just follow the Christian model. Characteristics of the Jewish primer are present too: following the Hebrew alphabet from 'aleph' to 'tav' we find the alphabet from 'tav' to 'aleph' and in 'atbash'. Thus, although little is known about the educational environment in which the codex was used, the method of learning displayed here, with its Jewish-Christian hybrid features, indicates that aspects from both didactic models were acceptable. If anything, the method reflects the cross-religious nature of the learning process itself.

Latin Going Hebrew and Judaeo-French

Very little research has been done on possible connections between the collection of Hebrew books and the works of known Christian Hebraists. So far, only Herbert of Bosham's commentary on the Psalms has been shown to contain shared readings with several of them. This commentary, completed in the late 1180s or early 1190s at the Cistercian abbey of Ourscamp in northern France where Bosham resided as a guest, combines a revision of Jerome's Latin translation of the Hebrew Psalms with an interpretation of the Psalms according to the literal sense of scripture. As the only literal exposition of the Psalms attempted by a Christian in the Latin West, it includes close paraphrases and critical assessments of Rashi's 'peshat' commentary on the Psalms, alongside some use, independent of Rashi, of the *Midrash Tehillim*, the Talmud, and the *Mahberet* by Menahem ben Saruq. Bosham cites over a hundred Hebrew words and phrases in transliteration, refers to aspects of Hebrew grammar and, as mentioned above, acknowledges at least one anonymous contemporary Jewish teacher who advised him on matters of literal exegesis. The commentary is extant, as far as we know, in only one copy, dating from the second quarter of the thirteenth century and it is unclear whether it had any direct *Nachleben*.

Bosham's text can be associated with five of the Hebrew manuscripts from the pre-expulsion period: three Psalters, a codex containing the Prophets, and the Hebrew-Latin-French dictionary.[27] Only one of the Psalters, Scaliger

---

identity, see K. A. Fudeman, *Vernacular Voices: Language and Identity in Medieval French Jewish Communities* (Philadelphia, 2010), pp. 1–59, esp. pp. 3–5.

[27] Leiden University Library, MS Codex Orientalis 4725 (Scaliger 8); CCC, MS 10; LPL MS 435; Bodl. MS Or. 46; Warminster, Longleat House, MS 21.

8, predates the composition of Bosham's commentary. The other Psalters, and the dictionary, have been dated between 1230 and 1250.[28] At first sight many of Bosham's revisions to the Latin text of the Psalms seem peculiar, and from a literary point of view the result presents little or no improvement on Jerome's translation made eight centuries earlier. The Hebrew is reflected very literally and Hebrew rather than Latin idiom adhered to: one example of many is 'kī y̲i̲t̲h̲ā̲m̲ē̲s̲ ləvavī' ('because my heart/soul was *embittered*') in Psalm 73(72). 21. Jerome's translation is 'quia cor meum <u>contractum</u> est' ('because my heart was *compressed*'), but Bosham changes the verb to 'fermentatum' ('leavened', 'fermented') because the Hebrew root 'ḥmṣ' means, in the first instance, 'ferment', 'be leavened'. Words from identical Hebrew roots tend to be matched in translation by words from the same Latin roots. For example 'šavita ševi' (literally 'you led captivity captive') in Psalm 68. 19 becomes 'captivasti captivitatem' as a reflection of the double use of the root 'šbh' instead of Jerome's 'captivum duxisti' ('you led captive'). Similarly, Bosham takes pains to find Latin grammatical equivalents for Hebrew phrases. 'Hif'il' (causative) verbs appear as a form of 'facio'+ *infinitive* and the construction 'lə' + *infinitive construct* becomes 'ad' + *gerund* as an expression of purpose. Bodl. MS Or. 46, in the Book of Ezra also uses the construction 'facio' + *infinitive* as a reflection of a 'hif'il' verb.[29]

While not being consistent throughout, the work does include passages in nearly every Psalm where Hebrew idiom is turned word for word into Latin, yielding, apart from grammatically incorrect sentence structures, several neologisms, or instances of language modernization. For example, 'nidəgol' ('we will lift banners') becomes 'vexillabimur' in Psalm 20 (19). 6, instead of 'ducemus choros'; 'haməqareh' ('[the one] laying beams') becomes 'trabeavit' ('he has laid beams') instead of Jerome's 'qui tegis' ('[you] who covers') in Psalm 104 (103). 3.[30] In the dictionary we find under the heading 'dəgol' (the imperative singular of 'dgl' 'carry a standard'), apart from the translation 'vexilla', also a cross-reference to Psalm 20 (19). 6 which states 'dicit ebreus '*in nomine Dei nostri uexillabimur'* ('the Hebrew says "*in the name of our God we will lift banners*"'), and the heading 'qəreh' (imperative singular of 'qrh', 'furnish with beams') lists, among other translations, 'trabesce'.[31] The identity of 'ebreus', which is attested around 1500 times, is not always clear. It seems to refer to the Hebrew biblical text in the majority of cases but may also cover a body of translations and cross-references, or may even refer to a Judaeo-French translation by an oral source, translated into Latin. It would

---

[28] Olszowy-Schlanger, *Manuscrits hébreux*, p. 16; Bale, 'Fictions of Judaism in England before 1290', in *The Jews in Medieval Britain: Historical, Literary, and Archaeological Perspectives*, ed. P. Skinner (Woodbridge, 2003), p. 144.

[29] Olszowy-Schlanger, 'Knowledge and Practice', p. 116; Ezra 1. 8.

[30] For other examples, see Goodwin, *'Take Hold of the Robe of a Jew'*, pp. 235–75.

[31] *Dictionnaire hébreu-latin-français de la Bible hébraïque de l'Abbaye de Ramsey (XIIIe siècle)*, ed. J. Olszowy-Schlanger and A. Grondeux (Turnhout, 2008), Dalet 10, p. 12; Qoph 57, p. 70.

not be a unique case of Judaeo-French finding itself absorbed into the corpus of Latin biblical translation. Bosham's revised Latin text of the Psalms borrows several 'le'azim', all in Latin translation, from Rashi and the Hebraico-French glossary tradition circulating in Jewish communities at the time. One example is Rashi's translation of 'ešet' as 'talpe' ('mole') in Psalm 58. 9; Bosham's translation is 'talpa' against Jerome's 'mulieris' ('of a woman').[32] From the anonymous glossary tradition he borrows 'déchalzét' ('buds'), latinizing it as 'discalcietur' as a translation for the Hebrew 'šeqadəmaṭ' ('grows', literally 'draws out') in Psalm 129. 6.

This deliberate and more or less methodical use of hebraized Latin presents a striking mirror image to the latinized language and sentence structure found in late thirteenth century Hebrew 'shetaroth' (private title deeds). Both examples form a wonderful demonstration of the sort of linguistic fluidity found at the time, where different languages were not just inherent to specific ethnic, social and religious spheres but were also, in some instances and to some degrees, allowed to merge and cross-fertilize. It seems likely that the process of latinization present in the 'shetaroth' was propelled by anxiety among English Jews about the deterioration of their social and economic status. In an environment marked by increasing anti-Jewish hostility and distrust, Jewish documents which in terminology closely resembled that of their Christian counterparts may have been seen as more acceptable and as a result were hoped to offer better legal protection.[33] Obviously, the reasons underlying Bosham's use of hebraized Latin, and of Hebrew words in transliteration, are, mostly, of a very different order. Although it could be argued that the appearance of Hebrew in Latin script may hold some motive of enforcing religious territory, and of perhaps avoiding the charge from fellow Christians of being a 'Judaizer', its main purpose was accessibility to Christian students who may or may not have known Hebrew, and readability to copyists. With this absorption of Jewish exegetical practice in a form accessible to his non-hebraist peers, Bosham unlocks for them the door to a largely unknown linguistic and theological world. It is easy to imagine a Christian biblical scholar resorting to the work, with its painstakingly literal translations, as a reference tool when tackling the Psalms in Hebrew.

Theoretically, the thirteenth-century Psalters and the dictionary could have sourced some of their glosses directly from Bosham's text. However since this group of glossed Psalters, while showing individual textual differences, share with one another a substantial number of readings variant to Jerome's *Hebraica*, it is likely that they are attestations of a larger Christian tradition of translating the Hebrew Psalms, reaching back to at least the twelfth century. Whether glossed by a developing Hebraist as a learning exercise in itself or offering a Latin translation commissioned for the benefit of Hebrew

---

[32] M. I. Gruber, *Rashi's Commentary on Psalms* (Leiden, 2004), p. 410 (English), 831 (Hebrew).
[33] Slavin, 'Hebrew went Latin', 306–25

students, these Psalters then could be passed on and become study tools for others. The fact that some of Bosham's readings overlap with certain translations offered in the Hebrew-Latin-French dictionary suggests that he relied on a twelfth-century or older prototype of the work, or that both sourced their readings from a Jewish corpus of French glosses ('ebreus'). It is probable that readings from the group of Hebrew-Latin Psalters found their way into the dictionary tradition and vice versa, and that twelfth-century prototypes of one or more Psalters, and of the dictionary, formed a reference base for Christian Hebraists such as Bosham. He, in turn, provided his readers with a close translation of the Hebrew Psalms and a commentary of literal exegesis combining clarifications of Hebrew grammar and idiom with selected and critically assessed paraphrases from Rashi and Midrash Tehillim.

The interplay of these different layers of textual and non-textual influences (Rabbinic exegesis, Hebraico-French glosses, which contemporary teachers made accessible via (Judaeo-) French translations, together with the Hieronymean Hebraist material already known to Christian scholars) results in a fascinating hybridity of Jewish and Christian interpretation. The method whereby at least some of these scholars learnt Hebrew reflects a similar hybridity of tradition and highlights another dimension to the Jewish-Christian dynamic in pre-expulsion England.

10

The Talmudic Community of Thirteenth-Century England

Pinchas Roth and Ethan Zadoff*

Introduction

The study of medieval law occupies a unique niche within traditional academic discourse. A concentration on philological precision, challenges pertaining to manuscript study, and the 'internal language' of jurisprudence have at times over-shadowed the consideration of the wider societal implications of medieval law and curtailed its use in the investigation of broad themes of social and cultural history. This is particularly true of the thirteenth-century Anglo-Jewish legal corpus, the study of which has been relegated to a select few articles and studies.[1]

Law can, however, serve as an important medium for understanding the social fabric and communal identity of a particular group. Numerous studies have utilized legal texts to explicate the wider terms of medieval European social and cultural history.[2] By studying the law and legal culture of the Anglo Jewish community, particularly the legal corpus of the thirteenth-century figure Elijah Menahem of London, this chapter aims to further expand our understanding of the already nuanced picture of the medieval English community. It explores the thirteenth-century Anglo-Jewish intellectual world as a localized domain with distinct regional identities, features, and

---

* The introduction and parts I–II are written by Ethan Zadoff. Parts III–IV are written by Pinchas Roth.

1 C. Roth, *The Intellectual Activities of Medieval English Jewry* (London, 1949); E. E. Urbach, *Baale Ha-Tosafot: Toldotehem, Hiburehem, ShiTatam*, 2 vols. (Jerusalem, 1955–86), II, 493–520; E. E. Urbach, 'Mitoratam shel Hakhmei Anglia Melifnei Hagirush', *Tiferet Yisrael: Likvod Harav Yisrael Brody* (London, 1967), pp.1–56; I. Ta-Shma, *Studies in Medieval Rabbinic Literature*, 4 vols. (Jerusalem, 2004–10), I, 371–87.

2 G. Austin, *Shaping Church Law around the Year 1000: The Decretum of Burchard of Worms* (Aldershot, 2009); E. Baumgarten, *Mothers and Children: Jewish Family Life in Medieval Europe* (Princeton, 2004); A. Grossman, *Pious and Rebellious: Jewish Women in Medieval Europe* (Waltham, 2004).

184

mentalities that was in debt to and negotiated with the reigning Tosafist culture of northern France and the continental mainland.

Evidence from both sides of the English Channel indicates that the English Tosafists engaged in a conversation with the continental centres of learning, covering a diverse range of legal topics. We aim to probe the scholarly workings of the thirteenth-century Anglo-Jewish community, locating within the work of Elijah Menahem the ways in which his intellectual and judicial identity was informed by both the local and the foreign. The first section of this study surveys what is known today about the thirteenth-century English Tosafists, as well as the general background to the family of Elijah Menahem. Part two is an investigation of Elijah's Commentary to Mishnah Berakhot and the conceptions and mentalities that stand at the core of this work. The third section takes up another element of Elijah's writings, his legal responsa, and provides a close reading of two specific responsa, pointing to glimmers of specifically English identity in his writings. Finally, the fourth section explores the afterlife of Elijah's work following the expulsion in 1290 and through the fourteenth and fifteenth centuries.

I: English Tosafists? The Jewish Intellectual Culture of Thirteenth-Century England

The foundations of the medieval Anglo-Jewish Talmudic community were laid primarily in the second half of the twelfth century by students of Jacob Tam of Ramerupt.[3] Two students, Jacob of Orléans and Yom Tob of Joigny, left Northern France and travelled to England, and Benjamin of Cambridge returned to his native land.[4] All three were known to later commentators through their legal decisions and writings. *Hagahot Mordekhai* records that Jacob of Orléans drew up a formula for loans, whereby the prohibition against usury could be circumvented.[5] According to Meir of Rothenburg, the practice of employing a non-Jew to heat houses on the Sabbath during the winter was introduced in France on Jacob's authority.[6] He composed *Tosafot* glosses on a number of Talmudic tractates and his commentary on the Pentateuch is extant in manuscript. Jacob was martyred in 1189 in London following the coronation of Richard I. Yom Tob of Joigny resided in the city of York and

---

3   According to Golb, Abraham the son of Rabbi Yosi of Rouen founded an academy in London during the middle decades of the twelfth century. See N. Golb, *The Jews in Medieval Normandy: A Social and Intellectual History* (Cambridge, 1998), 225–6; Richardson, *EJ*, p. 240; *JAE Docs.*, p. 236.

4   Roth, *Intellectual Activities*, p. 21, suggests that a number of known scholars may have visited England at the end of the twelfth century including Abraham ben Nathan of Lunel, the author of the *Sefer Hamanhig* as well as Joseph of Clisson.

5   See Samuel ben Aaron Schlettstadt, *Haghaot Mordekhai le-Masechet Bava Metzia*, para. 454–5.

6   Meir of Rothenburg, *Responsa of Meir of Rothenburg* (Prague, 1608), §92.

is purported in 1190 to have inspired the Jews to perform the act of *Kiddush Hashem* (to martyr themselves) in the face of an attacking Christian mob. His Halakhic decisions are reported *in Sefer Mordekhai* and in other compilations and he also commented on various sections of the Bible.[7] Several of his liturgical poems survive, including a ballad-like elegy on the Blois martyrs of 1171, *Yah Tishpokh Ḥamatkha.*[8] He is also the author of the hymn *Omnam Ken*, for the eve of the Day of Atonement.[9]

The third student, Benjamin of Cambridge, was born in England but travelled to Northern France to study.[10] Relatively few of Benjamin's legal opinions survive in later medieval texts and little is known about his life. *Sefer Mordekhai* records that he forbade the consumption of milk purchased from non-Jews unless a Jew had been present at the milking.[11] Two other legal opinions can be attributed to Benjamin. The first, recorded by Elijah Menahem of London, discusses women's dowry rights prescribed by Benjamin and the second relates to the monetary amount of damages paid as the result of libel. Benjamin is recorded in English rolls as 'Magister Benjamin' of Cambridge and probably maintained the local synagogue. He also served as a teacher of Moses of London, the father of Elijah Menahem.

Moses of London, the descendant of a prominent Jewish family that traced its lineage to the tenth-century *paytan* Simon ben Isaac of Mainz (and not to the Jewish communities of Normandy, like many other English Jews), was engaged in communal activities during the first decades of the thirteenth century.[12] He composed treatises on the cantillation marks of the Torah as well as on forbidden foods. Moses was familiar with the writings and opinions of Isaac of Dampierre as well Rashi, Rabbenu Tam, Judah of Paris, Isaac ben Abraham (RIZBA) and others and incorporated them into his legal decisions and glosses on a number of Talmudic tractates.[13] Moses

---

7   See Mordekhai ben Hillel, *Sefer Mordekhai le-Masechet Ketubot*, no. 198; Roth, *Intellectual Activities*, pp. 21–2.

8   S. L. Einbinder, Beautiful Death: Jewish Poetry and Martyrdom in Medieval France (Princeton, 2002); S. L. Einbinder, 'Meir b. Elijah of Norwich: Persecution and Poetry among Medieval English Jews', JMH 26 (2000), pp. 145–62.

9   Roth, *Intellectual Activities*, p. 22.

10 ibid., pp. 29.

11 See Mordekhai ben Hillel, *Sefer Mordekhai le-Masechet Avodah Zara*, no. 826; Roth, *Intellectual Activities*, pp. 31–2.

12 D. Kaufmann, 'Three Centuries of the Genealogy of the Most Eminent Anglo-Jewish Family before 1290', JQR o.s. 3 (1891), 555–66 (the manuscript described there is now Jerusalem, Schocken Institute, MS 19522); G. Vajda, 'De quelques infiltrations chrétiennes dans l'oeuvre d'un auteur anglo-juif du XIIIe siécle', in *Mélanges Georges Vajda: Études de pensée, de philosophie et de littérature juives et arabes*, ed. G. E. Weil (Hildesheim, 1982), pp. 313–31 (p. 314 n. 4); C. Roth, 'Elijah of London: The Most Illustrious Jew of the Middle Ages', JHSE Transactions 15 (1939–1945), 29–62 (pp. 30–1).

13 Urbach, *Baale Ha-Tosafot* II, 494-8, esp. p. 495, based on evidence taken from *Sefer Etz Hayyim* suggests that Moses of London may have been in contact with Isaac ben Samuel of Dampierre (RI Hazaken). However, the given dates of both Isaac and Moses's death, *c.* 1185 and

was the father of six sons, two of whom were actively involved in communal enterprises and the study of Halakha.[14] The first and most prolific was Elijah Menahem of London, the subject of this study, and the second was Berakhia of Nicole-Lincoln. Berakhia, 'Magister Benedictus filius magistri Mosei de Lincolnia', was an active member of the community, a businessman, as well as a legalist.[15] He married the daughter of Joseph ben Aaron, a relatively wealthy moneylender in the city of Lincoln and moved there shortly afterwards. Elijah quotes him a number of times in his own legal compositions as does Berakhia's student, Jacob bar Judah of London, throughout his late thirteenth century compendium, *Sefer Etz Hayym*.[16]

The Talmudic community of England was not limited to the family of Moses of London. A handful of scholars resided in the city of Lincoln, including Meir ben Elijah and Joseph of Nicole. Later scholars record a number of Joseph of Nicole's responsa and one in particular, on the subject of divorce, speaks to the engagement between England and the scholars of Northern France.[17] The town of Northampton was the home of Isaac ben Peretz and Aaron of Northampton.[18] Others who were part of the broader Talmudic community include Meir of England or Meir of London, as he was sometimes referred to, as well as the previously mentioned Jacob bar Judah of London who completed his wide-ranging and synthesizing work, *Sefer Etz Hayyim,* in the late 1280s.

Much of what was once the Anglo-Jewish Talmudic and legal corpus has not survived and we can only speculate regarding its breadth and scope. The material that has survived, however, is found in four general repositories; first, the legal responsa and Mishnah commentary of Elijah Menahem of London; second, *Sefer Etz Hayyim*, by Jacob bar Judah Hazan of London; third, Parma MS de Rossi 933, a manuscript with commentaries to various Talmudic tractates known as *Tosafot Hachmei Anglia;*[19] and fourth, various excerpts in later medieval texts such as *Sefer Mordekai* and Meir of Rothenburg's responsa, some of which are found in various manuscripts, including Bodl. MSS Neubauer 882 and 781.[20]

While the Talmudic community of thirteenth-century England was comparatively small, key figures and their writings can be identified and mined for important data about the nature of the community. The remnants of the medieval corpus point to England not as an intellectual desert but rather as a

---

1268 respectively, seem to preclude the possibility of actual contact.

[14] ibid., pp. 494–8.

[15] C. Roth, 'Rabbi Berechiah of Nicole (Benedict of Lincoln)', *Journal of Jewish Studies* 1 (1948–49), 67–81; Urbach, *Baale Ha-Tosafot* II, 506–9.

[16] Urbach, *Baale Ha-Tosafot* II, 518–520.

[17] M. of Zurich, *Sefer Hasemak mi-Zurich*, ed. I. J. Har-Shoshanim-Rosenberg, 3 vols. (Jerusalem, 1973), II, 130. For additional responsa see, pp. 269, 277, 280, 305.

[18] Urbach, *Baale Ha-Tosafot* II, 511–513

[19] See below, n. 30.

[20] On Bodl. MS Neubauer 781, see section IV below.

centre that fused approaches and methodologies common among the Jewish study houses on the Continent with local customs and laws. These writings serve as a valuable resource concerning the self-perception and social fabric of the Jewish community.

II: Elijah Menahem of London

Elijah Menahem of London, known in the Exchequer rolls as 'Magister Elias fil magistri Mossei', was born sometime around 1220.[21] Elijah's various business activities and his public life are well known and can be followed step by step in the surviving records.[22] He emerges in the various governmental rolls in the middle of the thirteenth century, engaging as a moneylender during the 1250s, 1260s and part of the 1270s while turning to trade in the 1270s when restrictions were placed on Jewish money lending activities.[23] His public life brought him into contact with officials from the Exchequer and with other public officials including Richard, earl of Cornwall, brother of King Henry III and eventual king of the Germans.[24] In addition to his economic activities Elijah was recognized as one of the leading members of the English Jewish community. He served as a witness on various judicial and governmental documents and played a significant role in the financial administration of the Jewish community.[25] He was a physician who may have had mystical tendencies as well.[26] In short Elijah was a prolific, dynamic, and active member of the thirteenth-century Jewish community.

Elijah Menahem is also one of the few pre-Expulsion English Jews whose writings on Jewish law have been preserved.[27] From their content, sources and terminology, it is clear that Elijah Menahem was a product of the North-

---

[21] Roth, 'Elijah of London', p. 34; Urbach, *Baale Ha-Tosafot* II, 500

[22] R. R. Mundill, 'Rabbi Elias Menahem: A Late Thirteenth-Century English Entrepreneur', *JHS* 34 (1994-6), 161–87; Roth, 'Elijah of London', pp. 40–4.

[23] R. R. Mundill, *England's Jewish Solution: Experiment and Expulsion, 1262–1290*, Cambridge Studies in Medieval Life and Thought, Fourth Series 37 (Cambridge, 1998), pp. 291–2.

[24] M. Page, 'Cornwall, Earl Richard, and the Barons' War', *EHR* 115 (2000), 21–38; B. Weiler, 'Matthew Paris, Richard of Cornwall's candidacy for the German Throne, and the Sicilian Business', *JMH* 26 (2000), 71–92; B. Weiler, 'Image and Reality in Richard of Cornwall's German Career', *EHR* 113 (1998), 1111–42.

[25] Roth, 'Elijah of London', pp. 44–5.

[26] ibid., pp. 52–5; J. Jacobs, 'Une lettre française d'un juif anglais au XIIIe siècle', *Revue des Études Juives* 18 (1889), 256–61; F. Getz, *Medicine in the English Middle Ages* (Princeton, 1998), pp. 22–3. The recent article by A. Leibowitz, 'Doctors and Medical Knowledge in Tosafist Circles', *Tradition: A Journal of Orthodox Jewish Thought* 42 (2009), 19–34, underscores this point with its unsuccessful attempt to find additional evidence for medical practice in Ashkenaz.

[27] N. Levy, *Nahalat Naftali* (Presburg, 1891), fol. 13r–13v; *JAE Docs.*, pp. 287–9. Most of his surviving corpus was published in *The Writings of Rabbi Elijah of London*, ed. M. Y. L. Sacks (Jerusalem, 1956).

ern French Tosafist movement, just as all of medieval English Jewry was an outgrowth of the Northern French community.[28] He studied with his father Moses of London.[29] Elijah composed a small corpus of writings including commentaries on *Mishnah Berakhot, Zeraim* and *Tehorot*, commentaries to various tractates of the Babylonian Talmud including *Tractate Berakhot*, and possibly *Shabbat* and *Shevuot*, a commentary to the Passover Hagadah and responsa.[30] Much of Elijah's writing is lost except for the commentary on *Mishnah Berakhot*, various *Pesakim* taken from the lost commentary on *Mishnah Zeraim*, the Haggadah commentary and a number of his responsa.

We can only be reasonably sure concerning the extent of Elijah's library and the earlier and contemporary works that he used. He cites a number of medieval Jewish legalists, commentators, and Tosafists including Rashi, Rashbam, Rabbenu Tam, Samson of Sens and more than a dozen others. The list is made up of predominantly French Tosafists but he also quotes various Geonim including Natronai Gaon, Amram Gaon, and Tzemah Gaon, although it is not clear that Elijah possessed any of these Geonic works.[31] The single quotation of Natronai Gaon, for instance, was taken from *Sefer ha-Itim* of Judah b. Barzillai, a text which Elijah seems to have possessed.[32] In addition Elijah also made use of the *Mishneh Torah* by Maimonides and Isaac Alfasi's glosses to the Babylonian Talmud. Elijah did not simply make sporadic use of the *Mishneh Torah*, citing when it was expedient, but rather made it the most frequently quoted source in the commentary to *Mishnah Berakhot*. Despite the ambivalence that a number of Northern French and German Tosafists and commentators exhibited towards the works of Maimonides and Alfasi during the thirteenth century, both the *Mishneh Torah* and Alfasi's glosses resonated with the Jewish community of England.[33]

---

28 Roth, *HJE*, p. 4.

29 It is unlikely that Elijah studied under Samson of Sens, as Roth posits, since Samson had probably left France to settle in the land of Israel by the time Elijah was born. See Roth, 'Elijah of London', pp. 34–5; Urbach, *Baale Ha-Tosafot* II, 507; E. Kanarfogel, 'The Aliyah of "Three Hundred Rabbis" in 1211: Tosafist Attitudes toward Settling in the Land of Israel', *JQR* 76 (1986), 191–215.

30 Urbach argues that the term "Mepi R. Eliyahu" found seven times in MS Parma de Rossi 933, on fol. 53d and elsewhere, refers to various statements of Elijah taken from his numerous Tosafot commentaries. In contrast, Ta-Shma points out that the term 'Mepi R. Eliyahu' does not necessarily refer to Elijah Menahem and that the English material collected in the manuscript makes up a small part of the overall text. See Urbach,'Mitoratam shel Hahkmei Anglia Melifnei Hagerush', pp. 1–50; Ta-Shma, *Studies in Medieval Rabbinic Literature* I, 371–87.

31 The works of the Geonim of Babylonia and Israel were an important resource for the Baalei Hatosafot of Northern France as well as their predecessors in Ashkenaz generally. A. Grossman, *The Early Sages of Ashkenaz: Their Lives, Leadership and Works (900–1096)* (Jerusalem, 1981), pp. 385–6, 424–35.

32 *Writings of Rabbi Elijah*, pp. 38.

33 A. Grossman, 'Ben Sefarad Le-Tzarfat: Hakesharim Ben Kehilot Yirael Shebesefarad Ha-Muslemit Uben Kehilot Tzarfat', in *Exile and Diaspora: Studies in the History of the Jewish People*, ed. A. Mirsky et al. (Jerusalem, 1988), pp 75–101; A. Grossman, 'Meandalusia Le-Eropa:

Moses of London may have composed glosses to Alfasi and incorporated Maimonides into his legal writings as well. On frequent occasions, Elijah agrees with Maimonidean legal opinion and the overarching conceptual goal of the *Mishneh Torah*.

The objectives of the Mishnah commentary can be best character-ized in two ways: first, as a systematic effort to explain the meaning of the Mishnaic dicta through summarizing the various discussions of the Babylonian Talmud as well as the views of a select number of Geonim, medieval Tosafists and legalists; second, to enumerate the practical law for communal (seemingly, mass) consumption. In essence, the principal *function* of the Mishnah commentary lies in a concerted effort to explain the simple meaning of the Mishnah, the laws, and requisite daily practices found in Tractate Berakhot, laws which pertain to the daily ritual, daily blessings and other important ritual matters. Included in the enumeration of the practical law are customs specific to the English community such as the practice of not reciting a prayer for the sick on the Sabbath day and the question of whether to recite the *Modim De-Rabanan* during the repeti-tion of the *Shemoneh Esreh*.[34] Notably absent from Elijah's commentary is a detailed discourse of theoretical dialectic of either the Talmudic or Tosafist type. In fact, the Mishnaic tract is a rather fluid explanation and enumera-tion of practical law. In a number of ways the objective of the commentary mirrors the wide-ranging goals enumerated in the continental Jewish legal codes of the thirteenth and fourteenth centuries, particularly the *Sefer Mitz-vot Gadol*, Sefer *Mitzvot Qatan*, *Kitzur Semag* and *Sefer ha-Niyar*.

The opening Mishnah of chapter four serves as a representative model of Elijah's exegetical and legal schema.[35] Mishnah Berakhot 4:1 enumerates the time constraints associated with the daily and Sabbath prayers. Elijah utilizes the related discussions in the Babylonian Talmud to unpack the de-tails of the Mishnaic law regarding the time when one should recite the daily liturgy. He condenses the Talmudic discussions, which occupy four folio pages in the Talmud, into their penultimate statements, excising the compli-cated discourse while presenting what he perceives to be the conclusion and requisite practice. Following the analysis of the proper time for reciting the four distinct prayers that the Mishnah discusses, Elijah turns to the prayer of *Neilah* – the final prayer on Yom Kippur. In discussing the *Neilah*, he follows Maimonides' pattern in *Mishneh Torah*, *Hilkhot Tefilah* which discusses the *Neilah* prayer in the context of the time constraints of the daily and Sabbath prayers.[36] Following this brief interlude, Elijah turns to another related topic,

---

Yahasam Shel Hakmei Ashkenaz Vetzarfat Bameot Ha-12–13 El Sifrei Hahalakha Shel Harif Ve-Harambam', *Peamim* 80 (1999), 14–32.

[34] *Writings of Rabbi Elijah*, p. 74.

[35] ibid., pp. 62–5.

[36] See M. Maimonides, *Mishneh Torah al pi Kitve Yad Teman im Perush Maqif*, ed. Y. Kafih, 23 vols. (Tel Aviv, 1983–84), Hilkhot Tefilah, ch. 1.

namely if one forgets to recite one of the daily prayers what course of action should one take? The discussion of this issue, which is dispersed among Talmudic passages, is brought together by Elijah in one cohesive 'essay', which glosses over much of the Talmudic dialectic and focuses on the practical elements of law. Elijah goes through the various combinations of forgetting a specific prayer and the actions one must take, for instance if one recited the weekday prayers on the Sabbath. Although the elements of law discussed and the conclusions reached are neither controversial nor path breaking, the the approach is significant. Elijah lays out the precise practice without resorting to complicated dialectical analysis. He also supplements the discussion with related laws not found in the immediate Talmudic context such as the issue of forgetting to add into the *Shemoneh Esreh* the special additional prayers for the celebration of Purim, Hanukkah, and the New Month.

The commentary on this particular Mishnah is but one example of Elijah's broader goal, to clarify the words of the Mishnah utilizing the legal observations stated in the Babylonian Talmud and to remove the complex debate so as to express the practical law and required practice. That Elijah composed a systematic study of practical law raises a string of questions pertaining to the areas of ritual knowledge among the thirteenth-century community. Did Elijah compose this commentary because the public was unaware of the proper practice or law? How did members of the English community learn these practices and laws of daily ritual and behaviour? Was it in a school environment or through practice in the synagogue? What can the Mishnah commentary tell us about Elijah's own perception of the level of practice of the Jewish community?

Members of the English community were familiar with areas of complex law and practice. A number of Jewish academies or schools functioned in medieval England. In a roll of 1236 Josce of Lincoln is called 'magistri scolarum Judeorum Linc' while Peytivin was in charge of a school in the same city during the 1250s. The fact that a number of academies are referred to as *scola* may indicate that they were not advanced Talmudic academies but perhaps a lower school geared towards younger students.[37] Yet, despite the existence of these primary schools, the extent of whose popularity or functionality remains unknown, it seems likely that the intention of Elijah's commentary was to guide the general population in the methods of practice and law. In this sense, the commentary displays a strong resemblance to the various codes of Jewish law produced in Germany and France during the twelfth century, such as the *Sefer ha-Trumah* and *Sefer Yeraim*, and even more closely to the *Sefer Mitzvot Gadol [SMA'G]*, *Sefer Mitzvot Qatan [SMA'K]* and *Sefer ha-Niyar* of the thirteenth and fourteenth centuries.[38]

---

[37] Golb, *Jews in Medieval Normandy*, pp. 195–6; Roth, *HJE*, pp. 117–18; E. Kanarfogel, *Jewish Education and Society in the High Middle Ages* (Detroit, 1992), p. 23.

[38] Urbach, *Baale Ha-Tosafot* II, pp. 132–40, 263, 286–99, 511–12; S. Emanuel, 'Biographical Data on R. Baruch b. Isaac', *Tarbiz* 69 (2000), 423–40. On SMA'G see I. Ta-Shma, 'On the SMA'G,

Sefer ha-Trumah and *Sefer Yeraim* were both composed with the purpose of emphasizing the practicality of the law, but they follow the internal cohesion of the Talmudic tractates for use by those engaged in the Tosafist enterprise. *SMA'G* and *SMA'K*, however, seem to have been written for dissemination among a wider audience. On the whole, the twelfth-century French Tosafists did not compose codes of Jewish law, while the thirteenth century marked a noticeable shift in focus. The impetus in compiling *SMA'G* seems to have been spurred on by Moses of Couçy's travels and preaching, particularly throughout Spain, as well as his dedication to Maimonides and the *Mishneh Torah*. The communities that heard his preaching asked for a legal collection in order to recall and practise the law.[39] The end result of Moses' endeavours was a compilation that was meant to be used not by the scholar of the Tosafist academy, but by the general populace. Moses also viewed Maimonides with reverence and respect not afforded to him by earlier French scholars and he adapted the style of the *Mishneh Torah*, to the Northern French milieu. Similarly, Isaac of Corbeil composed *Sefer Mitzvot Qatan* with a comparable audience in mind, as noted in the introductory section of the work. Its relative popularity is demonstrated by the high number of surviving thirteenth- and fourteenth-century manuscripts which number close to one hundred. The shift that materialized during the thirteenth century re-focused at least some of the writings of the Northern French Tosafists towards the general population. It would therefore be quite right to understand Elijah's composition in the context of this thirteenth-century shift. The striking similarity of focus on audience between Moses of Couçy, Isaac of Corbeil and Elijah Menahem of London suggests a like-minded concern with dissemination of the law among the general public for general and mass use. The goals adopted by Moses of Couçy for his *Sefer Mitzvot Gadol* from Maimonides and the *Mishneh Torah* seem to reflect the same direction as the intent of Elijah's commentary, which as we mentioned above quotes Maimonides more often than any other text. Maimonides and the *Mishneh Torah* seem to stand as the motivating focal point for both Moses of Couçy and Elijah Menahem of London. In this way, the geographical divide that separated the English Jews and those on the continent seems to have shrunk, at least in regards to their general conceptual goals.

An alternative way of understanding Elijah's commentary in light of the scholarly approach of thirteenth-century continental Jews is through its

---

Condensed SMA'G and Other Condensed Books', in I. Ta-Shma, *Studies in Medieval Rabbinic Literature*, 4 vols. (Jerusalem, 2004–10), IV, 259–68; J. Woolf, 'The Influence of the SMA'G on the Culture of Medieval Ashkenaz', *Sidra* 15 (1999), 31–49.

[39] Galinsky argues that Moses of Couçy sought to create a 'Mishneh Torah' for France through the promulgation of SMA'G. The purpose of SMA'G was not only to issue the law to a wider audience, but allow them to engage in the commandment of 'Talmud Torah'. Y. Galinsky, 'Come and Make a Sefer Torah from Two Parts: On Clarification of Rabbi Moses of Couçys' Intent in Writing the Sma'g', *Ha-Ma'ayan* 35 (1994), 23–31.

specific interpretive medium, a Mishnah commentary.[40] Mishnah commentaries were not a preferred mechanism of interpretation in twelfth- and thirteenth-century Ashkenaz and especially for those Mishnaic tractates that had a corresponding Babylonian Talmudic tractate. The few that were written, by Isaac ben Melchizedek of Siponto and Samson of Sens, focused on tractates in *Zeraim* and *Tehorot*, tractates on which Elijah composed commentaries as well. That Elijah was influenced by Samson of Sens's commentary is clear, particularly in regards to the methods of study.[41] Yet stark differences remain between the two commentaries. Samson composed a commentary on Seder Zeraim, but his comments on Tractate Berakhot are confined to his glosses on the Babylonian Talmud. In addition, Samson's Mishnah commentaries focus more on determining and correcting the text of the Mishnah and of its complementary texts such as the Tosefta, Yerushalmi, and various Midrashei Halakha. The determination of law is a secondary concern for Samson of Sens. These facts stand in contrast to Elijah Menachem's commentary, which in both the surviving Pesakim to Seder Zeraim and in the Berakhot commentary focuses primarily on the determination of practical law and observance. In a way Elijah's commentary to Berakhot parallels the intent of the Mishnah itself to clarify and systematize the relevant law.

Elijah's commentary to tractate Berakhot may represent an effort to form a judicial identity constructed through the medium and influence of the thirteenth-century northern French and continental intellectual culture. Elijah shaped a practical legal guide through the promulgation of a code of daily ritual law, often attuned to the specific English context, by combining the medium of the Mishnah commentary with the utility and purpose of the continental legal code along with the general context and intent of Maimonides and the Mishneh Torah. The combination of these different contexts speaks to the way in which Elijah, a geographical outsider, created a unique work informed by and negotiated with those on the continent.

III: Elijah Menahem and the 'Responsa' Literature: Ashkenaz and Identity

Medieval Jewish culture is generally divided into two major geographic cultures – Ashkenaz and Sefarad. Ashkenaz is the biblical name attached since Antiquity to Germany, and in a wider sense to Northern Europe in general.

---

40 On the attitude towards the Mishnah in Ashkenaz, see J. Sussman, 'Kitve-yad u-masorot nusah shel ha-Mishnah', in *Proceedings of the Seventh World Congress of Jewish Studies: Studies in the Talmud, Halacha and Midrash* (Jerusalem, 1981), pp. 215–54; R. Brody, *The Geonim of Babylonia and the Shaping of Medieval Jewish Culture* (New Haven CT, 1998), pp. 155–6.

41 J. N. Epstein, *Studies in Talmudic Literature and Semitic Languages*, II:2 (Jerusalem, 1988), pp. 751–66.

Sefarad refers to the geographic area of Spain, and since 1492 it connotes more generally the Jewish communities living in Islamic lands. The critical study of the history of Halakhah (Jewish law) has generated many insights into the differences, real and imagined, between these two cultures.[42] But it is only in recent decades that historians of Halakhah have begun to appreciate the more subtle differences and variations between the Halakhic cultures of different Jewish communities within these two groupings. Thus, though they both belonged to the same Ashkenazic culture, the medieval Jewish communities of Northern France and of the Rhineland are now known to have differed in important ways.[43] However, the role of smaller communities within these Halakhic cultures has not yet been explored. English Jewry was definitely a part of medieval Ashkenazic culture. It had family links to, and was influenced by, the Ashkenazic communities of France and Germany alike.[44] In view of this connection, did the Jews of England, like their Gentile compatriots, worry about their identity? [45]

Even a cursory glance at Elijah Menahem's life and work reveals striking aspects that set him apart from his Ashkenazic counterparts. In his Halakhic writings, Elijah made respectful reference to Maimonides – a figure who never played more than a marginal role in Ashkenazic rabbinic works.[46] Elijah Menahem wrote a commentary on the Mishnah – a text not normally studied in isolation from the Talmud in the Ashkenazic cultural sphere.[47] He was interested in Hebrew grammar, and wrote glosses on the grammatical work

---

[42] H. J. Zimmels, *Ashkenazim and Sephardim: Their Relations, Differences, and Problems as Reflected in the Rabbinical Responsa* (London, 1958); Malkiel, *Reconstructing Ashkenaz.*

[43] J. Sussman, 'The Scholarly Oeuvre of Professor Ephraim Elimelech Urbach', in *Ephraim Elimelech Urbach: A Bio-bibliography*, ed. D. Assaf (Jerusalem, 1993), pp. 7–116 (pp. 48–54); H. Soloveitchik, 'Catastrophe and Halakhic Creativity: Ashkenaz – 1096, 1242, 1306 and 1298', *Jewish History* 12 (1998), 71–85; Emanuel, 'Biographical Data on R. Baruch b. Isaac', pp. 423–40; E. Kanarfogel, 'Religious Leadership during the Tosafist Period: Between the Academy and the Religious Court', *Jewish Religious Leadership: Image and Reality*, ed. J. Wertheimer (New York, 2004), pp. 265–305; H. Soloveitchik, *Wine in Ashkenaz in the Middle Ages: Yeyn Nesekh – A Study in the History of Halakhah* (Jerusalem, 2008), pp. 122–124.

[44] See above, n. 12.

[45] R. C. Stacey, 'The English Jews under Henry III', in *JMB*, ed. Skinner, pp. 41–54 (pp. 47–8). Stacey's warning (at n. 39) not to overestimate the isolation of Anglo-Jewish scholars from the Continent is strengthened by the correspondence between Moses of London (Elijah Menahem's father) and some of the leading French rabbis of the mid-thirteenth century. See S. Emanuel, *Fragments of the Tablets: Lost Books of the Tosaphists* (Jerusalem, 2006), pp. 189–90.

[46] H. Soloveitchik, 'The Halakhic Isolation of the Ashkenazic Community', *Simon Dubnow Institute Yearbook* 8 (2009), 41–7; J. Woolf, 'Admiration and Apathy: Maimonides' Mishneh Torah in High and Late Medieval Ashkenaz', in *Be'erot Yitzhak: Studies in Memory of Isadore Twersky*, ed. J. M. Harris (Cambridge MA, 2005), pp. 427–53. Woolf declares that '[t]he first clear example of intensive study of the M[ishneh] T[orah, by Maimonides] … may be found in the Halakhic compendium *Sefer Etz Hayyim* by R. Jacob b. Judah Hazan of London' (p. 443). Jacob Hazzan was a student of Elijah Menahem.

[47] See above, n. 12.

Sefer ha-Shoham, authored by an earlier English Jew.[48] And, alone among medieval North European rabbis, he was a physician.[49] Besides Elijah's exegetical works described in section II, he composed many responsa, answering real-life questions in Jewish law.[50] His responsa were not collected systematically in his time, and those that survived were preserved haphazardly in manuscripts from the fourteenth century or later.[51] This section will consider two of his responsa, both of which were copied in the margins of a Hebrew manuscript held by the bishop's college library of Vercelli, in Piedmont in northern Italy.[52] The responsa concern marriage law, and are connected with Elijah's activity as the head of a rabbinic court. Some of the peculiar terms that Elijah uses in these responsa reveal much about the place he saw himself and his community occupying in the Jewish world.

The first responsum deals with the problem of Jewish men who died overseas, leaving the courts to establish their death in order to permit their wives to remarry. This was a common problem, especially when the man died in a remote location without Jewish witnesses to testify to his death.[53] If, however, he died in a Jewish community, the accepted practice was for the local court in the community where he died to prepare a document authenticating his death, and to send this court document to the man's home town, where it would be accepted by his own local court. As a general principle, Jewish courts accept testimony only from live witnesses, and not from transcripts of testimony.[54] But many rabbinical jurists recognized the difference between a witness who commits his testimony to writing instead of delivering it in court, as opposed to the situation just described where a competent court heard the oral testimony and the written document reflects the decision of that court – including a recounting of the testimony it heard. Once the first court has made its decision, the second court needs simply to be informed of that decision, and a written account is sufficient for that purpose. The text of the responsum reads:[55]

---

48   J. Olzsowy-Schlanger, 'Manuscrits hébreux et judéo-arabes médiévaux', *Annuaire de l'École Pratique des Hautes Études, Section des Sciences Historiques et Philologiques* 140 (2009), 43–5.

49   See above, n. 26.

50   Some of them have been published in German translation: H.-G. von Mutius, *Rechtsentscheide Mittelalterlicher Englischer Rabbinen, Judentum und Umwelt* 60 (Frankfurt, 1995), pp. 38–74.

51   Most of the known responsa of Elijah Menahem have been collected and published by A. Y. Havatselet in his: 'Piske Rabenu Eliyahu mi-Londres', in *Sefer ha-Zikaron li-khvodo ule-zikhro shel ha-gaon ha-gadol ha-dayan rabi Mosheh Svift*, ed. Y. Buksbaum (Jerusalem, 1986), pp. 15–40; and 'Piske ha-Ram mi-Londres', in *Sefer Zikaron Hesed le-Avraham*, ed. A. Berger (Bene Berak, 1989), pp. 40–6; A. Y. Havatselet, 'Pesakim be-inyane Pesah', *Moriah* 20 (1995), pp. 16–17.

52   L. M. Ottolenghi, 'Il manoscritto ebraico del seminario vescovile di Vercelli', in *Miscellenea di Studi in Memoria di Dario Disegni*, ed. E. M. Artom et al. (Turin, 1969), pp. 153–65.

53   J. A. Brundage, *Law, Sex, and Christian Society in Medieval Europe* (Chicago, 1987), pp. 292–5, 374–5; S. McDougal, 'Bigamy in Late Medieval France' (unpublished Ph.D. dissertation, Yale University, 2009), pp. 65–72.

54   Babylonian Talmud, Yevamot 31b; Gittin 71a.

55   Vercelli, Biblioteca Capitolare, Hebrew MS, fol. 287v.; Havatselet, 'Piske Rabenu Eliyahu',

[First the scribe explains:] Some of this is lacking because the copy I had before me was erased before the question. I think the question was how we permit remarriage on the basis of a witness who gives his testimony in writing and is not present before us.

I have often wondered how we allow [women] to remarry. [Here he quotes a passage from the Palestinian Talmud[56] which includes the statement 'if we find a document declaring that so-and-so has died, or so-and-so was killed, we do not allow his wife to remarry']. Now we must wonder, according to this opinion, why we allow [women] to remarry based on written testimony sent from there to here and from here to there ... I would suggest, in defen[c]e of our practice, that we distinguish between a report written independently, without reference to a specific legal need but simply for future reference – this is not a legal document. But documents which arrive because we sent for them in order to ascertain the truth, and which were investigated in court, and that court decided she could marry – we are simply carrying out the decision of that court, and allowing [the woman to remarry] based on their decision.

This was not a controversial opinion. Many, if not all, medieval rabbis who discussed this issue came to the same conclusion: a written account of the testimony given in a different court is acceptable.[57] Several rabbis utilized this same passage from the Palestinian Talmud.[58] What is unique, however, is the language that Elijah uses. It has already been noted by scholars that Elijah was very inventive and subtle in his re-use of words and phrases from earlier sources.[59] Consideration of the way in which he adapted legal terms may reveal additional aspects in his responsum.

First, the expression 'from there to here', משם לכאן. It sounds innocuous in English translation, but in the Talmuds it refers to a significant geographic Other.[60] In the Palestinian Talmud, composed in the Land of Israel, 'there' is

---

pp. 25–26. Part of the text, without the signature, appears in Hagahot Mordechai, Yevamot, ch. 2, paragraph 100.

[56] Palestinian Talmud, Yevamot 16, fol. 16a (*The Jerusalem Talmud – Third Order, Tractate Yebamot*, ed. H. W. Guggenheimer (Berlin, 2004), p. 658).

[57] e.g. Rothenburg, *Responsa*, § 550; E. E. Urbach, *Studies in Judaica* (Jerusalem, 1998), pp. 311–13.

[58] Eliezer ben Yoel ha-Levi, *Sefer Ra'avyah*, ed. D. Dablitsky (Bene Berak, 2005), III, §896, p. 20.

[59] *Writings of Rabbi Elijah*, pp. 12–13.

[60] The two Talmuds – the Palestinian Talmud and the Babylonian Talmud – were composed at approximately the same time, *c.* AD 200–400 . They were created by generations of rabbis living in, respectively, the Galilee and central Iraq. L. Moscovitz, 'The Formation and Character of the Jerusalem Talmud', in *The Cambridge History of Judaism IV: The Late Roman-Rabbinic*

Syria, a close neighbour but without the special legal status of the Land. And in the Babylonian Talmud, 'here' is Iraq and 'there' is Palestine. The Babylonian rabbis recognized the special status of the Land of Israel but when it came to matters of knowledge and expertise, they had, they were sure, a significant advantage over the Palestinian rabbis.[61]

The rivalry between the scholars of Palestine and Babylonia, with a history that continued into the Middle Ages,[62] infuses another term that Elijah deployed in this responsum. 'We are simply carrying out the decision of that court' translates the Aramaic words שליחותייהו קא עבדינן, literally 'we act on their agency'.[63] One aspect of the aura that accrued to the scholars of Palestine was that they received 'semikhah', a special conferral of authority that linked them to the chain of masters ostensibly beginning with Moses himself.[64] Babylonian scholars lacked this special authority. They believed that this ordination was necessary for carrying out certain judicial functions such as imposing fines and corporal punishment. Rather than give up on those judicial functions, the Babylonian rabbis created a legal fiction whereby they were acting in the Diaspora merely as messengers or subsidiaries of the ordained rabbis of Palestine. But the Babylonian rabbis had a much higher opinion of their own capabilities as jurists than they did of the Palestinian rabbis' skills. Their fictional subservience was a foil for their very real feelings of superiority.[65]

This is the 'us and them' and 'here and there' that Elijah encoded into his discussion. It helps us to understand why the question of testimonies being delivered by mail between England and the Continent was not simply a technical problem, as it was for his European contemporaries. It was a problem that Elijah had often wondered about, and which touched the sensitive depths of his communal identity. 'There', in Northern France, in the academies of the Tosafists, were scholars whose fame had spread throughout the Jewish world. What were the smaller Jewish communities of England, with barely a dozen notable Talmudists among them, but a pathetic backwater? Elijah felt that this outlook, though predictable, was unjust. Like the rabbis

Period, ed. S. T. Katz (Cambridge, 2006), pp. 663–77.

61 I. Gafni, 'How Babylonia became "Zion": Shifting Identities in Late Antiquity', in *Jewish Identities in Antiquity: Studies in Memory of Menahem Stern*, ed. L. I. Levine and D. R. Schwartz (Tübingen, 2009), pp. 333–48; S. Friedman, 'The Further Adventures of Rav Kahana: Between Babylonia and Palestine', in *The Talmud Yerushalmi and Graeco–Roman Culture*, ed. P. Schaefer, 3 vols. (Tübingen, 1998–2002), III, pp. 247–71.

62 Brody, *Geonim of Babylonia*, pp. 100–22.

63 Babylonian Talmud, Baba Kamma, 84b.

64 Semikhah' is the term used since the Middle Ages to refer to rabbinic ordination, but this use is secondary and does not carry the full authority that inhered to the Talmudic semikhah. J. Katz, 'Rabbinical Authority and Authorization in the Middle Ages', in his *Divine Law in Human Hands: Case Studies in Halakhic Flexibility* (Jerusalem, 1998), pp. 128–45.

65 I. Gafni, 'Talmudic Babylonia and the Land of Israel: Between Subservience and Assertiveness', *Te'uda* 12 (1996), 97–109.

of Babylonia, whose Talmud ultimately achieved supremacy in every Jewish community, the Talmudists of England deserved respect.

The second responsum also relates to the thorny question of authenticating a husband's death:[66]

> Reuben and Simeon, their wives and their children travelled in a time of war outside the city. At a distance of 3 or 4 parasangs from the city, Gentiles chased after them, beating and wounding the men, and leaving them dead. They did not wish to do anything to the women, but they wounded the boy. The women remained there with their husbands for more than half a day. Four years later they remarried. When we heard of this, we ordered that they be separated from their (new) husbands. We investigated the matter in the gate of our city and discovered that three idlers, false judges, had gone from our city to a small town and heard the evidence of the women. They didn't distinguish between wartime and peacetime, and they permitted them to remarry. We declared them ignorant small-town judges and condemned them to lashes, each according to his sin. We sent for the testifying women, interrogating them like R. Tarfon did (i.e., thoroughly)[67] because of the laxity of the generation, and found that their testimony was credible. They had stayed with their husbands for more than half the day, drumming on their hearts. They saw that one of them was dead and [his] brain spilled on the earth. We asked them how they knew it was brain, and they said 'We saw the white of the brain. When evening came, we took the wounded boy from there and led him to the edge of the city and placed a bandage upon him. The boy was thirsty so we gave him water and he fell asleep and died'. These were their words, no more and no less.

Elijah's conclusion, almost predictably, permitted the women to live with their new husbands. This story says something about those violent times.[68] But what is surprising about the violence is its highly localized nature. The attack occurred outside the city while within the city, peace reigned. The distinction between wartime and peace flows from the rabbinic sources, but Elijah made this distinction geographic.[69]

---

[66] Vercelli, Biblioteca Capitolare, Hebrew MS, fol. 302v; Havatselet, 'Piske Rabenu Eliyahu', pp. 26–8. Quoted partially in Hagahot Mordechai, Yevamot ch. 2, paragraph 123. German translation: Mutius, *Rechtsentscheide*, pp. 38–44.

[67] A reference to Babylonian Talmud, Yevamot 122b.

[68] For a similar story, see Zurich, *Sefer Hasemak mi-Zurich* II, 155.

[69] According to Mishnah Yevamot 15:1, a woman who testifies that her husband died is be-

This dichotomy between the city and the outside plays another role in the passage. When the 'idlers' wanted to engage in illicit justice they left the city and convened in a nearby village. Elijah Menahem branded them 'magosta' – a Talmudic term glossed by Rashi as 'villagers who do not know how to judge'.[70] In contrast, when Elijah himself investigated the case, he did so like a biblical judge, 'within the gate of our city'.[71] Royal authority might explain the higher security felt by Jews within the city walls,[72] but it does not explain the second issue. The three unofficial judges who aroused Rabbi Elijah's ire were not really country bumpkins. They too were Londoners; they held their tribunal outside the city precisely in order to escape R Elijah's reach.[73] In his rhetoric and apparently also in his actions, Rabbi Elijah used the prestige of the city, making it a part of his own judicial authority.

Perhaps local pride can account for some surprising omissions in Elijah Menahem's other writings. As noted above, his Mishnah commentary is extensively based upon the earlier commentary of Rabbi Samson of Sens. At a certain point, Samson's commentary refers to the lack of canvas in England. In Elijah's commentary, the sentence about England does not appear.[74] What caused him to drop this sentence from his commentary? It is possible, of course, that Samson of Sens was incorrect and that there was no lack of canvas in England.[75] But perhaps it was from a desire to eliminate potentially disparaging references to England in Halakhic literature.

One of the facts about England most widely known among medieval Halakhists was that its inhabitants drank beer. Medieval England produced very little local wine, and the Jewish community was too small either to produce its own or to import French wine regularly.[76] Most of the year, they got by with beer.[77] But beer is forbidden on Passover, just like bread. In ad-

---

lieved in peacetime but not in a state of war, since in such times people are liable to lose track of each other and to assume them dead.

[70] M. Sokoloff, *A Dictionary of Jewish Babylonian Aramaic of the Talmudic and Geonic Periods* (Ramat-Gan, 2002), p. 640, s.v. מגיסתא.

[71] O. Creighton and R. Higham, *Medieval Town Walls: An Archaeology and Social History of Urban Defence* (Stroud, 2005), pp. 170–1.

[72] Lipman, 'Jews and Castles', pp. 1–28.

[73] P. Tucker, *Law Courts and Lawyers in the City of London, 1300–1550* (Cambridge, 2007), pp. 43–6.

[74] *Writings of Rabbi Elijah*, p. 5.

[75] It seems that canvas was in fact produced in medieval England. See Epstein, *Studies in Talmudic Literature* II: 2, 761; J. Langdon, *Mills in the Medieval Economy: England, 1300–1540* (Oxford, 2004), p. 252. If this was the case, why did Elijah not take the opportunity to set the record straight?

[76] Soloveitchik, *Wine in Ashkenaz*, pp. 305–6. On the kosher wine trade between Cologne and England, see ibid., pp. 246–50. For Anglo-Jewish involvement in the wine trade, see R. R. Mundill, 'England: The Island's Jews and their Economic Pursuits', in *The Jews of Europe in the Middle Ages (Tenth to Fifteenth Centuries)*, ed. C. Cluse (Turnhout, 2004), pp. 221–32 (p. 228). But this involvement was on a very minor scale: H. Soloveitchik, *Principles and Pressures: Jewish Trade in Gentile Wine in the Middle Ages* (Tel Aviv, 2003), p. 74 n. 28.

[77] On the Halakhic disparity between wine, to which very strict laws adhere, and beer, which

dition, the Passover Seder requires that each participant consume four cups of wine. Moses of London, Elijah Menahem's father, composed instructions for Jews celebrating the Seder without wine, and versions of this list were included in the later English book Etz Hayyim and in the Vercelli MS.[78] Elijah Menahem himself composed a commentary on the Passover Haggadah.[79] One would have expected this commentary to be the perfect forum for discussing a wine-less Seder – but Elijah makes no mention of this situation in his commentary. He may not have considered it relevant. But in light of his father's treatment of the issue, it is surprising that it is not even hinted at.[80] Obviously, the imports and exports of England were not the responsibility of Elijah and his community. But nevertheless, for England to appear in Halakhic literature only as a French outpost where basic grocery products were lacking may have grated against his pride. Hence, he left them out.[81]

IV: Afterlife of Communal Identity

Another prism through which to examine the Halakhic identity of medieval Anglo-Jewry is its afterlife. How was the literary heritage of the English rabbis remembered and preserved over the course of the Middle Ages? The two responsa we have discussed are both found in the Vercelli manuscript, which was copied in Northern Italy in 1452 by an Italian rabbi of French descent – Netanel Trabot.[82] Trabot gathered an astonishingly wide variety of sources and incorporated them into his copy of *Sefer Mordechai* (composed by Mordechai ben Hillel, d. Germany 1298). *Sefer Mordechai* itself was composed as a series of glosses on an earlier work, the Halakhot Rabbati of R

could be consumed freely together with Gentiles, see Soloveitchik, *Wine in Ashkenaz*, pp. 311–14.

78 J. b J. Hazan, *The Etz Hayyim*, ed. I. Brodie, 3 vols. (Jerusalem, 1962–67), I, 371; Havatselet, 'Piske Rabenu Eliyahu', pp. 20–1.

79 The commentary is found in a single manuscript, Uppsala Universitetsbibliotek, MS O.Heb.22, published by J. D. Wilhelm, 'Seder Lel Pesah le-Rabenu Eliyahu Menahem b.r. Mosheh mi-Londres', *Tarbiz* 22 (1951), 43–52.

80 Robin Mundill kindly pointed out that Elijah's personal involvement in the import of kosher wine to England may have obviated the problem, *CCR* 1279–88, p. 60; Mundill, 'Elias Menahem', p. 170.

81 Perhaps one can find a similar example in the Ets Hayyim, composed by a student of Elijah Menahem. Isaac ben Samuel of Dampierre reported that in England butter is made from whey, but he concluded that this should not affect the kosher status of that butter (cited by Rabbi Eliezer ben Yoel ha-Levi, *Sefer Ra'avyah*, §1080 [ed. Deblitsky, IV, 65–6]). Hazan, *Etz Hayyim* II, 75, this is reported in a slightly different manner – 'Some believe it is forbidden because *there are those* in England who mix in whey'. Here it is not the universal English practice, but simply one of the techniques in use. Elijah Menahem and Yose of Lincoln both dismissed the concern regarding butter made from whey without mentioning England, Havatselet, 'Piske Rabenu Eliyahu', p. 39.

82 S. L. Einbinder, *No Place of Rest: Jewish Literature, Expulsion, and the Memory of Medieval France* (Philadelphia, 2009), pp. 137–57.

Isaac Alfasi (d. Lucena 1103). And it remained an open-ended book, with generations of scribes adding more and more additional material.[83]

Seen in this context, it does not seem especially surprising that almost all the surviving passages from responsa by Elijah Menahem of London are to be found in fourteenth- and fifteenth-century copies of *Sefer Mordechai* and similar works.[84] They demonstrate that English material was circulating in Germany and Italy in the late Middle Ages. But they do not reveal whether the medieval English rabbis carried any authority for later generations of European Jewry.

There exists only one manuscript containing Elijah Menahem's writings as a discrete unit. This manuscript, held by the Israel National Library in Jerusalem (MS 8°90), includes Elijah's Mishnah commentary and his accompanying legal discussions. It also contains a variety of other short Halakhic works, but Elijah's compositions occupy almost one third of the entire manuscript. This is doubly noteworthy as the largest preserved unit of Elijah's writings in any manuscript and the largest single unit within this manuscript.[85] Palaeographers have concluded that the Jerusalem manuscript was copied in the Eastern Mediterranean basin in the fifteenth century.[86] But there is no doubt that its roots lie in the West since a large number of responsa were authored by Catalonian rabbis of the thirteenth century.[87] The rulings of rabbis from Northern France (Corbeil and Landon) are collected here, along with those of a rabbi from Vienne, in south-eastern France.[88] The remaining items are from medieval Languedoc.[89] It is highly likely that the Jerusalem manuscript was copied from a Provençal archetype copied in

---

[83] I. Ta-Shma, 'The Open Book in Medieval Hebrew Literature: The Problem of Authorized Editions', in I. Ta-Shma, *Creativity and Tradition: Studies in Medieval Rabbinic Scholarship, Literature and Thought* (Cambridge MA, 2006), pp. 194–200.

[84] Besides the Vercelli manuscript, citations are found in the following manuscripts: Montefiore MS 108 (A. Marmorstein, 'Some Hitherto Unknown Jewish Scholars of Angevin England', *JQR* n.s. 19 (1928), 17–36 (pp. 28–9); Montefiore MS 129, fol. 39r (I. Ta-Shma, 'Seridim mi-Toratam shel Rishonim', *Moriah* 2 (1970), p. 64; cf. *Writings of Rabbi Elijah*, p. 148 and *Etz Hayyim*, ed. Brodie, I, 55–6); BN MS Héb. 1394, fol. 45v (Havatselet, 'Piske ha-Ram mi-Londres', p. 42–3).

[85] For a short description of the manuscript, which in its present state contains 119 folios, see B. I. Joel, *Catalogue of Hebrew Manuscripts in the Jewish National and University Library* (Jerusalem, 1934), pp. 22–3. Elijah Menahem's writings are on fols. 73v–111v (at 38 folios, over 30 per cent of the entire manuscript).

[86] According to the cataloguing information in the Israel National Library's Aleph system.

[87] Jerusalem, INL MS 8°90, fols. 17v–48r. Many of the responsa were authored by Solomon ibn Adret (Barcelona, died *c.* 1310).

[88] Solomon of Landon (MS 8°90, fols. 65r–67v; ed. M. J. L. Sacks, 'Piske ha-Rash mi-Landon', *Sinai* 13 (1943), 223–35); Isaac of Corbeil (fols. 67v–69r: ed. H. S. Sha'anan, 'Piske Rabenu Ri mi-Corbeil', in *Sefer Ner le-Shemayah* (Bene Berak 1988), pp. 5–32); Yakar of Vienne (fols. 69r–72v; ed. M. Herschler, 'Piske Rabenu Yakar mi-Vienne', in *Sefer ha-Zikaron for Rabi Hayim Shmulevitz*, ed. Y. Buksbaum (Jerusalem, 1980), pp. 283–91).

[89] MS 8°90, fols. 1r–16v, 49r–64v, 112r–119v. Much of this material is from Abraham ben Isaac of Narbonne (d. *c.* 1179) and his son-in-law Abraham ben David of Posquiéres (d. 1198).

1393.[90] Another manuscript with almost the same contents, Bodl. MS Mich. 46 (781), was copied in Avignon in 1391. It does not contain Elijah's Mishnah commentary, but it does include several citations from one of his compatriots, Yose of Lincoln.[91]

Jewish scribes in fourteenth-century Provence preserved Halakhic material from pre-Expulsion England that was neglected and forgotten by every other Jewish community. Similar hints to the special reception of English Halakhah in the south of France concern *Etz Hayyim*, probably the most famous Halakhic work from medieval England, completed by Jacob Hazan of London in 1286. *Etz Hayyim* was published by Israel Brodie from the autograph manuscript.[92] Recent research in Hebrew manuscript collections from the former Soviet Union has unearthed only one additional (fragmentary) manuscript of this work.[93] This page is written in Sefardic script, which was used by Jews in Spain and in the south of France.[94] And, while *Etz Hayyim* is quoted in a number of later medieval works, the only one to mention its author by name ("Rabbi Jacob") is Isaac de Lattes, a fourteenth-century Provençal rabbi.[95]

Demography provides a partial explanation for this link. Many of the Jews expelled from England in 1290 settled in the kingdom of France. When Philip the Fair expelled the Jews from his kingdom sixteen years later, many of them moved south to the County of Provence.[96] Among those French Jews were some English refugees. Joseph Shatzmiller has demonstrated that in the mid fourteenth century, some of the Jews in Manosque were still identified by their fellows as being English.[97] Some of those Jews who wandered from England through France to Provence probably brought their books with them. But there may also have been other reasons for a special affinity between the English exiles and their Provençal hosts. The history of Halakhah in southern France is a vivid example of how difficult it is for a small Halakhic community to preserve its identity. Bordered to the north by the robust Tosafist communities of Northern France, and to the south by the large and venerable centres of Spain, the rabbis of

---

90 A note on fol. 75r reads: 'Not from the book – in the year 5153 (= 1393 AD), it was the second year of the Sabbatical cycle and 30 years of the Jubilee cycle'. The words 'not from the book' (אינו מן הספר) make it clear that this calculation was a gloss in the original manuscript.

91 Roth, 'Rabbi Berechiah of Nicole', p. 79.

92 For a codicological description, see Olszowy-Schlanger, *Manuscrits hébreux*, pp. 243–46.

93 St Petersburg, Russian National Library, MS Evr. II A 744.

94 M. Beit-Arié, M., 'Hebrew Script in Spain: Developments, Offshoots and Vicissitudes', in *Moreshet Sefarad: The Sephardi Legacy*, ed. H. Beinart, 2 vols. (Jerusalem, 1992), I, pp. 282–317.

95 A. Neubauer, 'Miscellanea Liturgica: The עץ חיים', *JQR* o.s. 6 (1894), 348–54 (p. 354).

96 Some of the English refugees were forced to leave Royal France in 1291: R. Chazan, *Medieval Jewry in Northern France: A Political and Social History* (Baltimore, 1973), pp. 183–4.

97 J. Shatzmiller, 'Counterfeit of Coinage in England of the 13th Century and the Way It Was Remembered in Medieval Provence', in *Moneda y Monedas en la Europa Medieval*, ed. G. de Navarra (Pamplona, 2000), pp. 387–97; J. Shatzmiller, *Recherches sur la communauté juive de Manosque au moyen âge* (Paris, 1973), p. 17.

Provence and Languedoc took great pains to assert the legitimacy of their local traditions and customs.[98]

Medieval English Jewry found itself in a similar situation, culturally over-shadowed and overwhelmed by French influence. We have suggested some of the ways in which Elijah Menahem of London may have responded to the pressures of that influence. When, shortly after his death, the rabbi's compatriots were banished from England, some of them gravitated to the south of France, where they found communities of a cultural mindset similar to their own. Like the Jews in the south of France, they had hosted Abraham ibn Ezra during his wanderings, they held Maimonides in high regard as a Halakhist,[99] and they were influenced by German mysticism and Spanish poetry.[100] Having struggled to maintain their cultural identity as uniquely English Jews, they may have appreciated the similar efforts on the part of the Jews of the Midi. The study of these smaller Halakhic communities can provide fresh insights into the creation of identity in larger Jewish communities, while restoring a vital perspective on their host cultures as well.

[98] Y. Assis, '"Sefarad": A Definition in the Context of a Cultural Encounter', in *Encuentros and Desencuentros: Spanish-Jewish Cultural Interaction throughout History*, ed. C. C. Parrondo et al. (Tel Aviv, 2000), pp. 29–37; S. Schwarzfuchs, 'L'opposition Tsarfat-Provence: la formation du Judaisme du Nord de la France', *Hommage à Georges Vajda*, ed. G. Nahon and C. Touati (Louvain, 1980), pp. 134–54.

[99] On ibn Ezra in England and Provence, see U. Simon, 'Transplanting the Wisdom of Spain to Christian Lands: The Failed Efforts of R. Abraham ibn Ezra', *Simon Dubnow Institute Yearbook* 8 (2009), 139–89. On Maimonides in England, see above, n. 46. On Maimonides in the Midi, see J. T. Robinson, 'We Drink Only from the Master's Water: Maimonides and Maimonideanism in Southern France, 1200–1306', *Studia Rosenthaliana* 40 (2007), 27–60.

[100] The only person identified as belonging to the German mystical school of the 'Unique Cherub' is Elhanan ben Yakar of London (J. Dan, *The Unique Cherub Circle: A School of Mystics and Esoterics in Medieval Germany* (Tübingen, 1999), p. 46). Ashkenazic mysticism in Provence: M. Idel, 'The Intention of Prayer in the Beginning of Kabbalah: Between Germany and Provence', in *Porat Yosef: Studies Presented to Rabbi Dr. Joseph Safran*, ed. B. Safran and E. Safran (Hoboken NJ, 1992), pp. 5–14. On the influence of Spanish poetry in England: Einbinder, 'Meir b. Elijah of Norwich', p. 150.

11

Notions of Jewish Service in Twelfth- and Thirteenth-Century England

Anna Sapir Abulafia

'The King has provided and ordained etc.: That no Jew remain in England unless he do the King service, and that from the hour of birth every Jew, whether male or female, serve Us in some way', were the opening words of Henry III's *Statute concerning the Jews* of 1253.[1] Less than twenty-five years later in 1275 Edward I had forbidden moneylending, the very form of service with which Jews had paid for the privilege of residing in the kingdom.[2] In 1290 Edward expelled what was left of the rapidly depleting Jewish community in exchange for a magnificent sum from his Christian subjects to reward him for his action. Ironically, the last time the Jews served the king they did this through the cancellation of their very service and their expulsion from the land. Although Henry II had exploited them ruthlessly enough for much of his reign, the Jews of England had at least benefited from the way he had favoured their stake in the business of moneylending over that of their Christian competitors. How and why did the notion of Jewish service change from the time of Henry II to Edward I? How could the same notion lead to such different conclusions? And, crucially, what did the Jews themselves think about the serving role Christians had created for them?

The notion of Jewish service was largely premised on an Augustinian concept which had created space for Jews in Christian society. Augustine's (d. 430) own thinking was, naturally enough, embedded in the realities of Roman law, which recognized Judaism as a licit religion; all free Jews had been citizens of the Empire just like any other since AD 212. Theologically, Augustine's ideas were bound up in the Pauline expectation that Jews would convert at the end of time. Without Jews no such conversion could take place.

---

[1] *Select Pleas, Starrs and Other Records from the Rolls of the Exchequer of the Jews, 1220-1284*, ed. J. M. Rigg, Selden Soc. 15 (London, 1902), pp. xlviii–xlix, trans. on p. xlix. See also J. A. Watt, 'The Jews, the Law, and the Church: The Concept of Jewish Serfdom in Thirteenth-Century England', in *The Church and Sovereignty c. 590–1918*, ed. D. Wood (Oxford, 1991), pp. 153–72.

[2] *Statutes of the Realm* I, 221–2; R. R. Mundill, *England's Jewish Solution: Experiment and Expulsion, 1262–1290* (Cambridge, 1998), pp. 291–3.

But even more tellingly, Augustine made it his business to anchor the veracity of Christianity in its Jewish past. By preserving their own law, Jews witnessed to the truth of Christian teachings concerning Christ. As enemies of Christ they unwittingly served as his best advocates. Their dispersion meant that this kind of service was performed throughout the Roman Empire. Concomitantly, the fact that Jews had lost their own land proved how wrong they had been to reject Christ. Thus Augustine interpreted Psalm 58(9). 12, 'Slay them not lest they forget my law' as an explicit instruction to Christians not to murder Jews and to allow Jews to practise their religion. Others like Pope Gregory the Great (d. 604) would face the challenge of making legal sense of a continued presence of Jews in an increasingly Christian environment. In the spirit of Christian Roman law, that is to say Roman law as it developed under the Christian emperors, Gregory responded to incidents of anti-Jewish behaviour by stating that Jews should be left alone as long as they did not exceed what was deemed to be appropriate Jewish behaviour. This meant that they were allowed to maintain their synagogues and worship as Jews, but it emphatically prohibited them from owning Christian slaves. The idea that 'members of Christ' owed service to enemies of Christ was anathema to Gregory. Nor were Jews to build new synagogues. However fair-minded Gregory was towards Jews in a legal sense, he was as desirous as any for Jews to cease being Jews and convert to Christianity. But conversions had to be sincere; insincere conversions would only lead to converts returning to their vomit, to use the graphic term Gregory borrowed from II Peter 2. 22 (cf. Proverbs 26. 11). In Gregory's exegetical writings Jews served Christians by embodying the living proof of the kind of punishment meted out to those who rejected Christ: loss of land and dispersion. Jews, together with other 'undesirables', were supporters of Antichrist who together delayed the coming of the end of time to which Gregory looked forward with such keen anticipation.[3]

Augustinian and Gregorian ideas about Jews together with the vestiges of Roman law provisions concerning Jews found their way into Christian theological writings, decisions of ecclesiastical councils and collections of canonical material. Christian theological theory presented Christian princes with a complicated set of principles. Jews should be preserved but solely on Christian terms. Their presence must serve Christianity, not detract from it. Jews should not be put in authority over Christians. Jews should convert, but not under duress; on no account should Christian society be put at risk from insincere converts. But once baptism had taken place there was no return for the Jewish convert; the sacrament of baptism could not be undone

---

[3] P. Fredriksen, *Augustine and the Jews: A Christian Defense of Jews and Judaism* (New York, 2008); J. Cohen, *Living Letters of the Law: Ideas of the Jew in Medieval Christianity* (Berkeley CA, 1999), pp. 19–94; *The Jews in the Legal Sources of the Early Middle Ages*, ed. A. Linder (Detroit MI, 1997), nos. 703, 716, 719, 720, pp. 418–9, 433–4, 438–41; A. Sapir Abulafia, *Christian-Jewish Relations, 1000–1300: Jews in the Service of Medieval Christendom* (Harlow, 2011), pp. 1–25.

even if it had taken place unlawfully. It was up to princes to make sense of a theory that made Jews into mnemonic symbols of the past embodying cautionary lessons for present-day Christians and expectant signs of a future in which there would be no Jews.[4] How to deal with real Jews in the present was the conundrum the kings of England had to solve once they had been brought to the island by William the Conqueror.

William of Newburgh gives valuable insights into the ambiguous position of the Jews in England. As the 'king's usurers', to use his own terminology, they had served Henry II well through the taxes they paid out of the profits of the moneylending Henry had made so lucrative for them. (At this point it is important to interject that by twelfth-century theological standards the pejorative term 'usury' covered any form of interest, whether or not it was excessive.) But their very success or, to be more accurate, the success of the prosperous members of the Jewish community – we must remember that not all Jews of medieval England were rich! – had made them vulnerable. In Newburgh's eyes Jewish prosperity encapsulated the inversion of the correct relationship between Christians and Jews in England. Jews like Josce and Benedict of York were lording over their Christian debtors, living like princes. This was not meant to be: Jews were supposed to act like memorials; they were meant to serve , not benefit from them. Jews were supposed to invoke in Christian minds the same image crosses invoked: the image of the crucified Christ. How could Christ's crucifiers be allowed to dominate Christians through their economic resources? In other words, the very service present-day Jews provided for the king eroded the theological premise which had created a theoretical space for Jews in Christian society in the first place. Newburgh's exegetical work reinforced his views on the correct position of Jews with regard to Christians. His commentary on the Song of Songs reiterated the idea of Jewish theological service. But it would be a grave mistake to assume from this that Newburgh approved of the pogroms of 1189/90. He did not. He was appalled by the violence. His ruminations concerning the inversion of the correct relationship between Christians and Jews were, in fact, largely prompted by an attempt to understand how God could have allowed the murderous attacks on the Jews to have taken place. Newburgh emphatically endorsed the Augustinian principle of 'Slay them not'. Those who did slay Jews were mistaken in their religious zeal; attacking Jews was not what God intended.[5]

But Jews were also vulnerable vis-à-vis their royal master. For the more successfully they served the king the more exposed they became to the

---

4   Ideas concerning the status of a forced convert went back to canon 57 of the Fourth Council of Toledo of 633; see *Jews in the Legal Sources*, ed. Linder, no. 840, pp. 486–7; on the ambiguous status of Jews in temporal society see my *Christian-Jewish Relations*.
5   WN, ed. Howlett, I, 280, 293–322; *William of Newburgh's Explanatio sacri epithalamii in matrem sponsi*, ed. J. C. Gorman, Spicilegium Friburgense 6 (Fribourg, 1960), pp. 91, 228, 342; Kennedy, '"Faith"', pp. 139–52; J. Taylor, 'Newburgh', *ODNB* (2004).

king's exploitation of them. Already in 1186 Henry had taken for his own the vast estate of Aaron of Lincoln. It was the ruthless pursuit of Aaron's debts by the king that had sparked so much of the resentment against Jewish moneylending when Richard came to power. Henry's and Richard's collection of Aaron's debts initiated the introduction of special administrative procedures in the Exchequer which would become the Jewish Exchequer. This brings us full circle with the massacres that Newburgh tried to explain. Royal support of Jewish moneylending had a built-in time bomb. On the one hand, it allowed the medieval English Jewish community to become one of the wealthiest in Latin Christendom. On the other, it opened the door to particularly ruthless forms of royal exploitation which in turn could arouse menacing anti-Jewish sentiments among those who borrowed money from the Jews. And ever present was the stark reality that the raison d'être of Jews in England depended on a form of Jewish service which was at odds with ecclesiastical ideas concerning the correct position of Jews in Christian society.

This is not the place to attempt to analyse the overall trends in Jewish fortunes in the thirteenth century, leading to the eventual expulsion in 1290. Nor is it the place to scrutinize the varying circumstances in different Jewish communities throughout England. For our purposes one can say in general terms that the history of the Jews of medieval England was marked by a number of setbacks of different degrees of severity coupled with moments of remarkable recovery. John's heavy taxations and tallages together with the *captio* (seizure of Jews together with their bonds) of 1210, for example, followed on the rapid recovery of the Jewish life in England after the massacres at the start of Richard's reign. Attacks on synagogues in London, during the turmoil unleashed by the events surrounding Magna Carta, again revealed how royal pressure on Jews inevitably led to Jewish pressure on their Christians debtors who then turned on the Jews. The same sorry scenario was played out in the Barons' Wars against Henry III in the 1260s. Jewries throughout England were assaulted by Simon the Montfort and his followers. But huge Jewish fortunes had been made in the thirteenth century by the likes of Aaron of York (bankrupt in 1255) and Licoricia (impoverished by 1258). Interacting with these events was mounting ecclesiastical pressure concerning the correct positioning of Jews in England.[6]

---

6   See, for example, R. C. Stacey, 'The English Jews under Henry III', in *JMB*, ed. Skinner (Woodbridge, 2003), pp. 41–54 and his, 'Jewish Lending and the Medieval Economy', in *A Commercialising Economy: England 1086 to c. 1300*, ed. R. H. Britnell and B. M. S. Campbell (Manchester, 1995), 78–101; R. B. Dobson, 'A Minority within a Minority: The Jewesses of Thirteenth-Century England', in *Minorities and Barbarians in Medieval Life and Thought*, ed. S. J. Ridyard and R. G. Benson (Sewanee TN, 1996), pp. 27–48 (p. 44). On Licoricia, see S. Bartlet, *Licoricia of Winchester: Marriage, Motherhood and Murder in the Medieval Anglo-Jewish Community* (London, 2009).

Thomas of Chobham and Stephen Langton were both indebted to the teaching of Peter the Chanter (d. 1197) in Paris. Peter's forte was to apply scholastic thinking to moral issues of the day. One of those issues was, unsurprisingly, the question of usurious practices by both Christians and Jews, which he and his followers flatly condemned. As for the role of Jews in society, Peter explained that Psalm 58(9). 12 commanded Christians not to slay Jews because the Jews 'are our book carriers and the bearers of our texts and the witnesses to Christ's Passion, they must clean the streets of Christendom rather than be rich and they must perform public service to Christian society'.[7] Thomas pursued this approach in England in the manual he composed for confessors around 1216, when he had been subdean of Salisbury cathedral for some years. In his *Summa Confessorum* he expressed his strong disapproval of how princes benefited from the profits Jews made from moneylending, profits which derived indirectly from their Christian debtors. To his mind this made princes complicit in the sin of usury. Implicit in this statement was the strict ecclesiastical view that the only correct way to deal with usurious gains was to restore it to its rightful owners, who were the creditors who had wrongly been charged interest on the capital sums they had borrowed. Thomas evidently regretted that the Church was not strong enough to resist the practice. He did not seem at all convinced by the argument put forward by princes that they were collecting these monies in exchange for the protection they gave their subjects against the Jews and others who would drive them from the land if they could. (Thomas was writing at a time when England faced civil war and invasion by the French.) In Thomas's mind Jews should only be put up with if they accepted the yoke of Christian servitude, posed no threat to Christians or their religion and performed menial work so that their base condition would bear suitable witness to the truth of Christianity.[8] Royal conniving in their exalted position as

---

7   G. Dahan, 'L'Article *Iudei* de la *Summa Abel* de Pierre le Chantre', *Revue des Études Augustiniennes* 27 (1981), 105–26 (pp. 125–6); J. A. Watt, 'Parisian Theologians and the Jews: Peter Lombard and Peter Cantor', in *The Medieval Church: Universities, Heresy, and the Religious Life*, ed. P. Biller and B. Dobson, Studies in Church History, Subsidia s. 11 (Woodbridge, 1999), pp. 55–76 (p. 72).

8   J. Goering, 'Chobham, Thomas of', *ODNB* (Oxford, 2004); Thomas of Chobham, *Summa Confessorum* 7.6.11.4 and 7.4.6 (ed. F. Broomfield, Analecta Mediaevalia Namurcensia 25 (Louvain, 1968), pp. 434, 510); Watt, 'Parisian Theologians', pp. 72–4; I am trying to make sense of Thomas's words concerning the king's protection: 'Dicunt tamen principes quod quia ipsi defendunt subditos suos contra iudeos et alios qui eos expellerent a terra si possent, ideo possunt licite accipere tantam pecuniam de bonis eorum'. Baldwin rejected the reading given by Broomfield for a reading in a fifteenth-century edition which has the princes defending the Jews against his subjects and others: J. W. Baldwin, *Masters, Princes and Merchants: The Social Views of Peter the Chanter and his Circle*, 2 vols. (Princeton, 1970), I, 299; II, 204–5. J. A. Watt's reading in his, 'Grosseteste and the Jews: A Commentary on Letter V', in *Robert Grosseteste and the Beginnings of a British Theological Tradition*, ed. M. O'Carroll (Rome, 2003), pp. 201–16 (p. 214) concurs with Baldwin's; although his interpretation in 'Jews, the Law, and the Church', pp. 164–5 follows Broomfield's text.

usurers was clearly considered not just to be an inversion of the correct order of things, but immoral and detrimental to the fabric of Christian society.

Stephen Langton's exegetical work displays the interest he shared with others in Paris for the meaning of the original Hebrew of the Hebrew Bible. Andrew of St Victor's seminal work in this area which incorporated rabbinic commentaries in his historical explanations of the Old Testament also left its mark on him. An interest in Hebrew was, of course, perfectly compatible with Stephen's view that Jewish religious practices marked the Jews with the mark of Cain because it was on account of their religious observance that the Psalmist (58(9). 12) had said 'slay them not' and 'scatter them by thy power'. Christians saw in Jews the suffering of Christ; their dispersion proved that all the prophecies concerning Christ would be fulfilled.[9]

Stephen Langton's election to the see of Canterbury in 1206 was hotly contested by King John, and it was not until 1213 that he was able to spend some time in England. Stephen Langton tried, unsuccessfully, to impose on Jews the ruling of the Fourth Lateran Council (1215) that Jews should be distinguished from Christians by their clothing. In England this was to be done by means of a white badge of linen or parchment representing the tablets of the Law of Moses – the so-called *tabula*. The *tabula* had been introduced in 1218 during Henry III's minority in what Richardson has called a half-hearted way. In so far as it was enforced, Jews could easily buy the right not to wear it on behalf of themselves and their communities. This was clearly not to the taste of Langton, who was able to end his exile from England in May 1218. He was again absent from England between the latter part of 1220 and August 1221.[10]

In 1222 Langton convened a Council at Oxford at which he advocated many of the anti-Jewish canons of Lateran IV. The opening words of the first canon concerning Jews are illuminating for our topic:

> because it is absurd that the sons of the free woman [Sarah] should serve the sons of the slave [Hagar] and because considerable scandal regularly arises in God's Church [i.e. Christian society] on account of Jews and Christians living together, we decree that from now on Jews may not have Christian servants.

---

[9] G. Dahan, 'Exégèse et polémique dans les *Commentaires de la Genèse* d'Étienne Langton', in *Les juifs au regard de l'histoire: Mélanges en l'honneur de Bernhard Blumenkranz*, ed. G. Dahan (Paris, 1985), pp. 129–48 (pp. 132–6); Watt, 'Parisian Theologians', p. 73.

[10] C. Holdsworth, 'Langton, Stephen', *ODNB* (Oxford, 2004); Richardson, *EJ*, pp. 178–84; J. A. Watt, 'The English Episcopate, the State and the Jews: The Evidence of the Thirteenth-Century Conciliar Decrees', in *Thirteenth Century England II*, ed. P. R. Coss and S. D. Lloyd (Woodbridge, 1988), pp. 137–47 (p. 140).

The reference to the free woman and the bondwoman refers to the contrast between Sarah, the wife of the patriarch Abraham and the mother of Isaac, whose binding on the altar in Christian eyes prefigured the passion of Christ, and Hagar, Abraham's concubine who was sent into the wilderness with her son Ishmael. Paul had used the imagery in Galatians 4. 22-3 to contrast the liberty of Christianity with the bondage of Judaism. The image was a favourite in papal bulls. The canon went on to say that Christians were under no obligation to favour Jews beyond what the law required and that Jews, in fact, had shown themselves to be ungrateful to Christians through heinous actions. Therefore Jews should from now on not be allowed to build synagogues and they should pay the tithes they owe on church property to the relevant parishes. It is possible that the scandal of a deacon converting to Judaism lay at the back of the words concerning 'heinous actions' which ungrateful Jews supposedly had committed. The deacon was condemned at the Council and burnt without further ado by the temporal authorities. In Matthew Paris's typically colourful rendering of the incident in his *Historia Anglorum* the deacon not only converted, he urinated on a cross and defamed Mary in front of Archbishop Stephen; he also admitted that he had openly attended a sacrifice which the Jews had made of a crucified boy. Matthew Paris claimed that his witness for this story was John of Basingstoke, who was archdeacon of Leicester and one of Simon de Montfort's friends. Blasphemy against Christianity, defamation of Christian cult objects and ritual attacks on Christian children all remind us of the anti-Jewish elements of many Marian miracle tales and ritual murder accusations which disseminated from the middle of the twelfth century. Having said that, there was nothing new about a ruling against the construction of new synagogues; the prohibition entered Christian Roman Law in 415 and became a fixed item on the canonical anti-Jewish menu. Another Oxford canon emphasized the need for Jewish men and women to wear the *tabula* because there was hardly anything by which to distinguish Jews from Christians; plainly, sexual relationships like those of the deacon and his Jewish lover had to be avoided at all cost. Finally, Jews were not to enter churches unless they had a compelling reason to do so. On no account must they use churches as a place of safekeeping for their property. As Watt has pointed out, this last provision was peculiar to England; it was not present in contemporary canonical material.[11]

In 1231/2 Robert Grosseteste, who would become bishop of Lincoln in 1235, wrote a letter to Margaret, the countess of Winchester, who held lordship in St Margaret's parish in Leicester, to spell out how he thought Chris-

11 S. Grayzel, *The Church and the Jews in the XIIIth Century: A Study of their Relations during the Years 1198–1254*, revised edn (New York, 1966), no. XVI, pp. 314–15 (I have adapted the translation); *Councils and Synods with other documents relating to the English Church II: AD 1205–1313*, ed. F. M. Powicke and C. R. Cheney (Oxford, 1964), pp. 100–25; F. W. Maitland, 'The Deacon and the Jewess; or Apostasy at Common Law', *Law Quarterly Review* 2 (1886), 153–65; Paris, *Historia Anglorum* II, 254–5; Watt, 'English Episcopate', pp. 140–1.

tian rulers should apply theological ideas concerning Jewish service to real Jews living in their lands. Margaret had welcomed the Jews whom Simon de Montfort had expelled from his part of Leicester. Grosseteste elaborated on the salvific function of Jews in Christian society. Guilty as they were for Christ's death, guilty as they were for their continuing blasphemy against Christ and their ridicule of his passion, Jews had been subjected to serve Christian princes. These princes must endorse their divine punishment by making sure that Jews toiled on the land, while handing over to their lords any profit they might be able to make from their burdensome labour. On no account must princes allow Jews to oppress Christians with their usury. In the eyes of Grosseteste, usurers benefited from the misery of others. Any prince who permitted Jews to be moneylenders and who derived revenue from Jews was complicit in their crimes and 'live[d] by robbery and mercilessly [ate, drank, and clothed] themselves in the blood of those whom they were obliged to protect'. Grosseteste evidently shared Peter the Chanter's and Thomas of Chobham's view that the practical realities of Jewish existence were supposed to express unambiguously all of the things Jews were meant to embody in a theological sense; they were only kept alive to serve as Augustinian book carriers, as a reminder to Christians of the punishment they deserved for their lack of belief in Christ and for the part they played in the Passion and as harbingers of future conversion with the coming of the last days.[12] As Stow has demonstrated, it is striking how churchmen like Grosseteste took a much harder line against Jewish moneylending than the popes. Lateran IV had ruled against *immoderate* Jewish usury. It had not outlawed Jewish moneylending altogether.[13]

But however often numerous councils, churchmen and theologians tried to make sure that the realities of Jewish existence matched ecclesiastical theories about the correct relationship between Christians and Jews, consistent and effective royal support was needed to bridge the gulf between theological theories and temporal practice. To start off, the king countermanded ecclesiastical attempts to make Christians boycott Jews who did not conform to their idea of the correct relationship between Jews and Christians.[14] But by 1253 things had changed. Henry's *Statute concerning the Jews* absorbed and adapted many ecclesiastical concerns while confirming at the same time the king's ultimate power over 'his' Jews. Thus after stipulating that all Jews must serve the king, the *Statute* went on to legislate that Jews were not to

---

[12] *Roberti Grosseteste Epistolae*, ed. H. R. Luard, RS 25 (London, 1861), pp. 33–8; Watt, 'Grosseteste and the Jews', pp. 201–16; J. Goering, 'Robert Grosseteste and the Jews of Leicester', in *Robert Grosseteste and the Beginnings of a British Theological Tradition*, ed. M. O'Carroll (Rome, 2003), pp. 181–200 (pp. 194–7: Luard edition of letter; pp. 197–200: trans. of letter by F. A. C. Mantello and J. W. Goering); Watt, 'Jews, the Law, and the Church', pp. 165–71.

[13] K. R. Stow, 'Papal and Royal Attitudes toward Jewish Lending in the Thirteenth Century', *AJSR* 6 (1981), 161–84; Watt, 'Grosseteste and the Jews', p. 212.

[14] Watt, 'English Episcopate', pp. 140–2; Mundill, *England's Jewish Solution*, pp. 49–50.

build schools in places which did not have them in the time of King John; *scole* here must refer to synagogues. Royal awareness of the important role synagogues played in Jewish education is interesting in itself. Jews had to keep their voices down during synagogue services so that Christians could not hear them; Jews had to pay any tithes they owed on their houses to the appropriate rector; Christian wet nurses were not to suckle Jewish baby boys, nor were any Christians to serve Jews or eat with them or live in their houses. All Jews had to abstain from eating meat during Lent; no Jew was allowed to insult Christianity or dispute it in public. Christians and Jews were to have no sexual relations with each other; Jews had to wear the *tabula* badge. Jews were not to hang around churches as an insult to Christ. No Jew was allowed to prevent another Jew from converting to Christianity. Jews were not allowed to settle in new places unless they had a special royal licence. Finally, Jews would forfeit their possessions if these statutes were not kept.[15] Although it would be foolish to assume that all these provisions were necessarily always enforced, it is clear that much had changed since the times when Henry I and II and Richard I and John had granted the Jews 'the right to reside in [the king's] land freely and honourably'.[16] But for all of the clauses limiting interaction between Jews and Christians, Henry III continued to give his royal fiat to Jewish moneylending without saying so explicitly. The service he expected from 'his' Jews was the same service he had stipulated in the Jewry Statute of 1233 in which he had limited interest rates to two pennies per pound per week (which came to 43 per cent per annum) and prohibited compound interest.[17] It was the same service from which his increasingly punitive measures in the 1230s and 1240s attempted to draw ever more income for the royal treasury.[18]

It was Edward I who confronted the foundations of what constituted royal Jewish service head on. His *Statute of Jewry* of 1275 emphasized in no uncertain terms that it was the king who had the ultimate say over 'his' Jews' and that they were bound to the king through their service to him: 'Rey ky serfs yl sunt and il sunt taillable al Rey come ses serfs e a nul autres, for a Rey'. As Watt has shown, this is England's vernacular example of Jews being deemed as 'servi', the Latin equivalent which was used in Capetian France by 1230 and in Germany from 1236. The use of the term is the subject of a great debate which I cannot review here. Suffice it to say that I agree with those who have argued that the term refers to Jewish service rather than to Jewish serfdom *per se* in any legal sense. But Edward rewrote the rules of Jewish service in England by

---

[15] *Select Pleas*, ed. Rigg, pp. xlviii–xlix, *Councils & Synods* II, pp. 472–4; *Church, State, and Jew*, ed. Chazan, pp. 188–9; Watt, 'English Episcopate', pp. 143–4.

[16] *Church, State, and Jew*, ed. Chazan, pp. 67–9, 77–9.

[17] Richardson, *EJ*, pp. 293–4.

[18] Stacey, 'English Jews under Henry III', pp. 48–52; N. Vincent, 'Jews, Poitevins, and the Bishop of Winchester, 1231–1234', in *Christianity and Judaism*, ed. D. Wood, Studies in Church History 29 (Oxford, 1992), pp. 119–32.

demanding that henceforth Jews should cease from moneylending and earn their keep from 'lawful merchandise and their labour'. The stipulations of the *Statute* make it plain that Edward wanted to see whether this new definition of Jewish service would work in reality. For Jews, who could not manage to earn their keep from trade or labour, were allowed for the next fifteen years to buy farms or land on leaseholds of ten years or less and rent them out to Christians, as long as no acts of homage or fealty took place and no church advowsons were involved.[19] His *Statute* was reminiscent of similar rulings in France, where Louis IX had stipulated in 1254 that if Jews could not live without engaging in moneylending, they had to leave his kingdom. Because of multiple restrictions on Jewish economic activities both in France and England options for Jews to make a decent living outside moneylending were, in fact, slim. As Jordan has surmised with regard to Louis, the prohibition of moneylending was probably aimed at encouraging Jews to leave or, if they stayed, to force Jews to convert out of abject penury.[20] It is perhaps not for nothing that Charles II of Anjou's prohibition of usury was accompanied by the expulsion of the Jews from Anjou and Maine in 1289.[21] The Jews of England certainly saw the writing on the wall in 1275. In 1276 they petitioned the king to let them serve him as of old; they tried to impress upon him that the provision in the *Statute* concerning outstanding debts grossly disadvantaged Jewish creditors in favour of Christian debtors. They pointed out that restrictions on Jewish activities meant that Jews would not be able to compete with Christians as traders and make a living for themselves.[22] Their pleas fell on deaf ears and as Hannah Meyer's doctoral research has shown, it appears that Jews started to trickle out of England from 1275.[23] Those who remained were soon accused by ecclesiastics of continuing to engage in usury, whether through moneylending or through their activities in the trade of commodities.[24] But before we reach 1290, it is time we looked more carefully at the Jewish side of the story. How did the Jews of England react to the vulnerability of their position in the twelfth and thirteenth centuries? And how did they view the Christians whom they were meant to serve?

---

[19] *Statutes of the Realm*, I, 221–2; Mundill, *England's Jewish Solution*, pp. 118–20, 291–3; Watt, 'Jews, the Law, and the Church', pp. 153–72.

[20] W. C. Jordan, *The French Monarchy and the Jews: From Philip Augustus to the Last Capetians* (Philadelphia, 1989), pp. 148–50.

[21] *Church, State, and Jew*, ed. Chazan, pp. 314–17.

[22] *Select Cases in the Court of King's Bench*, ed. G. O. Sayles, 7 vols, Selden Society 55, 57–8, 74, 76, 82, 88 (London, 1936–71), III, cxiv; Mundill, *England's Jewish Solution*, pp. 120–1.

[23] H. Meyer, 'Female Moneylending and Wet-nursing in Jewish-Christian Relations in Thirteenth-Century England' (unpublished Ph.D. dissertation, University of Cambridge, 2009).

[24] *Councils & Synods* II, pp. 961–2; Grayzel, *Church and the Jews*, pp. 296–7. There is much debate on the exact nature of Jewish business activities after 1275 and whether or not their dealings in commodities involved usury. See Mundill, *England's Jewish Solution*, pp. 124–45; R. R. Mundill, 'Edward I and the Final Phase of Anglo-Jewry', in *JMB*, ed. Skinner, pp. 55-83 (pp. 62–70); Stacey, 'Jewish Lending', pp. 98–100.

What is immediately obvious is that Jews could not have prospered as they did for much of the twelfth and thirteenth centuries if there had been no lively interaction between Christians and Jews. Theory and practice are two very different matters; whatever churchmen said, Jews did employ Christians and Christians and Jews had dealings with each other on all levels. The fact that rabbis in England deliberated whether or not Jewish dietary laws permitted Jews to buy light pastries from Christians must indicate a considerable extent of contact. As their counterparts in France, they used the French word 'oublies' for these pastries. The question entailed a careful examination of the main components of 'oublies', eggs and flour. Flour was the easy one, because since Talmudic times Jews had been permitted to buy bread from non-Jews. The egg component was much trickier because eggs could derive from birds that Jews were not permitted to eat, or from permitted birds which somehow had become ritually unfit for Jewish consumption. They might also contain traces of blood, which was forbidden. The *Etz Hayyim*, the 'Tree of Life', a halachic compendium compiled by Jacob ben Judah Hazan of London just before the expulsion, ruled that there was no need to worry about the provenance of the eggs in 'oublies' or whether any of them might contain traces of blood. Following the majority principle, the fact that most eggs would be all right sufficed. Nor did one have to worry that the presence of eggs in 'oublies' meant that 'oublies' fell under the category of cooked foods which were not permitted to Jews if they were prepared by Gentiles. Following the opinion of Isaac ben Samuel of Dampierre (d. *c.* 1198) in opposition to the view of R. Tam (d. 1171), the illustrious grandson of Rashi (d. 1105), flour was considered the main ingredient of light pastries. And so the pastries were deemed permissible. It is only fair to add that Moses ben Jomtob of London (d. 1268) seems to have held a different view. Although at first he appeared not to be worried about Jews buying 'oublies' from Christians without concern about the provenance of the eggs he seems to have ended up by forbidding the practice because eggs seemed to be the main component of 'oublies'. This meant they could not be prepared by non-Jews for Jewish consumption. As for the *Etz Hayyim,* it also allowed Jews to eat fruit 'tartes' – the French word is transliterated into Hebrew – made by Christians, even if they were prepared in a non-Jewish oven where meat was being prepared. The smell of the meat did not render the tarts unsuitable, as long as there was no chance of any grease coming into contact with the cakes. Jacob Hazan's compendium was also lenient about permitting Jews to share a beer with Christians in their houses while remarking on Isaac of Dampierre's astonishment at the religious laxness of the English Jews in this respect.[25] The use of French terms for foodstuffs, the

---

[25] Hazan, *Etz Hayyim* II, 73–4, 64–5; Roth, 'Berechiah of Nicole', pp. 80–1; Von Mutius, *Rechtsentscheide*, pp. 14, 23–5, 72–3; Babylonian Talmud, Hullin 63b–64a, Babylonian Talmud, Avodah Zarah 31b, 37b–38a; *JAE Docs.*, pp. 269, 291–2. I am tempted to accept Von Mutius's assessment (p. 26) that R. Moses' ruling has come down to us in a corrupted form and that he did, in fact, allow the 'oublies'. I am very grateful to Pinchas Roth for helping me with this material.

efforts of rabbis to work out what they could and could not permit the members of their communities to do, all of this must point to significant interaction between Jews and Christians which, it has to be added, cannot always have conformed to the expectations of their leaders.

It is equally important to note that moneylending was at least as much of a problem to Jewish authorities as it was to their Christian counterparts. Particularly tricky was the question how Jews might borrow money from each other without falling foul of the biblical prohibition against charging interest. It is fascinating how Jacob of Orléans, a pupil of R. Tam, tried to work round the prohibition. Jacob, who was killed in the London riot of 1189, devised a loan contract by which the Jewish debtor would agree to *gift* his Jewish creditor a certain number of pennies per week if he could not pay back his interest free loan within fifteen days of being asked to do so. The loan would, in other words, have comprised something very similar to the penalty clause Christians used in an attempt to legalize moneylending. As Von Mutius has demonstrated, we know of the ruse on account of the horror with which it was received by Jacob's colleagues. The solution that Jews of England and France adopted was the straw man solution which Jacob Tam insisted was permissible: non-Jews were used as middlemen to make it seem that Jews were not lending money to each other. As for Jews lending money to Christians and charging them interest, Tam argued that that seemed to be inevitable because it was the only way Jews could feed their children.[26]

Christian polemic against Judaism was matched by Jewish comments on Christianity. Unsurprisingly, English Jews did not accept the religious premises Christians used to define Jewish service in Christian society. On the contrary, in common with French Jews they were accustomed to add to some of the prayers in their liturgy passages expressing their objections to Christianity and decrying the rough treatment they were receiving at the hands of those whom they were expected to serve. The *Etz Hayyim*, for example, contains an expanded form of the so-called *Alenu* prayer, the prayer which celebrates the election of Israel by God over all other peoples and looks forward to the time when all nations will accept God's rule. Different views exist about the dating of the *Alenu* prayer, but one view would place in the period when both Christianity and rabbinic Judaism were defining themselves after the destruction of the Temple in AD 70. The text of the prayer, which originally belonged to the liturgy of Rosh Hashanah, the Jewish New Year, contains the words:

[26] Von Mutius, *Rechtsentscheide*, pp. 6–8; S. Stein, 'The Development of the Jewish Law on Interest from the Biblical Period to the Expulsion of the Jews from England', *Historia Judaica* 17 (1955), 3–40 (pp. 22–4); H. Soloveitchik, 'Religious Law and Change: The Medieval Ashkenazic Example', *AJSR* 12 (1987), 205-21 (p. 219); H. Soloveitchik, 'Pawnbroking: A Study in Ribbit and of the Halakah in Exile', *Proceedings of the American Academy for Jewish Research* 38–39 (1970–71), 203–68 (pp. 251–3).

> It is our duty to praise the Lord of all ... for He has not
> made us like the nations of the lands ... for they prostrate
> themselves before vanity and emptiness, and pray to a god
> who cannot save ... But we bow down and prostrate our-
> selves before the King of the Kings of Kings, the Holy One,
> blessed be He.

El lo yoshia is the Hebrew for 'a god that cannot save'; the association between 'yoshia' and *Yeshu*, Jesus in Hebrew, seems obvious enough. The
phrase could easily be seen as deliberately insulting Christianity and was
commonly removed from Jewish prayer books by Christian censors in the
Middle Ages. In the *Etz Hayyim* the offending phrase is expanded to imply that those who worship *Yeshu* adore 'a man – ashes, blood, bile, flesh –
shame, stench, worms, etc. etc.'. During the twelfth and thirteenth centuries
the *Alenu* prayer was absorbed into the daily liturgy as the closing prayer
of the three main services of the day.[27] The harsh repudiation of the idea of
the Incarnation which these words reflect and which the Jews of England
would have used day-in-day-out brings out sharply the desperate irony of
dedicating the chapel of the 'Domus Conversorum' (The House of Converts)
in London to the Trinity and choosing the Virgin Mary for its patron saint.
The 'Domus' was founded in 1232 and was the brainchild of Henry III, who
did not just milk the Jews for what they were worth; he was also a keen
enthusiast for converting them to Christianity. As Robert Stacey has shown,
considerable numbers of Jews did convert in the latter part of Henry's reign,
if only because internal support systems within the Jewish community began to fail as the economic plight of the Jews increased.[28]

One of the highlights of the *Etz Hayyim* is a full *Seder* service (the service
on the eve of Passover held in the home), which English Jews shared with
the Jews of Normandy. The text includes a recipe for 'charoset', the ritual
paste made of nuts and fruit representing the mortar used by the Jews
when they were slaves in Egypt. The recipe calls for the use of all the fruits
mentioned in the Song of Songs. The section of the service preceding the
fourth cup of wine contains the passage pleading for God to redeem Israel
in the face of its persecutors. This custom seems to have been introduced
into the *Seder* ritual for the first time in the *Machzor Vitry*, a prayer book
from the circle of Rashi. The standard Ashkenazi version of the passage be-

---

[27] S. C. Reif, *Judaism and Hebrew Prayer: New Perspectives on Jewish Liturgical History* (Cambridge, 1993), pp. 208–9; *Encyclopaedia Judaica*, ed. C. Roth, 16 vols. (Jerusalem, 1971–72), II, 557–8; Hazan, *Etz Hayyim* I, 126 (an unexpanded form of *Alenu* is found on p. 98 in the section for Rosh Hashanah); I. J. Yuval, *Two Nations in Your Womb: Perceptions of Jews and Christians in Late Antiquity and the Middle Ages*, trans. B. Harshav and J. Chipman (Berkeley CA, 2006), pp. 119, 193–4; M. Halamish, 'An Early version of "Alenu le-Shabeah"', *Sinai* 110 (1992), 262–5.

[28] R. C. Stacey, 'The Conversion of Jews to Christianity in Thirteenth-Century England', *Speculum 97 (1992), 263–83.*

came: 'Pour out thy wrath upon the nations that know thee not, and upon the kingdoms that call not upon thy name. For they have devoured Jacob, and laid waste his dwelling place; let the fierceness of thine anger overtake them and destroy them in anger from under the heavens of the Lord'.[29] The *Etz Hayyim*'s version is considerably more elaborate. Texts from the Hebrew Bible railing against the foes of Israel and chastising the Israelites themselves for their own disobedience to God were knitted together in an all encompassing cry of distress.[30]

Violent language is difficult to assess. For a medieval historian it is important to remember that the Middle Ages were riddled with violence. What seems most important is to gauge the purpose and the effects of people's verbal raging. It seems to me that it is helpful to apply David Nirenberg's findings about violent Christian anti-Jewish rituals to Jewish vituperative language against Christians. Following Nirenberg one can posit that much of this evocative language must have helped Jews vent their frustration and let off steam in the same way as Christians would have done in their condemnation of Jews. The harsh rejection of the holiest concepts of the Christian faith, which had much in common with the anti-Christian invectives used in medieval Hebrew to describe any aspect of Christianity, must have been adopted in an attempt to strengthen Jewish identity in difficult circumstances. The constant repetition of these anti-Christian texts would also have been devised to try to programme Jews, as it were, to resist the temptation to convert to Christianity. The most crucial aspect of it all must, however, be to what extent violent language engendered violent actions. It goes without saying that Christian ritual and verbal violence were far more likely to turn into physical violence than Jewish verbal aggression, especially when Christian authorities resorted to violence themselves.[31]

The poet Meir ben Elijah of Norwich composed 'Put a curse on my enemy' in the late 1270s which gives us a poignant snapshot of English Jewry in its last decade in England. Although scholars have not been able to determine who Meir was with any precision, a great deal is known about Jewish business activities in Norwich, an important economic centre in this period. The poem is woven together from quotations from the Hebrew Bible. Indeed one can only wonder how many English Jews would have known their Bible well enough to capture the myriad of subtleties of the text. Susan Einbinder

---

29 Psalm 79. 6–7, Jeremiah 10. 25, Psalm 69. 25, Lamentations 3. 66.

30 Hazan, *Etz Hayyim* I, 329–30; Yuval, *Two Nations*, pp. 123–30; see also I. J. Yuval, 'Passover in the Middle Ages', in *Passover and Easter: Origin and History to Modern Times*, ed. P. F. Bradshaw and L. A. Hoffman (Notre Dame IN, 1999), pp. 127–60; D. Kaufmann, 'The Ritual of the Seder and the Agada of the English Jews before the Expulsion', *JQR* o.s. 4 (1892), 550–61; Roth, *Intellectual Activities*, p. 41.

31 Nirenberg, *Communities of Violence*; A. Sapir Abulafia, 'Invectives Against Christianity in the Hebrew Chronicles of the First Crusade', in A. Sapir Abulafia, *Christians and Jews in Dispute: Disputational Literature and the Rise of Anti-Judaism in the West (c.1000–1150)* (Aldershot, 1998), ch. XVIII, pp. 66–72; see also Abulafia, *Christian-Jewish Relations*, pp. 144–5, 198–201.

and others have pointed out that the poem shows interesting affinities to contemporary 'piyyutim' (Jewish liturgical poems) of France and Germany, as well as displaying interesting Spanish characteristics. Einbinder has carefully analysed the poem to show how it reflects the pain of the Jews in England at their financial plight after being taxed and fined far beyond their means: 'They make our yoke heavier, they are finishing us off. They continually say of us, let us despoil them until the morning light.' (ll. 13-14). The poem shows Jewish awareness of Christian resentment against their need to press Christian debtors for repayment: 'The land exhausts us by demanding payments, and the people's disgust is heard' (l. 10). It expresses grave concern about the inroads conversion had made on the Jewish community and the lack of effective communal authority: 'the words of the seer are garbled, for the foe has mocked Your children until they don't know which path is the one that gives off light' (ll. 7-8) and '… he has despaired of … Your ways of radiant light' (l. 26); 'the vision of His intimates tarries; the predicted time has passed' (l. 28); 'they scattered him with their horns, but he hoped in hidden prophecies' (l. 37). The poem pleads for God's intervention: 'Let the King bring home his banished one, let Him smell his savo[u]ry offer' (l. 22) and the closing lines of the poem: 'All his days, he [Israel] has surely hoped; day after day [he awaits] consolation. O Awesome and Mighty One in Heaven, who brings his justice into the light … If You have given me unto my enemy, rise up to plead my cause. Establish the Messiah's reign, [so that] light will be seen in your light' (ll. 46-50). The fervent expectation of divine deliverance is voiced in the refrain of his poem: 'You are might and full of light, You turn the darkness into light.'[32]

Delving into the biblical context of Meir's scriptural allusions allows us to gain an even greater insight into Meir's feelings about the state of English Jewry. The language of the very first line, 'every man supplants his brother ('kol ah acov jacov')' which derives from Jeremiah 9. 3, immediately brings to mind the passage in Genesis 25. 26 where Jacob gets his name because he tries to supplant his brother by beating him to the exit of his mother's womb. The metaphor of Jacob and Esau played a major role in the Jewish-Christian debate with both Jews and Christians claiming to be Jacob. This line would seem to evoke the damaging effects on English Jewry of the deep-rooted tensions between Christians and Jews. Line 2, 'When will You say to the house of Jacob, come let us walk in the light?' comes from Isaiah 2. 5. In the Bible this line follows Isaiah's words of messianic peace: 'They shall beat their swords into ploughshares … nation shall not lift up sword against nation'. But they are spoken to an Israel awash with treasures and riddled by the evils of idolatry. Again, might this not suggest that Meir had a dim view of the state of English

---

[32] Einbinder, 'Meir b. Elijah of Norwich', pp. 145–62 (analysis: pp. 153–6; translation with notes and biblical notations: pp. 156–9; Hebrew pp. 160–2). For Norwich see Lipman, *JMN*. Quotations from the poem with their biblical citations in this section and the following are from Einbinder's translation.

218

Jewry, whatever its wealth had been and could it reflect Meir's worries about the inroads conversion had made in the community? The refrain of the poem reads 'You are mighty and full of light, You turn the darkness into light'. The second part of the line comes from Isaiah 42. 16. Once again the prophetic message of redemption for suffering Israel is preached to the house of Israel which has been punished by God because it has been steeped in idolatry. This would seem to reflect the poet's attempt to explain why God is allowing his community to suffer so much, but it is surely also a criticism of the community for adopting the evil ways of their opponents. Line 5, 'When I hoped for good, evil arrived, yet I will wait for the light', comes from Job (30. 26), who is describing his changes of fortune. Could this be a commentary on the vagaries of fortune the Jews of England had experienced? Line 10 clearly denounces the hardships suffered by English Jewry, but the line would seem to say something over and above that. Einbinder has observed how 'The land exhausts us by demanding payments, and the people's disgust is heard' echoes passages in Nehemiah 5. What is remarkable is that the message of this part of Nehemiah constitutes a blistering criticism of the corruption engendered by the practice of lending money on pledges. Could we have here an expression of regret that the realities of the day had made English Jewry so dependent on moneylending? Could we have a glimpse here of Jewish reservations on the occupations Jews had been forced into by the circumstances of the diaspora? It certainly brings to mind Rabbi Tam's leniency concerning Jewish moneylending because he knew that in many regions it was the only way they could pay their taxes and make a living. This interpretation is reinforced by the following line: 'While we are silent and wait for the light', which comes from II Kings 7. 9. These words were spoken by the starving lepers who entered the camp of the Arameans, who were besieging Jerusalem. They discovered that the enemy had fled and they ate their fill on the food they found. They also hid the silver and gold they discovered in the camp. They became uneasy when they realized they were behaving badly towards their starving compatriots in the city by 'being silent and waiting for the light'. Again, could we have in these two lines a sombre view of the ill effects Jewish royal moneylending had had on the Jewish community?

Line 14 reads: 'They continually say of us, let us despoil them until the morning light'. This comes from I Samuel 14. 36 where King Saul was about to despoil the Philistines. What is so interesting here is the reversal of roles. Christians are taking on the role of the Israelites; Jews of the Philistines. This is reminiscent of countless cases in Christian writings where Christians see themselves as the true descendants of the Israelite heroes of the Bible.[33] Line

---

[33] A. Sapir Abulafia, 'Twelfth-Century Christian Expectations of Jewish Conversion: A Case Study of Peter of Blois', *Aschkenas* 8 (1998), 45–70 (p. 56); see also S. Menache, 'Faith, Myth, and Politics – the Stereotype of the Jews and their Expulsion from England and France', *JQR* n.s. 75 (1985), 351–74 (pp 360–3), where she speaks about English identification with Spiritual Israel in thirteenth-century political songs.

17, 'But she will be consoled for this; her lord will remain until light', plainly expresses the view that God will console Israel. This should be read as a refutation of Christian claims that God has deserted Israel. Line 19 in which the poet cries 'Have You forgotten to be gracious, My God?' is clearly a cry of frustration, begging God to take action on Israel's behalf. Finally, lines 34-5: 'Even if his [Israel's] sins have really enraged [You], why should his foes wage war [against him]? They whose mouths have spoken arrogantly, they are rebels against the light' would seem to continue the earlier idea that Jews are being punished by God, but it also clearly condemns Christian acts against the Jews, however sinful they might have been.[34]

The evidence we have cited from the *Etz Hayyim* and Meir b. Elijah's poem brings to life the conflicting realities of medieval English Jewry. On the one hand, English Jews, no different from Christians, did what they could do to pursue their business affairs and in so doing would have interacted perfectly well on a daily basis with their Christian neighbours. Underlying these relations, however, were the ever-present complexities of Christian thinking about the correct relationship between Christians and Jews and Jewish ideas about the turn their lives had taken in the diaspora. What ultimately governed these relations was, however, the political exigencies of the day as interpreted by the authority in whose hands the fate of English Jewry lay: the king whom the Jews served. And in 1290 Edward decided that his experiment had failed:

> whereas in ... the third year of our reign, We, moved by so-licitude for the honour of God and the wellbeing of the people of our realm, did ordain and decree that no Jew should henceforth lend to any Christian at usury upon security of lands, rents, or aught else, but that they should live by their own commerce and labour; and whereas the said Jews did thereafter wickedly conspire and contrive a new species of usury more pernicious than the old ... for which cause We, in requital of their crimes and for the honour of the Cruci-fied, have banished them [from] our realm as traitors ('tam-quam perfidos').[35]

The words 'tamquam perfidos' make one immediately think of the phrase of 'tamquam servi' which was used by popes and princes to express the theological and economic service Jews were deemed to owe to Christians. We have already seen how Edward had called Jews his 'serfs' in the 1275

---

[34] Einbinder wonders whether the foes could also refer to Jewish converts rather than to Christians (Einbinder, 'Meir b. Elijah of Norwich', p. 158 n. 63).

[35] *Select Pleas*, ed. Rigg, pp. xl–xlii; *Church, State, and Jew*, ed. Chazan, pp. 317–19; on whether or not Jews had engaged in 'a new species of usury' see n. 24.

Statute of Jewry.[36] The use of the term 'perfidus' to denote Jewish treachery echoes the theological use of the word which often implied that there was something menacing about Jewish lack of faith in Christ.[37] Divesting himself of Jewish service Edward insisted that the Jews who used to serve him had now betrayed him. The terminology seems to reflect well how Edward's antipathy to Jewish usury interacted with general Christian resentment of the role moneylending had given Jews in English society. That combined with the economic reality of an impoverished Jewry made expulsion seem the logical culmination of the two hundred and twenty-four year history of Jewish service in medieval England.[38]

---

[36] e. g. Innocent III's *Etsi Iudeos* bull of 1205 (Grayzel, *Church and the Jews*, no. 18, pp. 114–17) and Louis IX's ordinance of Melun (*tanquam proprium servum*: *Layettes du Trésor des Chartes*, ed. A. A. Teulet et al., 5 vols. (Paris, 1863–1909), II, no. 2083, pp. 192–3; *Church, State, and Jew*, ed. Chazan, pp. 213–15).

[37] See also Blumenkranz, 'Perfidia', 157–70.

[38] I would like to thank Hannah Meyer for reading this paper and giving me some useful comments.

12

Egyptian Days: From Passion to Exodus in the Representation of Twelfth-Century Jewish-Christian Relations

Heather Blurton

> Richard ... was consecrated king ... on the third day of the
> nones of September, a day which, from the ancient supersti-
> tion of the Gentiles, is called Evil, or Egyptian, as if it had
> been a kind of presage of the event which occurred to the
> Jews, and to be Egyptian rather than English; since England,
> in which their fathers had been happy and respected under
> the preceding king, was suddenly changed against them, by
> the judgment of God, into a kind of Egypt where their fa-
> thers had suffered hard things...[1]

The worst 'Egyptian day' suffered by the Jews of twelfth-century England
was undoubtedly the massacre at York in 1190 – an event that stunned contemporary onlookers, Jews and Christians alike.[2] Of contemporary chroniclers who discuss the violence at York, William of Newburgh provides the
most elaborated detail. He identifies the Egyptian day of Richard's coronation as something new for the Jews: events, he writes, were 'suddenly
changed against them'. Other chroniclers of the persecutions of the Jews that
followed the coronation of Richard the Lionheart in 1189 likewise noted that
they were novel: Ralph de Diceto, an eyewitness and participant in the coro-

---

[1] WN, Bk. IV, ch. 1: 'Ricardus ... est consecratus in regem ... tertio nones Septembris; qui
dies ex prisca gentili superstitione malus vel Ægyptiacus dicitur, tanquam quodam Judaici
eventus præsagio. Dies enim ille Judæis exitialis fuisse dignoscitur, et Ægyptiacus magis
quam Anglicus; cum Anglia, in qua sub rege priore felices et incliti fuerant, repente illis in
Ægyptum, ubi patres eorum dura perpessi sunt, Dei judicio verteretur'. Newburgh is cited
throughout from WN, trans. Stevenson, p. 555, with Latin from WN, ed. Howlett.

[2] Dobson, *JMY*, and the more recent discussion by J. D. Hosler, 'Henry II, William of Newburgh, and the Development of English Anti-Judaism', in *Christian Attitudes Toward the Jews
in the Middle Ages: A Casebook*, ed. M. Frassetto (New York, 2007), pp. 167–82 is also useful,
as is Susan Einbinder's account of Jewish memory of these events: S. L. Einbinder, *Beautiful
Death: Jewish Poetry and Martyrdom in Medieval France* (Princeton, 2002).

nation ceremony of Richard I, writes, 'the peace of the Jews, which they had always maintained since antiquity, had been severed by foreigners'.[3] And indeed, whereas Jews living on the continent had suffered at the hands of violent mobs particularly during the First Crusade, the Jews of England had survived safely through two crusades. Moreover, from the mid-twelfth century, the most troublesome discourse concerning the Jews of England did not involve violence against Jews, but rather against Christians. This, of course, was the accusation beginning in the 1140s and continuing through the end of the century that Jews would kidnap and ritually crucify Christian children.

There were apparently at least three of these accusations in twelfth-century England: of the martyrdom of William of Norwich in the 1140s, of Harold of Gloucester in 1168, of Robert of Bury St Edmunds in 1181 and perhaps also an unnamed boy in Winchester in 1192. One of the many things these accusations have in common is that none of them resulted in immediate, real violence. However, at the end of the twelfth century, for the first time in England, popular violence did break out against the Jews: on that 'Egyptian day' in London in 1189 at the coronation of Richard the Lionheart, and subsequently at Lynn, Bury St Edmunds, Stamford, and Lincoln among other places, including York.

While both the ritual crucifixion accusations and the pogroms of twelfth-century England can be read as part of a common narrative of the escalation of violent rhetoric and real violence against the Jews in the second half of the twelfth and the thirteenth centuries, as Anthony Bale has recently noted, 'Christian narratives of persecution by Jews did not translate simply or seamlessly into the Christian persecution of Jews'.[4] Indeed, as they appear in rhetorically aware historiography such as Newburgh's, although mutually constituting, these two tropes of persecution are informed by quite different discourses.[5] What I wish to suggest here is that as opposed to the ritual crucifixion narrative, which models Jewish-Christian relations through the lens of Christ's Passion, the late twelfth-century chronicles that describe the pogroms against English Jews are fundamentally informed by Biblical narratives of the destruction and expulsion of the ancient Israelites: for example (as Newburgh's reference to an Egyptian day befalling the Jews suggests), Exodus, but also the destruction of Jerusalem and the dispersal of the Jews

---

3 'pax Judaeorum, quam ab antiquis temporibus semper obtinuerant, ab alienigenis interrumpitur', Diceto, *Historical Works* II, 69.

4 A. Bale, *Feeling Persecuted: Christians, Jews, and Images of Violence in the Middle Ages* (London, 2010), p. 26. See also the seminal discussion in Rubin, *Gentile Tales: The Narrative Assault on Late Medieval Jews* (New Haven, CT, 1999).

5 In part, this difference can perhaps be accounted for by the different genres in which these episodes appear. *The Passion and Miracles of William of Norwich* is a hagiographic text, and as such depends on the standard tropes of saints' lives, modelled as they are on the life of Christ. Whereas, although Jocelin of Brakelond tells us that he has written a *Life* of Robert of Bury St Edmunds, that *Life* is no longer extant, and so we are dependent on chronicle sources for most of our knowledge of these events.

at Masada, and during the Babylonian exile, as expressed in Lamentations. The choice of these tropes, I will argue here, may be read as participating in an implicit argument for the expulsion of the Jews from England.[6]

The concern of this essay, then, will be to situate Newburgh's representation of what happened at York in 1190 in a literary history, noting just one aspect of the shifting tropes that articulate Jewish-Christian relationships over the course of the long twelfth century. It will consider first Newburgh's implicit dismissal of a nascent ritual murder cult in Stamford and his casting of the events of 1189-90 into a Biblical vocabulary of expulsion. That is to say, I will argue that Newburgh's treatment of these events marks a rhetorical shift from the use of the tropes of ritual crucifixion to those of exodus and expulsion to make sense of Christian violence against English Jews. I will argue further that if Newburgh relies on the tropes of exodus and expulsion in order to make sense of the violence of York 1190, in so doing he is joined by the majority of contemporary chroniclers who describe these events. Richard of Devizes, Roger of Howden, Ralph of Coggeshall and Ralph de Diceto all turn to the language of exodus and expulsion as a key narrative trope that makes sense of contemporary Jewish-Christian relations, and more specifically, of Christian violence against Jews.

In turning from Passion to Exodus, the chroniclers of 1189-90 are relying on very different tropes to make meaning out of contemporary events. The accusation of ritual crucifixion is fundamentally informed by the narrative and soteriological model of Christ's Passion. For example, in the earliest of the narratives of the ritual crucifixion accusation, Thomas of Monmouth's account of the 'martyrdom' of William of Norwich, William's death is emphatically modelled on that of Christ. Thus Thomas notes that the Jews patronized William:

> because, as I rather believe, by the ordering of divine provi-
> dence he had been predestined to martyrdom ('diuine nutu
> prouidentie ad martyrium') from the beginning of time, and
> gradually step by step was drawn on, and chosen to be made
> a mock of and to be put to death by the Jews, in scorn of the
> Lord's passion.[7]

---

6 M. J. Kennedy has previously discussed Newburgh's use of Exodus and other Old Testament tropes, seeing in Newburgh's historiography 'a puzzled man attempting to make some sense of events which deeply disturbed him' (p. 148), and in his commentary on the Song of Songs, Newburgh's 'confident hope … for Jewish repentance and conversion' (p. 151) (Kennedy, '"Faith"', pp. 139–52). While I do not disagree with Kennedy's articulation of William's relatively sympathetic treatment of the Jews (although I would argue for drawing a more clear distinction between the contemporary Jews of his *History* and the Biblical Jews of his *Commentary*), I read Newburgh and his contemporaries as making sense of events through the ideology of expulsion rather than conversion.

7 Thomas of Monmouth, *The Life and Miracles of St William of Norwich*, ed. and trans. A. Jessopp and M. R. James (Cambridge, 1896), p. 15.

Thomas places the murder during Passover, further bringing it into line with the death of Christ, and the man who comes to lure William away from his mother and deliver him to the Jews is characterized as 'the imitator in almost everything of the traitor Judas', and who, to drive the point home, betrays William into the hands of his enemies for three coins.[8] As Anthony Bale notes, although Thomas frames the martyrdom of William as an act of mockery, for its Christian audience it would have resonated most fully as a repetition of sacred history:

> Thomas says the Jews wanted to mock the Passion of Christ, but the sense and meaning of the entire project is based on rereading William's death as a heightened, clarified, remembered version of Christ's Passion. It might be said that the 'memory-work' a text like this performs is not to remember the Jewish murder of a Christian child, but to remember Christ's Passion.[9]

The Jews as imagined here are the perpetrators of violence against defenceless Christian bodies as they ceaselessly and timelessly re-enact their originary role in the Christian drama of sacrifice and salvation. In this role, they appear very differently to the Old Testament Israelite, the very model of the persecuted and oppressed, whose history is repeatedly inscribed as one of dispossession, expulsion, and diaspora.

Given Newburgh's clear interest in the place of the Jews in English society, it is paradoxical that he nowhere directly addresses rumours of ritual murder, as M. J. Kennedy points out:

> In twelfth-century England anti-Jewish sentiment manifested itself principally in allegations of Jewish complicity in the murders of a number of Christian children, and it is significant that William, who wrote more extensively on the Jews than any other English historian of his time, makes no reference to them.[10]

I want to suggest, however, that Newburgh does in fact obliquely address – but only in order to suppress – an incipient ritual murder cult, and that his

---

8   'ac fere per Omnia Iude traditoris imitator', Monmouth, *Life and Miracles of St William*, pp. 16–20. See also M. Otter, *Inventiones: Fiction and Referentiality in Twelfth-Century English Historical Writing* (Chapel Hill NC, 1996), p. 39 for a discussion of Thomas of Monmouth's use of the Easter narrative.

9   Bale, *Feeling Persecuted*, p. 55. For the continuing importance of the representation of Jews as killers of Christ see J. Cohen, 'The Jews as the Killers of Christ in the Latin Tradition, From Augustine to the Friars', *Traditio* 39 (1983), 1–27.

10 Kennedy, '"Faith"', p. 141.

treatment of it represents his narrative dismissal of an event which, at that time, was taking on another interpretation. The story to which I allude is set following an outbreak of rioting against the Jews of Stamford, one of the many riots following the coronation of Richard the Lionheart, begun by a group of young, foreign crusaders on their way to Jerusalem. These crusaders, annoyed that the Jews seemed to have so much money while they had so little and such a daunting adventure before them, attack and plunder the Jews of Stamford, who seek safety in the castle. The plunderers subsequently all leave town with their loot. As Newburgh recounts:

> One of these, by name of John, a most audacious youth (*ju-venis*), going to Hampton, deposited a part of his money with a certain man ('apud quendam'), by whom – from a desire to obtain that same money ('ejusdem pecuniae ambitu') – he was secretly murdered, and his body cast out of town at night. When it was found, and accidentally recognized by some people, the avaricious murderer took to secret flight. Soon after, some old women having had some visions, and some delusions of fallacious prophecies appearing there, these simple people ascribed to the murdered youth ('illi') the merit and glory of a martyr, and honoured his sepulchre with solemn watches. Roused by his reputation, the senseless common people ('vulgus') came at first from places in the neighbourhood, and afterwards poured in from different counties, in a curious spirit of devotion, desiring to witness the miracles of the new martyr, or to obtain his intercession; and no one came to his sepulchre empty handed. This was laughed at by prudent people; but it was agreeable to the clergy on account of the advantages that resulted from the superstition. (WN, Bk IV, ch. 8; trans. Stevenson, p. 565)

This popular nascent cult, however, is firmly repressed by the bishop, Hugh of Lincoln.

This story is most often called to witness the remarkable humanity, even modernity, of Hugh of Lincoln, a man, Newburgh writes, 'of exalted virtue' ('eximiæ virtutis virum').[11] But I would suggest that the incipient martyr cult that Newburgh describes must have been understood by the people of Stamford as a case of the ritual murder – or at least the murder – of a Christian by Jews. While the story opens as a classic double cross, it shares all the major

---

11 The 'John of Stamford' incident is also mentioned in the *Life* of Hugh of Lincoln: 'it is common knowledge that Hugh after a bitter struggle put a stop to the veneration paid to a robber at Northampton' ('Norhamtonia tamen latronis... Hugone acriter decertante, postposuisse noscuntur'), Adam of Eynsham, *Magna Vita Sancti Hugonis. The Life of Saint Hugh of Lincoln*, ed. and trans. D. L. Douie and H. Farmer, 2 vols., OMT (Oxford, 1985) II, 201.

elements of the ritual murder cult except the explicit statement that John was killed by Jews – rather, the identity of the murderer is coyly withheld. In any case, it is implicit in the telling that the 'senseless common people' understood John to have been murdered by Jews: this must be the point of situating the culting of a dead crusader in the context of violence against the Jews. This is why the recognition of the body is important, why this John is referred to as a 'youth', and why the incident is explicitly situated during Lent – the traditional time of year for ritual murder accusations, as in the ones at Norwich, Gloucester and Winchester.

Indeed, the story of 'John of Stamford' bears a remarkable resemblance to an incident of 1147 in Würzburg, where a murdered and dismembered man, discovered by a group of crusaders, was immediately assumed to have been martyred by the Jews. The 'martyr' was culted, and about twenty Jews were killed over this imagined crime. That cult also was put down by ecclesiastical authorities, acting along with the emperor.[12] The story of 'John of Stamford' also parallels that of William of Norwich, whose body is likewise discovered outside of the town, his sanctity announced by prodigies and women's visions, his martyrdom initially controversial. There seems to be general agreement that William's cult would have died out had not a new monk moved to town, Thomas of Monmouth, who became William of Norwich's biggest fan and, more importantly, his hagiographer.

In the final analysis, it seems that all 'John of Stamford' was missing was a keen hagiographer – the sort that William of Norwich found in Thomas of Monmouth. But Newburgh is not that hagiographer, and in reporting a promising ritual murder cult he simultaneously suppresses it. While this may be attributed to Newburgh's famed rationality and scepticism as an historian, it also reflects his understanding of the place of Jews in Christian society.[13] Indeed, his interest in framing the Jews as the murderers of Christ resides not so much in their potential danger to individual Christians, or in their ability to create new martyrs and saints. For Newburgh, the important theological lesson to be taken from the Jews' betrayal and murder of Christ is that it disqualifies them from the right to inhabit Jerusalem and condemns them to permanent exile. Newburgh is very clear on this point:

---

[12] R. C. Stacey, 'Crusades, Martyrdoms, and the Jews of Norman England, 1096–1190', in *Juden und Christen zur Zeit des Kreuzzüge*, ed. A. Haverkamp (Sigmaringen, 1999), pp. 233–51 (p. 236).

[13] Newburgh in general does not seem particularly interested in the culting of contemporary saints: he treats the incipient cult of William Longbeard very similiarly to that of the robber John. On Newburgh's treatment of Longbeard see N. F. Partner, *Serious Entertainments: The Writing of History in Twelfth-Century England* (Chicago, 1977), p. 24. On Newburgh's rationality and skepticism see ibid, pp. 51–52; Otter, *Inventiones*, p. 103; J. D. Hosler, 'Henry II, William of Newburgh, and the Development of English Anti-Judaism', in *Christian Attitudes Toward the Jews in the Middle Ages: A Casebook*, ed. M. Frassetto (New York, 2007), pp. 167-82 (p. 168).

> Other regions [than Jerusalem] … do not … swallow up or
> cast out their inhabitants, though they be more deeply de-
> based by transgressions, as that land afterward justly cast
> out even the seed of Abraham, to whom it was given as
> an heritage … But because they know not the time of their
> visitation, but by execrable infatuation killed their own Re-
> deemer, this same land, notable for the performance of the
> heavenly mysteries accomplished within it, cast [them] out
> with sorer judgment never to be recalled, while the Roman
> emperors Vespasian and Titus were the ministers of Divine
> vengeance. (WN, Bk III, ch. 15; trans. Stevenson, p. 534)

Written as much in response to the loss of Jerusalem to Saladin as to the Roman sack of Jerusalem in the first century, this passage nevertheless casts
Jerusalem as uniquely unwilling to be held by a morally corrupt people.[14]
The Jews, the Seed of Abraham, proved their moral corruption through the
murder of Christ, and have thus been rejected by Jerusalem. In Newburgh's
understanding, this exile is merited as much for the crusaders as for the
Jews, but the lesson is clear: Jewish perfidy implicitly and necessarily leads
to Jewish exile.

This theme of Jewish exile is revisited at the coronation of Richard the Lionheart where, in the passage that opened this essay, Newburgh frames the
experience of the Jews of England under their new king as 'Dies Ægyptiacus': an Egyptian day. Newburgh most likely borrows the idea of Richard's
coronation occurring on an 'Egyptian Day' from the text that is normally
assumed to be his most important source for this event, Roger of Howden's
Chronicle.[15] Howden seems simply to include the mention of an 'Egyptian
day' as a specifying element in his dating of the coronation: Richard 'was
consecrated and crowned King of England, at Westminster, in London, on
the third day before the nones of September, being the Lord's Day, and
the feast of the ordination of Saint Gregory, the pope (the same being also
an Ægyptian day ('die quoque Ægyptiaca')), by Baldwin, archbishop of
Canterbury'.[16] Howden's nineteenth-century translator notes

> Ægyptian days were unlucky days, of which there were said
> to be two in every month. It is supposed that they were so

---

[14] See the discussion of this passage in Hosler, 'Henry II, William of Newburgh, and the Development of English Anti-Judaism', pp. 173–5. Partner notes that this discussion of what
William calls 'the prerogative of the Land of Jerusalem' is not in his main source for these
years, the *Itinerarium Regis Ricardi* (Partner, *Serious Entertainments*, p. 105).

[15] On the relationship between Newburgh and Howden, see J. Gillingham, 'Two Yorkshire
Historians Compared: Roger of Howden and William of Newburgh', *Haskins Society Journal*
12 (2002), 15–37.

[16] Howden, *Annals* II, 116; Howden, *Chronica* III, 8.

called from an Ægyptian superstition, that it was not lucky
to bleed, or begin any new work, on these days.[17]

Newburgh seizes upon this theme and transforms it. For him, an Egyptian
day comes to signify not only misfortune, but a key to providential history.
In this moment, twelfth-century England is translated into the Biblical Egypt
of the new Pharaoh who persecutes the Jews, following the narrative of Exodus 1. 8-10:

> Then a new king, who did not know about Joseph, came to
> power in Egypt. 'Look', he said to his people, 'the Israelites
> have become much too numerous for us. Come, we must
> deal shrewdly with them or they will become even more
> numerous'.

With a single stroke, the English under Richard I are thus cast as the new
Egyptians in the drama of destruction and exodus that Newburgh is script-
ing. With Richard I as the Pharaoh, the expulsion of the Jews becomes inevitable. While this may seem an odd casting, as Newburgh himself notes: 'the
Omnipotent may frequently execute His will (which is most good) by the
will and the acts (which are most evil) of men even the most wicked' (WN,
Bk. IV, ch. 1; trans. Stevenson, p. 558).

Newburgh further particularizes his theme of Jewish expulsion through
his elaboration of the connection drawn by Howden between contemporary Jewish suicide at York and ancient Jewish suicide at Masada.[18] In
Howden's *Chronicle*, the connection of events at York to the historical siege
and destruction of the Jews at Masada by the Romans is implicit in a speech
that echoes that of Eleazar at the siege of Masada: 'Men of Israel, listen to
my advice. It is better that we should kill one another, than fall into the
hands of the enemies of our law', as recounted in Josephus's *History of the
Jewish War*.[19] Newburgh makes the connection more explicit: he includes
an elaborated version of the speech, and he adds a citation lest a careless
reader miss the reference:

> whoever reads the *History of the Jewish War* by Josephus, un-
> derstands well enough, that madness of this kind, arising
> from their ancient superstition, has continued down to our
> own times, whenever any very heavy misfortune fell upon
> them (WN, Bk. IV, ch. 10; trans. Stevenson, p. 570).

---

[17] Howden, *Annals* II, 116 n. 21.
[18] See also the important discussion by Vincent in this volume about Newburgh's use of Josephus and the circulation of the Josephus tradition in twelfth-century England, pp. 000-000.
[19] Howden, *Annals* II, 138.

Historically, the siege of Masada was a desperate last stand after the fall and destruction of Jerusalem, and so in staging York as an erstwhile Masada, Newburgh imagines a historical connection between York and Masada that emphasizes the destruction and dispersal of the Jews.[20] Indeed, in so doing, both Howden and Newburgh may have been elaborating on a theme that already had a certain amount of cultural currency. At least one of the versions of Josephus's text circulating in twelfth-century England already encoded fantasies of Jewish expulsion. Thus Newburgh's Masada reference, in Ruth Nisse's words:

> evokes a specific nexus of interpretations of the historical fall of Jerusalem and its relation to Europe. In particular, Pseudo-Hegesippus's late fourth-century Christian 'adaptation' of Josephus's *Jewish War* to new ideological ends assigns the meaning of the Jewish diaspora to Jesus as 'he whose death is the destruction of the Jews'. In this widely circulated work, sometimes called the *De excidio Hierosolymitano*, a version of the zealot Eleazar's speech urging the Jews to suicidal martyrdom becomes the final death knell for Judaism within a Christian world.[21]

Through the citation of Eleazar's speech, and the invocation of the days of Egypt and Masada more generally, Newburgh is insistently reminding his readers that the history of the Jews is characterized by a series of expulsions and encouraging them to imagine a connection between that past and the English present.[22]

A similar rhetoric is at work in the *Cronicon* of Richard of Devizes, which, like Book Four of Newburgh's *Historia,* begins with the coronation of Richard the Lionheart and ends with the failure of his crusade. Indeed, like Newburgh, the only scene from the coronation that Devizes actually describes is the violence that erupted against the Jews of London:

[20] In so doing, William strangely elides the massacres of the Rhineland Jews by crusading armies during the First Crusade that produced scenes of mass suicide analogous to that at York. The extent to which news of those massacres had travelled to England is not clear, but the Jews of York certainly knew of them and commemorated them (Einbinder, *Beautiful Death*, pp. 29–3, 51).

[21] R. Nisse, '"Your Name Will No Longer Be Aseneth": Apocrypha, Anti-martyrdom, and Jewish Conversion in Thirteenth-Century England', *Speculum* 81 (2006), 734–53 (p. 739). For Newburgh's use of the Masada trope see also E. N. van Court, '"The Siege of Jerusalem" and Augustinian Historians: Writing about Jews in Fourteenth-Century England', *Chaucer Review* 29 (1995), 227–48.

[22] See Kennedy for Newburgh's similar construction of the Jews in his *Commentary on the Song of Songs,* where he emphasizes the culpability of the Jews for the crucifixion, but also that they are included in its promise of salvation. Kennedy, '"Faith"'. For the text of the *Commentary* see *William of Newburgh's Explanatio sacri epithalamii in matrem sponsi,* ed. J. C. Gorman, Spicilegium Friburgense 6 (Fribourg, 1960).

> On that same coronation day, at about the hour of that so-
> lemnity in which the Son was immolated to the Father, they
> began in the city of London to immolate the Jews to their Fa-
> ther, the Devil. It took them so long to celebrate this mystery
> that the holocaust was barely completed on the second day.
> The other towns and cities of the country emulated the faith
> of the Londoners, and with equal devotion they dispatched
> their bloodsuckers bloodily to hell. To some degree, but not
> everywhere the same, this storm against the incorrigible
> people raged throughout the kingdom. [23]

Winchester does not participate in the anti-Jewish riots that follow, but, Devizes notes:

> Because Winchester should not be deprived of its just praise
> for having kept peace with the Jews, as is told at the begin-
> ning of this book, the Jews of Winchester, zealous, after the
> Jewish fashion, for the honour of their city (although what
> was done greatly lessened it), brought upon themselves, ac-
> cording to the testimony of many people, the widely known
> reputation of having made a martyr of a boy in Winchester.[24]

Like Newburgh with his narration of the death and culting of John in Stamford, Devizes – with his hyperbolic language and satirical tone – may be
read here as casting doubt on the facticity of the ritual murder accusation.[25]
Where Newburgh seems to refuse the trope of ritual murder as a narrative
model for making sense of Jewish-Christian relations, Richard of Devizes
does recount a tale of ritual murder – but he articulates it through the tropes
of exodus and expulsion. And while the *Cronicon*'s modern editor notes that
this passage is heavily indebted to classical authors – Horace, Virgil, Ovid
and Lucan – it draws equally on Biblical tropes.[26] In the tale Devizes tells
about the Winchester ritual murder accusation. The martyred boy is a poor
French cobbler's apprentice who is convinced to leave France and travel to

---

[23] Devizes, *Chronicle*, p. 3.

[24] ibid., p. 64.

[25] The incident that Richard of Devizes describes almost certainly never occurred, although scholars have been hesitant to dismiss it completely since Cecil Roth's identification of a contemporary fine levied against some Winchester Jews that suggested to him that the ac-cusation might be accepted (Roth, *HJE*, p. 134). On this episode as satire see R. Levine, 'Why Praise Jews: Satire and History in the Middle Ages', *JMH* 12 (1986), 291–6; I have ar-gued elsewhere for reading the tropes of Menippean satire in Richard's *Cronicon*: H. Blurton, 'Richard of Devizes's *Cronicon*, Menippean Satire, and the Jews of Winchester', *Exemplaria* 22 (2010), 265–84. For the discovery of an important literary analogue see A. Bale, 'Richard of Devizes and Fictions of Judaism', *Jewish Culture and History* 3 (2000), 55–72.

[26] Devizes, *Chronicle*, p. 64 n. 2.

England by a French Jew who assures him that Winchester is 'the Jerusalem of the Jews' (*Iudeorum Ierosolima*) and that England is 'a land of milk and honey' ('terram lacte et melle');[27] echoing God's words to the Israelites in Exodus 3. 17: 'I will bring you up out of the affliction of Egypt ... unto a land flowing with milk and honey' ('ad terram fluentem lacte et melle'). This same French Jew also refers to the young Christian boy as a 'scapegoat' and lays hands on him, evoking the complex rites of sin and expiation of Leviticus 16, where the scapegoat is to be exiled into the wilderness carrying the sins of the Israelites.[28]

Moreover, the narrative of ritual murder recounted by Devizes is rather anticlimactic: when the French boy goes missing on Good Friday, his friend is troubled by bad dreams and searches everywhere, including at the house of the French boy's Jewish employer. Turned roughly away, the friend breaks out in shrill accusations, shouting: 'You son of a dirty whore ... you thief, you traitor, you devil, you have crucified my friend!'. When a crowd gathers, he continues: 'This Jew is a devil; this man has torn the heart out of my breast; this man has cut the throat of my only friend, and I presume he has eaten him too'. This rant hardly draws upon the typology or the imagery of Christ's Passion at all, but it does quote Lamentations 1. 12, as the boy addresses the gathering crowd: 'O you men who gather together ... see if there is a grief like unto my grief':[29] a passage for which the greater context is precisely that of exodus and exile – the lamentation of the prophet Jeremiah over the destruction of Jerusalem by Nebuchadnezzar:

> How does the city sit solitary that was full of people! How is the mistress of the Gentiles become as a widow ... Judah has removed her dwelling place because of her affliction, and the greatness of her bondage: she hath dwelt among the nations and she has found no rest (Lamentations 1. 1; 3).

Richard of Devizes's narrative of the (purported) 1192 accusation of ritual murder in Winchester seems more interested in framing the relationship between Jews and Christians in the language of exodus and exile than of the Passion, although paradoxically here *England* is framed as the promised land – the 'Jerusalem of the Jews': a suggestion that is surely intended ironically given the preceding description of the 'storm' that raged against the Jews following the coronation of the new king.[30]

The rhetoric of exodus and expulsion used by both Richard of Devizes and William of Newburgh similarly informs other commentary on the events

---

[27] ibid., p. 67.
[28] ibid., p. 65: 'ac si esset hircus emissarius'.
[29] ibid., p. 68.
[30] Although the text of Lamentations is part of the liturgy for Holy Week, suggesting also a connection to remembering Christ's Passion.

of 1189-90. As discussed above, Newburgh's text elaborates the suggestions found in Roger of Howden's *Chronicle*, identifying in it the references to both the 'Egyptian day' and to Masada that he subsequently draws out to their full potential. Ralph de Diceto, who, like Newburgh, deplores the violence at York,[31] follows his account of the massacres with a list of the 'several humiliations of Jerusalem' – by Pharaoh Necho, by Nebuchadnezzar, Antiochus, Pompey, Titus, and ultimately by the Saracens, the Crusaders, before 'Saladinus Jerusalem subjugavit'.[32] This list recalls Newburgh's identification of Jerusalem as a region that refuses to submit to those morally unworthy to hold it, and which is thus subject to repeated conquest. Contextualizing the massacre at York within the list of the conquests of Jerusalem also suggests a connection between the destruction of the Jews in York and the destruction of the Jews in Jerusalem, narrating once again the history of the Jews as one of destruction and dispossession.

One historian of the York massacre of 1190 to assert his opinion that the Jews got precisely what they deserved was Ralph of Coggeshall, who writes that because Jewish usury had brought many men of all stations to poverty, 'such a cruel persecution by Christians was not unmerited'.[33] While Coggeshall does not speak explicitly of expulsion, he does suggest that the Jews have become too numerous in England, juxtaposing his opinion that such misfortunes would not have befallen the Jews 'without divine disapproval' ('sine divina animadversione') to a comment that 'this nefarious people spread all throughout England under King Henry II'.[34] This suggestion of the numerousness of the Jews in England may also be underwritten by Exodus 1. 8: 'the Israelites have become much too numerous for us'. Like Newburgh and Devizes, the consensus response of contemporary historians to the pogroms of 1189-90 – even of those who refuse to condone violence against Jews – is to remind their readers of the Jewish history of dispersal and diaspora.

In drawing on the store of Biblical imagery depicting the expulsion of the Jews from various lands in their depictions of the violence of 1189-90, twelfth-century chroniclers were hardly originating a mode of representa-

---

[31] Kennedy highlights the ways in which Ralph de Diceto's language refuses to condone the violence: 'Yet in this brief reference his disapproval is clear. The Norwich Jews were "trucidati", at Stamford "occisi sunt multi", and Bury fifty-seven "jugulati sunt"', Kennedy, '"Faith"', p. 144.

[32] Diceto, *Historical Works*, p. 77. The edition notes that 'this enumeration appears as a separate article in the MS Tiberius A. 9 fol. 25', ibid., p. 76 n. 1.

[33] 'unde non immerito tam crudelis persecutio a Christianis eis illata est'. R. Coggeshall, *Radulphi de Coggeshall Chronicon Anglicanum*, ed. J. Stevenson, RS 66 (London, 1875), p. 28. See also discussion in Kennedy, '"Faith"', p. 144, although I disagree with Kennedy's assessment that Coggeshall is 'less reflective' than his contemporaries on this topic. It seems to me to be possible that he has reflected fully and come to an ungenerous conclusion.

[34] 'gens illa nefaria per regnum Angliae circumquaque dispersa sub Henrico rege secundo'. *Radulphi de Coggeshall Chronicon*, ed. Stevenson, p. 28.

tion. The appropriation of these Biblical models clearly relates to calls for the expulsion of the Jews that had begun as early as the 1180s. In 1182 King Philip of France had expelled all the Jews from the Île de France (although they were subsequently readmitted), and Robert Stacey has remarked on the case of Roger de Asterby, a knight from Lincolnshire who warned, rather dramatically, that 'if Henry did not expel the Jews, he would die miserably within four years'.[35] Stacey further argues that there may have been a general expectation that the new king, Richard the Lionheart, a famous crusader, would expel the Jews from his kingdom upon assuming the throne.[36] Suggestions of an expulsion of the Jews from England existed even earlier and alongside tales of ritual crucifixion, as evidenced in Thomas of Monmouth's *Life and Miracles of St William of Norwich*, which portrays the Jews who have (purportedly) crucified Newburgh as worrying that 'our race will be utterly driven out from all parts of England ... we shall be delivered up to death, we shall be exterminated'.[37] In stark contrast to the language of 'extermination' used here by Monmouth, the language of Exodus, such as Newburgh's invocation of an 'Egyptian day', is especially interesting because Exodus is a particular kind of expulsion that is simultaneously a liberation: Exodus signifies not only the escape from bondage in Egypt, but the establishment of the Covenant of the Law between God and the Israelites.[38] The recollection of Exodus here, alongside that of other, more menacing expulsions, may simply indicate that Exodus is the most obvious Biblical model for the dispersal of a people. Or, it perhaps signifies an ambivalence concerning the politics and ethics of the expulsion of the Jews: an ambivalence that will ultimately be resolved over the course of the thirteenth century, ultimately in the Expulsion of 1290.

Nevertheless, all these historians ultimately follow Saint Augustine – who influentially argued that the Jews are like Cain, who because of his sin is cursed to wander, but who may not be killed.[39] To late twelfth-century historians, both aspects of Cain's punishment are important: even as they seem willing to espouse the dispersal of the Jews, they are nevertheless quick to

---

[35] Stacey, 'Crusades, Martyrdoms, and the Jews', p. 244. Roger de Asterby's predictions are reported by Gerald of Wales in *De principis instructione liber*, ed. G. Warner (*Giraldi Cambrensis Opera*, VIII, 186).

[36] Stacey, 'Crusades, Martyrdoms, and the Jews', pp. 246, 250.

[37] 'genus nostrum tunc ab Anglie partibus funditus exterminabitur... repiemur ad mortem, dabimur et exterminium', Monmouth, *Life and Miracles of St William*, p. 25.

[38] The Exodus of the ancient Israelites was also a common trope through and in which medieval Christians identified their own place in the world. A standard allegorical sense of Exodus, for example, was redemption through Christ (P. S. Hawkins and B. D. Schildgen, 'Introduction: Paul's Letter to the Romans in the Middle Ages', in *Medieval Readings of Romans*, ed. W. S. Campbell et al. (London, 2007), pp. 1–10 (p. 2)). For a sampling of the variety of its uses, see also, Nicholas Howe's discussion of the Old English *Exodus* in N. Howe, *Migration and Mythmaking in Anglo-Saxon England* (New Haven CT, 1989).

[39] Kennedy, '"Faith"', p. 141.

remind their readers of Augustine's influential reading of Psalm 59 (Psalm 58 in the Vulgate): 'Slay them not, lest my people forget'.[40] In his commentary on this Psalm, Augustine draws the parallel between the Jews and Cain, and he argues further that unconverted Jews have been tolerated to remain as living witnesses to the truth of Biblical history. Thus Ralph de Diceto points out that: 'it is incredible that so grievous and deadly a murder of Jews should be pleasing to prudent men, since that text of David, "Do not kill them" comes frequently to our own ears'.[41] William of Newburgh likewise quotes Psalm 59, and he remarks:

> The perfidious Jew that crucified the Lord Jesus Christ is suffered to live amongst Christians, from the same regard to christian utility, that causes the form of the cross of the Lord to be painted in the church of Christ; that is to say, to perpetuate the highly beneficial remembrance of the passion of the Lord amongst all the faithful; and while in the Jew we execrate that impious action, in that sacred form we venerate the Divine majesty with due devotion. The Jews ought to live among Christians for our own utility; but for their own iniquity they ought to live in servitude. (WN, Bk. IV, ch. 9; trans. Stevenson, p. 568)[42]

Here, the Jews' place in Christian society is not to make martyrs or to make money or to make trouble – their job is simply to be looked at; like the crucifix, a silent, passive witness.

Augustine's influential interpretation of Psalm 59, that not only does the misfortune of the Jews reflect divine punishment, but that the Jews are a necessary reminder to Christian society of the truth of its past, present and future, both explained and endorsed the continued presence of unconverted Jews in Christian society throughout the Middle Ages. However, Jeremy Cohen has suggested that a shift in thinking about Augustinian theology on the Jews is key to the twelfth century. Cohen argues that over the course of the twelfth century Christian thinkers throughout western Europe began to reconsider the relevance of Augustine's doctrine of Jewish witness to their practical policy concerning the continued toleration of the Jewish communities in their midst. Increasing knowledge and access to post-Biblical, Talmudic Judaism brought sharply to Christian attention the fact that the Jews had not remained, as in Bernard of Clairvaux's influential formulation 'living letters of Scripture', but that Judaism, like Christianity, had continued to change and develop. Cohen further notes

---

[40] See Augustine, *Sancti Aurelii Augustini Enarrationes in Psalmos*, ed. J. Fraipont and E. Dekkers, 3 vols. (Turnhout, 1956) and the discussion at Kennedy, '"Faith"', p. 141.

[41] Diceto, *Historical Works*, pp. 68–9, 75–6; quoted in Kennedy, '"Faith"', p. 144.

[42] See also the discussion by Vincent in this volume.

that: 'the new ideas never displaced the old ones; rather, they took their place beside them'.[43]

In reading the fourteenth-century poem, *The Siege of Jerusalem*, Elisa Narin Van Court has influentially set what she reads as a particularly Yorkshire 'tradition of violently enacted anti-Judaism' against Yorkshire's 'tradition of Augustinian historicism and toleration', exemplified by Newburgh's treatment of the massacre of 1190.[44] Where she sees the beginning of a genealogy of Augustinian toleration, however, I read a darker vision. By aligning the Jews of York with the Jews of Masada, and condemning the violence against them, Newburgh does sympathize with their plight. Nevertheless, by aligning contemporary Jews with ancient Jews, he is also expressing a profoundly conservative desire to see the Jews perform their role as 'living letters of Scripture' rather than as actors in a contemporary world. Likewise Newburgh's insistence that the Jews are primarily meant to be looked at 'from the same regard to Christian utility that causes the form of the cross of the Lord to be painted in the church of Christ' – that is, Newburgh prefers to see the Jews as the object of Christian action rather than actors in their own right. It is significant that Newburgh's most fully articulated expression of sympathy for the Jews of York is reserved for those whose desire for Christian baptism was genuine.

Both William of Newburgh and Richard of Devizes engage with cultural anxiety about the continued relevance of the Augustinian doctrine of Jewish witness with their juxtaposition of the narratives of ritual murder and pogrom. In the ritual murder accusation, the Jews are seen timelessly to re-enact their crime, while in the pogroms they are seen to suffer the consequences. While these historians share a scepticism about Jewish violence against Christian children and an abhorrence of Christian violence against Jews, they nevertheless also share an interest in thinking about the presence of Jews in Christian society through the tropes of dispersal and expulsion, as well as an anxiety that England should not become, as in Devizes's facetious formulation, 'the Jerusalem of the Jews'. This turn from Passion narrative to Exodus in chronicle representations of the violence suffered by English Jews in 1189-90 strikes me as significant in this context not least because it frames a representational shift from imaginary violence against Christian bodies to violence against Jewish bodies. It also marks a shift from representing the individual to representing the corporate body: if narratives of ritual crucifixion focus attention on the single and singular body of the boy / saint / Christ, the Exodus narrative requires a larger view, which considers peoples, rather than individuals, in conflict. And finally, of course, this literary rhetoric of exodus and expulsion is useful to read as an early articulation of the cultural

---

43 Cohen, *Living Letters*, p. 16.
44 Court, '"Siege of Jerusalem"', p. 239. See also pp. 241–3 for her very interesting tracing of a genealogy of Augustinian historians from William of Newburgh to the fourteenth century sympathetic to the Jews.

climate that leads both to the Expulsion of 1290, as well as to the smaller expulsions that preceded it in the thirteenth century, of the Jews from certain towns, and from the queen's dower lands.[45] The rhetoric of expulsion that characterizes these texts of the 1190s is ultimately an attempt to reconstitute national identity following the coronation, which itself followed the loss of Jerusalem to Saladin. Following that disaster, it may have been no longer enough to think about the way in which individual Christian bodies might be threatened by the continued presence of Jews in Christian society, rather the health of the entire Christian body politic may have seemed to demand the more immediate concern.

[45] Mundill, *England's Jewish Solution*, pp. 25, 265.

13

'De Judaea, muta et surda':
Jewish Conversion in Gerald of Wales's
*Life of Saint Remigius**

Matthew Mesley

Jews are confined to the periphery in twelfth- and thirteenth-century literature. When they do appear within Christian texts, their actions and behaviour are restricted and circumscribed. Viewed as living symbols of Christ's
suffering on the cross, and as actors within the wider Christian drama, their
performance was interpreted through the Church's teachings. Within a literary context, as Stephen Kruger has argued, 'Jews and Judaism can be quite
easily rendered "virtual," reduced to a non-presence, even a non-being that
functions to reconfirm a real, present Christianity'.[1] In this way, representations of Jews were used to define the nature of Christianity, and to police the
boundaries that separated each faith.

Gender roles and ideals played an important function in this respect. Jewish men were aligned with a variety of negative stereotypes, and they were
frequently attributed the role of perpetrator in stories of host desecration or
ritual murder. Jewish women, in contrast, were more ambiguously placed in
Christian discourse.[2] They could appear as beautiful or exotic seductresses,
but also featured in a more passive respect, considered susceptible to Christian conversion, even assimilation.[3] As such, Jewish women often walked a

---

* I would like to thank Sarah Hamilton and Julia Crick for their comments after reading earlier drafts of this chapter.

[1] S. Kruger, *The Spectral Jew: Conversion and Embodiment in Medieval Europe* (Minneapolis,
2006), p. xx. Kruger's own notion of the spectral Jew is, 'related and indebted to notions like
the "hermeneutical," "theological," "paper," and "virtual"'. Such notions share the idea that
the Jew-within-the-text was an ideological construction used as a tool by Christian writers.

[2] For the Christian tradition, see L. Lampert, *Gender and Jewish Difference from Paul to Shakespeare* (Philadelphia, 2004); A. Bale, 'The Female "Jewish" Libido in Medieval Culture', in
The Erotic in the Literature of Medieval Britain, ed. A. Hopkins and C. Rushton (Cambridge,
2007), pp. 94–104. For the male perpetrator see M. Rubin, *Gentile Tales: The Narrative Assault
on Late Medieval Jews* (New Haven CT, 1999), pp. 71–3.

[3] I. G. Marcus, 'Jews and Christians Imagining the Other in Medieval Europe', *Prooftexts* 15
(1995), 209–26, and R. Perez, 'Next-Door Neighbors: Aspects of Judeo-Christian Cohabita-

tightrope; depending on the narrative context they could be seen as either more or less threatening to the faithful than their male counterparts. To take one example, the Jewish woman in the twelfth-century *Life of Christina of Markyate*, who was 'intent on harming Christina with particularly powerful magic', is used by the author to demonstrate that even a wicked Jewish 'witch' saw that her efforts would fail, protected as Christina was by angels.[4] Indeed, Christian writers employed the Jew-within-the-text as a hermeneutic device, in order to reinforce or make plain their point or to support a wider didactic edifice.[5] In hagiography, where an author's intention was to emphasize the sanctity of his subject, the Jew could offer a perfect foil, and provided a way into discussions concerning salvation, conversion and faith. By examining how Jews were placed within specific narrative settings, we can explore the ways in which such depictions were used to strengthen Christian identity.

Here I investigate a neglected miracle story found in the twelfth-century *Life of Remigius*, written by the archdeacon and secular canon Gerald of Wales (*c.* 1146–*c.* 1220). This posthumous miracle describes the cure of a Jewish woman from Lincoln and her subsequent baptism by Alexander, bishop of Lincoln (d. 1148).[6] Although this is one of the few literary examples of a Jewish woman converting to Christianity, it is missing from both D'Blossier Tovey's eighteenth-century *Anglia Judaica* and Joseph Jacobs' important contribution to Anglophone scholarship, *The Jews of Angevin England*.[7] More recently, however, Haidee Lorrey used the source in a discussion of the ways in which converted Jews were represented within the literature of post-con-

---

tion in Medieval France', in *Urban Space in the Middle Ages and the Early Modern Age*, ed. A. Classen (Berlin, 2009), pp. 309–30 (p. 326).

4   *The Life of Christina of Markyate*, trans. C. H. Talbot et al., rev. edn (Oxford, 2009), p. 24. The earlier translation by Talbot (1987) reads: '[She] wanted to harm Christina with tricks which were more powerful than the rest'. Jews were often aligned with magic: C. Watkins, *History and the Supernatural in Medieval England* (Cambridge, 2007), p. 161.

5   J. Cohen, *Living Letters of the Law: Ideas of the Jew in Medieval Christianity* (Berkeley CA, 1999), pp. 1–17.

6   Gerald of Wales, 'Vita Sancti Remigii', in *Giraldi Cambrensis Opera*, ed. J. S. Brewer et al., 8 vols., RS 21 (London, 1861-91), VII, 1-80 [herein *VSR*], p. 24. For a discussion of the *vita's* composition, see M. Mesley, 'The Construction of Episcopal Identity: The Meaning and Function of Episcopal Depictions within Latin Saints' Lives of the Long Twelfth Century' (unpublished Ph.D. dissertation, University of Exeter, 2010), pp. 181–3. For Gerald, see R. Bartlett, *Gerald of Wales: A Voice of the Middle Ages* (Stroud, 2006).

7   Tovey, D'Blossiers, *Anglia Judaica: Or the History and Antiquities of the Jews in England* (Oxford, 1738) and *JAE Docs*. Jacobs does, however, refer to a section of the *Vita Sancti Remigii* where Robert de Chesney (d. 1166), one of Remigius's successors at Lincoln, was censured for taking out a loan of £300 from Aaron of Lincoln. Later in the narrative Geoffrey of York (*c.* 1151–*c.* 1212), briefly bishop-elect of Lincoln, is praised for correcting his predecessor's errors: *VSR*, p. 35. Tovey's omission of the miracle may result from only having had access to Wharton's seventeenth-century edition of the *Vita Sancti Remigii*, in which this specific miracle was not included. See H. Wharton, *Anglia Sacra*, 2 vols. (London, 1691), II, 408–34.

quest England.[8] Lorrey argued that the miracle was employed by Bishop Alexander, and later also by Gerald of Wales, as a way of convincing Jews to convert to Christianity.[9] I suggest that Gerald's account has little to do with efforts to proselytise to the Jewish community at Lincoln. Instead, this *exemplum* would have been directed to and read by a Christian audience, primarily the secular canons at Lincoln Cathedral. This particular miracle demonstrates how representations of Jews often relied on the audience's expectations of how Jews were supposed to behave or act; this was very much influenced by an intellectual tradition in which they were typically portrayed in a stereotyped and generic fashion. Stories set in a familiar environment were still retold with an eye to their allegorical and moral message.

The current emphasis upon the 'literary' or 'narrative' Jew within contemporary historiography reflects an interest in how textual representations of Jews were framed, and how such depictions evolved in subsequent revisions or later recensions of the texts.[10] Anthony Bale has argued that we should understand and interpret Christian depictions of Jews within a cultural and literary framework and, in particular, take into account the specific contexts of textual production.[11] By tackling the text in such a way it is possible to avoid, as one scholar recently put it, 'trying to find the literal in the literary'.[12] Contemporary gender expectations may have also played some part in this miracle account, yet it is worth taking heed of Hannah Meyer's criticism of recent works that use literary depictions of medieval Jewish women and assume such representations reflect Christian-Jewish interaction.[13] In this instance, Gerald of Wales's selection of 'topoi' in his depiction of a Jewish woman who converts likely reflects the wider cultural assumptions and beliefs that Christians held of *all* Jews. Yet, as will be argued, the conversion fulfilled a purpose within the text, and the fact that it was a woman who converted could be used to reflect upon the relationship between Christianity and its progenitor.[14] The following analysis places the

---

8 H. Lorrey, 'Religious Authority, Community Boundaries and the Conversion of Jews in Medieval England', in *Authority and Community in the Middle Ages*, ed. D. Mowbray et al. (Stroud, 1999), pp. 85–100 (p. 91).

9 Lorrey states that the *Vita* is a chronicle, yet Gerald's hagiographical *proemium* (a type of prologue or introduction) suggests it is rather a saint's life.

10 See E. N. van Court, 'Socially Marginal, Culturally Central: Representing Jews in Late Medieval English Literature', *Exemplaria* 12 (2000), 292–326.

11 See A. Bale, *The Jew in the Medieval Book: English Antisemitisms, 1350–1500* (Cambridge, 2006); A. Bale, 'Fictions of Judaism in England before 1290', in *JMB*, ed. P. Skinner, pp. 129–44; A. Bale, '"House Devil, Town Saint": Anti-Semitism and Hagiography in Medieval Suffolk', in *Chaucer and the Jews: Sources, Contexts, Meanings*, ed. S. Delany (New York, 2002), pp. 185–212.

12 P. Skinner, 'Introduction' in *JMB*, ed. Skinner, pp. 1–12 (p. 9).

13 H. Meyer, 'Female Moneylending and Wet-nursing in Jewish-Christian Relations in Thirteenth-Century England' (unpublished Ph.D. dissertation, University of Cambridge, 2009).

14 There will be little attempt at assessing the story in relation to Gerald of Wales's specific intellectual world, or of trying to decipher his beliefs about Judaism. Gerald had studied at the Paris Schools and would have been aware of the use of the 'hermeneutic Jew' in Christian

text within its compositional and historical context, and then considers the miracle story's discursive function.

The miracle occurs in chapter IX of the *Life of Remigius* and is entitled 'Of the Jewess, deaf and mute, [who was] in that same place [Remigius's tomb] made healthy'.[15] It recounts how a disabled Jewish woman enters Lincoln Cathedral and stumbles across the tomb of St Remigius; gazing at the tomb, she is suddenly cured and so can hear and begins to speak in French.[16] Afterwards, she is baptised by Bishop Alexander. The story ends with both on a publicity tour – they travel through cities and towns, the Jewish woman used as a prop to promote Remigius's miracle-working powers.[17] The story is the only evidence for this Jew. No further details are forthcoming – nothing about the woman's family, marital status or age, not even her name; we are only told that she lived in Lincoln.

An extant version of the *Vita Sancti Remigii* is found in Cambridge, Corpus Christi College MS 425.[18] Dated to *c.* 1209–1214, the *Vita* (fols. 6r–44v) is placed before a *Life of Hugh of Avalon* (fols. 46r–79r), also composed by Gerald of Wales.[19] Gerald describes this treatise as containing two parts: 'Volumen hoc bipartitum, duorum quippe virorum illustrium vitas … complectens'.[20] Nevertheless, the *Vita* was composed independently of, not in conjunction with, the *Life of Hugh*. Indeed, evidence from an inventory of donations to the Lincoln Cathedral library suggests that an earlier version of the *Life of St Remigius* was written a decade before the text found in MS 425.[21] The *Vita* was composed at some point between 1197 and 1199, during which time Gerald was studying at Lincoln's nascent theological school.[22] We can, therefore, place the text at the end of the decade in which English Jewish communities had suffered increasingly violent attacks by their Christian neighbours. Although the *Vita* comprised the life and miracles of the eleventh-century Lincoln bishop, Remigius (d. 1092), an account of his successors to the see, and a component entitled *De episcopis Angliae tergeminis*, here, we will focus on the second part of the *Vita Sancti Remigii*,

theology, as well as the tradition of Christian-Jewish disputation – for the latter see A. Sapir Abulafia, *Christians and Jews in the Twelfth-Century Renaissance* (London, 1995).

15 *VSR*, p. 24: *De Judaea, muta et surda, sana ibidem effecta.*

16 K. A. Fudeman, *Vernacular Voices: Language and Identity in Medieval French Jewish Communities* (Philadelphia, 2010). Fudeman suggests that French was the primary spoken language of the Jewish communities of England.

17 For Alexander, see D. Smith, 'Alexander (d. 1148)', *ODNB* (Oxford, 2004).

18 M. R. James, *A Descriptive Catalogue of the Manuscripts in the Library of Corpus Christi College Cambridge*, 2 vols. (Cambridge, 1912), II, 330–2; *VSR*, pp. ix–x.

19 An inscription appears at the beginning of the manuscript: 'Libellus de divercis [sic] miraculis, G. De Barri dictus archidiaconus sancti Dauid': MS 425, fol. 1r.

20 *VSR*, p. 2.

21 R. Woolley, *Catalogue of the Manuscripts of Lincoln Cathedral Chapter Library* (Oxford, 1927), pp. v–ix; see also *VSR*, app. C, pp. 165–71; other evidence is discussed in Mesley, 'Construction of Episcopal Identity', pp. 186–9.

22 *The Autobiography of Giraldus Cambrensis*, ed. H. E. Butler (London, 1937), pp. 127–8.

the 'miracula', and ask what possible sources Gerald may have used in composing this section.[23]

The 'miracula' comprise chapters VI-XX, which can be divided into two parts.[24] Gerald describes chapters VI-XIII, which includes the account of the female Jew (cap. IX), as Remigius's more ancient miracles ('antiquiora miracula').[25] The last seven chapters (cc. XIV-XX) refer to the saint's recent miracles, most of which had occurred during repairs to the roof of Lincoln Cathedral following an earthquake in 1185. Gerald admits that we can be more certain of these latter miracles as they are supported by verifiable testimony.[26] It is unclear how Gerald would have found out about the earlier miracles, but since they all occurred at Remigius's tomb, Gerald may have taken his information from a register of the miracles, documented by the tomb's custodians.[27] Gerald might have also used an old martyrology, now lost, which is mentioned in a 1312 dispute between the canons of Lincoln and the cathedral dean. In a register that documented the disagreement, the canons used a set of *Consuetudines* from 1214; the author noted how the earlier canons had, prior to 1214, recorded their *customs* at the end of an 'antiquum Martirologium'.[28] It is possible that this martyrology included details concerning Remigius's postmortem miracles. Yet even if Gerald had access to written material, it is more probable that the early miracles were disseminated through oral tradition.[29] Working with few specifics, Gerald could take some artistic license in his account of the Jewish woman. Before we examine the miracle proper, however, it is worth briefly considering how even dating the miracle is problematic.

Although not explicit, Gerald implies a date for when the woman was cured. Most significant is the role of Bishop Alexander, who features in the events following her cure. The miracle must be situated between his consecration and death, 1123–1148. Following the conversion account (cap. X) the author describes a fire that took place thirty-two years after Remigius's death in 1092 – that is 1124.[30] If Gerald was writing down or copying these miracles chronologically, which of course presupposes that he knew when all these miracles took place, then the miracle involving the Jewish woman would have had to have occurred in the first year of Alexander presiding over the

---

[23] *VSR*, p. 13: 'In quatuor itaque particulas libellus iste distinguitur'. For Remigius see D. Bates, *Bishop Remigius of Lincoln, 1067–92* (Lincoln, 1992) and H. E. J. Cowdrey, 'Remigius (d. 1092)', *ODNB* (Oxford, 2004).

[24] *VSR*, pp. 22–30.

[25] ibid., p. 27.

[26] ibid., p. 30: 'Certiora tamen, et evidentioris fulta testimonio veritatis, stili officio comprehendimus'.

[27] Dimock's suggestion: *VSR*, p. xxii.

[28] Mesley, 'Construction of Episcopal Identity', pp. 192–4.

[29] One reason why Gerald wished to now record these miracles in written form was to secure a tradition previously only acknowledged through oral accounts.

[30] *VSR*, pp. 25–6.

see in 1124.[31] However, the text also mentions that the Jewish woman lived in Lincoln, offering an extremely early date for Jewish habitation. Richardson, for instance, has argued that it is unlikely that Jewish settlements outside of London would have commenced until after Henry I's reign.[32] For Lincoln, Francis Hill claimed that 'the earliest known reference to the Jews in Lincolnshire occurs in 1159',[33] referring to the pipe roll of that year, which records that a 'donum' of 60 marks was collected from Lincoln's Jewish community. More recently, Kevin Streit, citing the pipe roll of 31 Henry I and two brief entries in the *Leges Edwardi Confessoris*, suggested that the argument against early settlements is not definitive.[34] Streit argues that it was under Stephen's (1135–54) initiative and direction that Jewish communities began to spread to English towns outside of London.[35]

The suggested date of 1123–24 is still, therefore, problematic. It also relies on Gerald having accurate information of a fire occurring at Lincoln in 1124. Dimock, the editor of the *Vita*, was not convinced, pointing out that Gerald was the sole source for this particular date. Earlier witnesses, including the Peterborough version of the Anglo-Saxon chronicle and the Annals of Margam Abbey, give dates of 19 May 1123 and 1122 respectively, placing the fire before Alexander's prelacy. If true, it would suggest that our miracle story either was not placed chronologically within the *Vita*, or that Gerald got his dates wrong.[36] Nevertheless, Gerald may have purposefully conflated this earlier fire with one that took place later. Henry of Huntingdon (*c.* 1088–*c.* 1157), the archdeacon and author of the *Historia Anglorum*, stated that in 1145 the church at Lincoln had been 'gutted by fire'. Henry, who makes no mention of the earlier fire, states further that Alexander subsequently restored the church so that 'it seemed more beautiful than when it was newly built'.[37] By dating it to before 1124, perhaps Gerald suggested that Alexander had, even in his first days as bishop, sought to disseminate Remigius's sanctity. More cynically, a correlation between a natural disaster and Alexander's sudden interest in Remigius was avoided. Clearly, if such an event had occurred, a date nearer to the 1140s appears more probable, especially considering the meagre evidence for Jewish settlement at Lincoln in the 1120s.

---

[31] Lorrey, 'Religious Authority', p. 91.

[32] Richardson, *EJ*, pp. 8–9.

[33] J. W. F. Hill, *Medieval Lincoln* (Cambridge, 1948), p. 217.

[34] K. T. Streit, 'The Expansion of the English Jewish Community in the Reign of King Stephen', *Albion* 25 (1993), 177–92 (pp. 177–8).

[35] More sceptical is J. Hillaby, 'Jewish Colonisation in the Twelfth Century', in *JMB*, ed. Skinner, pp. 15-40 (pp. 22–3).

[36] *VSR*, pp. xxix–xxxii, 25 n. 2. Peter Kidson has argued for an earlier fire, but does not refer to the conversion miracle. See P. Kidson, 'Architectural History', in *A History of Lincoln Minster*, ed. D. M. Owen (Cambridge, 1994), pp. 14–46 (pp. 22–4).

[37] Huntingdon, *Historia*, pp. 748–9. Gerald also states that Alexander built a stone vault for the church after a fire. Gerald provides no date for the fire, but it does appear at the end of his description of Alexander's time in office: *VSR*, p. 33.

Of course, to some extent, it is more worthwhile thinking about how Gerald's contemporary audience would have reacted to this story, and how this interesting miracle acts as a window into Christian attitudes of the Jewish 'Other'. Indeed, even if based upon an actual Lincoln resident, the female Jew is portrayed, within the context of this conversion story, as a stereotypical member of what Gerald calls 'her faithless and perverse people'.[38] It is made clear at the outset that the woman entered the church in order to commit an act of sacrilege. She is not described as being interested in Christianity or wanting to convert, and neither is she there seeking a cure for her disability. The motives of the Jewish woman, as defined here, reinforce the image of a 'malevolent' and 'polluting' Jew. The text highlights this fear of contamination; indeed, accounts of Jews entering churches remained a familiar topos of medieval 'exempla', such as the story of a Jew who disguised himself to enter a church unnoticed in order to steal the Eucharist.[39] Here her sex, too, may have reinforced the sense of intrusion. By entering the church, the Jewish woman encroached upon a space that gained its legitimacy through male spiritual authority.[40] We should also recognise that as a consequence of the 'Gregorian' reforms, there was a tendency to see women's bodies as polluting, and increasingly clerical concerns about impurity shaped ideas about gender and sexuality.[41] Such clerical understandings would have been applied to all women, whether Christian or Jewish, yet here the Jewish woman was shown to defile the entire Christian community.

In our miracle story, Gerald accuses the woman of blasphemy.[42] Gerald relates that due to her disability, the woman could not blaspheme vocally, so she demonstrated her contempt through her disposition and with bodily gestures.[43] The actual stereotypes used reflected images found in Christian depictions of Jews, which emphasized their wild gesticulations and lack of self-control.[44] These characteristics were directed at women too;

---

[38] *VSR*, p. 24: 'gentis suae perfidae et perversae'. See also Hyams in this volume on 'perfidia' in characterizing the Jews.

[39] M. Rubin, 'Imagining the Jew: The Late Medieval Eucharistic Discourse', in *In and Out of the Ghetto: Jewish-Gentile Relations in Late Medieval and Early Modern Germany*, ed. R. Po-Chia-Hsia and H. Lehmann (Cambridge, 1995), pp. 177–208 (pp. 182–3); Rubin, *Gentile Tales*, pp. 7–39.

[40] The 1222 Council of Oxford decreed that Jews should not enter churches: J. Edwards, 'The Church and the Jews in Medieval England', in *JMB*, ed. Skinner, pp. 85–95 (p. 91).

[41] See *Medieval Purity and Piety: Essays on Medieval Clerical Celibacy and. Religious Reform*, ed. M. Frassetto (New York, 1998); D. Elliott, *Fallen Bodies: Pollution, Sexuality, and Demonology in the Middle Ages* (Philadelphia, 1999).

[42] Accusations increased over the course of the twelfth and thirteenth centuries. Canon 68 of Lateran IV stipulated punishment for Jews who blasphemed: *Decrees of the Ecumenical Councils*, ed. N. Tanner, 2 vols. (London, 1990), II, 266.

[43] *VSR*, p. 24: 'etsi non verbis, mente tamen et gestu … miserrima blasphemaret'.

[44] Christian artists often portrayed Jews with negative bodily gestures: D. Strickland, *Saracens, Demons, and Jews: Making Monsters in Medieval Art* (Princeton, 2003), pp. 120–2. See also Bradbury's essay in this collection.

their 'excitable speech' and unruly bodies were often conceived as dangerous or threatening to social norms. In this miracle account both Judaism and femininity are associated with carnality, as opposed to a Christian (and male) spirituality.[45]

The idea that Jews sought to actively mock the Christian faith was a recurring theme in medieval 'exempla' and sermon stories, and played upon fears that Jews sought to deride Christian rituals and practices – for instance, the account of a Jewish boy who apparently mocked the Christian participants of the St Frideswide's day procession in Oxford.[46] The fear of disruption caused by inter-religious tensions would come to influence ecclesiastical policies; Lateran IV (1215) acted to restrict Jews appearing in public during Easter, thus avoiding the possibility that disrespect was shown during Christian festivities.[47] Narrative accounts could therefore have been reacting or contributing to a wider antisemitic discourse that combined popular and intellectual elements.

The specific disabilities that Gerald ascribes to the Jewish woman, deafness and the inability to speak, probably had a symbolic function. Along with blindness, these conditions were frequently attributed to Jews.[48] Jews were thought to have no ears to hear the teachings of Christ, neither could they see the divinity of Christ, and as such they were believed to be spiritually blind. Christian artists often represented Judaism itself as a blindfolded woman, Synagoga.[49] The fact that Jews ignored Christian teachings, and failed to hear or see what was evidently true, was at times considered a fault and, at other times used in an apologist manner. Christian writers argued that Jews could not help but be spiritually blind and deaf, as that was their nature.[50] A good example of how such tropes were combined is found in an eleventh-century miniature from a manuscript of Monte Cassino. Here the Jews are depicted as stopping their ears with their fingers, and turning their backs on an apostle who is preaching the Gospels.[51]

It is likely that for his educated readers, Gerald wanted to draw an analogy with the biblical stories in which Jesus performed miracles involving

---

[45] For such associations Bale, 'Female "Jewish" Libido', esp. pp. 101–3; and J. Gregg, *Devils, Women, and Jews: Reflections of the Other in Medieval Sermon Stories* (New York, 1997), pp. 18–22.

[46] *Acta Sanctorum*, 8 October (1853), pp. 567–7. Ritual murder myths were also predicated on the belief that the Jews were re-enacting and mocking the Crucifixion of Christ: Bale, 'Fictions of Judaism', p. 131.

[47] See *Decrees of the Ecumenical Councils*, ed. N. Tanner, 2 vols. (London, 1990) I, 266.

[48] E. Wheatley, '"Blind" Jews and Blind Christians: Metaphorics of Marginalization in Medieval Europe', *Exemplaria* 14 (2002), 351–82 and Cohen and Bradbury in this volume.

[49] Lampert, *Gender and Jewish Difference*, pp. 43–7.

[50] Influenced by an Augustinian tradition: K. R. Stow, *Alienated Minority: The Jews of Medieval Latin Europe* (Cambridge MA, 1992), pp. 17–21.

[51] Cited in A. Oisteanu, *Inventing the Jew: Antisemitic Stereotypes in Romanian and Other Central-East European Cultures* (Lincoln NE, 2009), p. 276.

the blind and the deaf. Significantly, such stories often involved those who later were baptised and became the first of Jesus's early adherents. In the Scriptures, physical and spiritual transformation went hand-in-hand. In the miracle account, Gerald states that the Jew was cured at the same time as a passage was being read from the Gospels, specifically Luke 11. 14: 'And Jesus was casting out the demon, and that demon was mute: and when he had cast out the demon, the person spoke, and the multitudes were in admiration of it'.[52] Clearly, the reader was expected to draw an analogy with the cure of a deaf and mute Jewish woman, and the exorcism by Jesus of a man possessed by a mute demon. Yet Gerald's readers would have also been aware that this story ended with a woman in the crowd calling out to Jesus: 'Blessed is the womb that bore you and the breasts that nursed you!'. To which Jesus had responded, 'Blessed rather are those who hear the word of God and obey it!'. In the context of the Jewish woman's conversion, readers may have linked the miracle with this latter passage.[53] Thus on one level the woman's demon was here interpreted and conflated with her religion; curing her disability, Remigius had exorcised the very root of her problem – her Jewishness. But by reading this alongside Luke 11 in its entirety, Gerald perhaps raised a broader point about the relationship between Judaism and Christianity. While the former could be viewed as the mother religion, Jews, like the woman in the miracle account had wilfully chosen to ignore the Good News of the New Testament. Only a sign brought about their conversion.

So how do we situate this account alongside other hagiographical texts where conversion or former Jews appear?[54] Although the inclusion of the 'Jewish convert' is a rare figure in twelfth- and thirteenth-century saints' lives, when included within a text authors did so for a purpose. As Anna Abulafia has suggested Jews were made to serve Christian aims and needs – and this can be demonstrated on a textual level.[55] For example, in the mid twelfth-century *Life of William of Norwich* the author, Thomas of Monmouth, claimed that Theobald, a former Jew and now monk of Norwich Cathedral, had stated that William's murder was part of a Europe-wide Jewish conspiracy, centred at Narbonne. According to Theobald, Jewish elders would meet annually and

---

52 *VSR*, p. 24: 'Erat Jhesus ejiciens daemonium, et illud erat mutum: et cum ejecisset daemonium, locutus est mutus, et admiratae sunt turbae'.

53 William of Newburgh had even written a sermon based on the verse. See *The Sermons of William of Newburgh*, ed. A. Kraebel (Toronto, 2010), pp. 61–83. I would like to thank Dr Abulafia for directing me to this text.

54 For conversion within other narrative contexts see H. Hames, 'The Limits of Conversion: Ritual Murder and the Virgin Mary in the Account of Adam of Bristol', *JMH* 33 (2007) 43–59; R. Nisse, '"Your Name Will No Longer Be Aseneth": Apocrypha, Anti-martyrdom, and Jewish Conversion in Thirteenth-Century England', *Speculum* 81 (2006), 734–53.

55 Abulafia, *Christian-Jewish Relations, 1000–1300: Jews in the Service of Medieval Christendom* (Harlow, 2011), and see her essay in this volume.

decide on where a Christian child would next be killed.[56] Theobald's assertion presumably was thought to add an extra level of verisimilitude to the text: who better to convince Christian sceptics of Jewish culpability than a former Jew? Likewise, in the thirteenth-century account of little Hugh, a convert is also used within the text to point to the complicity of his former brethren.[57]

The relative lack of Jewish converts within saints' lives goes against the grain of contemporary trends. In the thirteenth century, there were increasing attempts to convert the Jewish populace through 'persuasion'; the friars, in particular, were used in their capacity as missionaries.[58] These efforts were partially successful: Robert Stacey has estimated that by the late 1250s, 5–10 per cent of Jews in England had been converted.[59] Whether this had an impact upon literary representations is difficult to assess. In the mid-thirteenth century *Life of St Richard*, bishop of Chichester (d. 1253), there is a very brief account of a Jew's conversion.[60] We are told that at Westminster Abbey the convert was baptised by Richard with great solemnity. The hagiographer does, however, situate this example within what appears to be a wider authorial agenda, stressing Richard's attempts to preach to and convert the Jewish community within his diocese. The tone of the work certainly reflects the increasingly confrontational environment of the thirteenth century; in line with early thirteenth century canons, Richard refused a request for the Jews to build a synagogue.[61] Conversion here occurred not from a miracle, but through Richard's proselytising and so fitted neatly into contemporary episcopal ideals; as an active pastor, Richard sought to educate and administer those within his care, but also to persuade those outside the faith.

Why is there such a silence about conversion through miracles in the hagiographical literature of twelfth and thirteenth century England? Notwithstanding Augustine's assertion that a miracle was the most efficacious tool for converting Jews to Christianity, such miracles frequently appear in episcopal hagiography of early medieval Europe.[62] Considering the popularity

---

56 Thomas of Monmouth, *The Life and Miracles of St William of Norwich,* ed. and trans. A. Jessopp and M. R. James (Cambridge, 1896), pp. 93–4; G. I. Langmuir, 'Thomas of Monmouth: Detector of Ritual Murder', *Speculum* 59 (1984), 820–46 (pp. 835–7).

57 G. I. Langmuir, 'The Knight's Tale: Young Hugh of Lincoln', *Speculum* 47 (1972), 459–82.

58 R. C. Stacey, 'The Conversion of Jews to Christianity in Thirteenth-Century England', *Speculum* 97 (1992), 263–83, and F. D. Logan, 'Thirteen London Jews and Conversion to Christianity: Problems of Apostasy in the 1280s', *BIHR* 45 (1972), 214-29. For the friars' impact, see J. Cohen, *The Friars and the Jews: The Evolution of Medieval Anti-Judaism* (Ithaca NY, 1982).

59 R. C. Stacey, 'The English Jews under Henry III', in *JMB,* ed. Skinner, pp. 41-54 (p. 51).

60 *Saint Richard of Chichester: The Sources for his Life,* ed. D. Jones, Sussex Record Society 79 (Lewes, 1995), pp. 133–4 (Latin), pp. 209–11 (trans.).

61 J. A. Watt, 'The English Episcopate, the State and the Jews: The Evidence of the Thirteenth-Century Conciliar Decrees', in *Thirteenth-Century England II: Proceedings of the Newcastle upon Tyne Conference 1987,* ed. P. R. Coss and S. D. Lloyd (Woodbridge, 1988), pp. 137–47.

62 See M. Goodich, *Miracles and Wonders: The Development of the Concept of Miracle, 1150–1350* (Aldershot, 2007), pp. 9–10; M. Toch, 'The Jews in Europe 500–1050', in *The New Cambridge Medieval History I: c. 500–c. 700,* ed. P. Fouracre (Cambridge, 2005), pp. 547–70 (p. 553).

of the cult of saints in twelfth- and thirteenth-century England, one wonders whether Christian devotion towards the saints had an effect on their Jewish neighbours. Certainly, Ephraim Shoham-Steiner, who has investigated medieval Jewish 'exempla', has argued it was likely that some Jews did visit Christian saints' shrines, because there is evidence of Jewish elders warning of the perils of such encounters.[63] In contrast, Christian authors may have been reluctant to include such accounts unless there was evidence of conversion. In the miracles of Thomas Becket, in a chapter entitled 'the result of entering a Jewish house', a certain Christian woman called Godeliva, skilled in charms, attempts to cure a Jewish woman's leg with water blessed from the saint's shrine.[64] Thomas, presumably displeased with the way his holy water was being used, made the bucket Godeliva carried explode on entering the Jewish woman's house. Here a broader warning against Christian-Jewish relations was also being made. The writer made clear that Godeliva had often looked after the Jewish woman's health using charms, suggesting a level of familiarity, even neighbourliness. Yet, the saint's actions caused Godeliva to understand her error, the text stating that she never returned to the Jewish woman's house. Returning to Gerald's account, what was made clear here was that the Jewish woman was baptised after her cure. And even if given typically negative traits, there was still a possibility of reconciliation available here. The door was not firmly closed.

If she is not represented as a model pilgrim, there is a purpose behind Gerald's depiction. Having blasphemed against Christ, she stumbles across the tomb of Remigius and without any wish on her part is miraculously cured; at no point does she seek Remigius's intercessory power. Yet, returning to Gerald's analogy of demonic possession, the woman's actions could be explained as a consequence of her nature. Gerald was able to demonstrate that her error had, through her cure and baptism, been replaced with enlightenment. She was shown, however, to lack responsibility for this conversion; the cure revealed, Gerald argued, that 'it is not always on account of merits, or devotion that miracles occur, but so that the glory of God is made manifest'.[65]

Gerald's account of the cure and conversion of the Jewish woman is unusual in the context of late twelfth and thirteenth-century Latin hagiography. The outcome – which could on one level be construed as a happy ending – did not conform to an increasingly bellicose attitude towards Jews.[66] How-

---

[63] S. Shoham-Steiner, 'Jews and Healing at Medieval Saints' Shrines: Participation, Polemics, and Shared Cultures', *Harvard Theological Review*, 103 (2010), 111–29.

[64] *MTB* II, 71.

[65] *VSR*, p. 24: 'quia non propter merita semper, aut devotionem, sed ut manifestetur gloria Dei, miracula fiunt'.

[66] R. Chazan, 'The Deteriorating Image of the Jews – Twelfth and Thirteenth Centuries', in *Christendom and its Discontents: Exclusion, Persecution, and Rebellion, 1000–1500*, ed. S. L. Waugh and P. D. Diehl (Cambridge, 2002), pp. 220–33.

ever, Gerald still situated the woman's actions within a traditional and pejorative framework, attributing to her a number of customary Jewish tropes
that interacted with gendered associations. Depicting the Jew as a malevolent intruder would not have helped reach out to Jews, convincing them of
Christianity's message. Certainly we should be careful in suggesting that an
account of conversion necessarily had, as its rationale, a desire to convert.
Neither was the actual practice of conversion essential to construct identity; written accounts of conversion could work just as well. Here, the tale
of a Jewish woman, who was cured and baptised, conveyed a message that
confirmed and validated the Christian faith and identity of Gerald's readers,
primarily the secular canons at Lincoln. These same canons might in their
daily life interact with members of the Jewish community living in Lincoln.
This anonymous woman may have represented the stereotyped view of the
perfidious Jew, but she also stood for those Jews living and working within
Lincoln, alongside yet always outside the Christian community. As Sylvia
Tomasch has pointed out, Jewish bodies were at the same time 'imagined
constructions and actual people'.[67] While there may have been a reading of
the account that led to uneasiness over what was a tale of an 'undeserving'
Jew being rewarded, perhaps such a story was itself a strength, emphasizing
the possibility of redemption for those considered the most unworthy. On
one level readers of the *Life* could celebrate St Remigius's efficacy in healing
the Jew and bringing her into the Christian fold. Yet even in a conversion
story, contempt for Christianity came before reconciliation. Such a reconciliation was only ever partial too – as a Christian, the woman is described as
re-enacting her conversion – reminding people that she had once been Jewish. As Christians, Jews continued to fulfil their role.

---

[67] S. Tomasch, 'Postcolonial Chaucer and the Virtual Jew', in *The Postcolonial Middle Ages*, ed. J.
Cohen (New York, 2000), pp. 243–60 (p. 252).

14

Dehumanizing the Jew at the Funeral of the Virgin Mary in the Thirteenth Century (c. 1170–c. 1350)

Carlee A. Bradbury

Before and after the expulsion of the Jews from England in 1290, artists made and audiences understood pictured Jews as embodiments of opposition to the Christian norm, as the quintessential other. Such visual dehumanization of the Jew has been widely considered elsewhere,[1] so this essay will focus on one topos that recurs at York: the Jew in visualizations of the Funeral of the Virgin. Both the textual and visual narratives of this tale depend on the moment when a Jew tries to overturn the platform on which Mary's body is being carried during her burial procession. Upon contact with the pall covering her body, his hand becomes dried, withered and stuck, while his companions in the crowd are struck blind. What makes medieval English images of this event so interesting is the intensity with which artists visually demonize this particular Jew.

Vilification of this figure in English art begins just after the York Massacre in 1190 and escalates long after the expulsion in 1290. Artists developed and articulated a new purely visual character to accommodate the complexities of this narrative, as well as iconographic connections with animals. Audiences read, understood, and accepted this new character in a variety of media. The most compelling examples of the Funeral of the

---

1   Recent interdisciplinary scholarship on the visual dehumanization of the Jew by Debra Higgs Strickland, Sara Lipton, and Anthony Bale builds on the foundations laid in classic works by Ruth Mellinkoff, Heinz Schreckenberg, and Bernard Blumenkranz: D. Strickland, *Saracens, Demons, & Jews*; S. Lipton, *Images of Intolerance: The Representation of the Jews and Judaism in the Bible Moralisée* (Berkeley CA, 1999); A. Bale, *Feeling Persecuted: Christians, Jews, and Images of Violence in the Middle Ages* (London, 2010); R. Mellinkoff, *Outcasts: Signs of Otherness in Northern European Art from the Later Middle Ages*, 2 vols. (Berkeley CA, 1993): H. Schreckenberg, *The Jews in Christian Art: An Illustrated History* (London, 1996); B. Blumenkranz, *Le juif médiéval au miroir de l'art chrétien* (Paris, 1966). My specific focus on the topos of the Jew at the Virgin's Funeral fills a gap in existing scholarship. Prior to the present study the most comprehensive treatment of the subject, as it appears in the Taymouth Hours, is in A. Bale's, 'The Jew's Hand and the Virgin's Bier: Tangible Interruption', in Bale, *Feeling Persecuted*, 90–117.

Virgin appear in manuscripts, mostly psalters and books of hours, and stained glass, particularly windows from York Minster. The Funeral can be found in both the marginal space of the 'bas de page' as well as the main space of the full page miniature or window light. Instead of presenting a catalogue of each appearance of the Funeral, my focus is on key manuscript illuminations that will contextualize the most visually alarming illustrations of the scene that are found in stained glass from York Minster.[2] Analysis of this selection of examples shows that fluid understanding of the Jew at the Funeral, whether on the margin or in the centre, depended on the knowledgeable medieval audience being willing to accept and perpetuate antisemitism through a new lens.

The scene of the Jew at the Funeral is part of a cycle of events surrounding the Death and Assumption of the Virgin that originated with early texts of the Apocryphal New Testament by writers such as St John the Theologian and Melito of Sardis.[3] In early Coptic texts of the legend, the Jews plot to burn Mary's body and are struck with blindness, while other texts in Greek and Latin describe a moment after Mary's death, when a cloud of singing angels appears above her body and attracts crowds of people.[4] Melito writes,

> And behold, one of them who was the prince of priests of the Jews was filled with fury and wrath and said to the rest, 'Behold the tabernacle of the man who troubled us and all our nation, what glory it has received.' And he came near and tried to overthrow the bier and cast the body on the earth. And forthwith his hands dried up from his elbows and stuck to the bier. And when the apostles lifted the bier, part of him was hanging loose and part stuck to the bier, and he was wrung with extreme torment as the apostles went on and sang. But the angels who were in the clouds smote the people with blindness.[5]

---

[2] Indeed my focus is on possible origins for the iconography found in the York windows. Other late medieval English illustrations of the Jew at the Funeral of the Virgin include: The Luttrell Psalter (BL MS Add. 42130) fol. 99; Canticles, Hymns, and Passion (Cambridge, St John's College Library, MS 262, K21) fol. 64; wall paintings from Wimborne Minster in Dorset, Croughton Church in Northamptonshire, Chalgrove Church in Oxfordshire; and stained glass from St Peter Mancroft in Norwich, North Moreton Church in Berkshire, and Gresford Church.

[3] *The Apocryphal New Testament: A Collection of Apocryphal Christian Literature in an English Translation*, ed. J. K. Elliott (Oxford, 1993), pp. 691–723. Scholarship on the Death and Assumption of the Virgin is vast, but see the following for key interpretations: S. J. Shoemaker, *The Ancient Traditions of the Virgin Mary's Dormition and Assumption* (Oxford, 2006); M. Clayton, 'The Transitus Mariae: The Tradition and Its Origins', *Apocrypha* 10 (1999), 74–98.

[4] *Apocryphal New Testament*, ed. Elliot, p. 712.

[5] ibid., p. 712.

The Jew, named Jephonias by St John, then implores St Peter for help and, upon conversion, the sight of the other Jews in the crowd is restored.[6] The basic pre-conversion plot points are delivered in a clear, straightforward manner in the earliest image of the Funeral in England, the Wirksworth slab.[7] This Anglo-Saxon relief, dating to around AD 800, now at the church of St Mary the Virgin in the village of Wirksworth (Derbs.), is striking for its visual simplicity. The Funeral procession is led by John (with his palm), observed from above by a group of six angels, and disrupted by the Jew who is being dragged under the Virgin's body.

Popularity of the ancient textual narratives continued further into the Middle Ages, potentially providing artists in England with an addition to the standard iconography of the Virgin. Yet other early visual examples are rare, and only one pre-1200 image can be identified: in a Psalter of *c.* 1170.[8] The folio is divided into two parts, the top showing the Death of the Virgin; the bottom showing the funeral procession. Three bareheaded apostles lead the procession, while a group of five people follow. In the foreground a bearded figure wearing a blue hat reaches out to touch the body on the platform; the three figures in front look back at him while two angels swoop under the Virgin's body as if to prevent her from falling. The artist does not make this Jew particularly threatening; he has no emotion on his face and, though reaching, seems entirely stationary. There is no Passion cycle in this manuscript, and thus, no earlier visual precedent within its pages of Jews as tormentors. Like the Wirksworth slab, the image from the Psalter is both exceptional and isolated.

By contrast, the de Brailes Hours contains an extended cycle of the Virgin and the Doubting Jews, which fits squarely within a well-articulated visual and textual language of antisemitism. The Oxford artist William de Brailes

---

6   ibid., p. 707.
7   Jane Hawkes identified the eight scenes on the slab as scenes from the Infancy and Passion. She made the connection between the Funeral scene on this relief and a possible Eastern model, connecting the uniqueness of this work to accounts of the sacred geography of Jerusalem recounted in Anglo-Saxon England by pilgrims such as Willibald. J. Hawkes, 'The Wirksworth Slab: An Iconography of Humilitas', *Peritia: The Journal of the Medieval Academy of Ireland* 9 (1995), 246–89 (pp. 252–3). For earlier interpretations of the Wirksworth Slab see B. Kurth, 'The Iconography of the Wirksworth Slab', *Burlington Magazine for Connoisseurs* 86 (1945), 114–21 (pp. 116–21); M. Clayton, *The Cult of the Virgin Mary in Anglo-Saxon England* (Cambridge, 1990), pp. 153–5.
8   Glasgow, Hunterian Library, MS Hunter U.3.2(229), fol. 18r. The provenance of this manuscript is still under debate. Historically the Psalter was known as the York Psalter, owing to a supposed Northern pictorial style as well as the inclusion of Northern saints including Oswarld of Northumbria in the calendar and litany. Recently Jonathan James Greenland suggested that the book might have been commissioned by Roger de Mowbray (d. 1188), a wealthy magnate from Yorkshire. Though tempting, firm evidence proving the York connection is still lacking and now the Psalter is known primarily as the Hunterian Psalter, due to its present location in Glasgow, T. S. R. Boase, *The York Psalter in the Library of the Hunterian Museum, Glasgow* (London, 1962); C. M. Kauffmann, *Romanesque Manuscripts, 1066–1190* (London, 1975), pp. 117–18; J. J. Greenland, *The Iconography of the Hunterian Psalter: University of Glasgow MS Hunter 229*, 2 vols. (Cambridge, 1996).

created the de Brailes Hours, possibly the earliest book of hours to be made in England, around 1240.[9] The Death, Assumption, and Burial of the Virgin are illustrated in an elaborate marginal structure that frames the text of Psalm 42, *Judica me*, in the hour of Compline.[10] The vertical element contains two semi-roundels: in the middle of the folio, an angel transports the Virgin up to heaven where, at the top of the folio, Christ places a crown on her head. The vertical and horizontal narratives meet in a roundel bearing an illustration of the Virgin on her deathbed. The Virgin's burial procession is in the center of the bottom section.

The reader's comprehension of the Funeral image on folio 61 depends not only on de Brailes' exploitation of visual contrast within the image, but a specific knowledge of the visual typing and textual labelling from the Passion cycle earlier in the book. Over the course of the Passion cycle, de Brailes deploys three visualizations of Jews (a tormentor, a witness, and a priestly judge) alongside different words in his captions: 'iudes' (Jews), 'felons' (felons), or 'giues' (Jews). Despite difference in the meaning of terms 'iudes' and 'felons', de Brailes' visualization of these figures is identical. The 'iudes' and 'felons' are the tormentors and they all have grey skin, expressive grimacing mouths, and dark curly hair. In contrast to the monstrous 'iudes' and 'felons', the Jews as witnesses, whom de Brailes labels as 'giues' (Jews), appear human.[11]

Returning to the Funeral on folio 61, two identical haloed figures carry Mary's shrouded body, while two Jewish figures try to overturn the funeral bier. One stands at the left shaking the handles, as a second more tenacious figure attempts to pull the shroud from the body. The latter receives punishment immediately, and his hand becomes stuck. In comparison to the haloed and graceful apostles, the Jews appear dark, dirty, and crude. William de Brailes crafted these Jews to heighten their contrast to the apostles (they are physically smaller, they wear shoes, and have mask-like grimaces on their faces) and deepen their connection to the earlier tormenting Jews from the Passion cycle.

As the cycle for Compline continues, in three historiated initials, de Brailes transforms his Jews on both a spiritual and physical level. One initial, on folio 61v, shows nine Jews who are struck blind for their lack of faith after their desecration of Mary's bier. In another, on folio 62v, one of the blinded Jews begs St Peter to be cured with the pall from the Virgin's coffin. Finally, the Jew's sight is restored not by his contact with the relic, but rather by his pro-

---

9   BL MS Add. 49999, fol. 61r – 62v. For a codicological study of the manuscript see C. Donovan, *The De Brailes Hours: Shaping the Book of Hours in Thirteenth-Century Oxford* (London, 1991). For an extended discussion of the latent antisemitism present in both text and image of the de Brailes Hours, see C. A. Bradbury, 'Imaging and Imagining the Jew in Medieval England' (unpublished Ph.D. dissertation, University of Illinois, 2007), pp. 110–72.

10 The caption, at the top of the folio, reads, 'ce est l'asumpsiun nr dame quant les apostels la porterent al val de iosafaz'.

11 Though 'iude' and 'giue' have slightly different etymological origins, the words are identical in meaning; yet de Brailes chose to visualize them in different ways.

fession and declaration of faith in the powers of the relic. De Brailes maintains control of his pictured Jews by visually manipulating their humanity. First, he negates their human nature at the Funeral, associating them with the Jewish, animal-like tormentors which he depicted in the Passion cycle, earlier in the book. Second, he restores the body of the Jew who verbally accepts Christianity, aligning him instead with one of the other earlier Jewish types: the benevolent figures of the 'giues'.

The Funeral narrative continued to gain popularity into the thirteenth century, culminating in its inclusion in the Golden Legend compiled around 1263–67 by Jacobus da Voragine (Iacopo da Varazze).[12] Roughly contemporary to this influential and popular text is the first of three representations of the Funeral of the Virgin at York Minster. The earliest, dating to before 1280 or 1290, appears in a Chapter House window showing events from the Life of the Virgin.[13] (Fig. 1) The three apostles, with expressive faces dominated by large, sad eyes set under furrowed brows, carry the Virgin's body while two smaller figures cling to the pall. Even though the bodies of the Jews are a tangle of shapes, it is impossible to discern clothing and their faces are blank, one can see their hands clearly. Viewing this panel from the ground, the scene is easily identifiable, affirming recognition of the story but also its inclusion with traditional iconography of the Virgin. Yet because only one scene from the story appears in the window, there can be no hope of conversion and re-humanization for this Jew in the Chapter House window. His companions' punishment of being struck blind, illustrated in the de Brailes Hours is, though, alluded to in the painting of the blindfolded Synagogue that once adorned the Chapter House ceiling.[14]

Examining the Jew at the Virgin's Funeral as it appears in two further books of hours suggests possible contextual influences for the scene in two elaborate windows from York Minster. The de Lisle Hours was made between 1316 and 1331 for the wife or one of the daughters of Robert de Lisle, possibly in or near York.[15] Here, the Funeral of the Virgin appears between her Death and her As-

[12] J. de Voragine, *The Golden Legend: Readings on the Saints*, trans. by W. G. Ryan, 2 vols. (Princeton, 1993), II, 80–81. On the date, see T. Kaeppeli and A. Panella, *Scriptores Ordinis Praedicatorum Medii Aevi*, 4 vols. (Rome, 1975-93), II, 350.

[13] The date of the York Chapter House has been the subject of much debate. The Chapter House glass is frequently identified as being the oldest in the Minster but lack of documentary evidence makes assigning a specific date the subject of much debate. Succinct overviews of the history and scholarship pertaining to its glass are found in: N. Coldstream, 'York Chapter House', *Journal of the British Archaeological Association*, 3rd s. 35 (1972), 15–23; D. E. O'Connor and J. Haselock, 'The Stained and Painted Glass', in *A History of York Minster*, ed. G. E. Aylmer and R. Cant (Oxford, 1977), pp. 313–93 (pp. 334–41); S. Brown, *Stained Glass at York Minster* (London, 1999), pp. 23–31.

[14] The painted panel bearing an image of *Synagoga* is contemporary with the Chapter House glass, *c.* 1285, as well as another image of the blindfolded figure from a window in the Chapter House vestibule, *c.*1290. The wooden panels were removed from the Chapter House in 1798. Brown, *Stained Glass at York Minster*, pp. 29–30; C. Norton, 'The Medieval Paintings in the Chapter House', *Friends of the York Minster Annual Report* 67 (1996), 34–51.

[15] New York, Pierpont Morgan Library, MS G.50, fol. 161r.; L. F. Sandler, *Gothic Manuscripts*,

Figure 1: 'The Funeral of the Virgin', The Chapter House at York Minster. © Dean and Chapter of York: Reproduced by kind permission of the Dean and Chapter and Hilary Moxon.

cension to Heaven. The artist shows the two elements of the Funeral procession by representing the same Jew twice. In the first instance the Jew appears in the centre of the image, seeming to have jumped up from the group and pushing, with both hands, the Virgin's covered body; while below he appears, moments later, with his hand stuck, and so being dragged along the ground. All the while ten tall and elegant apostles, wearing long, lightly coloured robes that reveal their bare feet, peacefully carry the bier. The Jew wears a bright red orange tunic that falls above his knees, revealing bare legs and black shoes. The Jews are, at most, half the height of the apostles, and they are visual opposites: the apostles stand tall and walk peacefully ahead while the artist pre-

1285–1385, 2 vols. (London, 1986), II, 83. See also L. F. Sandler, *The Psalter of Robert de Lisle in the British Library* (London, 1982), p. 11.

sents the Jew as a tangle of bent arms and legs. Just as William de Brailes constructed a visual association between the Jews at the Funeral of the Virgin and the tormentors at the Passion in his book of hours, in the de Lisle Hours we can compare the Jews at the Funeral with its earlier figures who blindfold and torment Christ. The same reliance on contrast exists in images from both books of hours: the tall, elegant figure of Christ is set against the angular and awkward tormentors. Readers of each of these books would recognize the figures from the Passion cycle in the later Funeral image as universal tormentors, always in the same costume and always violating the space of the Christian bodies of both the Virgin and Christ, by grabbing, pushing, and pulling.

This visual connection between the Jewish tormentor and the Christian body is strongest in the Taymouth Hours, made in or near London for a female member of the Neville family between 1325 and 1335.[16] The Funeral of the Virgin appears in a cycle of images along the 'bas de page' illustrating the events from the Death to the Coronation of the Virgin in the Penitential Psalms. Here we find two scenes from the story, first the Jew attacks the body and second he converts and takes baptism. Indeed, the Taymouth image of the Funeral is striking in its focus on this singular figure. The artist shows the moment when the Jew touches the Virgin's body and he seems to scream out with pain. Everything about the Jew's body is in contrast with the apostles: his body is smaller, twisted and angular; his legs are bent revealing the skin of his knees. Most visually shocking is his face, shown in an exaggerated profile: his eyes are deeply set black creases above his upturned nose, dominating his face over his open mouth. Overall, his face is tight and compact, mirroring the pattern of his tight curls. He fits squarely in line with a host of tormentors from the Passion cycle in the Taymouth Hours. Though not a direct copy of any of these earlier figures in the manuscript, the Jew at the Funeral is a clear allusion to the tormentor-type established by the Taymouth artist. Turning the folio, we see the end to the story. St Peter baptises the Jew, but while he wears the same short red tunic the artist has given him two key costume changes. He now wears blue leggings, to cover his bare legs and mimic the blue of Peter's robes, and his black shoes have been replaced with lighter tan ones to mimic Peter's bare feet. These two changes, coupled with the relaxing of his caricatured face, humanize the Jew as the baptismal waters wash over him.

The artist's visualization of the Jew at the Funeral, as well as these earlier figures from the Passion, calls on another group of images in this manuscript for inspiration and association. Late in the Office of the Dead are a series of illustrations of 'animal tales', inspired by bestiary and folklore traditions, along the 'bas de page'. These images do not relate to the text and do not contain inscriptions. Within this cycle there are three scenes containing apes.[17] In the first, an ape pushes a wheelbarrow full of other apes, mimicking Noah and

---

the Ark. In the second, an ape mother, chased by a lion, is about to drop her favourite child while her least favourite clings to her back. In the third, the culmination of this common bestiary tale, the ape mother is in a tree with her child hiding from the lion. The Taymouth artist consistently illustrates the apes in profile, with wide mouths and sunken eyes. Apes or monkeys were very common in all media of medieval art and they almost always behave badly, showing audiences what not to do.[18] In the Taymouth Hours, audiences could read the Jew at the Funeral of the Virgin, in terms of both the Passion figures and the worst of beasts, the ape. The artist makes the association so visually strong in terms of the Jew's change in physical appearance before and after his conversion that when the baptismal water touches him, the artist restores physical humanity to this monstrous tormentor.

With the establishment of an iconography dependent on the Jew's hands remaining stuck to the pall, artists could deny any hope for the Jew's re-demption, physical or spiritual. Particularly in the illustrations from the de Brailes Hours and the Taymouth Hours, artists exercised complete physi-cal and spiritual control over the Jews they constructed, creating situations where audiences comfortably watch the Jew shift from animal-like monster to human. This concept is most fully articulated in two final examples from York Minster. In these cases, the private experience of reading the Jew in a small book of hours moves into the public sphere of a cathedral window.

The first comes from the popular scene of the Monkeys' Funeral from the Pilgrimage Window from the north side of the nave (Fig. 2). This window dates to around 1325, making it roughly contemporary to the Taymouth Hours.[19] The window's six main lights show scenes from the Crucifixion as well as a knight and lady going on pilgrimage. There are three small panels running along the bottom of the window.[20] The left panel is the most elaborate: on the left a fox reads from a lectern to a cock; on the right a monkey exam-ines a urine flask. In the centre of the panel, we see an elaborate procession of monkeys, the first rings a white bell, the second carries a gold cross and then a bier is carried by four monkeys while a smaller monkey hangs in the center with his hands stuck to the body. This scene of the Monkeys' Funeral is widely read as a parody and recently by Paul Hardwick as a meditation on humility.[21] I read this scene as fitting squarely into our progression of imagery, where the Jew has officially left the realm of humanity. In the larger space of this one win-dow, the monkey can take one of two roles outside of the Funeral, as a mock

---

[18] The authority on this subject remains H. W. Janson, *Apes and Ape Lore in the Middle Ages and Renaissance* (London, 1952).

[19] O'Connor and Haselock, 'Stained and Painted Glass', pp. 354–7; Brown, *Stained Glass at York Minster*, pp. 42–3; J. Toy, *A Guide and Index to the Windows of York Minster* (York, 1985), p. 17.

[20] The centre panel shows a scene from Reynard the Fox of a woman beating a fox with her distaff while a monkey holding an owl watches from the corner. The right panel contains a continuous hunting scene.

[21] P. Hardwick, 'The Monkeys' Funeral in the Pilgrimage Window, York Minster', *Art History* 23 (2003), 290–9.

Figure 2. 'The Monkeys' Funeral', detail from the Pilgrimage Window, the north aisle of the nave of York Minster. © Dean and Chapter of York: Reproduced by kind permission of the Dean and Chapter and David O'Connor.

doctor or sitting quietly with an owl. The latter recalls the monkey as the worst beast in the Taymouth Hours, for the owl is the bird most associated with the Jews by bestiary authors and artists.[22] Though the Funeral appears at the margins of the main window, just as most of the examples from manuscripts appeared along the 'bas de page', its meaning should not be seen as secondary to the main lights of the window. The Monkeys' Funeral is the easiest part of the window to see and continues to offer audiences a possible example of medieval antisemitism thinly veiled as a joke or parody.

There is nothing veiled about the last example of the Funeral from York Minster. Now in the high clerestory windows above the south aisle of the Lady Chapel, the Funeral of the Virgin lies between the Death and Coronation of the Virgin. These windows are difficult because they are literally out of place, since they were originally made around 1340–50 for another smaller chapel dedicated to the Virgin – either the chapel of St Mary and All Angels (off the northwest part of the Minster) or a local parish church owned by the Dean and Chapter. They were installed so high up, and out of order, in about 1370.[23] The

22 M. Miyazaki, 'Misericord Owls and Medieval Anti-Semitism', in *Mark of the Beast: The Medieval Bestiary in Art, Life, and Literature*, ed. D. Hassig (New York, 1999), pp. 23–50.
23 Toy, *Guide and Index to the Windows*, p. 36; Brown, *Stained Glass at York Minster*, pp. 52–4; O'Connor and Haselock, 'Stained and Painted Glass', pp. 378–85. For studies of these problematic windows, their original location and association with the Lady Chapel see: T. W. French, 'The Dating of the Lady Chapel in York Minster', *Antiquaries Journal* 52 (1972), 309–19; T. W. French, 'Observations on Some Medieval Glass in York Minster', *Antiquaries Journal* 51 (1971), 86–93; J. A. Knowles, 'Notes on Some Windows in the Choir and Lady Chapel of York Minster', *YAJ* 39 (1956), 91–118; A. H. Thompson, 'The Chapel of St Mary and the Holy

Figure 3. 'Lady Chapel Window', from the south side of the choir clerestory of York Minster. Reproduced by kind permission of the Dean and Chapter of York. © W. J. Green: Reproduced by kind permission of English Heritage.

window pre-dates the Funeral of the Virgin as it was performed in the York Mystery Plays.[24] This Funeral of the Virgin is the culmination of our story (Fig. 3). Here the Jew appears tiny, almost shrunken, next to the tall and elegant apostles, two of which seem about to crush him as they turn to stare at him. He wears a short tunic that looks almost like a kilt that draws attention to his legs trying to get free. We see the moment his hands get stuck and he seems to howl in pain. A flattened nose, dark eyes set in a furrowed brow, and a gaping void of a mouth, dominate his face. The complete exaggeration of this figure's face is what makes this panel so visually successful.[25]

This unknown glass artist thus brings everything together in this one image. Earlier manuscript images called on inscriptions, as in the de Brailes Hours, or association with tormentors in the Passion to create the Jew in the Funeral. They were overt visual connections that would have been easily read by medieval audiences. This glass artist makes the audience work a bit harder,

Angels, otherwise known as St Sepulchre's Chapel at York', *YAJ* 36 (1944), 63–77.

24 The Funeral of the Virgin with the Jew, with Fergus attacking the bier, was part of the late fourteenth and fifteenth-century cycle of mystery plays performed on the streets of York. *York Mystery Plays: A Selection in Modern Spelling*, ed. R. Beadle and P. M. King (Oxford, 1984), pp. xii–xiv; A. E. Nichols, 'The Hierosphthitic Topos, or the Fate of Fergus: Notes on the N-Town *Assumption*', *Comparative Drama* 25 (1991), 29–41.

25 In his drawing of the Jew at the Funeral for his 1956 article, Knowles re-humanizes the Jew, giving him a longer, more elegant body and a sweet, almost cherubic face. Knowles, 'Notes on Some Windows in the Choir and Lady Chapel', p. 94.

creating a more covert antisemitic message. Viewers had to read the image on its own and then connect the Jew in the story with this new creature in the window. The artist does not give any hints, he creates a character who was identifiable to medieval audiences as a Jew through association with the remembered story. The viewer's connection of tale and text perpetuated medieval antisemitism by moving the Jew further and further from reality into the realms of inhumanity.

15

Massacre and Memory: Ethics and Method in Recent Scholarship on Jewish Martyrdom

Hannah Johnson

History, it seems, must always suffer the impositions of second guessing. If this is true of historical events, the traditional content of historical accounts, it is no less true of historiography, that higher order analysis which is itself a venerable form of retrospective re-examination. We continuously revise our understanding of historical explanations as well as events. In a volume dedicated to revisiting the massacre at York in 1190 and its legacy, I take it as given that part of our task is to consider what kinds of tools we have in our scholarly arsenal in the early twenty-first century for evaluating that moment and its context, in terms that encompass contemporary historiographical trends as well as medieval documents. My own small part in this project is to reflect on the intellectual moment in which we find ourselves, and to consider briefly how this context might offer some new resources as well as new challenges for engaging with the events at York.

A critical aspect of our current intellectual climate is what I will call an emergent paradigm shift in medieval Jewish studies that is at once methodological and ethical. Recently we have seen the development of competing historiographical views of the phenomenon of Jewish self-martyrdom in medieval Europe that I will try to summarize clearly, if rather schematically. On the one hand are those interpretations that fall within a tradition that might be described as memorializing, and tend to frame acts of medieval Jewish self-sacrifice primarily as heroic demonstrations of communal self-assertion. This perspective is prominently represented by Robert Chazan, though his work is part of a longstanding post-Holocaust historiographical tradition.[1]

---

[1] See, for example, Jeremy Cohen's insightful overview of the historiography on the martyrdoms of 1096 in *Sanctifying the Name of God: Jewish Martyrs and Jewish Memories of the First Crusade* (Philadelphia, 2004), pp. 31–54, as well as his earlier article, 'A 1096 Complex? Constructing the First Crusade in Jewish Historical Memory, Medieval and Modern', in *Jews and Christians in Twelfth-Century Europe*, ed. M. A. Signer and J. van Engen (Notre Dame IN, 2000), pp. 9–26. David Nirenberg also offers an astute analysis of Yitzhak Baer's evolving work in the wake of the Holocaust, in 'The Rhineland Massacres of Jews in the First Crusade:

But increasingly, scholarship on this fraught subject is moving toward a perspective that emphasizes aspects of contingency, ambivalence, and uncertainty in accounting for these events. Here I include work by scholars such as Israel Yuval and Jeremy Cohen as prominent exemplars.[2] I will argue that what is visible in these competing paradigms is not simply a methodological shift, but a historiographical move that carries with it – whether explicitly or implicitly – a set of ethical claims about the meaning or cultural significance of this history. What follows is by no means an exhaustive review of the literature in this dynamic field; considerations of space alone would prohibit such an ambitious undertaking. Instead, I propose to offer a reading of a few influential recent discussions about the appearance of a medieval Jewish martyrological tradition as a way of elucidating some of the ethico-methodological tensions that haunt conversation on this topic. And I believe we can better understand the implications of this ongoing discussion for scholarship on the events of 1190 if we see this scholarly turn as an ethical move from an emphasis on memorialization to an emphasis on the experience of contingency, rather than if we see it as solely methodological.[3]

Of course invoking a word like ethics in this fraught context carries its own substantial risks of misunderstanding. When I speak of ethics, I refer to a specific attitude of engagement with historical materials that assumes certain obligations on the part of the historian and, by implication, his audience. I invoke the language of the ethical – as opposed to the moral – both because ethics is the more capacious conceptual category, and because I see the nature of the obligations entailed by certain historiographical perspectives as being open to both dispute and exploration, rather than operating as closed or settled imperatives.[4] It is far from true that methodological ques-

Memories Medieval and Modern', in *Medieval Concepts of the Past: Ritual, Memory, Historiography*, ed. G. Althoff et al. (Cambridge, 2002), pp. 279–310 (pp. 299–303). In addition to Nirenberg, Arnold J. Band presents a reading of Shalom Spiegel's *The Last Trial* as a scholarly lament that addresses historiographical questions through the lens of modern memory: A. J. Band, 'Scholarship as Lamentation: Shalom Spiegel on "The Binding of Isaac"', *Jewish Social Studies* n.s. 5 no. 1/2 (1998/99), 80–90. Also see Chazan's own analysis of historiographical trends in the synthesis he produced for a broad audience, *In the Year 1096: The First Crusade and the Jews* (Philadelphia, 1996), pp. 107–70. Below I analyse Chazan's arguments in *European Jewry and the First Crusade* (Berkeley CA, 1987) and *God, Humanity, and History: The Hebrew First Crusade Narratives* (Berkeley CA, 2000).

2   Cohen, *Sanctifying the Name*, and I. J. Yuval, *Two Nations in Your Womb: Perceptions of Jews and Christians in Late Antiquity and the Middle Ages*, trans. B. Harshav and J. Chipman (Berkeley CA, 2006).

3   I am not the first scholar to observe a change in the weather where studies of medieval Jewish martyrdom are concerned. Others have commented on the methodological shift; I am interested in what might be defined as a shifting ethics of memory that is linked in complex ways with methodological questions. I do, however, acknowledge that ideology is bound up with such issues (see below). In addition to the references above, see the broader survey offered in I. G. Marcus, 'Israeli Medieval Jewish Historiography: From Nationalist Positivism to New Cultural and Social Histories', *JSQ* 17 (2010), 244–85.

4   Though philosophers and ethicists have parsed these terms in a number of ways, I rely

tions somehow precede or elude the concerns of ethical deliberation. Instead the two issues are implicated in one another in complex ways. To consider how particular historical events were experienced by specific human actors is at the same time to consider the problem of the meaning we assign to those events. To ask about causality is also to entertain questions of responsibility. A key ethical question at stake in recent discussions of the medieval phenomenon of Jewish self-martyrdom, or *Kiddush ha-Shem*, concerns the nature of our obligation to acknowledge and examine the historical reality of persecution and atrocity; that is, how we are to come to terms with the past in a way that clarifies events, but also makes them amenable to *ethical* comprehension and analysis. I invoke the category of memory here because I believe that this felt sense of obligation to recollect and even commemorate historical acts of injustice operates as one ethical presupposition within which contemporary historians pursue their interpretive projects, and it is in these terms that their claims are registered as affirming within existing contexts of collective memory or, on the contrary, understood as controversial.[5] These questions are bound up with the critical issue of the meaning or cultural impact of historical events in the present. For the moment, my goals are modest: to articulate two very different interpretive paradigms for understanding medieval Jewish acts of self-sacrifice, and to demonstrate how both ethical and methodological considerations are tied up in such projects of interpretation.

on Paul Ricoeur's useful distinction between the ethical aim and the moral norm, which he defines as the difference between 'that which is *considered to be good* and of that which *imposes itself as obligatory*. It is, therefore, by convention that I reserve the term "ethics" for the *aim* of an accomplished life and the term "morality" for the articulation of this aim in *norms* characterized at once by the claim to universality and by an effect of constraint.' P. Ricoeur, *Oneself as Another*, trans. K. Blamey (Chicago, 1992), p. 170 (author's emphasis). The historians whose work I survey below would probably all agree on some version of the claim that it is ethically desirable, even necessary, to remember and reconstruct historical moments of Jewish suffering – this might be described as a broadly shared ethical aim. They would probably disagree, however, about the best and most satisfactory way to go about achieving this aim. What interests me is how an ethics of memory that appeared self-evident to earlier generations of historians – even sometimes approaching the compulsory status of a moral norm – is no longer understood as binding by recent historians and is in fact being actively renegotiated.

5   A specifically Jewish communal memory is obviously relevant in this context, but I do not mean to suggest that the impulse to memorialize such events is limited to Jewish scholars alone. Although Yerushalmi's *Zakhor* remains the *locus classicus* for discussions about the relation between memory and history in Jewish culture, this essay is neither a commentary on nor a continuation of his. See Y. H. Yerushalmi, *Zakhor: Jewish History and Jewish Memory* (Seattle, 1982).

Method and Memory

To explain what I mean about the complex entanglement of ethical and methodological concerns in this corner of historiography, it is useful to revisit a well-known historiographical dispute between Robert Chazan and Ivan Marcus in the late 1980s and early 90s. This debate was an early barometer of a tension that has become more obvious over time, between an explicitly memorializing perspective and an emphasis on historical contingency and uncertainty. In his book, *European Jewry and the First Crusade*, Chazan uses surviving Hebrew accounts as a major component of his effort to reconstruct crusader attacks on Jewish communities along the Rhine. He chooses to give the Hebrew testimonies priority for quite traditional historicist reasons:

> They were composed fairly close in time to the events depicted, are based on first-hand testimony, are committed to a portrayal of a variety of patterns of Christian and Jewish behavior, and are written in a plain and unadorned style.[6]

The documents' status as privileged witnesses, according to Chazan, is underwritten by their straightforward delivery and their interest in expressing diverse aspects of the reality they depict. Chazan argues that by reading these texts carefully, it should be possible to reconstruct a reliable and fairly transparent picture of historical reality from them. This is a traditional view of how the historian ought to proceed, sifting surviving evidence for key facts and discarding merely narrative material as unreliable or primarily useful for adding a sense of local colour. Yet, as I hope to show, these well-worn methodological guidelines are also imbricated in complex ways with questions of memory and, more specifically, the responsibilities that devolve upon the historian who seeks to revisit this difficult ground or even reimagine the historical context in which acts of Jewish martyrdom unfolded.

In his review of Chazan's book in *Speculum*, Marcus seems to critique any use of the Hebrew narratives to produce a straightforward reconstruction of events: 'Variety of detail in the sources does not prove that the detail is in the events themselves and not in the narrators' minds. Chazan's argument is circular, and his insistence on looking for detailed "facts" in these sources is futile.'[7] The facts of the case, Marcus argues, are secondary to the larger

---

6   Chazan, *European Jewry*, p. 3. Chazan's valorization of the 'plain, unadorned' style recalls Nancy Partner's remark that modern historians seem to like medieval historians best, and trust them most, when they sound most like modern historians. See N. F. Partner, *Serious Entertainments: The Writing of History in Twelfth-Century England* (Chicago, 1977), p. 25.

7   I. G. Marcus, 'Review: *European Jewry and the First Crusade*', *Speculum* 64 (1989), 685–8 (p. 687). In a related article, Marcus remarks, 'it is not that events and "facts" do not exist out there "behind" these texts, but they are not "in" them, and the persistent assumption that

persuasive agenda of the texts. The needs and attitudes of the original audience are the matter we may infer from our reading of these documents, while the status of facts is far more complicated. Beliefs and attitudes appear as the secure ground for the historian's work; stable facts are more insecure, since they are filtered through the needs and preoccupations of the narrators who present them. Though Marcus does not directly acknowledge the influence of structuralist and poststructuralist theory, his arguments register the force of debates about the impossibility of achieving direct access to the past through the referentiality of historical documents.[8] The past, he argues, is ineluctably mediated by the language and cultural context preserved in the documents that form the historian's evidentiary base, and our acts of interpretation must always be attentive to this mediation. Yet in Marcus's arguments, as in much recent historiography on Jewish self-martyrdom, these methodological claims strongly correlate with a subtle ethical directive that bears on questions of meaning as well as method.[9] Our ethical obligation as readers and interpreters of history, from this point of view, lies in uncovering the ambivalence and indeterminacies surrounding the medieval Jewish community's effort to understand these acts of martyrdom.

In his response to Marcus's critiques, Chazan seems hard-pressed to account for the difference between his approach and his colleague's, and is clearly stung at being categorised as a backward-looking positivist.[10] 'Both Marcus and I agree', he writes,

> that the Hebrew First Crusade narratives are highly tendentious, addressing a variety of issues ranging from political advice through halakhic justification of the martyrs and on to theological rationalization for the catastrophe. We both agree that the presentation of Christian and Jewish behav-

---

they are leads to few positive results and, more significantly, avoids a more appropriate analysis that would make historical sense of what that type of source can tell us.' I. G. Marcus, 'History, Story and Collective Memory: Narrativity in Early Ashkenazic Culture', *Prooftexts* 10 (1990), 365–88 (p. 367).

8   In his 1990 article, Marcus presents a metaphor of the historian as anthropologist that often seems to operate as a stand-in for such critiques, 'History, Story and Collective Memory', pp. 365–6. See Gabrielle Spiegel's well-known examination of these issues in the context of medieval historiography, G. M. Spiegel, 'History, Historicism and the Social Logic of the Text in the Middle Ages', *Speculum* 65 (1990), 59–86. For a follow-up discussion, see G. M. Spiegel, *The Past as Text: The Theory and Practice of Medieval Historiography* (Baltimore, 1999). These debates are widely known in the field, so I will refrain from summarizing them again here.

9   See also I. G. Marcus, 'The Representation of Reality in the Narratives of 1096', *Jewish History* 13:2 (1999), 37–48.

10   Chazan suggests that, 'Marcus treats all efforts at identifying historical realities in narrative sources as "positivist", a designation surely intended as pejorative'. R. Chazan, 'The Facticity of Medieval Narrative: A Case Study of the Hebrew First Crusade Narratives', *AJSR* 16 (1991), 31–56 (p. 55).

iors in the Hebrew First Crusade narratives is highly styl-
ized both in language and in imagery.[11]

Like Marcus, in other words, Chazan is prepared to account for both cultural
and individual bias in the production of the historical texts he analyses. The
sticking point remains the nature and ascertainability of historical reality, an
issue that was being discussed with some urgency at the time, but which has
been allowed to fade quietly into the background since then. Even if Marcus's theories about the literary structure of the Hebrew narratives of 1096
are correct, Chazan asks,

> would this necessarily mean that such a [narrative] sequence
> was a product of the author's imagination? Would it not be
> possible that the author was profoundly impressed with
> the reality of a striking sequence that forced itself upon his
> consciousness?[12]

Chazan continues to press home the claim that where an author is not imitat-
ing previous textual models, and where the narrative seems to speak in an
original voice, even to the point of contradicting itself or incorporating un-
flattering details, these are signs of the true, the real, and can form the basis
of a legitimate reconstruction of events.[13]

But for Chazan, a determination about historical reality is also, critically,
a determination about intelligibility and meaning. Reality is what makes
sense, or what can be made to make sense with the proper interpretive grid,
and in that linkage between reality and meaning lies a hint of Chazan's ethics of memory. There is a plaintive quality near the end of his article, when,
considering Marcus' critiques, he writes,

> I am much interested in what Jews 'thought, felt, and wrote
> about the past.' That, however, is not 'the very goal' that I
> seek. I am also very much concerned with *what happened*
> during the First Crusade. While in no sense denying the de-
> sirability and possibility of extracting insight on [*sic*] how
> subsequent Jews viewed the past, I am, at the same time,
> vitally interested in *the realities* of that past.[14]

---

11 Ibid., p. 41.
12 Ibid., p. 43. This is a possibility that Paul Ricoeur would appear to leave open , though for a
    critic like Hayden White, the idea that narrative patterns would somehow 'inhere' in events
    'themselves' is dubious at best, a product of the historian's perception—or wishful think-
    ing. See, in particular, P. Ricoeur, *Time and Narrative I*, trans. K. McLaughlin and D. Pellauer
    (Chicago, 1990) and H. White, *The Content of the Form: Narrative Discourse and Historical Rep-
    resentation* (Baltimore, 1987).
13 Chazan, 'Facticity of Medieval Narrative', esp. pp. 44–6.
14 ibid., p. 54 (emphasis is mine).

It is in this precise sense that Marcus characterizes his fellow historian as a positivist, though Chazan himself might prefer the more neutral designation 'historical realist'. Yet his methodological arguments fundamentally reinforce a broadly memorializing impulse already visible in his work. Certainly a message of elegiac meaning – even an echo of the very collective memory enshrined in the Hebrew narratives of 1096 themselves – is detectable in the moving eulogistic prose of Chazan's later work:

> Survivors [of the events of 1096] needed to maintain their recollection of the Jews who stretched forth their necks before the swords of the crusaders and burghers, the Jews who threw themselves off the ramparts overlooking the Rhine River or who plunged daggers into their stomachs, and the Jews who took up swords against their own flesh and blood.[15]

The bare gestures of these tragic historical actors are testimony to a desperation that is not soon forgotten, and they impose a specific obligation of memory that implies a particular evaluation of events. When Chazan argues that the medieval work of memory requires a factual account of real events in order to accomplish its communal goals, he says more than he may know, since his own analysis, rooted in a memorial impulse, also requires a full, factual, and referential account in order to do the work of memory so clearly important to him. Chazan's analysis reproduces the memorial trajectory of the sources he analyses.

The image Chazan creates is of a community heroic in its martyrdom, speaking to itself as spiritually whole, whose doubts or moments of ambivalence are of relatively less importance than some recent scholars have suggested.[16] Chazan has continued to pursue a variant of his 'facticity' thesis across three books on the events of 1096, culminating in a project published in 2000, *God, Humanity, and History: The Hebrew First Crusade Narratives*. Here he articulates a distinction between what he calls the 'time-bound' objectives of the Hebrew chronicles, which are directed toward communicating vital information and articulating strategies for avoiding or mitigating violence, and the 'timeless' objectives of commemorating the martyrs' deaths.[17] In this way he has kept the category of facticity sacrosanct, while making some allowances for critiques (like Marcus's) that invoke the terms of recent theoretical debates. But again we can see a process of transference at work

---

[15] R. Chazan, *God, Humanity, and History: The Hebrew First Crusade Narratives* (Berkeley CA, 2000), pp. 122–3.

[16] I do not intend to imply that Chazan himself is deaf to the internal contradictions or inconsistencies these sources present. Certainly he is not. However, he does not attribute the same importance to such textual cruxes that many of his colleagues do.

[17] Chazan, *God, Humanity and History*, esp. pp. 1–18, 112–56.

in the structure of the analysis itself, since the categories of the timeless and the time-bound actually echo some structures of Jewish observance. Judaism divides *mitzvot*, or commandments, into those which are time-bound and those which are not, and offers an exemption from the categories of the time-bound to women and those who are ill. In Chazan's work, the logic of this distinction is reversed, but it still acts to preserve a critical nexus of meaning-making. The non-time-bound elements of the Hebrew chronicle accounts, according to Chazan, apply to the larger spiritual needs of the Jewish community, while the time-bound objectives are meant to address – and provide a guide for – specific temporal problems of survival. There appears to be an unconscious mapping of a Jewish ritual paradigm onto a set of historiographical problems that reveals something of the author's deep ethical investment in a communal, memorial narrative of medieval Jewish suffering.

Yet I do not wish to suggest that Marcus's arguments about the mediation of historical reality simply succeed without qualification as methodologically neutral guidelines while Chazan's work falls short of such goals. Nor would I wish to disparage the ideals that inform Chazan's analysis. While I may appear to single him out, my emphasis on Chazan's work is one indication of his importance in the field as well as the continuity of perspective his work displays over time. My point is not that we might somehow simply divest historiography of any ethical investment; as I have suggested, where there is meaning, there also is ethics. Instead, I want to argue that we must be aware of the ethical implications of history as a meaning-making enterprise, and consider how the 'neutral' claims of method remain fundamentally bound up in such concerns. I also want to avoid creating the impression that historiography may be neatly divided between two binary interpretive systems. Certainly we can imagine a contingent view of historical reality that yields a memorializing interpretation, or a set of claims about the transparency of a given set of historical events that nevertheless registers uncertainty about the proper way to evaluate them. However, in the debate between Chazan and Marcus, these methodological and ethical factors track together in revealing ways. An ethics of memorialization that seeks a sense of closure and fullness of meaning in history is not merely 'associated' with a referential view of historical reality in Chazan's case; the former virtually requires the latter. Transparency and meaning reinforce one another so that questioning narrative transparency can seem like a threat to meaning itself. In a complementary sense, an emphasis on the experience of contingency makes sense in the context of a definition of historical reality that draws attention to the loose ends, unfinished business, or uncertainties that a historiographical narrative of closure leaves behind. What is more, these are points on a continuum, rather than absolute positions, and these paradigms carry within them a complex politics of meaning.

Marcus may be more reticent than Chazan to make strong claims about historical reality; nevertheless, it cannot be said that he makes *no* claims on reality. In fact, some such claims animate, even supply the unspoken foundations for, his arguments about the mentalities that describe, characterise, and shape the historical reality represented in the texts he examines. More importantly, Marcus's methodological claims are also bound up in an implicit ethical evaluation that speaks to vital questions of meaning. Some critiques of more traditional historiography on medieval Jewish self-sacrifice speak to the investments at stake quite clearly. David Myers, for instance, writes that,

> Modern Jewish historiography provides an interesting laboratory to explore and refine the distinction between history and memory. When dealing with the Crusades, modern scholars have often produced narratives that burst forth with impassioned descriptions of, and implicit prescriptions for, Jewish history.[18]

Many recent scholars have obviously reacted against such 'prescriptions', but with a vision of experience in view that privileges division, contingency, and uncertainty as the fundamental vectors for evaluating the historical experience of Jewish suffering. In his recent book, David Malkiel describes such a project in terms of what he calls the 'human face' of medieval Jewish communities, perhaps particularly when it comes to the experience of martyrdom. He writes:

> I argue that medieval Ashkenaz was not a community of saints and martyrs but simply of people, with both the heroism and the foibles found in other eras and locales. Lowering Ashkenazic Jewry from its pedestal complicates the picture of the Middle Ages as an era of a purer religious life, and by implication it may grant strength to contemporary Jews as they face their own challenges to religious fidelity, for although one can admire saints and martyrs, it is difficult to identify with them.[19]

Malkiel's remarks hint at the possibility that he has another kind of memorial project in mind when he suggests that merely human, historical sufferers may offer more possibilities for identification and empathy for modern audiences. Rather than some clearly delineated view of communal solidarity,

---

[18] D. N. Myers, '"*Mehabevin et ha-tsarot*": Crusade Memories and Modern Jewish Martyrologies', *Jewish History* 13:2 (1999), 49–64 (p. 51).

[19] D. Malkiel, *Reconstructing Ashkenaz: The Human Face of Franco-German Jewry, 1000–1250* (Stanford CA, 2009), p. xi. Malkiel participates in the vision of a historical community that is 'less heroic and therefore more human', one that is 'heterogeneous and hence both credible and human', ibid., p. xiii. He devotes considerable attention to nonconformers, apostates, and dissidents within the Jewish community. One of his desired aims, he writes, is to establish 'a less fraught, more normal image of Jewish-Christian relations in place of one that recognizes only alienation and confrontation', ibid., p. xii.

much recent scholarship reframes medieval acts of Jewish self-martyrdom in open-ended ethical terms that stress difficulty and uncertainty as authentic to the experience of persecution and suffering. Both Malkiel and Jeremy Cohen, for instance, emphasize the ambivalence and complexity of medieval Jewish discourse about martyrdom rather than the clear moral claims that later historical memory attached to the events. We are not asked to valorize Jewish martyrs, but to understand their experiences in terms that recognize not only the impossible choices confronting them, but also the contradictions and deep ambivalence legible in their behaviour. What is at stake is the question of meaning, which has an irreducibly ethical dimension.

Reading Persecution

I would like to consider these perspectives in relation to a particularly fraught story of martyrdom drawn from the Hebrew chronicles that describe the events of 1096. The narrative I have chosen to highlight concerns the martyrdom of Isaac ben David and his family around the time of the attack on Mainz.[20] Isaac's is a complex case: he submitted to forced baptism, we are told, in order to be sure that his children would not be adopted and raised as Christians after his death. His wife, Skolaster, had already been killed by crusaders, and his mother was seriously injured by them. After the immediate danger of violence had subsided, Isaac suffered remorse and despair over his baptism as well as the loss of his community. We are told that he decided to make a gesture of atonement and expiation. This response in fact replicates the traumatic force of the violence he had witnessed. Isaac locks his mother in the family house and sets it on fire, assuring her death. He then kills his children within the confines of the local synagogue before setting it on fire with himself inside. When Christians try to pull him from the fire, Isaac refuses to be rescued, and is killed in the flames.[21]

This is a difficult story by any measure. How should we evaluate this profound act of martyrological violence, accomplished after the major attacks

---

20 The story of Mistress Rachel of Mainz and her four children is another example often discussed as a particularly fraught case. Chazan, *European Jewry*, pp. 111–13; Chazan, *God, Humanity and History*, pp. 166–67, 180–84; Cohen, *Sanctifying the Name*, pp. 106–29; Marcus, 'Representation of Reality'.Yuval refers to this story as exemplifying the emphasis on child sacrifice in the Hebrew chronicles, without lengthy discussion of its themes, *Two Nations*, pp. 158–9.

21 The story appears in the chronicle of Eliezer bar Nathan and that of Solomon bar Samson, from which it is extracted and analysed in Cohen, *Sanctifying the Name*, pp. 91–4, and Chazan, *European Jewry*, pp. 103–5. Chazan also includes an appendix featuring his own translations of two Hebrew chronicles, ibid., pp. 223–97. Also see the three major modern editions of the Hebrew chronicles: *The Jews and Crusaders*, ed. Eidelberg (Madison, WI, 1977); *Sefer Gezerot Ashkenaz ve-Tsarfat*, ed. A. Habermann (Jerusalem, 1945); *Hebräische Berichte über die Judenverfolgungen während der Kreuzzüge*, ed. A. Neubauer and M. Stern (Berlin, 1892).

had already subsided? How would an early twelfth century Jewish audience have evaluated the story? We know, for instance, that most of the Jews who were forcibly converted in 1096 returned to Judaism with support from their temporal lords. But for Isaac ben David, and perhaps for others like him, the shame and the cost of such survival were too high. His death may be read as a self-chosen statement in a high stakes religious conflict with the Christian majority. If the phenomenon of *Kiddush ha-Shem* in relation to Christian persecution already prompts complex responses where scholarship intersects with the drives of memory, what are we to do with such a difficult example as this? Isaac's martyrdom is frequently discussed in the scholarly literature, in part because of its problematic status as a martyrdom after the fact, and one involving family members who do not appear to have been implicated in guilt-inducing acts of forced conversion. As a test case, it offers a useful paradigm for thinking about the ways in which ethical presuppositions inform interpretation.

Chazan's evaluation of this episode evolves over time within a distinct memorializing tradition. In his early discussion of the episode in 1987, he presents a long extract from a chronicle account of Isaac's martyrdom, and then remarks:

> This portrait is one of the most vivid that has survived from this intense period. It is the portrait of a man maddened by suffering, pain, and guilt and consumed by a powerful drive for repentance and atonement. The act of conversion shattered Isaac, leaving him possessed by the desire to undo the sin which he felt he had committed.[22]

This summary of the stakes of Isaac's sacrifice speaks to the power of the story, and Chazan's own emphasis on the strong sense of religious identity that motivated acts of self-sacrifice. In his 2000 discussion of this same episode, his description suggests that the best response to such difficult episodes may be reverential silence. 'Here again', he writes, 'the complexity of the matter can hardly be avoided', and goes on to summarize the difficult circumstances of Isaac's initial conversion followed by his agonizing death, prompting Chazan to ask, [23]

> What precisely made his earlier decision [to convert] erroneous and his later decision [to martyr himself] correct? Again, our author does not set forth an argument. Rather, he makes his case through the force of his powerful tale. The suicide

---

[22] Chazan, *European Jewry*, p. 105. Chazan's brief discussion of the episode draws attention to the evidence corroborating the intensity of medieval Jewish resistance to conversion, and a firm commitment to their faith (ibid., pp. 105–7).

[23] Chazan, *God, Humanity and History*, p. 122.

of Isaac and his friend Uri ben Joseph (by burning the synagogue) and the murder of Isaac's aged mother and young
children are told in a manner that hardly brooks rational ob-
jection. ... The best—indeed the only—justification for the
radical forms of Jewish martyrdom in 1096 was the persuasive recounting of the martyrs' stories.

In this way, Chazan argues, the author of the account dispenses with the
need to justify the martyrs' actions in terms of Jewish religious law (*halakha*).
The medieval writer's goals were rather different:

Part of the motivation for telling these powerful and haunting
stories was the author's sense of obligation to those whose
heroism demanded memorialization. ... [This was] a need
above and beyond either the need to rationalize some of their
extreme actions or the need to comprehend the tragedy.[24]

Chazan argues that this need to memorialize actually constitutes an argument in favour of the historical accuracy of such stories, since part of doing justice to the martyrs – perhaps particularly in cases where their actions
were difficult to understand – involved remembering them accurately. Yet
I would underscore the way Chazan's account of the chronicler's interests
dovetail with his own. Chazan's discussion of this episode leaves one with
the impression that to delve too deeply into the complex circumstances of
a martyr 'maddened' by pain and grief would be unseemly. In contrast to
scholars like Jeremy Cohen and Israel Yuval, who draw attention to the con-
tradictory currents in the story, Chazan reads it as continuous with ideals
of medieval Jewish identity and memory. 'The glory of these behaviors', he
remarks, 'could not be allowed to dissipate, and re-creating these acts of
heroism became a moral and religious obligation.'[25]

For Cohen, however, as for Malkiel, the human face of medieval Jewish
communities is also fundamentally an ambivalent one, and he devotes considerable space to a consideration of the Isaac ben David account. In his recent book on the martyrdoms, Cohen stresses that the Hebrew chronicles
commemorating acts of martyrdom were designed to meet the emotional
and religious needs of early twelfth century survivors, many of whom may
have felt guilt about the mechanisms that enabled their survival of the attacks, including temporary forced conversion to Christianity. Cohen thus
reads the Hebrew narratives as documents riven by internal contradiction,
ambivalence, and anxiety. They are not the records of a community united
by a fully integrated ideology of defiance; instead, the documents show a

24 ibid., p. 122.
25 ibid., p. 123.

community struggling to survive and resolve a profound crisis. In his interpretation of Isaac's story, Cohen calls attention to aspects of doubt or uncertainty in the narrator's account of events, and attributes these to the needs of survivors, an audience bearing a certain amount of guilt, but also bitterness. When Isaac's would-be Christian rescuers call out, 'Wicked man, get out of the fire!', Cohen reads the ambivalence of the survivors themselves:

> we recall that to get out of the fire is exactly what Isaac did two days earlier [when he initially escaped the crusaders by converting]. Did that make him a wicked man? Or did killing himself, his mother, and his children make him wicked?[26]

The terms of the question recall Chazan's, and speak to the puzzling challenges the story represents. In Cohen's reading, Isaac's martyrdom represents a series of painful choices, many of them also faced by those who originally encountered his story. If his choices represent that audience's dilemma as well as its doubts, Cohen argues that Isaac also gives voice to their struggle with God. Like Isaac, whose story evokes both 'pity and ridicule', according to Cohen, the survivors struggle with the realities of their survival:

> From the perspective of early twelfth-century German Jewry, distinguished by its self-confidence, firmly convinced of the perfection of its collective piety, God and history had shortchanged them in 1096; their massacre at the hands of the crusaders constituted nothing less than desecration of the first order.[27]

The traumatized martyr thus becomes representative of the traumatized community that hears his story. From this point of view, the narrator's claim that Isaac falls as a whole-hearted and willing sacrifice to God can only appear as a dark irony, since he sacrifices himself to a God who appears not to react. If Chazan's memorializing trajectory influences his claims about the medieval Jewish community's needs, Cohen's presuppositions about the meaning of traumatic experience no less concretely shape his arguments about the Hebrew chronicle accounts commemorating acts of self-martyrdom.

Yuval's work represents another aspect of what I might term a scholarly ethics of contingency, though he takes a very different position on the surviving Jewish community's struggle with God from Cohen. In his study, Yuval characterizes Isaac's death as an activist's death, since his interpretation revolves around the motif of vengeance. Jewish martyrs in 1096, he writes,

---

[26] Cohen, *Sanctifying the Name*, p. 103.
[27] ibid., pp. 104, 105.

are engaging God in a 'messianic holy war' and their acts of sacrifice, deliberately modelled on the now defunct animal sacrifices in the ancient Temple, are not just martyrdoms but a 'sacrificial ritual', 'blood ritual' or 'blood rite'. He even refers to a 'martyr's cult of blood and sacrifice'.[28] Yuval has argued that the dramatic acts of martyrdom that occurred in 1096 were part of a coherent ideology of vengeance, in which the spilled blood of the Jewish victims was understood to call down the wrath of a God who will eventually take revenge for the deaths of his people. 'The purpose of these acts and of their telling', he writes, 'is to shock and horrify not only the reader, but God himself.' Later he adds that, 'Rhetorically, one might sharpen the point by saying more specifically that the chronicles were not intended to shape earthly public opinion, but heavenly public opinion, the World on High'.[29] In this way, the martyr's suicide and sacrificial killing of his family becomes a kind of activism, since he hopes to spur God to action. Yuval writes: 'The martyrs are soldiers in the heavenly army who fell in a cosmic war … Their death was not in vain because, by virtue of their sacrifice, they arouse the wrath of the avenging God and bring deliverance closer.'[30]

Like Cohen, Yuval calls attention to the specific rhetoric of this account of martyrdom, and the ways it complicates our image of the scene of Jewish persecution. This is in part because Yuval refuses to accede to the idea that the Jewish martyrological response to persecution was merely reactive. Instead, he insists that we understand Jewish martyrdom as a phenomenon rooted in a sustained medieval Jewish religious ideology – developed in relation to Christian theological claims, certainly, but not suddenly spurred into existence by the traumatic events of 1096.[31] In this picture, medieval Jewish communities emerge as assertive and self-directed, but also as more aggressive than traditional historiographical accounts might suggest. These written martyrdoms appear not only as acts of desperation, but as polemical affirmations of Jewish identity. Though Yuval's picture of communal solidarity might seem to place him out of step with the trends I have been discussing, he is attentive to the ruptures and difficulties of this evolving rhetoric of inter-religious conflict. Yuval emphasizes that these historical events are suffused by more dynamic and less predictable forms of inter-religious communication than the traditional historiographical picture of utterly divided communities of persecutors and victims would lead us to believe. The acts of persecution are no less real, but the image of the suffering community that endured them is rendered considerably more complex. What is for Malkiel

---

[28] Yuval, *Two Nations*, esp. pp. 139–40 and 143.
[29] ibid., pp. 152, 154.
[30] ibid., p. 139.
[31] See, for example, Yuval's explicit refusal of the idea that what he describes as anti-Christian hostility within the Jewish community was merely a spontaneous response to particular acts. Instead, he sees Jewish (and Christian) religious polemics as the fruit of a longstanding negative dynamic between communities. See ibid., pp. 120–3.

the 'human face' of the medieval Jewish community becomes in Yuval's account a view of a community in crisis that accommodates anger and vitriol as well as saintly suffering. Within such a framework, projects of historical memory (medieval and modern) become considerably more fraught.

Politics and Memory

The historiographical developments I have characterized in terms of competing paradigms of ethical meaning have also been characterized (and criticized) in terms of ideology. Yuval's insistence on the motif of Jewish vengeance, for instance, has provoked more than a little discomfort and even anger. Johannes Heil, summarizing some of Yuval's early critics, writes that such claims of 'deep enmity' are 'more than delicate, since "Jewish enmity" was, and still is today, a central argument in every kind of anti-Jewish polemic'.[32] Cohen, too, writes that certain audiences who heard his early work on the Hebrew chronicles at conferences and lectures accused him of approaching a perilous historical revisionism.[33] Those audiences seemed worried, most of all, about scholarship's potential effects in the arena of popular discourse. But other scholars, such as David Nirenberg and, more recently, Elliott Horowitz, have also been critical of an ethics of memorialization on essentially ideological grounds, suggesting that a defensive rhetoric which insists upon the holiness of suffering Jewish communities in the past is linked with very modern concerns about antisemitism or fractured Jewish identities.[34] As Cohen suggests, there is certainly a kind of 'myth-wrecking' quality to recent work, a conscious decision to revise or contest many of the claims of communal memory.[35]

Here again Yuval in particular has been a lightning rod for criticism. His analysis rather pointedly highlights the tragic consequences when deeply rooted oppositions between communities become mutually sustaining. In this context, his work may be understood by some readers as a kind of political exemplum or allegory for the twenty-first century, one that is deeply implicated in contemporary Israeli politics. He highlights the ideological uses of memory itself, and the ways in which ancient conflicts can be mobilized to perpetuate ideological divisions and propel them into the future. The perfect symmetry of Jewish-Christian relations in Yuval's account, painstak-

---

[32] J. Heil, '"Deep Enmity" and/or "Close Ties"? Jews and Christians before 1096, Sources, Hermeneutics, and Writing History in 1096', *JSQ* 9 (2002), 259–306 (p. 269).

[33] Cohen, *Sanctifying the Name*, p. ix.

[34] D. Nirenberg, 'The Rhineland Massacres of Jews in the First Crusade: Memories Medieval and Modern', in *Medieval Concepts of the Past: Ritual, Memory, Historiography*, ed. G. Althoff, J. Fried, and P. Geary (Cambridge, 2002), pp. 279-310; E. Horowitz, *Reckless Rites, Purim and the Legacy of Jewish Violence* (Princeton, 2006).

[35] Cohen, *Sanctifying the Name*, p. 43.

ingly elaborated over the centuries of the Common Era, illustrates the ways an oppositional construction of communities' self-identities can come to be deeply codependent. At least one early critic of his work in the Israeli journal *Zion* accused him of violating the memorial order specifically, arguing that his historical account of Jewish-Christian relations effectively blamed the victims for their own persecution.[36] Horowitz's book invokes the spectre of Jewish Purim violence in Israel, and includes a cover photo of a young Orthodox man reading a Hebrew book (probably the Book of Esther) while using a toy machine gun as a pointer.[37] More explicitly than Yuval, he is concerned about modern as well as pre-modern politics.

Yet such connections are easier to identify than they are to diagnose. If I have invoked ethics and method as key terms here rather than ideology, it is in part because ideology is a term capable of overwhelming other issues, and of acquiring a peculiarly deterministic power when applied as an interpretive lens. It is all too easy to see historiography as the product of ideology alone, when a concatenation of scholarly interests, investments, and concerns are at stake. Competing methodologies and ethical evaluations of historical events are only two such factors.[38] I would no more wish to deny that ideology matters in historical interpretation than I would wish to say that it is the only term that matters. I have sought to de-prioritize such questions here in order to emphasize the specifically ethical stakes of scholarly paradigms for remembering and depicting medieval Jewish martyrs in contemporary historiography. My primary concern has been to bring to light some questions that are often overlooked when ideology comes into more explicit view.[39]

The uneasy coexistence of such different ethical paradigms is an issue that future historiography on the events at York in 1190 will have to confront. I have argued for an important relationship between memory and method in recent scholarship on medieval Jewish self-martyrdom, but studies of the events at York in 1190 must necessarily follow a rather different path from that outlined above, if for no better reason than that the records – certainly the records of Jewish communal response – are sparse in this case. Yet the interpretive paradigms I have described are likely to make themselves felt nevertheless. How should we write about the victims of 1190, or their per-

---

36 Ezra Fleischer's criticism was impassioned on this score see his 'Christian-Jewish Relations in the Middle Ages Distorted', [Hebrew] *Zion* 59 (1994), 267–313.
37 For the references to the modern Israeli context, see particularly Horowitz, *Reckless Rites*, pp. 1–12.
38 The historian's own national identity and the context of his educational training are other factors not addressed here. Some of the historians whose work I discuss live and work in Israel, a few as immigrants; most were trained in Western universities. Though these biographical details might be discussed further, they are not my focus here.
39 My book on the historiography of the ritual murder accusation, *Blood Libel: The Ritual Murder Accusation at the Limit of Jewish History* (Michigan, 2012), addresses this concatenation of ethical, methodological, and ideological concerns – and their implications for medieval Jewish studies – in greater depth.

secutors? Knotty difficulties of representation and understanding remain. The events at York have generated their own modest memorial tradition,[40] and the desire to do justice to the historical victims of persecution is no less real in this case than in others. Again, I am not arguing that we might simply dispense with this felt sense of obligation – nor that we should. My hope is simpler, though perhaps also more difficult: I hope that by making the ethical stakes of our scholarship more transparent to ourselves, we might be in a better position to examine the ways method and ethics track together, and what the larger implications of such questions may be. Will we lay claim to this ethical work, or disown it, and what are the costs of that decision? If we acknowledge our own implication in ethical questions as well as methodological ones, then how might this change the shape of our scholarship? Is it simply a matter, as some recent trends in historiography seem to suggest, of acknowledging our personal ties to a subject, an identity, or a community we are discussing? Or should our questions, and our inquiry, extend further, to encompass the structures of historical interpretation itself, and the disciplinary assumptions and codes that guide that work? In closing, I would like to suggest that it is the latter, more ambitious project that is the more important one, and that it has special bearing on cases like that at York in 1190. One of the obligations of memory is recalling to conscious attention our own assumptions about the work of memory itself.

---

[40] In addition to ghost tour tales about the reddish glow of Jewish blood on the walls of Clifford's Tower (actually the result of a much later munitions explosion), the site inspires memorial gestures, sometimes with unusual results. At the 1990 commemoration of the massacre, for instance, one participant wrote that, 'one of the few remaining descendants of the arch-villain of the events of 1190—the infamous Richard Malebisse of Acaster Malbis—acknowledged the wickedness of his ancestor; at the unveiling ceremony [of the plaque at Clifford's Tower in 1978] the Archbishop read a note he had received which apologized for his ancestor and just said "sorry."', G. Hunter, et al., *Clifford's Tower Commemoration, York, 15-18 March 1990: A Programme and Handbook* (York, 1990), p. 15.

16

The Future of the Jews of York

Jeffrey Cohen

William of Newburgh's *History of English Affairs* grants an access to the troubling events of 1190 unmatched by other sources. It is difficult to resist portal analogies when speaking of the world we glimpse in his vigorous Latin prose. Detailed and wide-ranging, Newburgh's narrative enables the reader to feel a witness to unfolding incidents. He creates a sense of privileged access to a vivacious world of complicated human actors, of local and national forces on the move. Yet the story Newburgh tells is partial, framed by the doorway he constructs around its contours to give the tale coherence. His narrative is shaped by his reading, his desires. Sometimes, moreover, within this metaphorical ingress into English history a literal door will swing open, proffering an unexpected invitation to consider the stories Newburgh does not recount.

Towards the close of the first book of the *History*, such a gateway suddenly appears in rural Yorkshire.[1] A drunken traveller is returning home late at night when the noise of revelry issues from what had been a familiar landmark, a roadside tumulus: 'He heard voices singing, as though people were feasting in celebration ('quasi festive convivantium').'[2] Newburgh assures us that he knows this mound himself, having viewed its topographical ordinariness numerous times. Though the hill has never before offered anything other than a grassy slope, this evening a doorway has opened into its side, revealing 'a large, well-lit dwelling ('domum amplam et luminosam') crowded with men and women reclining at table as at a formal feast'. A servant at the threshold observes the traveller and offers him a drink. Rather than enter the mound and join the banquet, however, the man empties the liquid from the cup, leaps onto his horse and gallops home.

The stolen drinking vessel is in every way unfamiliar, 'of unknown material, unusual colour, and strange shape' ('vasculum materiae incognitae,

---

1   I have considered this story rather differently in 'Introduction: Infinite Realms', in *Cultural Diversity in the British Middle Ages: Archipelago, Island, England*, ed. J. Cohen (Basingstoke, 2008), pp. 1–16.

2   WN, Bk. I, ch. 28. Citations here from WN, ed. Walsh & Kennedy, I; from later books, WN, ed. Howlett; trans. from WN, trans. Stevenson, silently emended.

coloris insoliti, et formae inusitate'). Though the pilfered goblet could have functioned as the key to another world, the entry into a mystery demanding explication, theft removes the cup from knowability, transforming it into a decontextualized curiosity, interesting for its aesthetics rather than its history.[3] To flee the beckoning feast is to refuse the story of that community which has invited the traveller to commensality. What would happen, though, if the man had joined the celebration? Had he risked conviviality with the subterranean congregants, would one of these congenial revellers have spoken the tale of who they were and what they honoured at their banquet? Glimpsed but spurned by an English man who preferred the security of his home over the startling anomalousness of an unlooked-for communal table, this invitation to tell the story is also refused by Newburgh. Beyond the threshold of the open door Newburgh discerns not a living narrative, but an irrecoverably lost one. He suggests the revelry was staged by demons and is content to offer no particulars, leaving the event to its silent mysteries.

The two great historians who preceded Newburgh, William of Malmesbury and Henry of Huntingdon, were children of mixed parentage. Each possessed an English mother and Norman father. Malmesbury tries to make a virtue of this dual blood, asserting that because the heritage of conqueror and native dweller belongs to him equally he can narrate English history with impartiality. As it turns out, however, Malmesbury creates a text full of what I have called difficult middles: agonizing and desire-filled spaces where hybridity cannot be so placidly resolved.[4] Henry of Huntingdon fares similarly, creating a text more discordant than he intends. Newburgh writes in an England secure in its collective identity. He instigates his text with the flat and unselfconscious statement that his book offers 'historiam gentis nostrae, id est Anglorum' ('a history of our race, that is, the English'). The mound in Yorkshire figures a dissonant story that Newburgh embeds within this 'history of our race' but cannot quite tell. As textual archaeologists we can excavate a fragment of the narrative, we can admire its beauty and strangeness, but we cannot assimilate it into something known. Like the goblet this narrative is 'formae inusitate', 'rare' as well as 'lacking in use-value'. It is difficult to know what to do with this unexpected door that opens into a mound in the English countryside, a portal and an invitation that Newburgh, like his traveller, refuses.

Newburgh narrated in detail the events of 1189-90, a story he culminates with the massacre in York. Although Jews figure prominently in only a few chapters of Book Four of the *History*, they ought not to be immured within so small a space. By looking into unexpected architectures like that Yorkshire

---

[3] Monika Otter analyses the cup's diminution into ordinariness in M. Otter, *Inventiones: Fiction and Referentiality in Twelfth-Century English Historical Writing* (Chapel Hill NC, 1996), p. 105.

[4] See my *Hybridity, Identity and Monstrosity in Medieval Britain: On Difficult Middles* (New York, 2006).

mound, by detaching Newburgh's Jewish story from a narrative that climaxes in fire and obliteration, by reading the events in the tower as something more than a second Masada – by freeing William's Jews from the cement of familiar history – we might give them something they too infrequently attain: an unpredetermined future.

The Jewish Challenge

Gerald of Wales proves the venerable lineage of dark Jewish humour through a narrative in his *Gemma ecclesiastica* (*Jewel of the Church*), composed during his studies at Lincoln towards the close of the twelfth century. At this time Jews and Christians were living in the city together, sometimes quite peacefully, sometimes not.[5] In 1190, Bishop Hugh faced down a 'raging and riotous mob' intent on violence against the city's Jewish population. When the crowd raised their swords against him, the fearless bishop scolded so severely that they backed down. Unlike Lynn, Stamford, Norwich, Bury St Edmunds, and York, Lincoln did not suffer a pogrom that year. Lincoln's Jews remained fond of the bishop until his death, at least according to Hugh's medieval biographer, who records that they wept at his funeral. This same bishop also put the brake on a cult that effloresced around one of the plunderers of Jewish homes in Northampton in 1190. An accomplice had murdered the man for his loot. The local people reported miracles and the nearby clergy reaped profits. Through a 'bitter struggle' Hugh ended the veneration of the robber, a worship that he (as well as Newburgh, who also tells the story) condemned as a 'superstitious abomination'.[6]

Gerald, writing perhaps during Hugh's reign, tells a somewhat similar tale about veneration, miracles, clerical profits, and 'cultus'. A young Jew in Oxford ridicules the worship of the local saint, Frideswside. The event takes place 'in modern times', as the body of the city's patron was translated to a shrine church.[7] Civic celebration was accompanied by an outbreak of mira-

---

5   See Gerald of Wales, *The Jewel of the Church, a translation of* Gemma ecclesiastica *by Giraldus Cambrensis*, ed. J. J. Hagen (Leiden, 1979), p. xi, whose translations are used here. For the Latin see *Giraldi Cambrensis Opera*, ed. J. S. Brewer, J. Dimock and G. Warner, 8 vols., RS 21 (London, 1861-91), II, 1.51. Gerald was friends with Hugh of Avalon, the bishop of Lincoln, who oversaw a thriving intellectual community in the city.

6   Adam of Eynsham, *Magna Vita Sancti Hugonis. The Life of Saint Hugh of Lincoln*, ed. and trans. D. L. Douie and H. Farmer, 2 vols., OMT (Oxford, 1985), II, 4.4, 5.17, 5.20. On the cult of the robber of Northampton, see also R. Bartlett, *England under the Norman and Angevin Kings, 1075–1225* (Oxford, 2000), p. 472. Newburgh tells the story as well (WN, Bk II, ch. 8); Partner describes it as an example of his 'intellectual fastidiousness' in her *Serious Entertainments: The Writing of History in Twelfth-Century England* (Chicago, 1977), pp. 73–4. See also Hillaby and Blurton in this volume.

7   The event took place in 1180, and may have been witnessed by Gerald himself. *Jewel of the Church*, ed. Hagen, p. 308n.

cles worked by the Anglo-Saxon virgin, drawing streams of worshippers. The Jewish youth infiltrated the crowd, hands and legs tied by cords to seem paralysed. After begging the saint for help 'mockingly' (*ironice*), he would unbind his ropes and declare himself healed, shouting 'Behold, what great miracles the holy Frideswide can work! She has cured others in the same way as she has just now cured me.' This nameless young Jew, in other words, undermined through histrionic excess the marvels supporting the saint's revitalized cult. The Jew's parody of saintly healing was meant to cast doubt on the veracity of the Oxonian efflorescence of cures, articulating a critique likely on more than Jewish minds: can an obscure virgin from five hundred years ago really be so conveniently powerful 'in modern times'?[8]

Bishop Hugh's scepticism was reserved for unofficial cultic practices and is lauded. Our Jewish doubter, however, eventually hangs himself in his father's cellar by the same cords with which he faked a divinely given mobility. He dies uttering an unspecified blasphemy, a last and a lost protest against the narrative vengeance machine that swallows him. Although his parents attempt to conceal their son's suicide, the event is quickly made public by 'the Jewish family's servants and nurses, who were Christians.'[9] The Jew, in other words, does not live an isolated life. The young man's prank is directed at those with whom he shares urban and domestic space. His humour challenges; it is dark; it is directed towards the complicatedly multicultural world in which he lived. He pays for his little piece of performance art with his life. But he does not die unnoticed, or unrecorded.

By the twelfth century Ashkenazic Jewish communities cohabitated with Christians in cities across France, Germany, and England. As in Gerald's narrative, literary and historical texts suggest that these Jews could offer through their rituals and their words a sharp challenge to Christian self-assurance. Pulled into contemporary deliberations over epistemology and religious faith, the Jews became a community intimately involved in questions of orthodoxy and unbelief.[10] In his groundbreaking 1974 essay, 'The Jewish Minority in Mediaeval England', Paul Hyams observed that 'No devout Christian could see a Jew at Eastertide ... without an uneasy feeling that his very presence cast doubt on the fundamental dogma that the Messiah had come.'[11] Christians

---

[8] Hagen notes that the Jew's name is given as 'Deus-cum-crescat' in the version of the story by Prior Philip of the monastery of St Frideswide in his *Appendix ad acta S. Frideswidae, de libro miraculorum ejus* (c. 1180). The story differs only in the details of the discovery of the young Jew's death. In his translation of the *Gemma ecclesistica*, Hagen suggests that Philip may have been Gerald's source (*Jewel of the Church*, ed. Hagen, p. 308n).

[9] Giraldi Cambrensis, *Opera*, II, 1.51; trans. p. 118.

[10] I use that word as John H. Arnold does, as a term more flexible than heresy: unbelief is 'the absence of something expected ... divergent, "superstitious", heretical and skeptical viewpoints ... intriguingly varied forms of dissent and divergence from the orthodox norm', J. H. Arnold, *Belief and Unbelief in Medieval Europe* (London, 2005), p. 4.

[11] P. Hyams, 'The Jewish Minority in Medieval England, 1066–1290', *Journal of Jewish Studies* 25 (1974), 270-93 (p. 280). Hyams provides another episode of Jewish unbelief involving St

were fascinated with Jewish irony and 'incredulitas', partly because Jews got to say what Christians sometimes suspected but could not safely express.

Medieval Jews really did disparage Jesus as 'the Hanged One'. They questioned Mary's virginity. They insisted that God had engendered no son, that the Messiah had yet to arrive. But we likely do not possess in examples like the one Gerald provides cases in which Christians were listening attentively to their Jewish neighbours. The mocker of St Frideswide's miracles perishes, after all, with his final imprecation unrecorded. For Gerald it suffices that his dying words constituted a blasphemy. Their specific content is irrelevant. The Jew of Unbelief is mainly a Christian fantasy. A timeless and petrified type rather than a historical person, he exists within and for the Christian imagination. Immobile, existing only to be mobilized, he possesses no future other than perfunctory self-immolation.

Coinhabited Space (Love Thy Neighbour)

In the Prioress's Tale Chaucer imagines an Asian city shared by Jews and Christians, but composed of segregated neighbourhoods. The religious quarantine that he describes was never the historical experience of the England in which he wrote.[12] Until the Expulsion of 1290, Christians and Jews shared urban space. They lived alongside each other and were domestic intimates. Though separation might not have existed geographically, however, it was in theory achieved through a kind of temporal segregation. Anti-Judaic medieval narratives were addicted to their binaries, with Jews figuring a superseded, frozen and lethal temporality, Christians a vibrant if Jew-endangered modernity. Jews were living fossils, lingering remnants of a surpassed history; they carried the bloody stain of deicide as if they had just crucified Jesus, and therefore were likely to prove once more Christianicidal ('christianicidarum iudeorum', to use Thomas of Monmouth's neologism).[13]

Frideswide when in describing Jewish anger against Christians he writes 'Incidents such as that which occurred at Oxford in 1268, when a Jew threw down and then trampled upon a crucifix as it was being carried in a solemn University procession towards the shrine of St Frideswide were to be expected from time to time' (ibid., p. 284). Sabina Flanagan quotes Herbert of Bosham, a renowned Hebraist, as wondering in his Life of St Thomas, 'What if it is as the Jews say and the Messiah has not yet come?'. See S. Flanagan, *Doubt in an Age of Faith: Uncertainty in the Long Twelfth Century* (Turnhout, 2008), p. 176. On Christian doubt and projection of uncertainty onto Jews, compare Gavin I. Langmuir, who invokes a similar thesis throughout his work: G. I. Langmuir, *Toward a Definition of Antisemitism* (Berkeley CA, 1996) and *History, Religion, and Antisemitism* (Berkeley CA, 1993). For an important reevaluation of Langmuir's work, see Flanagan, *Doubt in an Age of Faith*, pp. 162–83.

[12] This partitioning is not, however, stable: Anthony Bale attentively maps the ways in which the boundaries are violated in the tale in *The Jew in the Medieval Book: English Antisemitisms, 1350–1500* (Cambridge, 2006), pp. 85–6.

[13] I explore Thomas of Monmouth's vocabulary of anti-Judaism at great length in *Hybridity, Identity and Monstrosity in Medieval Britain,On Difficult Middles* (New York, 2006), ch. 5.

Behind these reductive narratives, though, can often be glimpsed more complicated stories of co-inhabitance. According to Gerald of Wales, the suicide of the Jew who cast doubt upon saintly efficacy is revealed in the most ordinary of ways: by the Christian servants and nurses who form a part of his family's household. Gerald's tale of Jewish-Christian difference is also a story of Christian-Jewish inter-reliance. Within Gerald's text exists oblique acknowledgement of a mixed if stratified household, one in which Jews and Christians tangibly and mutually depend upon each other. Anti-Judaic stories often reveal a fuller domain than they intend to depict, a world in which we might witness, however fleetingly, narratives of *convivencia* more intricate and more vivacious than the reductive, hostile, and historically petrified representations at their surfaces.[14] So, to return to the household employees who betrayed the parents in Gerald's account: did the Christian nurses, servants and neighbours who dwelled with and alongside the Jews see their employers and business relations and acquaintances as locked in another time, a time that is not (as Gerald would say) 'in tempore moderno'? At Oxford, Lincoln, York, Norwich, London – in all of those cities of Jewish and Christian adjacency, where the two peoples shared more than simply space – could something happen between Christian and Jew that might yield a story other than the timeless one provided by the temporally rigidified Jew, whose narrative is by, for and about Christians?

Moments of non-hostile coinhabitance are discernible but rare. It is especially difficult to discover such scenes of neighbouring in the textual record we possess for the York massacre. Newburgh enacts a strict partitioning of worlds, well articulated when he cites the papal council now known as Lateran III (1179):

> No Jews or Saracens shall be permitted to have Christian servants in their houses, either under the pretence of educating their children, or as slaves, or for any other purpose whatsoever. Moreover, let those be excommunicated who presume to live with them ... Jews ought to be subject to Christians. (WN, Bk. III, ch. 3; trans. Stevenson, p. 508)

This pronouncement imagines a segregation that had clearly not obtained in England in 1144, when a Christian maid employed within a Jewish household offered her supposedly eyewitness narrative of the ritual murder of William of Norwich, an account with a keen sense of domestic detail, even if the interior described is used for nailing a boy to a pillar in

---

[14] Arguing that northern Europe saw a '*convivencia* in a minor key', Jonathan Elukin surveys contemporary work on *convivencia* that stresses its coexistence, cultural interpenetrations, rivalry, friction, jealousies, violence, and mutual creative influences via affection and infection. See J. Elukin, *Living Together, Living Apart: Rethinking Jewish-Christian Relations in the Middle Ages* (Princeton, 2007), pp. 135–8, quotation at p. 136.

mockery of Christ. Nor is the Council's wished-for partition any more evident in the Oxford described by Gerald of Wales, or the Lincoln of 1255 narrated by Matthew Paris when he recounts the story of little Hugh. Yet Newburgh writes as if such separation always holds, rarely allowing Christians and Jews to share anything but spaces of contest, struggle and violence. Newburgh sunders into separate spheres what was likely to have been a tangled social reality. Elites may have lived in the solitude of castles and manor houses, bishops within a palace or cathedral close, but urban houses opened to the street. Jews did not dwell in ghettoes. Civic space was heterogeneous, gregarious.[15] A dirty word in the Christian medieval vocabulary was *Judaizer*: come too close to the Jew, neighbour the Jewish world without erecting sufficient partition, and both of you may change as a result. Both of you may enter an imaginary space – albeit, perhaps, a temporary one – where what has always been need no longer hold. Recent scholarship makes clear that Judaizing and Christianizing happened more frequently, more quietly than has previously been acknowledged.[16]

We are used to the massacre of 1190 standing as the inevitable future of the Jews of York, the logical outcome of an endemic rivalry. The Expulsion of 1290 seems an inexorable rendezvous. Such defining moments exert their aura of ineluctability because they are familiar. They differentiate the past into the same binaries that anti-Judaic narrative envisions, with the Jews always having been different, out of place, their residence inherently temporary. The Jews who followed William the Conqueror from Rouen become interchangeable with those who lived in Norwich in 1144, those who perished in 1190, those who vanished into the 'Domus Conversorum' in 1253, that remnant who sailed for other shores in 1290. Yet a teleological narrative that culminates in catastrophe does not allow for medieval Jews who may have been irreverent punks, who may have considered themselves citizens of York and England as well as rootless cosmopolitans, who may have carried with them identities that only at a first and cursory glance seem timeless, set in stone.

---

15 Hyams explores this propinquity in his essay in this volume.
16 The bibliography is too immense to list exhaustively here, but representative work includes D. Biale, *Blood and Belief: The Circulation of a Symbol between Christians and Jews* (Berkeley CA, 2007); D. Boyarin, *Border Lines: The Partition of Judaeo-Christianity* (Philadelphia, 2004); E. Horowitz, *Reckless Rites: Purim and the Legacy of Jewish Violence* (Princeton, 2006); D. Malkiel, *Reconstructing Ashkenaz: The Human Face of Franco-German Jewry, 1000–1250* (Stanford CA, 2009); I. G. Marcus, *Rituals of Childhood: Jewish Acculturation in Medieval Europe* (New Haven CT, 1996); and I. J. Yuval, *Two Nations in Your Womb: Perceptions of Jews and Christians in Late Antiquity and the Middle Ages*, trans. B. Harshav and J. Chipman (Berkeley CA, 2006).

Jews of Stone

Matthew Paris's account of the events surrounding the ritual murder of little Hugh of Lincoln is chilling.[17] A Christian boy and nineteen Jews perish. Sustained, national attention comes to an accusation that had previously been local, sporadic. Yet Matthew's lethal story also contains a minor remark that quietly gestures towards a reality different from the eternal Christian-Jewish enmity that underwrites his main narrative. Made on a street in Lincoln where Jewish and Christian homes adjoin, the sentence opens another world, suggests another possible reality, a potential community. Hugh's mother enters a Jewish home because she realizes that her son likely did the same thing. She has 'been told by the neighbours that they had last seen [Hugh] playing with some Jewish boys of his own age'. Her son may have drowned in the basement well of the residence because he was playing with friends there. Rather than focus only upon his death, however, we might ask a question of his life. What would happen if we followed Hugh across that unexpected threshold, into a Jewish household offering not a fatal promise, but amity, maybe even commensality? This might be Hugh's narrative, an alternate history glimpsed when his friendship with nearby and non-Christian boys enables him to cross a boundary that in anti-Judaic tales marks utter difference, not affiliation. Matthew writes of the Lincoln Jews carted to London for their supposed participation in Hugh's murder: 'And if they were perchance pitied by any Christians, they did not excite any tears of compassion amongst the Caursins, their rivals.' This statement leads us in two directions, one historicist (the allusion is explained through context, and the Jews become figures whose meaning is determined by history), and the other more local, more contingent, more possibility-laden.

Matthew acknowledges a Christian economic reliance upon the Jews. Lincoln's cathedral was, after all, constructed through a loan made by Aaron, a Jewish financier who at his death in 1186 was second in wealth only to England's king. The city depended on its Jewish population in tangible ways, as anyone who knew the history of the magnificent cathedral was reminded each time its soaring architecture came into view. This financial reliance is stressed when the Jews merit no compassion from the Caursines, their Christian rivals in moneylending, who are happy to see their competition transported to their doom.[18] Yet before the Jews dissolve into political critique, existing only to tell a story about a contemporary regent, another phrase is

---

[17] *Matthew Paris's English History from the year 1235 to 1273 translated from the Latin,* ed. J. A. Giles, 3 vols. (London, 1852–4), II, pp. 138–41; *Paris, Chronica Majora* V, 516–19.

[18] The Caursines, or Cahorsin (from Cahors) money lenders, are condemned by Matthew Paris early in his history (in 1235). He writes that 'there was hardly anyone in England, especially among the bishops, who was not caught in their nets. Even the king himself was held indebted to them for an incalculable sum of money.' (*Matthew Paris's English History,* ed. Giles, I, 2).

worth attention, one easy to overlook because it of its brevity: 'And if they were perchance pitied by any Christians'. The line suggests, in its small way, that more than one Jewish portal was open in hospitality to neighbours, that some Christian doors might likewise be unbolted, that Hugh was not the only resident of the city to stride across a threshold that could make the strange familiar and the familiar strange.

Matthew's narrative of little Hugh of Lincoln unexpectedly reveals a more intricate story of coinhabitance, of lived spaces between Christian and Jew where orthodox partition breaks down into heterodox quotidian praxis. Here in this mixed space a lived practice of propinquity unfolds. The frozen-in-time theological figures who enact in the modern day a script inherited from the New Testament Passion might become the adaptive, limited, human Jewish neighbour. As a Christian fantasy, the Jew is a figure consigned to segregated and superceded space-time. Just as biblical Jews disbelieved and murdered Christ, modern ones will repudiate and perhaps sacrifice the children of Christ. The Jew as neighbour, on the other hand, is the near-dweller, he whose door may be open to Elijah, but whose door may also be ajar so that the Christian boy from across the street can find his way inside.

Little Hugh of Lincoln's story unfolds across an open doorway, a threshold of possible welcome. William of Newburgh's Jewish narrative arc begins in Book Four with some inauspiciously closed doors. Having come to London to witness the coronation of Richard, the leading men among the English Jews are barred from the church at which the king is to be crowned and forbidden to enter the palace for the celebratory feast (Bk IV, ch. 1). The Jews mingle outside with the gathered crowd. When a group surges forward some find themselves unwillingly conveyed through the gates into the royal residence. They and those who linger by the doors are attacked by indignant Christians with clubs and stones. Violence escalates, fanned by a rumour that the king has ordered all Jews destroyed. A massacre ensues: death by trampling, swordpoint, conflagration. When the Jews barricade themselves inside their houses, a mob sets fire to their roofs. 'Knowing no distinction' the flames catch 'the nearest houses of the Christians also'. In describing this irruption of hostility destined to spread quickly northward, William speaks of the 'novel confidence of the Christians against the enemies of the Cross of Christ'. Even as these ravages are new, even as Newburgh has much difficulty interpreting what their unprecedented advent might signify, he in the end returns to stabilities and hoary verities. 'Divine vengeance' precipitates the brutality against these 'stiff-necked' and 'perverse' 'blasphemers'. Benedict of York, forced into baptism, renounces his new identity immediately and speaks of having always been a Jew in his soul, 'and he would rather die as such': a statement at once heroic and indicative of a Christian tendency to place racial stubbornness, a resistant Jewish identity, in the very flesh.

Back to those doors Richard closed against the Jews bearing gifts in his honour. Other than to make the minor point that the conflagrations of the mob do not discriminate, illuminating in their burning the urban adjacency

of Christian and Jew, there seems no way across this royally barred threshold other than unwilling conveyance. No future here. Rather than follow a
body that crosses a portal and perhaps tells a story rather different from the
dominating narrative in which it appears, as we could with Hugh of Lincoln,
we may move to the end of Newburgh's Jewish story of 1190 and try another tack, following a stone as it tumbles through the air and crushes a mad
hermit. This lethal projectile – foundational, elemental, ambiguous – is, in a
strange way, the protagonist of the narrative. The scene is the siege of York's
royal tower. The Jews of the city have taken their last refuge against a crowd
intending their destruction:

> [The Jews] kept off the besiegers with stones alone, which
> they pulled out of the wall in the interior. The castle was
> actively besieged for several days; and at length engines
> were got ready and brought up. That hermit of the Premon-
> stratensian order ... urged onward the fatal work more than
> any one else. Roused by the rumour, he had lately come
> to the city, and in his white frock was sedulously engaged
> among the besiegers of the castle, repeating often: "Down
> with the enemies of Christ!" with loud shouts ... When the
> engines were moved forward, he fervently helped with all
> his strength. Whence it came to pass that, approaching the
> wall incautiously, and not observing a large stone which
> was falling from above ('saxum grande desuper veniens non
> caveret'), he was crushed by it; he fell forward, and when
> he was lifted up, he instantly expired. It thus became mani-
> fest that, either by reason of his profession, or of his order, a
> greater judgment fell upon him than upon any other, for he
> was the only one of our people who happened miserably to
> die there. (Bk IV, ch.10; trans. Stevenson, pp. 568-9)

The agent of the hermit's destruction is textually uncertain: was it the Jews
dropping a rock upon him as he incautiously drew within range? Or did the
stone tumble from one of the siege machines brought forward by the Christians? The former seems most likely, given his proximity to the wall, but
Newburgh's Latin is not entirely clear. Yet the result is the same: the rock's
plunge silences a vociferous critic for the Jews. Yet the 'mentally blind' man
in white who rails against the entrapped Jews says nothing that William in
his own voice does not also say.

The hurtling stone allows the Jews to score a small victory by silencing
the hateful hermit. Yet the engines are in place; the tower will be breached at
dawn. The stones they hurl are torn from the foundation of the architecture
in which they find themselves imprisoned. It's hard to resist reading this
physical confinement metaphorically as well: a living people imprisoned
within a structure of someone else's devising, doors shut fast, their only way

of escape through death. But the tower is also a bluntly historical architecture, constructed during the Norman reconfiguration of York, rendering it a structure that is in some ways as alien to York as the Jews are *and* a structure in some ways as intimate to York as the Jews are.[19] By 1190 the Normans may have disappeared into an adopted Englishness, but the tower was one of many memorials to how profoundly the city had been altered at their hands. The Normans had many strategies for announcing their enduring possession of England, massive lithicization among them, with cathedrals and castles of towering stone. In York the new archbishop's precinct and two emerging castles profoundly reshaped urban space, including the Roman network of roads, and destroyed almost a thousand tenements.[20] In most cities much of the Norman colonization of space by stone, especially as an ecclesiastical project, was made possible through Jewish moneylending.

Social change was ongoing, as the arrival and partial assimilation of the Jewish community makes clear. Still, it seems the end of the rock's trajectory brings us to a stopping point, an impasse. Once embedded in the ground, the stone has come to the limit of its movement and the termination of its narrative. Likewise, the Jews are stuck: as confined in the tower as they are by William's text –Jews who have no future, and so in fire and with sword will re-enact a deadly past.

Thinking the New

Futurity is Newburgh's preoccupation. He records his events for transmission to posterity. Yet his language is unfailingly past-looking, especially in his limited vocabulary for Jewishness. Uncritical repetition of timeworn terms is Newburgh's typical method for describing non-English peoples: the Welsh, Scots, and Irish are given the same feral descriptors that abound in Henry of Huntingdon and William of Malmesbury (or even, in the case of the Welsh, Bede). His Muslims are not crusade caricatures, but neither are they anything more than uncomplex and unremitting enemies. Even though Jewish presence in England was only as old as the Conquest, the terms of Newburgh's anti-Judaism are familiar because inherited: nothing original about stressing Jewish perfidy, unbelief, racial distinctiveness, impiety. What is striking about Newburgh's Jewish story, though, is his recurring mention of Jewish economic prosperity (the Jews attend Richard's coronation to ensure the continuation of the affluence they experienced under Henry), and

---

[19] As V. D. Lipman observes, both castles and Jews were Norman imports: 'Jews and Castles in Medieval England', *JHSE Transactions* 28 (1984), 1-28 (p. 1).

[20] Fleming gathers copious evidence for the systematic seizure and destruction of urban property and architectures to make room for Norman edifices in R. Fleming, *Kings and Lords in Conquest England* (Cambridge, 1991), pp. 194–204; my description of the changes in York are based on pp. 195–6.

his stating that the Christian-Jewish violence he records is novel. The *economic* gains made by the Jews and the English *newness* of what unfolded obsess him throughout his narrative, even as he attempts to play down the latter.

Newburgh will often turn to the past, nervously, to discover reassurance in precedent, to imagine some principle of repetition and therefore of order. To comprehend the Jewish choice of self-sacrifice over conversion during those desperate moments in the besieged tower, he invokes Josephus and the *History of the Jewish War*, as if York were Masada and Jewish 'madness' and 'superstition' as eternal as their legendary intransigence (Bk IV, ch. 10).[21] Yet what unfolds in York is not the same as what transpired in that distant desert a millennium previous, a narrative of martial and rebel Jews, a story without Christian content. Newburgh's twin preoccupations – economic prosperity, discomforting novelty – are inter-related: what bothers Newburgh about Jewish affluence, for example, is the Jews' ability to mimic newly prosperous Christians by living like them and among them in impressive stone houses.[22] Newburgh states the Augustinian position that the 'perfidus Judaeus' lingers among Christians 'pro utilitate nostra vivere,' as eternal reminders of the Passion (Bk IV, ch. 9). The living Jew is like a crucifix painted in a church: a beneficial reminder of sacred history.

The problem for Newburgh is that these functional and timeless Jews, who ought to be decorative spurs to memory, were the ones finding Christians to be useful. They were adapting to modernity instead of remaining locked in a narrative 1,157 years old. The Jews of England had the audacity to participate within and accelerate financial and economic systems, becoming in Newburgh's words 'happy and famous above the Christians' (Bk IV, ch. 9) - but more accurately, becoming prosperous in a way that some Christians had likewise become. Though he will condemn Richard Malebisse and his compeers for their blatantly financial reasons for instigating the massacre of York's Jews, Newburgh shares their anti-Judaic hostility. His violence is textual rather than physical. Jews gall Newburgh because they are highly visible catalysts to and signs of a reallotment of wealth. They seem to have integrated themselves not only into the contemporary economy, but into present community, especially through their sometimes opulent housing in the midst of the city.

Newburgh's preoccupations of Jewish wealth and unprecedented Jewish identities find expression in what might be called Newburgh's poetics of stone. Trapped in the tower at York, the Jews excavate and hurl rocks.

---

[21] Cf. A. Bale, 'Fictions of Judaism in England before 1290', in *JMB*, ed. Skinner, pp. 129–44, p. 139, on Newburgh's use of the Masada story and Vincent in this volume.

[22] Cf. A. Sapir Abulafia: 'Unease about the [Christian] making of money was often expressed by Christians by attacking the Jews for doing just that,' in her, 'Bodies in the Jewish-Christian Debate', in *Framing Medieval Bodies*, ed. S. Kay and M. Rubin (Manchester, 1994), pp. 123–37 (p. 129).

The hermit is crushed by a stone from the sky. The tumbling rock resonates with the geology of medieval antisemitism according to which Jews are stone-hearted. Christian interpreters hijacked Ezekiel 36. 26 ('And I will take away the stony heart out of your flesh, and will give you a heart of flesh'). Thus Peter the Venerable wonders, 'I really do not know whether a Jew is a man ... I know not, say I, whether he is a man from whose flesh the stony heart has not yet been removed.'[23] Peter's Jews are of 'inveteratam duritiem', congenital in their obduracy, their stony hardness. For William of Newburgh, the Jews live a kind of petrified life, re-enacting Masada in northern climes because time is incapable of altering their unyielding nature, of providing them with anything but the same old script to re-enact. Newburgh repeatedly returns to the affluence and the lithic materiality of Jewish homes: in London they are 'of strong construction' (Bk IV, ch. 1) and therefore almost impregnable; their domiciles in Lynn (Bk IV, ch. 7) and Stamford (Bk IV, ch.8) are replete with riches; York Jews 'built houses of the largest extent in the middle of the city, which might be compared to royal palaces; and there they lived in abundance and luxury almost regal' (Bk IV, ch. 9). Josce, a Jew who had been present in London during Richard's coronation, possesses a house in the city 'which, from the magnitude and strength of its construction, might be said to be equal to a castle of no small size' (Bk IV, ch. 9). These invariably stone houses seem to partition the Jews, set them apart; but they also bring them intolerably close to the Christians. Or, at least, to *some* Christians: those for whom each rock of these little castles (*castella*) materializes the transformation of liquid, Christian wealth via Jewish usury into Jewish holdings; those who were not pleased to see petrifying Christian typology challenged by the mobility of contemporary Jewish identities. Newburgh metaphorizes Jewish intransigence through unyielding rock. Figuratively, stone was supposed to keep the Jews in place. In fact, though, the material is more protean than carceral.

Lapidary Tales

The narratives that medieval Christians told about Jews tended to petrify them temporally: the figural Jew is immutable, an intrusion into modernity of an eternally repeating past. The Jew performs his stubbornness, carnality, literal-mindedness and enmity against Christians in tiresome repetitions. Yet when examined carefully, many anti-Judaic narratives betray their stark and rigid segregations, yielding partial views of effervescent quotidian practice, of potentially affirmative Christian-Jewish neighbouring. Coinhabitation sometimes fostered alliance, sharing, and becoming, contravening a narrative ar-

---

23 'Petri Venerabilis adversus Iudeorum inveteratam duritiem' 3, lines 564–70. Cited in Abulafia, 'Bodies in the Jewish-Christian Debate', p. 127. An excellent discussion of Peter and the Jews can be found in Flanagan, *Doubt in an Age of Faith*, pp. 164–7.

dour for ghettoization, abjection, and fossilization. Physical neighbouring and the improvised confederations it could engender might leave their traces as mutually lived spaces that effervesce quietly within a text. We know that Jews and Christians residentially intermingled because narratives like William of Newburgh's tell us they did. These stories convey something of shared history into the present. They are also a performance of that reality itself. Can we not glimpse in the very form of these narratives (narratives that insist on segregation but are quietly undone by co-dwelling, neighbouring) another kind of living-together? William of Newburgh conceptually segregates space that is in fact plurally inhabited. Yet he also places his Jewish stories in the heart of a Christian narrative, and makes them resonate with themes that haunt the whole of his work. Jewish houses of stone abut Christian houses of stone. Jewish identities, which can at first glance appear fashioned of immutable, typological stone, abut Christian identities, and are just as dynamic.

The Middle Ages inherited an ambivalent lapidary vocabulary from the Bible. Stone could be foundational (Peter is the rock upon which the Church is built), inert and useless materiality (Matthew 4. 3-4), a material to convey memory into the future (Jacob erects a stone to mark the place where he beheld the Gate of Heaven), a weapon (Goliath dies from a stone to the head), the door to a tomb (Lazarus, Jesus), a substance that can cry out (Luke 19. 40), a symbol of ruin (Matthew 24. 1-2), a mute idol (Habakkuk 2. 19). Stone in medieval texts is not nearly so inert a substance as it might at first seem. In the lapidaries it is often the hero of its own narratives, journeying the world in the mouths of fabulous beasts or the pockets of exotic merchants, radiating its innate *vertu* to vanquish poison or preserve chastity. According to the *Book of John Mandeville*, some rocks possess a promiscuous sexuality: male and female diamonds copulate to bring baby diamonds into the world. Stone seems immobile only when viewed anthropocentrically. As Chaucer points out in the Knight's Tale, given enough time stone is as protean as any substance.

Neither will stone stay in its place in William of Newburgh's narrative. Book One includes a stone architecture erected upon the field of Hastings that exudes fresh gore after each rain; the walls of Ramsey abbey run with real blood ('verum sanguinem sudarunt') when seized; green children emerge from the earth near Woolpit, and one of them refuses assimilation to a new English life. In one quarry, a huge rock is split open, revealing two smelly, hairless greyhounds living inside; in another workmen discover a beautiful 'double-stone' ('lapis formosus duplex') with an even more marvellous creature within:

> While they were digging very deep for materials for building, there was found a beautiful double stone, that is, a stone composed of two stones, joined with some very adhesive matter ('ex duobus subtili agglutinatione compactus lapidibus'). Being shown by the wondering workmen to the bishop, who was at hand, it was ordered to be split, that its

> mystery (if any) might be developed. In the cavity, a little animal ('bestiola'), called a toad, having a small gold chain ('cathenulam auream', a pet's chain) around its neck, was discovered. When the bystanders were lost in amazement at such an unusual occurrence, the bishop ordered the stone to be closed again, thrown into the quarry, and covered up with rubbish for ever. (Bk I, ch. 28; trans. Stevenson, p. 437)

The nameless bishop disdains the astonishment that seizes the workmen upon discovery of the doubled stone, the amazement that possesses them when the conjoined rock is cracked open to reveal dwelling at its secret interior a creature of art (the gold chain) and danger (toads were considered venomous). He orders the stone resealed – but with what? Once broken, can the doubled stones be restored, can they contain the unprecedented and living phenomena which has been revealed as inhabiting their secret interior? A toad with a golden chain, sent into the future as the gift of two mutually dependent spheres, received by an uncomprehending yet wonderstruck audience, returned to the depths of the ground by a bishop cannot thereby end the life of the astonishing story that has already escaped from that rock, even as the being at its interior is consigned to the prison of the earth: what message might this prodigy convey about the future of the Jews of York? What message does it yield about history as discovery, *inventio*? Why intentionally destroy the beauty and challenge of that which arises when worlds acknowledge their agglutination, their generative and irrevocable conjoining?

Giving the Jews of York a future means not just de-coupling their narrative from lachrymose history, which always knows its destinies in advance, but also allowing their narratives to live within a wider, more capacious context: here, by not isolating the Jewish section of William of Newburgh's narrative from its embeddedness in his whole *History*. Just as Christian-Jewish neighbouring unfolded in shared urban space, coinhabitance must be textual: neighbouring is literal as well as literary. Jews share space in William's book with Scots, Saracens, Welsh. His world is wide. They also textually touch Other Worlds, where we behold stones yielding wonders, green children from a distant land who do not eat English food, sport English skin, wear English dress, utter English words … and yet, when they do speak, prove not wholly alien.

Might these lapidary tales, like the quarry rocks, hold the promise of some strange beauty, some unfamiliar future, that the dominant narrative will not yield? Let us return to the story of stone with which we began: the Yorkshire hill within which an uncanny people celebrate their nocturnal feast. The familiar landmark is rendered queer when the passerby observes through an open door (*januam patentam*) a banquet in progress, men and women reclining 'as at a formal feast'. When the servant spots him at the doorway and offers him a cup, the man takes the goblet and flees, leaving himself only a story of an invitation declined. The feast not enjoyed is a refusal by William to recognize another possible narrative, one in which a passing Christian *might* have shared an alien table. Could we witness at the table in the mound an invitation to Christian-Jewish commensality?[24] A door left ajar, reclining at formal table, a ready cup: all that seems missing is *matzoh* and bitter herbs. Does this feast not seem to be a *seder*, the door and the goblet ready to welcome Elijah? Of course it could not be, the mound's banquet is Welsh or Irish but not Jewish … yet this unexpected possibility opens in Yorkshire in a space William knows well, opens in the heart of William's own story to perplex him, to attract him to what he already knows, an invitation not so much refused as misrecognized, an invitation that endures.

Does this open door not still proclaim, *Another world is possible?*

---

[24] David Malkiel treats Jewish-Gentile sharing of wine (*yeyn nesekh*) in *Reconstructing Ashkenaz*, pp. 203–4. Pinchas Roth and Ethan Zadoff explore the challenges posed by England's beer-drinking culture in their paper in this volume.

Afterword

Violence, Memory and the Traumatic Middle Ages

Anthony Bale

The events surrounding the violent death of the Jews of York in March 1190 continue to exert a strong fascination: accounts of these events demand a radical and troubling act of empathy and imagination. How could something so horrible, so bloody, and so resonant in its foreshadowing of future horrors, happen *in this place*, at this sturdy bailey under grey northern skies? The setting is at once familiar, a corner of a beautiful small city, and obscene: a Yorkshire Masada, a place where a lethal combination of lucre, zeal and vengeance made a perfect deadly storm. Clifford's Tower is a deeply affecting site, and has been profoundly generative, as the essays in this volume show. This volume of essays demonstrates just how broad the ramifications of that day in 1190 are: from the specifics of the moment itself, to the religious, financial, cultural and political issues which surround it and came to be attached to it.

However, the hard facts of the 1190 massacre are hard to locate: neither the bodies nor the twelfth-century buildings survive, records and witnesses from the time are scant and predictably partial. When the remains of the medieval Jewish cemetery at York were excavated in the 1980s, as the Jewbury burial-ground site was prepared for a new life as a supermarket car-park, it was hoped that physical evidence of the massacre would emerge, but no such evidence presented itself. The events at Clifford's Tower are, then, largely memorial: made out of, and enduring through, memory, put together from the few narratives we have available. The stone tower currently standing postdates the 1190 attack on the Jews, in which the wooden castle was burned too, but memory and trauma inhere in ideas not places: Clifford's Tower (its name recalling the hanging there in the 1320s of one Robert de Clifford, a local felon) has become a potent emblem of the persecution of medieval Jewry by its neighbours and, more generally, a metonym of medieval cruelty and bloodiness.

In this afterword I would like to offer some reflections on the kinds of memory at work concerning the events at York: not in a Freudian key of 'witnessing', 'trauma' and 'forgetting', but in terms of the aesthetics and politics of memory, medieval and modern. In fact, the archaeological excavations at Jewbury did reveal some arresting remnants of medieval vi-

294

olence in all its unmediated horror: a teenaged girl stabbed at least five times in the head; a man in his forties stabbed repeatedly through the leg so that the bone had sheared; a man in his twenties, stabbed in the head and then operated on.[1] However, this violence seems to have been of a specific kind – one person committing violence against another, the grim, quotidian, ugly striking of blows and tearing of flesh; not the cosmic, martyrological kind, not the trans-historical battle between Christian and Jew, as at Clifford's Tower.

Clifford's Tower: A Souvenir of the Middle Ages

The present building at Clifford's Tower, a heritage tourist site with plaques, pamphlets and websites calling attention both to its bloodied past and its present interest, can be seen as a perfect souvenir: a token of remembrance, a thing that helps us to remember. The tower now standing, a quatrefoil stone keep, probably dating from Henry III's reign (d. 1272), is quite different, in size and shape, stone not wood, and, of course, now replete with comfortable first-world tourists, not people in desperate fear for their lives from what it was that early spring day in 1190. Clifford's Tower fulfils the most fundamental terms of Susan Stewart's illuminating discussion of the souvenir as a memory-cue which replaces the lived lives of bodies with a 'nostalgic myth of contact and presence';[2] Clifford's Tower, as a souvenir, reflects a kind of second-hand experience, both inauthentic and strangely absent of material history. Moreover, 'the souvenir is by definition always incomplete', in that the object (Clifford's Tower) is a metonym for something else and something much bigger, and in that it is not 'homomaterial' (the current tower is, in every sense, in a different medium from the 'original'): it can 'still exist as a sample of the now-distanced experience, an experience which the object can only evoke and resonate to, and can never entirely recoup'. The key points about the souvenir I wish to pick up here are that the souvenir 'is not a narrative of the object; it is a narrative of the possessor ... Furthermore, the souvenir is often attached to locations and experiences that are not for sale.' Thinking about Clifford's Tower as a marker of the past, a site of formal and public history which is 'not for sale', helps us understand the identity politics at work in our construction of the events of 1190, a material object which, at its moment of inauthenticity, serves as a trace of bloodied, awful, violent history. The souvenir can 'envelop the present within the past',[3] as the place where we take what we need from the past, a place where our empathy for, and horror of, the past can rest in a public peace.

---

1   J. M. Lilley et al., *Jewish Burial Ground at Jewbury*, The Archaeology of York 12:3 (London, 1994), pp. 480–2.
2   S. Stewart, *On Longing: Narratives of the Miniature, the Gigantic, the Souvenir, the Collection* (Durham NC, 1993), p. 133
3   The preceding quotations are from ibid., pp. 136, 151.

What *effect* is Clifford's Tower now supposed to have on us? What kind of witness or historian – amateur or professional – is appealed to here? Eight hundred and twenty-one years (to the day) after the massacre, the tower's custodian, English Heritage, includes no information on the Jews' fate on the Clifford's Tower website: instead, its 'History of Clifford's Tower' briefly mentions the role of the bailey in William the Conqueror's fortification of York, the thirteenth-century building of the stone keep in its 'unusual four-lobed design', its role in the Pilgrimage of Grace (1536) and in the Civil War siege of York (1644), and its nineteenth-century incorporation into York pris-on.[4] However, visitors to the tower are greeted by a handsome memorial plaque commemorating the 1190 massacre, set into the base of the mount. Placed there in the late 1970s, the plaque reads:

> On the night of Friday 16 March 1190 some 150 Jews and Jewesses of York having sought protection in the Royal Castle on this site from a mob incited by Richard Malebisse and others chose to die at each other's hands rather than renounce their faith. ישימו לד כבוד ותהלתו באיים
>
> Isaiah XLII 12

The final line, engraved in Hebrew but not translated into English, cites Isaiah, 'Let them do honour [or respect] [to the Lord], and tell His glory in the coastlands [or islands]'. In this way the plaque carefully makes both a devotional-martyrological 'Jewish' sense and a historical-contextual 'sense' of the 1190 massacre: the historical circumstances of the Jews' persecutor and debtor, Malebisse, combine with the biblical sentiments of Isaiah 42, a chapter which has within it a description of exilic suffering ('Opening eyes deprived of light,/ Rescuing prisoners from confinement, From the dungeon those who sit in darkness'). However, the pious diaspora sentiments of Isaiah 42. 12 are joined in the biblical text by violent vengeance articulated in the verse which follows: 'The Lord goes forth like a warrior,/ Like a fighter He whips up His rage' (Isaiah 42. 13). The plaque is then, succinctly, situated between histories: at once the cosmic Jewish-devotional time of Isaiah and the specific medievalism of 'mob' violence, incitement and faith in York.

Whilst what happened at York in 1190 was undoubtedly an event of shocking bloodshed, by the standards of its own times as well as ours, it was not without European precedent (far from it) and there had been numerous violent attacks on the English Jews which go unmemorialized. The attack at York can be seen as the culmination of a chain of attacks which were launched at Richard I's coronation in the autumn of 1189, and spread, as Joe Hillaby describes above, through eastern England before reaching York. These other

---

4 English Heritage, 'The History of Clifford's Tower'. http://www.english-heritage.org.uk/daysout/properties/cliffords-tower-york/history/ [accessed 16 March 2011].

cities – London included, but also Lynn, Stamford and Bury St Edmunds – have no such memorials to their slain Jews. How do we chose which sites to make into what Pierre Nora has influentially called 'lieux de mémoire', sites of memory, valorized sites which incarnate national narratives?[5]

Horrible Histories or Positively Medieval?

The plaque at Clifford's Tower is not unusual: in fact, plaques have sprung up, since the early twentieth century, at many sites of medieval Anglo-Jewish interest. There are two main streams in this flood of plaques: one might be termed 'religious' (prayerful, pious, apologetic, concerned with religious relations), the other 'historical' (archaeological, invested in specific materials and sites, concerned with context). All these plaques display a fascination with vestiges of medieval Anglo-Jewish life but, less optimistically, less benignly, they also speak to our fascination with the traces of violence and narratives of disappearance, the idea that in this place, on this spot, occurred something horribly medieval.

The Clifford's Tower plaque is, in fact, more or less a riposte to the plaque in Lincoln Cathedral (1955), unveiled for the seven-hundredth anniversary of the murder of Little Hugh of Lincoln. This plaque read:

> Trumped up stories of 'ritual murders' of Christian boys by Jewish communities were common throughout Europe during the Middle Ages and even much later. These fictions cost many innocent Jews their lives. Lincoln had its own legend and the alleged victim was buried in the Cathedral in the year 1255. Such stories do not redound to the credit of Christendom, and so we pray: Lord, forgive what we have been,/ amend what we are,/ and direct what we shall be.

Placed in a cathedral, it is hardly surprising that the Lincoln plaque sought to make a Christian sense of the story of Little Hugh: emphasizing prayerfulness, begging for forgiveness, the Lincoln plaque was a curious combination of aporia ('even much later', within a decade of the Holocaust), legalistic refutation ('trumped up stories', 'innocent Jews', 'alleged victim') and a solipsistic concern for the 'credit of Christendom'. Just as the Hebrew prayer at Clifford's Tower addresses memory to observant Jews, the Lincoln plaque spoke to contrite Christians, through the language of Protestant penitential liturgy ('forgive what we have been' etc., a prayer often used on Ash Wednesday): neither plaque can be said either to indulge the ostensibly secular and impartial eye of most historical scholarship or to see religious

---

[5] P. Nora, 'Between Memory and History: *Les Lieux de Mémoire*', *Representations* 26 (1989), 7-24.

conflict as human, rather than sectarian, tragedies. New signage was erected at Lincoln *c.* 2002, very different in tone but equally fraught with what the Middle Ages means to us today:

> This fabrication is a shameful example of religious and racial hatred, which, continuing down through the ages, violently divides many people in the present day. Let us unite, here, in a prayer for an end to bigotry, prejudice and persecution.

Elisa Narin van Court has written comprehensively and provocatively about the politics and silences of 'Jewish' plaques in York, Lincoln and Norwich, and her academic work on this politics of memory informed the new signage at Lincoln Cathedral.[6] Aggressively ecumenical ('many people', 'let us unite') and boldly transhistorical ('a shameful example', 'continuing down through the ages', 'in the present day'), the contemporary Lincoln signage attests, explicitly, to the public and current ownership of the medieval past. Fictions of 'collective identity', explored above by Jeffrey Jerome Cohen, continue to animate these narratives around medieval England. The Lincoln signage little considers context, or the medieval victims, and does not mention Judaism and Christianity, preferring instead universals of 'religious and racial hatred'. Here, the medieval past is a useful lens through which to refract our own troubled times. Similarly, at Norwich Cathedral a 'chapel of reconciliation' has been established by the site of William of Norwich's medieval shrine, originally established in the wake of the boy's disappearance in 1144.

The other main manner of commemoration is historical, foregrounding the medieval topography or built environment of Anglo-Jewry. Egregious examples include St Aldate's, Oxford: 'THIS STREET KNOWN TILL 1300 AS GREAT JEWRY CONTAINED MANY HOUSES OF THE JEWS/ INCLUDING THE SYNAGOGUE WHICH LAY TO THE NORTH OF TOM TOWER 1931' and the adjacent plaque on Blue Boar Street ('This extension to the Townhall stands on land at the centre of the Anglo-Saxon town, later the heart of the Medieval Jewish quarter'); the Jew's House at Lincoln, 'THE NORMAN HOUSE FORMERLY KNOWN AS AARON THE JEW'S HOUSE'; and the Jew's Court at Lincoln, 'Building of medieval origins by tradition used as a synagogue – Supported by the Heritage Lottery Fund'. Whilst not always entirely accurate, such plaques are formal markers of heritage and thus largely steer clear of the devotional-interpretative energies of the 'religious plaques'. In doing so, they might be seen to endow the medieval Jews (and Christians) with a greater sense of subjectivity or agency, if not empowerment, in as much as such plaques emphasize con-

---

6   E. N. van Court, 'Invisible in Oxford: Medieval Jewish History in Modern England', *Shofar* 26 (2008), 1–19.

textual and archaeological uniqueness rather than religious macrohistory. Still others mark sites of Anglo-Jewish historical interest, but do not make this explicit: the plaque at the Music House (Norwich) merely records: 'Music House. The oldest dwelling house in Norwich. Home of the Jurnet family *c.* 1170–1240; Sir John Paston after 1478; and Lord Chief Justice Coke from 1613', whilst the well at Bristol, now thought by many to be a medieval 'mikveh', simply states 'Jacob's Well 1089'. Such plaques are points of civic interest, but they trust the viewer to interpret them. Whilst van Court has seen such plaques as articulating Jewish 'invisibility', we might also see them as honestly integrating Anglo-Jewish sites into the urban fabric of what were, or remain, mixed communities never entirely defined by their Jewish associations.

Not far from York, in the castle town of Knaresborough (N. Yorks.), this historical impetus to memorialize has resulted in a plaque, erected in 2008, commemorating the small medieval Jewish community which once resided there. It reads:

> In the thirteenth-century a Jewish community lived and worshipped in Knaresborough. The Synagogue was situated at the end of Synagogue Lane, at the rear of these buildings, the exact location is unknown. It is believed the Knaresborough Jewish community was dissolved in 1275, before all of the Jewish faith were expelled from England in 1290. Knaresborough Civic Society 2008.

The plaque functions, on the surface, to explain the incongruous presence of a street called Synagogue Lane in this small northern town; what is equally incongruous, in a way, is that the plaque commemorates what seems to have been barely a Jewish community, more of an occasional Jewish presence, a sub-community of that at York.[7] Far from being an admission of civic pride, the Knaresborough plaque seems to be a civic apology, albeit one in a place not even noted for its anti-Jewish violence in the middle ages.

A similarly small-scale commemoration is afforded by the discreet plaque at Guildford (Surrey), placed on the Monsoon/Accessorize shop in the late 1990s:

> In 1995 archaeologists from Guildford Museum discovered an unusual stone chamber beneath this High Street shop. It was suggested that it might have been a medieval synagogue dating back to the twelfth-century.

---

7   The Knaresborough community is only recorded in the third quarter of the thirteenth century. See R. R. Mundill, *England's Jewish Solution: Experiment and Expulsion, 1262–1290* (Cambridge, 1998), p. 157.

The plaque is welcome, not least because so much of Guildford's medieval history has been obscured or destroyed by later building, and because the site is highly unusual. The building in question was the subject of extensive archaeological investigation, and Mary Alexander's survey and study suggests a rather greater degree of certainty than the plaque that this undercroft was indeed a synagogue.[8] Rumours continue to circulate that the commercial owners of the site wished, but were not able, to put a glass floor into the shop in order that shoppers might gaze, perhaps rather jarringly, onto the site where the local Jews prayed some eight hundred years previously. Real commitment to the unusual stone chamber might have re-opened it as a historical exhibition about the medieval town, but, in an area of commercially-desirable property, this is unrealistic. Thus the plaque now suggests something hidden, something unavailable: a recalcitrant memory of the town's Jews, the actual site unable to be put on show but equally unable to be disregarded altogether. Similarly, in London, the site of a mid thirteenth century *mikveh* (ritual bath) in the heart of what is now the heart of the City is not marked publicly (unless the signs on Milk Street bearing the legend 'Dry Riser Rising Main' and 'Dry Riser Falling Main' are understood as cryptic indicators of the proximity of flowing water required for such a bath!). The blocks of Reigate stone from the Milk Street *mikveh* are now exhibited at the new Jewish Museum in Camden, north London, the heartland of a modern rather than medieval Jewish community. Yet the medieval London Jewry is commemorated in earlier plaques: at the church of St Lawrence Jewry, a gilded sign explains:

> St Lawrence Jewry is so called because the original Twelfth Century Church stood on the Eastern side of the City, occupied by the Jewish Community. That Church, built in 1136, was destroyed in the Great Fire of London of 1666. The building which replaced it was designed by Sir Christopher Wren in 1680. Almost completely destroyed by fire in 1940, this time as a result of action by the King's enemies, it was restored in 1957 in the tradition of Wren's building. St Lawrence Jewry is now the Church of the Corporation of London.

The sign is obviously alert to the traumas of London history, but remains silent on the fate of the 'Jewish Community' with which the church once shared its neighbourhood. Nearby, on Old Jewry, a Corporation of London ceramic plaque records 'The Great Synagogue stood near this site until 1272'. Again, what happened in 1272 is left to the passer-by to surmise. Such acts of oblique memorialization are mirrored in the fact that the street Old Jewry

---

8   M. Alexander, 'A Possible Synagogue in Guildford', in *Religion and Belief in Medieval Europe. Papers of the Medieval Europe Brugge 1997 Conference IV* ed. G. de Boe et al. (Zellik, 1997), pp. 201–12.

(London, EC2) was known as Colechurch Lane until the fourteenth century: in the decades after the Jews' expulsion it became a kind of memorial, a souvenir, of the Jews' vanished presence.

What are such plaques commemorating: life or death? What are they attempting to memoralize: rupture or continuity? Carved in stone or cast in clay, often underwritten with some formal 'heritage' or 'civic' mandate, they suggest the past's immovable presence and its social ownership (or regulation). Are they aimed at a specific group, or intended to have a specific effect? Like any text, these plaques can mean different things to different audiences: to empathetic global citizens and historically-literate tourists, they offer a site for reflection; for other viewers, in particular a kind of ideally-constructed Jew and Englishman or Englishwoman, I suggest these plaques do articulate quite precise historical and emotional agendas, which are strikingly similar to the agendas present in the medieval construction of the Jewish and English communities. I do not think it is going too far to suggest that these plaques represent our own historical trauma, our desire, need and failure to make sense of the medieval past, as they do the traumatic experience of the Jews in medieval England.

However, these plaques often seem to be functioning as ways of formulating and articulating moral universals about past, and present, tolerance: in other words, the Jew as a hermeneutic device for understanding the national narrative, just as the Jew was in Middle Ages.[9] Dewy-eyed references to bigotry, combined with hopeful declarations of tolerance and peace, are designed to act as markers not so much of historical events but of the moral superiority of the present day over both the Middle Ages and, as at Lincoln, of previous twentieth-century plaque-makers. These sites are burdened with gravitas, as making a plaque to mark such murders and expulsions also marks a progressive distance, through public atonement, from the Middle Ages. The plaques seem to be saying not only 'look what we come from', but 'look how different we are now', 'look how far we have come'. Such memorializations then might be seen as part of the twentieth- and twenty-first-century construction of the Middle Ages as a barbaric period of unthinking, constant bloodshed in which representations of violence are seamlessly elided with their supposed horrific contexts.[10]

The obvious connection here – a connection some of the plaques encourage us to make – is with Holocaust memorials and the resulting dark tourism which has sprung up in the last two or three decades in central and eastern

---

[9] As Matthew Mesley comments in his essay, above, this 'hermeneutic Jew' could 'reinforce or make plain [a writer's] point or to support a wider didactic edifice'. On the Jew as medieval hermeneutic device see also S. Kruger, *The Spectral Jew: Conversion and Embodiment in Medieval Europe* (Minneapolis, 2006).

[10] For a provocative discussion of the relationship between violence and historical otherness, see R. Mills, *Suspended Animation: Pain, Pleasure and Punishment in Medieval Culture* (London, 2005), pp. 8–18.

Europe. Ruth Ellen Gruber has written extensively about this phenomenon, observing that 'fashion, commercialism, and what can be described as post-Holocaust necrophilia' all play a role in this 'exploitative kitsch'; yet, Gruber goes on, this accompanies 'thoughtful reevaluations of history, culture, and identity' as 'sincere attempts to make up for the past', in fascinatingly diverse manifestations of 'third generation' syndrome, in which 'memory – memory of Jews – is employed as a vehicle for self-discovery and self-exploration'.[11] In the present context, Gruber usefully describes the 'almost familiar exotica', a 'pseudonostalgia for stereotypes', staged by Jewish sites which, I suggest, is echoed in the English plaques of Anglo-Jewry: stereotypes not of Jews, but of the past that we seek when we look back to the Middle Ages.

The Aesthetics of Remembering

Plaques recording violence and discord wrestle with the same issue medieval writers had in describing such events: that is, the 'dilemma of uniqueness' within patterns of hatred and social violence.[12] As Nicholas Vincent describes above, William of Newburgh used Josephus' account of the massacre at Masada to evoke sacred martyrdom; modern and contemporary plaques have sought to make violent confrontation the public reference point for the historically-aware visitor or tourist to English cities. Just as Newburgh's use of Josephus in a 'historical' text indicated the exemplary pastness of the events he described, so too plaques declare their own 'pastness' (to use van Court's word): plaques are concerned with the past and label something as *of* the past – but there is too the strong sense that it is through plaques that the present chooses the past it wants. However, as Narin van Court makes clear, plaques also function as an important *public* face for history: where history breaks out of its dusty ruins into a textual, durable, and singularly public form.

An honest history of medieval England must include Jews and their interactions with their Christian neighbours, but we must not forget that the Jews never lived in isolation from these neighbours, and the Jewish experience must not be reduced to a shapeless, thousand-year history of 'antisemitism'. Medieval texts about massacres, communal violence, the expulsion from a town of people who had been living and working side by side – seem to demand of the modern critic a 'turn to the human'; as Hannah Johnson comments above, 'To consider how particular historical events were experienced by specific human actors is at the same time to consider the problem of the meaning we assign to those events'.

---

[11] R. E. Gruber, *Virtually Jewish: Reinventing Jewish Culture in Europe* (Berkeley CA, 2002), pp. 8–9.
[12] The phase 'the dilemma of uniqueness' comes from the illuminating essay by J. C. Alexander, 'On the Social Construction of Moral Universals: The "Holocaust" from War Crime to Trauma Drama', in J. C. Alexander et al., *Cultural Trauma and Collective Identity*, (Berkeley CA, 2004), pp. 196–263 (p. 253).

The sources we have by which to understand the events at York – and, indeed, the violent experience the English Jews had in England from the 1190s until their expulsion – demand that we try to consider the humanity not only of the protagonists and victims, but also the medieval audiences of the surviving accounts. Or, to put it another way, much more attention has been paid to considering what the available sources tell us about what happened and why, and much less attention has been paid to considering how and why these accounts were written. Or, to put it yet another way, martyrologies tell us more about martyrologists than they do martyrs.

The essays in this volume speak to the critical importance of the 1190 massacre: a critical turn both in the fortunes of the English Jews, and in the ways contemporary scholarship negotiates the Middle Ages. But what we are also dealing with is a crisis of fact, of perspective, of paltry materials and documentary remains. Violence leaves its own traces not necessarily because of humanitarian concern for the victims, but because violence equates to secure remembering.[13] Indeed, the very definition of trauma is of something witnessed and repeated, which necessitates testimony. However, following the work of Pierre Nora and Dominick LaCapra, psychoanalytically-inflected descriptions of trauma and memory have become familiar concepts in Jewish and Holocaust studies.[14] Memory has vaguely been suggested to stand in for history; but memory is absolutely crucial to how we approach Clifford's Tower, because almost all the sources we have by which we know anything about it are, in one way or another, explicitly memorial: monastic chronicles (which narrate a 'universal' Christian history in which the local is within a cosmic pattern) and Hebrew liturgical poems and prayers (which narrate the specific through the general and biblically-resonant diction of Jewish experience) were designed to be memory-aids for their medieval audiences.[15]

The plaques discussed above relate directly to the medieval accounts of Jewish-Christian violence in that they perform violent memorial work for their audiences. I want to close by briefly mentioning a final plaque, on the outskirts of Oxford, on Mill Street, in the tumbledown remains of the great medieval Augustinian abbey at Osney:

> Near this stone in Osney Abbey Robert of Reading otherwise
> Haggai of Oxford suffered for his faith on Sunday 17 April
> 1222 AD corresponding to 4 Iyyar 4982 AM.

---

[13] On the relation of violence to memory see M. Carruthers, *The Book of Memory. A Study of Memory in Medieval Culture*, 2nd ed. (Cambridge, 2008), pp. 168–71.

[14] See Nora, 'Between Memory and History'; D. LaCapra, *Representing the Holocaust: History, Theory, Trauma* (Ithaca NY, 1996).

[15] See S. L. Einbinder, *Beautiful Death: Jewish Poetry and Martyrdom in Medieval France* (Princeton, 2002), pp. 29–31.

The plaque, inaccessible on private property, was erected by the city council in 1931 at the same time as the plaque marking the synagogue site on St Aldate's. The Osney plaque refers, confusedly, to the first public burning in medieval England: Robert had studied Judaism, fallen in love with a Jew, been circumcised and converted to Judaism.[16] This memorial is unusual, prosaically eloquent but profoundly marginal, at the edge of the city, on a vestigial wall of the medieval abbey. It does not allude clearly to Robert/ Haggai's death, and thus allows the reader-viewer to make their own connection between physical pain and socio-religious suffering. In describing how Robert/Haggai 'suffered for his faith' this plaque simply describes both a living, sensate body and the tradition of martyrdom it inaugurates. Indeed, the death by burning here was used, as Roth reports, as the common-law precedent for the 1401 act, *De haeretico comburendo*, which begot that most horribly 'medieval' of punishments, burning at the stake for religious dissent.[17] What I find most eloquent about the Osney plaque is its careful but unobtrusive balancing of Christian and Jewish; that, unlike many of the other plaques, it refrains from imagining 'a segregation that had clearly not obtained in England', to quote Jeffrey Cohen's essay in this volume: both names, both dates, equally present, a Christian Jew and a Jewish Christian, burned to death at an abbey, a diaspora world of intricate, malleable, interpenetrating, and difficult identities. The Osney plaque makes no mention of moral responsibility, instead allowing us to make of our own sense of Robert/Haggai's story, and thus points to both the unstable status of England's medieval Jewish community and the abiding memories, medieval and modern, surrounding it.

---

[16] For images and a brief discussion, including a history of the plaque itself, see: Oxford Jewish Heritage Committee, 'The Robert of Reading Plaque'. http://www.oxfordjewishheritage. co.uk/projects/osney-abbey-first-public-burning-in-england/137-the-robert-of-reading-plaque [accessed 26 April 2011]. In fact, as Cecil Roth observed, the plaque conflates two narratives: one of the unnamed Dominican monk who converted to Judaism in 1222, arousing 'the most violent passions' at the Oxford Council of the Province of Canterbury in that year, and the similar story of Robert of Reading, dating from the 1270s. Roth, *HJE*, p. 41, esp. n. 4.

[17] Roth, *HJE*, p. 41.

BIBLIOGRAPHY

Manuscripts

Cambridge, Gonville and Caius College
MS 404/625

Cambridge, St John's College Library
 MS 262, K21

Cambridge University Library
MS Dd.1.4
MS Dd.1.28

Glasgow, Hunterian Library
MS Hunter 229 (U.3.2): The Hunterian Psalter

Hereford, Herefordshire Record Office
MS AH81/34

Kew, The National Archives
SC 6/708
C 52/21
E 9/43
E 101/249/10
E 101/250/3
E 101/249/29
E 101/250/5
E 159/60
E 368/13

Leiden University Library
MS Codex Orientalis 4725 (Scaliger 8)

London, British Library
Additional MS 42130: Luttrell Psalter
Additional MS 49999: de Brailes Hours
Additional Charter 10636
MS Cotton Claudius B. III: Cartulary of York Minster
MS Cotton Claudius D. XI: Cartulary of Malton Priory
MS Cotton Nero D. III

MS Royal 4 D. VII: Petrus Comestor, Historia Scholastica
MS Royal 13 D. V
MS Royal 13 D. VI: Works of Flavius Josephus
MS Royal 13 D. VII: Works of Flavius Josephus
Yates Thompson 13: Taymouth Hours
London, Lambeth Palace Library
MS 435: Psalterium Hebraicum

London, St Paul's Cathedral Library
MS 2: Psalterium cum commento

Manchester, John Rylands University Library
MSS 220-1: Cartulary of St Mary's Abbey, York

New York, Pierpont Morgan Library
MS G.50: de Lisle Hours

Oxford, Bodleian Library
MS Dodsworth 7
MS Or 3
MS Or 46
MS Or 621

Oxford, Corpus Christi College
MS 7
MS 10

Paris, Bibliothèque nationale de France
MS Héb. 113
MS Héb. 1394

Warminster, Longleat House
 MS 21

Westminster, Westminster Abbey Muniments
WAM 6106
WAM 6278
WAM 6686
WAM 6687
WAM 6693
WAM 6698
WAM 6719
WAM 6744
WAM 6889
WAM 6906

WAM 6921
WAM 6968
WAM 6976
WAM 6983
WAM 6986
WAM 6997
WAM 9002
WAM 9006
WAM 9009
WAM 9012
WAM 9028
WAM 9077
WAM 9079
WAM 9080
WAM 9081
WAM 9112
WAM 9113

York, York City Archives
A1
G16

York, York Minster Archives
Cartulary of St Mary's Abbey, York
L2/1
MS XVI.A.7

Printed Primary Sources

Abstracts of the Charters and Other Documents contained in the Chartulary of the Cistercian Abbey of Fountains in the West Riding of the County of York, ed. W. T. Lancaster, 2 vols. (Leeds, 1915)

Advance Contracts for the Sale of Wool c. 1200–c. 1327, ed. A. R. Bell, C. Brooks and P. Dryburgh, List and Index Society 315 (Kew, 2006)

Ambroise, *The History of the Holy War: Ambroise's Estoire de la Guerre Sainte*, ed. M. Ailes and M. Barber, 2 vols. (Woodbridge, 2003)

Ancient Charters, Royal and Private, prior to A.D. 1200, ed. J. H. Round, PRS 10 (London, 1888)

Annales Monastici, ed. H. R. Luard, 5 vols., RS 36 (London, 1864-69)

The Apocryphal New Testament: A Collection of Apocryphal Christian Literature in an English Translation, ed. J. K. Elliott (Oxford, 1993)

Augustine, Saint, *Sancti Aurelii Augustini Enarrationes in Psalmos*, ed. J. Fraipont and E. Dekkers, 3 vols., Corpus Christianorum. Series Latina 38-40 (Turnhout, 1956)

Bracton, Henry of, *On the Laws and Customs of England*, ed. S. E. Thorne, 4 vols. (Cambridge MA, 1968-77)

Brakelond, Jocelin of, *The Chronicle of Jocelin of Brakelond, concerning the acts of Samson, Abbot of the Monastery of St Edmund*, ed. H. E. Butler, Nelson's Medieval Classics (London, 1949)

British Borough Charters, 1042–1216, ed. A. Ballard (Cambridge, 1913)

Burton, Geoffrey of, *Life and Miracles of St Modwenna*, ed. R. Bartlett, OMT (Oxford, 2002)

Calendar of Close Rolls, Edward I, 5 vols. (London, 1900-8)

Calendar of the Fine Rolls of the Reign of Henry III: Preserved in the National Archives, ed. P. Dryburgh and B. Hartland, 3 vols. (Woodbridge, 2007-9)

Calendar of Patent Rolls, Henry III-Edward I, 10 vols. (London, 1893-1913)

Calendar of the Plea Rolls of the Exchequer of the Jews, ed. J. M. Rigg et al., 6 vols. (London, 1905-2005)

Canterbury, Gervase of, *The Historical Works of Gervase of Canterbury*, ed. W. Stubbs, 2 vols, RS 73 (London 1879-80)

Cartularium abbathiæ de Whiteby, Ordinis S. Benedicti fundatæ anno MLXXVIII, ed. J. C. Atkinson, 2 vols., SS 69 and 72 (Durham, 1879-81)

The Cartulary and Historical Notes of the Cistercian Abbey of Flaxley, otherwise called Dene Abbey, in the County of Gloucester, ed. A. W. Crawley-Boevey (Exeter, 1887)

A Cartulary of the Hospital of St John the Baptist, ed. H. E. Salter, 3 vols., Oxford Historical Society 66, 68-9 (Oxford, 1914-17)

La Chanson de Roland, ed. G. Brault, student edn (University Park PA, 1984)

Le Charroi de Nîmes: chanson de geste du XIIe siècle, ed. D. McMillan, Bibliothèque française et romane. Série B: Éditions critiques de texts 12 (Paris, 1972)

Chartres, Fulcher of, *Fulcheri Carnotensis Historia Hierosolymitana (1095-1127)*, ed. H. Hagenmeyer (Heidelberg, 1913)

Charters of the Honour of Mowbray, 1107–1191, ed. D. E. Greenway, Records of Social and Economic History, New Series 1 (London, 1972)

Charters of the Vicars Choral of York Minster, ed. N. Tringham, 2 vols., YAS, Record Series 148 and 156 (Leeds, 1993-2002)

Chobham, Thomas of, *Thomae de Chobham Summa Confessorum*, ed. F. Broomfield, Analecta Mediaevalia Namurcensia 25 (Louvain, 1968)

Chronicles and Memorials of the Reign of Richard I, ed. W. Stubbs, 2 vols., RS 38 (London 1864-5)

Chronicles of the Reigns of Stephen, Henry II., and Richard I, ed. R. Howlett, 2 vols., RS 82 (London, 1884-89)

The Church Historians of England, ed. J. Stevenson, 5 vols. (London, 1853-8)

Church, State, and Jew in the Middle Ages, ed. R. Chazan (New York, 1980)

Coggeshall, Ralph of, *Radulphi de Coggeshall Chronicon Anglicanum*, ed. J. Stevenson, RS 66 (London, 1875)

Councils and Synods with other documents relating to the English Church II: AD 1205–1313, ed. F.M. Powicke and C.R. Cheney (Oxford, 1964)

Coventry, Walter of, *The Historical Collections of Walter of Coventry*, ed. W.

Stubbs, 2 vols., RS 58 (London, 1872-3)

Curia Regis Rolls, Richard I–Henry III, 20 vols. (London, 1922-2006)

Decrees of the Ecumenical Councils, ed. N. Tanner, 2 vols. (London, 1990)

Devizes, Richard of, *The Chronicle of Richard of Devizes of the Time of King Richard the First*, ed. J. T. Appleby (London, 1963)

Diceto, Ralph de, *The Historical Works of Master Ralph de Diceto, Dean of London*, ed. W. Stubbs, 2 vols., RS 68 (London, 1876)

Dictionnaire hébreu-latin-français de la Bible hébraïque de l'Abbaye de Ramsey (XIIIe siècle), ed. J. Olszowy-Schlanger and A. Grondeux, Corpus Christianorum. Continuatio Mediaevalis. *Lexica Latina medii aevi* 4 (Turnhout, 2008)

Durham, Lawrence of, *Gottes Heilspan – verdichtet: Edition des Hypognosticon des Laurentius Dunelmensis*, ed. S. Daub (Erlangen, 2002)

Early Charters of the Augustinian Canons of Waltham Abbey, Essex (1062–1230), ed. R. Ransford, Studies in the History of Medieval Religion 2 (Woodbridge, 1989)

Early Yorkshire Charters, ed. W. Farrer and C. T. Clay, 13 vols., YAS, Record Series, Extra Series 1-10 (Edinburgh and Wakefield, 1914-65)

Early Yorkshire Families, ed. C. T. Clay, YAS, Record Series 135 (Leeds, 1973)

Écrits théologiques de l'École d'Abélard, ed. by A. Landgraf, Spicilegium Sacrum Lovaniense 14 (Louvain, 1934)

English Historical Documents, II: 1042–1189, ed. D. C. Douglas and G. W. Greenaway, 2nd edn (London, 1996)

English Historical Documents, III: 1189–1327, ed. H. Rothwell (London, 1975)

English Lawsuits from William I to Richard I, ed. R. C. van Caenegem, 2 vols., Selden Soc. 106 and 107 (London, 1990-1)

Evangelia Apocrypha, C. von Tischendorf, 2nd edn (Berlin, 1876)

Eye Priory Cartulary and Charters, ed. V. Brown, 2 vols., Suffolk Charters 12-13 (Woodbridge, 1992)

Eynsham, Adam of, *Magna Vita Sancti Hugonis. The Life of Saint Hugh of Lincoln*, ed. and trans. D. L. Douie and H. Farmer, 2 vols., OMT (Oxford, 1985). First published in 1961 in Nelson's Medieval Classics, 1985 is a 'corrected reprint'.

Fantosme, Jordan, *Chronicle of the War between the English and the Scots in 1173 and 1174*, ed. F. Michel, SS 11 (London, 1840)

Feet of Fines of the Reign of Henry II and of the First Seven Years of the Reign of Richard I, A.D. 1182 to A.D. 1196, PRS 17 (London, 1894)

Fitznigel, Richard, *Dialogus de Scaccario: The Course of the Exchequer*, ed. C. Johnson, OMT, revised edn (Oxford, 1983)

Foedera, Conventiones, Litterae, et Cujuscunque Generis Acta Publica, ed. T. Rymer, 20 vols., (London, 1704-35)

The Gesta Normannorum Ducum of William of Jumièges, Orderic Vitalis and Robert of Torigni, ed. E. M. C. van Houts, 2 vols., OMT (Oxford 1994-95)

Glanville, Ranulf de, *The Treatise on the Laws and Customs of the Realm of England commonly called Glanvill*, ed. G. D. G. Hall, OMT, revised edn (Oxford, 1993)

Grosseteste, Robert, *Roberti Grosseteste Epistolae,* ed. H. R. Luard, RS 25 (London, 1861)

_____, *The Letters of Robert Grosseteste, Bishop of Lincoln,* ed. F. A. C. Mantello and J. Goering (Toronto, 2010)

Great Roll of the Pipe for 31 Henry I, ed. J. Hunter, Record Commission (London, 1833)

Great Rolls of the Pipe for 2, 3 and 4 Henry II, ed. J. Hunter, Record Commission (London, 1844)

Great Rolls of the Pipe, Henry II–Richard I, 56 vols., PRS (London, 1884-1964)

Hazan, J. b J., *The Etz Hayyim,* ed. I. Brodie, 3 vols. (Jerusalem, 1962-67)

Hebräische Berichte über die Judenverfolgungen während der Kreuzzüge, ed. A. Neubauer and M. Stern, Quellen zur Geschichte der Juden in Deutschland 2 (Berlin, 1892)

Hegesippi qui dicitur Historiae Libri V, ed. V. Ussani, 2 vols., Corpus Scriptorum Ecclesiasticorum Latinorum 66 (Vienna, 1932-60)

Howden, Roger of, *The Annals of Roger de Hoveden: Comprising the History of England and of other Countries of Europe from A.D. 732 to A.D. 1201,* ed. H. T. Riley, 2 vols. (London, 1853)

_____, *Gesta Regis Henrici Secundi et Gesta Regis Ricardi: The Chronicle of the Reigns of Henry II and Richard I, AD 1169-1192,* ed. W. Stubbs, 2 vols., RS 49 (London, 1867)

_____, *Chronica Magistri Roger de Houedene,* ed. W. Stubbs, 4 vols, RS 51(London, 1868-71)

Huntingdon, Henry of, *Historia Anglorum: The History of the English People,* ed. D. Greenway, OMT (Oxford, 1996)

The Jerusalem Talmud – Third Order, Tractate Yebamot, ed. H. W. Guggenheimer (Berlin, 2004)

The Jews and the Crusaders: The Hebrew Chronicles of the First and Second Crusades, ed. S. Eidelburg (Madison WI, 1977)

The Jews in the Legal Sources of the Early Middle Ages, ed. A. Linder (Detroit, MI, 1997)

The Jews of Angevin England: Documents and Records from the Latin and Hebrew Sources, Printed and Manuscripts, ed. J. Jacobs (London, 1893)

Josephus, F., *Flavii Iosephi patria Hierosolymitani, religione Iudaei, inter Graecos historiographos, cum primis facundi, Opera quaedam Rvffino presbytero interprete* (Basle, 1524)

_____, *The Latin Josephus I: Introduction and Text:* The Antiquities, *Books I-V,* ed. F. Blatt, Acta Jutlandica 30 (Aarhus, 1958)

Landulphus, Sagax, *Landolfi Sagacis Historia Romana,* ed. A. Crivellucci, 2 vols. (Rome, 1912-13)

Leiston Abbey Cartulary and Butley Priory Charters, ed. R. Mortimer, Suffolk Charters 1 (Woodbridge, 1979)

Letters of Jews through the Ages, from Biblical times to the middle of the Eighteenth Century, ed. F. Kohler, 2 vols. (London, 1952)

The Life of Christina of Markyate: A Twelfth Century Recluse, ed. and trans. C. H.

Talbot, OMT (Oxford, 1987)

The Life of Christina of Markyate, trans. C. H. Talbot and ed. S. Fanous and H. Leyser, revised edn, Oxford World Classics (Oxford, 2009)

The Life of King Edward Who Rests at Westminster, ed. F. Barlow, OMT, 2nd edn (Oxford, 1992)

Losinga, Herbert de, *Epistolae Herberti de Losinga, primi episcopi Norwicensis*, ed. R. Anstruther (Brussels, 1846)

_____, *The Life, Letters and Sermons of Bishop Herbert de Losinga*, ed. E.M. Goulburn and H. Symonds, 2 vols. (Oxford, 1878)

Maimonides, M., *Mishneh Torah al pi Kitve Yad Teman im Perush Maqif*, ed. Y. Kafih, 23 vols. (Tel Aviv, 1983-84)

The Making of Kings Lynn: a Documentary Survey, ed. D. M. Owen, Records of Social and Economic History, New Series 9 (London, 1984)

Malmesbury, William of, *Gesta Regum Anglorum*, ed. R. M. Thomson and M. Winterbottom, 2 vols., OMT (Oxford 1998-99)

Map, Walter, *De Nugis Curialium: Courtiers' Trifles*, ed. M. R. James, C. N. L. Brooke and R. A. B. Mynors, OMT (Oxford, 1983)

Materials for the History of Thomas Becket Archbishop of Canterbury, ed. J. C. Robertson and J. B. Sheppard, 7 vols., RS 67 (London 1875-85)

Medieval English Jews and Royal Officials: Entries of Jewish Interest in the English Memoranda Rolls, 1266–1293, ed. Z. E. Rokéah (Jerusalem, 2000)

The Medieval European Stage, 500–1550, ed. W. Tydeman (Cambridge, 2001)

Medieval Jewish Documents in Westminster Abbey, ed. A. Causton (London, 2007)

The Memoranda Roll for the Michaelmas Term of the First Year of the Reign of King John (1199-1200), ed. H. G. Richardson, PRS 59 (New Series 21) (London, 1943)

The Memoranda Roll of the Tenth Year of the Reign of King John (1207-8), ed. R. A. Brown PRS 69 (New Series 31) (London, 1957)

Memorials of St. Edmund's Abbey, ed. T. Arnold, 3 vols., RS 96 (London, 1890-96)

Menahem, E., *The Writings of Rabbi Elijah of London*, ed. M. Y. L. Sacks (Jerusalem, 1956)

Missale ad usum insignis ecclesiae Eboracensis, ed. W. Henderson, 2 vols., Publications of the Surtees Society 59-60 (Durham, 1872-74)

Monmouth, Geoffrey of, *The History of the Kings of Britain*, trans. L. Thorpe, Penguin Classics (Harmondsworth, 1966)

_____, *The Historia Regum Britannie of Geoffrey of Monmouth I: Bern Burgerbibliothek, MS. 568*, ed. N. Wright (Cambridge, 1985)

_____, *The History of the Kings of Britain: An Edition and Translation of* De gestis Britonum (Historia regum Britanniae), ed. M. D. Reeve and transl. N. Wright (Woodbridge, 2007)

Monmouth, Thomas of, *The Life and Miracles of St William of Norwich*, ed. and trans. A. Jessopp and M. R. James (Cambridge, 1896)

Neckam, Alexander, *Alexandri Neckam De Naturis Rerum Libri Duo*, ed. T. Wright, RS 34 (London, 1863)

Newburgh, William of, *Guilielmi Neubrigensis Historia sive Chronica Rerum Anglicarum*, ed. T. Hearne, 3 vols. (Oxford, 1719)

_____, 'Historia Rerum Anglicarum', in *The Church Historians of England*, ed. J. Stevenson, 5 vols. (London, 1853-58), IV, pt. 2, 397-672

_____, *Historia Rerum Anglicarum Willelmi Parvi de Newburgh*, ed. H. C. Hamilton, 2 vols. (London, 1856)

_____, 'Historia Rerum Anglicarum', in *Chronicles of the Reigns of Stephen, Henry II and Richard I*, ed. R. Howlett, 4 vols., RS 82 (London, 1884-89), I-II

_____, *William of Newburgh's Explanatio sacri epithalamii in matrem sponsi*, ed. J. C. Gorman, Spicilegium Friburgense 6 (Fribourg, 1960)

_____, *The History of William of Newburgh*, reprint of Stevenson's translation, (Felinfach, 1996)

_____, *The History of English Affairs, Books 1 and 2*, ed. P. G. Walsh and M. Kennedy, 2 vols. (Warminster and Oxford, 1988-2007)

_____, *The Sermons of William of Newburgh : Edited from Oxford, Bodleian Library, MS Rawlinson C.31, London, Lambeth Palace Library, MS 73, and London, British Library, MS Stowe 62*, ed. A. Kraebel, Toronto Medieval Latin Texts 31 (Toronto, 2010)

Niger, Ralph, *Radulfi Nigri Chronica*, ed. R. Anstruther, Caxton Society 13 (London, 1851)

The Original Acta of St Peter's Abbey, Gloucester, c. 1122 to 1263, ed. R. B. Patterson (Gloucester, 1998)

Paris, Matthew, *Matthew Paris's English History from the year 1235 to 1273 translated from the Latin*, ed. J. A. Giles, 3 vols. (London, 1852-54)

_____, *Historia Anglorum*, ed. F. Madden, 3 vols., RS 44 (London, 1866-9)

_____, *Chronica Majora*, ed. H. R. Luard, 7 vols., RS 57 (London, 1872-83)

Patrologiae Cursus Completus. Series Latina, ed. J.-P. Migne, 221 vols. (Paris, 1844-64)

Patrologiae Cursus Completus. Series Graeco-Latina, ed. J.-P. Migne, 162 vols. (Paris, 1857-1912)

Pleas before the King or his Justices, 1198–1202, ed. D. M. Stenton, 4 vols., Selden Soc. 67-8 and 83-4 (London, 1952-67)

Poitiers, William of, *The Gesta Guillelmi of William of Poitiers*, ed. R. H. C. Davis and M. Chibnall, OMT (Oxford 1998)

Recueil des actes de Henri II, ed. L. Delisle, 3 vols. (Paris, 1916-27)

Red Book of the Exchequer, ed. H. Hall, 3 vols., RS 99 (London, 1896)

Rigord, *Oeuvres de Rigord et de Guillaume le Breton, historiens de Philippe-Auguste*, ed. H. F. Delaborde, 3 vols. (Paris, 1882-85)

Rolls of the Justices in Eyre: Being the Rolls of Pleas and Assizes for Yorkshire in 3 Henry III (1218-19), ed. D. M. Stenton, Selden Soc. 56 (London, 1937)

Rothenburg, Meir of, *Responsa of Meir of Rothenburg* (Prague, 1608)

Rotuli Chartarum in Turri Londinensi Asservati: Ab Anno 1199-1216, ed. T. D. Duffy, Record Commission (London, 1837)

Rotuli Litterarum Clausarum in Turri Londinensi Asservati, ed. T. D. Hardy, 2

vols., Record Commission (London, 1833-44)

Rotuli Litterarum Patentium in Turri Londinensi Asservati, 1201-1216, ed. T. D. Hardy, Record Commission (London, 1835)

Rotuli de Oblatis et Finibus in Turri Londinensi Asservati, tempore regis Johannis, ed. T. D. Hardy, Record Commission (London, 1835)

Saint Richard of Chichester: The Sources for his Life, ed. D. Jones, Sussex Record Society 79 (Lewes, 1995)

Salisbury, John of, *Ioannis Saresberiensis Policraticus*, ed. K. S. B. Keats-Rohan, Corpus Christianorum Continuatio Medievalis 118 (Turnhout, 1993)

The Sarum Missal in English, trans. F. E. Warren, 2 vols., Alcuin Club Collections 11 (London, 1913)

The Sarum Missal: Edited From Three Early Manuscripts, ed. J. Wickham Legg (Oxford, 1916)

Sefer Gezerot Ashkenaz ve-Zarfat, ed. A. Habermann (Jerusalem, 1945)

Select Cases in the Court of King's Bench, ed. G. O. Sayles, 7 vols., Selden Soc. 55, 57-8, 74, 76, 82, 88 (London, 1936-71)

Select Charters and Other Illustrations of English Constitutional History from the earliest times to the Reign of Edward the First, ed. W. Stubbs, rev. by H. W. C. Davis, 9th ed. (Oxford, 1913)

Select Pleas, Starrs and Other Records from the Rolls of the Exchequer of the Jews, 1220-1284, ed. J. M. Rigg, Selden Soc. 15 (London, 1902)

Seville, Isidore of, *The Etymologies of Isidore of Seville*, trans. S. A. Barney, W. J. Lewis et al. (Cambridge, 2006)

Shetaroth: Hebrew Deeds of English Jews before 1290, ed. M. D. Davis, Publications of The Anglo-Jewish Historical Exhibition 2 (London, 1888)

Statutes of the Realm, 1101-1713, 11 vols., Record Commission (London, 1810-28)

Three Rolls of the King's Court in the Reign of King Richard I, AD 1194-1195, PRS 14 (London, 1891)

Tyre, William of, continuation of, *Die lateinische Fortsetzung Wilhelms von Tyrus*, ed. M. Salloch (Leipzig, 1934)

Venerable, Peter the, *Petri Venerabilis Adversus Iudeorum inveteratam duritiem*, ed. Y. Friedman, Corpus Christianorum. Continuatio Mediaevalis 58 (Turnhout, 1985)

The Visitation of Shropshire, taken in the year 1623, ed. G. Grazebrook and J. P. Rylands, 2 vols., Harleian Society Publications 28 and 29 (London, 1889)

Vitalis, Orderic, *The Ecclesiastical History of Orderic Vitalis*, ed. M. Chibnall, 6 vols. OMT (Oxford, 1968-80)

Voragine, Jacobus de, *The Golden Legend: Readings on the Saints*, trans. by W. G. Ryan, 2 vols. (Princeton, 1993)

Wales, Gerald of, *Giraldi Cambrensis Opera*, ed. J. S. Brewer, J. Dimock and G. Warner, 8 vols., RS 21 (London, 1861-91)

———, *The Autobiography of Giraldus Cambrensis*, ed. H. E. Butler (London, 1937)

_____, *The Jewel of the Church, a translation of* Gemma ecclesiastica *by Giraldus Cambrensis*, ed. J. J. Hagen (Leiden, 1979)

_____, 'Vita Sancti Remigii', in *Giraldi Cambrensis Opera*, ed. J. S. Brewer, J. Dimock and G. Warner, 8 vols., RS 21 (London, 1861-91), VII, 1-80

Wendover, Roger of, *The Flowers of History*, ed. H. G. Hewlett, 3 vols., RS 84 (London, 1886-9)

York Minster Fasti: Being Notes on the Dignitaries, Archdeacons and Prebendaries in the Church of York prior to the year 1307, ed. C. T. Clay, 2 vols., YAS, Record Series 123 and 124 (Wakefield, 1958-9)

York Mystery Plays: A Selection in Modern Spelling, ed. R. Beadle and P. M. King (Oxford, 1984)

Yorkshire Deeds, ed. W. Brown, C. T. Clay and M. J. S. Price, 10 vols., YAS, Record Series 39, 50, 63, 65, 69, 76, 83, 102, 111, 120 (Leeds, 1909-55)

Zurich, M. of, *Sefer Hasemak mi-Zurich*, ed. I. J. Har-Shoshanim-Rosenberg, 3 vols. (Jerusalem, 1973)

Secondary Works

Abrahams, I., 'The Northampton *Donum* of 1194', *JHSE Miscellanies* 1 (1925), pp. lix-lxxiv

Abrahams, M., 'Leaf from an English *Siddur* of the Twelfth Century', *Jews' College Jubilee Volume* (London, 1906)

Abulafia, A. Sapir, 'Jewish Carnality in Twelfth-Century Renaissance Thought', in *Christianity and Judaism*, ed. D. Wood, Studies in Church History 29 (Oxford, 1992), pp. 59-75

_____, 'Bodies in the Jewish-Christian Debate', in *Framing Medieval Bodies*, ed. S. Kay and M. Rubin (Manchester, 1994), pp. 123-37

_____, *Christians and Jews in the Twelfth-Century Renaissance* (London, 1995)

_____, 'Invectives against Christianity in the Hebrew Chronicles of the First Crusade', in A. Sapir Abulafia, *Christians and Jews in Dispute: Disputational Literature and the Rise of Anti-Judaism in the West (c.1000–1150)* (Aldershot, 1998), ch. XVIII, pp. 66-72.

_____, 'Twelfth-Century Christian Expectations of Jewish Conversion: A Case Study of Peter of Blois', *Aschkenas* 8 (1998), 45-70

_____, *Christian-Jewish Relations, 1000–1300: Jews in the Service of Medieval Christendom* (Harlow, 2011)

Addyman, P. V., 'Excavations at Baile Hill, York', *Château Gaillard. Etudes de Castellogie Médiévale* 5 (1972), 7-12

_____, and Priestley, J., 'Baile Hill, York', *Archaeological Journal* 134 (1977), 115-56

Adler, M., 'Benedict the Gildsman of Winchester', *JHSE Miscellanies* 4 (1942), 1-8

Agus, I. A., *Urban Civilization in Pre-Crusade Europe: A Study of Organized Town-Life in Northwestern Europe during the Tenth and Eleventh Centuries based on the Responsa Literature*, 2 vols. (New York, 1965)

Alexander, J. C., 'On the Social Construction of Moral Universals: The "Holocaust" from War Crime to Trauma Drama', in J. C. Alexander et al., *Cultural Trauma and Collective Identity* (Berkeley CA, 2004), pp. 196-263

Alexander, M., 'A Possible Synagogue in Guildford', in *Religion and Belief in Medieval Europe: Papers of the 'Medieval Europe Brugge 1997 Conference'* IV, ed. G. de Boe and F. Verhaeghe, I.A.P. rapporten 4 (Zellik, 1997), pp. 201-12.

Arnold, J. H., *Belief and Unbelief in Medieval Europe* (London, 2005)

Assis, Y., '"Sefarad": A Definition in the Context of a Cultural Encounter', in *Encuentros and Desencuentros: Spanish-Jewish Cultural Interaction throughout History*, ed. C. C. Parrondo et al. (Tel Aviv, 2000), pp. 29-37

Aurell, M., *The Plantagenet Empire, 1154–1224* (Harlow, 2007)

Austin, G., *Shaping Church Law around the Year 1000: The Decretum of Burchard of Worms*, Church, Faith and Culture in the Medieval West (Aldershot, 2009)

Ayers, B., 'The Urban Landscape', in *Medieval Norwich*, ed. C. Rawcliffe and R. Wilson (London, 2004), pp. 1-28

Baldwin, J. W., 'The Intellectual Preparation for the Canon of 1215 against Ordeals', *Speculum* 36 (1961), 613-36

_____, *Masters, Princes and Merchants: The Social Views of Peter the Chanter and his Circle*, 2 vols. (Princeton, 1970)

Bale, A., 'Richard of Devizes and Fictions of Judaism', *Jewish Culture and History* 3 (2000), 55-72

_____, '"House Devil, Town Saint": Anti-Semitism and Hagiography in Medieval Suffolk', in *Chaucer and the Jews: Sources, Contexts, Meanings*, ed. S. Delany (New York, 2002), pp. 185-212

_____, 'Fictions of Judaism in England before 1290', in *The Jews in Medieval Britain: Historical, Literary, and Archaeological Perspectives*, ed. P. Skinner (Woodbridge, 2003), pp. 129–44

_____, *The Jew in the Medieval Book: English Antisemitisms, 1350–1500* (Cambridge, 2006)

_____, 'The Female "Jewish" Libido in Medieval Culture', in *The Erotic in the Literature of Medieval Britain*, ed. A. Hopkins and C. Rushton (Cambridge, 2007), pp. 94-104

_____, *Feeling Persecuted: Christians, Jews, and Images of Violence in the Middle Ages* (London, 2010)

Band, A. J., 'Scholarship as Lamentation: Shalom Spiegel on "The Binding of Isaac"', *Jewish Social Studies* n.s. 5 (1998/99), 80-90

Barrow, G. W. S., 'The Bearded Revolutionary: The Story of a Twelfth-Century London Student in Revolt', *History Today* 19 (1969), 679–87

Bartlet, S., *Licoricia of Winchester: Marriage, Motherhood and Murder in the Medieval Anglo-Jewish Community* (London, 2009)

Bartlett, R., *England under the Norman and Angevin Kings, 1075–1225* (Oxford, 2000)

_____, *Gerald of Wales: A Voice of the Middle Ages* (Stroud, 2006)

Bate, K., 'Exeter, Joseph of', *ODNB*, online edn (Oxford, 2004)

Bates, D., *Bishop Remigius of Lincoln, 1067–92* (Lincoln, 1992)

Baumgarten, E., *Mothers and Children: Jewish Family Life in Medieval Europe* (Princeton, 2004)

Bautier, R.-H., 'Le cheminement du sceau et de la bulle', *Revue française d'héraldique et de sigillographie* 54-59 (1984-89), 41-84

Bedos-Rezak, B., 'Les sceaux juifs français', in *Art et archéologie des juifs en France médiévale*, ed. B. Blumenkranz (Toulouse, 1980), pp. 207-28

_____, 'Les Juifs et l'écrit dans la mentalité eschatologique du Moyen Age chrétien occidental (France, 1000-1200)', *Annales. Économies. Sociétés. Civilisations* 49 (1994), 1049-63

Beit-Arié, M., 'Hebrew Script in Spain: Developments, Offshoots and Vicissitudes', in *Moreshet Sefarad: The Sephardi Legacy*, ed. H. Beinart, 2 vols. (Jerusalem, 1992), I, pp. 282-317

Bell, A. A., 'Josephus and Pseudo-Hegesippus', in *Josephus, Judaism and Christianity*, ed. L. H. Feldman and G. Hata (Leiden, 1987), pp. 349-61

Bell, D. N., 'The Books of Flaxley Abbey', *Analecta Cisterciensia* 43 (1987), 92-110

_____, *The Libraries of the Cistercians, Gilbertines and Premonstratensians*, Corpus of British Medieval Library Catalogues 3 (Oxford 1992)

Bennett, J. M., *Ale, Beer and Brewsters in England: Women's Work in a Changing World 1300–1600* (Oxford, 1996)

Berger, B.-D., *Le drame liturgique de pâques du Xe au XIIIe siècle: Liturgie et théâtre*, Théologie Historique 37 (Paris, 1976)

Beveridge, W. H., 'The Yield and Price of Corn in the Middle Ages', *Economic History* 1 (1927), 155–67

Biale, D., *Blood and Belief: The Circulation of a Symbol between Christians and Jews* (Berkeley CA, 2007)

Biddle, M and Keene, D., 'Winchester in the Eleventh and Twelfth Centuries', in *Winchester in the Early Middle Ages: An Edition and Discussion of the Winton Domesday*, ed. M. Biddle, Winchester Studies 1 (Oxford, 1976), pp. 241-448

Biller, P., 'Words and the Medieval Notion of "Religion"', *Journal of Ecclesiastical History* 36 (1985), 351-69

_____, 'William of Newburgh and the Cathar Mission to England', in *Life and Thought in the Northern Church c.1100–c.1700: Essays in Honour of Claire Cross*, ed. D. Wood, Studies in Church History, Subsidia Series 12 (Woodbridge 1999), pp. 10-30

Blackburn, M., 'Coinage and Currency', in *The Anarchy of King Stephen's Reign*, ed. E. King (Oxford, 1994), pp. 145-205

Blumenkranz, B., 'Perfidia', *Archivium Latinitatis Medii Aevi, Bulletin Du Cange* 22 (1952), 157-70

_____, *Le juif médiéval au miroir de l'art chrétien* (Paris, 1966)

Blurton, H., 'Richard of Devizes's *Cronicon*, Menippean Satire, and the Jews of Winchester', *Exemplaria* 22 (2010), 265-84

Boase, T. S. R., *The York Psalter in the Library of the Hunterian Museum, Glasgow* (London, 1962)

Bowers, R. H., 'From Rolls to Riches: King's Clerks and Money Lending in Thirteenth-Century England', *Speculum* 58 (1983), 60-71

Boyarin, D., *Border Lines: The Partition of Judaeo-Christianity* (Philadelphia, 2004)

Brand, P., *The Origins of the English Legal Profession* (Oxford, 1992)

_____, 'Jews and the Law in England, 1275–1290', *English Historical Review* 115 (2000), 1138-58

_____, 'Aspects of the Law of Debt, 1189–1307' in *Credit and Debt in Medieval England, c.1180–c.1350*, ed. P. R. Schofield and N. J. Mayhew (Oxford, 2002), pp. 19-41

_____, 'The Jewish Community in the Records of Royal Government', in *Jews in Medieval Britain: Historical Literary and Archaeological Perspectives*, ed. P. Skinner (Woodbridge, 2003), pp. 73-83

_____, 'Introduction', in *Plea Rolls of the Exchequer of the Jews preserved in the National Archives (formerly the Public Record Office) VI: Edward I, 1279-81*, ed. P. Brand (London, 2005), pp. 1-73

Britnell, R. H., *The Commercialisation of English Society, 1000–1500*, 2nd edn (Manchester, 1996)

Brody, R., *The Geonim of Babylonia and the Shaping of Medieval Jewish Culture* (New Haven CT, 1998)

Brooke, C. N. L., *London, 800–1216: The Shaping of a City* (London, 1975)

Brown, D., *Vir Trilinguis: A Study in the Biblical Exegesis of Jerome* (Kampen, 1992)

Brown, G. H., 'The Psalms as the Foundation of Anglo-Saxon Learning', in *The Place of the Psalms in the Intellectual Culture of the Middle Ages*, ed. N. van Deusen (Albany NY, 1999), pp. 1-24

Brown, R. A., 'Framlingham Castle and Bigod, 1154–1216', *Proceedings of the Suffolk Institute of Archaeology and Natural History* 25 (1950), 128-48

_____, *Castles from the Air* (Cambridge, 1989)

Brown, S., *Stained Glass at York Minster* (London, 1999)

Brundage, J. A., *Law, Sex, and Christian Society in Medieval Europe* (Chicago, 1987)

Büntgen, U. et al., '2500 Years of European Climate Variability and Human Susceptibility', *Science* 331 (2011), 578–82

Burrow, J. A., *Gestures and Looks in Medieval Narrative* (Cambridge, 2002)

Carpenter, D., *The Minority of Henry III* (London, 1990)

_____, *The Struggle for Mastery. Britain 1066–1284* (Oxford, 2003).

Carruthers, M., *The Book of Memory: A Study of Memory in Medieval Culture*, 2nd edn (Cambridge, 2008)

Castaigne, E., 'Note sur le sceau que l'on apposait du temps du roi Philippe Auguste sur les obligations dues aux Juifs', *Bulletin de la Société Archéologique et Historique de la Charente* (1863), 53-8

Chazan, R., *Medieval Jewry in Northern France: A Political and Social History* (Baltimore, 1973)

_____, ed., *Church, State, and Jew in the Middle Ages* (New York, 1980)

_____, *European Jewry and the First Crusade* (Berkeley CA, 1987)

_____,'The Facticity of Medieval Narrative: A Case Study of the Hebrew First Crusade Narratives', *AJSR*16 (1991), 31-56

_____, 'Ephraim ben Jacob's Compilation of Twelfth-Century Persecutions', *Jewish Quarterly Review* 84:4 (1994), 397-416

_____, *In the Year 1096: The First Crusade and the Jews* (Philadelphia, 1996)

_____, *God, Humanity, and History: The Hebrew First Crusade Narratives* (Berkeley CA, 2000)

_____, 'The Deteriorating Image of the Jews – Twelfth and Thirteenth Centuries', in *Christendom and its Discontents: Exclusion, Persecution, and Rebellion, 1000–1500*, ed. S. L. Waugh and P. D. Diehl (Cambridge, 2002), pp. 220-33

Cheney, C. R., *Hubert Walter* (London, 1967)

Cheney, M. G., *Roger, Bishop of Worcester, 1164–1179* (Oxford, 1980)

_____, 'Inalienability in Mid-Twelfth-Century England: Enforcement and Consequences', in *Proceedings of the Sixth International Congress of Medieval Canon Law, Berkeley, California, 28 July–2 August 1980*, ed. S. Kuttner and K. Pennington, Monumenta Iuris Canonici Series C: Subsidia 7 (Vatican City, 1985), pp. 467-78

Cheyette, F. L., *Ermengard of Narbonne and the World of the Troubadours* (Ithaca NY, 2001)

Childs, W. R., *Anglo-Castilian Trade in the Later Middle Ages* (Manchester, 1978)

Clanchy, M. T., *From Memory to Written Record: England 1066–1307*, 2nd edn (Oxford, 1993)

Clark, J., *Clifford's Tower and the Castle of York* (London, 2010)

Clark, J., and Field Archaeology Services, *Historic Buildings Analysis: Clifford's Tower, York, Report for English Heritage* (London, 2005)

Clayton, M., *The Cult of the Virgin Mary in Anglo-Saxon England* (Cambridge, 1990)

_____, 'The Transitus Mariae: The Tradition and Its Origins', *Apocrypha* 10 (1999), 74-98.

Cohen, J., *The Friars and the Jews: The Evolution of Medieval Anti-Judaism* (Ithaca NY, 1982)

_____, 'The Jews as the Killers of Christ in the Latin Tradition. From Augustine to the Friars', *Traditio* 39 (1983), 1-27

_____, *Living Letters of the Law: Ideas of the Jew in Medieval Christianity* (Berkeley CA, 1999)

_____, 'A 1096 Complex? Constructing the First Crusade in Jewish Historical Memory, Medieval and Modern', in *Jews and Christians in Twelfth-Century Europe*, ed. M. A. Signer and J. van Engen (Notre Dame IN, 2000), pp. 9-26

_____, *Sanctifying the Name of God: Jewish Martyrs and Jewish Memories of the*

First Crusade (Philadelphia, 2004)

Cohen, J. J. , *Hybridity, Identity and Monstrosity in Medieval Britain: On Difficult Middles* (New York, 2006)

_____, 'Introduction: Infinite Realms', in *Cultural Diversity in the British Middle Ages: Archipelago, Island, England*, ed. J. Cohen (Basingstoke, 2008), pp. 1-16

Coldstream, N., 'York Chapter House', *Journal of the British Archaeological Association*, 3rd s. 35 (1972), 15-23

Colvin, H. M., *The White Canons in England* (Oxford, 1951)

_____, ed., *The History of the King's Works*, 6 vols. (London, 1963-82)

Connolly, D. K., *The Maps of Matthew Paris: Medieval Journeys through Space, Time and Liturgy* (Woodbridge, 2009)

Constable, G., 'Introduction', in *Apologiae Duae*, ed. R. B. C. Huygens, Corpus Christianorum, Continuatio Mediaevalis 62 (Turnhout, 1985), pp. 47–130

Cooper, T. P., *York: The Story of its Walls, Bars and Castles* (London, 1904)

_____, *The History of the Castle of York from its Foundation to the Present Day* (London, 1911)

Court, E. N. van, '"The Siege of Jerusalem" and Augustinian Historians: Writing about Jews in Fourteenth-Century England', *Chaucer Review* 29 (1995), 227-48

_____, 'Socially Marginal, Culturally Central: Representing Jews in Late Medieval English Literature', *Exemplaria* 12 (2000), 292-326

_____, 'Invisible in Oxford: Medieval Jewish History in Modern England', *Shofar* 26 (2008), 1-19

Cowdrey, H. E. J., 'Martyrdom and the First Crusade', in *Crusade and Settlement*, ed. P. Edbury (Cardiff, 1985), pp. 46-56.

_____, 'Remigius (d. 1092)', *ODNB*, online edn (Oxford, 2004)

Cramer, A. C., 'The Jewish Exchequer: An Inquiry into its Fiscal Functions', *American Historical Review* 45 (1940), 327-37

_____, 'The Origins and Functions of the Jewish Exchequer', *Speculum* 16 (1941), 226-9

Creighton, O. and Higham, R., *Medieval Town Walls: An Archaeology and Social History of Urban Defence* (Stroud, 2005)

Crick, J., *The Historia Regum Britannie of Geoffrey of Monmouth IV: Dissemination and Reception in the Later Middle Ages* (Cambridge, 1991)

Crook, D., *Records of the General Eyre* (London, 1982)

_____, 'The Earliest Exchequer Estreat and the Forest Eyres of Henry II and Thomas fitz Bernard, 1175–80', in *Records, Administration and Aristocratic Society in the Anglo-Norman Realm*, ed. N. Vincent (Woodbridge, 2000), pp. 29-44

Crosby, A., *A History of Thetford* (Chichester, 1986)

Crouch, D., *The Reign of King Stephen 1135–1154* (Harlow, 2000)

Curschmann, F., *Hungersnöte im Mittelalter: ein Beitrag zur deutschen Wirtschaftsgeschichte des 8. bis 13. Jahrhunderts*, Leipziger Studien aus dem Gebiet der Geschichte 6.1 (Leipzig, 1900)

Dahan, G., 'L'Article *Iudei* de la *Summa Abel* de Pierre le Chantre', *Revue des Études Augustiniennes* 27 (1981), 105-26

_____, 'Exégèse et polémique dans les *Commentaires de la Genèse* d'Étienne Langton', in *Les juifs au regard de l'histoire. Mélanges en l'honneur de Bernhard Blumenkranz*, ed. G. Dahan (Paris, 1985), pp. 129-48

_____, *Les intellectuels chrétiens et les juifs au moyen âge* (Paris, 1999)

_____, 'Deux Psautiers Hébraïques Glosés en Latin', *Revue des Études Juives* 158 (1999), 61-87

Dalton, P., *Conquest, Anarchy and Lordship: Yorkshire, 1066–1154*, Cambridge Studies in Medieval Life and Thought, Fourth Series 27 (Cambridge, 1994)

Dan, J., *The Unique Cherub Circle: A School of Mystics and Esoterics in Medieval Germany* (Tübingen, 1999)

Davies, R., 'The Medieval Jews of York', *YAJ* 3 (1875), 147-97

Davis, G. R. C., *Medieval Cartularies of Great Britain: A Short Catalogue* (London, 1958)

Davis, J., 'Baking for the Common Good: A Reassessment of the Assize of Bread in Medieval England', *Economic History Review* 57 (2004), 465–502

Davis, R. H. C., *King Stephen, 1135–58*, 3rd edn (London, 1990)

Dean, E. T., *Shook over Hell: Post-Traumatic Stress, Vietnam and the Civil War* (Cambridge MA, 1997)

Dobson, R. B., *The Jews of Medieval York and the Massacre of March 1190*, Borthwick Papers 45 (York, 1974)

_____, 'The Decline and Expulsion of the Medieval Jews of York', *JHSE Transactions* 26 (1979 for 1974), 34-52

_____, 'The Jews of Medieval Cambridge', *JHS* 32 (1993 for 1990-2), 1-24

_____, 'A Minority within a Minority: The Jewesses of Thirteenth-Century England', in *Minorities and Barbarians in Medieval Life and Thought*, ed. S. J. Ridyard and R. G. Benson, Sewanee Mediaeval Studies 7 (Sewanee TN, 1996), pp. 27-48

_____, The Jewish Communities of Medieval England: The Collected Essays of R.B. Dobson, ed. H. M. Birkett, Borthwick Texts and Studies 39 (York, 2010)

_____, 'The Medieval York Jewry Reconsidered', in *The Jews of Medieval Britain: Historical, Literary and Archaeological Perspectives*, ed. Patricia Skinner (Woodbridge, 2003), pp. 145-56

Donovan, C., *The De Brailes Hours: Shaping the Book of Hours in Thirteenth-Century Oxford* (London, 1991)

Duffy, E., *The Stripping of the Altars: Traditional Religion in England, 1400–1580* (New Haven CT, 1994)

Dyer, C., *Standards of Living in the Later Middle Ages: Social Change in England c. 1200–1520* (Cambridge, 1989)

Edwards, J., 'The Church and the Jews in Medieval England', in *The Jews in Medieval Britain: Historical, Literary and Archaeological Perspectives*, ed. P. Skinner (Woodbridge, 2003), pp. 85-95

Einbinder, S. L., 'Meir b. Elijah of Norwich: Persecution and Poetry among Medieval English Jews', *JMH* 26 (2000), 145-62

_____, *Beautiful Death: Jewish Poetry and Martyrdom in Medieval France* (Princeton, 2002)

_____, *No Place of Rest: Jewish Literature, Expulsion, and the Memory of Medieval France* (Philadelphia, 2009)

Elliott, D., *Fallen Bodies: Pollution, Sexuality, and Demonology in the Middle Ages* (Philadelphia, 1999)

Ellis, C., *Hubert de Burgh: A Study in Constancy* (London 1952)

Elukin, J., *Living Together, Living Apart: Rethinking Jewish-Christian Relations in the Middle Ages* (Princeton, 2007)

Emanuel, S., 'Biographical Data on R. Baruch b. Isaac', *Tarbiz* 69 (2000), 423-40

_____, *Fragments of the Tablets: Lost Books of the Tosaphists* (Jerusalem, 2006)

Emmerson, R. K., *Antichrist in the Middle Ages: A Study of Medieval Apocalypticism, Art, and Literature* (Manchester, 1981)

Epstein, J. N. *Studies in Talmudic Literature and Semitic Languages* II, pt 2 (Jerusalem, 1988)

Feldman, L. H., *Josephus and Modern Scholarship, 1937–1980* (Berlin, 1984)

Fellows-Jensen, G., 'The Anglo-Scandinavian Street-Names of York', in *Aspects of Anglo-Scandinavian York*, ed. R. A. Hall et al., The Archaeology of York 8:4 (York, 2004), pp. 357-71

Flahiff, G. B., 'Ralph Niger: An Introduction to his Life and Works', *Mediaeval Studies* 2 (1940), 104-36

Flanagan, S., *Doubt in an Age of Faith: Uncertainty in the Long Twelfth Century* (Turnhout, 2008)

Fleischer, E., 'Christian-Jewish Relations in the Middle Ages Distorted', *Zion* 59 (1994), 267-313

Fleming, R., *Kings and Lords in Conquest England*, Cambridge Studies in Medieval Life and Thought, Fourth Series 15 (Cambridge, 1991)

_____, 'Bones for Historians: Putting the Body back into Biography', in *Writing Medieval Biography, 750–1250: Essays in Honour of Professor Frank Barlow*, ed. D. Bates, J. Crick and S. Hamilton (Woodbridge, 2006), pp. 29-48

Fogle, L., 'Between Christianity and Judaism: The Identity of Converted Jews in Medieval London', *Essays in Medieval Studies* 22 (2005), 107-16

Frassetto, M., ed., *Medieval Purity and Piety: Essays on Medieval Clerical Celibacy and Religious Reform* (New York, 1998)

Fredriksen, P., *Augustine and the Jews. A Christian Defence of Jews and Judaism* (New York, 2008)

French, T. W., 'Observations on Some Medieval Glass in York Minster', *Antiquaries Journal* 51 (1971), 86-93

_____, 'The Dating of the Lady Chapel in York Minster', *Antiquaries Journal* 52 (1972), 309-19

Friedman, S., 'The Further Adventures of Rav Kahana: Between Babylonia and Palestine', in *The Talmud Yerushalmi and Graeco-Roman Culture*, ed. P. Schaefer, 3 vols., Texte und Studien zum antiken Judentum 71, 79, 93 (Tübingen, 1998-2002), III, pp. 247-71.

Fudeman, K. A., *Vernacular Voices: Language and Identity in Medieval French Jewish Communities* (Philadelphia, 2010)

Gafni, I., 'Talmudic Babylonia and the Land of Israel: Between Subservience and Assertiveness', *Te'uda* 12 (1996), 97-109

_____, 'How Babylonia became "Zion": Shifting Identities in Late Antiquity', in *Jewish Identities in Antiquity: Studies in Memory of Menahem Stern*, ed. L. I. Levine and D. R. Schwartz (Tübingen, 2009), pp. 333-48

Galinsky, Y., 'Come and Make a Sefer Torah from Two Parts: On Clarification of Rabbi Moses of Couçy's Intent in Writing the Sma'g', *Ha-Ma'ayan* 35 (1994), 23-31

Gameson, R., *The Manuscripts of Early Norman England (c.1066–1130)* (Oxford, 1999)

Geremek, B., *Poverty: A History*, trans. A. Kolakowska (Oxford, 1994)

Gershon, S. W., *Kol Nidrei: Its Origins, Development, and Significance* (Northvale NJ, 1994)

Gervers, M. and Hamonic, N., '*Pro Amore Dei*: Diplomatic Evidence of Social Conflict during the Reign of King John', in *Law as Profession and Practice in Medieval Europe: Essays in Honor of James A. Brundage*, ed. K. Pennington and M. H. Eichbauer (Farnham, 2011), pp. 231-62

Getz, F., *Medicine in the English Middle Ages* (Princeton, 1998)

Gieysztor, A., 'The Genesis of the Crusades: The Encyclical of Sergius IV (1009–1012)', *Medievalia et Humanistica* 5 (1948), 1-25; 6 (1950), 3-34

Gillingham, J., *Richard I* (New Haven CT, 1999)

_____, 'Historians without Hindsight: Coggeshall, Diceto and Howden on the Early Years of John's Reign', in *King John: New Interpretations*, ed. S. D. Church (Woodbridge 1999), pp. 1-26

_____, 'Royal Newsletters, Forgeries and English Historians: Some Links Between Court and History in the Reign of Richard I', in *La Cour Plantagenêt (1154-1204): Actes du colloque tenu à Thouars du 30 avril au 2 mai 1999*, ed. M. Aurell (Poitiers, 2000), pp. 171-85

_____, *The Angevin Empire*, 2nd edn (London, 2001)

_____, 'William of Newburgh and Emperor Henry VI', in *Auxilia Historica: Festschrift für Peter Acht zum 90*, ed. W. Koch et al. (Munich, 2001), pp. 51-71

_____, 'Two Yorkshire Historians Compared: Roger of Howden and William of Newburgh', *Haskins Society Journal* 12 (2002), 15-37

Godding, P., and Pycke, J., 'Le Paix de Valenciennes de 1114: Commentaire et édition critique', *Bulletin de la Commission Royale pour la Publication des Anciennes Lois et Ordonnances de Belgique* 29 (1981), 1-142

Goering, J., 'Robert Grosseteste and the Jews of Leicester', in *Robert Grosseteste and the Beginnings of a British Theological Tradition. Papers delivered at the Grosseteste Colloquium held at Greyfriars, Oxford on 3ʳᵈ July 2002*, ed.

M. O'Carroll, Bibliotheca Seraphico-Capuccina 69 (Rome, 2003), pp. 181-200

_____, 'Chobham, Thomas of', *ODNB*, online edn (Oxford, 2004)

Le Goff, J., 'Le rituel symbolique de la vassalité', in J. Le Goff, *Pour un autre moyen âge* (Paris, 1977), pp. 349-419

Golb, N., *The Jews in Medieval Normandy: A Social and Intellectual History* (Cambridge, 1998)

Goldin, S. *The Ways of Jewish Martyrdom*, trans. Yigal Levin (Turnhout, 2008)

Goodich, M., *Miracles and Wonders: The Development of the Concept of Miracle, 1150–1350* (Aldershot, 2007)

Goodwin, D., *'Take Hold of the Robe of a Jew': Herbert of Bosham's Christian Hebraism* (Leiden, 2006)

Grayzel, S., *The Church and the Jews in the XIIIth Century: A Study of their Relations during the years 1198–1254*, revised edn (New York, 1966)

Green, J., 'King Henry I and Northern England', *TRHS* 6th s. 17 (2007), 35-55

Greenland, J. J., *The Iconography of the Hunterian Psalter: University of Glasgow MS Hunter 229*, 2 vols. (Cambridge, 1996)

Gregg, J., *Devils, Women, and Jews: Reflections of the Other in Medieval Sermon Stories* (New York, 1997)

Grierson, P., 'Weights and Measures', in *Domesday Book Studies*, ed. A. Williams and R. W. H. Erskine (1987), pp. 80-5

Groot, R., 'When Suicide became Felony', *Journal of Legal History* 21 (2000), 1-20

Gross, C., 'The Exchequer of the Jews of England in the Middle Ages', in *Papers Read at the Anglo-Jewish Historical Exhibition*, ed. J. Jacobs and L. Wolf (London, 1888)

Grossman, A., *The Early Sages of Ashkenaz: Their Lives, Leadership and Works (900–1096)* (Jerusalem, 1981)

_____, 'Ben Sefarad Le-Tzarfat: Hakesharim Ben Kehilot Yirael Shebesefarad Ha-Muslemit Uben Kehilot Tzarfat', in *Exile and Diaspora: Studies in the History of the Jewish People Presented to Professor Haim Beinart on the Occassion of his Seventieth Birthday*, ed. A. Mirsky, A. Grossman and Y. Kaplan (Jerusalem, 1988), pp. 75-101

_____, 'Meandalusia Le-Eropa: Yahasam Shel Hakmei Ashkenaz Vetzarfat Bameot Ha-12-13 El Sifrei Hahalakha Shel Harif Ve-Harambam', *Peamim* 80 (1999), 14–32

_____, *Pious and Rebellious: Jewish Women in Medieval Europe* (Waltham, 2004)

Gruber, M. I., *Rashi's Commentary on Psalms* (Leiden, 2004)

Gruber, R. E., *Virtually Jewish: Reinventing Jewish Culture in Europe* (Berkeley CA, 2002)

Halamish, M., 'An Early Version of "Alenu le-Shabeah"', *Sinai* 110 (1992), 262-5

Hall, R., *English Heritage Book of Viking Age York* (London, 1994)

_____ and K. Hunter-Mann, ed., *Medieval Urbanism in Coppergate: Refining a Townscape*, The Archaeology of York 10:6 (York, 2002)

Hames, H., 'The Limits of Conversion: Ritual Murder and the Virgin Mary in the Account of Adam of Bristol', *JMH* 33 (2007) 43-59

Hamilton, B., *The Leper King and His Heirs: Baldwin IV and the Crusader Kingdom of Jerusalem* (Cambridge, 2000)

Hardison, O. B., *Christian Rite and Christian Drama in the Middle Ages: Essays in the Origin and Early History of Modern Drama* (Baltimore, 1965)

Hardwick, P., 'The Monkeys' Funeral in the Pilgrimage Window, York Minster', *Art History* 23 (2003), 290-9

Hardy, T. D., *Descriptive Catalogue of Materials Relating to the History of Great Britain and Ireland*, 3 vols., RS 26 (London, 1862-71)

Harvey, P. D. A., 'The English Inflation of 1180–1220', *P & P* 61 (1973), 3–30

Hatcher, J., and Miller, E., *Medieval England: Rural Society and Economic Change, 1086–1348* (Harlow, 1978)

Havatselet, A. Y., 'Piske Rabenu Eliyahu mi-Londres', in *Sefer ha-Zikaron li-khvodo ule-zikhro shel ha-gaon ha-gadol ha-dayan rabi Mosheh Svift*, ed. Y. Buksbaum (Jerusalem, 1986), pp. 15-40

————, 'Piske ha-Ram mi-Londres', in *Sefer Zikaron Hesed le-Avraham*, ed. A. Berger (Bene Berak, 1989), pp. 40-46

————, 'Pesakim be-inyane Pesah', *Moriah* 20 (1995), pp. 16-17.

Haverkamp, E., *Hebräische Berichte über die Judenverfolgungen während des Ersten Kreuzzugs* (Hannover, 2005)

Hawkes, J., 'The Wirksworth Slab: An Iconography of Humilitas', *Pernitia: The Journal of the Medieval Academy of Ireland* 9 (1995), 246-89

Hawkins, P. S. and Schildgen, B. D., 'Introduction: Paul's Letter to the Romans in the Middle Ages', in *Medieval Readings of Romans*, ed. W. S. Campbell, P. S. Hawkins and B. D. Schildgen, (London, 2007), pp. 1-10

Heer, F., *The Medieval World: Europe, 1100–1350* (New York, 1962)

Heil, J., '"Deep Enmity" and/or "Close Ties"? Jews and Christians before 1096, Sources, Hermeneutics, and Writing History in 1096', *JSQ* 9 (2002), 259–306

Heiser, R. R., 'Richard I and his Appointments to English Shrievalties', *EHR* 112 (1997), 1–19

Helmholz, R. H., *The Oxford History of the Laws of England: Volume 1: The Canon Law and Ecclesiastical Jurisdiction from 597 to 1640* (Oxford, 2004)

Herschler, M., 'Piske Rabenu Yakar mi-Vienne', in *Sefer ha-Zikaron for Rabi Hayim Shmulevitz*, ed. Y. Buksbaum (Jerusalem, 1980), pp. 283-91

Hill, J. W. F. *Medieval Lincoln* (Cambridge, 1948)

Hillaby, J., 'The London Jewry: William I to John', *JHS* 33 (1995 for 1992-94), 1-44

————, 'Jewish Colonisation in the Twelfth Century', in *The Jews in Medieval Britain: Historical, Literary, and Archaeological Perspectives*, ed. P. Skinner (Woodbridge, 2003), pp. 15-40

Hilton, R. H., 'Freedom and Villeinage in England', *P & P* 31 (1965), 3–19

Holdsworth, C., 'Langton, Stephen', *ODNB*, online edn (Oxford, 2004)

Holt, J. C., *King John*, Historical Association Pamphlets, General Series 53 (London, 1963)

_____, *'Ricardus Rex Anglorum et Dux Normannorum'*, in J. C. Holt, *Magna Carta and Medieval Government*, Studies presented to the International Commission for the History of Representative and Parliamentary Institutions 68 (London, 1985), pp. 67–83

_____, *The Northerners: A Study in the Reign of King John*, 2nd edn (Oxford, 1992)

_____, *Magna Carta*, 2nd edn (Cambridge, 1992)

Horowitz, E., *Reckless Rites, Purim and the Legacy of Jewish Violence* (Princeton, 2006)

Hosler, J. D., 'Henry II, William of Newburgh, and the Development of English Anti-Judaism', in *Christian Attitudes Toward the Jews in the Middle Ages: A Casebook*, ed. M. Frassetto (New York, 2007), pp. 167-82

Hourihane, C., *Pontius Pilate, Anti-Semitism and the Passion in Medieval Art* (Princeton, 2009)

Howe, N., *Migration and Mythmaking in Anglo-Saxon England* (New Haven CT, 1989)

Hudson, J., 'Glanville, Ranulf de (1120s?–1190)', *ODNB*, online edn (Oxford, 2004)

_____, 'L'écrit, les archives et le droit en Angleterre (IXe-XIIe siècle)', *Revue Historique* 315 (2006), 3-35

Hughes, A., *Medieval Manuscripts for Mass and Office: A Guide to their Organization and Terminology* (Toronto, 1982)

Hunt, R.W., *The Schools and the Cloister: The Life and Writings of Alexander Neckam, 1157–1217*, ed. M. Gibson (Oxford, 1984)

Hunter, G. et al., *Clifford's Tower Commemoration, York, 15-18 March 1990: A Programme and Handbook* (York, 1990)

Huscroft, R., *Expulsion: England's Jewish Solution* (Stroud, 2006)

Hyams, P., 'The Jewish Minority in Medieval England, 1066–1290', *Journal of Jewish Studies* 25 (1974), 270-93

_____, 'Trial by Ordeal: The Key to Proof in the Early Common Law', in *Of the Laws and Customs of England: Essays in Honor of Samuel E. Thorne*, ed. T. A. Green, M. Arnold, S. Scully and S. D. White (Chapel Hill NC, 1981), pp. 90-126

_____, 'The Charter as a Source for the Early Common Law', *Journal of Legal History* 12 (1991), 173-89

_____, 'The Jews in Medieval England, 1066–1290', in *England and Germany in the High Middle Ages*, ed. Alfred Haverkamp, Hanna Vollrath and Karl Leyser (Oxford, 1996)

_____, 'The End of Feudalism?', *Journal of Interdisciplinary History* 27 (1997), 655-62

_____, 'Homage and Feudalism: A Judicious Separation', in *Die Gegenwart des Feudalismus*, ed. N. Fryde, P. Monnet and O. G. Oexle (Göttingen, 2003), pp. 13-49

_____, 'Afterword: Neither Unnatural nor Wholly Negative: The Future of Medieval Vengeance', in *Vengeance in the Middle Ages: Emotion, Religion, and Feud*, ed. S. Throop and P. R. Hyams (Farnham, 2010), pp. 203-20

_____, 'The Legal Revolution and the Discourse of Dispute in the Twelfth Century', in *The Cambridge Companion to Medieval English Culture*, ed. A. Galloway (Cambridge, 2011), pp. 43-65

Idel, M., 'The Intention of Prayer in the Beginning of Kabbalah: Between Germany and Provence', in *Porat Yosef: Studies Presented to Rabbi Dr. Joseph Safran*, ed. B. Safran and E. Safran (Hoboken NJ, 1992), pp. 5-14.

Jacobs, J., 'Une lettre française d'un juif anglais au XIIIe siècle', *Revue des Études Juives* 18 (1889), 256-61

Jahncke, R., *Guilelmus Neubrigensis: Ein pragmatischer Geschichtsschreiber des zwölften Jahrhunderts* (Bonn, 1912)

James, M. R., *On the Abbey of St Edmund at Bury*, Publications of the Cambridge Antiquarian Society, Octavo Series 28 (Cambridge, 1895)

_____, *A Descriptive Catalogue of the Manuscripts in the Library of Corpus Christi College Cambridge*, 2 vols. (Cambridge, 1912)

Janson, H. W., *Apes and Ape Lore in the Middle Ages and Renaissance*, Studies of the Warburg Institute 20 (London, 1952)

Jeffery, K., *Clifford's Tower and the Jews of Medieval York* (London, 1995)

Jenkinson, H., 'The Records of Exchequer Receipts from the English Jewry', *JHSE Transactions* 8 (1915-17), 19-54

Joel, B. I., *Catalogue of Hebrew Manuscripts in the Jewish National and University Library* (Jerusalem, 1934)

Jolliffe, J. E. A., *Angevin Kingship*, 2nd edn (London, 1963)

Jones, M., Stocker, D., and Vince, A., *The City by the Pool: Assessing the Archaeology of the City of Lincoln* (Oxford, 2003)

Jordan, W. C., *The French Monarchy and the Jews: From Philip Augustus to the Last Capetians* (Philadelphia, 1989)

_____, 'Jews, Regalian Rights, and the Constitution in Medieval France', AJSR 23 (1998), 1-16

Kanarfogel, E., 'The 'Aliyah of "Three Hundred Rabbis" in 1211: Tosafist Attitudes toward Settling in the Land of Israel', *JQR* 76 (1986), 191–215

_____, *Jewish Education and Society in the High Middle Ages* (Detroit, 1992)

_____, 'Religious Leadership during the Tosafist Period: Between the Academy and the Religious Court', *Jewish Religious Leadership: Image and Reality*, ed. J. Wertheimer (New York, 2004), pp. 265-305

Katz, J., *Exclusiveness and Tolerance: Studies in Jewish-Gentile Relations in Medieval and Modern Times* (London, 1961)

_____, 'Rabbinical Authority and Authorization in the Middle Ages', in J. Katz, *Divine Law in Human Hands: Case Studies in Halakhic Flexibility* (Jerusalem, 1998), pp. 128-45

Kauffmann, C.M., *Romanesque Manuscripts, 1066–1190*, A Survey of Manuscripts Illuminated in the British Isles 3 (London, 1975)

Kaufmann, D., 'Three Centuries of the Genealogy of the Most Eminent An-glo-Jewish Family before 1290', *JQR* o.s. 3 (1891), 555-66

——, 'The Ritual of the Seder and the Agada of the English Jews before the Expulsion', *JQR* o.s. 4 (1892), 550-61

Keene, D., *Survey of Medieval Winchester*, 2 vols. (Oxford, 1985)

Kemp, E. W., *Canonization and Authority in the Western Church* (Oxford, 1948)

Kennedy, M. J. '"Faith in the One God Flowed Over You from the Jews, the Sons of the Patriarchs and the Prophets": William of Newburgh's Writ-ings on Anti-Jewish Violence', *Anglo-Norman Studies* 25 (2003), 139-52

Ker, N. R., ed., *Medieval Libraries of Great Britain: A List of Surviving Books*, 2nd edn (London 1964)

Kermode, J., *Medieval Merchants: York, Beverley and Hull in the Later Middle Ages*, Cambridge Studies in Medieval Life and Thought, Fourth Series 38 (Cambridge, 1998)

Kidson, P., 'Architectural History', in *A History of Lincoln Minster*, ed. D. M. Owen (Cambridge, 1994), pp. 14-46

King, E., ed., *The Anarchy of King Stephen's Reign* (Oxford, 1998)

Knowles, D., Brooke, C. N. L. and London, V. C. M. ed., *Heads of Religious Houses, England and Wales I: 940–1216* (Cambridge, 1972)

Knowles, J. A., 'Notes on Some Windows in the Choir and Lady Chapel of York Minster', *YAJ* 39 (1956), 91-118

Kruger, S., *The Spectral Jew: Conversion and Embodiment in Medieval Europe* (Minneapolis, 2006)

Kurth, B., 'The Iconography of the Wirksworth Slab', *Burlington Magazine for Connoisseurs* 86 (1945), 114-21

LaCapra, D., *Representing the Holocaust: History, Theory, Trauma* (Ithaca NY, 1996)

Lampert, L., *Gender and Jewish Difference from Paul to Shakespeare* (Philadel-phia, 2004)

Langdon, J., *Mills in the Medieval Economy: England, 1300–1540* (Oxford, 2004)

Langmuir, G. I., 'The Knight's Tale: Young Hugh of Lincoln', *Speculum* 47 (1972), 459-82

——, 'Thomas of Monmouth: Detector of Ritual Murder', *Speculum* 59 (1984), 820-46

——, *History, Religion, and Anti-Semitism* (Berkeley CA, 1993)

——, *Toward a Definition of Antisemitism* (Berkeley CA, 1996)

Latimer, P., 'Early Thirteenth-Century Prices', in *King John: New Interpreta-tions*, ed. S. D. Church (Woodbridge, 1999), pp. 41-73

——, 'The English Inflation of 1180–1220 Reconsidered', *P & P* 171 (2001), 3-29

Leibowitz, A., 'Doctors and Medical Knowledge in Tosafist Circles', *Tradi-tion: A Journal of Orthodox Jewish Thought* 42 (2009), 19-34

Levine, R., 'Why Praise Jews: Satire and History in the Middle Ages', *JMH* 12 (1986), 291-6

Levy, N., *Nahalat Naftali* (Presburg, 1891)

Lewy, H., 'Josephus the Physician: A Mediaeval Legend of the Destruction of Jerusalem', *Journal of the Warburg Institute* 1 (1937-8), 221-42

Lilley, J. M., et al., *The Jewish Burial Ground at Jewbury*, The Archaeology of York 12:3 (London, 1994)

Lipman, V. D., *The Jews of Medieval Norwich* (London, 1967)

_____, 'The Anatomy of Medieval Anglo-Jewry', *JHSE Transactions* 21 (1968 for 1962-67) 64-77

_____, 'Jews and Castles in Medieval England', *JHSE Transactions* 28 (1984), 1-28

Lipton, S., *Images of Intolerance: The Representation of the Jews and Judaism in the Bible Moralisée* (Berkeley CA, 1999)

Little, A. G., 'Friar Henry of Wodstone and the Jews', in *Collectanea Franciscana II*, ed. C. L. Kingsford (Manchester, 1922), pp. 150-6

Little, L. K., *Benedictine Maledictions: Liturgical Cursing in Romanesque France* (Ithaca NY, 1993)

Loewe, R., 'Herbert of Bosham's Commentary on Jerome's Hebrew Psalter', *Biblica* 34 (1953), 44-77, 159-92, 275-98

_____, 'The Mediaeval Christian Hebraists of England: Herbert of Bosham and Earlier Scholars', *JHSE Transactions* 17 (1953), 225-49

_____, 'The Mediaeval Christian Hebraists of England: The "superscriptio" Lincolniensis', *Hebrew Union College Annual* 28 (1957), 205-52

_____, 'Alexander Neckam's Knowledge of Hebrew', *Mediaeval and Renaissance Studies* 4 (1958), 17-34

Logan, F. D., 'Thirteen London Jews and Conversion to Christianity: Problems of Apostasy in the 1280s', *BIHR* 45 (1972), 214-29

Lorrey, H., 'Religious Authority, Community Boundaries and the Conversion of Jews in Medieval England', in *Authority and Community in the Middle Ages*, ed. D. Mowbray, R. Purdie and I. Wei (Stroud, 1999), pp. 85-100

Lot, F., *Études critiques sur l'abbaye de Saint-Wandrille* (Paris, 1913)

McEwan, J., 'William FitzOsbert and the Crisis in London in 1196', *Florilegium* 21 (2004), 18-42

McGinn, B., *Antichrist: Two Thousand Years of the Human Fascination with Evil* (New York, 2000)

McKane, W., *Selected Christian Hebraists* (Cambridge, 1989)

McNall, C., 'Some Aspects of the Business of Statutory Debt Registries, 1283–1307', in *Credit and Debt in Medieval England c.1180–c.1350*, ed. P. R. Schofield and N. J. Mayhew (Oxford, 2002), pp. 68-88

Maddicott, J. R., *Simon de Montfort* (Cambridge, 1994)

Madox, T., *The History and Antiquities of the Exchequer of the Kings of England*, 2 vols., 2nd edn (London, 1769)

Maitland, F. W., 'The Deacon and the Jewess; or Apostasy at Common Law', *Law Quarterly Review* 2 (1886), 153-65

_____ and Pollock, F., *History of English Law before the time of Edward I*, 2 vols., 2nd edn (Cambridge, 1898)

Malkiel, D., *Reconstructing Ashkenaz: The Human Face of Franco-German Jewry, 1000–1250* (Stanford CA, 2009)

Marcus, I. G., 'Review: *European Jewry and the First Crusade*', *Speculum* 64 (1989), 685-8

_____, 'History, Story and Collective Memory: Narrativity in Early Ashkenazic Culture', *Prooftexts* 10 (1990), 365-88

_____, 'Jews and Christians Imagining the Other in Medieval Europe', *Prooftexts* 15 (1995), 209-26

_____, *Rituals of Childhood: Jewish Acculturation in Medieval Europe* (New Haven CT, 1996)

_____, 'The Representation of Reality in the Narratives of 1096', *Jewish History* 13 (1999), 37-48

_____, 'Israeli Medieval Jewish Historiography: From Nationalist Positivism to New Cultural and Social Histories', *JSQ* 17 (2010), 244-85

Markowski, M., 'Peter of Blois and the Conception of the Third Crusade', in *The Horns of Hattin*, ed. B. Z. Kedar (Jerusalem, 1992), pp. 261-9

Marmorstein, A., 'Some Hitherto Unknown Jewish Scholars of Angevin England', *JQR* n.s. 19 (1928), 17-36

Meekings, C. A. F., 'Justices of the Jews, 1216–68: A Provisional List', *BIHR* 28 (1955), 173-88

Mellinkoff, R., *Outcasts: Signs of Otherness in Northern European Art from the Later Middle Ages*, 2 vols., California Studies in the History of Art 32 (Berkeley CA, 1993)

Menache, S., 'Faith, Myth, and Politics – the Stereotype of the Jews and their Expulsion from England and France', *JQR* n.s 75 (1985), 351-74

Miller, E., 'Medieval York', in *A History of the County of York: The City of York*, ed. P. M. Tillot, Victoria History of the Counties of England (Oxford 1961), pp. 25-116

_____ and Hatcher, J., *Medieval England: Rural Society and Economic Change, 1086–1348* (Harlow, 1978)

_____ and Hatcher, J., *Medieval England: Towns, Commerce and Crafts, 1086–1348* (London, 1995)

Mills, R., *Suspended Animation: Pain, Pleasure and Punishment in Medieval Culture* (London, 2005)

Miyazaki, M., 'Misericord Owls and Medieval Anti-Semitism', in *Mark of the Beast: The Medieval Bestiary in Art, Life, and Literature*, ed. D. Hassig (New York, 1999), pp. 23-50

Mollat, M., *The Poor in the Middle Ages: An Essay in Social History* (New Haven CT, 1986)

Moor, C., *Knights of Edward I*, 5 vols., Harleian Society Publications 80-4 (London, 1929-32)

Moore, R. I., *The Formation of a Persecuting Society: Power and Deviance in Western Europe, 950–1250* (Oxford, 1987)

Mortensen, L. B., 'The Texts and Contexts of Ancient Roman History in Twelfth-Century Western Scholarship', in *The Perception of the Past in Twelfth-Cen-*

tury Europe, ed. P. Magdalino (London, 1992), pp. 99-116

Moscovitz, L., 'The Formation and Character of the Jerusalem Talmud', in *The Cambridge History of Judaism IV: The late Roman-Rabbinic Period*, ed. S. T. Katz (Cambridge, 2006), pp. 663-77

Mossop, H. R., *The Lincoln Mint c. 890–1279* (Newcastle-upon-Tyne, 1970)

Mozley, J. H., 'Susanna and the Elders: Three Medieval Poems', *Studi Medievali* n.s. 3 (1930), 27-52

Mundill, R. R., 'Anglo-Jewry under Edward I: Credit Agents and their Clients', *JHS* 31 (1990), 1-21

_____, 'Rabbi Elias Menahem: A Late Thirteenth-Century English Entrepreneur', *JHS* 34 (1994-6), 161-87

_____, *England's Jewish Solution: Experiment and Expulsion, 1262–1290*, Cambridge Studies in Medieval Life and Thought, Fourth Series 37 (Cambridge, 1998)

_____, 'Clandestine Crypto-Camouflaged Usurer or Legal Merchant? Edwardian Jewry, 1275–90', *Jewish Culture and History* 3 (2000), 73-97

_____, 'Christian and Jewish Lending Patterns and Financial Dealings during the Twelfth and Thirteenth Centuries', in *Credit and Debt in Medieval England c.1180–c.1350*, ed. N. J. Mayhew and P. R. Schofield (Oxford, 2002), 42-67

_____, 'Edward I and the Final Phase of Anglo-Jewry', in *The Jews in Medieval Britain: Historical, Literary, and Archaeological Perspectives*, ed. P. Skinner (Woodbridge, 2003), pp. 55-83

_____, 'England: The Island's Jews and their Economic Pursuits', in *The Jews of Europe in the Middle Ages (Tenth to Fifteenth Centuries)*, ed. C. Cluse, Cultural Encounters in Late Antiquity and the Middle Ages 4 (Turnhout 2004), pp. 221-32

_____, *The King's Jews: Money, Massacre and Exodus in Medieval England* (London, 2010)

_____, 'Out of the Shadow and into the Light – The Impact and Implications of Recent Scholarship on the Jews of Medieval England 1066–1290', *History Compass* 9:8 (2011), 572-601

Mutius, H.-G. von, *Rechtsentscheide Mittelalterlicher Englischer Rabbinen*, Judentum und Umwelt 60 (Frankfurt, 1995)

Myers, D. N., '"*Mehabevin et ha-tsarot*": Crusade Memories and Modern Jewish Martyrologies', *Jewish History* 13 (1999), 49-64

Neubauer, A., 'Miscellanea Liturgica: The Etz Chayim', *JQR* o.s. 6 (1894), 348-54

Nichols, A. E., 'The Hierosphthitic Topos, or the Fate of Fergus: Notes on the N-Town *Assumption*', *Comparative Drama* 25 (1991), 29-41

Nirenberg, D., *Communities of Violence: Persecution of Minorities in the Middle Ages* (Princeton, 1996)

_____, 'The Rhineland Massacres of Jews in the First Crusade: Memories Medieval and Modern', in *Medieval Concepts of the Past: Ritual, Memory, Historiography*, ed. G. Althoff, J. Fried, and P. Geary (Cambridge, 2002), pp. 279-310

Nisse, R., '"Your Name Will No Longer Be Aseneth": Apocrypha, Anti-martyrdom, and Jewish Conversion in Thirteenth-Century England', *Speculum* 81 (2006), 734-53

Nora, P., 'Between Memory and History: *Les Lieux de Mémoire*', *Representations* 26 (1989), 7-24

Norgate, K., 'The Date of Composition of William of Newburgh's History', *EHR* 19 (1904), 288–97.

Norton, C., 'The Medieval Paintings in the Chapter House', *Friends of the York Minster Annual Report* 67 (1996), 34-51

O'Brien, B., *God's Peace and King's Peace: The Laws of Edward the Confessor* (Philadelphia, 1999)

O'Connor D. E. and Haselock, J., 'The Stained and Painted Glass', in *A History of York Minster*, ed. G. E. Aylmer and R. Cant (Oxford, 1977), pp. 313-93

Oisteanu, A., *Inventing the Jew: Antisemitic Stereotypes in Romanian and Other Central-East European Cultures* (Lincoln NE, 2009)

Olszowy-Schlanger, J., 'The Knowledge and Practice of Hebrew Grammar among Christian Scholars in Pre-expulsion England: The Evidence of "Bilingual" Hebrew-Latin Manuscripts', in *Hebrew Scholarship and the Medieval World*, ed. N. de Lange (Cambridge, 2001), pp. 107-28

_____, *Les manuscrits hébreux dans l'Angleterre médiévale: Étude historique et paléographique*, Collection de la Revue des Études Juives 29 (Paris, 2003)

_____, 'Learning to Read and Write in Medieval Egypt: Children's Exercise Books from the Cairo Geniza', *Journal of Semitic Studies* 48 (2003), 47-69

_____, 'A Christian Tradition of Hebrew Vocalisation in Medieval England', in *Semitic Studies in Honour of Edward Ullendorff*, ed. G. Khan (Leiden, 2005), pp. 126-46

_____, 'Christian Hebraism in Thirteenth-Century England: The Evidence of Hebrew-Latin Manuscripts', in *Crossing Borders: Hebrew Manuscripts as a Meeting-Place of Cultures*, ed. P. van Boxel and S. Arndt (Oxford, 2009), pp. 115-22

_____, 'Manuscrits hébreux et judéo-arabes médiévaux', *Annuaire de l'École Pratique des Hautes Études, Section des Sciences Historiques et Philologiques* 140 (2009), 43-5

Orme, N., *Medieval Children* (New Haven CT, 2001)

_____ and Padel, O. J., 'Cornwall and the Third Crusade', *Journal of the Royal Institution of Cornwall* (2005), 71-7

Ottaway, P. and Rogers, N., *Craft, Industry and Everyday Life; Finds from Medieval York. The Archaeology of York* 17:15 (York, 2002)

Otter, M., *Inventiones: Fiction and Referentiality in Twelfth-Century English Historical Writing* (Chapel Hill NC, 1996)

Ottolenghi, L. M., 'Il manoscritto ebraico del seminario vescovile di Vercelli', in *Miscellenea di Studi in Memoria di Dario Disegni*, ed. E. M. Artom et al. (Torino, 1969), pp. 153-65

Bibliography

Owen, D. M., 'Bishop's Lynn: The First Century of a New Town?', in *Proceedings of the Battle Conference on Anglo-Norman Studies II, 1979*, ed. R. A. Brown (Woodbridge, 1980), pp. 141-53

Page, M., 'Cornwall, Earl Richard, and the Barons' War', *EHR* 115 (2000), 21-38

Page, W., 'Hospitals: York', in *A History of the County of York*, ed. W. Page, 3 vols., Victoria History of the Counties of England (1907-74), III, pp. 336-52

Painter, S., *The Reign of King John* (Baltimore, 1949)

Palliser, D. M., 'The Medieval Street-Names of York', *York Historian* 2 (1978), 2-16

_____, *Domesday York*, Borthwick Papers 78 (York, 1990)

_____, 'The Birth of York's Civic Liberties, c. 1200–1354', in *The Government of Medieval York : Essays in Commemoration of the 1396 Royal Charter*, ed. S. Rees Jones, Borthwick Studies in History 3 (York, 1997), pp. 88-107

_____, Slater, T. R., and Dennison, E. P., 'The Topography of Towns 600–1300', in *The Cambridge Urban History of Britain I: 600–1540*, ed. D. M. Palliser (Cambridge, 2000), pp. 153-86

Parente, F., 'Sulla doppia transmissione filologica ed ecclesiastica del testo di Flavio Giuseppe: un contributo alla storia della ricezione della sua opera nel mondo Cristiano', *Rivista di Storia e Letteratura Religiosa* 36 (2000), 3-51

Parker, E. C., and C. T. Little, *The Cloisters Cross: Its Art and Meaning* (London, 1994)

Parkes, J., *The Jew in the Medieval Community: A Study of his Political and Economic Situation* (London, 1938)

Partner, N. F., *Serious Entertainments: The Writing of History in Twelfth-Century England* (Chicago, 1977)

Patschovsky, A., 'The Relationship between the Jews of Germany and the King (11th–14th Centuries): A European Comparison', in *England and Germany in the High Middle Ages*, ed. A. Haverkamp and H. Vollrath (London, 1996), pp. 193-218

Perez, R., 'Next-Door Neighbors: Aspects of Judeo-Christian Cohabitation in Medieval France', in *Urban Space in the Middle Ages and the Early Modern Age*, ed. A. Classen (Berlin, 2009), pp. 309-30

Phillips, T., 'On the Cartulary of Flaxley Abbey, in Gloucestershire', *Transactions of the Royal Society of Literature of the United Kingdom* 1 (1829), 53-6

Plucknett, T. F. T., *Legislation of Edward I* (Oxford, 1949)

Pollock, F., and Maitland, F. W., *History of English Law before the time of Edward I*, 2 vols., 2nd edn (Cambridge, 1898)

Postan, M. M., 'Private Financial Instruments in Medieval England', *Vierteljahrschrift fur Sozial und Wirtschaftsgeschichte* 23 (1930), 26-75

Prescott, E., *The English Medieval Hospital, c. 1050–1640* (London, 1992)

Prestwich, J. O., 'The Military Household of the Norman Kings', *EHR* 96 (1981), 1-35

Prynne, W., *A Short Demurrer to the Jewes long discontinued barred Remitter into England* (London, 1656)

Pugh, R. B., 'Prisons and Gallows', in *A History of the County of York: The City of York*, ed. P. M. Tillot, Victoria History of the Counties of England (Oxford 1961), pp. 491-8

_____, 'The Seals, Insignia, Plate and Officers of the City', in *A History of the County of York: The City of York*, ed. P. M. Tillot, Victoria History of the Counties of England (Oxford 1961), pp. 544-6

RCHME, *An Inventory of the Historical Monuments in the City of York*, 5 vols. (London, 1962-81)

Rees Jones, S., 'The Historical Background', in J. M. Lilley et al., *The Jewish Burial Ground at Jewbury*, The Archaeology of York 12:3 (London, 1994), pp. 301-12

_____, *The Database of Medieval Title Deeds for the City of York: A Guide for Users*, University of York Occasional Papers in History 3 (York, 1996)

_____, 'York's Civic Administration, 1354–1464', in *The Government of Medieval York: Essays in Commemoration of the 1396 Royal Charter*, ed. S. Rees Jones, Borthwick Studies in History 3 (York, 1997), pp. 108-40

_____ with Daniell, C., 'The King's Pool', in *Medieval Urbanism in Coppergate: Refining a Townscape*, ed. R. Hall and K. Hunter-Mann, The Archaeology of York 10:6 (York, 2002), pp. 696-8

_____, 'Building Domesticity in the City: English Urban Housing before the Black Death', in *Medieval Domesticity: Home, Housing and Household in Medieval England*, ed. M. Kowaleski and P. J. P. Goldberg (Cambridge, 2008), pp. 66-91

_____, 'The Cults of St William of York and St Kenelm of Winchcombe', in *Cities, Texts and Social Networks 400–1500: Experiences and Perceptions of Medieval Urban Space*, ed. C. Goodson et al. (Farnham, 2010), pp. 193-214

_____, *Medieval York, the Making of a City, 1068–1350* (Oxford, forthcoming)

Reif, S. C., *Judaism and Hebrew Prayer: New Perspectives on Jewish Liturgical History* (Cambridge, 1993)

Richardson, H., *Medieval Fairs and Markets of York*, St Anthony's Hall Publications 20 (York, 1961)

Richardson, H. G., *The English Jewry under Angevin Kings* (London, 1960)

Riché, P., *Education et culture dans l'occident médiévale*, Variorum Collected Studies Series CS420 (Aldershot, 1993)

Ricoeur, P., *Time and Narrative I*, trans. K. McLaughlin and D. Pellauer (Chicago, 1990)

_____, *Oneself as Another*, trans. K. Blamey (Chicago, 1992)

Riley-Smith, J., 'Christian Violence and the Crusades', in *Religious Violence between Christians and Jews: Medieval Roots, Modern Perspectives*, ed. A. Sapir Abulafia (Basingstoke, 2002), pp. 3-20

Robinson, J. T., 'We Drink Only from the Master's Water: Maimonides and Maimonideanism in Southern France, 1200–1306', *Studia Rosenthaliana* 40 (2007), 27-60

Roche, T., '"Des conventions infiniment variées" : normes et coutumes dans les concordes des moines de Saint-Wandrille (XIe-XIIe siècles)', in *Coutumes, doctrine et droit savant*, ed. V. Gazeau and J.-M. Augustin (Poitiers, 2007), pp. 13-42

Roth, C. 'Elijah of London: The Most Illustrious Jew of the Middle Ages', *JHSE Transactions* 15 (1939-1945), 29-62

_____, 'Rabbi Berechiah of Nicole (Benedict of Lincoln)', *Journal of Jewish Studies* 1 (1948-9), 67-81

_____, *England in Jewish History* (London, 1949)

_____, *The Intellectual Activities of Medieval English Jewry*, British Academy, Supplemental Papers 8 (London, 1949)

_____, *A History of the Jews in England*, 3rd edn (Oxford, 1964)

_____, ed., *Encyclopaedia Judaica*, 16 vols. (Jerusalem, 1971-72)

Round, J. H., 'Richard the First's Change of Seal (1198)', in J. H. Round, *Feudal England: Historical Studies on the XIth and XIIth Centuries* (London, 1895), pp. 539–51

Rubin, M., 'Imagining the Jew: The Late Medieval Eucharistic Discourse', in *In and Out of the Ghetto: Jewish-Gentile Relations in Late Medieval and Early Modern Germany*, ed. R. Po-Chia-Hsia and H. Lehmann (Cambridge, 1995), pp. 177-208

_____, *Gentile Tales: The Narrative Assault on Late Medieval Jews* (New Haven CT, 1999)

Rutledge, E. and Rutledge, P., 'Kings Lynn and Great Yarmouth, Two Thirteenth-Century Surveys', *Norfolk Archaeology* 37 (1978), 92-114

Sacks, M. J. L., 'Piske ha-Rash mi-Landon', *Sinai* 13 (1943), 223-35

Saltman, A., 'John of Salisbury and the World of the Old Testament', in *The World of John of Salisbury*, ed. M. Wilks, Studies in Church History, Subsidia Series 3 (Oxford 1984), 343-63

Sanders, I. J., *English Baronies: A Study of their Origin and Descent, 1086–1327* (Oxford, 1960)

Sandler, L. F., *The Psalter of Robert de Lisle in the British Library* (London, 1982)

_____, *Gothic Manuscripts, 1285–1385*, 2 vols., A Survey of Manuscripts Illuminated in the British Isles 5 (London, 1986)

Sargeant, F., 'The Wine Trade with Gascony', in *Finance and Trade under Edward III*, ed. G. Unwin (Manchester, 1918), pp. 257-311

Schmidt, H. D., 'The Idea and Slogan of "Perfidious Albion"', *Journal of the History of Ideas*, 14 (1953), 604–16

Schramm, P. E., *A History of the English Coronation* (Oxford, 1937)

Schreckenberg, H., *Die Flavius-Josephus-Tradition in Antike und Mittelalter*, Arbeiten zur Literatur und Geschichte des hellenistischen Judentums 5 (Leiden, 1972)

_____, *Rezeptionsgeschichtliche und Textkritische Untersuchungen zu Flavius Josephus*, Arbeiten zur Literatur und Geschichte des hellenistichen Judentums 10 (Leiden, 1977)

_____, *The Jews in Christian Art: An Illustrated History* (London, 1996)

Schwarzfuchs, S., 'L'opposition Tsarfat-Provence: la formation du judaisme du nord de la France', *Hommage à Georges Vajda*, ed. G. Nahon and C. Touati (Louvain, 1980), pp. 134-54

Seidel, L., 'Images of the Crusades in Western Art: Models as Metaphors', in *The Meeting of Two Worlds: Cultural Exchange Between East and West During the Period of the Crusades*, ed. V. P. Goss (Kalamazoo, 1986), pp. 377-91

Sha'anan, H. S., 'Piske Rabenu Ri mi-Corbeil', in *Sefer Ner le-Shemayah* (Bene Berak, 1988), pp. 5-32

Shatzmiller, J., *Recherches sur la communauté juive de Manosque au moyen âge* (Paris, 1973)

_____, 'Counterfeit of Coinage in England of the 13ᵗʰ Century and the Way It Was Remembered in Medieval Provence', in *Moneda y Monedas en la Europa Medieval*, ed. G. de Navarra, Semana de Estudios Medievales 26 (Pamplona, 2000), pp. 387-97

Shay, J., *Achilles in Vietnam: Combat Trauma and the Undoing of Character* (New York, 1994)

Shoemaker, S. J., *The Ancient Traditions of the Virgin Mary's Dormition and Assumption* (Oxford, 2006)

Shoham-Steiner, S., 'Jews and Healing at Medieval Saints' Shrines: Participation, Polemics, and Shared Cultures', *Harvard Theological Review*, 103 (2010), 111-29.

Simon, U., 'Transplanting the Wisdom of Spain to Christian Lands: The Failed Efforts of R. Abraham ibn Ezra', *Simon Dubnow Institute Yearbook* 8 (2009), 139-89

Sirat, C., *Hebrew Manuscripts of the Middle Ages*, ed. and trans. by N. de Lange (Cambridge, 2002)

Skinner, P., 'Introduction: Jews in Medieval Britain and Europe', in *The Jews in Medieval Britain: Historical, Literary and Archaeological Perspectives*, ed. P. Skinner (Woodbridge, 2003), pp. 1-12

Slavin, P., 'Hebrew Went Latin: Reflections of Latin Diplomatic Formulae and Terminology in Hebrew Private Deeds from Thirteenth-Century England', *Journal of Medieval Latin* 18 (2008), 306-25

Smalley, B., *Hebrew Scholarship among Christians in 13ᵗʰ Century England: As Illustrated by some Hebrew-Latin Psalters*, Lectiones in Vetere Testamento et in Rebus Iudaicis 6 (London, 1939)

_____, 'A Commentary on the *Hebraica* by Herbert of Bosham', *Recherches de théologie ancienne et médiévale* 18 (1951), 29-65

_____, *The Study of the Bible in the Middle Ages*, 2nd edn (Oxford, 1952)

Smith, A. H., *The Place-Names of the East Riding of Yorkshire and York*, English Place-Name Society 14 (Cambridge, 1937)

Smith, D., 'Alexander (d. 1148)', *ODNB*, online edn (Oxford, 2004)

Sokoloff, M., *A Dictionary of Jewish Babylonian Aramaic of the Talmudic and Geonic Periods* (Ramat-Gan, 2002)

Soloveitchik, H., 'Pawnbroking: A Study in *Ribbit* and of the Halakah in Exile', *Proceedings of the American Academy for Jewish Research* 38-39 (1970-1), 203-68

_____, 'Catastrophe and Halakhic Creativity: Ashkenaz - 1096, 1242, 1306 and 1298', *Jewish History* 12 (1998), 71-85

_____, 'Religious Law and Change: The Medieval Ashkenazic Example', *AJSR* 12 (1987), 205-21

_____, *Principles and Pressures: Jewish Trade in Gentile Wine in the Middle Ages* (Tel Aviv, 2003)

_____, *Wine in Ashkenaz in the Middle Ages: Yeyn Nesekh – A Study in the History of Halakhah* (Jerusalem, 2008)

_____, 'The Halakhic Isolation of the Ashkenazic Community', *Simon Dubnow Institute Yearbook* 8 (2009), 41-7

Spiegel, G. M., 'History, Historicism and the Social Logic of the Text in the Middle Ages', *Speculum* 65 (1990), 59-86

_____, *The Past as Text: The Theory and Practice of Medieval Historiography* (Baltimore, 1999)

Stacey, R. C., 'Royal Taxation and the Social Structure of Medieval Anglo-Jewry: The Tallages of 1239-42,' *Hebrew Union College Annual* 56 (1985), 175-249

_____, 'The Conversion of Jews to Christianity in Thirteenth-Century England', *Speculum* 97 (1992), 263-83

_____, 'Jewish Lending and the Medieval Economy', in *A Commercialising Economy: England 1086 to c. 1300*, ed. R. H. Britnell and B. M. S. Campbell (Manchester, 1995), 78-101

_____, 'Parliamentary Negotiation and the Expulsion of the Jews from England', in *Thirteenth Century England* vi (1997), ed. M. Prestwich, R. H. Britnell and R. Frame, pp. 77-101

_____, 'Crusades, Martyrdoms, and the Jews of Norman England, 1096–1190', in *Juden und Christen zur Zeit des Kreuzzüge*, ed. A. Haverkamp (Sigmaringen, 1999), pp. 233-51

_____, 'Jews and Christians in Twelfth-Century England: Some Dynamics of a Changing Relationship', *Jews and Christians in Twelfth-Century Europe*, ed. M. A. Signer and J. van Engen, Notre Dame Conferences in Medieval Studies 10 (Notre Dame IN, 2001), pp. 340-53

_____, 'The English Jews under Henry III', in *The Jews in Medieval Britain: Historical, Literary and Archaeological Perspectives*, ed. P. Skinner (Woodbridge, 2003), pp. 41-54

Staley, L., 'Susanna and English Communities', *Traditio* 62 (2007), 25-58

Stein, S., 'The Development of the Jewish Law on Interest from the Biblical Period to the Expulsion of the Jews from England', *Historia Judaica* 17 (1955), 3-40

Stephenson, C., 'The Aids of English Boroughs', *EHR* 34 (1919), 457-73

Stewart, S., *On Longing: Narratives of the Miniature, the Gigantic, the Souvenir, the Collection* (Durham NC, 1993)

Stokes, H. P., *Studies in Anglo-Jewish History* (Edinburgh, 1913)

Stow, K. R., 'Papal and Royal Attitudes toward Jewish Lending in the Thirteenth Century', *AJSR* 6 (1981), 161-84

_____, *Alienated Minority: The Jews of Medieval Latin Europe* (Cambridge MA, 1992)

Streit, K. T., 'The Expansion of the English Jewish Community in the Reign of King Stephen', *Albion* 25 (1993), 177-92

Strickland, D. H., *Saracens, Demons, and Jews: Making Monsters in Medieval Art* (Princeton, 2003)

Sussman, J., 'Kitve-yad u-masorot nusah shel ha-Mishnah', in *Proceedings of the Seventh World Congress of Jewish Studies: Studies in the Talmud, Halacha and Midrash* (Jerusalem, 1981), pp. 215-54

_____, 'The Scholarly Oeuvre of Professor Ephraim Elimelech Urbach', in *Ephraim Elimelech Urbach: A Bio-bibliography*, ed. D. Assaf, Supplement to Jewish Studies 1 (Jerusalem, 1993), pp. 7-116

Ta-Shma, I., 'Seridim mi-Toratam shel Rishonim', *Moriah* 2 (1970), pp. 60-64

_____, *Studies in Medieval Rabbinic Literature*, 4 vols. (Jerusalem, 2004-10)

_____, 'On the SMA'G, Condensed SMA'G and Other Condensed Books', in I. Ta-Shma, *Studies in Medieval Rabbinic Literature*, 4 vols. (Jerusalem, 2004-10), IV, 259-68

_____, 'The Open Book in Medieval Hebrew Literature: The Problem of Authorized Editions', in I. Ta-Shma, *Creativity and Tradition: Studies in Medieval Rabbinic Scholarship, Literature and Thought* (Cambridge MA, 2006), pp. 194-200

Tabuteau, E., *Transfers of Property in Eleventh-Century Norman Law* (Chapel Hill NC, 1988)

Tait, J., *The Medieval English Borough: Studies on Its Origins and Constitutional History* (Manchester, 1936)

Taitz, E., *The Jews of Medieval France: The Community of Champagne* (Westport CT, 1994)

Taylor, J., 'Newburgh, William of', *ODNB*, online edn (Oxford, 2004)

Thomas, H. M., *The English and the Normans: Ethnic Hostility, Assimilation, and Identity 1066–c.1220* (Oxford, 2003)

_____, 'Portrait of a Medieval Anti-Semite: Richard Malebisse *vero agnomine Mala Bestia*', *Haskins Society Journal* 5 (1993), 1–15

_____, 'Mowbray, Sir Roger (I) de (d. 1188)', *ODNB*, online edn (Oxford, 2004)

Thompson, A. H., 'The Chapel of St. Mary and the Holy Angels, otherwise known as St. Sepulchre's Chapel at York', *YAJ* 36 (1944), 63-77

Thrupp, S., *The Merchant Class of Medieval London, 1300–1500* (Chicago, 1948)

Toch, M., 'The Jews in Europe 500–1050', in *The New Cambridge Medieval History I: c. 500-c. 700*, ed. P. Fouracre (Cambridge, 2005), pp. 547-70

Tomasch, S., 'Postcolonial Chaucer and the Virtual Jew', in *The Postcolonial Middle Ages*, ed. J. Cohen (New York, 2000), pp. 243-60

Tovey, D'Blossiers, *Anglia Judaica: Or the History and Antiquities of the Jews in England* (Oxford, 1738)

Toy, J., *A Guide and Index to the Windows of York Minster* (York, 1985)

Tucker, P., *Law Courts and Lawyers in the City of London, 1300–1550* (Cambridge, 2007)

Turner, R. V., *Men Raised from the Dust: Administrative Service and Upward Mobility in Angevin England* (Philadelphia, 1988)

Tyerman, C., *England and the Crusades, 1095–1588* (Chicago, 1988)

Urbach, E. E., *Baale Ha-Tosafot: Toldotehem, Hiburehem, ShiTatam*, 2 vols. (Jerusalem, 1955-86)

_____, 'Mitoratam shel Hahkmei Anglia Melifnei Hagirush', *Tiferet Yisrael: Likvod Harav Yisrael Brody* (London, 1967), pp. 1-56.

_____, *Studies in Judaica* (Jerusalem, 1998)

Vajda, G., 'De quelques infiltrations chrétiennes dans l'oeuvre d'un auteur anglo-juif du XIIIe siècle', in *Mélanges Georges Vajda: Études de pensée, de philosophie et de littérature juives et arabes. In memoriam*, ed. G. E. Weil (Hildesheim, 1982), pp. 313-31

Vaughan, R., 'The Handwriting of Matthew Paris', *Transactions of the Cambridge Bibliographical Society* 1 (1953), 376-94

_____, *Matthew Paris*, 2nd edn (Cambridge, 1979)

Vielliard, F., 'Richard Coeur de Lion et son entourage normand: Le témoignage de l'Estoire de la Guerre Sainte', *Bibliothèque de l'École des Chartes* 160 (2002), 5-52

VCH, *A History of the County of York*, ed. W. Page, 3 vols., Victoria History of the Counties of England (London, 1907-74)

_____, *A History of the County of York: The City of York*, ed. P. M. Tillot, Victoria History of the Counties of England (Oxford 1961)

_____, *A History of the County of York: East Riding*, 8 vols. Victoria History of the Counties of England (London, 1969-2002)

Vincent, N., 'Jews, Poitevins, and the Bishop of Winchester, 1231–1234', in *Christianity and Judaism*, ed. D. Wood, Studies in Church History 29 (Oxford, 1992), pp. 119-32

_____, *Peter des Roches: An Alien in English Politics, 1205–1238* (Cambridge, 1996)

_____, 'The Pilgrimages of the Angevin Kings of England 1154–1272', in *Pilgrimage: The English Experience from Becket to Bunyan*, ed. C. Morris and P. Roberts (Cambridge 2002), pp. 12-45

_____, 'The Court of Henry II', in *Henry II: New Interpretations*, ed. C. Harper-Bill and N. Vincent (Woodbridge 2007), pp. 278-334

_____, 'Stephen Langton, Archbishop of Canterbury', in *Etienne Langton: Prédicateur, bibliste, théologien*, ed. L.-J. Bataillon et al., Bibliothèque d'Histoire Culturelle du Moyen Age 9 (Turnhout, 2010), pp. 51-123

Visscher, E. De, 'Putting Theory into Practice? Hugh of Saint Victor's Influence on Herbert of Bosham's Psalterium cum commento', in *Bibel und Exegese in der Abtei Saint-Victor zu Paris: Form und Funktion eines Grundtextes im europäischen Rahmen*, ed. R. Berndt, Corpus Victorinum. Instrumenta 3 (Münster, 2009), pp. 491-502

_____, '"Closer to the Hebrew": Herbert of Bosham's Interpretation of Literal Exegesis', in *The Multiple Meaning of Scripture: The Role of Exegesis in Early-Christian and Medieval Culture*, ed. I. van 't Spijker (Leiden, 2009), pp. 249-72

_____, 'Cross-Religious Learning and Teaching', in *Crossing Borders: Hebrew Manuscripts as a Meeting Place of Cultures*, ed. P. van Boxel and S. Arndt (Oxford, 2009), pp. 123-32

Warren, W. L., *King John*, 2nd edn (New Haven CT, 1997)

_____, *Henry II*, new edn (New Haven CT, 2000)

Watkins, C., *History and the Supernatural in Medieval England* (Cambridge, 2007)

Watt, J. A., 'The English Episcopate, the State and the Jews: The Evidence of the Thirteenth-Century Conciliar Decrees', in *Thirteenth-Century England II: Proceedings of the Newcastle upon Tyne Conference 1987*, ed. P. R. Coss and S. D. Lloyd (Woodbridge, 1988), pp. 137-47

_____, 'The Jews, the Law, and the Church: The Concept of Jewish Serfdom in Thirteenth-Century England', in *The Church and Sovereignty c. 590–1918: Essays in Honour of Michael Wilks*, ed. D. Wood, Studies in Church History, Subsidia Series 9 (Oxford, 1991), pp. 153-72

_____, 'Parisian Theologians and the Jews: Peter Lombard and Peter Cantor', in *The Medieval Church: Universities, Heresy, and the Religious Life. Essays in Honour of Gordon Leff*, ed. P. Biller and B. Dobson, Studies in Church History, Subsidia Series 11 (Woodbridge, 1999), pp. 55-76

_____, 'Grosseteste and the Jews: A Commentary on Letter V', in *Robert Grosseteste and the Beginnings of a British Theological Tradition: Papers delivered at the* Grosseteste *Colloquium held at Greyfriars, Oxford on 3rd July 2002*, ed. M. O'Carroll, Bibliotheca Seraphico-Capuccina 69 (Rome, 2003), pp. 201-16

Weiler, B., 'Image and Reality in Richard of Cornwall's German Career', *EHR* 113 (1998), 1111-42

_____, 'Matthew Paris, Richard of Cornwall's Candidacy for the German Throne, and the Sicilian Business', *JMH* 26 (2000), 71-92

Wharton, H., *Anglia Sacra*, 2 vols. (London, 1691)

Wheatley, E., '"Blind" Jews and Blind Christians: Metaphorics of Marginalization in Medieval Europe', *Exemplaria* 14 (2002), 351-82

White, H., *The Content of the Form: Narrative Discourse and Historical Representation* (Baltimore, 1987)

White, S. D., 'Imaginary Justice: The End of the Ordeal and the Survival of the Duel', *Medieval Perspectives* 13 (1998), 32-55

Wilhelm, J. D., 'Seder Lel Pesah le-Rabenu Eliyahu Menahem b.r. Mosheh mi-Londres', *Tarbiz* 22 (1951), 43-52

Wilmart, A., 'Les Mélanges de Matthieu, préchantre de Rievaulx au début du XIII siècle', *Revue Bénédictine* 52 (1940), 15-84

Woolf, J., 'The Influence of the SMA'G on the Culture of Medieval Ashkenaz', *Sidra* 15 (1999), 31-49

_____, 'Admiration and Apathy: Maimonides' Mishneh Torah in High and Late Medieval Ashkenaz', in *Be'erot Yitzhak: Studies in Memory of Isadore Twersky*, ed. J. M. Harris (Cambridge MA, 2005), pp. 427-53

Woolley, R., *Catalogue of the Manuscripts of Lincoln Cathedral Chapter Library* (Oxford, 1927)

Wright, S. K., *The Vengeance of Our Lord: Medieval Dramatization of the Destruction of Jerusalem*, Pontifical Institute of Mediaeval Studies, Studies and Texts 89 (Toronto, 1989)

Yerushalmi, Y. H., *Zakhor: Jewish History and Jewish Memory* (Seattle, 1982)

Young, C. R., *The Royal Forests of Medieval England* (Leicester, 1979)

Young, K., 'Observations on the Origin of the Medieval Passion-Play', *Publications of the Modern Language Association of America* 25 (1910), 309-54

Yuval, I. J., 'Passover in the Middle Ages', in *Passover and Easter: Origin and History to Modern Times*, ed. P. F. Bradshaw and L. A. Hoffman (Notre Dame IN, 1999), pp. 127-60

_____, *Two Nations in Your Womb: Perceptions of Jews and Christians in Late Antiquity and the Middle Ages* (Berkeley CA, 2006)

Yver, J., *Les contrats dans le très ancient droit normand (xie-xiiie siècles)* (Domfront, 1926)

Zimmels, H. J., *Ashkenazim and Sephardim: Their Relations, Differences, and Problems as Reflected in the Rabbinical Responsa*, Jews' College Publications, New Series 2 (London, 1958)

Unpublished Works

Bradbury, C. A., 'Imaging and Imagining the Jew in Medieval England' (unpublished Ph.D. dissertation, University of Illinois, 2007)

Cohen, S., 'Plea Rolls of the Exchequer of the Jews, Michaelmas 1277–Hilary 1279' (unpublished Ph.D. dissertation, University of London, 1951)

Kletter, K. M., 'The Uses of Josephus: Jewish History in Medieval Tradition' (unpublished Ph.D. dissertation, University of North Carolina, 2005)

Lieberman, S. T., 'English Royal Policy towards the Jews' Debtors, 1227–1290' (unpublished Ph.D. dissertation, University of London, 1983)

McDougal, S., 'Bigamy in Late Medieval France' (unpublished Ph.D. dissertation, Yale University, 2009)

Mesley, M., 'The Construction of Episcopal Identity: The Meaning and Function of Episcopal Depictions within Latin Saints' Lives of the Long Twelfth Century' (unpublished Ph.D. dissertation, University of Exeter, 2010)

Meyer, H., 'Female Moneylending and Wet-nursing in Jewish-Christian Relations in Thirteenth-Century England' (unpublished Ph.D. dissertation, University of Cambridge, 2009)

Rees Jones, S., 'Property, Tenure and Rents: Some Aspects of the Topography and Economy of Medieval York', 2 vols. (unpublished D.Phil. dissertation, University of York, 1987)

Websites

Le *Centre national de la recherche scientifique*, 'Chartae Burgundiae Medii Aevi Project'. http://www.artehis-cnrs.fr/La-base-de-donnees-CBMA [accessed 12 April 2012]

Chipp, J., 'Recognizance for Solomon Gidney, 1828', New Paltz, Ulster County, New York. http://www.co.ulster.ny.us/archives/documents/recog.html [accessed 12April 2012]

English Heritage, 'The History of Clifford's Tower'. http://www.english-heritage.org.uk/daysout/properties/cliffords-tower-york/history/ [accessed 16 March 2011]

McNabb, N., 'Anglo-Scandinavian, Medieval and Post-Medieval Urban Occupation at 41–49 Walmgate, York, UK', The Archaeology of York, Web Series 1 (York, 2003). http://www.iadb.co.uk/wgate/main/discuss. php [accessed 1 July 2012]

Oxford Jewish Heritage Committee, 'The Robert of Reading Plaque'. http:// www.oxfordjewishheritage.co.uk/projects/osney-abbey-first-public-burning-in-england/137-the-robert-of-reading-plaque [accessed 12 April 2011]

University of Toronto, 'Documents of Early England Data Set (DEEDS) Research Project'. http://res.deeds.utoronto.ca:49838/research/ [accessed 12 April 2012]

York Archaeological Trust, York Archive Gazetteer, '44, Coney Street/Feasegate, York. Site Code: 1998.2 YORYM, SE60305182', http://www.iadb. co.uk/gaz/gaz_details.php?SiteID=1055 [accessed 1 July 2008]

INDEX

of people, places and texts

YORK MEDIEVAL PRESS: PUBLICATIONS

God's Words, Women's Voices: The Discernment of Spirits in the Writing of Late-Medieval Women Visionaries, Rosalynn Voaden (1999)

Pilgrimage Explored, ed. J. Stopford (1999)

Piety, Fraternity and Power: Religious Gilds in Late Medieval Yorkshire 1389-1547, † David J. F. Crouch (2000)

Courts and Regions in Medieval Europe, ed. Sarah Rees Jones, Richard Marks and A. J. Minnis (2000)

Treasure in the Medieval West, ed. Elizabeth M. Tyler (2000)

Nunneries, Learning and Spirituality in Late Medieval English Society: The Dominican Priory of Dartford, Paul Lee (2000)

Prophecy and Public Affairs in Later Medieval England, Lesley A. Coote (2000)

The Problem of Labour in Fourteenth-Century England, ed. James Bothwell, P. J. P. Goldberg and W. M. Ormrod (2000)

New Directions in Later Medieval Manuscript Studies: Essays from the 1998 Harvard Conference, ed. Derek Pearsall (2000)

Cistercians, Heresy and Crusade in Occitania, 1145-1229: Preaching in the Lord's Vineyard, Beverly Mayne Kienzle (2001)

Guilds and the Parish Community in Late Medieval East Anglia, c. 1470-1550, Ken Farnhill (2001)

The Age of Edward III, ed. J. S. Bothwell (2001)

Time in the Medieval World, ed. Chris Humphrey and W. M. Ormrod (2001)

The Cross Goes North: Processes of Conversion in Northern Europe, AD 300-1300, ed. Martin Carver (2002)

Henry IV: The Establishment of the Regime, 1399-1406, ed. Gwilym Dodd and Douglas Biggs (2003)

Youth in the Middle Ages, ed. P. J. P Goldberg and Felicity Riddy (2004)

The Idea of the Castle in Medieval England, Abigail Wheatley (2004)

Rites of Passage: Cultures of Transition in the Fourteenth Century, ed. Nicola F. McDonald and W. M. Ormrod (2004)

Creating the Monastic Past in Medieval Flanders, Karine Ugé (2005)

St William of York, Christopher Norton (2006)

Medieval Obscenities, ed. Nicola F. McDonald (2006)

The Reign of Edward II: New Perspectives, ed. Gwilym Dodd and Anthony Musson (2006)

Old English Poetics: The Aesthetics of the Familiar in Anglo-Saxon England, Elizabeth M. Tyler (2006)

The Late Medieval Interlude: The Drama of Youth and Aristocratic Masculinity, Fiona S. Dunlop (2007)

The Late Medieval English College and its Context, ed. Clive Burgess and Martin Heale (2008)

The Reign of Henry IV: Rebellion and Survival, 1403-1413, ed. Gwilym Dodd and Douglas Biggs (2008)

Medieval Petitions: Grace and Grievance, ed. W. Mark Ormrod, Gwilym Dodd and Anthony Musson (2009)

St Edmund, King and Martyr: Changing Images of a Medieval Saint, ed. Anthony Bale (2009)

Language and Culture in Medieval Britain: The French of England c.1100-c.1500, ed. Jocelyn Wogan-Browne et al. (2009)

The Royal Pardon: Access to Mercy in Fourteenth-Century England, Helen Lacey (2009)

Texts and Traditions of Medieval Pastoral Care: Essays in Honour of Bella Millett, ed. Cate Gunn and Catherine Innes-Parker (2009)

The Anglo-Norman Language and its Contexts, ed. Richard Ingham (2010)

Parliament and Political Pamphleteering in Fourteenth-Century England, Clementine Oliver (2010)

The Saints' Lives of Jocelin of Furness: Hagiography, Patronage and Ecclesiastical Politics, Helen Birkett (2010)

The York Mystery Plays: Performance in the City, ed. Margaret Rogerson (2011)

Wills and Will-Making in Anglo-Saxon England, Linda Tollerton (2011)

The Songs and Travels of a Tudor Minstrel: Richard Sheale of Tamworth, Andrew Taylor (2012)

Sin in Medieval and Early Modern Culture: The Tradition of the Seven Deadly Sins, ed. Richard G. Newhauser and Susan J. Ridyard (2012)

Socialising the Child in Late Medieval England, c. 1400-1600, Merridee L. Bailey (2012)

Barking Abbey and Medieval Literary Culture: Authorship and Authority in a Female Community, ed. Jennifer N. Brown and Donna Alfano Bussell (2012)

York Studies in Medieval Theology

I   *Medieval Theology and the Natural Body*, ed. Peter Biller and A. J. Minnis (1997)

II   *Handling Sin: Confession in the Middle Ages*, ed. Peter Biller and A. J. Minnis (1998)

III   *Religion and Medicine in the Middle Ages*, ed. Peter Biller and Joseph Ziegler (2001)

IV   *Texts and the Repression of Medieval Heresy*, ed. Caterina Bruschi and Peter Biller (2002)

York Manuscripts Conference

Manuscripts and Readers in Fifteenth-Century England: The Literary Implications of Manuscript Study, ed. Derek Pearsall (1983) [Proceedings of the 1981 York Manuscripts Conference]

Manuscripts and Texts: Editorial Problems in Later Middle English Literature, ed. Derek Pearsall (1987) [Proceedings of the 1985 York Manuscripts Conference]

Latin and Vernacular: Studies in Late-Medieval Texts and Manuscripts, ed. A. J. Minnis (1989) [Proceedings of the 1987 York Manuscripts Conference]

Regionalism in Late-Medieval Manuscripts and Texts: Essays celebrating the publication of 'A Linguistic Atlas of Late Mediaeval English', ed. Felicity Riddy (1991) [Proceedings of the 1989 York Manuscripts Conference]

Late-Medieval Religious Texts and their Transmission: Essays in Honour of A. I. Doyle, ed. A. J. Minnis (1994) [Proceedings of the 1991 York Manuscripts Conference]

Prestige, Authority and Power in Late Medieval Manuscripts and Texts, ed. Felicity Riddy (2000) [Proceedings of the 1994 York Manuscripts Conference]

Middle English Poetry: Texts and Traditions. Essays in Honour of Derek Pearsall, ed. A. J. Minnis (2001) [Proceedings of the 1996 York Manuscripts Conference]

Manuscript Culture in the British Isles

I   *Design and Distribution of Late Medieval Manuscripts in England*, ed. Margaret Connolly and Linne R. Mooney (2008)

II   *Women and Writing, c.1340–c.1650: The Domestication of Print Culture*, ed. Anne Lawrence-Mathers and Phillipa Hardman (2010)

III *The Wollaton Medieval Manuscripts: Texts, Owners and Readers*, ed. Ralph Hanna and Thorlac Turville-Petre (2010)

IV   *Scribes and the City: London Guildhall Clerks and the Dissemination of Middle English Literature, 1375–1425*, Linne R. Mooney and Estelle Stubbs (2013)

Heresy and Inquisition in the Middle Ages

Heresy and Heretics in the Thirteenth Century: The Textual Representations, L. J. Sackville (2011)

Heresy, Crusade and Inquisition in Medieval Quercy, Claire Taylor (2011)